COMPANION TO CONTEMPORARY BLACK BRITISH CULTURE

COMPANION TO CONTEMPORARY BLACK BRITISH CULTURE

Edited by Alison Donnell

London and New York

First published 2002
by Routledge
11 New Fetter Lane, London EC4P 4EE

Simultaneously published in the USA and Canada
by Routledge
29 West 35th Street, New York, NY 10001

Routledge is an imprint of the Taylor & Francis Group

© 2002 Routledge

Typeset in Baskerville by Taylor & Francis Books Ltd
Printed and bound in Great Britain by TJ International Ltd, Padstow,
Cornwall

British Library Cataloguing in Publication Data
A catalogue record for this book is available from the British Library

Library of Congress Cataloging in Publication Data
Companion to contemporary black British culture/
edited by Alison Donnell

Includes bibliographical references and index
1. Blacks–Great Britain–History–20th century–Handbook, manuals, etc.
2. Great Britain–Race relations–History–20th century–Handbooks,
manuals, etc. 3. Blacks–Great Britain–Civilization–Handbooks, manuals,
etc. 4. Great Britain–Civilization–20th century–Handbooks, manuals, etc.
I. Donnell, Alison, 1966–
DA125.N4 C63 2001
941.00496–dc21   2001019658

ISBN 0–415–16989–5 (hbk)

FOR PAULINE POLKEY (1958–99) AND THE JOY OF INSPIRATIONAL FRIENDSHIPS

Fifteen years ago we didn't care, or at least I didn't care, whether there was any black in the Union Jack. Now not only do we care, *we must*.

(Stuart Hall, 1987)

Extraordinary new forms have been produced and much of their power resides in their capacity to circulate a new sense of what it means to be British. . . . The seemingly trivial forms of youth sub-culture point to the opening up of a self-consciously post-colonial space in which the affirmation of difference points forward to a more pluralistic concept of nationality and perhaps beyond that to its transcendence.

(Paul Gilroy, 'The peculiarities of the black English', 1993)

For me the fact that it's so difficult to pin down blackness in Britain is a positive thing, it leaves me freer.

(Lola Young, 1998)

Where is the integration? Blacks as radio and television presenters, as MPs, as arts wallahs means nothing if the lives of ordinary Black people at the bottom of the pile have not improved.

(A. Sivanandan, 2000)

Unlike their parents, the second generation of Black youth did not see themselves as 'temporary guests' of Her Majesty's government. They were not here to work and eventually return 'home' to the Caribbean or Africa. Britain was their home, and according to one of the symbolic political slogans of the time, they were 'Here to Stay!' Consequently, they had little choice but to engage the class- and race-laden structures of British society.

(Owusu, 2000)

Contents

Editorial team

General editor

Alison Donnell
Nottingham Trent University, UK

Advisers

David A. Bailey
University of East London, UK

Satinder Chohan
Freelance writer, UK

William Henry
Goldsmiths College, UK

D. Keith Peacock
University of Hull, UK

James Procter
University of Stirling, UK

Karen Ross
Coventry School of Art and Design,
Coventry University, UK

Kadija Sesay
Editor/publisher of *Sable*, UK

Yinka Summonu
Goldsmiths College

Carol Tulloch
Royal College of Art, UK

Lynnette Turner
Oxford Brookes University, UK

Andy Wood
Dundee University, UK

List of contributors

Margaret T. Andrews
Teacher and educator, UK

An'Yaa Anim-Addo
James Allen's Girls' School, UK

Joan Anim-Addo
Goldsmiths College, UK

Rebecca Arnold
Central St Martins College of Art and Design, UK

Elaine Aston
Lancaster University, UK

David A. Bailey
University of East London, UK

Derek A. Bardowell
Freelance journalist, UK

Andrea D. Barnwell
Spelman College of Fine Arts, USA

Ian Baucom
Duke University, USA

Dipti Bhagat
Royal Holloway College, University of London, UK

Suman Bhuchar
Tamasha Theatre Company, UK

Christopher Breward
London College of Fashion, UK

Huw Bucknell
Freelance writer, UK

Eleanor Byrne
Manchester Metropolitan University, UK

Gavin Carver
University of Kent at Canterbury, UK

Janice Cheddie
Goldsmiths College, UK

Gail Ching-Liang Low
University of Dundee, UK

Satinder Chohan
Freelance writer, UK

Sandra Courtman
Staffordshire University, UK

Susan Croft
Theatre Museum, London, UK

Pauline de Souza
Universities of East London and Birmingham, UK

Alison Donnell
Nottingham Trent University, UK

Tobias Döring
Freie Universität Berlin, Germany

Oliver Double
University of Kent at Canterbury, UK

Andrea Enisuoh
Freelance journalist/literature consultant, UK

Raymond Enisuoh
Journalist, *New Nation* newspaper, UK

Diana Omo Evans
Freelance journalist, UK

Len Garrison
London, UK

Lynette Goddard
University of London, UK

Donna Griffiths
Freelance writer, UK

William Henry
Goldsmiths College, UK

Peter James
Birmingham Central Library, UK

Doreth Jones
London, UK

Kris Knauer
University of Silesia, Poland, and WriteOnLine, UK

David Knight
University of Central Lancashire, UK

Paola Marchionni
Commonwealth Institute and *Wasafiri*, UK

Pinkie Mekgwe
University of Sussex, UK

Shaheen Merali
University of Westminster and Central St Martins College of Art and Design, UK

Cynthia Moody
Keeper Ronald Moody Estate, UK

Susanne Mühleisen
Universität Frankfurt am Main, Germany

Nyantah
PR consultant, London, UK

Paul O'Kane
Goldsmiths College, UK

D. Keith Peacock
University of Hull, UK

Anita Naoko Pilgrim
Goldsmiths College, UK

Sandra Ponzanesi
University of Amsterdam, the Netherlands

Tracy J. Prince
Portland State University, USA

James Procter
University of Stirling, UK

Ruvani Ranasinha
Oxford University, UK

Niru Ratnam
The Open University, UK

Karen Ross
Coventry University, UK

Sara Salih
University of Kent at Canterbury, UK

Linda Sandino
Camberwell College of Arts, UK

Suzanne Scafe
South Bank University, UK

Asha Sen
University of Wisconsin–Eau Claire, USA

Kadija Sesay
Editor/publisher of *Sable*, UK

Alpana Sharma
Wright State University, USA

Jane Sillis
Freelance arts consultant, UK

Gareth Stanton
Goldsmiths College, UK

Mark Stein
Universität des Saarlandes, Germany

Francis Summers
Sleazenation magazine, UK

Rafiel Sunmonu
St Olaves, UK

Yinka Sunmonu
Goldsmiths College, London

Debbie Thacker
Cheltenham and Gloucester College of Higher Education, UK

Alex Tickell
University of York, UK

Carol Tulloch
Royal College of Art, UK

Lynnette Turner
Oxford Brookes University, UK

Catherine Ugwu
Freelance curator and producer

Leon Wainwright
SOAS, London University, UK

Sam Walker
Black Cultural Archives, UK

Tracey L. Walters
Stony Brook University, USA

Pawlet Warner
Cambridge Cultural Planning, UK

Patrick Williams
Nottingham Trent University, UK

Andy Wood
Dundee University, UK

Samina Zahir
Nottingham Trent University, UK

Introduction

In the second half of the twentieth century, notions of what constitute Britishness, blackness and culture have all been opened up and fiercely debated in a post-imperial nation that has experienced the collapse of Empire, large-scale immigration from its former colonies, the mass women's movement, black power and nationalist movements, institutionalised racism, Thatcherism and multiculturalism. This book charts black British cultural production from 1970 to 2001 and documents the creative and intellectual achievements of the second generation of black Britons.

The focus of this *Companion* on the contemporary period is in no way a denial of earlier black British cultural production but simply an indicator of the necessary limitations of the project as a single-volume publication. Indeed, the historical life of black people in Britain goes back at least four centuries and there is much to say about this history, as well as more to be researched. Perhaps, though, 1970 does offer a useful starting point as it marks a historical moment from which black as an identificatory category began to establish itself within Britain, reconstructing ideas of community and difference around a political signifier. As Kobena Mercer describes, 'When various peoples – of Asian, African and Caribbean descent – interpellated themselves and each other as /black/ they invoked a collective identity predicated on political and not biological similarities... alliance and solidarity among dispersed groups of people sharing common historical experiences of British racism' (1994: 291). For the purposes of this *Companion*, black signifies this collectivity and alliance under a political identity, and encompasses people of African, Caribbean and South Asian

descent. The debates about for whom and to whom black as an identity category should refer are well documented. Nevertheless, given the problematic nature of black British as a proposed cultural category (where does it begin and end?) and the fact that it is a cultural identity that is often expressed as ambivalent, conflicted and deeply felt, it seems important to offer some discussion of the issues and debates that have shaped its discursive and political currency.

Stuart Hall describes Britain in the 1970s as 'the land which they are *in* but not *of*, the country of estrangement, dispossession and brutality' (1978: 357) and the conscious orchestration of identity around blackness at this time was crucially concerned with the need to express resistance and protest against a white national British culture that appeared fairly definable and monolithic. The politicisation of black consciousness in the 1970s – when the media cocktail of race riots, mugging and carnival led to a powerful and damaging representation of black youth as criminalized and subcultural – was clearly a reaction and opposition to state racism and offered a vital, if limited, platform for self-representation. Nevertheless, the relationship between street politics and acts of representation was mutually beneficial to many of the cultural practitioners and products of this decade, and continued the intellectual traditions of black Britain that, like those in the Caribbean and other ex-colonial regions, have always been engaged with political and rights movements. There was very much the sense that artists, practitioners and cultural activists were providing intellectuals and theorists with what Stuart Hall has termed 'a new vocabulary and syntax of rebellion' (Hall 1978). Moreover, this cross-fertilisation between acts of political representation and those in the cultural sphere, the reciprocation between the street and the study, and the need to pursue questions of representation alongside those of rights was always an organic process, as many of the key figures from this period, such as C.L.R. James, Farrukh Dhondy, and John La Rose, had a firm footing in both spaces.

However, as well as a joining of forces across generational and cultural lines, there was also an important shift taking place across this decade in terms of an engagement with a specifically black British identity. Many of those who had been influential in setting the early agendas around black politics and consciousness in Britain, such as Kamau Brathwaite and other members of the Caribbean Artists Movement, had provided a valuable link between black communities and activities in the USA, the Caribbean and Britain, but many of their works and their inspirations had a focus beyond Britain, which was re-interpreted by the second generation in more urgently localised tones. In many areas of cultural production an articulation of specifically black British concerns was emerging in the late 1970s with writers Linton Kwesi Johnson, James Berry and Buchi Emecheta; film-makers Horace Ové and Menelik Shabazz; musicians Dennis Bovell and Jah Shaka; dance companies MAAS Movers and Company 7; the playwright Mustapha Matura and the theatre companies Tara Arts and Temba Theatre Company. The 1970s had delivered a far more visible and definable notion of black British culture by the decade's end, and it was very much a culture concerned with issues of race, representation, resistance, empowerment and justice.

The cultural and political projects of the 1970s had enabled a shift in terms of identification and representation, from being perceived as the black presence in Britain to the black dimension of Britain by the 1980s. Although the catalyst for mainstream public exposure in this decade was still police racism and the civil disturbances that followed (1981, 1985), there was a more consolidated profile of commentators from within the black community and an established and accomplished set of practitioners in film, visual arts, music, writing and performance works. The generation of artists David A. Bailey, Ingrid

Pollard, Rasheed Araeen; writers John Agard, Grace Nichols, Merle Collins, Benjamin Zephaniah; film directors John Akomfrah, Isaac Julien, Hanif Kureishi and Maureen Blackwood; organisations Ten.8, Black Audio Film Collective, Black Theatre Co-operative and Asian Women Writer's Workshop demonstrated the strength of their work and a determination to be received on their own terms.

However, if black British culture now had a more visible and coherent profile within the national culture, within itself fractures were beginning to be felt and, by the mid-1980s, there was also a more sustained questioning of the usefulness of black as an organising category. This came from the voices of an emergent black British cultural studies, in many ways initiated by the important work of Stuart Hall. The collective commitment to achieving cultural recognition, voice and visibility did not necessitate conformity or ideological consensus. The fact that there were tensions, conflicts and serious differences among key thinkers, practitioners and commentators was publicly highlighted by the now notorious exchange between Salman Rushdie, Stuart Hall and Darcus Howe, in January of 1987, over the representational strategies and aesthetic value of the film *Handsworth Songs*. Also, a number of interventions by women scholars such as Hazel Carby and Amrit Wilson drew attention to the need to account for gender politics, and work by Isaac Julien and Kobena Mercer highlighted the significance of sexuality in the constitution of cultural identities. Cultural production began to reflect the need to articulate the multiple imbrications of identity.

The need to acknowledge multiple perspectives and the pluralisation of cultural forms and positions within the arena of black British culture was an almost inevitable consequence of the growth of interest and work being done in this area. However, there was also the sense that this opening out was crucial in terms of the expectations and constraints under which black artists were working. In his important article, 'Black art and the burden of representation', Kobena Mercer outlined the problematic status of the black artist: 'burdened with the impossible task of speaking as "representatives", in that they are widely expected to "speak for" the marginalized communities from which they come' (1994: 235). In a sense, the success of the 1980s meant that black culture could now afford to entertain internal disputes and controversies without being under threat.

Indeed, despite inevitable tensions, in the 1990s there was a strong sense that these differences within the black community were both important and enabling to articulations of identity and creative works. Cultural and scholarly interests were less directed towards collective definition in the face of an unknowing or unwilling host culture than towards more complex and diverse acts of self-definition, and participation in reconfigurations of national culture. As Gilroy documents: 'Extraordinary new forms have been produced and much of their power resides in their capacity to circulate a new sense of what it means to be British' (1993: 61–2). Although less optimistic about the receptiveness of British society, Stuart Hall seems to echo Gilroy's perception of black British culture's recognition of its own value and cultural capital in his observation that: 'Black British culture is today confident beyond its own measure in its own identity – secure in a difference which it does not expect, or want, to go away, still rigorously and frequently excluded by the host society, but nevertheless not excluding itself in its own mind' (Hall 1997, in Owusu 2000: 127). However, it is in this same article, 'Frontlines and backyards: the terms of change', that Hall also argues that black no longer works as an identificatory category for African, Caribbean and Asian communities in Britain because of the 'internal cultural segmentation'. The proposition that cultural and ethnic differences have now become so pronounced as to make the idea of collective identity untenable is an issue that Kwesi Owusu raises in interview with the editor of *Race and Class*, and intellectual, A. Sivanandan. Sivanandan responds with the statement that 'recognizing cultural segmentation is not to accept it...my preoccupation is with racial justice and a political culture that can deliver racial justice...political culture tends to cut across such segmentation' (Owusu 2000: 423).

While the racially motivated murders of Stephen Lawrence and Michael Menson testify to the fact that racial justice remains an urgent political cause, many of the works, organisations, practitioners and artists included within this volume attest to the achievements and the continued realities of cutting across the segmentation. Black British culture and black British cultural studies have had a considerable impact on acknowledged conceptions of cultural and national identity over the last thirty years and hopefully they will continue to do so, as both the subject and the subject positions of national culture remain a site of struggle and contestation. To date, it has remained a usefully dynamic and self-reflexive field, which is constantly re-opening discussions on the difficult cultural issues around identity, representation and rights. As difference becomes both more marketable and more nuanced, the notion of black as an identificatory category will surely both demand and seek constant re-definition; nevertheless, while institutionalised racism persists, it would seem that for many in Britain black remains a politically resonant and historically significant sign of alliance.

Looking across the diverse and culturally plural composition of this *Companion*, it would appear reasonable to conclude that while difference has remained both an academic and a political focus for cultural workers, the conceptualisation of difference has moved on and there has been a reconstruction of positions on agency and authenticity. Not only is there a stronger sense of the recognition of difference within the communities that had elected to identify through the category 'black', but there is an acknowledgement that black may not be the necessary starting point for self-articulation – black may now be seen as one identity category alongside that of artist; or writer; or woman; or Muslim; or gay. It is still important to ask what it means to refer to Jackie Kay's poetry as black British rather than as Scottish or as lesbian, but it is perhaps less urgent to do so now that black culture is less restrained by the burden of representation and Kay's poetry is well known for its autobiographical power, its interrogation of Scottishness and its articulations of sexuality.

The scrutiny of whiteness and Englishness as dominant ethnicities, indeed as ethnicities at all, which has been occasioned by the cultural and ethnic diversity of contemporary Britain, as well as the devolution of Scotland and Wales, suggests a recognition of the way in which cultural identities are formed through complex patterns of difference and alliance, in the context of a nation in which definitions of nationality are now more mobile and multiple. From a point at the twentieth century's end, it is possible to see cross-cultural and inter-cultural interactions that are constantly challenging and refining our ideas of cultural identity. I am not just referring to the historically important borrowings and crossings of black cultural forms, such as music and fashion, by white youth groups, which can be traced back to the 1950s, but rather to newer forms of cross-cultural interaction. The recent study of white Englishness by Darcus Howe in his television series *White Tribes* (2000) suggests a horizontal expression of political engagement and human interest that in turns helps to re-write possibilities for cross-cultural representations. Donald MacLellan's photographic exhibition 'Black Power', which showed at the National Gallery in 1998, also offers new ethical models of representation by returning to the relationship of white photographer/black subject with an awareness of its historical dimensions and a strategy of empowerment, allowing subjects to enunciate their own subject positions through statements that appear alongside the photographic representations. The phenomenal success of the Asian comedy series *Goodness Gracious Me*, which satirises both South Asian and white British cultural traits alongside each other, speaks of a certain confidence to address the issues of cultural sensitivities and idiosyncrasies across, as well as within, cultural and ethnic communities.

It is the very nature of working in the contemporary period that we do not know how history will record our age but it seems significant to make representations that work against conventional historical biases and it is in this spirit that the *Companion* makes a gesture towards recording the immense and yet often unrecognised talent and significance of contemporary black British culture. The *Companion* is designed to be one starting point within the project to fully describe and annotate the field of post-1970 black British cultural production. It covers seven major overlapping areas: writings; performance works; visual and plastic arts; intellectual life; television; film and cinema; and music. However, entries as diverse as 'hairdressing' and 'new racism' point to the fact that cultural forms need to be recognised as having a social and political context that has both shaped

them and which they in turn shape. While restrictions on space have meant that categories such as politics and sport have not been able to be included, the aim has been to open up each chosen field beyond the familiar names and known achievers. The entries are listed in alphabetical order for ease and simplicity, and cross-references are made by following those terms marked in bold type. Those wishing to search a particular specialist area can consult the subject listings at the front of the book, but it is my aim that this book might encourage browsing, and exploratory reading as unfamiliar names, organisations and works appear.

The overview entries for each of the main areas are designed to suggest the broad contours and wider pictures of each field, as well as to gesture towards those names and works that could not be represented by individual entries in this first volume. Indeed, in some cases, our list of potential entries was so extensive, for example that from David A. Bailey of over 300 artists, that selection seemed impossible to reconcile with representation. Of course, these issues are always at the forefront of edited collections of any sort but with reference to black British culture, which has suffered from both blatant and subtle forms of neglect and marginalisation, the arguments concerning the issues and burdens of representation seemed both urgent to address and impossible to fulfil.

As I have sought to outline, contemporary black British culture is both complex and unstable, and it is the objective of this *Companion* as a whole to trace some of those complexities and instabilities rather than to offer any kind of resolution or settlement. The *Companion* is in no way designed to be definitive or authoritative; rather, contributors have been encouraged to offer individual perspectives and confront contentious issues. This approach seemed particularly important given the dearth of publications in the field and the particular nature of the historical engagement of reference works with black culture that has shaped this work as a *Companion*, rather than the more imperial and definitive form of an encyclopaedia. Indeed, it is designed to be read as a consciously provisional and frustratingly partial beginning.

This *Companion* began life several years ago, as an endnote on a book report that I wrote for a volume on post-colonial cultures. I made the comment that, once again, black British culture had not been recognised or attended to under this designation and that there was very little in the way of reference books to document the black British dimension. When this observation was taken up by Routledge in the form of a contract to edit a multi-disciplinary reference work on contemporary black British culture, I was given the opportunity to set this record a little straighter, at least. I realised then that editing any reference work would be a challenge simply because of the issues around scope, coverage and accessibility, and I was aware that I would have few previous volumes to refer to, review or raid. However, I was not aware of how difficult it would be to resource and harness all of the available information, or of how little information had previously been collated and recorded in certain subject areas. The struggle to compile a balanced and broad selection has been significant and the project has been a total education in terms of how archives, organisations, academies and just plain old folk work. Although I am aware that much more work needs to be done in this field, perhaps this *Companion* will inspire others by its inclusions as well as its omissions.

The issue of selection and representation has been taken very seriously by the whole advisory team. In the end, word limits and deadlines have been the final deciders, and I am aware that, as I hand this work over for publication, its blind spots are far more glaring than any of its visions. Although the tendency is always for reference works to appear somehow definitive or descriptive of a field, I would want to finish this piece of introductory writing by working in the opposite direction and making a serious invitation to scholars, researchers, academics, students, practitioners and other interested parties to help take this project forward by making contact with any works, individuals and organisations that are not currently listed and which merit inclusion. If this book is designed to be a starting-point and a place of signposts that others may follow and elaborate on, then I hope that some of them may point back here.

References

Gilroy, P. (1993) *Small Acts: Thoughts on the Politics of Black Cultures*, London: Serpent's Tail.

Hall, S. (1997) 'Frontlines and backyards: the terms of change', in Kwesi Owusu *Black British Culture and Society: a Text Reader*, pp. 127–30.

Hall, S., Critcher, C., Jefferson, T., Clarke, J. and Roberts, B. (1978) *Policing the Crisis – Mugging, the State, and Law and Order*, London: Macmillan.

Mercer, K. (1994) *Welcome to the Jungle: New Positions in Black Cultural Studies*, London: Routledge.

Owusu, K. (2000) *Black British Culture and Society: a Text Reader*, London: Routledge.

Acknowledgements

I would like to thank all those who were involved with this project; it has been a long and difficult, but rewarding, experience. I am extremely grateful to my final team of over seventy contributors, especially to Yinka, David, Lynnette and James, who were there until the almost bitter end. All of my advisers deserve special thanks for their endurance, guidance and brilliance in their fields. Stephanie Rogers, my editor at Routledge, merits the highest praise for making the *Companion* seem an achievable and real publication after all. As ever, my love and thanks go to my mother and my extended family, and to my friends, particularly Caroline and Dracaena. Most especially and most deservedly I am thankful to Jeremy for all things great and small, and to Max and little Asher for being such compelling and lovable distractions.

Alison Donnell
Nottingham Trent University

Thematic entry list

Fashion and design

Asian fashion
Bakare, Ade
Boateng, Ozwald
Bradford art galleries and museums
Campbell, Naomi
Casely-Hayford, Joe
Chic
Edge, Nina
fashion and design
funky dreds
hairdressing
Joe Bloggs
Jones, Adebayo
Lilliard, Derek Alvin
lovers' rock style
Natt, Sarbjit
Nehru Gallery
Oldfield, Bruce
raggamuffin
Rana, Mah
Rastafari
Shah, Fahmida
Wek, Alek

Film and cinema

Adefarasin, Remi
Akomfrah, John
Amin, Ruhul
Andrews, Naveen
Attille, Martina
Auguiste, Reece
Babymother
Bhaji on the Beach
Bhattacharjee, Paul

Black Audio Film Collective
Black Film Bulletin
Blackwood, Maureen
Bollywood
British Film Institute
Burning an Illusion
Campbell, Topher
Chadha, Gurinder
cinemas
Dehlavi, Jamil
East is East
Electric Cinema
film and cinema
Givanni, June Ingrid
Grewal, Shani
Handsworth Songs
Henriques, Julian
Hussein, Waris
Jaffrey, Madhur
Jaffrey, Saeed
Jamal, Ahmed
Jamal, Mahmood
Jean-Baptiste, Marianne
Julien, Issac
Kapur, Shekhar
Khan, Shaheen
Kureishi, Hanif
Laird, Trevor
Lester, Adrian
Looking for Langston
McQueen, Steve
Marsh-Edwards, Nadine
My Beautiful Laundrette
My Son the Fanatic
Newton, Thandie
Nubian Tales/b3 Media
Onwurah, Ngozi

Joi
Jones, Fae
jungle
Kaliphz
Knight, Beverly
Lewis, Shaznay
Loose Ends
lovers' rock
LTJ Bukem
Macka 'B'
Mad Professor
Massive Attack
Mau/Earthling/Cuba
Mel B
Mercury, Freddie
Mishra, Jyoti
Misty in Roots
music
Mwelwa, Hilary
Nation Records
Nelson, Shara
Nelson, Trevor
Ocean, Billy
Oriental Star Agencies
Outcaste
Paris, Mica
Parvez
Pine, Courtney
post-bhangra
Priest, Maxi
Quaye, Finley
Rebel MC
reggae
Reneau, Francis
Richards, Derek
Sade
Sagoo, Bally
Sawhney, Nitin
Seal
Shri
Siffre, Labi
Singh, Talvin
Singh, Tjinder
Size, Roni/Reprazent
ska
Small, Heather
Smiley Culture
soul
Soul II Soul

sound system DJs
Sutherland, Luke
Tippa Irie
Transglobal Underground
Tricky
Trojan Records
Wee Papa Girl Rappers
White Town
WOMAD

Organisations

African Cultural Exchange
Afro-Caribbean Education Resource Project
arts funding bodies
Asian Women Writers' Collective
Autograph: the Association of Black Photographers
Black Arts Alliance
Brixton Black Women's Group
Camden Black Sisters
Caribbean Artists' Movement
Caribbean Women Writers' Alliance
Centerprise Women's Café
Commission for Racial Equality
Drum, the
Greater London Authority
Greater London Council
Institute of Contemporary Arts
Institute of International Visual Arts
Live Art Development Agency
Minority Arts Advisory Service
Mosaic
New Playwrights Trust
Newham Asian Women's Project
Nia Centre for African and Caribbean Culture
Organisation of Women of Asian and African Descent
Panchayat
Radical Alliance of Poets and Players
Rock against Racism
Southall Black Sisters
Ten.8
Working Group against Racism in Children's Resources

Others

Black British Englishes
Lawrence, Stephen

Television and broadcasting

Visual and plastic arts

List of websites

The 1990 Trust
www.blink.org.uk
UK site for ethnic-minority issues

Africa Centre
www.africacentre.org.uk

Apples and Snakes
www.applesandsnakes.org
Premier poetry organisation

Aviva – women's world-wide web
www.aviva.org
The international women's listings magazine

Black About
www.blackabout.com

Black Art Alliance
www.baas.demon.co.uk

Black Books and Stuff
communities.msn.co.uk/BlackBooksStuff
For people of African heritage who are interested
in personal and spiritual development

Black Britain
www.blackbritain.co.uk
Wide scope of information on black Britain

Black Filmmaker
www.blackfilmmakermag.com

Blacknet
www.blacknet.co.uk
Entertainment and news

Blackpresence
www.blackpresence.co.uk

BLU Magazine
www.blumagazine.net
Edutainment

Darker than Blue
www.darkerthanblue.com
Home of black music

Ethnic Media Group
www.ethnicmedia.co.uk

Griot World
www.griotworld.demon.co.uk
UK's site for African World Culture

IC3
www.penguin.co.uk

Man Mela Theatre Company
www.man-mela.dircon.co.uk

Moti Roti
www.motiroti.com

Nubian Tales
www.2359.com
Black British arts, culture and entertainment
listings and magazine

Paublo Books
www.multiculturalbooks.co.uk

Precious Online
www.preciousonline.co.uk
Online magazine for black women

Saltpetre
www.saltpetre.com
Poetry

Stephen Lawrence Charitable Trust
www.stephenlawrence.org.uk

The Voice
www.voice-online.co.uk

WriteOnLine
www.write-on-line.co.uk
Publisher of electronic books

198 Gallery

Founded in 1988 by Zoe Linsley-Thomas, the 198 Gallery is named after its location at Railton Road in Brixton. The gallery's initial policy was to promote the work of contemporary Asian, Afro-Caribbean and African artists whose expressions represent the cultural diversity of British society. The policy has since changed to include artists from outside Britain. Bisi de Silvia was the gallery's first black curator in 1991, followed by Julian Barnes. Between 1993 and 1995, Linsley-Thomas ran the exhibition programme and then invited artists Godfried **Donkor**, Maria Amdu and Faisal **Abdu'Allah** to form an exhibition committee. In 1989 the gallery's first commission 'The First Child' project was awarded to the Nigerian artist David Matusa. However, due to various problems the project continued for ten years, finally being completed in 1999 by Raymond Watson.

In 1995, as part of the AFRICA 95 festival, the gallery held 'Winds of Change', a series of three exhibitions by African artists working in Europe. In the following year the exhibition 'Revelations' showed the dramatic work of Faisal Abdu'Allah and Kofi. The gallery's self-sufficiency remains evident in its Exhibition Support Fund, which has been running since 1990. The gallery's Contemporary Art Sale, organised by Linsley-Thomas, at Letherby Gallery in the Central School of Art was the first commercial enterprise for the support fund.

Further reading

Howard, P. and Linsley-Thomas, Z. (eds) (1997) *198 Gallery Review*, London: 198 Gallery.

Porter, C. (1989) 'Black artists in new guise' *South London Press*, 12 May.

PAULINE DE SOUZA

2nd Generation

'Second generation' is a term that has increasingly been applied to the children of migrants, and the magazine *2nd Generation* draws heavily upon this theme. *2nd Generation* was launched in 1997 by editor-in-chief Imran Khan and editor Rahul D. Singh. In 1998, after just one year in print, *2nd Generation* was given the Youth in Media award by the **Commission for Racial Equality**, specifically for its efforts to promote a multicultural UK. Khan has commented that part of the problem in editing a magazine such as *2nd Generation* is defining what or who the term actually applies to. The difficulty lies in categorising groups as belonging to specific cultures or cultural forms, when, in fact, there are no acknowledged parameters. *2nd Generation* therefore draws on the youth and club scene culture, with some issues-based articles, although these are more lifestyle than politically led. The magazine also concentrates on 'multicultural' elements that reflect a sense of the fusions which are taking place. In *2nd Generation*, Khan stresses British relevance, with articles discussing the group Kula Shaker and Madonna's use of *mehndi*, as well as those people deemed 'second generation', such as **Cornershop**, **Asian Dub Foundation** and Morcheeba.

SAMINA ZAHIR

A

A Guy Called Gerald

b. 1967, Manchester, UK

artist, producer, remixer, DJ

Gerald Simpson has been an innovative figure at the forefront of the UK dance scene since the late 1980s. He first came to prominence as a founder member of 808 State, but it is as a solo artist recording as A Guy Called Gerald that he has made his best-known work. From *Voodoo Ray* in 1988, which made the transition from underground club hit to number twelve in the charts, to the ground-breaking album *Back Secret Technology* in 1995, which featured contributions from **Goldie**, 4 Hero and Finley **Quaye**, Simpson has always managed to keep at least one step ahead of his peers in the innovative field of dance music. Moving from the Chicago and Detroit house-influenced sounds of his early albums, *Hot Lemonade* (1988) and *Automanik* (1990), to the hard edged jungle of *28 Gun Bad Boy* (1993) and the more reflective experimentation of *Black Secret Technology* (1995) has meant that Simpson has yet to repeat the commercial success of his first solo release. *Essence* was released in 2000 and Simpson runs his own label, Juicebox, and is also a stalwart of Radio 1's *One In The Jungle* show.

ANDY WOOD

Abani, Chris

b. 1966, Afikpo (now Ebonyi State),
    Nigeria

writer, poet, saxophonist

In Nigeria in 1985, Chris Abani was arrested and imprisoned after his first published novel *Masters Of The Board* was considered to be a blueprint of the failed political *coup* involving General Vasta. Abani also published the critically acclaimed novel *Sirocco* (1987) in Nigeria. After settling in Britain and dividing his time between London and the USA, Abani eventually became a creative writing teacher in Hackney. He is regarded as one of the most talented and understated writers of the black British arts scene and has also taken an active role in London's Black Literature Development Project. Abani has contributed to the acclaimed black writing anthologies *Burning Words, Flaming Images* and *The Fire People*, and was a section editor of the black arts community journal **Calabash**. In 2000, Abani published his acclaimed political poetry collection *The Kalkuta Republic*, inspired by the torture he underwent during his time as a political prisoner, and by the legendary Nigerian musician Fela Kuti. Abani is also an accomplished saxophonist.

Select bibliography

Abani, C. (2000) *The Kalkuta Republic*, London: Saqui Books.

Further reading

Lemn, S. (ed.) (1998) *The Fire People*, Edinburgh: Payback Press.

Newland, C. and Sesay, K. (eds) (2000) *IC3: the Penguin Book of New Black Writing in Britain*, London: Penguin.

Sesay, K. (ed.) (1998) *Burning Words, Flaming Images*, London: SAKS Publications.

RAYMOND ENISUOH

AbbaKush

Formed in 1981, AbbaKush was the first mainly female **reggae** band in the UK. The quintet was formed by 1983 and they began their musical career by supporting **Misty in Roots**. Their music reflects their strong commitment to **Rasta-fari** ideals of love, peace and unity, and their work draws strongly on Jamaican reggae rhythms but also incorporates other African diasporic forms such as jazz and soca. Among their best-known tracks are 'Batta Dem' and 'Strong, Cultural and Black'. They have performed at reggae festivals internationally and, in March 2000, joined with Akabu, Thriller Jenna, Aisha and Jayzik to form 'Sista', a female reggae collective, to celebrate International Women's Day.

ALISON DONNELL

Abdu'Allah, Faisal

b. 1969, England

visual artist

Educated at the Royal College of Art, Abdu'Allah converted to Islam in 1991, an event that has greatly affected his artistic output. His conversion attests to the growing relevance of Islam to the black British community, and reflects the variety of concerns for young black British artists. Abdu'Allah has explored the links between religion and contemporary urban experience in works such as *The Last Supper*, in which eleven black men and women sit in Islamic costume around a table, while the figure corresponding to Judas stands with a gun

behind his back, which is only visible to the viewer. Other works feature portraits of young black men, such as *Silent Witnesses*. The accompanying sound-track of rap, prayer and interviews suggests the confluence of discourses surrounding the contemporary black subject. Abdu'Allah's use of light-boxes can be read as referring to Islam (Allah as 'the light that shines within us') or purely formally, heightening the isolation and unworldliness of his subjects. Everyday urban violence is another theme that preoccupies Abdu'Allah, who explores this through images of morgues and guns.

Further reading

Glasgow Gallery of Modern Art (1997) *Out of the Blue*, exhibition catalogue.

NIRU RATNAM

Adebayo, Diran

b. 1968, London, England

novelist, journalist

Of Nigerian descent, Adebayo was born in North London. He read law at Oxford and has since worked as a journalist for both newspapers (he regularly contributes to the *Nation*) and television (BBC and LNT). He is best known as a writer, and his first novel, *Some Kind of Black*, won the **Saga Prize**. He has since adapted the book for radio. The book was regarded as a 'major step in black British literature' (Sesay), especially in its use of language and characterisation. The protagonist, Dele, rebounds between London and university, as well as between different accents and social roles, while he self-consciously dons personalities that range as wide as his stylish garb. This navigation across a continuum of black British identities reveals an irreverence for ethnic or cultural purity. However, his sister's particular vulnerability (she suffers from sickle cell anaemia) shows Dele the tangible limits of this ideal when a brutal police arrest sends the young black woman into a coma. Coming to terms with being black in an often hostile and predominantly white society – an important thematic concern of black British literature – Dele has to juggle racism and counter-racism, the demands of peers and parents, and of groupings that opportunistically seek to co-opt his sister as a *cause célèbre*. A second novel, *My Once upon a Time*, was published in 2000.

Select bibliography

Adebayo, D. (2000) *My Once upon a Time*, London: Abacus.

—— (1996) *Some Kind of Black*, London: Virago.

MARK STEIN

Adebayo, Dotun

b. 1959, Nigeria

publisher, journalist

Adebayo moved from his home in Lagos, Nigeria to London at the age of six to join his parents. He developed a thirst for reading as a young child and was guided by his father, an academic, to the works of the Black Panthers and contemporary US fiction. He studied at Stockholm and Essex Universities, but also worked as a music journalist, later taking a job with the *Voice* newspaper. It was while at the *Voice* that he first worked with Steve Pope, then editor of the newspaper, with whom he later established **X Press**, a black British publishing house specialising in popular fiction and reprints of classic black texts. His brother Diran **Adebayo** is a novelist.

ALISON DONNELL

Adefarasin, Remi

b. England

cinematographer

Adefarasin excels in a profession that is hardly mentioned by cultural thinkers in black arts – cinematography. He developed an interest in photography through his English grandfather (his father is Nigerian) and went on to study film and photography at Harrow Technical College. He won a place on the renowned BBC Camera Training Scheme and now works in film and television producing mini-series and television films. He has the respect of his peers and works in Hollywood. In 1998, he won an Oscar for Best Cinematographer for the multi-award-winning film *Elizabeth*. Other accolades for the same film included an American Society of Cinematographers Award and a Fennecus award for Cinematography composition and lighting. Other credits are for *The House of Mirth* (2000), with *X Files* star Gillian Anderson, *Sliding Doors* (1998), starring Oscar-winning actress Gwyneth Paltrow, and the acclaimed film *Truly, Madly, Deeply* (1991), with Juliet Stevenson and Alan Rickman. Among his **television** credits is his work for BBC 2 *Playhouse* and *Grown Ups*, which starred Oscar-nominated actress Brenda Blethyn (who co-starred with Marianne **Jean-Baptiste** in *Secrets and Lies*). In 2001, he worked on *Unconditional Love*.

YINKA SUNMONU

Adrus, Said

b. 1958, Kampala, Uganda

visual artist

Adrus, born in Kampala of Indian descent, trained in English art schools, graduating from Trent Polytechnic in 1983. His early work echoes the brash, often racist, urban graffiti he witnessed in the North of England and involves layered imagery, words, bright colours and aerosols while sharing characteristics with 1980s neo-expressionists like Basquiat or Guston. After graduating, he visited family in Switzerland where he learned more about the plight of immigrant workers and their experience of racism and inequality. He then travelled to India where Gujurati imagery and cinema posters enhanced his already bright palette. Adrus's complex cultural make-up, spanning India, Uganda, Britain and Switzerland, influenced him to pursue threads of 'colour'-as-identity woven through official national distinctions. Later works embraced an equally vivid potential of computer imagery and, at Bracknell Gallery in 1995, Adrus used video and sound to produce a 'challenging environment'. Adrus thinks of the world as a collage of imports, exports and migrations and cites Warhol and Rauschenberg as influences. His exhibitions include: 'Creativity, Knowledge and Faith' (1987), 'History and Identity – Seven Painters' (1991) and 'Transition of Riches' (1993), which toured Birmingham, Southampton and Stirling.

PAUL O'KANE

African and Asian Visual Arts Archive

The African and Asian Visual Arts Archive (AAVAA) is an arts organisation founded in 1989 by Eddie **Chambers** and originally based in Bristol. In 1995, the archive was re-housed at the University of East London. It is now co-ordinated by David A. **Bailey** and Sonia **Boyce**. AAVAA is designed to be a 'living' archive, in that it aims to foster links between its clients – both the artists who contribute and those who visit it. The archive contains over 6,000 slides of artwork by black British artists and detailed information on over 200 individual artists. It also holds relevant books and exhibition catalogues, and information about other British arts organisations, art historians, cultural critics and curators, especially those involved in post-colonial debates. As an archive, AAVAA is a key source of information on the history of black British **visual artists**, as well as contemporary developments. It is a key resource for students, curators and writers, among others, with information on 1980s exhibitions that is hard to find elsewhere. In addition, under the banner 'AAVAA Creative Forum', it aims to help shape contemporary debates around post-colonial issues through artists' commissions and round-table discussions.

NIRU RATNAM

African Cultural Exchange

African Cultural Exchange (ACE) was founded in Birmingham in October 1996. The company members, formerly of Kokuma Dance Theatre, have included Joanne Bernard (dancer), Gail Claxton-Parmel (dancer), Ian Parmel (musician), Stuart Thomas (dancer) and Skibu (musician). A major facet of the company's work involves educational and outreach work in, for example, schools and community venues. ACE stresses the need to enable African and Caribbean musicians and dancers to access arts provision, stimulating and encouraging long-term development and recognition of such performance arts forms.

Their key aims are to highlight African and Caribbean dance and music, exploring old and new performance-based art forms while developing them within the context of the contemporary black British experience. ACE consider themselves to be developing a black dance technique for the future, influenced by the traditions of the past. In 1997, the company devised *The Path*, a performance piece that toured nationally. *The Path* contained four elements, fear, hope, laughter and change, and was supported by RJC Dance Company. In 1998 ACE worked on a number of pieces, including *Loss* and *Vibe*.

SAMINA ZAHIR

AFRICAN PEOPLE'S HISTORICAL MONUMENT FOUNDATION *see* Black Cultural Archives

Afrobeat

Afrobeat (1999), edited by Patsy Antoine, is an anthology of black British writing. In the 1990s, such anthologies started to be produced because of a growing interest in black British writing and **literature**. This collection features contributions from new writers and from **Saga Prize** winners Joanna **Traynor** and Judith Bryan, as well as works by Kadija **Sesay**, Yinka **Sunmonu** and others. The stories cover topics such as HIV, racism, confession-style **television** shows, obsession and **new racism**. Although it is generally noted that more women take up fiction writing than men, it is still surprising to note that twelve of the fifteen contributors are women. *Afrobeat* and *IC3: the Penguin Book of New Black Writing* both showcase new and established writers, some of whom may well make their mark on the UK's literary establishment.

RAFIEL SUNMONU

Afro-Caribbean Education Resource Project

The Afro-Caribbean Education Resource Project (ACER) was established in 1978 by Len Garrison in order to produce learning materials that challenged the Eurocentric approach common in British schools in the 1970s and 1980s. This was the same education system that ignored the positive features and attributes of black children's ethnic and cultural heritage, and which diverted African-Caribbean children from mainstream schools into Education-ally Sub-Normal schools in alarming proportions (Coard 1971). ACER provided materials that treated black children as valued equals in the culture of the school curriculum and which became the cornerstone of ILEA's Multi-Cultural Policy in the late 1970s and 1980s. The project team devised, piloted and developed learning materials for children aged three to seven at primary level (ACER *Myself*, 1978) and the seven to twelve age range (ACER *Ourselves*, 1981) for the multi-cultural as well as the all-white classroom. The learning materials reinforced ILEA's objective: 'to ensure that, with a society that is cohesive not uniform, cultures are respected, differences are recognised and indivi-duals' identities are secure' (Malik 1996: 149). ACER staff ran special courses for teachers in centres and schools across London, as well as presentations to conference workshops and tea-chers' centres in other parts of the country.

An equally important part of ACER's work was its research library and its information service. ACER's library holding runs to over 10,000 books, journals and papers on African, African-Carib-bean, multi-cultural and anti-racist reference materials, which provides a unique resource base in the community. ACER's work has also been influential in Europe and the Anne Frank Founda-tion (Schellekens 1995) incorporated the spirit of ACER's learning materials in a comprehensive Inter-Cultural Education scheme for children in the Netherlands. These packs are being published in Dutch and will be translated into German and Danish for use in those countries.

References

ACER (1981) *Ourselves*, London: ACER.
—— (1978) *Myself*, London: ACER.
Coard, B. (1971) *How the West Indian Child is Made Educationally Sub-Normal in the British School System*, London: New Beacon Books.
Malik, K. (1996) *The Meaning of Race*, London: Macmillan.
Schellekens, E. (1995) *This Is Me*, Amsterdam: Anne Frank House.

LEN GARRISON

Agard, John

b. 1949, Guyana

poet, editor

Agard wrote poetry from the age of sixteen but began his career teaching English, French and Latin, and later working in a library. While in Guyana he joined the performance troupe 'All ah We'. In 1977, he came to the UK, where he has lived since. Although Agard has published nearly a dozen volumes of poetry, and his writing is widely anthologised, performance is still crucial to his work. His poetry has covered an enormous range of subjects and is direct, complex, humor-ous and moving – sometimes all at once, as in 'Half Caste', one of his best-known verses. In 1982, he won the Casa de las Americas prize for his collection *Man to Pan* and he was shortlisted for the Smarties Prize in 1987 for his children's collection *Lend Me Your Wings*. Some of his works focus directly on the Caribbean, such as *The Calypso Alphabet* (1989), *No Hickory, no Dickory, no Dock* (1995) and *A Caribbean Dozen* (1994), the last two which he edited with his wife Grace **Nichols**. After a residency with London's South Bank Centre, Agard was engaged as the BBC's first poet-in-residence and he played a key role in their **Windrush** season.

Select bibliography

Agard, J. (1990) *Lovelines for a Goat-born Lady*, London: Serpent's Tail.
—— (1989) *The Calypso Alphabet*, London: William Collins Sons and Co.
—— (1985) *Mangoes and Bullets: Selected and New Poems 1972–1984*, London: Pluto Press.
Agard, J. and Nichols, G. (1991) *No Hickory, no Dickory, no Dock: Caribbean Nursery Rhymes*, London: Penguin Viking.

ALISON DONNELL

Agbabi, Patience

b. 1965, London, England

poet, performer, workshop facilitator

Patience Agbabi is British-born Nigerian, her family are from the Ijaw community; she also remains close to her white foster family. She read English language and literature at Pembroke College, Oxford. Agbabi is one of the foremost artists on the performance scene. She has toured nationally and abroad, has appeared on radio and television, and has been published in fifteen anthologies. Her first collection, *R.A.W.*, was published by Gecko Press in 1995 and reprinted in 1997. Agbabi has worked extensively with young people in schools and youth clubs. She has performed at venues ranging from Ronnie Scott's to the Royal Albert Hall, and at the Glastonbury Festival, Edinburgh Book Festival and Europride. In 1994, she toured South Africa. Together with Adeola Agbebiyi and Dorothea **Smartt**, she performed *Fo(u)r Women* at the **Institute of Contemporary Arts** in 1996. She appeared on BBC 2's Def II in 1992 and **Channel 4**'s LITPOP in 1998. In 1997, she won the Excelle Literary Award. Her second collection *Transformatrix* was published by Payback Press in Autumn 1999. From August 1999 to April 2000 she was in-house poet in Flamin' Eight, funded by the Poetry Society's Poetry Places scheme. In 2001 she took up a joint residency with the School of Healthcare and the School of Humanities at Oxford Brookes University.

Select bibliography

Agbabi, P. (2000) *Transformatrix*, Edinburgh: Payback Press.
—— (1995) *R.A.W.*, London: Gecko Press.

Select discography

Agbabi, P. (1994) *One Hell of a Storm*, Tongue and Groove Records.

ANITA NAOKO PILGRIM

Agbenugba, Gbenga

b. 1966, London, England

novelist, journalist, editor

The experience of his return to London from Nigeria and reading Sam **Selvon**'s *The Lonely Londoners* inspired Agbenugba's first novel, *Another Lonely Londoner* (1991). He was the first young Nigerian-British author to reflect a West African viewpoint, writing about the experience of living within the Nigerian youth circuit in London, writing in a mixture of English and Nigerian pidgin. Agbenugba came to England to study scriptwriting for screen and stage, and this is his central interest. He was editor of the Nigerian lifestyle magazine *Ovation* (1996–7), and in 1999 became the editor of the Nigerian lifestyle magazine *Omega*. He is the Media Consultant to African Independent Television. Agbenugba wrote his second novel, *Many Rivers to Cross* (1997), under his own name, Ola Opesan.

Select bibliography

Agbenugba, G. (1991) *Another Lonely Londoner*, London: Ronu Books.
Opesan, O. (2000) 'The proliferation of African businesses in the UK: will Africans be the new Asians of UK business', in C. Newland and K. Sesay (eds) *IC3: the Penguin Book of New Black Writing in Britain*, London: Penguin, pp. 197–206.
—— (1997) *Many Rivers to Cross*, London: X Press.

KADIJA SESAY

Ahmad, Aijaz

academic

Aijaz Ahmad is a cultural theorist and Professorial Fellow at the Centre of Contemporary Studies, Nehru Memorial Museum and Library, New Delhi. His polemic and erudite work *In Theory: Classes, Nation, Literatures* provides a Marxist re-reading of a range of iconic authors and positions in literary theory, engaging with issues of empire, post-colonialism and migrancy. *In Theory* created much debate and discussion in the field of post-colonial theory, largely through its critique of arguments such as Fredric Jameson's in 'Third World literature in the era of multinational capitalism': that all Third World literary texts are national allegories and that the individual story cannot be anything except the telling of the collectivity. Ahmad challenges the ideologies behind the break-up of the globe into First, Second and Third Worlds. He argues that, while the division between the 'First' and 'Second' Worlds is defined in terms of production systems (capitalism or socialism), the definition of the 'Third World' only refers to externally inflicted phenomena such as colonialism and imperialism. Thus the 'Third World' is defined not by relations of production but rather by internal domination. Ahmad is particularly outspoken on the theoretical and political incompatibility between Marxist and post-colonial positions, and bemoans the fact that very few critics have continued with an exclusively Marxist interrogation of empire. He argues that most have turned towards post-structuralism, which he believes grossly overlooks capitalist modernity. He particularly challenges established post-colonial critics such as Edward Said, Salman **Rushdie** and Homi **Bhabha**, whom he regards as profiting from high-profile careers in Western academia while pretending to speak for extant colonial peoples. Ahmad's 2000 publication *Lineages of the Present* traces the complex histories of right-wing nationalist movements currently gaining prominence in many regions across the globe.

Select bibliography

Ahmad, A. (2000) *Lineages of the Present*, London: Verso.
—— (1992) *In Theory: Classes, Nation, Literatures*, London: Verso.

SANDRA PONZANESI

Ahmad, Rukhsana

b. 1948, Karachi, Pakistan

writer, translator, artistic director

Rukhsana Ahmad taught English at Karachi University and came to England after her marriage in 1973. She has four Masters degrees and finds it stimulating to learn something new. Ahmad is motivated by a feminist activism. She was a founder member of the **Asian Women Writers' Collective**, and began the Kali Theatre Company, which she co-founded with Rita **Wolf** in 1990, to draw more Asian women to the theatre. She wrote Kali's first play, *Song for a Sanctuary*, which was nominated for the Susan Blackburn Smith Award. Ahmad also writes for radio and the radio version of *Song for a Sanctuary* was shortlisted for the **Commission for Racial Equality** Race in the Media Award in 1993. Her adaptation of Jean Rhys's *Wide Sargasso Sea* was runner-up for both the Writer's Guild Award for 'best radio dramatisation' and the CRE Race in the Media Award in 1994. She also worked on the World Service drama series *Westway*. Ahmad edited and translated a popular and important collection of feminist Urdu poetry, entitled *We Sinful Women*. Her play *River on Fire* was toured by Kali in 2000/2001.

Select bibliography

Ahmad, R. (1996) *The Hope Chest*, London: Virago.
—— (ed.) (1991) *We Sinful Women*, London: the Women's Press.
Ahmad, R. and Gupta, R. (eds) (1994) *Flaming Spirit: Stories from the Asian Women Writers' Collective*, London: Virago.

SUMAN BHUCHAR

AHMED, SHAMI *see* Joe Bloggs

Ajamu

b. 1963, Huddersfield, England

fine-art photographer

A self-taught photographer, Ajamu has been a practising artist since 1990. His work has been exhibited in London, New York, Frankfurt, São Paulo, Amsterdam and Paris. His first solo exhibition was at Centerprise Community Centre in London in 1991. In 1994, Camerawork, London, showcased his work in the exhibition 'Black Bodyscapes'. Among other group exhibitions, he has taken part in the first 'Open Gay Pride Show' (London, 1991), Arles Photographic Festival (1993), 'Kissing the Dust: Artists' Working Collections' (Huddersfield, Oldham and Oxford, 1997) and 'Africa by Itself' at the Musée Européene de la Photographie (Paris, 1998). His work is featured in several books, including Sue Golding's *The Eight Technologies of Otherness* (1997, London: Routledge), Emmanuel Cooper's *Fully Exposed: Male Nude in Photography* (1995, London: Routledge), Kobena Mercer's *The Camera as Kinky Machine* (catalogue for 'Black Bodyscapes' exhibition) and Lloyd Vega's *In Our Own Image: the Art of Black Male Photography* (1993, Vega Press). In 1995, Ajamu was the subject of Topher Campbell's film *The Homecoming: a Short Film about Ajamu*.

Further reading

Bright, D. (1998) *The Passionate Camera*, London: Routledge.

ANITA NAOKO PILGRIM

Akomfrah, John

b. 1957

film-maker

John Akomfrah is best known for the films he has directed as part of the **Black Audio Film Collective**: ***Handsworth Songs*** (1987), *Testament* (1988), *Seven Songs for Malcolm X* (1992) and *Mothership Connection* (a.k.a. *Last Angel of History*) (1995). The collective received financial backing from **Channel 4** and, before that, the **Greater London Council**, which enabled them to make independent and experimental works. *Handsworth Songs*, which won the Grierson Prize, is now regarded as a crucial landmark of black British cultural production of the 1980s, addressing questions of representation, identity and politics through a distinctive and innovative documentary format that drew on news footage of the 1985 Handsworth riots and disturbances in Birmingham, as well as earlier moments, to present an alternative history. *Seven Songs for Malcolm X* continued Akomfrah's stylised documentary work, this time focused on the African American civil rights leader. The film was awarded Best Use of Archive Footage in a Documentary at the Chicago Film Festival in 1993. *Mothership Connection* works with science fiction imagery and powerful digital effects.

Further reading

Fusco, C. (1988) 'An Interview with Black Audio Film Collective', in Mercer, K. and Julien, I. (eds) *Black Film, British Cinema*, ICA Documents 7, London: ICA/BFI, pp. 60–2.

ALISON DONNELL

Ali, Arif

b. 1935, British Guyana

publisher

After pursuing several lines of work in Guyana, Ali came to the UK in 1957 and founded the monthly *West Indian Digest* in 1971. A relaunched *West Indian World* followed in 1973, and in 1979 the *Asian Digest*. In 1981 he launched two newspapers, *Caribbean Times* and *Asian Times*. He founded **Hansib Publishing** Ltd in 1973, the largest of Britain's specialist black **publishing houses**. Ali, known as a pioneer in the field of black publishing (see **publishing, books**), was an Outstanding Merit Award Finalist in the ***Windrush*** Achievements Awards, 2000. He collaborated with Catherine Hogben and James **Berry** on *Grassroots in Verse*

(1988, London: Hansib) and wrote *1992*, published as a leather-bound book.

ALISON DONNELL

alternative minority media: cable and satellite

Increasingly, minority viewers who are disillusioned with the offerings of mainstream **television**, even from those departments ostensibly set up to meet their needs, are turning to minority cable and satellite. The developments in cable technology, and its growing availability, have opened up new possibilities for black viewers and black media professionals working in broadcasting. That there is a vibrant and enthusiastic audience for popular black-originated work can be seen by the success of the US cable network Black Entertainment Tele-vision (BET), which was valued at between $220 million and $250 million in 1992. When Robert Johnson conceived the project in 1979, his objective was for the company to become the primary producer-distributor of black-oriented cable programming, as well as the most significant vehicle through which to reach black consumers (Salmas, 1992). Fifteen years later BET remained the only cable channel of its kind, reaching 31.9 million households with a schedule of entertain-ment, music, news, current affairs and sport. In 1990, the British-made ***Desmonds*** was the first British show to be broadcast on BET. The politico-economic aspects of broadcasting and distribution are outside the scope of this unit but clearly, as Downing points out, the development of some ethnic minority media is simply 'good' business – niche marketing rather than good community relations (Downing, 1992).

The success of BET in exploiting the potential of an eager black audience eventually made the transatlantic crossing to Britain and Identity Television (IDTV), marketed as Britain's first black entertainment channel, was launched in June 1993. IDTV was backed by BET and began transmitting on the London Interconnect system to approxi-mately 150,000 homes. The publicity material for the channel boldly says: 'it's your identity – get to know it!' The schedule was a mix of programmes from the USA, the Caribbean, Africa and the UK, and included soaps, music, comedy and current affairs programmes. When launched, IDTV in-tended to raise awareness among all those who at the time received cable – about 600,000 nationally – although the total market was thought to be in the region of 2.9 million homes. However, after very few years in operation, IDTV was wholly taken over by its parent company BET, and in 1997 BET pulled out of the UK market to be replaced with BET on Jazz, a 24-hour rolling jazz sister channel, largely because it was most 'mobile internationally' (Sutherland 1998: 40).

Namaste TV has been broadcasting since 1992 and aims to cater to the new second and successive generations of UK-born Asians. Namaste is promoted as 'truly East greets West' and, unusually for a minority channel, over 40 per cent of the channel's output is produced by UK crews, but only 20 per cent of their output is broadcast in English, although much of the programming is sub-titled. The range of genres includes Asian music, soaps, light entertainment, drama and business programmes, and more recently the channel has launched a youth-oriented strand called TeenAsia. More recent entrants into this particular niche market include AsiaVision and AsiaNet.

In 1997, the UK-based African Broadcasting Corporation (ABC) was launched, aiming to become 'the first black television channel to serve the UK black TV consumer market, particularly in London' (Sutherland, 1998: 39). In June 1998, ABC was granted a licence from the ITC to begin broadcasting and Mine TV was open for business, confident that it would succeed where its pre-decessor, IDTV, had failed. ABC's managing director, Alistair Soyode, argues that it is important to have a menu that reflects the interests of Britain's black communities, not simply a regular and monotonous diet of US-imports (Soyode cited in Sutherland 1998: 40). He also believes that the channel needs to be of interest to non-black audiences and envisages that at least 20 per cent of his audience will be cross-over.

The constant search for resourcing, particularly from advertisers, has the inevitable result that, despite these new channels' potential to run more challenging material, entertainment-based programmes become their principal output. In addition, the stated aim of many minority channels is to produce programmes in-house or at least to commission UK-based companies, but too often channels rely on cheap(er) imports to bulk out their schedules. As Ismond argues, 'one of the consequences of low-level investment in domestic production is that it does not augur well for the promotion of cable as a showcase for innovative and experimental (read "risky") material' (Ismond cited in Cottle 1997: 205–6). Hopefully, though, over time, as consumers get more switched on to the opportunities for alternative products, channels will be able to produce the range of output that really does begin to challenge the normative versions of 'race' and ethnicity, which are such a commonplace everywhere else in the media.

References

Becker, E. (1992) 'One smart BET', *Emmy* 14(3): 58–62.

Cottle, S. (1997) *Television and Ethnic Minorities: Producers' Perspectives*, Aldershot: Avebury Salmas.

Downing, John D.H. (1992) 'Spanish-language media in the Greater New York region during the 1980s', in S.H. Riggins (ed.) *Ethnic Minority Media: an International Perspective*, Newbury Park, London, New Delhi: Sage Publications, pp. 256–75.

Sutherland, F. (1998) 'Mine the gap', *Cable and Satellite Europe*, October: 39–40.

White, J. (1998) 'Digital diversity: going back to my roots', *Cable and Satellite Europe*, October: 37–8.

KAREN ROSS

Alvi, Moniza

b. 1954, Lahore, Pakistan

poet, teacher

Alvi's first collection of poems, *The Country at My Shoulder*, was published by Oxford University Press in 1993. Selected poems from this collection had already appeared in a pamphlet in 1991, for which Alvi was judged joint winner of the Poetry Business Competition. Her second collection, *A Bowl of Warm Air*, appeared, to equal acclaim, in 1996, and, in 2000, Bloodaxe Books published a new series of her poems, *Carrying My Wife*, which included both of Alvi's previous works. She reads poems from all three collections on *The Poetry Quartets 6* audio cassette series (the British Council/Bloodaxe Books). She has also co-edited the *Poetry London Newsletter*.

The daughter of a South-Asian father and a British mother, Alvi grew up in Hertfordshire, and her poetry shows a sophisticated engagement with migrancy, **cultural hybridity** and self-remaking. Her poems focus equally on personal, familial connections with the subcontinent, and on the English landscapes of her own childhood. Alvi now lives and teaches in London.

Select bibliography

Alvi, M. (2000) *Carrying My Wife*, Newcastle upon Tyne: Bloodaxe Books.

—— (1996) *A Bowl of Warm Air*, Oxford: Oxford University Press.

—— (1993) *The Country at My Shoulder*, Oxford: Oxford University Press.

Alvi, M. and Daniels, P. (1992) *Peacock Luggage*, Huddersfield: Smith/Doorstop Books.

ALEX TICKELL

Ama, Shola

b. 1979, London, England

R'n'B singer and songwriter

While chart success for UK R'n'B and soul artists had been sporadic since **Soul II Soul**'s initial impact in 1989, Shola Ama's rendition of Randy Crawford's 'You Might Need Somebody' in 1997 helped open up the market again. Discovered by Kwame of D-Influence while waiting at Hammersmith tube station in 1995, 'You Might Need Somebody' sold almost 350,000 copies in the UK and reached number four in the national charts. Ama's follow up-single 'You're the One I Love' went to number three and her debut album *Much Love* reached number six in the album charts. *Much Love*, an album of accessible soul rhythms behind Ama's winsome vocals, featured Ama as a co-writer on the majority of the tracks. Such success helped her win a Brit Award for Best British Female Solo Artist. For the next two years, Ama split her time touring with the Fugees and 3T while recording new material for an album. In 1999, she kept herself in the spotlight by collaborating with WEA label mate Glamma Kid on his Top 10 hit 'Taboo'. Her second album, *In Return* (1999), did not match her previous success.

DEREK A. BARDOWELL

Amin, Ruhul

b. Bangladesh

film-maker

Amin is an East London Bangladeshi film-maker whose films reflect his assertion that: 'By birth, I am a Bengali. By naturalisation, I am a British subject and, spiritually, I am an East Ender.' From documentaries such as *Purbo London* (1978) and *Flame in My Heart* (1983) to short films *Moviewallah* (1992) and *Rhythms* (1994), Amin has created emotionally resonant, humanistic portraits of Asian migrants – particularly, migrants from a displaced Bengali community living in the UK. Loss and longing for the homeland are primary tropes in his early work, as demonstrated in Amin's 1986 debut feature *A Kind of English*. In Amin's film (see **film and cinema**), 9-year-old Samin assists his grandmother in re-creating the village back home to overcome their family's over-riding feelings of isolation in London. In the highly lyrical vignette *Rhythms*, Amin again represents the healing generational bonds between Bengali migrants and their British-born descendants through an old man and young boy's love of Bengali **music**. Amin deploys a neo-realist aesthetic, his films inhabiting visually expressive realms where dialogue is sparse and lingering silences punctuate evocative images. His use of non-professional actors from the Bengali community in films such as *A Kind of English* contribute to the drama-documentary atmosphere, while his representations of women foreground their oft-unspoken grievances and innermost concerns. A British-Bengali, thoroughly art-house director who helped design a multimedia installation at the Arts Worldwide Bangladesh Festival

2000, Amin's films bespeak the resilient spirit of Bengali East London.

SATINDER CHOHAN

Andrews, Naveen

b. 1969, Balham, England

actor

Naveen Andrews was born and brought up in South London. He attended the Guildhall School of Music and Drama, and his peers included Ewan McGregor and David Thewlis. At the end of his studies, Andrews was offered the part of Bike in Hanif **Kureishi**'s *London Kills Me* (1991). One of his memorable early performances was as Zaf, a wild and enthusiastic leader of a Southall Country and Western band, in *Wild West* (1992), a film (see **film and cinema**) written by Harwant **Bains**. This role earned him a nomination for the most promising newcomer in the Evening Standard Drama Awards, 1993. Andrews went on to play Karim Amir, in the **television** series of Kureishi's *The Buddha of Suburbia* (1993), which fell foul of television watchdogs for depicting a six-minute sex orgy. However, it was his role of Kip, the Sikh bomb disposal expert, who won the heart of Hana, played by Juliette Binoche in Anthony Minghella's *The English Patient* (1996), that brought him international fame. He went to Bombay and worked on Kaizad Gustad's debut feature, *Bombay Boys* (1998). Other credits include Mira Nair's *Kama Sutra* (1996), where he played the dissolute king, Raj Singh, and the television drama, *The Peacock Spring* (1995). Andrews is now living and working in the USA, where his credits include *The Chippendales Murder* (2000) and *Blessed Art Thou* (2000).

SUMAN BHUCHAR

Anim-Addo, Joan

b. 1948, St George's, Grenada

lecturer, writer, editor

Anim-Addo is Head of the Caribbean Centre at Goldsmiths College, University of London, where she teaches literature, Caribbean studies and creative writing. She is also Founder/Chair of the **Caribbean Women Writers' Alliance** (CWWA) and editor of the magazine *Mango Season*. Her writing interests are varied and include poetry, short stories, literary criticism, libretto, drama and history. She first came to the attention of a wider audience as a cultural historian through two works: *Longest Journey: a Black History of Lewisham* (1995) and *Sugar Spices and Human Cargo: an Early Black History of Greenwich* (1996). Both works document a history of black people's belonging to Britain dating back, with individual records, to the sixteenth century. History is an important dynamic in much of Anim-Addo's creative writing. *Haunted by History: Poetry* (1998), her first collection of poetry, configures the 'here and there and in-between of diaspora primarily as trajectories of history' (deCaires Narain 1999). Her first play, *At Gulley's Edge*, which tells a family-focused story of US naval forces in Grenada in 1983, was first read at the Oval House Theatre in October 1996. This was followed by the libretto, *Imoinda*, which rewrites Aphra Behn's seminal seventeenth-century work *Oroonoko* and was first performed in workshop at the Oval House Theatre, London, in 1998.

References

deCaires Narain, D. (1999) *Wasafiri* 29 (spring): 92–3.

Select bibliography

Anim-Addo, J. (ed.) (2000) *Centre of Remembrance*, London: Mango Publishing.

—— (ed.) (1998) *Another Doorway: Visible inside the Museum*, London: Mango Publishing.

—— (1998) *Haunted by History: Poetry*, London: Mango Publishing.

—— (ed.) (1996) *Framing the Word*, London: Whiting & Birch.

—— (1995) *Longest Journey: a History of Black Lewisham*, London: Deptford Forum Publishing.

ALISON DONNELL

Anjali

singer

Anjali Bhatia fronted the early 1990s Asian British all-girl band Voodoo Queens. The Voodoo Queens were signed to Wiiija Records at the same time as **Cornershop** and their sound was abrasive and guitar based with lyrics dealing with gender issues such as body fascism – their debut single was called 'Supermodel superficial' – and consequently Voodoo Queens were lumped in with the nascent riot grrrl scene. The band were concerned with being portrayed as a novelty act, with Bhatia commenting that the media saw them as a gimmick: 'Asians, women as well, what a brilliant press angle'. After releasing their only album *Chocolate Revenge* the band split and Anjali began learning the basics of the technology involved in producing electronic **music**, preferring to experiment herself rather than relying upon the help of a producer, and immersed herself in the expanding club scene. In 1998, Anjali released her debut solo single, 'Maharani', which was an inspired mix of **hip hop** beats, seductive vocals and Indian film (see **film and cinema**) samples. A second single, *Aquila*, also has a drum and bass feel to it and Anjali's debut album, released in 1999, is the culmination of her ambitious first steps into a solo career. Her second album, *Anjali*, was released in 2000.

ANDY WOOD

Anokha

Anokha began as a Sunday afternoon club in North London in 1995, showcasing mainly drum and bass-influenced music but with a distinctly Asian British slant. The club's founder, producer and instrumentalist Talvin **Singh**, then oversaw the move of Anokha to the fashionable East London venue, the Blue Note. Anokha, along with **Outcaste**, provides a focal point for a burgeoning and innovative Asian British **music** scene outwith the **bhangra** scene, and has attracted large crowds as well as interest from the mainstream media and music industry. In addition to DJ sets, performers such as State of Bengal and Amar have been showcased at the club. In 1997, Singh's Omni label released a compilation through Island Records entitled *Anokha – Soundz Of The Asian Underground*, which highlighted both the common threads shared and the diversity of contemporary Asian British dance music. Singh contributed two songs, as did Anokha regulars State Of Bengal and Amar. Along with similar albums including *Untouchable: Outcaste Beats* and *Eastern Uprising – Dance Music from the Asian Underground*, released around the same time as *Anokha*, these helped create huge interest in what had previously been an underground scene.

ANDY WOOD

Apache Indian

b. 1967, Birmingham, England

musician

Although of Indian parentage, Apache Indian is strongly associated with **reggae** sound systems. Growing up in Handsworth, Birmingham (born Steven Kapur), he experienced an era when the city was being celebrated as a musical melting pot. Apache's first single 'Move Over India' was released in 1990, a ragga tune containing elements of **bhangra**, and it led to him being heralded as representing a cross-cultural fusion of **music**. He went on to hit the headlines, in 1992, with the release and chart success of the single 'Arranged Marriage' and the album *No Reservations* (Island, 1993). In this album he raised issues traditionally not discussed within the Asian community, with songs such as 'Drink Problems' and 'Aids Warning' as well as a comment, in 'Moving On', against the election of a BNP member to a council seat in Tower Hamlets. His second album *Make Way for the Indian* followed in 1995. His subsequent success, seven hit singles in the Top 40, drew criticism from the more 'traditional' sphere of the reggae business and he eventually lost his 'ragga' audience. The commercial success has since eluded him and he has been dropped by Island Records. *Real People* was released with Coalition in 1997, and was

followed in 2000 by *The Best of Apache Indian* (Universal/Spectrum) and *Karma* (Sunset).

SAMINA ZAHIR

Araeen, Rasheed

b. 1935, Karachi, Pakistan

visual artist, curator, writer

As an artist, curator and writer, Araeen has had an enormous influence within black British culture. Araeen moved to the UK in 1964 and his work at this time initially explored what would come to be termed 'minimalism', before later introducing moving and time-based elements. In the early 1970s, Araeen became interested in anti-racist politics, becoming a Black Panther. Subsequently his work became more politicised. In 1975, Araeen started writing and co-founded *Black Phoenix*, a black art magazine. At this time he was working with Artists for Democracy. As the 1980s movement of black art grew, Araeen was a senior figure, although he did not agree with many of the premises of black art. His curating and writing stressed the role artists who had been designated 'other' had played within modernism, and he explored this in **The Other Story**, which he curated. As well as curating other important exhibitions, exhibiting and writing, Araeen founded the art journal **Third Text** in 1987. During the 1990s, Araeen has continued to exhibit, edit and give papers, with solo exhibitions at the South London Gallery and on the Serpentine lawn.

Select bibliography

Araeen, R. (1984) *Making Myself Visible*, London: Kala Press.

NIRU RATNAM

Arif, Saleem

b. 1949, Hyderabad, India

visual artist

Arif came to the UK in 1966, having grown up in a family with Sufi origins. He studied sculpture at the

Birmingham College of Art but also produced drawings that drew on Indian eroticism and surrealism. Subsequently he took up a place at the Royal College of Art, and was influenced by Matisse, Klee and the Indian miniatures in the Victoria and Albert Museum. He continued to draw rather than to sculpt, and developed a particular interest in Dante's *Inferno*, researching the affinities between Dante and Islamic texts. Arif developed a style of cut-outs in-between sculpture and drawing, which consist of coloured panels that fit together like a large, abstract jigsaw. The panels are usually abstract, but animal and human figures, usually highly symbolic, also appear, sometimes overlapping with each other. Additionally, Arif incorporates areas of negative space in-between panels, adding depth to the picture plane. The texture of the pieces is often uneven as Arif uses combinations of materials such as sand and acrylic, the effect of which is to give each piece a highly individual quality.

Further reading

Hubbard, S. 'The art of Saleem Arif', *Third Text* 27: 37–44.

NIRU RATNAM

ARIWA LABEL *see* Mad Professor

art forms

The steadily expanding body of works by contemporary British artists of a range of cultural backgrounds is both widely varied and richly textured. Although some commentators and curators have chosen to subdivide them into themes (for example: cultural politics, race and ethnicity, myth and belief) great care is always taken not to reduce the scope of their works to a final and definitive formal categorisation. With equal force, these artists themselves have consistently questioned the desirability and tenability of the frames of reference used within conventional and contemporary art history and criticism. Yet, within the critical space opened up by these efforts, it is still possible to

notice in their art the presence of key formal and thematic interests. Modernism, for instance, forms the founding fabric for the work of a number of artists, predominantly, although not entirely occupied with painting and sculpture. The figurative canvases of painters Uzo Egonu and Balraj Khanna, and abstract works by Frank **Bowling**, artists connected to Africa, South Asia and the Caribbean respectively, are typical of this attachment to modernism. During the late 1970s and early 1980s, an exploration of modernist sculpture played a defining role in geometric, minimalist outdoor projects by Rasheed **Araeen**, and a subsequent return to natural materials in the work of Avtarjeet **Dhanjal**.

A greater number of artists have chosen to orient their works towards vigorously debated political questions, such as those around ideas of homeland, nationhood and belonging. Picturing these artists as political subjects, these works implicitly emphasise gender, race and ethnicity as crucial to an understanding of the composite and negotiated nature of culture and identity. From the early 1980s, the work of Ingrid **Pollard**, Keith **Piper**, Lubaina **Himid**, Eddie **Chambers** and Sonia **Boyce** engaged directly with the politics of identity, as did others such as Veronica **Ryan**, Claudette **Johnson** and Donald **Rodney**. The late 1980s and 1990s saw a move beyond a radical questioning of the politics of nation, representation and difference, towards a new focus on issues as varied as sexual politics and desire, internationalism in art criticism and curating, and the role of the new digital technologies.

While some have argued that black political art works ideally demand a realist format in order to be understood (Mercer 1994: 56), many of the most dynamic realist projects of the period developed alongside if not beyond the arena of political discussion. A broad range of realist works has emerged based on figuration, portraiture, self-portraiture and realist **photography**. Photographs by Vanley **Burke** exploring black British urban life, and the work of others such as Pogus Caesar, Lesley **Sanderson**, Faisal **Abdu'Allah** and Brenda Agard, demonstrates a strident confidence in the appeal of the realist genre. At the same time, their diverse attention to realism has contributed significantly to the breadth of critical debates aimed at dismantling the supposed transparency and mimetic properties of realist visual practices (Young 1993: 81).

Narrative works such as the drawings of Manjeet Lamba, and painting and murals by Shanti **Panchal**, take up figuration as a medium for articulating personal, collective, historical and often art historical narratives, reinstating their artists' origins and influences. The early pastel drawings of celebrated artist Sonia **Boyce**, using visual devices of continuity and sequence, present an extended exploration of memory and cultural retention through her narratives of childhood and family. Interactive multimedia works by Keith Piper capture imaginative narratives as diverse as the histories of anthropological encounters with the non-West, urban police surveillance, masculinity, slavery and the black Church. The relaying of narratives in a great number of works is also sharply underlined by an abundant use of textual references, where a juxtaposition of image and text help to probe and ultimately to fix their visual meanings. Perhaps the most complex example of this is a monochrome photo-essay of 1990 by Zarina **Bhimji**, dealing with gender codes within Hindu marriage (Bhimji 1990: 127).

There is also an array of visual references to iconographic schemes in ritual, performance and religious art from Africa, Asia and the Caribbean. Kinetic sculpture by Sokari **Douglas Camp**, invoking Nigerian masquerade, and the play of Hindu signifiers in the sculpture of Dhruva **Mistry**, and of the Hindu deity Kali in the painting and collage of Sutapa **Biswas**, are each characteristic of this ongoing conversation with visual languages distinct from those of Western art. These and other works, such as the cut-out collage and painted work of Saleem **Arif**, Uzo Egonu's dialogue with cubism and primitivism, and monumental wooden sculpture by Juginder **Lamba**, offer instances of deep familiarity with historically, spatially and culturally diverse systems of visual meaning.

Finally, perhaps the most entertaining of all their works are the great many satirical images and objects that have punctuated exhibitions throughout the period. Political satire has offered a detached look at the various dimensions of struggle faced by these artists, the graffitti and photographs of Rasheed Araeen for instance, or Keith Piper's cutting, witty critiques of white liberalism and Thatcherite politics. Others such as Rotimi **Fani-Kayode**, turning the camera on himself to ridicule the art world fetishism of the black male body, or Yinka **Shonibare**'s cameo appearance as a Victorian gentleman or 'dandy', orchestrate an explosive combination of mimicry and irony. Turner Prize winner, Chris **Ofili** has played with eroticised 'Afro' images, and even balls of elephant dung gathered from London zoo, in an elaborate and colourful inversion of popular receptions of black material and visual culture, and the conventions of modernist painting and gallery display.

Taken together, the diverse technical and thematic interests of these artists present a range of innovative and developed formal concerns. From the dynamic surface of their works emerges a close engagement and understanding of the visual.

References

Bhimji, Z. (1990) 'Live for Sharam and die for Izzat', in J. Rutherford (ed.) *Identity: community, culture, difference*, London: Lawrence & Wishart.

Mercer, K. (1994) *Welcome to the Jungle: New Positions in Black Cultural Studies*, London: Routledge.

Young, L. (1993) 'Identity, Realism and Black Photography', in M. Sealy (ed.) *Vanley Burke: a Retrospective*, London: Lawrence & Wishart.

Further reading

Sirmans, M.F. (ed.) (1998) *Transforming the Crown: African, Asian and Caribbean Artists in Britain 1966–1996*, New York: Caribbean Cultural Center.

LEON WAINWRIGHT

Artrage

A quarterly inter-cultural arts magazine, *Artrage* was first published by the **Minorities' Arts Advisory Service** (MAAS) in 1983. Its remit was to provide a specialised publication reflecting the work of MAAS, a training organisation that served as a leading advocate of cultural diversity and equal access to arts provision In 1993, the high cost and low sales of producing two black arts publications led to *Artrage* incorporating *Black Arts in London*, including its essential listings element, and publishing bi-monthly. With the reorganisation of MAAS to the Artrage Intercultural Advisory Service in 1994, the magazine was reincarnated. It became a full-colour, monthly, black arts listings publication, distributed by *Time Out*, effectively attracting a more contemporary audience. It lasted until April 1995, when the organisation was put into voluntary liquidation. LAB recognised the need for such a publication to continue and accepted the bid from Nubian Tales (see **Nubian Tales/b3 Media**) to produce a print and on-line magazine, *24/59*. *Artrage* nurtured contributors that have since become internationally renowned in the arts, culture and media fields, including E.A. **Markham**, Fred **D'Aguiar**, James **Berry**, Dionne St Hill, Kwesi **Owusu**, Rukhsana **Ahmad**, Jacob **Ross** and Aamer Hussein.

KADIJA SESAY

arts funding bodies

The past twenty years have seen a rapid shift of perception both among black arts themselves, and within funding bodies, over horizons and interpretations of the situation. Arts funding bodies have operated under what is notoriously considered, by many black arts groups, inherent structural racism; the unproportional distribution of resources is just one example of this. Funding bodies, such as the Arts Council of England, have persistently encouraged black arts organisations to buy into their categorisations. Hence, rather than articulating black arts in a manner with which they felt comfortable, black arts groups were forced to express themselves in the 'acceptable format' of funding bodies.

The Arts Council made little attempt to increase provision to black arts prior to Walter Baker's report 'The Arts of Ethnic Minorities – Status and Funding' (1985), which highlighted the low levels of funding received by black arts groups; in 1985, Regional Arts Board funding of black arts stood at just 0.5 per cent. Following on from this, the Arts

Council of England's 'Ethnic Minority Action Plan' (February 1986) recommended that, within two years, funding of black arts should reach 4 per cent. Unsurprisingly, this did not happen, and it was not until the early 1990s that Arts Council funding reached this amount.

In the early 1980s, the **Greater London Council**'s Arts and Recreation Committee acknowledged as one of its priorities the development of London's multi-ethnic communities arts. The first Ethnic Arts Sub-Committee was subsequently elected and grants to black arts groups increased from the previous £300,000 budget to £2 million. Section 11, although only in temporary existence, allowed groups to apply for funds under the Section of the Local Government Act 1966. While the grants funded a range of arts-based projects, they inevitably collapsed when the scheme ended.

Applying for National Lottery funding continues to prove difficult since applications adhere to Arts Council categorisations. Additionally, only a few black arts groups or organisations have buildings that could profit from capital funds, while many find it hard to raise the necessary proportion of 'match' funding required as a basic condition of application. Even the Arts Council of England acknowledged, in 1997, that the possibility of business sponsorship for black arts was slight. Black arts projects still have less access to prestigious venues and are less attractive to investors, having a shorter life-span with greater risks.

SAMINA ZAHIR

Asian Age, The

The *Asian Age* is a broadsheet English-language daily newspaper, which began publication in 1994. Set up by Indian journalist, editor and author, M.J. Akbar, the idea was to create a paper that appeared simultaneously in London, Delhi and Bombay. Since then it has expanded to Calcutta, Bhubaneswar, Bangalore and Ahmedabad. Each edition operates as an independent franchise. The London edition is owned by the Dolphin Media group, which includes the Indian movie fanzine *Cineblitz*. M.J. Akbar is the overall managing editor. The paper aims to provide Indian and South Asian news, primarily for the Indian population living abroad. However, it has encountered a problem in covering domestic British news, because, due to the different time zones, the news has already appeared in the British papers and is therefore not new. The paper has not been able to resolve this because there are not enough resources to have stringers around Britain. Although the paper has failed to take off in the UK, in India it has expanded but has been unable to make inroads against the more established newspaper groups, but the space it is able to devote to foreign news is a positive difference.

SUMAN BHUCHAR

Asian Dub Foundation

Asian Dub Foundation (ADF) formed in 1993, beginning as a sound system and mutating into a band. They released their first album *Facts and Fictions* on the **Nation Records** label in 1995. ADF met through the London-based collective, Community Music Workshops, where two founder members were tutors. ADF's music is a reflection of their roots in various sound systems and workshops, taking inspiration from sources such as **jungle**, dub, rap and punk to produce a hard, rhythm-driven sound that adapts well to live performance. In France, ADF have a huge following but their debut album did less well in the UK due to a combination of media preconceptions as to what exactly constitutes an 'Asian band' and the lack of resources at their label, Nation. Subsequently, the band signed a major deal and released a series of singles culminating in the release of their second album *Rafi's Revenge* (1998). ADF were shortlisted for the 1998 Mercury Awards but their growing commercial appeal has not softened their political approach, with the band continuing to support community workshops and the campaign to release Satpal Ram from prison. A third album, *Community Music*, was released in 2000.

ANDY WOOD

Asian fashion

It may be argued that popular British culture has discovered both the aesthetic and the commercial potential of Asian fashion (see **fashion and design**) and that designers such as Jean-Paul Gaultier, Stella McCartney, Jade Jagger and John Galliano have been inspired by Asian designs and have brought them on to the catwalk. In terms of an instantly recognisable fashion item, the influence of the *pashmina* (shawl) cannot be under-estimated. Also, the increase in cross-cultural interaction means that ethnic and Western clothes can be mixed and matched by both British Asian and British white youth on the street. The *atchkan* (tunic) or *choli* (blouse) can be used with jeans or trousers and self-adhesive *bindis* and henna tattoos can be bought from high-street chains. This fashionable mixing of styles by both designers and consumers may suggest that Asian fashions are already part of the British cultural scene. But does that mean that it is too late for Asian British designers to take ownership and establish themselves? It is fair to say that Asian British designers have only made their mark in fusion or traditional fashion in this country towards the end of the twentieth century. In the past, this could be attributed to the way in which Asian families saw fashion as a career, and dress as a means through which to preserve cultural identity and regional distinctiveness. Yet there has been a shift in attitudes among second- and third-generation Asian British people, who are more open to the fashion spectrum and willing to embrace both East and West.

There is now a growing awareness of the move of Asian fashion towards the mainstream, as well as a recognition of the creative design challenges it presents with the use of vibrant and subtle colours, and fine materials such as silk. The different Asian fashion markets are also leading business interests and Paul Garrod is the owner of Chandni Chowk, a group of shops selling 'Europeanised' Asian wear. Moreover, Asian designers are now making their impact within the British fashion scene. Bashir Ahmed, who trained at St Martin's, is a design director for Apartment Clothes. Babs Mahil has designed Asian-style outfits for Cherie Blair QC, while Ffion Hague has worn clothes created by

Raishma Islam. There is also more encouragement for an upcoming generation and young British Asian students at fashion school talk of establishing couture houses and shops. In 2000, BBC Haymarket Exhibition MD Simon Kimble announced plans to launch, with the participation of Indian supermodel Farheen Khan, the first British Asian Fashion Awards at Clotheshow 2001. One category is the Young Designer of the Year Award to recognise emerging talent.

Further reading

Khan, N. (1992) 'Asian women's dress: from Burqah to Bloggs – changing clothes for changing times', in J. Ash and E. Wilson (eds) *Chic Thrills: a Fashion Reader*, London: Pandora Press.

YINKA SUNMONU

Asian radio comedy

Unrepresented within an effective 'closed shop' of radio comedy performance (and a principally white, male, middle-class comedy-writing culture), Asian voices have been virtually unheard within British radio comedy for almost the entire duration of its history. Lacking the more globally aware perspectives of the BBC Radio Drama department, Asian characters within Light Entertainment output have been most frequently played by white performers speaking with the 'curry-flavoured English' epitomised by *The Goon Show*'s Lalkaka and Banerjee.

Following decades of marginalisation, however, the recent pioneering work of British Asian comedy writers and performers represents one of the broadcasting phenomena of the late 1990s. Two series, first broadcast within weeks of one another in 1996, are largely responsible for this turnaround. Meera **Syal**'s *Masala FM* was heralded as 'the first Asian sitcom', and chronicled the fortunes of an Asian radio station and its largely eccentric employees. The series combined a bold statement of contemporary British Asian identity and clear feminist sentiments with a broad comedic agenda, and was a modest success with the Radio 4 listenership. All the parts were played by the four cast members (Syal, plus Nina **Wadia**, Sanjeev

Bhaskar and Nitin **Sawhney**), a *tour de force* in ensemble acting, while Sawhney's musical contributions (largely in the form of Masala FM jingles) afforded the series a distinct identity within the Radio 4 schedules.

The impact of *Masala FM* was, however, dwarfed by that of the sketch show **Goodness Gracious Me** (featuring the same cast, but with the addition of Kulvinder **Ghir**). Initially intended by producer Anil Gupta to be a cheap 'pilot' for a prospective **television** series, it enjoyed three very successful series in its original radio incarnation. The formula was largely standard sketch show fare – stock characterisations, catch-phrases, sitcom-styled domestic family units – but situated within a specifically British Asian context. In its wickedly funny Asian re-appropriation of archetypally British comedic situations, the series spoke volumes about the contemporary dynamics of both cultures. Its defining moment occurred in a sketch concerning a group of young Bombay friends ending a night on the tiles by 'having an English'. They taunt the waiter; ask for more chips than they could possibly hope to eat; and as a final statement of machismo request 'the blandest thing on the menu!' The show's pan-religious/pan-cultural approach ensured its broadest possible acceptance among the 'young British Asians' whom Gupta had initially hoped would form its audience. Also a hit with the broader Radio 4 listenership, *Goodness Gracious Me* none the less elicited an ambivalent response from the more conservative elements of Britain's Asian communities.

Following the success of the series (which eventually led to a national **theatre** tour), Asian writers and performers have maintained a small but notable presence within mainstream BBC radio comedy. A veteran contributor to Radio 4 comedy prior to *Goodness Gracious Me*, Syal's subsequent radio work included the all-woman sketch show *Five Squeezy Pieces* (1998), while Bhaskar lent his talents to the topical late-night sketch series *The Way it is* (1998). However, the most consistent ongoing Asian contribution to BBC radio comedy comes in the form of 'dramedy' (a conflation of 'drama' and 'comedy' used within the BBC's Light Entertainment department). Low-key 'gentle' dramedy series such as Philip Afshar's *Eastern Mix* (1997) and Shaheen

Khan and Sudha **Bhuchar**'s *Girlies* (1997) represent distinctive elements of Radio 4's daytime schedules, and continue to be periodical (albeit criminally under-exposed) outlets for British Asian writing and performing talent.

HUW BUCKNELL

Asian Times

A weekly tabloid published by the Ethnic Media Group (EMG) and launched in 1981, *Asian Times* claims to be 'Britain's leading Asian newspaper'. Like the *Voice*, it was established to present news of interest to a specialist ethnic population, this time the Asian community in Britain, as well as to provide information on current affairs nationally and internationally. The paper has covered issues that were previously inaccessible to Asians in Britain and highlighted festivals and events. Selling at fifty pence, it has a readership of 114,000. *Asian Times* does not have the popular feel of *Eastern Eye*, also published by EMG. Its front-page story for the end of February 2001 was 'Ceasefire extended – Pakistan rejects Indian overture as a ploy', written by the editor Emenike Pio. By contrast, *Eastern Eye* had a 'showbiz exclusive' on the **Bollywood** oscars with a photograph of Hrithik Roshan, who won the Best Actor award. *Public Sector*, created and launched by Joy **Francis** in 1999, is a weekly newspaper supplement for African Caribbean and Asian public-sector professionals that accompanies *Asian Times*. It is now edited by Denise Malcolm, while subbing is done by Jacob **Ross**. *Public Sector* was shortlisted by, and commended in, the **Commission for Racial Equality** Race in the Media Awards for Best Specialist Publication, only six months after its launch. Sections on charity and community news cover health, education and crime. The notice board provides information from different public bodies on initiatives and reports.

YINKA SUNMONU

Asian Women Writers' Collective

The Asian Women Writers' Workshop (AWWW) was founded in 1984, mainly due to the efforts of writer/activist Ravinder **Randhawa**, who managed to enlist the support of Black Ink and the **Greater London Council**. The London-based workshop was designed to increase the visibility of South Asian women writers and to give them access to **publishers**. The workshop provided women writers with a supportive community and addressed critical issues such as the evaluation of minority **literature**. The transition from workshop to collective resulted in much debate over the group's name. Some members were in favour of calling themselves 'black' to show their solidarity with Afro-Caribbean women, while others felt discriminated against by certain dominant Afro-Caribbean women's groups. Another set felt that there were too many cultural differences between Asian and Afro-Caribbean writing to make it possible for the groups to respond critically to each other. The title 'Asian Women Writers' Collective' (AWWC) was finally agreed upon on the grounds that there had hitherto been no forum for Asian women writers to express themselves. It was decided that the collective would work closely with black women's groups and participate in events for black women writers. AWWC members also preferred the choice of 'woman' over 'feminist' as they felt the latter was too closely associated with the needs of middle-class white women.

In addition to helping Asian women to develop their writing skills and maintaining the other goals of the workshop, the AWWC encourages its members to get involved in performance poetry, media and the **visual arts**. The group has expanded from eight to over forty members. Although its current membership is predominantly South Asian, it seeks to include all women who have roots in Asia. At the outset, group members were committed to working in their mother tongues as a way of reaching first-generation, working-class women who did not know English, but the wider interpretation of 'Asianness' has come to mean that English is used more often. However, the group continues to maintain links with working-class women and helps them to use the collective's networks in productive ways.

The AWWC also tries to negotiate the pressures of age, class, religion and language that influence its membership and to connect with women in the outer-London boroughs. Despite recent financial problems, most significantly the loss of funding from the Greater London Arts Association, the collective managed to collect and publish its own work. *Read on* appeared in 1990, followed by *If I Say 'No'* in 1991. Earlier the AWWW had published an anthology of writing entitled *Right of Way* (1988) and in 1994 Virago brought out another anthology by the collective called *Flaming Spirit*. The collective continues to plan other anthologies, and a measure of their success can be seen in the increasing number of AWWC members who are being published and performed, and in their liberal representation in high-profile, national black arts forums.

Select bibliography

Asian Women Writers' Collective (1994) *Flaming Spirit*, London: Virago
Asian Women Writers' Workshop (1988) *Right of Way*, London: Women's Press.

ASHA SEN

ASIAN WOMEN WRITERS' WORKSHOP *see* Asian Women Writers' Collective

Aswad

Aswad was formed in 1974 in London and is made up of the trio of Brinsley 'Dan' Forde, Angus 'Drummie Zeb' Gaye and Tony 'Gad' Robinson. Taking the Amharic word for black as their name, Aswad was one of the first British groups to compete successfully with the Jamaican reggae scene for attention in the UK. Also, Aswad was the only British group to perform and record with top Jamaican artists of the time. Their debut release 'Back to Africa' went to number one in the UK reggae charts in 1976. Their album *Love Fire*, released in 1981, is now considered part of the **reggae** canon. In the 1980s, they kept their musical style in step with new forms and fused the different genres of **dancehall**, **hip hop** and dub. Their most popular hit came in 1988 with 'Don't Turn Around', which took the number one place in the UK charts. In 1994, Aswad enjoyed their first Grammy nomination for Best Reggae Album of the Year with *Rise and Shine*. In 1995, they released *DUB: the Next Frontier*, their fifteenth album, taking their musical career into its third decade.

ALISON DONNELL

Attille, Martina

b. 1959, St Lucia

film-maker

Throughout her distinguished career Martina Attille, a film-maker who has lived in London since 1961, has examined the rituals of remembrance and the complex narratives of identity, sexuality and desire among blacks who reside in Britain, the Caribbean and the US South. Beginning in the mid-1980s she became an advocate for black artists and film-makers. In 1984, due to the lack of intellectual freedom for, and the few opportunities allotted to, black students studying communications in Britain, Attille, along with Isaac **Julien**, Nadine Marsh-Edwards and Maureen **Blackwood**, formed **Sankofa Film Collective**.

In her award-winning film (see **film and cinema**) *Dreaming Rivers* (1988), Attille investigated central concerns, including inter-racial relationships, longing, black subjectivity, West Indian migration to England and the intersection of western and African religions. Set in the main character's bedroom, this film explores, through flashbacks, the sustaining impact of death, the memory, dreams and desires of the female protagonist and her family.

Attille, a contributor to important publications such as *The Fact of Blackness: Frantz Fanon and Visual Representation* (1996) and *Rhapsodies in Black: the Art of the Harlem Renaissance* (1997), has also lectured at the University of California, San Diego; Duke University, Durham, North Carolina; and Goldsmiths College, University of London.

Select bibliography

Attille, M. (1997) 'Still', in R. Powell and D. Bailey *Rhapsodies in Black: the Art of the Harlem Renaissance*, Berkeley: University of California Press, pp. 154–9.

Attille, M. and Blackwood, M. (1986) 'Black women and representation', in C. Brundson (ed.) *Films for Women*, London: British Film Institute.

ANDREA D. BARNWELL

Auguiste, Reece

director, writer

A director with **Black Audio Film Collective**, Auguiste has directed their film (see **film and cinema**) *Twilight City* (1989), which looks at a relationship between an estranged mother and daughter against the backdrop of London as postcolonial city. His other credits include *Mysteries of July* (1991), which he wrote and directed.

ALISON DONNELL

Autograph: the Association of Black Photographers

Founded in London in 1988, and currently under the directorship of Mark **Sealy**, Autograph is an international bureau dedicated to the promotion of black photographic practices. Autograph has developed new strategies and methods in order to achieve both national and international representation for black photographers and, although it has been aided by public funding, it has also been keen to develop the commercial potential of its work within the international market-place. Autograph organises a variety of activities including exhibitions and festivals, residency programmes and the commissioning of new works. It also makes superb use of the new media of website, database and CD-ROM. It has produced interactive CD-ROMs: *Party-line* (1997), with Arts Council funding, and *Autograph: Virtual Gallery* (1996). Its work is always strongly informed by a political and intellectual context and the *Party-line* CD-ROM features critical essays by David A. **Bailey** and Stuart **Hall**, Kobena **Mercer**, and Clementine Deliss and Mark Sealy.

The majority of Autograph's exhibitions have explored issues relating to identity politics, such as their first exhibition 'Autoportraits', at Camerwork in 1991. Autograph has also celebrated its collaboration with other photographic institutions both at home and abroad. In 1993 it organised 'Recontres Au Noir 20 British Black Photographers' at the XXIV Recontres International Festival de la Photographie in Arles, France and, in 1996, 'Distant Relations: Roy Mehta', shown at the Cambridge Darkroom Gallery. In 1999, Autograph moved to new premises in Hoxton Square and Richard **Hylton** took on the role of part-time curator, becoming full-time in 2000.

PAULINE DE SOUZA

Aziz, Lisa

b. Totnes, England

presenter

After graduating from Goldsmiths College, London, Aziz began her career in broadcasting when she joined Radio City Liverpool. However, she was keen to work in **television** and eventually secured a job with BBC TV West, from where she was talent-spotted by HTV and then TV-AM. She is probably best known as the newsreader on the breakfast television show TV-AM.

ALISON DONNELL

B

BLAK (UK) *see* Glynn, Martin

Baadass TV

Baadass TV, a youth-orientated fashion (see **fashion and design**) and culture series, presented by Andrea Oliver and US rapper Ice-T, was aired on **Channel 4** in 1994. Although the series came under heavy criticism from black figureheads, including Trevor **Phillips**, for reinforcing black stereotypes of 'gangsters, pimps, whores and freaks' it was also acknowledged as the first British series to explore the wilder side of black culture. The show featured soft-pornography, rapping dwarves, paintings made from elephant droppings and fitness fanatics Juicy Julia and the Raggaerobics crew. **Reggae** legend Lee 'Scratch' Perry also made a memorable appearance on the critically acclaimed series. When *Baadass TV* was launched, it aimed to capture an alternative, contemporary audience who were interested in **hip hop** music, the 'blackploitation' movies of the 1960s and African American culture. Although the show was eventually taken off the air for its lack of political correctness, in its inclusion of Ice-T as a presenter, *Baadass TV* made history by giving British music fans the opportunity to view a famous US rap star headline a British TV programme.

RAYMOND ENISUOH

Babylon Zoo

b. 1971, Dudley, England

singer

Babylon Zoo is the artist Jas Mann. The name of the band stems from the vivacious 'Babylonian' colours of his childhood in India contrasted with the bleak urban 'zoo' of his adolescence in Wolverhampton. Mann was born in the UK to Sikh parents. His childhood was spent between countries: at the age of three he spent some time in India with his grandfather; and he spent a year on a ranch in the USA with his mother's Sioux Indian family. The remainder of his childhood to adolescence was spent in Wolverhampton. Mann says of his Asian British identity, 'I think I took all the positive things from both cultures rather than taking the negative side. . . . I liked the fact that it wasn't one-dimensional' (Roger Morton, 1996).

Babylon Zoo's first single 'Spaceman' (1996) sold a quarter of a million copies in its first week, making it the fastest selling British debut ever, undoubtedly aided by the fact that it appeared in a Levis advert. Mann went on to debut with the album *The Boy with the X-Ray Eyes* (1996), so named because of his blue eyes.

SAMINA ZAHIR

Babymother

Babymother (1998) was the first feature film (see **film and cinema**) directed by Julian **Henriques** and produced by Parminder **Vir**, though both had previously done successful work in **television** and documentaries. The film, deliberately aimed at the mainstream according to Henriques, is the story of Anita, a single mother bringing up two children in Harlesden, and her struggle to succeed not only as a parent but also as an independent woman and a singer. **Music** provides both the sphere where Anita most wants to succeed and the principal hook for audience pleasure. For Anita, success involves not just gaining credibility for her act with her two 'rude girl' friends, but overcoming rivals, both male and female, including Byron, the father of her children and an already established performer. Of greater social importance is the theme of female lone parents, and the generational change in attitudes to being a single mother at a very young age. Anita's song, with its repeated invocation, 'babymother, be a mother to your child', is a message to all the women in her position, but it also marks the understandable failure of the older generation, including Anita's own mother, to offer that kind of parenting.

PATRICK WILLIAMS

Badawi, Zenab

b. 1959, Sudan

broadcaster

An Oxbridge graduate, Badawi was one of the first black women newscasters on **television**. It is fair to say that she built her reputation in terms of viewer recognition on the *Channel 4 News*, which she joined in 1989 as a reporter and presenter of the news belt section of the programme. Three years later she became Jon Snow's deputy on *Channel 4 News*, anchoring the programme in his absence. Badawi's television journalism career started with Yorkshire Television. She joined BBC Manchester in 1987 and went on to work as a reporter on the BBC 2 series *Brass Tacks*, compiling five thirty-minute reports on diverse issues including domestic violence and the privatisation of the National Health Service. After a decade, she returned to the BBC where she worked as a freelance broadcaster on the live political programme, *BBC World Service News and Current Affairs*. A versatile professional, she has presented a four-part series on Africa for **Channel 4** examining political, economic and social issues through short films and discussion. Badawi also found herself on location in Ghana, Kenya and Zambia for the programme, interviewing heads of state. While working as a newscaster on the new ITN night-time and incoming services, she enrolled for a one-year Masters degree at London University. Badawi was a member of the Government Committee Panel, 2000, and was appointed to the Hansard Commission into Parliamentary Scrutiny.

YINKA SUNMONU

Badmarsh

b. Yemen

DJ, record producer

Born in Yemen but brought up in East London, Badmarsh took his name from the Urdu for trickster. He began working with dub **reggae** sound systems before starting out as a house DJ. At one point he was involved in the setting up of a pirate radio station, Ali FM, before the Department of Trade and Industry and the police closed it down. While continuing to DJ, Badmarsh began to record and produce his own **music** and set up his own label. He released his debut single 'I am that type Of Badmarsh' on **Outcaste** in 1996. The follow-up single 'I am that type Of Badmarsh 2', released the following year, was a massive underground hit and was picked up for airplay on several Radio 1 programmes. Although offers of record deals came in from more established record companies, Badmarsh remains a core member of the Outcaste roster. In 1998 the label released *Dancing Drums*, Badmarsh's collaborative debut album with fellow Outcaste recording artiste, **Shri**. *Dancing Drums*, which mixes up Badmarsh's urban influences and club-influenced beats with Shri's classical instrumentation, was well received by audiences and DJs. A second Badmarsh and Shri album *Tribal* was released early in 2001.

ANDY WOOD

Bailey, David A.

b. 1961, London, England

photographer, writer, curator, lecturer, archive director

Bailey has been central to black cultural production, debate and publication from the early 1980s. His earliest contribution, in diverse ways, was the establishment of a strong black presence in the British visual arts (see **visual and plastic arts**) scene. Bailey was a member of the **D-Max** photography group, and he designed the catalogue for their show, in which he also exhibited, at Birmingham's Ikon Gallery in 1987. He also worked with **Sankofa Film Collective**, documenting and advising on numerous productions, including *The Passion of Remembrance* (1986) and *Looking for Langston* (1988). As well as being a practising photographer, he has published widely on black art and culture. In 1992, with Stuart **Hall**, he co-edited the *Ten.8* issue, 'The critical decade: black British photography in the 1980s'. In 1995, he curated the season 'Mirage: Enigmas of Race, Difference and Desire' at the **Institute of Contemporary Arts**. In 1997, he curated the hugely successful exhibition 'Rhapsodies in Black: Art of the Harlem Renaissance' at the Hayward Gallery. His board membership has included the ICA, **Institute of International Visual Arts**, **Autograph: the Association of Black Photographers** and the Arts Council of Great Britain, and he also has editorial roles in *Third Text* and *Ten.8*. He is co-director of AAVAA (**African and Asian Visual Arts Archive**).

Select bibliography

Bailey, D.A. and Hall, S. (eds) (1992) 'Critical decade: black British photography in the 1980s', special issue, *Ten.8* 2(3).

ELEANOR BYRNE

Bains, Harwant

b. 1963, England

writer

Brought up in a predominantly Sikh community in Southall, West London, writer Harwant Bains has infused his work with a British Asian urban male understanding of the immigrant and cross-cultural experience. In November 1987, his debut play *The Fighting Kite* dealt with issues of race and racism, and was staged at the Theatre Royal Stratford East. Bains later co-edited the book *Multi-Racist Britain*, in which he penned an essay about Southall youth. *The Fighting Kite* was followed by *Blood* at the Royal Court Theatre, where Bains was appointed writer-in-residence, the play evoking both the blood and violence of Sikh history and the dramatic contours of a Jacobean tragedy. His next, *True Love Stories*, preceded a screenplay for the **Channel 4**-funded film (see **film and cinema**) *Wild West* (directed by David Atwood, 1992), which analysed British Asian culture and identity through the madcap adventures of an aspiring country and western band in Southall. Focusing on pioneer and immigrant dreams, the film analogises the frontiers-people who conquered the American West with the frontiers-people who migrated from the Indian subcontinent to the West. In 1995, Bains scripted the BBC drama *Two Oranges and A Mango* about a brother and sister who suffer a culture shock when they return to India for their father's funeral. Ensuing radio plays have included *Learning The Language*, *Tutti Frutti Holy Man* and the comedy drama *Grease Monkeys*.

Select bibliography

Bains, H. (1989) *Blood*, London: Methuen.
Cohen, P. and Bains, H. (eds) (1988) *Multi-Racist Britain*, London: Macmillan.

SATINDER CHOHAN

Bakare, Ade

b. 1966, Midlands, England

fashion designer, couturier

Bakare graduated with a BA (Hons) degree in history (education) in 1987 from Lagos University. He then embarked on a fashion (see **fashion and design**) course (his first love) at Salford University College, Manchester, where he gained an HND in fashion design three years later. While studying there he obtained second place in the National Bridal Student Competition. Success led to his work being screened on the **television** show *This Morning*. On graduation, Bakare became a design assistant for the couturier Christina Stambolian. This was followed by work at Victor Edelstein's couture house.

Bakare set up his own business in 1991 with the aid of a loan from the Prince's Youth Business Trust, creating the Ade Bakare Couture Label. His early designs were showcased at premier collections in Birmingham and Vienna. With a solid background and a good reputation, he opened a salon in Mayfair. A versatile designer famed for bridal wear, Bakare designs for **theatre** and television. He added to his specialities in 1997 with the launch of a hat line and is working on ADE, designs for the younger market. Two years later, he became one of the first black British designers to launch his own perfume, Breeze. Bakare now has a salon in Chelsea. His work appears in national and international publications. Bakare, who works with numerous charity organisations, has lectured at University College, Salford, and St Martins, London, and has worked as a design consultant for the Design Council, Haymarket.

YINKA SUNMONU

Bancil, Parv

b. 1967, Moshi, Tanzania

writer

Bancil, who came to the UK aged two, grew up in Hounslow, West London. He left school at fifteen, and joined Hounslow Arts Co-operative

(HAC), a professional Asian **theatre** company. He began writing without any formal training. His work is hard-hitting and exposes the hypocrisies of the Asian community and the underbelly of Asian life. His first play *Curse of the Dead Dog* (co-written by Ravinder Gill) tells of three young Asian men who waste their time drinking beer. They are encouraged to set up a sound system and mount a benefit gig, which goes badly wrong when one of them informs the local Southall gang of this and the performance is sabotaged. After the HAC theatre closed in 1990, Bancil became a freelance writer. He enjoys a base at Watermans Arts Centre and has also completed a residency at the Royal Court.

Bancil is a founder member of *One Nation Under a Groove, Innit'*, a comedy revue circuit and is part of a comedy band known as the Dead Jalebis. To date, he has written seventeen plays. *Nadir* was the winner of the BBC Radio 4 Young Playwrights Festival in 1991 and *Papa Was a Bus Conductor*, first performed in 1995, has had many revivals. The last is a surreal satirical comedy and is generally acknowledged as the inspiration for much of the second-generation Asian comedy.

Select bibliography

Bancil, P. (1997) *Crazyhorse*, London: Faber & Faber Stagescripts.

SUMAN BHUCHAR

Bandele, Biyi

b. 1967, Kafanchan, Nigeria

novelist, playwright, poet

Educated in Nigeria, Bandele studied drama at Obafemi University, Ile-Ife, and moved to London in 1990. His work for the stage includes *Howling, Death Catches the Hunter* (1995) and *Rain*, which won the thirteenth international Student Playscript Competition in 1988. *The Female God and Other Forbidden Fruit* was broadcast on the BBC World Service in 1991. He was awarded an Arts Council Writer's Bursary in 1992, and *Marching for Fausa* was performed at the Royal Court in 1993. Recent work for **theatre** includes adaptations of Chinua Achebe's novel *Things Fall Apart* for the Performance Studio Workshop of Nigeria, and Aphra Behn's novella *Oroonoko* for the Royal Shakespeare Company. His first novel, *The Man who Came in from the Back of Beyond* was published in 1991, and it is a story about storytelling in West African culture. Other prose works include *The Sympathetic Undertaker and Other Dreams* (1991) and a novella *Incantation on the Eve of an Execution*. A third novel *The Street* was published in 1999. Film (see **film and cinema**) and **television** work includes *Not Even the Gods are Wise Enough* and *Bad Boys*.

Select bibliography

Bandele, B. (1994) *Two Horsemen*, Charlbury: Amber Lane Press.
—— (1993) *Marching for Fausa*, Oxford: Amber Lane Press.
—— (1991) *The Man who Came in from the Back of Beyond*, London: Bellew.
—— (1991) *The Sympathetic Undertaker and Other Dreams*, London: Bellew.

SARA SALIH

Bandung File

A **Channel 4** programme launched in 1991 and dedicated to issues relevant to black British communities, *Bandung File* was named after the 1955 conference of the same name that brought together African and Asian states in Indonesia. It was the successor to the current affairs programme *Black on Black*. The programme sought to raise issues that were relevant to being black in Britain, such as discrimination and **new racism**. It also gave space to current debates and contentious issues such as political correctness and multiculturalism, as well as to promote the historical significance of African and Asian cultures and their impact on Western cultural development. Darcus **Howe** and Tariq Ali were frequent contributors. Channel 4 launched their latest current affairs programme on black issues, *Black Bag*, in 1992.

ALISON DONNELL

Beaton, Norman

b. 1934, Georgetown, Guyana; d. 1994, Georgetown, Guyana

actor, recording artist

Norman Lugard Beaton made his debut as an actor in Guyana in the 1950s while studying at teacher training college. He also enjoyed success as a singer, becoming Guyana calypso champion in 1956. In 1960, Beaton migrated to Britain where he progressed from regional theatre to lead roles at the National Theatre and the Royal Court Theatre. In 1997, Beaton also founded the Black Theatre of Brixton, which was instrumental in introducing black **theatre** to Britain. Beaton soon became one of Britain's prominent **television** actors, landing roles in Britain's first all-black soap opera **Empire Road** (1978–9), *Dead Head* (1986) and *Little Napoleons* (1993), among many others. He also appeared alongside Denzel Washington in the movie *The Mighty Quinn* (1989). From 1989 to 1994, Beaton enjoyed unprecedented popularity on British television with **Channel 4**'s highly successful sitcom **Desmonds**. In the series, Beaton played the owner of a South London barber shop. As a result of Beaton's popularity, African American comedian Bill Cosby invited him to the USA in 1991 to make appearances in *The Cosby Show*. Shortly after Beaton died in 1994, aged sixty, Channel 4 showed the film *Shooting Stars* (1994) as a special tribute to the thespian, with an appearance by Beaton reading a Shakespearean sonnet.

Further reading

Beaton, N. (1996) *Beaton but Unbowed* (autobiography), London: Methuen.
Bourne, S. (1996) *Black in the British Frame – Black People in British Film and Television 1896–1996*, London: Cassell.

RAYMOND ENISUOH

Being Here I, II and III

A series of exhibitions of photographic collections, the first being held in Birmingham Art Gallery in

1996. This remarkable collection presented photographs taken during the period of 1950 to the late 1970s to evidence the arrival of African, Asian and Caribbean migrants to Birmingham. Peter James (Birmingham Central Library's Head of Photography) rescued the doomed contents of the Dyche studio from a council skip, removing them to the Reference Library as an archive of black settlement. The photographs were the work of two white commercial studio photographers who operated from premises at 354 Mosely Road, Balsall Heath: Ernest Dyche (1887–1973) and, from the late 1940s, his son Malcolm, who died in 1990. The Dyches' subjects were anonymous studio visitors, and the public display of such private documents is undoubtedly one of the most disturbing aspects of the exhibition. Local and national newspaper articles that have sought to identify the subjects have had limited success and the majority of the subjects are destined to remain as 'missing persons'. However, their value as 'alternative' historical records lies in what Stuart **Hall** argues is a 'democratisation of representation. They are poor-person's "portraits".' Ernest Dyche studied the techniques of theatrical and cinema photographers, and was highly experienced in constructing a desirable portrait within the generic practices of Edwardian studio conventions, with their properties and costumes. The result is an ethereal quality in the photographs enhanced by his use of backcloths and props, which had been in service since the studio opened in the 1920s. These 'fantasy' settings mean that the photographs are loaded with well-chosen signifiers, with some portraits of the migrant subjects not unlike glamorous actors posed against a theatrical backdrop. The photographs suggest a double form of 'writing back' to an inhospitable metropolis and to concerned loved ones back home; 'the costume' was contrived to signal advanced status. Equally, many photographs were taken in uniforms (bus conductor's or nurse's) to convey the confidence of a respectable trade or profession. However, the historical reality of material racism, which meant that many migrants failed to gain equivalent working conditions to indigenous workers, must acknowledge the contradictions that this photographic evidence presents.

Further reading

Hall, S. (1991) 'Reconstruction work: images of post-war black settlement', in J. Spence and P. Holland (eds) *Family Snaps: the Meanings of Domestic Photography*, London: Virago, pp. 152–65.

James, P. (1998) 'Under exposed: snapshots of the history of photography and photographic collections in Birmingham 1839–1998', in *Coming To Light: Birmingham Photographic Collections*, Birmingham: Birmingham Libraries and Birmingham Museums and Art Gallery.

SANDRA COURTMAN

BERESFORD, ROMEO *see* Jazzie B

Berry, James

b. 1924, Boston, Jamaica

poet, editor

Born in Jamaica, Berry spent a brief period in the USA in the early 1940s, before moving to London in 1948. Working as a telegraphist from 1951, Berry did not become a full-time writer until 1977, when he was awarded the C. Day Lewis Fellowship. He won the Poetry Society's National Poetry Competition in 1981, and his collections of poetry include *Fractured Circles* (1979), *Lucy's Letters and Loving* (1982), *Chain of Days* (1985) and *Hot Earth Cold Earth* (1995). Some of Berry's most important contributions to the field, however, have been as editor of the *Bluefoot Traveller* (1976) and *News for Babylon* (1984) anthologies, which have proved to be influential early collections of black British writing. A Committee Member of the **Caribbean Artists' Movement**, Berry has played an active role as a performance poet and broadcaster on **television** and radio. Committed to multicultural education, he has also worked as writer-in-residence at Vauxhall Manor School and has written a number of books for children. He was awarded the OBE in 1990.

Select bibliography

Berry, J. (ed.) (1984) *News for Babylon*, London: Chatto & Windus.

—— (1979) *Fractured Circles*, London: New Beacon Books.

—— (ed.) (1976) *Bluefoot Traveller*, London: Lime-house Publications.

JAMES PROCTER

Bhabha, Homi K.

b. 1949, Bombay, India.

post-colonial theorist, literary and cultural critic

Bhabha's work in the post-colonial field has had a huge international impact on current debates about identity, migrancy and nation. He grew up in the small Parsee community in Bombay, his early reading falling under the Anglocentric influence of his mother. His father was a lawyer who spent some years at Lincoln's Inn, London, in the 1950s. He attended Elphinstone College, Bombay, as an English Literature undergraduate and then Oxford, writing an M.Phil. on V.S. **Naipaul**.

He subsequently became a lecturer at Sussex University. His early research focused on what he termed 'the ambivalence of colonial discourse'. It drew on post-structuralist narrative theories and the work of Edward Said, and transformed critical understandings and approaches to colonial and post-colonial texts. He then went on to develop work on concepts of mimicry, hybridity and the third space. Bhabha was also at the forefront of supporters for Salman **Rushdie** in the late 1980s, following the proclamation of the *fatwa*, organising the group 'Black Voices in Defense of Salman Rushdie' in 1989.

His work on nation includes the collection of essays he edited, *Nation and Narration* (1990), featuring his seminal piece, 'DissemiNation: time, narrative and the margins of modernity', a complex, wide-ranging and fascinating meditation on the relationship of narrative to nation. In 1994, a collection of his essays, *The Location of Culture*, brought together work published over the previous decade alongside his current research. His work has subsequently moved into an area which he

terms 'minoritarian cosmopolitanism'. In 1997, he edited a special edition of the journal *Critical Inquiry*, 'Front lines/border posts'. In 1994, he was appointed Chester D. Tripp Professor in the Humanities at the University of Chicago.

Select bibliography

Bhabha, H.K. (1994) *The Location of Culture*, London and New York: Routledge.

—— (ed.) (1990) *Nation and Narration*, London and New York: Routledge.

ELEANOR BYRNE

Bhaji on the Beach

With a screenplay by Meera **Syal** and directed by Gurinda **Chadha**, *Bhaji on the Beach* (1993) was a key film (see **film and cinema**) of the early 1990s, which was well received both in the independent and mainstream cinematic fields, combining a social-realist mode with an interweaving of psychological, fantastical and surreal aspects. Three generations of Asian women go for a day trip to Blackpool where they discover what binds them together, as well as the radical differences between them. The film was important in centring its focus on Asian women's experiences in Britain and exploring issues such as inter-racial relationships, sexuality, abortion and domestic violence from this perspective. Alternating between a serious investigation of these social issues and a mixture of slapstick and darker humour, the film managed to negotiate a balance between being what Sarita Malik calls 'a cinema of duty' and a playful and intelligent exploration of contemporary Asian British culture. *Bhaji on the Beach* also engaged with stereotypes of English civility, focused through the character of Ambrose Waddington, an archetypal straw-boatered English gentleman, who turns out to be an unemployed pantomime actor. The film consciously engaged with questions of identity by examining the performance of racial and national stereotypes in the carnivalistic atmosphere of Blackpool pleasure beach. It signalled a dissatisfaction with essentialist notions of either British or

Asian identities and emphasised the provisionality of these norms.

Further reading

Malik, S. (1996) 'Beyond "the cinema of duty"? The pleasures of hybridity: black British film of the 1980s and 1990s', in A. Higson (ed.) *Dissolving Views. Key Writings on British Cinema*, London and New York: Cassell, pp. 201–10.

ELEANOR BYRNE

Bhamra, Kuljit

b. 1959, Nairobi, Kenya

musician, composer

Kuljit Bhamra is a skilled *tabla* player, composer and record producer. He is one of the most influential musicians in the creation of the **bhangra** sound as we know it in the UK. He grew up in Southall and is a qualified civil engineer, and worked for Richmond Council for fifteen years before taking up **music** full time in 1993. A self-taught musician, Bhamra learnt by imitation and does not follow any particular Indian tradition or school. His inspiration comes from his mother, Mohinder Kaur Bhamra, a gifted singer who sang at weddings before turning professional and asking her son to accompany her. During his early days, he arranged, wrote and produced albums, such as *Chamak Jehi Mutiar Da* (1983), for the band Premi. This album was repeatedly played on Sina Radio, becoming a hit, and Bhamra's career took off. He has worked with virtually all of the big names in the bhangra field, including Heera, Gurdas Maan and Chirag Pechan. He set up his own record company, Keda Records, and began managing artists as well. After the bhangra craze peaked, he stepped out as a performer and collaborated with many Western musicians. To date, he has composed, produced and recorded more than 1,000 songs, many of which have been international hits on the Asian music circuit. He has composed for the films **Bhaji on the Beach** (1993) and *Monkey Bone* (provisional title, forthcoming), and most recently

for the stage play *The Ramayana*, by Indhu **Rubasingham**, at the Birmingham Repertory Theatre, 2000, and Royal National Theatre, April 2001.

SUMAN BHUCHAR

bhangra

While bhangra's origins lie in the Punjab region of India, its importance and influence in Britain lies in its role as a catalyst in the development of a sense of cultural identity and visibility for Asian British youth since around the mid-1980s. Prior to this, bhangra music and performers largely fulfilled the same role as they would have traditionally done in the Punjab over the past 200 years. Bhangra was, and still is, a **dance** music performed at celebrations and gatherings such as weddings, birthdays and harvest celebrations. Musically, bhangra had changed little; the *dhol* drum remained prominent but modern instruments had been introduced to help adapt to the needs of modern performances. This was not an event peculiar to the performance of bhangra in Britain, as the performers in rural Punjab had continually introduced traditional and more modern instruments to the music over the years.

In 1984, Alaap, a traditional bhangra band who had mainly performed at family gatherings in Southall, began work on an album with the producer Deepak Kazanchi. Kazanchi had previously worked with an array of artists encompassing the spectrum of popular music, from mainstream Western pop to **reggae**, and did not seem to be an obvious choice for Alaap, a band who had already recorded several bhangra albums on the Birmingham-based Multitone label. This was borne out by the resulting album, which was very different from Alaap's previous recordings. *Teri Chunni De Sitare*, while still a bhangra album, introduced elements of contemporary electronic dance music into Alaap's sound. In the wake of the album's release, Alaap began to perform to larger audiences outwith traditional gatherings and a number of newer, more professional bhangra acts began to emerge, including Heera and Holle Holle. By late 1986, these newcomers could command audiences of around 3,000 in Central London and the music of Alaap and their contemporaries was dubbed the 'Southall sound' as media interest in bhangra grew.

Bhangra music continued to develop as a newer generation of bands came through, including Achanak, Safri Boys and Eshara, who were able to take on board and expand upon the pioneering work of their predecessors and contemporaries, introducing elements of reggae, ragga, techno and rap to their sound. Bally **Sagoo**'s influence, initially as a bhangra artist and producer, and later as a remixer, is important as he continually re-vamped bhangra hits with collaborations and impressive remixes on albums such as *Bally Sagoo on the Mix* and the *Star Crazy* compilations. In many ways these artists reflected the multitude of sounds and styles of music that they grew up with, including black British musical styles.

Despite the growing popularity of bhangra and an increasing media profile, the music impinged only marginally upon popular consciousness. Excluding specialist Radio 1 DJs such as John Peel and Andy Kershaw, bhangra was only played on local stations and received very little **television** coverage, although the Joi Bangla sound system were featured in a two-part BBC documentary *Big City: the Hidden Sounds of London* in 1992. One major reason that is often cited for bhangra's lack of impact on the charts and radio is the method of distribution for the majority of bhangra acts. Most of the acts and labels distributed the music, mainly in the form of cassettes, through a network of Asian stores; moreover, larger shops were unwilling to stock such products due to the minuscule profit margins involved. The small profit margins on bhangra albums also meant that only bigger labels such as Multitone and Nachural could afford to invest in bigger-scale studio productions and bhangra albums were rarely recorded for more than £10,000, far less than the cost of the average pop album. The best selling bhangra artists could achieve sales of between 60,000 and 75,000 copies of each album, yet these sales were not recorded for the charts. In 1992, a Billboard survey highlighted the failure of the attempts by several bhangra producers to break out of the 'price-trap', showing that, despite such attempts, 90 per cent of bhangra's sales still occurred in the network of Asian stores. The report concluded that bhangra was still predominantly an 'ethnic underground economy' (Mitchell: 62). Despite such problems, Multitone and Nachural were still able to sign licensing deals with major record companies and bhangra acts continued to perform to growing audiences at more established venues.

Although bhangra artists had always shown an enthusiasm for adding new styles and influences to their music, the breathrough of artists such as **Apache Indian** in the 1990s heightened tensions between those who believed that bhangra was a traditional music with a set sound and style, and those who were experimenting with a fusion of sounds. Apache Indian's music was mainly influenced by reggae forms, especially ragga, to which he added influences such as bhangra. His impact upon the music scene was extensive, providing an example of the 'commercial viability of westernized Indian, rather than Indianised western pop music' (Sabita Banerji, in Mitchell). The prominence of Apache Indian gave rise to a renewed interest in Asian British popular culture but by the middle of the 1990s attention was moving away from the bhangra scene to the **post-bhangra** sounds being produced, performed and consumed by a new generation of artists, bands and audiences.

Further reading

Banerji, S. and Baumann, G. (1990) 'Bhangra 1984–8: fusion and professionalization in a genre of South Asian dance music', in P. Oliver (ed.) *Black Music in Britain: Essays on the Afro-Asian Contribution to Popular Music*, London: Open University Press, pp. 137–52.

Mitchell, T. (1996) *Popular Music and Local Identity*, London: Leicester University Press.

Sharma, S., Hutnyk, J. and Sharma, A. (eds) *Disorienting Rhythms: the Politics of the New Asian Dance Music*, London: Zed Books.

ANDY WOOD

Bhaskar, Sanjeev

b. 1964, London, England

writer, presenter, comedian

Sanjeev Bhaskar grew up in West London and went to Hatfield Polytechnic to read marketing, where he met musician Nitin **Sawhney**. Together they performed comedy sketches and sang in the college bar. After leaving college, they set up the comedy duo Secret Asians and toured on the London fringe **theatre** circuit. It was here that the catch-phrase 'Kiss my chuddies' was born. Bhaskar wanted to be an actor, but lacked confidence, so he worked, first, with the Asian Music Circuit and, then, at the Tom Allen Centre. In 1995, he got the opportunity to perform as part of the education work undertaken by **Tara Arts** and decided to take it. He also presented one series of the BBC Asian magazine show *Network East* and the last series of *Bollywood or Bust*. The comedy work continued, however, and a pilot for a live comedy show with Sawhney, which was to become ***Goodness Gracious Me***, was recorded at Riverside studios after they were spotted by the BBC's Anil Gupta and Sharat Sardana. *Goodness Gracious Me* was then produced for two Radio 4 series before moving on to television for three series. Nitin Sawhney pulled out shortly before the television show began, in order to concentrate on his musical career, leaving Bhaskar with colleagues Kulvinder **Ghir**, Meera **Syal** and Nina **Wadia**. Bhaskar has commented of *Goodness Gracious Me* that 'there was nothing on TV that as a British Asian I had any ownership over... *Goodness Gracious Me* was unapologetic about being Asian'. With the success of *Goodness Gracious Me* behind him, Bhaskar developed a one-man show, which he launched at the Queen Elizabeth Hall in London. Although relatively well received, it was not considered to be of the same quality as *Goodness Gracious Me*. Bhaskar has appeared in the **Channel 4** sitcom *Small Potatoes* and in 1999 Bhaskar worked alongside Kenneth Branagh in the short film *Dance with Shiva*, a true story about Indian soldiers in the First World War, as well as in *Notting Hill* with Julia Roberts and Hugh Grant.

SUMAN BHUCHAR AND SAMINA ZAHIR

Bhattacharjee, Paul

b. 1960, London, England

actor

Paul Bhattacharjee is an actor who is passionate about **theatre**. He began in young people's theatre working with a company called Young Theatre. He met Jatinder **Verma** after spotting an advert in *Time Out*, where Verma was seeking people interested in being part of an Asian theatre company. They met in 1979, and Paul started performing with **Tara Arts** during their community years. He believed that the company should become a professional theatre company and drafted the constitution to begin the process of this change. The radical approach of Tara Arts fitted Paul's politics and he never went to drama school but got his equity card through Tara. His first performance as a professional was in the play *Lion's Raj*. In 1983, he took a year out from Tara and went to work as an assistant director at Riverside Studios. Other credits at Tara include: *The Little Clay Cart*, *Ancestral Voices* and *Meet Me*.

His **television** break came with a BBC play and he appeared in the Granada soap *Albion Market* (1985) as Jaz, a character who ended up being charged for the manslaughter of a racist. His career in television grew and he has been in BBC's drama serial *Shalom Salaam*. He has also appeared in the films *Love Birds* (1987) and *My Sister Wife*. Later on he was in *Murmuring Judges*, one of the David Hare trilogy at the Royal National Theatre and the overseas tour of *Arabian Nights*. A highlight of his career was taking over Art Malik's role in Tom Stoppard's *Indian Ink*, playing opposite Niamh Cusack.

SUMAN BHUCHAR

Bhimji, Zarina

b. 1963, Uganda

visual artist

Bhimji's early photographic work examines the exotic and the status of traditional Indian artefacts, although her approach is far from sociological, instead relying on allusive, poetic imagery. Personal objects and mementoes often appear in the early work as a way of exploring identity and place. Emerging at the end of the 1980s, Bhimji's lyrical style pointed one way forward for black artists increasingly realising the limits of more didactic work, and in this sense she can be seen as a transitional figure between 1980s and 1990s practices. The vulnerability of Bhimji's photographic imagery is developed in later installations, particularly in her use of burnt and charred fabric. More recently, Bhimji's interest in place has led her to explore institutions for her work, including Leighton House and the British Museum. Her locations are often associated with regimes of knowledge, but Bhimji's interrogation of them is a subtle one. Her interest in Orientalism and ciphers of exoticism has remained as an abiding theme through her career, as has her fusion of personal imagery with cultural and religious iconography.

Further reading

Ikon Gallery (1992) *Zarina Bhimji: I Will Always Be Here*, exhibition catalogue, Birmingham: Ikon Gallery.

NIRU RATNAM

Bhuchar, Sudha

b. 1962, Tanga, Tanzania

actor, writer, artistic director

Sudha Bhuchar was born and brought up in East Africa, but has lived in the UK for over twenty-five years. She is a maths and sociology graduate from Roehampton University, London. She began her acting career with **Tara Arts**, performing in their community and professional productions, such as *The Little Clay Cart* (1986, Black Theatre Season remount), *Meet Me* and *Chilli in Your Eyes*. Her other theatre credits include *Prem, Torpedoes in the Jacuzzi* and Salman **Rushdie**'s *Haroun and the Sea of Stories* at the Royal National Theatre. In 1989, Bhuchar and Kristine **Landon-Smith** set up **Tamasha Theatre Company** and she has since acted in,

adapted and produced many of the company's plays. In addition to her stage work, she has acted widely in **television**, including in *Shalom Salaam*, *Billy Webb, Lovejoy, Dangerfield* and *Boon*. She played Meena in the BBC soap opera *Eastenders*, where her character courted controversy by having an affair with her brother-in-law, Sanjay (played by Deepak **Verma**). She also co-presented three series of *Network East*, the BBC Asian magazine programme. In 1993, Bhuchar became the first Asian character to settle in Ambridge, when she was chosen to play the solicitor, Usha Gupta, in Radio 4's, *The Archers*. She played the part for a year until actress Souad Faress took over. In 1995, Bhuchar turned to writing after participating in the Royal Court International Summer School, because she realised that 'there were no good parts for thirty-something women'. She teamed up with Shaheen **Khan** and has written several plays for BBC Radio 4, including the very successful series *Girlies*, about the travails of four thirty-something Asian women. Their first original stage play, *Balti Kings*, a pungent 'slice of life' comedy, drawn from research into the balti restaurants so prevalent in Birmingham, was produced by Tamasha in 1999–2000.

SUMAN BHUCHAR

Bhuller, Darshan Singh

b. 1961, Punjab, India

dancer, choreographer, film-maker

Bhuller lived in the Punjab until the age of six when he came to England. His interest in **dance** began while a pupil at Harehills Middle School, Leeds, where a dance module based on the Laban method was programmed. He has danced with the London Contemporary Dance Theatre, Richard Alston Dance Company, Phoenix Dance Company and Siobhan Davies Company. Bhuller draws heavily on Martha Graham's technique, a US choreographer who frequently worked with the late Robin Howard. Bhuller began to choreograph while working with the London Contemporary Dance Theatre and further developed this area when working with other companies. He went on to choreograph *Once Upon a Time in England* for

CandoCo, a dance company with both able-bodied and wheelchair-using dancers. In the late 1990s, Bhuller set up his own company, Singh Productions, enabling him to choreograph, direct and continue film-making. In 1998, he worked on *Planted Seeds*, a dance piece based around the experiences of those in the Bosnian war. He went over to Bosnia to meet people who lived with traumatic experiences and drew on his own family's experiences of India and partition when relating to them and re-telling their stories.

SAMINA ZAHIR

Bildungsroman

Many recent black British novels such as Diran **Adebayo**'s *Some Kind of Black* (1996), David **Dabydeen**'s *The Intended* (1991), Hanif **Kureishi**'s *The Buddha of Suburbia* (1990) and *The Black Album* (1995), and Andrea **Levy**'s first three novels can be read as *Bildungsromane*. They are stories about one or more protagonists developing from childhood or adolescence into adulthood in a culture that does not necessarily recognise and support their growth.

Levy's first novel, *Every Light in the House Burnin'*, features a very articulate central character whose quiet-mannered parents urge her to be inconspicuous. Having partly internalised the host society's notion that as immigrants they should not reside in Britain, they tried to 'blend in' and remain silent: 'My parents' strategy was to keep as quiet as possible in the hope that no one would know that they sneaked into this country' (Levy 1994: 88). In opposition to this, Angela, who is born in Britain, is determined to stand her ground. As is typical of the *Bildungsroman*, the central character of *Some Kind of Black* cannot choose a pre-determined route. Dele can lead neither his parents' life nor the one they have in mind for him, but needs to chart his own journey. His path of growing up is also less clear than that of his white peers. In his case, growing away from his Nigerian parents entails distancing himself from one of his own cultural backgrounds, a difficult choice in the face of an inhospitable society. The black British *Bildungsroman* thus often implies generational conflict. In many cases this is a conflict between a generation that migrated to Britain and one that was born here.

As well as airing issues related to the protagonists' identity formation, this genre is also about voicing this identity, a feature that points to the genre's closeness to autobiographical writing. Bernardine **Evaristo**'s *Lara*, in the verse novel of that name, deplores:

> Home. I searched but could not find myself,/ not on the screen, billboards, books, magazines,/ and first and last not in the mirror, my demon, my love/ which faded my brownness into a Bardot likeness/ [. . .] I longed for an image,/ a story, to speak me, describe me, birth me whole.
>
> (Evaristo 1997: 69).

The gendered and adolescent pressures of fashioning her body in accordance with the icons of the day make it harder for Lara than her white peers to come upon images that can represent her intact. Wishing to feel unbroken, she seeks a rebirth by being represented in her entirety through an image or a story. Lara imagines 'home' as the location of self-identity, of assured self-knowledge, and in the course of the novel tries to find this 'home'.

Not feeling adequately represented (in the media, in school, in politics, in **literature**) is a problem experienced by many protagonists of the black British *Bildungsroman*. However, the narratives of growing up that are already in circulation are supplemented and remade by the very genre itself, to include stories of British youths with an Asian, African or Caribbean background. Such acts of inscription can accumulate to a transformative force, which reaches out, beyond the text. In this sense, the black British *Bildungsroman* can be said to have a dual function: it is about the formation of its protagonists and at once about the transformation of the 'national script' for growing up. By describing and inciting cultural changes in Britain, the *Bildungsroman* reinforces heterogeneity, and crucially contributes to its acceptance. In this way, the black British *Bildungsroman* does not only feature the formation of an individual: instead the text is also a symbolic act of carving out space, and of creating a public sphere. These writers pursue the project of their inscription into a literary tradition and of 're-writing' Britain, a project to which the *Bildungsroman* is well-suited. In the context of African-Caribbean literature, Geta LeSeur has suggested that the 'Black *bildungsroman*' (her term) does not follow European literary models but relates to Olaudah Equiano's autobiography from 1789; this claim for a black literary ancestor is significant as it would displace J.W. Goethe's *Wilhelm Meister*, published a few years later (1795–6), as the foundational narrative of the *Bildungsroman*.

Select bibliography

Adebayo, D. (1996) *Some Kind of Black*, London: Virago.

Dabydeen, D. (1991) *The Intended*, London: Secker & Warburg.

Evaristo, B. (1997) *Lara*, Tunbridge Wells: Angela Royal.

Levy, A. (1994) *Every Light in the House Burnin'*, London: Headline Review.

Kureishi, H. (1995) *The Black Album*, London: Faber & Faber.

—— (1990) *The Buddha of Suburbia*, London: Faber & Faber.

Further reading

LeSeur, G. (1995) *Ten is the Age of Darkness: the Black Bildungsroman*, Columbia and London: University of Missouri Press.

Schoene-Harwood, B. (1999) 'Beyond (t)race: *Bildung* and *proprioception* in Meera Syal's *Anita and Me*', *JCL* 34(1): 159–68.

Stein, M. (1998) 'The black British *Bildungsroman* and the transformation of Britain: connectedness across difference', in B. Korte and K.-P. Müller (eds) *Unity in Diversity Revisited? British Literature and Culture in the 1990s*, Tübingen: Gunter Narr, pp. 89–105.

MARK STEIN

Biswas, Anup Kumar

b. 1957, West Bengal, India

musician

Biswas's musical ability was first nurtured at the Oxford Mission School in Calcutta. He began playing the cello at the age of ten and by sixteen had made his concert debut and had recorded for radio and **television**. In 1974, Biswas came to London to study at the Royal College of Music and has since played at the Royal Albert Hall, the House of Commons and St James's Palace. In 1994, he made his debut at the Carnegie Hall, New York. However, Biswas, who also studied classical Indian music, still performs annually in India and in 1983 was made Director of the Mathieson Music School in Calcutta.

ALISON DONNELL

Biswas, Sutapa

b. 1962, Bolpur, India

visual artist

Almost immediately after graduating, Biswas became involved with the Black Women group of artists, taking part in the exhibition *The Thin Black Line*. She also became associated with the wider circle of black art, taking part in a number of group exhibitions. Her early work was confrontational and her *Housewives with Steak-knives* is one of black art's most iconic pieces. The piece is a good example of Biswas's highly satirical, straightforward early style. As black art became a less useful organising principle, Biswas, like many of her contemporaries, started making more reflexive, layered work. Biswas turned to other media such as **photography**. She retained her interest in exploring the legacy of her Indian cultural heritage in works such as her *Synaspe* series, but the emphasis in these works is more on memory and the fragmentary nature of identity. The shift in Biswas's work might be seen as embodying the move away from anti-racist didacticism, which characterised 1980s black visual culture, to the questioning of identity, which characterised 1990s practices.

Further reading

The Photographer's Gallery (1992) *Synaspe: Sutapa Biswas*, exhibition catalogue.

NIRU RATNAM

Black and White Power Plays

Black and White Power Plays was the title given to a series of **theatre** productions arranged through the **Institute of Contemporary Arts** in 1970 in line with their objective to strengthen the profile of black arts in Britain. In keeping with their historical moment, a number of the plays looked to the ascendant black politics across the Atlantic and explored the Black Power and civil rights movements in the USA. The series also included *Black Pieces*, the first play by Mustapha **Matura**.

ALISON DONNELL

Black Art Gallery

Founded at Finsbury Park, North London, in 1983 by the Organisation for Black Art Advancement and Leisure Activities, the gallery stood for the defence of fine art and other cultural activities created by artists with African roots, at a time when the promotion of ethnic arts was dominating funding policies. Its purpose was to support contemporary artists whose works challenged preconceptions of black culture. 'Hearts in Exile' was the inaugural show, which included works by Eddie **Chambers** and Keith **Piper**. In 1984 the exhibition 'Black Art Now' coincided with the conference of the same name. Both events set out to document and discuss the situation of black art in the mid-1980s. This was followed by the seminar 'What Next?' in September 1985. Negative responses towards black identity remained the same and 'The Black Bastard as a Cultural Icon' was exhibited in 1985, including 'From Generation to Generation'.

Sonia **Boyce**, Uzo Egonu and Lubaina **Himid** had solo exhibitions in 1986. Towards the end of the 1980s financial concerns caused problems for the gallery. One of the last exhibitions held was 'Ask Me No Questions and I Tell You No Lies'.

Further reading

Araeen, R. (1987) *The Essential Black Art*, London: Chisenhale Gallery.

Chambers, Eddie (ed.) (1988) *Black Art: Plotting the Course*, Oldham: Oldham Art Gallery.

PAULINE DE SOUZA

Black Art Group

Founded in 1980 by Eddie **Chambers**, the Black Art Group was first known as the Wolverhampton Young Black Art Group. However, it became the Black Art Group in 1981 to emphasise the radical political and social concerns of the black art students living in Britain. The 'Black Art Group' was the title of the first exhibition curated by Chambers in 1981 at the Wolverhampton Art Gallery. Members of the group participating in the exhibition included Dominic Daves, Ian Palmer, Andrew Hazel and Keith **Piper**. The exhibition provided space for members to criticise Western art practice and its definitions of history, identity and culture. Originally the group's conception of black art derived from Eric Pemberton's interest in the use of political meanings in artworks, but over the years the attitude of the group was informed by Harlem Renaissance leaders such as Marcus Garvey and the civil rights leaders Martin Luther King and Malcolm X. This association with other black historical events was displayed in their first touring exhibition, the 'Pan-Afrikan Connection', curated by Chambers at the African Centre in London in 1982. The confrontational approach to Western colonialism and post-colonialism stimulated debates and received considerable media attention. It led directly to the First National Black Art Convention at Wolverhampton in the same year, organised by the Black Art Group. Other black artists' exhibitions followed and the final exhibition, 'Radical Black Art', was held in London in 1984.

Further reading

Chambers, E. (ed.) (1988) *Black Art: Plotting the Course*, Oldham: Oldham Art Gallery, Wolverhampton: Wolverhampton Art Gallery, Liverpool: Bluecoat Gallery.

—— (ed.) (1990) *Let the Canvas Come to Life With Dark*

Faces, Sheffield: Herbert Art Gallery and Museum.

PAULINE DE SOUZA

Black Art: Plotting the Course

One of two major survey shows of 1988 that indicated the fracturing of black art, *Black Art: Plotting the Course* was curated by Eddie **Chambers**, partly as an answer to *The Essential Black Art* curated by Rasheed **Araeen** earlier in the year. While Araeen's exhibition had showcased the leading figures of black art, Chambers's show consisted of young, upcoming artists whom he thought fitted the parameters of black art. Chambers accepted that the term black art was misused and misunderstood; however, unlike Araeen, he felt it was still useful. Central to Chambers's understanding of it was perceived links to black art practices in the USA such as the Harlem Renaissance. At times Chambers's theory seemed at odds with his curatorial practice, particularly with the question of whether black was ethnically specific and excluded Asians. He later admitted in interview that he had been pressurised into accepting black as an umbrella term that encompassed Asians, against his own judgement.

Further reading

Archer-Straw, P. (1999) 'Interview with Eddie Chambers', in V. Clarke and G. Tawadros (eds) *Run through the Jungle: Selected Writings by Eddie Chambers*, London: inIVA.

Oldham Art Gallery (1988) *Black Art: Plotting the Course*, exhibition catalogue.

NIRU RATNAM

Black Arts Alliance

Black Arts Alliance (BAA) has been established since 1985. With a high reputation for delivering quality arts projects, including workshops, performances, exhibitions, seminars, colloquiums and conferences, BAA boasts a membership of 350 artists including mainland Africans and African Americans.

In its formative years, and without an office base, BAA managed to co-ordinate a wide range of activities that brought its membership into the most prestigious galleries and theatres. In 1998 BAA finally moved into a suite of five offices that includes a library resource, a base large enough to reflect the profile of its work. 'ArtBlacklive' is now recognised nationally and internationally for its work in **live art** conferences, training and commissions. 'Let the Talking Commence' brings small groups of artists and speakers together for informal mentoring and inspiring gatherings. *Four for More*, released in 2001, will be the first in a series of in-house publications. Every year BAA celebrates its survival as no other black organisation has lasted so long, and for that it acknowledges all members past, present and future

Further reading

Black Arts Alliance Report (1999) Manchester.

PAULINE DE SOUZA

black arts movements

Britain's black arts movements took shape against a changing social, political and cultural backdrop, being heavily influenced by post-war emigration from the Caribbean, Asia and Africa. While black arts movements experienced considerable prejudice to their work, there were a number of institutions that succeeded in offering support. Both the **Institute of Contemporary Arts**, established in the late 1940s, and Gallery One and the New Vision Centre Gallery, both set up in the early to mid-1950s, targeted international but nationally unknown artists and took some of the first steps in promoting and developing both international and national black artists in the UK.

In 1976, Naseem **Khan**'s Ethnic Minority Report, ground-breaking in its day, defined black arts in terms of their difference from the dominant host – British – culture. However, Khan's report undoubtedly opened out debate, instigating the setting up of the **Minorities' Arts Advisory**

Service (MAAS), which developed arts advisory services countrywide and produced the first publication of the London register of artists and performers. MAAS also published *Echo*, its monthly bulletin, which was later succeeded by ***Artrage***. The 1970s saw the gradual increase in arts movements such as the **Caribbean Artists' Movement** and Indian Artists: United Kingdom. 'Into the Open', held in Sheffield in 1984, was the first national exhibition of black artists in the UK. The report, *The Arts of Ethnic Minorities*, from the **Commission for Racial Equality**, stressed the contribution that 'ethnic arts' could offer community arts in the 1980s. Also, the Black Visual Artists Forum was set up in London by the **Greater London Council**, who previously established the first Ethnic Arts Sub-Committee.

In the 1990s, access to black arts played an increasingly pivotal role as Regional Arts Boards were encouraged to prioritise and develop arts access and cultural diversity work. In 1997, the Arts Council collaborated with the British Council over its plans for 'Re-inventing Britain'. The conference centred on challenging traditional notions of Britishness and a 'pure' culture. In 1998, the **Drum** hosted the Arts Council's yearly conference. The conference theme, 'Correcting the Picture', examined new perspectives on cultural diversity in arts management. The conference highlighted how a lack of representation of black employees in senior or middle arts management continues.

Further reading

Khan, N. (1976) *The Arts Britain Ignores: the Arts of Ethnic Minorities in Britain*, London: Arts Council of Great Britain

Owusu, K. (1986) *The Struggle for Black Arts in Britain: What Can We Consider Better than Freedom?*, London: Comedia.

SAMINA ZAHIR

black Atlantic, the

A concept based upon the premise that since the time of slavery black people's experiences of their interaction with the West have been marked by travel (in diverse forms), transcultural influences and international dialogues that have been a result of the African diaspora. Paul **Gilroy** uses the term 'black Atlantic' when outlining his model for the development of a wide variety of black cultural production in the USA and Europe. He proposes that in order to appreciate the transnational influences on the production of black musical forms, painting, poetry or fiction we need a model that transgresses the different nationalist paradigms for thinking about cultural history, which, he claims, ultimately fail when confronted by the history of intercultural and transnational formations that he sees as marking black experiences of modernity in the West. He offers the model of the 'black Atlantic' as one that will counter what he sees as a depressing affiliation to ideas of cultural nationalism, which, to him, fail to recognise the fundamentally syncretic ways in which black cultures have developed in the USA and Europe.

Gilroy cites a range of cultural and political figures whose experiences of migration involved movement to and from both sides of the Atlantic, and who were also influenced by or had connections with Africa, making them particularly good early examples of this phenomenon: Martin Delany, Frederick Douglass, W.E.B. Du Bois and Richard Wright. He then goes on to demonstrate how this phenomenon is useful when discussing popular cultural forms in the present, in the USA, the Caribbean and Europe. His model also proposes a new way of understanding identity. He comments, ' The history of the black Atlantic yields a course of lessons as to the instability and mutability of identities which are always unfinished, always being remade.' Hence, the phenomenon of the black Atlantic, according to Gilroy, is marked by creolisation, metissage (see **métis(se)/ mixed race**) and hybridity. These concepts challenge the notion of essential and originary identities based on a notion of national purity and instead focus on the ways in which multiple cultural, national and political influences have worked to produce black cultures in the West.

Further reading

Gilroy, P. (1993) *Small Acts*, London: Serpent's Tail.

—— (1993) *The Black Atlantic: Modernity and Double Consciousness*, London and New York: Verso.

ELEANOR BYRNE

Black Audio Film Collective

The Black Audio Film Collective (BAFC) was one of a number of independent black film (see **film and cinema**) workshops and collectives that emerged during the 1980s, and which produced independent black films. The members of the collective were John **Akomfrah**, Reece **Auguiste**, Lina Gopaul and Avril Johnson. Like other film collectives at this time, they were crucially shaped by the cultural politics of the early 1980s and by the provision of arts subsidies in the UK during the Thatcher years. The provision of funding both from the **Greater London Council** and from **Channel 4** specifically for collective productions has, as Reece Auguiste noted, had a significant impact on the emergence of black independent film-makers in the UK, who became a phenomenon following the first wave of new black arts graduates from British universities. As a grant-aided collective operating in the public sector they, like others, were committed to 'integrated practice', entailing activities around training, education, developing audience outreach and networks of alternative distribution and exhibition, working through collectivist methods.

Expeditions (1983), their first cultural project, used text and images to explore cultural assumptions and racist ideologies surrounding representations of race, and offered an archaeology of the black diaspora through a post-colonial lens. Reece Auguiste has described this project as a contribution to debates about a pan-Africanist vision that were prevalent in the early 1980s, which was informed by theorists such as Frantz Fanon and Michel Foucault. The film challenged the positive/negative terms of the then current debates about race and representation, using a theoretically informed approach to colonial discourse, the colonial archive and constructions of nation.

The BAFC made their most notable impact on the British political and cultural scene with their production *Handsworth Songs* (1987). Directed by John Akomfrah, this was BAFC's most renowned film. It received critical attention well beyond the independent cinema circuit, and has been described as one of the most significant documentaries of the 1980s, although it had a very mixed critical reception. The film addressed the rioting and civil disobedience that took place in London and Birmingham from 1981 to 1985. It involved documentary footage from the 1985 Handsworth riots interwoven with archival newsreels of black historiography. Its experimentation with narrative forms and questions of representation led to some questioning whether the film was 'too avant-garde'. It developed several non-linear narratives, deploying alternative viewpoints from traditional documentary forms using a cut and mix editorial style.

In 1992, the BAFC completed *Seven Songs for Malcolm X*, directed by John Akomfrah, which held its own as an independent film alongside the release of Spike Lee's *Malcolm X*. Offering the familiar fragmented editorial and narrative style that marks their earlier work, this film explores the significance of the man and his legacy, from a range of narrative positions.

Further reading

Auguiste, R./Black Audio Film Collective (1989) 'Black independents and third cinema: the British context', in J. Pines and P. Willemen (eds) *Questions of Third Cinema*, London: BFI, pp. 212–17.

Fusco, C. (1988) 'An interview with Black Audio Film Collective', in K. Mercer (ed.) *Black Film, British Cinema*, ICA Documents 7, London: ICA/BFI, pp. 60–2.

Mbye, B.C. and Andrade-Watkins, C. (eds) (1988) *BlackFrames: Critical Perspectives on Black Independent Cinema*, London and Cambridge, MA: MIT Press.

ELEANOR BYRNE

Black Beauty and Hair

The only black magazine (see **publishing, newspapers and magazines**) to have an ABC circulation, *Black Beauty and Hair* retains a certain professionalism in its presentation and style. Edited since its launch in 1982 by fashion (see **fashion and design**) graduate Irene Shelley, it has grown and developed over the years to become a magazine that black British women can be proud of. Its departments are split into hair, looks and regulars consisting of beauty advice, health updates, new products and horoscopes. There are exclusives and features, which in the past have covered how celebrities manage to keep the almost perfect shape, and information on how to plan towards a wedding. Readers have the chance to interact by putting themselves forward for make-overs and giveaways. The magazine has a comprehensive directory of black hairdressers nationwide and a salon profile, which is useful to people who find themselves living in areas where such hairdressers are inaccessible. *Black Beauty and Hair* has produced five hairstyle books and is about to launch a bridal magazine. It organises the annual Black Beauty/Wahl Hair awards, sponsored by Wahl Europe Ltd to showcase the talent and professionalism of black hairdressing. There are ten categories to the award including stylist of the year, styling team, barber, avant-garde and braids (plaits). On inspection, *Black Beauty and Hair* lives up to its claim of catering 'for the beauty conscious black woman'. Published by Hawker Consumer Publications, the magazine is innovative in the way that it keeps ahead of the trends by launching related events and encouraging reader and industry participation.

YINKA SUNMONU

Black Britain

The **television** programme *Black Britain* was launched by the British Broadcasting Corporation (BBC) in 1995 as part of its News and Current Affairs programming. It aired on BBC 2 as a magazine programme that would cover wide-ranging issues relevant to black Britons that were not necessarily being covered in the main news agenda. Politics, business and community news achieved prominence, while stars from the world of sport and entertainment were profiled, including footballer Ian Wright and All Saints singer Shaznay **Lewis**. *Black Britain* obtained the first ever television interview with Melanie Brown a.k.a. Scary Spice (see **Mel B**).

Black Britain has won awards for its journalism and production, winning the Rima award for news in 1996–7 and 1998. It also won the RTS journalism award for the *Black Britain* special, 'Why Stephen?', on the Stephen **Lawrence** case. The show has received honours in Europe for reports on mental health. *Black Britain* has now changed from a magazine format to a documentary programme. The Olympic special, 'The faster race', highlighted the myths about, and reported on, race and sport. Another special, 'Bands apart', featured the journey of jazz musician Courtney **Pine** as he searched through South Africa for a unique music archive. Maxine Watson is the series producer.

YINKA SUNMONU

black British

The term 'black British' gained currency in the mid-1970s and was used primarily as a political signifier. Within the British context, the word 'black' has been used to refer to African, Caribbean and South Asian settlers. This contrasts with the use of the term 'black' in North America, where it refers solely to African and Caribbean settlers. In Britain, the umbrella term 'black British' facilitated a political alliance across second-generation immigrants from very different cultures who came together to organise collectively against their common experiences of institutional and individual racism. Institutional racism manifested itself in education, employment, housing, immigration policies and in police harassment of young black people. Although, for decades, there has been a strong presence of **ethnic minorities** in Britain, the post-war period has been a time of intense racial conflict. When increased immigration set off anxieties among the white majority population, an immigration control act was initiated (1962), and the government formed a 'crisis management' plan. The policy, agreed to by both the Labour and Conservative leadership, aimed to reduce the number of 'coloured' immigrants yet foster integration. As Fielding and Geddes point out, the result of this policy was the political marginalization of black immigrants – 'they and their offspring were treated as '"objects of" policy' (1998: 61). *The Empire Strikes Back* shows that, in the 1960s, the belief that 'the nation' was diseased and slowly destroying itself came to be conceptualised as a 'threat' from the changing racial demographics of the country, from the 'enemy within'. One response to the perceived 'threat' against what was often articulated as 'all that is English and wholesome' was a re-working of the concepts of 'nation' and 'citizen' that aimed 'to deny even the possibility that black people can share the native population's attachment to the national culture – God, Queen and country' (Centre for Contemporary Cultural Studies 1982: 29) This, of course, had profound implications for the way black people were viewed and treated. The racist ideas articulated in these debates over immigration and in official policies found their way into educational institutions, social services, employment practices and many other facets of everyday life. With the new political alliances of the 1960s and with Malcolm X's visit to England in 1965 and Stokely Carmichael's visit in 1967, the 'Black Power' movement began to take hold in Britain to resist the entrenched racism.

Many people found solidarity against such racism and attempted to answer these questions by becoming active in black British political alliances. As *The Empire Strikes Back* points out, the general feeling was that whether people were called 'blacks, browns, coloureds, darkies, nig-nogs, or Pakis' there was little difference in the point being made and collective action against such pervasive racism was thought a more powerful political force than many separate efforts (Centre for Contemporary Cultural Studies 1982: 66). Thus, in the 1970s and 1980s, there was increased political representation of black interests, and attention paid to the culture and significance of black arts in post[-]colonial Britain. However, the alliances formed under the rubric of black British collectivity were often fragile, and in the late 1980s black British began to lose its original purpose of a strong common political identification and was replaced by more specific ethnic identities. In Hanif

Kureishi's *The Buddha of Suburbia* we see confusion over the designation as the protagonist states: 'Two of us were officially "Black" (though truly I was more beige than anything)' (1990: 167.) Many found that 'black' identities were not, in themselves, enough to unite a disparate set of interests and cultural identities. Stuart **Hall**'s pioneering essay, '**New ethnicities**' expands upon this cultural shift in the 1980s. 'New ethnicities' draws attention to the way in which 'black' has become a pluri-signifying category that is de-stabilised by other cultural affiliations to class, gender, sexuality and ethnicity. However, although Hall problematises the label 'black British', he argues that it is important not to reject it because the political and ideological struggle over 'blackness' continues. The persistence of institutional racism and **new racism** indicates the need to continue organising together, despite an increased sensitivity towards cultural differences. This is most strikingly revealed in the murder of Stephen **Lawrence** by five youths and the apparent indifference by police. Stephen's parents took the police to court, and this resulted in the McPherson Report, released in 1999, which indicated that racism is still prevalent at all levels of British institutions. Thus, the issues forefronted in the 1970s collaborative organisation against racism under the umbrella 'black British' are still quite pertinent today. However, black British is still an awkward designation, a fact made clear in the ambiguity it has always evoked. As Pratibha **Parmar** indicates: 'This united us in a fragile alliance against racism, since we experienced British institutional racism in very similar ways. However, in recent years this strategic use has lost its currency as questions of ethnic differences and national identities begin to take primacy' (Parmar *et al.* 1993: 6).

References

Centre for Contemporary Cultural Studies (1982) *The Empire Strikes Back: Race and Racism in 70s Britain*, London: Hutchinson.

Fielding, S. and Geddes, A. (1998) 'The British Labour Party and "ethnic entryism": Participation, integration and the Party context', *Journal of Ethnic and Migration Studies* 24(1) (January): 57–72.

Parmar, P., Gever, M. and Greyson, J. (1993) *Queer*

Looks: Perspectives on Lesbian and Gay Film and Video, Toronto: Between the Lines.

Further reading

Gilroy, P. (1987) *There Ain't no Black in the Union Jack*, London: Hutchinson.

Layton-Henry, Z. (1992) The Politics of Immigration, Oxford: Blackwell.

Mohan, L. (1997) *Britain's Black Population: Social Change, Public Policy and Agenda*, Aldershot: Ashgate Pub Ltd.

TRACY J. PRINCE

black British Englishes

Notwithstanding earlier black presences in Britain, it was mainly the large post-war immigration movements that marked the beginning of a notable black linguistic impression on the British Isles. The multiple facets of black British culture are well-reflected in the wealth of languages spoken in Britain today. Some of them have been restricted to particular speech communities, such as those of West African languages (Yoruba, Twi, Ibo, Ga and Fante) or Kwéyòl from the Eastern Caribbean islands of St Lucia and Dominica, where this French-lexicon creole is spoken by a large population. There is a sizeable number of South Asian speech communities, some of the most significant ones being Bengali, Gujarati, Hindi (often spoken as a second language), Urdu, Punjabi, Tamil and Sinhala (cf. Alladina, S. and Edwards, V. (1991) *Multilingualism in the British Isles*).

Those language varieties brought by the first generation of West Indian immigrants from the 'anglophone Caribbean', i.e. Jamaica, Trinidad and Tobago, Guyana, Barbados, Belize, Bahamas, St Kitts-Nevis, Montserrat, Antigua and Barbuda, Anguilla, Grenada, St Vincent and the Grenadines, have made the biggest impact on a wider British society and black British culture. As the result of a common British colonial history, their official language is English. The mother tongue of the majority of the population – called 'patois' or 'dialect' by most of its speakers, and 'English-lexicon creole' by linguists – is, despite a largely shared vocabulary, significantly different from metropolitan English. The various regional English-lexicon creoles themselves are not identical; however, they bear enough similarities in their social history and their structure to be grouped together. It has taken some transformations, shifts and appropriations of these Caribbean creole origins before they became black British Englishes with a distinctly British usage. Their vigorous and exciting impact on many aspects of contemporary black British culture cannot be overestimated.

The nature of Caribbean creole languages as well as their cultural representation has to be explored from a historical point of view. Their origin lies in the multilingual language contact situations on the Caribbean plantations during the seventeenth and eighteenth centuries. The languages involved in this situation were the European languages of the respective colonial powers and the different languages of the Niger-Kongo group spoken by the enslaved West Africans. While a large part of the vocabulary was taken from the socially dominant European languages, many of the phonological and grammatical features can be traced back to influences from West African languages, as has been shown, for instance, in Mervyn Alleyne's *Comparative Afro-American* (1980). In linguistic theory, creoles are thus seen as socially and linguistically autonomous languages and not as dialectal variants of their lexifiers. In actual practice, this was often not acknowledged by either outsiders or speakers. The language had a low prestige because of its connection with slavery and colonialism, and moreover the source of differences to standard metropolitan English was often obscured by a Eurocentric concept of language. Studies on attitudes towards English-related creoles in the Caribbean, like John Rickford's *Standard and Non-Standard Language Attitudes in a Creole Community* (1983), based on Guyana, have shown them to be largely ambiguous: on the one hand, they evoke feelings of solidarity and identity, on the other hand, their lexical similarity to English has often led to the notion that they are simply a dialect or even an 'inferior' form of English.

The majority of those approximately 200,000 West Indians arriving in Britain between 1955 and 1961 were from Jamaica. However, the maintenance of the different regional varieties, like

Trinidadian creole, Guyanese creole, etc., spoken by the first generation of West Indians was at first aided by distinct settlement patterns according to island affiliation. Examples for this would be the large percentage of Jamaicans among the West Indian population in Brixton, or the Caribbean 'settlements' in High Wycombe, which were almost exclusively Vincentian. The 'West Indian accent', however, as it was interpreted by the wider society, often added to the many difficulties this first generation and their children were faced with. Early research in the 1970s on creole in Britain mainly focused on these negative aspects. Studies like Viv Edwards's *The West Indian Language Issue in British Schools* (1979) exhibit the results of a mixture of linguistic misconceptions, negative language attitudes in connection with racist tendencies and cultural stereotypes. Failure rates of students of West Indian background were exceedingly high in the 1960s and 1970s, and compared unfavourably not only with achievements of white British school children but also with those of other immigrant groups. At this time, creole thus was the language of disadvantage: it was not different enough to be recognised as a distinct language, in the same way that Punjabi, Chinese or Greek would be, with second-language programmes to support their speakers. In addition to regional differences, creoles vary also in terms of distance or approximation to standard English, often described as the 'creole continuum'. Systematic differences between creole and standard English are thus often obscured. Alternatively, creole forms were not accepted as 'proper English' either.

The pressure for second-generation West Indians to change their speech was therefore at least as great as for other immigrant groups. However, this seems to have resulted more in bilingualism than in a language shift in the generation of those who first grew up in Britain and received their education in the British school system. There are incongruous reports about patois usage in the late 1970s: one large-scale report, Rosen and Burgess, *Languages and Dialects of London School Children* (1980), suggests that creole is used regularly only by a small proportion of British-born blacks. In a different survey conducted in Bedford by David Sutcliffe, in *British Black English* (1978, 1982), on language use of British- and Caribbean-born West Indians, the vast majority (over 90%) of his participants reported that they used some patois. Viv Edwards's study on patois use in Dudley, West Midlands, *Language in a Black Community* (1986), shows that the frequency of patois usage and the competence in patois in the 1980s correlates significantly with the extent of integration into a black community.

Largely undisputed is a shift in linguistic orientation, towards Jamaican creole, in the patois used by the second and third generation of West Indians: Jamaicans have been dominant among Afro-Caribbeans in Britain, not only numerically but also in terms of cultural attractiveness. The rise of popular music forms with their origins in Jamaica, such as **reggae**, toasting and dub, as well as the association of **Rastafari** with that particular culture can be seen as largely responsible for a 'Jamaicanisation' of West Indians in Britain. Mark Sebba, in his study on creole in London, *London Jamaican. Language Systems in Interaction* (1993), sees this as one of the main reasons why Jamaica has also served as a linguistic role model for West Indian youths of the second and third generation. In consequence, the linguistic diversity of different regional creoles has given way to a variety Sebba terms 'London Jamaican'. This variety, which is formed out of Jamaican Creole and elements from standard British English, London English and Jamaican Standard English, has undergone significant transformations in form and function to the heritage languages the first-generation immigrants brought with them.

Sebba's study also illustrates that for most of these second- to third-generation speakers, a form of British English (here London English) is their first language. Their uses of creoles/patois are often quite restricted and London Jamaican is always used in conjunction with British English in a code-switching style. The functions of creole are therefore limited: its communicative purpose is not as important as its symbolic significance as a marker of black identity. Sebba identifies the use of creole, or 'talking black', as a social rather than an informational activity. The extent to which creole is used is highly dependent on the speakers' own perceptions of their language rather than on a purely formal identification of linguistic features. Thus, for the second- and third-generation West Indians, creole is not the mother tongue that fulfilled most communicative functions any longer, but a (variable) set of phonological, lexical and grammatical features that are used out of choice to negotiate and symbolise black identity and culture.

This symbolic value then has another effect, again a transformation creole has undergone, which this time reflects the group of its users. While for the first generation, creole was spoken by exclusively West Indians of all ages and ethnic groups, creole in Britain has since become the language of Afro-Caribbeans and, more generally, of black youth culture. Alternatively, cross-cultural use of creole by adolescents of non-Caribbean heritage has become quite common: although there are no detailed studies of patois spoken by adolescents of African background, observation suggests that this is a customary practice, especially in peer groups of both African and Afro-Caribbean adolescents. Roger Hewitt describes the use of patois by black and white youths in two London neighbourhoods in *White Talk Black Talk. Inter-racial Friendship and Communication amongst Adolescents* (1986). Because creole in Britain is so much inscribed as the language of black culture, the use of creole by white kids is highly marked and has to be seen again as a symbolic act of identity. However, Hewitt also shows that this verbal behaviour is often not accepted by the group the speakers want to identify with: independent of individual proficiencies of both black and white youths, white creole use such as described above is often regarded with suspicion and hostility, although more recently remade in comic form by Ali G. In its representation of black culture and identity creole may, however (especially in adolescent contexts), stand for a counter-culture to the mainstream with 'subversive' potential in a more general way. This also becomes evident when looking at the one case where white creole use is commonly accepted by their black peers: when it is used to defy and obscure communication, as a kind of 'anti-language'. This association of creole with an opposition to hierarchical authority is also documented in Ben Rampton, *Crossing. Language and Ethnicity among Adolescents* (1995), where his group of respondents, school kids of East Indian background, seem to incorporate creole features in their talk for oppositional purposes.

The structure and usage of creole in Britain has thus shifted considerably since the first post-war immigrants from the West Indies arrived with the *SS Empire Windrush* in 1948: the distinct island varieties have been creatively transformed into black British Englishes where creole elements are used in a code-switching style with British Englishes. The communicative function creole had for the first generation has given way almost exclusively to a symbolic function, also crossing community boundaries. These developments are best reflected and represented in the use of patois in all areas of black British culture that involve verbal art. It is here that creole/patois/Jamaican/talking black has its most public and most visible or audible presence.

Further reading

Alladina, S. and Edwards, V. (eds) (1991) *Multilingualism in the British Isles. Vol. II: Africa, the Middle East & Asia*, London: Longman.

Alleyne, M. (1980) *Comparative Afro-American*, Ann Arbor: Karoma.

—— (1986) *Language in a Black Community*, Clevedon: Multilingual Matters.

Edwards, V. (1979) *The West Indian Language Issue in British Schools: Challenges and Responses*, London: Routledge and Kegan Paul.

Hewitt, R. (1986) *White Talk Black Talk. Inter-racial Friendship and Communication amongst Adolescents*, Cambridge: Cambridge University Press.

Rampton, B. (1995) *Crossing. Language and Ethnicity among Adolescents*, London: Longman.

Rickford, J. (1983) *Standard and Non-Standard Language Attitudes in a Creole Community*, Trinidad: Society for Caribbean Linguistics (Occasional paper No. 16).

Rosen, H. and Burgess, T. (1980) *Languages and Dialects of London School Children*, London: Ward Lock Educational.

Sebba, M. (1993) *London Jamaican: Language Systems in Interaction*, London: Longman.

Sutcliffe, D. (1982) *British Black English*, Oxford: Blackwell.

Sutcliffe, D. with Figueroa, J. (1992) *System in Black Language*, Clevedon: Multilingual Matters.

Sutcliffe, D. and Wong, A. (eds) (1986) *The Language of the Black Experience*, Oxford: Blackwell.

SUSANNE MÜHLEISEN

Black Cultural Archives

In 1981, a group of black parents, educationalists and other concerned individuals established the African People's Historical Monument Foundation (APHMF). The Foundation was established to set up a black cultural archive and museum in Brixton (the pioneer settlement of **Windrush** arrivants after the Second World War), which would undertake to collect, document and disseminate the culture and history of peoples of African and Caribbean ancestry living in Britain. The archive procures documents, artefacts, photographs, oral history interviews, newspaper cuttings, books and other archival records. The collected information is disseminated as an essential part of British history, culture and heritage. The archive director is Sam Walker.

The urgent need for such an institution emerged during the late 1960s when children of African and Caribbean ancestry were deemed to be under-achievers in the British education system and were therefore categorised as educationally sub-normal (ESN). Early research conducted by the founders of this organisation revealed an absence in the school curriculum of black people's contribution in the arts, sciences, **literature**, classical **music** and in the social, economic and political development of Britain. It also became evident that the absence of historical documentation, and social data of verifiable quality of the historical presence and achievements of black people in Britain, contributed towards a sense of frustration and alienation from society, which militated against their participation in wider community interests.

Black Cultural Archives and Middlesex University have embarked on a partnership programme to create a new charitable entity that will develop a 'National Museum and Archives of Black History and Culture', based on the foundations already laid by Black Cultural Archives. This new entity will arrange and use current and new archival collections for the purposes of research, education and interpretation of all aspects of the history of peoples of African ancestry in Britain. The partnership with Middlesex University will increase access to the collection for the benefit of primary- and secondary-school pupils, and students both nationally and internationally. It will also impact on the development of on-line and other remote access to the collections and their use in pathways into further and higher education in a life-long learning perspective. Access will also be expanded for the local community and community groups throughout London and the country. The ultimate objective of the APHMF is a purpose-built museum and archives, which will serve as a repository for black British history and culture, and which will represent for the very first time in Britain a tangible asset of black British heritage.

Further reading

Garrison, L. (1990) 'The black historical past in British education', in P. Stone (ed.) *The Excluded Past*, London: Routledge, pp. 231–44.

Philips, M. and Phillips, T. (1998) *Windrush: the Irresistable Rise of Multi-racial Britain*, London: HarperCollins.

Walker, S. (1997) 'Black cultural museums in Britain', in E. Hooper Greenhill (ed.) *Cultural Diversity: Developing Museum Audiences in Britain*, Leicester: Leicester University Press.

SAM WALKER

Black Film Bulletin

The *Black Film Bulletin* came out of the temporary existence of the African and Caribbean Unit at the **British Film Institute** (BFI). After operating for four years, the BFI closed the unit as part of a large restructuring programme. Four issues a year were produced by the editors, June **Givanni** and Gaylene Gould. When the unit closed, they were replaced in the autumn of 1996 by part-time editors, Andrea Stewart and Onyekachi Wambu. The last edition to come from the BFI was in the summer of 1996. The *Black Film Bulletin* continues to exist and is currently produced at the Department of Humanities and Cultural Studies at the University of Middlesex. The *Black Film Bulletin* offered that very rare space, an opportunity to address issues that affect black film (see **film and cinema**) practitioners and theorists. It provided the context for discussion, networking, information and updates on funding, festivals and up-and-coming films, particularly independent films. There were frequent contributions from both researchers and practitioners, as the *Bulletin* was one of the few magazines that truly sought to profile the work being done within 'black film' and to open out debate around relevant issues at both a theoretical and practical level. It was a rare cross-over magazine where researchers conversed with practitioners.

Unsurprisingly, the *Bulletin* built up a strong reputation for its excellent contribution to, and coverage of, media and black arts and culture. Contributors as diverse as Kobena **Mercer**, Jim Pines, Mike **Phillips** and Menelik **Shabazz** were placed alongside interviews with practitioners, including Ruhul **Amin**, Alrick Riley and Gurinder **Chadha**, and theorists, such as Horace **Ové** and bell hooks. Typical articles included reviews of new independent works, updates on films being distributed direct to video, film festivals specifically featuring black films, and problems faced by regional film and video workshops. These were accompanied by theory-led articles that examined identity-led film-making, black film in the 1990s and hybrid films and the experiences of mixed cultures. Regular interviews offered profiles on black British film-makers who discussed their experiences of making films from a black British perspective and the problems that they experienced.

In her last edition as editor June Givanni commented on her concerns regarding the manner in which black culture was being pushed out of what she termed 'minority spaces' to make way for issues surrounding 'new technologies'. It seemed, she suggested, that there was only sufficient space for one minority issue. Black concerns were considered part of a pre-modern 'politically correct' world and did not, therefore, feature in the future world of new technology.

SAMINA ZAHIR

Black Londoners

A radio programme that aired from 1974 until 1988, *Black Londoners* was developed and produced by Alex **Pascall** for Radio London. Its aim was to establish a black presence in the British media and, using a magazine format of interviews, overseas reports and special features on individuals and events, to create a microcosm of the larger Caribbean community in the UK. Initially, the BBC ran a test series of six programmes; the manager of Radio London, Peter Redhouse, was reported as saying that there would not be enough material to fill regular one-and-a-half-hour slots. However, as a result of the success of the test series, the programme developed into a one-and-a-half-hour, then one-hour, weekly programme. The earliest programmes had a strong community focus, and prominent community activists were asked to contribute. In 1978, *Black Londoners* was scheduled to run as a daily one-hour programme; guests included prominent British and Caribbean politicians, Mohammed Ali, Alex Haley and entertainers such as the Mighty Sparrow (1979). Pascall, the programme's main journalist, was later joined by reporters Juliette Alexander, Sonia Fraser and Vince Herbert; the producers were Keith Yeomans and Barry Clayton.

Further reading

Harris, R. and White, S. (1999) *Changing Britannia*, London: New Beacon Books

SUZANNE SCAFE

Black Mime Theatre Company

Black Mime Theatre Company was founded in 1984 by Sarah Cahn and David Boxer to 'encourage the emergence of Black performers in mime'. Between its inception and 1997, when the company folded, it toured over eighteen shows throughout Britain and abroad. Black Mime became renowned for presenting issue-based dramas of relevance to the black community in a distinct physically based visual style. They would present their shows in a sketch/comic book style, which meant that they were accessible to both black and non-black audiences. The emphasis on visual, rather than verbal, imagery meant that barriers based on age, race, class and so on could, to an extent, be overcome. Thus, the productions toured to schools and community centres, as well as established **theatre venues** such as the Young Vic in London, and other regional venues. The success of the Men's Troupe meant that the company earned the recognition of theatre funding bodies, and were awarded Arts Council three-year revenue funding in 1990. At this point, Black Mime's Women's Troupe was established to devise pieces that were pertinent to women. Their first show, *Mothers* (1990), which explored the mother–daughter relationship received great critical acclaim for its portrayal of black British female identity, and *Drowning* (1991), which dealt with women and alcoholism, based on case studies uncovered during research, was similarly praised. In 1993, the Black Mime Ensemble was formed, and their first show explored the contentious dynamic of communication between men and women. *Heart* (1993) explored the many issues that contribute to misunderstandings and breakdowns in communications between women and men. The mixed ensemble went on to devise shows on black experiences of the prison system (*E.D.R – Earliest Date of Release*, 1993) mixed-race relationships, (*Dirty Reality II, 1995)* and mourning in black communities (*Mourning Song, 1996)*. Black Mime attempted to redefine mime away from the associations with white gloves and white faces; theirs was a new mime – a black mime – which redefined the boundaries of the art form on black terms. Mainly relying on sounds and vision, Black Mime's mime also invoked the spoken word, as well as songs, poetry and prose. The company therefore became renowned not only for what they had to say but also for the way that they chose to say it. They made a vast contribution to black theatre in Britain, remaining the only black mime-based company in Europe until they folded in 1997.

Further reading

Aston, E. (1995) *An Introduction to Feminism and Theatre*, London: Routledge.

Goodman, L. (1993) *Contemporary Feminist Theatres: to Each Her Own*, London: Routledge.

LYNETTE GODDARD

Black on Black

A **television** series that aired from 1982 until 1985. Following the success of LWT's *Babylon*, a series on the Afro-Caribbean community, and *Skin*, devised in 1970 to provide information on social issues affecting the Afro-Caribbean and Asian communities in Britain, **Channel 4** commissioned LWT to produce *Black on Black*. Using a magazine format, the series aimed to cover all aspects of black life in Britain. The country's first team of black journalists was led by producer Trevor **Phillips**, who said in a 1982 interview: 'British audiences are used to seeing blacks as rebels, criminals, or victims. We make a positive impact as statesmen, writers, artists, musicians and just real people.' The programme's director was Trevor Hampton; it was presented by Beverly Anderson, who was joined by Pauline Black in the 1985 series. The reporters included Julian **Henriques**, Simi Bedford, Kim Gordon, Elaine Smith and Victor Romero Evans, alias 'Moves', who presented the programme's media gossip items. A number of special feature programmes were commissioned, including 'Ethiopa Special', which reported on the Ethopian famine, and 'After the Invasion', which reported on the aftermath of the invasion of Grenada, both in 1983. *Black on Black* ceased production in 1985 amid much media speculation and commentary.

SUZANNE SCAFE

Black Perspectives

'Black Perspectives' took place at the South London Gallery from 22 May to 11 June 1987. It was selected and organised by the 'Sojourner Truth Association' in collaboration with Southwark Arts and Greater London Arts to provide a 'window' to the talent of black artists in Southwark. Its stated aims were to 'create...opportunities...increase awareness...and stimulate...development of black arts in Southwark'. It was unusual in bringing together artists with diverse experiences into 'a collection of works from trained and untrained artists from our area'. The catalogue provided an interesting forum for some refreshingly straightfor-ward artists' statements displaying passion, com-mitment and variety. Artists featured were: Simone Alexander, A. Davey 'Birdlegs', Tyrone Evelyn, Sandra Gowie, Gordon Vivian De La Mothe, Jamie Boroughs, Peter Hammond, Amanda **Holi-day**, Ian Joseph, Meekel, Iusi Miyo, Mowbray **Odonkor**, Joel Loughlin, Eileen Siley, Barry Simpson, Winston Walker, Canal Head Work-shops, Eugene **Palmer**, O. Scharsmidt, Barry Simpson and Winston Antonio Walker.

PAUL O'KANE

Black Power

'Black Power', an exhibition by photographer Donald MacLellan, was first shown at the National Portrait Gallery, London, from February to June 1998. The exhibition featured twenty-four portraits of black Britons who have made historic achieve-ments. The striking black and white photographs were accompanied by thought-provoking narra-tives that enabled the subject to remark on their experiences of living and striving to achieve in Britain. In undertaking the project MacLellan aimed to 'challenge the perception of black achievers as only sports personalities and pop musicians', and the exhibition featured a wide range of professions in which black people have made important contributions to British society, including academia, politics, the Church, medi-cine, the sciences and the arts. Those featured included: Transport and General Workers Union leader Bill Morris; the Bishop of Stepney, the Rt. Revd Dr John Mugabi; civil-servant Barbara Tomlin-Lindsay; editor-publisher Margaret **Busby**; Professor Lola **Young**; cultural theorist Stuart **Hall**; barrister and member of the House of Lords, Baroness Scotland of Asthal; Chief Inspec-tor Dalton McConney; sculptor Sonia **Boyce**; and broadcaster/politician Trevor **Phillips**. Since debuting at the National Portrait Gallery, the exhibition has toured various galleries and com-munity venues, including Centerprise and the Freedom Forum European Centre Gallery.

ANDREA ENISUOH

Black Star Liner

Black Star Liner formed in Leeds in 1993, taking their name from Marcus Garvey's 1930s organisa-tion to aid the return of blacks from America to Africa. They released two independent singles 'Smoke the prophets' and 'High Turkish influence' on the local Soundclash label before signing to the now defunct EXP, who released their debut album *Yemen Cutta Connection* in 1996. Although Black Star Liner had received an impressive amount of critical acclaim for their music, including being invited to perform at Radio 1's *India 5–0* celebration of independence, broadcast along with Talvin **Singh** and **Cornershop**, problems with their label saw the album disappear. Black Star Liner signed to Warners and released a second album *Bengali Bantam Youth Experience* in early 1999. Black Star Liner front-person Choque Hussein has been vocally opposed to the mixed-race band being lumped in with the hype of the new 'Asian cool' and the band have a sound that embraces influences such as Arabic music and dub. Hussein remixed Cornershop's 'Jullander Shere 6 a.m.' single in 1997 and Tjinder Singh co-wrote 'Duggie Dhol'. Black Star Liner have also remixed a track by the late Nusrat Fateh Ali Khan, 'Star rise', and Dreadzone's 'Little Britain'.

ANDY WOOD

Black Theatre Co-operative

Black Theatre Co-operative was founded in 1979 by Mustapha **Matura** and Charlie Hanson, and is one of a core of professionally recognised black theatre companies in Britain. The company has toured over forty plays, with an emphasis on encouraging new writing by black British play-wrights. Significant achievements in their history include the commissioning of *No Problem* (1982), a London Weekend Television sitcom with Judith Jacobs and Chris Tummings, and the acclaimed national touring production of Ray Shell's *Iced* (1997), a collaboration with the Nottingham Play-house, which had a sell-out run at the Tricycle Theatre. Black Theatre Co-operative have been producing black theatre for longer than any other black company in Europe, and their existence has been significant to the careers of many of Britain's renowned black actors, actresses and playwrights. At the end of the twentieth century, when so many other black companies had lost the funding battle, Black Theatre Co-operative remained the only revenue (three-year) funded nationally touring black theatre company in Britain. The company was renamed Nitro in 1999.

Further reading

Rees, R. (1992) *Fringe First*, London: Oberon Books.

LYNETTE GODDARD

Black Women Time Now

One of two exhibitions in 1983 to signal the rise of black women as a distinct artistic group, *Black Women Time Now* was an exhibition of fifteen artists who termed themselves Black Women in order to critique the patriarchy of black cultural politics and the Eurocentrism of **feminism**. The artists included Sonia **Boyce**, Chila **Burman**, Claudette Johnson, Lubaina **Himid**, Ingrid **Pollard** and Veronica **Ryan**, and was held at the Battersea Arts Centre, London. An accompanying programme of **theatre**, film (see **film and cinema**), **music**, poetry and **dance** took place, indicating a multidisciplinary approach to black culture. Boyce, Himid, Johnson, and Ryan also participated in *5 Black Women* in the same year at the Africa Centre, London, and came to be regarded as core Black Women artists; Himid was the organiser of both exhibitions. It is more useful to look at Black Women as an active community of artists rather than a movement. There were strong links with the black art movement, itself very much in its infancy; Johnson was a member of the Pan-Afrikan Connection, responsible for the first black art shows.

Further reading

Sulter, M. (ed.) (1990) *Passion: Discourses on Black-*

women's Creativity, Hebden Bridge: Urban Fox Press.

NIRU RATNAM

BLACK WOMEN'S GROUP *see* Brixton Black Women's Group

Blackgrounds

Blackgrounds was jointly established in 1998 by the **Theatre Museum Archive** and **Talawa Theatre Company** as a project to record the oral history of black, African-Caribbean and Asian performers working in Britain, a history rendered invisible by existing accounts of the period. It began the process with five video recordings of interviews with black professionals working in British theatre in the immediate post-war era: Earl Cameron, Pearl Connor Mogotsi, Cy Grant, Barry Reckord and Alaknanda Samarth. Pearl Connor Mogotsi's account describes her beginnings in the Little Carib Theatre in Trinidad, which under Beryl McBernie began to explore the folk history of the island. She goes on to describe her arrival in Britain in 1948 and involvement in the West India Service of the BBC, the career of her husband, actor and singer Edric Connor, who was the first black man to perform Shakespeare at Stratford-upon-Avon with the title-role in *Pericles*, as well as their establishment in 1963 of the Negro Theatre Workshop, staging several plays in London and Senegal. Centrally she describes the importance of the agency she and Edric jointly set up in gaining recognition, Equity membership and better pay for black performers when existing agencies refused to recognise them. Barry Reckord was one of the first black playwrights (with Errol John) to have work staged at the Royal Court with six plays in all, including *You in Your Small Corner*, *Flesh to a Tiger* and *Skyvers*; the last, against his wishes, was staged in 1963 with all white performers playing its schoolboy characters, as it was claimed that no appropriate black actors could be found. Reckord describes his pessimism about contemporary black writing: both the demise of black theatre companies and the 'horrible cosiness' of representations of black people in series like **Desmonds** and *Porkpie*. Both Earl Cameron and Cy Grant describe successful, sometimes overlapping, careers as actors, Grant also addressing the encounters with racism which made him give up the Bar and turn to the theatre. He also describes his popular success performing nightly on the *Tonight* programme with calypsos based on the day's news and his establishment of the Concorde festival of cultural diversity. Bermuda-born Cameron describes his experiences touring India with ENSA and voice-training with Amanda Aldridge, daughter of the great black Shakespearean actor Ira Aldridge. Alaknanda Samarth's career has moved constantly between Britain and India, and she discusses her position as a performer between cultures, doing Western theatre in India and playing the Asian 'other' in British **theatre** and **television**, including her role in Tony Harrison's 1976 adaptation of *Phèdre*, set in the British Raj. She also addresses her relationship to language, identity, cultural memory and the emergence of hybrid forms, as in the Black Theatre Forum's seasons and in collaborations with visual artists and musicians, where cultures collide.

Blackgrounds tapes and transcripts are available to view at the Theatre Museum and have been used for educational work and conference presentations.

Further reading

Reckord, B. (1966) *Skyvers* , London: Penguin.

SUSAN CROFT

Blackman, Malorie

b. 1962, London, England

writer

Blackman is one of the most prolific writers of **children's literature** in Britain, with the ability to write for all age groups. As a child, she wanted to be a teacher and in a sense her books have an educative role. She attended Honor Oak Grammar School and then took a Computer Science degree at Thames Valley University. Blackman became a database manager and remained in the computing

profession until she decided to become a full-time writer in 1990. She is a recipient of numerous awards. Her first book, *Hacker*, won both the W.H. Smiths Mind Boggling Book Award (1994) and the Young *Telegraph*'s Fully Booked Award (1994). She became the only writer to win the *Telegraph* award twice, when *Thief* won in 1996. Blackman writes for children and young people, and she has adapted *Whizzywig* for **Channel 4** and *Pig-Heart Boy* for the BBC. The latter won a BAFTA award for Best Children's Drama. *Thief* was televised for Book Box for Channel 4 Schools, along with a book for younger readers entitled *Space Race*. Raised at a time when reading about black children in books was almost a rarity, Blackman's protagonists are always black and she has written over forty books in the past decade. Her latest book, *Noughts and Crosses*, was published in 2001.

Select bibliography

Blackman, M. (2001) *Noughts and Crosses*, London: Corgi.
—— (1993) *Hacker*, London: Corgi.
—— (1995) *Operation Gadgetman*, Yearling Books.
—— (1998) *Pig-Heart Boy*, London: Collins Educational.

Further reading

Stone, R. (ed.) (1999) *A Multicultural Guide to Children's Books*, Books for Keeps.

YINKA SUNMONU

Blackwood, Maureen

writer, film-maker

In 1983, Maureen Blackwood was one of the founder members, along with Isaac **Julien**, Martina **Attille** and Nadine Marsh-Edwards, of **Sankofa Film Collective**, part of the black British film workshop movement that emerged in the 1980s. As a writer, Blackwood's vision is expansive – 'We need stories that reference the totality of who we are. I want to be writing material that puts black actors in dramatic or comic situations which actually allow them to fulfil their craft' – though as director she acknowledges more constraints, not least on the urge to represent all black people: 'I've always said that there are a wealth of stories to be told, but I don't think it's up to me, or the handful of Black women directors out there.' After working as co-director on *The Passion of Remembrance* (1987) with Isaac Julien, Blackwood turned to directing on her own, with the documentary *A Family Called Abrew* (1992) and the short feature *Home away from Home* (1993), commissioned by British Screen and **Channel 4**. Beautifully filmed and entirely without dialogue, *Home away from Home*, loosely based on real-life events, tells the story of Miriam, lone parent and cleaner at Heathrow Airport. Her desire for links with her African culture, rejected by her Westernised eldest daughter, takes shape when she builds a traditional African house in the garden. The racist reactions of the white neighbours, culminating in the night-time destruction of the mud house, create a powerful bond between mother and daughter.

PATRICK WILLIAMS

Blackwood, Richard

b. 1972, London

comedian, presenter, singer

Blackwood was brought up by his grandparents in London and took a degree in business studies. After a one-off gig at Covent Garden's the Spot, Blackwood went on to appear in *The A Force* and in sketches on *The Real McCoy* and *Five Night Stand*. He was spotted by MTV and asked to host their *Select* programme and *Singled out*, which has since moved to Channel 5. Blackwood is only the second black British comedian, after Lenny **Henry**, to have his own programme, *Club Class* with Channel 5. His most recent **television** programme, *The Richard Blackwood Show* on **Channel 4**, combines comedy and the chat-show formula to good effect. In 2000, he launched his vocal career with a sample based on a remix of his uncle's famous hit 'Mama – Who Dat Man?', which went straight into the UK charts at number three. He has since released two singles, '1, 2, 3, 4 – Get with the

Wicked' and 'Someone There for Me', and his debut album, *You'll Love to Hate This*.

ALISON DONNELL

Bloom, Valerie

b. 1956, Jamaica

poet, performer

Bloom trained as a teacher and taught English, speech and drama in Jamaica until she came to the UK in 1979 to study for a degree in English, African and Caribbean studies at the University of Kent. As a child she would perform 'Miss Lou's' poems, and her work has been both inspired and influenced by Louise Bennett and the other great Jamaican performing poet, the late Mikey Smith. Bloom has worked as a Multicultural Arts Officer as well as pursuing a career in writing and performing. Her first poetry collection *Touch Mi; Tell Mi* was published in 1983 and established her as a confident voice drawing on a strong and vibrant Caribbean oral tradition within a British context. More recently she has published *A Soh Life Goh* and *Let Me Touch The Sky*. She is well known for her writing for young people and has many publications that bring Caribbean culture, language and landscape to children's attention, such as *Ackee, Breadfruit, Callaloo: an Edible Alphabet* and *Fruits*, a Caribbean counting poem.

Select bibliography

Bloom, V. (2000) *Let Me Touch the Sky*, Basingstoke: Macmillan's Children's Books.
—— (2000) *The World is Sweet*, Basingstoke: Macmillan's Children's Books.
—— (1997) *Fruits*, Basingstoke: Macmillan's Children's Books.
—— (1994) *A Soh Life Goh*, London: Bogle L'Ouverture.
—— (1994) *Ackee, Breadfruit, Callaloo: an Edible Alphabet*, London: Bogle L'Ouverture.
—— (1983) *Touch Mi; Tell Mi*, London: Bogle L'Ouverture.

Further reading

Ncgobo, L. (ed.) (1988) *Let it Be Told*, London: the Women's Press.

ALISON DONNELL

Boakye, Paul

b. 1963, London, England

writer, editor, online publisher

Boakye has written for **theatre**, radio, film (see **film and cinema**), academia and magazines (see **publishing, newspapers and magazines**). His debut play *Jacob's Ladder* (1986) took the UK Student Playscript Award. In 1991, *Hair*, portraying the cultural gap between a Jamaican single mother and her British-born son, received the BBC Radio Drama Young Playwrights' Award. In his self-produced *Boy with Beer* (1992), Boakye chooses to deal with hitherto taboo subjects including the making of a black gay couple, bisexuality and AIDS (as in the commissioned dramas *No Mean Street* (1994) and *Safe* (1995)). His provocative and existential writing comes of age in *Wicked Games* (1997), a dramatisation of contemporary post-colonial British identity (and 'being in the world') as experienced by Londoners enacting the 'social structures we live' on a holiday in Ghana. The conflict between the British, American and African Dream is also explored in *Darker Than Blue: Black British Experience of Home and Abroad* (2000). He is Director of the WriteOnLine Publishing Company.

Select bibliography

Boakye, P. (2000) 'Darker than blue', in K. Knauer and S. Murray (eds) *Britishness and Cultural Studies: Continuity and Change in Narrating the Nation*, Katowice, Poland: Slask, pp. 188–212.
—— (1997) *No Mean Street*, in *The Best Stage Scenes of 1996*, New York: Smith and Kraus.
—— (1995) *Boy with Beer*, in *Black Plays 3*, London: Methuen Drama.

Further reading

Knauer, K. (2001) '*Wicked Games*: Boakye, British-ness and "the structures we live"', in *Reciprocity and Multicultural Imagination*, Katowice, Poland: University of Silesia Press, pp. 95–130

KRIS KNAUER

Boateng, Ozwald

b. 1967, London, England

tailor, couturier

Born in London, the son of Ghanaian parents, Boateng studied computing before progressing on to a fashion (see **fashion and design**) course at Southgate College. While still a student he demonstrated his entrepreneurial skills by selling his designs to the stores Acrobat and Sprint. At the age of twenty, having previously entered into partnership with the store Academy, Boateng developed his first menswear collection as an independent designer. His signature style combined the traditional attention to detail of Savile Row tailoring with the vibrant colour and sharp sensibility of his Ghanaian heritage. In 1994, Boateng became the first tailor to show on the catwalk at Men's Fashion Week in Paris. He opened his own store in London's Vigo Street the following year, specialising in what he has termed 'bespoke couture', a fusion of innovative design principles with traditional construction techniques. In 1996 Boateng won Best Male Designer Award at the Trophées de la Mode in Paris. Following financial uncertainty arising from the 1998 recession in the Far East, Boateng consolidated his enterprises and launched the first British 'Couture House' for men, in Wimpole Street. Clients for his distinctive brand include lawyers, financiers, politicians and international artists.

CHRISTOPHER BREWARD

BOBB, LOUISE GABRIELLE *see* Gabrielle

Bogle L'Ouverture

A black radical publishing house, Bogle L'Ouverture was started by Jessica and Eric Huntley in

1969. As an organisation, they have been active in the founding of other political and cultural activities. Their London home hosted the original discussions that became the **Caribbean Artists' Movement** and Bookshop Joint Action, after racist and fascist attacks against their bookshop in 1997. In 1997, their home also hosted early meetings of the storytelling organisation, the Ananse Society. In 1974, they opened The Bogle L'Ouverture bookshop, renamed the Walter Rodney bookshop, after he was murdered in Guyana in 1981. It was also a performance and discussion space until it closed in 1992. Bogle L'Ouverture Publications went into voluntary liquidation in 1989 but, with the help of Friends of Bogle, re-emerged the following year as Bogle L'Ouverture Press. Their authors have been culturally and politically ground-breaking. Their first publication in 1969 was *The Grounding with My Brothers* by Walter Rodney, later publishing his *How Europe Underdeveloped Africa* (1972). They published the first collection of poetry by Linton Kwesi **Johnson** and Lemn **Sissay**'s second collection, which helped establish both poets nationally.

KADIJA SESAY

Bollywood

The origins of India's 'Bollywood' film (see **film and cinema**) industry date back to the 1890s, when a number of short films were shown in Mumbai (formerly Bombay). Although the term Bollywood is a derivation of Hollywood, there are more films produced in Bollywood than Hollywood. Mumbai is India's film capital and home to the second largest film industry in the world. It is said to have a gross turnover in excess of £200 million. Film production is prolific and it is estimated that over 500 films are made each year. Traditionally, the films are characterized by **music**, song and **dance**, and follow a set formula where good overcomes evil and everybody lives happily ever after. Films are released in Hindi and other regional languages. Often, the songs are released before the films and become major hits. However, there is a gradual shift away from that

image and formula, and the first feature-length cartoon film is about to be released in Bollywood.

The British Tourist Authority and the British Film Commission in India have carried out an information-gathering exercise to assess the potential value of the Indian film industry to Britain. Britain is one of the major overseas markets for Bollywood films, which are shown at many cinemas across the country including a selection of UCI cinemas and Cineworld, Bexleyheath. Although in general the films offer escapism and entertainment, they can also be seen as providing a cultural link for British Asians. Moreover, the link does not end there. According to a BBC report, the Indian film industry is increasingly attracted to Britain as a film location, with Scotland a favoured area. Also, London became host to the first International Indian Film Awards (IIFA) ceremony at the Greenwich Millennium Dome in June 2000. Aishwarya Rai, a former Miss World, was nominated twice for a Best Actress award. Six months later, Bollywood star Amitabh Bachchan became the first Indian actor to have a waxwork model at Madame Tussauds. The industry's influence is felt beyond the world of films with the opening of a café bar in Newham called Bollywood's.

YINKA SUNMONU

Booker Prize

Since its inception in 1969, many debates have surrounded the selections for the Booker Prize. In the past decade, when authors from various margins of the former empire and black British authors started receiving more attention, the argument shifted to there being too few white authors on the shortlist, although rarely stated as explicitly as this. The following comment by Merritt Moseley of the *Sewanee Review* is typical of those views that have been voiced frequently in the 1980s and 1990s:

> [T]he selection and award process for the UK's Booker Prize for novels is cumbersome, biased against English entries and open to significant errors by the judges.... The novels reflected a multicultural background that, while politically

correct, did not include native, non-minority British authors.

(1995: 473)

This very public angst over the lack of white British authors selected has allowed deeply held and often unacknowledged racism to surface and expose beliefs in an Anglo-English vision of Britain. Increasingly, in post-war British **literature**, the Booker Prize has begun to shape canonical structures with its economic power and the increasing media attention given to the award. This has also added difficulty to the question of defining what the British canon is. With the Booker pool coming from authors throughout the world who are writing in English, there is no need for a writer's 'Britishness' or lack of it to be considered. Yet, the heated debates over the shortlists, and even news coverage of the intense wagering over the top choice, sometimes result in sweeping media commentary over 'the state of British literature today', which includes writers from the UK, the Commonwealth, the Republic of Ireland, Pakistan or South Africa under the British literary flag. Graham Huggan points out in the essay 'Prizing otherness' that 'the Booker might be seen...as remaining bound to an Anglocentric discourse of benevolent paternalism' (1997: 412), since the central figure always remains the Mother Country. Kazuo Ishiguro also talks about the central position British issues and novels have held in Booker discussions over the years:

> [T]here was a feeling that British society was so important in the world that if you wrote about it you were automatically writing about big themes. And if people in Kuala Lumpur weren't interested in British values, well, they damn well should be, and they could learn a lot by reading about British life.
>
> (Wilson 1995: 100)

In the 1980s and 1990s, when the shortlists began to include more black authors, headlines and public debates about the Booker Prize focused on the lack of 'British' novels on the lists. This debate also seemed to bring out deeply held resentments about the changing nature of Britishness, often voiced in terms of anger over multi-

cultural politics and political correctness. Paul **Gilroy** talks about such national tensions in *'There Ain't no Black in the Union Jack'*, where he details the prevalent perception of the power that the alleged 'anti-racist autocracy' hold over the allegedly 'tolerant population' (1987: 236). In this sort of logic, it was often proposed that the choices for the shortlist were influenced by the judges' overly zealous attention to having a diverse, 'politically correct' selection of authors. As Gilroy points out, the anger over political correctness has created a climate where 'the right to be prejudiced' is perpetuated, since people think they are merely resisting 'the anti-racist autocracy' and those people who are too focused on political correctness. These tensions reveal themselves time and again in discussions concerning the race, ethnicity and nationality of the shortlisted Booker authors. Pat Barker, 1995's winner, made inflammatory comments along these lines when she pronounced:

> I think that there is a certain amount of unacknowledged resentment among...white native British writers, on the ground that the additional tinge of exoticism when it comes to the Booker Prize does a writer no harm at all...there's a sort of resentment that the Booker judges are so obviously straining to be unparochial and exotic...the homegrown English novel is really rather undervalued now.
>
> (Wilson 1995)

Comments such as these remind us of the sad persistence of colonial binarisms such as 'homegrown English' and 'exotic' even within the exciting multi-ethnic and culturally diverse society of contemporary Britain and its literary outputs; they also situate the Booker Prize as an interesting and provocative catalyst to discussions about what happens when the empire writes back.

References

Gilroy, P. (1987) *'There Ain't no Black in the Union Jack'*, London: Hutchinson.

Huggan, G. (1997) 'Prizing "otherness": a short history of the Booker', *Studies in the Novel* 29(3) (fall): 412–32.

Moseley, M. (1995) 'Battle of the books', *The Sewanee Review* (summer) 103(3): 473.

Wilson, J. (1995) 'A very English story', *The New Yorker* (6 March): 96–106.

Further reading

Todd, R. (1996) *Consuming Fictions: the Booker Prize and Fiction in Britain Today*, London: Bloomsbury.

TRACY J. PRINCE

Bowling, Frank

b. 1936, Bartica, Guyana

artist

Bowling moved to London in 1950. He studied at the Slade School of Fine Art and the Royal College between 1956 and 1962. He moved to New York in 1966. His abstract paintings are expressions of instinctive creative forces, but in later paintings semi-abstract images rest on the two dimensional surface. Bowling states that his work has a dialogue with the issues of non-figurative painting. His strength as an abstract painter was recognised at 'Commonwealth Art Today' (1962) where his works were hung alongside Henry Moore, Victor Passmore and Aubrey **Williams**. In 1965 he won the Grand Prize for Contemporary Art at the First World Festival of Negro Art (Senegal). In 1968 his work was on display in the **Institute of Contemporary Arts**'s exhibition 'The Obsessive Image' and in 1971 at the Whitney Museum of American Art.

Bowling returned to London in 1976 and in the following year his work was in 'London, 25 Years of Painting' held at the Royal Academy. He was continuously identified as a Caribbean artist. In 1979 he exhibited at the 'Contemporary Caribbean Artists…African Expressions' at the Studio Museum in Harlem (USA). He took part in '**The Other Story**' (1989) and in 1997 he had a solo show 'Frank Bowling: Bowling on through the Century' at the Bracknell Gallery curated by Eddie **Chambers**.

Further reading

Araeen, R. (1989) *The Other Story*, London: Hayward Gallery.

PAULINE DE SOUZA

Boyce, Sonia

b. 1962, London, England

artist, archive director

Boyce's contribution to black visual arts in the UK has been substantial. She first exhibited her work alongside Lubaina **Himid** and others in two exhibitions: 'Five Black Women' (1983), at the Africa Centre, and '**Black Women Time Now**' at the Battersea Arts Centre in the same year. Her first solo exhibition, called 'Sonia Boyce Recent Work', was at the Whitechapel Art Gallery in 1988. She exhibited in '**The Other Story**', at the Hayward Gallery in 1989, and has exhibited widely in group and solo exhibitions since, including 'The British Art Show' (1990) and the launch of inIVA (**Institute of International Visual Arts**). She is co-director of the **African and Asian Visual Arts Archive** at the University of East London. Her work has moved through three distinct phases: in the 1980s, crediting Frida Kahlo's influence, she produced some of her best-known pastel drawings, often involving self-portraiture, such as *Big Woman Talk*, and *She Ain't Holding Them up She's Holding on*. She subsequently moved into collage work and then into installation. These projects have included an extended exploration of hair, as in *Afro Wigs*, and an interest in museum culture, such as the installation at Brighton Museum, *Peep*, in 1995. In 1998, she was artist in residence at Manchester University.

Further reading

Tawadros, G. (1997) *Sonia Boyce: Speaking in Tongues*, London: Kala.

ELEANOR BYRNE

Bradford art galleries and museums

Purchasing for Bradford's transcultural collection at Cartwright Hall began in 1986, with a commitment to collecting fine and decorative arts in four broad categories of contemporary fine arts and crafts, calligraphy in the Muslim world, gold/silver, and textiles. All of these are related to the Indo-Pakistan subcontinent and reflect the multi-ethnic composition of West Yorkshire. As such it is the first non-colonial collection of its kind in the UK. Objects directly from the subcontinent derive from 1900 onwards, celebrating the quality of twentieth-century craftsmanship. Contemporary fine arts and crafts are primarily focused on artists of subcontinental origin living in the UK, commencing in the 1930s with Jamini Roy, and including artists such as Anish **Kapoor**, Dhruva **Mistry**, Nina **Edge**, Sutapa **Biswas** and Salima Hashmi. The collection thus holds the work of radical artists who took part in the public social protest and anger under the broad umbrella of 'black art' of the 1980s, as well as artists of the 1990s whose works more subtly negotiate a private exploration of dual heritage. Furthermore, these collections have been certain to reiterate that those artists who speak of the experience of marginality are, however, central to British mainstream art activity.

DIPTI BHAGAT

Brah, Avtar

b. Punjab, India

academic

Born in the Punjab, India, Brah grew up in Uganda and was educated at the Universities of California, Wisconsin and Bristol. She now teaches at Birkbeck College, University of London. Brah has published extensively on questions of '**difference**' and 'identity' through a focus on the intersections of ethnicity, racism, gender, sexuality and class. One major area of her research is youth, diaspora and cultural change. She has published widely on young British South Asians, concentrat-

ing on gender, intergenerational relations and their position in the labour market. Her major publication is *Cartographies of Diaspora. Contesting Identities*, which fuses both empirical and theoretical material to map issues such as 'diversity', 'difference' and 'commonality' as relational concepts. Particular attention is given to South Asian Muslim women in Britain and how they deal with gendered and racialised discourses. The concept of diaspora is central to the framework of analysis Brah proposes, since it marks the simultaneous articulation of migration, race, ethnicity and class. Her latest work *Hybridity and its Discontents* (edited with Annie Coombes) explores the history and experience of hybridity in North and South America, Latin America, the UK and Ireland, South Africa, Asia and the Pacific.

Select bibliography

Brah, A. (1996) *Cartographies of Diaspora. Contesting Identities*, London and New York: Routledge.

Brah, A., Hickman, M.J. and Mac an Ghaill, M. (eds) (1999) *Global Futures: Migration, Environment and Globalisation*, Basingstoke: Macmillan.

—— (eds) (1999) *Thinking Identities: Ethnicity, Racism and Culture*, Basingstoke: Macmillan.

Brah, A. and Coombes, A. (eds) (2000) *Hybridity and its Discontents*, London: Routledge.

SANDRA PONZANESI

Braithwaite, E.R.

b. 1920, Guyana

author, teacher, lecturer, ambassador

During the Second World War, Edward Ricardo Braithwaite left the West Indies after volunteering for a post in the RAF. Having settled in Southampton, he graduated from Cambridge University and became a schoolteacher in London's East End. Here, due to his colour, he had a complex relationship with his students and, in 1958, Braithwaite published his debut novel *To Sir with Love*, based upon his teaching experiences, which went on to become a national best-seller and was also adapted into a Hollywood movie. Braithwaite is still regarded as the only black person in Britain to have a cinema film (see **film and cinema**) based on his life. After becoming a social worker for London's County Council in 1962, Braithwaite also published *Paid Servant* in an attempt to change the change the attitudes of his fellow social workers. Braithwaite later became an ambassador for the Guyanese Government in 1965 and a lecturer for New York University in the early 1970s. It was during this period that he published the acclaimed works *Reluctant Neighbours* (1972) and *Honorary White* (1975). He is now retired.

RAYMOND ENISUOH

Breeze, Jean 'Binta'

b. 1956, Sandy Bay, Jamaica

performance poet

Breeze's performance poetry is rooted in her rural, Jamaican upbringing and, although she still identifies as a Jamaican artist, her work has been strongly influential within the black British context. Poetry for Breeze came not from reading books but from her mother, and all of her work is strongly voice- and performance-related. In 1978, after a time spent teaching, Breeze joined the Jamaican School of Drama and went on to become the first woman to write and perform dub poetry. Her first published poetry appeared in *Answers* (1982). In 1985 Breeze moved to London, where she still lives, writing and performing in Jamaican English. In 1988 Breeze appeared with Ntozake Shange on the 'Women of the Word' tour and in 1992 she performed Shange's choreopoem *The Love Space Demands* at **Talawa Theatre Company**'s Cochrane Theatre, London. Her poetry is also recorded on the dub poetry album *Word Sound Ave Power* (1985) and on *Tracks* (1988), under Linton Kwesi **Johnson**'s LKJ label. Her latest collection of poems, *The Arrival of Brighteye and Other Poems*, was published in 2000.

Select bibliography

Breeze, J.B. (2000) *The Arrival of Brighteye and Other Poems*, Newcastle upon Tyne: Bloodaxe.

—— (1997) *On the Edge of an Island*, Newcastle upon Tyne: Bloodaxe.

—— (1992) *Spring Cleaning*, London: Virago.

—— (1988) *Riddym Ravings and Other Poems*, ed. M. Morris, London: Race Today.

—— (1988) 'Interview', *Spare Rib* 195: 6–9.

Cooper, C. (1990) 'Words unbroken by the beat: the performance poetry of Jean 'Binta' Breeze and Mikey Smith', *Wasafiri* 11: 7–13.

ELAINE ASTON

Brewster, Yvonne

b. 1938, Kingston, Jamaica

director

Yvonne Brewster is the acclaimed director of the London-based black company **Talawa Theatre Company**. Brewster's early life was spent in Jamaica, which she left in 1956 in order to study at the Rose Bruford College and at the Royal Academy of Music, England. Having trained as a performer, Brewster returned to Jamaica to work in radio and **television**, presenting and producing. Back in London in the 1970s, she furthered her directing skills in projects aimed at black communities. In 1982 she was the first black woman drama officer to be appointed to the Arts Council, a position she held for two years, and in 1985 she founded Talawa. Brewster's numerous directing credits for Talawa include productions by black writers Derek Walcott, Ola Rotimi and Wole Soyinka, as well her direction of black performers in white 'classics', such as Shakespeare's *Antony and Cleopatra*. In 1993 Brewster was awarded an OBE.

Select bibliography

Brewster, Y. (ed.) (1995) *Black Plays: Three*, London: Methuen.

—— (1991) 'Drawing the black and white line: defining black women's theatre', interview, *New Theatre Quarterly* 7(28): 361–8.

—— (ed.) (1989) *Black Plays: Two*, London: Methuen.

—— (ed.) (1987) *Black Plays*, London: Methuen.

ELAINE ASTON

British Film Institute

The British Film Institute (BFI) was founded in 1933 to cover all aspects of film (see **film and cinema**) and **television** from an educational, cultural and theoretical perspective. The collection covers printed material, films, videos and other forms of new technology. It has an extensive collection of archives for people interested in the moving image.

A collection of material documenting the black British experience through the years represents the positive and negative images of ethnic minority (see **ethnic minorities**) groups in film. Information is also available on black film from a global perspective. In 1993, the BFI launched the quarterly journal **Black Film Bulletin** to inform readers on developments in film and production. In January 2000, the BFI offered a journalism scholarship to black and Asian students on one of its specially run courses. Six months later, it published a draft report *Towards Visibility*, outlining its cultural diversity plans for black and Asian groups to 2003. One of its key publications, by Onyekachi Wambu, examines the black British film industry from a commercial perspective, looking at six films and interviewing producers including Parminder **Vir**. The BFI continues to take the lead with its publications. **Black and Asian Film Research** was specially commissioned to seek the views of ethnic minority audiences in Britain in order to help inform strategy.

The BFI runs the National Film Theatre and is a leader in the preservation of the country's screen heritage. It provides an archival viewing service for researchers and historians, and holds the world's largest filmographic databases, SIFT. A special collections service provides working papers and programmes, newspaper cuttings, autographed material and unpublished scripts.

Further reading

Ashbury, R., Helsby, W. and O'Brien, M. *Teaching African Cinema*, resource book and videos, London: BFI.
Wambu, O. (1999) *A Fuller Picture*, London: British Film Institute.

(2000) 'Be black and buy', *Sight and Sound* (December).
Sight and Sound, BFI monthly magazine.

YINKA SUNMONU

Brixton Black Women's Group

The Brixton Black Women's Group (BWG), which existed from 1973 until 1985, identified itself as a socialist feminist organisation, and was one of the first black women's groups to be established in the UK. The aim of the BWG was to create a distinct space where women of African and Asian descent could meet to focus on political, social and cultural issues as they affected black women. The Mary Seacole Craft Group joined with the BWG to establish the Mary Seacole House, renamed the Black Women's Centre in 1979. The centre was managed by the Black Women's Group and became a focal point for the meeting of black and Asian women's groups and political organisations across London. BWG published its own newsletter *Speak Out*, which kept alive the debate about the relevance of **feminism** to black politics and provided a black women's perspective on immigration, housing, health and culture. BWG had strong links with other women's groups nationally and internationally, and provided support for radical political groups, particularly in the Caribbean and Central America.

Further reading

Bryan, B., Dadzie, S. and Scafe, S. (1985) *The Heart of the Race: Black Women's Lives in Britain*, London: Virago.
Wander, M. (1972) *The Body Politic*, London: Stage 1 Publishers.

SUZANNE SCAFE

Buffong, Jean

b. 1943, Grenada

novelist, poet

After settling in Britain and working full time as a

lawyer, Jean Buffong began writing fiction in her early forties. After striking her first mainstream book deal, Buffong wrote the novels *Under the Silk Cotton Tree* (1992) and *Snowflakes in the Sun* (1995). Her work, which centres heavily around her Grenadian childhood, consists of poetry, short stories and plays, and is noted for giving positive images of West-Indian immigrants and black female professionals. Buffong has also been published in the anthologies *The Women's Press Book Of Myths and Magic* (1993), *Mango and Spice* and the poetry collection *Hearsay* (1994). She is also the co-editor of the anthology *Just A Breath Away* (1991). As well as being the welfare officer of the West Indian Standing Conference, Buffong is an active member of the **Caribbean Women Writers' Alliance** and the Chairperson of the Ananse Society. She now divides her time between London and the Gambia.

Select bibliography

Buffong, J. (1995) *Snowflakes in the Sun*, London: the Women's Press.
—— (1992) *Under the Silk Cotton Tree*, London: the Women's Press.
Buffong, J. and Payne, N. (1995) *Jump-up-and-Kiss-Me*, London: the Women's Press.

RAYMOND ENISUOH

BULSARA, FAROK *see* Mercury, Freddie

Burford, Barbara

b. 1944, Jamaica

writer, scientist

Barbara Burford came to the UK from Jamaica with her parents and sisters at the age of ten, and attended a girls' school. She later read zoology at King's College, London and studied further to qualify as a medical laboratory scientific officer. Burford has worked at Great Ormond Street Hospital, where she was part of the research team working on heart and lung transplants for children. She is now Director for the Equal Opportunities

Unit of the National Health Service Executive. Although Burford has always written, her commitment to her scientific career has inevitably slowed down her publication profile. *The Threshing Floor* (1986) is a collection of stories about women's work. Her poems have appeared in several collections and she was commissioned by 'Changing Women's Theatre' to write a play, *Patterns*, which was performed at the Oval Theatre in 1984. Although Burford's work often engages with science fiction, it is also informed by her own complex cultural identity 'as a descendent of three different diasporas: African, Jewish and Scots', as well as her lesbian identity.

Select bibliography

Burford, B. (1986) *The Threshing Floor*, London: Sheba Feminist Publishers.
Burford, B., Kay, J., Pearse, G. and Nichols, G. (1985) *A Dangerous Knowing: Four Black Women Poets*, London: The Women's Press.

Further reading

Hutton, E. (ed.) (1998) *Beyond Sex and Romance? The Politics of Contemporary Lesbian Fiction*, London: The Women's Press.
Mason-John, V. (ed.) (1995) *Talking Black: Lesbians of African and Asian Descent Speak Out*, London: Cassell.

ALISON DONNELL

Burke, Vanley

b. 1951, Jamaica

photographer

Vanley Burke came to England from Jamaica in 1965 with a much loved camera and began thirty years of distinguished photo-documentary work. His photographic subjects range from sensitive portrayals of the ebb and flow of a black diaspora in Handsworth, Birmingham, to the bitter record of liberation struggles in South Africa. In 1998, his Birmingham exhibition 'NKUNZI: Photographs from Birmingham and South Africa, 1993–1997' consolidated his reputation and his work has received the critical acclaim of Stuart **Hall**, Lola **Young** and Mark **Sealy**. Burke has exhibited in the UK, and was one of four Birmingham photographers whose work was shown in the 1993 '**From Negative Stereotype to Positive Image**' exhibition. In 1997, he exhibited in New York as part of '**Transforming the Crown**: African, Asian and Caribbean Artists in Britain, 1966–1996'. His photographs have been used in the music videos of UB40, televised as illustrations for the BBC's programme *Ebony* and as images to accompany the BBC's **Windrush** celebrations. Burke is markedly respectful of private family baptisms and funerals, and these images remain as compelling as his front-line photographs of racial conflict. As Sealy has commented, Burke's ability to focus equally on the personal moment and the political event characterises an unobtrusive and expertly tuned historiographic vision.

Further reading

Sealy, M. (ed.) (1993) *Vanley Burke: a Retrospective* London: Lawrence & Wishart.

Bailey, D.A. and Hall, S. (eds) (1992) 'The vertigo of displacement: shifts within black documentary practices', in 'Critical decade: black British photography in the 80s', special issue, *Ten.8* 2(3): 14–31.

Merchant, U. (1998) 'Interview with Vanley Burke', *Praxis* 1: 16–19.

SANDRA COURTMAN

Burman, Chila Kumari

b. 1957, Liverpool, England

visual artist

Chila Kumari Burman, the daughter of a Hindu-Punjabi family who emigrated to Britain in the 1950s, grew up in a working-class community in Liverpool. Burman studied art at Leeds Metropolitan University and gained an MA degree in printmaking from the Slade School of Fine Art, London, in 1982. Burman was one of the first British Asian women artists to study at art school

and produce political work. From early on, Burman curated exhibitions of black artists; wrote criticism; participated in residencies in education and community settings and collaborated on murals. Burman is principally a printmaker, but also uses a variety of other media such as **photography** and text to create two-dimensional works and installations. Her works explore the complexities of female cultural identity, frequently using images of herself. Burman refuses to be constrained by any tradition and has created multiple identities for herself, drawing on the tradition of the goddess Kali, Hindi screen actresses and contemporary **music**. Burman's work was included in two seminal exhibitions of black women artists in the early 1980s '**Black Women Time Now**' and '**The Thin Black Line**'. She has had solo exhibitions in Europe, Canada and Pakistan, shown widely in group exhibitions, and was included in the 1995 Johannesburg Biennale and the 1994 5th Bienal de la Habana, Havana, Cuba.

Further reading

Nead, L. (1995) *Chila Kumari Burman: Beyond Two Cultures*, London: Kala Press.

JANE SILLIS

Burning an Illusion

Burning an Illusion (1981) was the first film produced and directed by Menelik **Shabazz**, with funding from the **British Film Institute**. The film starred Cassie McFarlane as the central character, Pat Williams, and Victor Romero as her boyfriend, Del Bennett. Shabazz was particularly interested in film realism and shot the film in and around Notting Hill and Ladbroke Grove in London in order to provide 'street' credibility, filming one scene during the **Notting Hill Carnival**. The film tells the story of a young black woman's coming of age, highlighting a time when she questions her middle-class aspirations and search for security through marriage. Her realisation of her status, both in her personal relationships and within a society that is shown as racist, gradually leads her to political enlightenment and the possibility of a new response to the problems and pressures she encounters – that of black consciousness.

Pat's changing political stance is represented by her shift in reading matter, from Mills and Boon novels to works on Malcolm X. Towards the end of the film we see her taking a boxful of Mills and Boon novels to be burnt, hence the film's title.

SAMINA ZAHIR

Busby, Margaret

b. Ghana

publisher, editor, journalist

Busby graduated in English at Bedford College, University of London, in 1967 and soon put her literary interests to use as co-founder of the publishing house Allison and Busby, which published many significant black writers, such as C.L.R. **James**, George **Lamming**, Buchi **Emecheta** and Roy **Heath**. In 1987, she moved on to take the position of editorial director of Earthscan Publications, which specialised in Third World non-fiction. Since 1990, Busby has worked as a freelance journalist, editor and broadcaster, and has acted as a judge on many literary prize panels. She has served on the boards of the African Centre, the Royal Literary Fund and the Arts Council. In 1993, she won the Pandora Prize for the most positive contribution to the status of women in publishing and is widely regarded as an accomplished and inspirational figure.

ALISON DONNELL

Butt, Hamad

b. 1962, Lahore, Pakistan; d. 1994, London, England

visual artist

Butt graduated from Goldsmiths' School of Art in 1990 with one of the highest grades ever to be awarded by the institution. His graduation show 'Transmission' was subsequently re-made for the Milch Gallery. His largest installation 'Substance Sublimation Units' was first shown in 1992. The installation took the form of three sculptures, each containing one of the three major halogens, iodine, chlorine and bromine, and explored the themes of alchemy, the nature of scientific discourse and death. The installation was later exhibited at the acclaimed 1995 Tate exhibition 'Rites of Passage'. Before his premature death in 1994 from an AIDS-related illness, Butt was widely regarded as one of the most promising artists of his generation – which included his contemporaries at Goldsmiths such as Damien Hirst and Gary Hume. His small *œuvre* has attracted acclaim from leading critics and academics such as Stuart Morgan, Sarat Maharaj and Jean Fisher. His inclusion in 'Rites of Passage' alongside international artists such as Joseph Beuys, Bill Viola and Louise Bourgeois was indicative of the critical attention his work commanded.

Further reading

Foster, S. and Tawadros, G. (eds) (1996) *Hamad Butt: Familiars*, London: inIVA.

NIRU RATNAM

C

Calabash

Established in 1996 by Kadija George **Sesay**, then Literature Development Officer for Centerprise Trust in Hackney, *Calabash* is the only literary broadsheet serving writers and readers of African, Caribbean and Asian literature in Britain. It is published tri-yearly by the Black Literature Development project at Centerprise, and is funded by the London Arts Board and the London Borough of Hackney. Since its inception, *Calabash* has grown from a voluntarily produced publication with a 2,000-strong circulation, to a quality international (Europe, USA and West Africa) accessory to black **literature** serving 5,000 readers. Distributed through the West Midlands and London central library systems, universities, literary venues and community organisations, such as Working Group against Racism in Children's Resources and East London Black Women's Organisation, it features reviews and interviews with major writers, among them Ben **Okri**, Walter Mosely, Susan L. Taylor and Courttia **Newland**. Because of its commitment to encouraging aspiring writers with the hope of seeing more black authors published in Britain, each issue of *Calabash* also includes a wealth of practical advice and information on writing techniques and genres, methods towards getting published, workshops, writing competitions and literary events. As such, it has become a valuable and inspirational instrument in the development of contemporary black British literature.

DIANA OMO EVANS

Camden Black Sisters

Camden Black Sisters was formed by Lee Kane and Yvonne Joseph during an **Organisation of Women of Asian and African Descent** conference in 1979 and is still in active existence. The group continues to provide a library for black women wishing to explore black history, offers rooms for groups to meet, and arranges performing art workshops, conferences and seminars. Camden Black Sisters works with other similar organisations to celebrate particular black historical events, such as Black History Month in October of each year and Martin Luther King Day.

PAULINE DE SOUZA

Campbell, Bill

b. 1948, St Elizabeth, Jamaica

vocalist, producer

Campbell began singing as a member of his church choir in Jamaica during the mid-1950s. After migrating to the UK, he settled in Nottingham. At the age of fifteen he entered and won a music showcase, hosted by **reggae** legend Jimmy Cliff. Campbell relocated to London in 1970, where both he and his brother Pete signed with Trojan Records and released their single 'Come on Home Girl'. Five years later Bill signed a single deal with EMI. In 1985, Campbell was approached and signed to one of the biggest independent labels during the 1980s, Stiff Records. He recorded a light soca reggae track 'Nearest to My Heart', which was a huge success in the USA. Later that year Campbell launched his own production outfit, Worldsound Records. He has since produced a number of national and international artists, as well as touring South America, Ghana and Nigeria. His albums have sold in excess of 1 million in Nigeria, Ghana and Brazil. Campbell's music arrangements have also been used in the BBC's popular soap *Eastenders*. Campbell has taken an active step in promoting up-and-coming British artists and became the Chairperson of the charity organisation Caribbean Culture in 1991.

DORETH JONES

Campbell, Naomi

b. 1970, London, England

supermodel

Campbell entered the world of modelling young, at fifteen, and was signed to Elite. By 1988, she had appeared on the front cover of British *Vogue* and had been the first black cover girl for French *Vogue*. By 1989, she was on the cover of American *Vogue*. In 1996, Campbell was the only black woman to appear in a league table of the world's top twenty-five cover girls, at twelfth place; in 1999, she shared an appearance with Alek **Wek** and Iman, two of the extremely few high-profile black models. She has often accused the fashion world of prejudice, particularly the editors of glossy magazines (see **publishing, newspapers and magazines**). Although she avoided the term 'racism', she commented that blonde and blue-eyed girls are what sells and has frequently suggested that, because she is black, she loses out on some of the extremely lucrative advertising contracts. During 1994 she was particularly active outside the world of modelling, with the release of her novel *Swan*, ghost written by Caroline Upcher, and her debut album *Babywoman*.

Further reading

Jones, L.A. (1993) *Naomi Campbell, the Rise and Rise of the Girl from Nowhere*, London: Mandarin.

SAMINA ZAHIR

Campbell, Topher

b. 1965, London, England

film-maker, theatre director

Campbell has been directing and producing plays for more than ten years, including world premières by black and Asian British writers, such as Paul **Boakye**'s *Wicked Games* and *No Mean Street*, Tariq Ali's *Necklaces* and Cheryl West's *Jar the Floor*. In 1996, he set up Gorgeous Films for which he wrote and directed *The Homecoming* a short film about photographer **Ajamu** and his quest for a place called home. This documentary features commentary by Stuart **Hall** and Kobena **Mercer** on representation of the black male body. *A Mulatto Song*, another of his poetic short films, tells of the eighteenth-century Polish-Barbadian slave George Polgreen Bridgetower, who played first violin in the Prince of Wales's private orchestra. Campbell is also a founder member of rukus! (a black Queer arts organisation created to profile the best work by black gay men, lesbians and transgender people). He was Artistic Director of Urban Mass, an eight-day festival that featured HIP-HOP Theatre, contemporary **dance**, film (see **film and cinema**), fashion (see **fashion and design**), politics and club-based events. He is Artistic Director Designate of Talawa Theatre.

KRIS KNAUER

Carby, Hazel

academic

Hazel V. Carby is Professor of African and American Studies at Yale University. Working alongside Prabitha **Parmar** and Stuart **Hall** at the **Centre for Contemporary Cultural Studies**, University of Birmingham, England, Carby published her much cited and influential essay 'White woman listen! Black feminism and the boundaries of sisterhood'. In this essay she describes how the processes of racism and sexism are simultaneously activated in society, and calls for **feminism** to account for this. Carby is concerned that black women are subjected to the simultaneous oppression of patriarchy, class and race, and argues that the structures of power relationship this creates between white and black women must be addressed and accounted for. In 1987 Carby published her landmark study *Reconstructing Womanhood: the Emergence of the Afro-American Woman Novelist*, in which she sketches a historiography of black feminist criticism alongside the emergence of black American women as novelists. *Race Man* appeared in 1998 and criticises the various dimensions of black masculinity, manifested through such genres as **music**, **literature**, film (see **film and cinema**), politics and **photography**, in the work of progressive historical figures ranging from W.E.B. Du Bois, to C.L.R. **James**, Miles Davis, Martin Luther King and Malcolm X. Carby constructs a historical context for understanding both the inherent male-centredness of black race leaders in the twentieth century and the manner in which oppressive masculinities permeate black politics and culture today, continuing to undermine the cause of black liberation. *Cultures in Babylon: Black Britain and African America*, a collection of Carby's essays on multiculturalism, was published in 1999.

Select bibliography

Carby, H. (1999) *Cultures in Babylon: Black Britain and African America*, London: Verso.
—— (1998) *Race Man*, Cambridge, MA: Harvard University Press.
—— (1987) *Reconstructing Womanhood: the Emergence of the Afro-American Woman Novelist*, Oxford: Oxford University Press.
—— (1982) 'White woman listen! Black feminism and the boundaries of sisterhood', in Centre for Contemporary Cultural Studies (eds) *The Empire Strikes Back: Race and Racism in 70s Britain*, London: Routledge, pp. 212–35.

SANDRA PONZANESI

Caribbean Artists' Movement

While the Caribbean Artists' Movement's (CAM) official existence spanned only six years (1966–72), its members advanced Caribbean and black British writing, art, criticism and publishing (see **publishing, books**) in a far-reaching way. By the time CAM was formed, Caribbean arts were already established through a substantial quantity of fiction, poetry, plays and art exhibitions in the UK. Nevertheless, the production of new material was not matched by the critical attention that it warranted and CAM grew out of a growing need for 'an aesthetic which was no longer tied to European Art'. In publishing her literary history of the Caribbean Artists' Movement, Anne Walmsley (an original member) challenged the movement's otherwise 'curious absence' from cultural histories of the period in the UK and in the Caribbean. The book charts the movement, from its formation in December 1966, at Edward and Doris Brathwaite's London flat, through its subsequent public readings, critical debates, exhibitions, conferences and publications. The founder members were (Edward) Kamau Brathwaite, John **La Rose** and Andrew **Salkey** but many well-known writers, critics and artists were associated with the movement: C.L.R. **James**, Stuart **Hall**, Wilson **Harris**, Ronald **Moody**, Aubrey **Williams**, Orlando Patterson, Kenneth Ramchand, Gordon Rohlehr, Louis James, Ivan Van Sertima, James **Berry**, Donald Hinds, Linton Kwesi **Johnson**, Christopher Laird and Errol **Lloyd**. CAM was not exactly the exclusively male 'club' that is. suggested by the preceding list of key participants. Walmsley documents the contributions of the women involved, either directly as artists, writers and performers, or more indirectly as wives and partners of CAM leading lights. Intellectual enquiry was also encouraged through CAM debates on the groundbreaking scholarship of Merle Hodge, Lucille Mathurin-Mair and Elsa Goveia. Although the movement grew out of the collective dissatisfaction of West Indian students, artists and intellectuals who found themselves in London during the political and cultural ferment of the 1960s and early 1970s, CAM's activities were extended through its members' travels back and forth between the UK and the Caribbean. CAM's journal *Savacou*, edited by Kamau Brathwaite, provided a necessary 'platform for the new creative writing' and criticism. The movement also strongly influenced the formation of specialist publishing houses **New Beacon Books** and **Bogle L'Ouverture**.

CAM's most important achievement lies in its nurturing of talented new Caribbean writers and artists, and in disseminating work that would otherwise have been produced in a critical void. By 1972, the impossibility of managing an organisation with members fragmented throughout the Caribbean, the UK, the rest of Europe and North America meant that official activities declined, although unofficial networks continued to be effected through its members who, like Andrew Salkey, maintained a bureau of Caribbean artists, activists and intellectuals throughout the world.

Further reading

Walmsley, A. (1992) *The Caribbean Artists' Movement 1966–1972*, London: New Beacon Books.

SANDRA COURTMAN

Caribbean Women Writers' Alliance

Caribbean Women Writers' Alliance (CWWA) is a membership organisation with an international profile. The CWWA was formally established following the first London-based Caribbean Women Writers' Conference organised its by founder members, most notably Joan **Anim-Addo**, and held at Goldsmiths College in July 1994. Its beginnings are rooted in a shared interest in writing by women that draws upon a Caribbean heritage. The CWWA aims to develop access to and debate about Caribbean women's writing, while also creating opportunities for women of Caribbean heritage and allies to develop creative writing skills and publication possibilities. A regular termly publication, *Mango Season*, has subsequently developed. It offers a window on creative writing by published and first-time writers, alongside discussion about writing by Caribbean heritage writers within the UK and abroad, and the black British literary scene. In addition, *Mango Season* disseminates information about CWWA's wide ranging activities, including classes, workshops, performances, writers' support groups, occasional publications and conferences.

ALISON DONNELL

carnival

Public festivals of masking, cultural display, feasting and comedy, often including reversal and transgression, have been performed by cultures for at least the last 6,000 years, the first recorded perhaps being the festival of Osiris in Egypt. These celebrations, which often marked significant calendar events, such as the end of one year and the beginning of the next, acted both as a magical invocation for prosperity and fertility of the land, and as a form of social catharsis, allowing emotional and social release from normal, often enforced, patterns of behaviour. Christianity sought to capitalise on these rituals, which existed in various forms throughout Europe, and incorporated many of the customs into 'official' winter celebrations, most notably Carnival, a festival of indulgence and licence, before the coming of Lent, at the end of a three-month cycle of winter fetivities. This was a festival of reversal *par excellence*: the low becomes high, not just in terms of the social order but also in the body, where carnal pleasures and images are privileged over the cerebral. During this time the fool is wise and the natural order is briefly held in obeisance. It was a festival that opposed fixity and closure, and ridiculed authority. It was, however, a licensed time, for order was reimposed with the coming of Lent, and all transgressions were in one way or another authorised – this is the paradox of carnival.

The term carnival itself is probably derived from the Latin, *Carne Vale*, which literally means 'farewell to flesh', but more metaphorically 'farewell to the sins of the flesh': a last 'blow out' before abstinence. During the early Renaissance, Carnival was celebrated within the Church, although this period of indulgence was increasingly opposed by Rome, while at the same time being absorbed into the more acceptable and genteel activities of the nobility and upper classes. It was this restrained and aesthetic re-working of Carnival that was celebrated by the French plantation owners and colonists in Trinidad, the island perhaps most associated with the history of carnival. During this time, the colonists wore lavish costumes and masks, the men often blacking their faces in imitation of the *negue jardin* and carrying burning canes and drums into the fields, mocking the activities of slaves during a plantation fire. Women were more likely to dress as coloured 'mulattos', bestowing upon themselves the sexual allure that they imagined their husbands found in these women. Although carnival was celebrated shortly after Christmas, a festivity in which some freedom to **dance** and celebrate was given to the slaves, carnival itself, officially at least, excluded them as anything other than subjects of the plantation owners' games, although this in itself was a change from the normal work routine. For the British, following the French in Trinidad, Christmas rather than carnival was the most significant annual festival, although carnival was celebrated by all whites and free coloureds throughout the period prior to emancipation. Unofficially, the slaves certainly did indulge in comic and festive rituals (although these were unlicensed), parodying those of the colonists, although these were as likely to be at Christmas time as carnival. Indeed, although carnival traditionally has a fixed place in the calendar, it is the nature of the activity rather than its calendar location that marks it out. In Christmas, 1805, for example, a slave conspiracy was unmasked in which the participants, using elaborate costumes and satiric songs, played out roles of kings, queens, dauphines and so on. Perhaps this was not carnival in the strict sense, but it was a parodic fantasy of freedom none the less.

After emancipation, carnival became a focus for celebrations of freedom and, in apprehension of what might have occurred, carnivals immediately post-emancipation were heavily restricted. This was because carnival as a time of licence did not sit comfortably with major social changes. The upper classes swiftly withdrew from what became a less decorative but more popular festival. Although initially tentative throughout the nineteenth century, attendance from the working classes grew and the event came to include, among other things, West African traditions of **music** and dance

alongside mockeries of Roman Catholic Carnival, processions, the satirical songs of calypso, masking in white, costumes depicting kings, queen, pirates and South American 'Indians', and the wearing of chains. The festive ritual of Canboulay (later replaced by the Jouvay or '*jour ouvert*'), originally celebrated on 1 August, was moved to become the midnight opening of the carnival season and re-enacted the burning of cane in the fields, both as a pastiche of the colonists' own festive tradition and as a reflection of the past activities of the enslaved. This carnival was far closer in spirit to the origins of the festival than were the balls of the colonists.

Various colonial governors made efforts to restrict the excesses of carnival, which, by 1870, had come to be seen as vile, bawdy and disreputable by the white media, and certainly became the focus of oppositional performances at times of crisis. By the last decade of the nineteenth century, the carnival had once again become a contained and largely acceptable spectacular performance, albeit with undercurrents referencing its history. This condition of carnival is largely that which exists in Trinidad today and it is that which has been brought into the diasporic carnivals such as the **Notting Hill Carnival**.

Modern West Indian carnival is based largely on this heritage, refining artistic aspects while still having at its heart the notion of carnival as a celebration of freedom and culture. Naturally, additions have been made to the repertoire of carnival images and performances but there remain three key elements. The first is mas, or masquerade, which is the element of costume and procession; derived from the parodic costumes of the early tradition, these spectacular sculptures are now at the heart of the Trinidad and diasporic events. Each mas band, of which there may be in excess of fifty in a large procession, will construct one or two large costumes, often effectively giant puppets, which will be surrounded by their court, clothed in simpler evocations of a common theme, variously ranging from the decorative (*The Sea*, *Butterflies*), to the mildly political (*Rituals of the Sioux Indians*) and to the more clearly positioned (*Me, Myself, Warrior*). A second constituent element of contemporary carnival is calypso, derived from aggressive satirical African songs, which in Trinidad were initially sung in French patois and later in

English; the lyrics were often irreverent and satirised the dominant classes. More recently, calypso has become fused with soul to create a separate musical form, soca, an Indian-influenced form, which is commonly used to accompany the mas processions. Both of these forms keep political debate and controversy alive in contemporary Trinidad. The third essential element is the steelband, using instruments that clearly reference the cultural origins of the carnival, where the poverty of the participants meant that festive props were often collected from recycled material. The steel drum was originally created from oil drums stolen from plant sites and then tuned using intense heat and quick cooling. Ironically, it was the popularity of the steel drum in the UK that led to its revival in Trinidad.

Contemporary British carnival has also tended to include static sound systems (see **sound system DJs**), principally a Jamaican contribution, which generally play a range of music from soca through **reggae** to **jungle** and **hip hop**, the last, like the steel drum, being a re-working and appropriation of extant music, but originally using topical and usually oppositional lyrics. West Indian carnival was first celebrated in the UK in 1966 at Notting Hill, initially a small event but becoming one of the largest European street festivals and diasporic carnivals. The event, both in Notting Hill and in other major cities, such as Bradford, utilises the traditional constituent disciplines in a spectacular celebration of culture. Moreover, these carnivals have also necessarily acted as a focus for racial discourse, as carnival always has. At various times, the carnivals have articulated both a liberal, colour-blind position, as when an event is conscripted to be an exercise in race relations, and (particularly at Notting Hill) a clear statement against the oppression of racial minorities. These conflicting texts of carnival have often resulted in an uneasy alliance between the two positions, but when a balance is not met carnivals may be constructed as either, at one extreme, simply decorative spectacles or, at the other, locations of social disruption and violence. This duality is, of course, the essence of the paradox of carnival.

Further reading

Carr, A. (ed.) (1988) *Trinidad Carnival* [a republication of the *Caribbean Quarterly Trinidad Carnival* (1956) 4(3–4)], Port of Spain: Prara Publishing Company.

Cohen, A. (1993) *Masquerade Politics*, Oxford: Berg.

Orloff, A. (1981) *Carnival*, Wörgl, Austria: Perlinger.

GAVIN CARVER

Casely-Hayford, Joe

b. 1956, Kent, England

fashion designer, stylist, curator, artist, writer

Since the mid-1980s, Casely-Hayford has contributed extensively to the avant-garde in style and fashion (see **fashion and design**). A graduate of St Martin's College of Art (1979), he established the label Joe Casely-Hayford in 1983. The range consisted of a mainline collection of men's and womenswear, until 1999 when Joe Casely-Hayford 'Denim' was launched for Spring/Summer 2000. The established reputation of the designer earned him the nomination of Designer of the Year in 1989 and a number of freelance commissions, as in the range of womenswear he designed exclusively for Top Shop in 1993.

Casely-Hayford's styling career began in 1984. He was commissioned by the Clash to produce clothing for the album *Combat Rock*. Between 1984 and 1986, Casely-Hayford was styling consultant at Island Records, working with such artists as **Aswad** and Black Uhuru, also working on the launch of Mica **Paris**. In 1991, one of his most high-profile commissions came from the Irish rock band U2. Casely-Hayford designed and produced all the stage outfits for their two world tours, the albums *Achtung Baby* and *Zooropa*, and a number of associated videos. In the same year, Joe Casely-Hayford designs were used in the film *Edward II* and the play *The Year of the Family*. His design acumen has led him to contribute to a number of art-based projects. Casely-Hayford produced a quilt for the 'Quilts of Love' exhibition (1994) and he designed the exhibition 'The Art of African Textiles: Technology, Tradition and Lurex' at the Barbican Centre, London. In honour of his work, the retrospective exhibition 'Through the Ages' was held in Tokyo in 1996.

CAROL TULLOCH

Centerprise Women's Café

The first Word Up Women's Café at the Centerprise Community Centre in Hackney was started in February 1991. The aim was to offer an intimate, dynamic setting for new and established writers, and the Centerprise café quickly established itself as the only women-only space in London for writers, performers, musicians, dancers and comics. Women from across the country and abroad performed there. Bernadette Halpin suggested the idea following the demise of the lesbian reading sessions at the London Women's Centre. When Dorothea **Smartt** joined Halpin at Centerprise six months later, as the Black Literature Worker, they dedicated the first Friday of every month for black women performers. In 1993, Smartt and Halpin co-edited an anthology featuring lesbian poets who had performed at Word Up from its inception until March 1992, *Words From the Women's Cafe* (Centerprise Publications). Performers who first appeared there include Patience **Agbabi**, Maya **Chowdhry**, and Valerie **Mason-John**. The last café was in 1994 after both Smartt and Halpin had left Centerprise.

KADIJA SESAY

Centre for Contemporary Cultural Studies

The Centre for Contemporary Cultural Studies (CCCS) at the University of Birmingham has played a leading role, perhaps *the* leading role, in institutionalising, defining and shaping the projects of cultural studies in Britain since it was founded in 1964. First directed by Richard Hoggart, and charged with the task of studying 'cultural forms, practices, and institutions and their relation to society and social change' (Turner, p. 70), the

CCCS has effected a series of crucial shifts in the history of British cultural studies. In its early years, under Hoggart's directorship, it helped to synthesise and systematise the work of some of the 'founding' figures of cultural studies (Raymond Williams, E.P. Thompson and Hoggart himself), in large part by examining the cultural complexity of the everyday, lived experiences of working-class Britons.

Under the directorship of Stuart **Hall**, who succeeded Hoggart, the work of scholars at the centre increasingly began to focus on the mass media and the capacity of the media to structure dominant representations of social life. A central element of that turn to media and communications analysis was a heightened interest in the general problem of ideology and the ideological determination, through media representations, of normative models of social behaviour and political life. In introducing ideology-critique to the ongoing project of British cultural studies, the CCCS, particularly through the writings of Hall, helped wed the British Marxist tradition of Williams and Thompson to the structural Marxism of Louis Althusser, Continental semiotics, various strands of poststructural thought (especially a Lacanian psychoanalysis) and the political writings of Antonio Gramsci. Under Hall's directorship, the CCCS also began to focus attention on 'subcultures' (alternative or oppositional cultural formations counter-hegemonically present within the dominant culture), particularly youth subcultures.

Since the late 1970s and early 1980s the CCCS, while continuing to sponsor such forms of research, has also been home to a number of probing auto-critiques of the dominant form of cultural studies work in Britain. In 1978 the Women's Studies Group at the centre published a volume entitled *Women Take Issue: Aspects of Women's Subordination*, critical of the implicit masculinisation of cultural life in much cultural studies research. Also, in 1981, the CCCS volume *The Empire Strikes Back: Race and Racism in 70s Britain* followed up on the 1978 text *Policing the Crisis: Mugging, the State, and Law and Order* by issuing a double critique of the racial exclusiveness of the British polity and state, and the narrow, racially homogenous nationalism of much preceding cultural studies analysis of a 'common' British culture. Taken together, *Policing the Crisis* and *The*

Empire Strikes Back can be seen as crucial originary texts in a black British cultural studies enterprise both at odds with the CCCS's prior organisation of cultural studies in Britain and crucially indebted to the centre's shaping of the field. A centre for publishing, research and postgraduate teaching throughout its existence, the CCCS has recently been re-organised as a Department of Cultural Studies with an undergraduate programme.

Further reading

Davies, I. (1995) *Cultural Studies and Beyond: Fragments of Empire*, London and New York: Routledge.

Dworkin, D. (1997) *Cultural Marxism in Postwar Britain: History, the New Left, and the Origins of Cultural Studies*, Durham: Duke University Press.

Turner, G. (1990) *British Cultural Studies: an Introduction*, London and New York: Routledge.

IAN BAUCOM

Chadha, Gurinder

b. 1960, Kenya

film-maker, actor

Gurinder Chadha is a British Asian film-maker whose successful feature film (see **film and cinema**) *Bhaji on the Beach* (1994) documents the excursions of a group of South Asian women in Blackpool and celebrates women's solidarity in the face of racism and domestic violence. Chadha's other films were also made in response to the media's tendency to ignore the role played by the South Asian community in Great Britain. *I'm British, but...* (1990) examines the perspectives of second-generation British immigrants, *A Nice Arrangement* (1991) provides glimpses of a British-born Indian girl's wedding day, *Acting Our Age* (1993) is made up of interviews with inhabitants of a South Asian shelter for the elderly, and *What Do You Call an Indian Woman Who's Funny?* (1994) tells the stories of four women comedians. Chadha celebrates the multiple identities of her Indian subjects by incorporating **bhangra** into the soundtracks of her films and by juxtaposing Indian

actors and iconography against the natural landscape of Great Britain.

Select bibliography

Chadha, G. (1994) *Bhaji on the Beach*, London: Umbi.

—— (1993) *Acting Our Age*, London: Umbi.

ASHA SEN

Chambers, Eddie

b. 1960, Wolverhampton, England

visual artist, archivist, curator, writer

Eddie Chambers is a pivotal figure in the history of black art in the UK. As an artist, Chambers was a member of the Pan-Afrikan Connection, the group of young artists responsible for the first formulation of black art as a programme with a manifesto. Chambers's artwork, like the others in the group, was direct and confrontational; perhaps his best-known image was the simple but effective 'Destruction of the National Front', which depicted the break-up of an icon made up from the Union Jack and the swastika. By the mid-1980s, Chambers's collection of cuttings and photographs was forming the basis of what would become **African and Asian Visual Arts Archive**, an important archive and resource. He had also started curating with the exhibition '**D-Max**' in 1987. He went on to curate several important shows including '**Black Art: Plotting the Course**' and 'Four × 4'. Furthermore, he had also started publishing articles, most notably on black art, but also exhibition reviews on a regular basis for a number of magazines, in particular *Art Monthly.*

Further reading

Clarke, V. and Tawadros, G. (eds) (1999) *Run through the Jungle: Selected Writings by Eddie Chambers*, London: inIVA.

NIRU RATNAM

Chandra, Avinash

b. 1931 Simla, India; d. 1991, London, England

painter

Chandra came to the UK in 1956, and quickly gained critical attention for his highly decorative and expressive works. Along with Francis **Souza** he was included in the 1958 Gallery One show, *Seven Indian Painters*, and went on to have solo shows at the Bear Lane Gallery, Oxford and the Molton Gallery in London. The erotic imagery of his mature work led many critics to draw a direct line between Chandra and Khajuraho, but this ignored the more international and local imagery in his work, such as his use of the gothic. Chandra faced the problem that confronted many black British artists – he was either perceived as being 'Indian' and thus exoticised, or he was accused of being derivative of Western styles. Like Souza, Chandra enjoyed a period of acclaim in the early 1960s before slipping into obscurity. The exhibition, 'Six Indian Artists', at the Commonwealth Institute in 1965, which featured both painters, can be seen as the end of this first phase of black British visual art (see **visual and plastic arts**).

Further reading

Araeen R. 'Conversation with Avinash Chandra', *Third Text* 3–4: 69–96.
Horizon Gallery, London (1987) *Avinash Chandra*, exhibition catalogue.

NIRU RATNAM

Channel 4

Channel 4 was established in 1981 as a public broadcasting service to inform, educate and entertain. Unlike the British Broadcasting Corporation (BBC), the station was commercial. It went on air in November 1982 and currently celebrates nineteen years of diversity.

One of the remits of the television station was to be innovative and inclusive, covering multiculturalism, education and disabilities. From the start,

Channel 4's importance was that it had a policy giving access of opportunity to ethnic minority (see **ethnic minorities**) people who hoped to work on screen and behind it. Sue Woodford became the channel's first commissioning editor for multicultural programming. The magazine programmes *Eastern Eye* and *Black on Black* were produced, gaining a late evening slot on Tuesday nights. The slant of these programmes was to look at issues of concern to the black community that did not always reflect racism *per se*. In the early years, the broadcasting channel was criticised for being tokenistic. The 1990s saw the emergence of **television** programmes with a slant towards sex. In October 1993, Channel 4 transmitted the three-part series *Doing it with You...Is Taboo*, an adult-type programme looking at relationships. Towards the end of the 1990s, the way in which multicultural programmes were presented changed again. They became an important part of Channel 4's primetime schedule in 1999 with the 'Untold' season of black history programmes, launched with the screening of Trevor **Phillips**'s *Slave Trade*. Channel 4 also has a successful film (see **film and cinema**) channel: launched in November 1998, FilmFour has established an impressive reputation. One of its critical and commercial successes is the comedy *East is East*, about an Anglo-Indian family in 1970s Salford. The film also won a BAFTA Award as the outstanding film of the year. Hollywood film star and director Forest Whitaker set up a unit within Film Four to promote black British and Asian film-makers and producers in the industry.

Documentaries formed an important part of multicultural programming. The award-winning *Dispatches* screened shows on private fostering and transracial adoption, topical subjects within the black community. Other documentaries included *Raj Love* in Bombay, *Lagos Airport* and *Love in Leeds*, focusing on the lives of a group of young, single, Asian, black and white women. *Sex Warriors and the Samuri*, produced for Channel 4 by Parminder **Vir**, won the Best Documentary Award at the Mondial Film and Video Festival in Brussels. In terms of light entertainment, comedian Richard **Blackwood** got his own self-titled show, while the *Hip Hop Years* and *The MOBO Awards* showed Channel 4's commitment to **music**. Channel 4 challenges cultural taboos with its *Positions Impossible* series, an exploration of the Kama Sutra presented by Sanjeev **Bhaskar**. The multicultural programming department under commissioning editor Yasmin Anwar received an Oscar nomination for the Best Documentary Feature for *The Farm: Angola, USA*, a film that appeared in the Ba Ba Zee series. In October 2000, Channel 4 marked Black History Month with the launch of the Black and Asian History Map on its website: a link to historical projects throughout Britain.

Further reading

Anwar, M. and Shang, A. (1982) *Television in a Multi Racial Society*, London: Commission for Racial Equality.

Ross, K. (1996) *Black and White Media: Black Images in Popular Film and Television*, Oxford: Press.

YINKA SUNMONU

Charles, Faustin

b. 1938, Toco, Trinidad

poet, novelist, children's writer, storyteller

Charles came to London in 1962 to further his education, as well as his creative writing ambitions, obtaining a degree in African and Caribbean studies from the University of Canterbury in 1980. He has held three writer in residence posts, including one at the University of Warwick in 1986. Charles has taught colonial and Caribbean history and culture, and Caribbean **literature**, at adult education institutions throughout England, and is a popular storyteller, both for children and adults. His operetta, *Anancy Man*, was staged in a London primary school in 1994. He has published books on Caribbean literature for schools in the Caribbean; collections of poetry, novels and children's books.

Select bibliography

Charles, F. (1998) *The Selfish Crocodile*, London: Bloomsbury.

—— (1997) *Wilkie and the Bakoo*, London: Longman.

—— (1994) *Uncle Charlie's Crick Crack Tales*, London: Karia Press.

—— (ed.)(1991) *The Kiskadee Queen*, London: Blackie.

—— (ed.) (1989) *Under the Storyteller's Spell*, London: Viking.

—— (1986) *Days and Nights in the Magic Forest*, London: Bogle L'Ouverture.

—— (1985) *The Black Magic Man of Brixton*, London: Karnak House.

—— (1981) *Signposts of the Jumbie*, London: Bogle L'Ouverture.

KADIJA SESAY

(charles), Helen

academic

As a lesbian feminist philosopher (charles)'s research has consistently interrogated the concealed conceptual elements in identity politics. The essay 'Whiteness', which first appeared in 1992, drew attention to the occlusions and instabilities surrounding 'white' as a marker of ethnicity and/or identity. (charles) developed a series of workshops on the white/non-white binary and invited participants to interrogate the meanings of their perceptions of their skin colour, focusing in particular on the ramifications for 'white' participants of considering themselves white. This attention to conceptual language, nominal definitions and power characterises (charles)'s scrutiny of the codes and languages of blackness within gay politics and queer theory. (charles)'s research interests are visually represented in her last name, which draws immediate attention to the problematics of the surname. In foregrounding the otherwise naturalised patriarchal assumptions embedded in the conventional surname, (charles)'s act of re-inscription highlights the fact that the family names of many African Caribbean people derive from slave-owning patronymics.

Select bibliography

(charles), H. (1996) '"White" skins, straight masks', in D. Jarrett-Macauley (ed.),*Reconstructing Womanhood, Reconstructing Feminism*, London: Routledge.

—— (1995) '(Not) compromising: inter-skin colour relations', in L. Pearce and J. Stacey (eds), *Romance Revisited*, London: Lawrence & Wishart.

—— (1993) 'Queer nigger: theorizing "white" activism', in J. Bristow and A.R. Wilson (eds) *Activating Theory: Lesbian, Gay, Bisexual Politics*, London: Lawrence & Wishart.

—— (1992) 'Whiteness? The relevance of politically colouring the "non"', in Hilary Hinds, Ann Phoenix, Jackie Stacey (eds) *Working out: New Directions for Women's Studies*, Falmer: University of Brighton Press.

LYNNETTE TURNER

Chatterjee, Debjani

b. 1952, Delhi, India

poet, activist

Since coming to Britain in 1972, Chatterjee has been playing an important role as an activist in community relations, women's movements and the promotion of **literature**. After finishing her Ph.D. in 1977, she worked in education and served as Director of Sheffield Racial Equality Council (1984–94). She is now a full-time writer and committee member of the National Association of Writers in Education. A founding member of the Bengali Women's Support Group, Chatterjee has edited a number of the group's bilingual anthologies, among which *Barbed Lines* was the winner of the Raymond Williams Community Publishing Prize. The recipient of many poetry prizes, Chatterjee's collections include *I Was that Woman* (1989) and *Albino Gecko* (1998), in which the richness of her different cultural backgrounds is woven together in her original use of the English language. She is also a translator from Bengali and Urdu into English, and the author of **children's literature** inspired by Hindu mythology. In 2000 she published *Animal Antics* and edited *The Redbeck Anthology of British South Asian Poetry*.

Select bibliography

Chatterjee, D. (2000) *Animal Antics*, Hebden Bridge: Pennine Pens.

—— (ed.) *The Redbeck Anthology of British South Asian Poetry*, Bradford: Redbeck Press.

—— (1998) *Albino Gecko*, Salzburg: University of Salzburg.

—— (1989) *I Was That Woman*, Frome: Hippopotamus Press.

—— (1989) *The Elephant-headed God and other Hindu Tales*, Cambridge: Lutterworth Press.

PAOLA MARCHIONNI

Chaudhuri, Amit

b. 1962, Calcutta, India

writer, essayist, singer, editor

Amit Chaudhuri grew up in Bombay and was educated at University College, London, and Balliol College, Oxford, where he completed his doctorate. He has written four novels. The first, *A Strange and Sublime Address*, published in 1991, won the Betty Trask Award, and Commonwealth Writer's Prize. The second, *Afternoon Raag* (1993), was highly acclaimed and won the Society of Authors and Southern Arts Literature Prizes. His third novel, *Freedom Song*, was published in 1998, and his most recent work, *A New World*, came out in 2000. He has edited the *Picador Book of Modern Indian Literature* and has contributed criticism and fiction to literary journals such as *Granta* and the *New Yorker*. Chaudhuri is also a singer trained in the Hindustani classical tradition, an interest that recurs as a motif in works such as *Afternoon Raag*. He was initiated into **music** by his mother, the singer Bijoya Chaudhuri, and has performed internationally.

Select bibliography

Chaudhuri, A. (2000) *A New World*, London: Picador.

—— (1999) *Freedom Song: Three Novels* [omnibus volume], New York: Knopf.

—— (1998) *Freedom Song*, London: Picador.

—— (1993) *Afternoon Raag*, London: Picador.

—— (1991) *A Strange and Sublime Address*, London: Picador.

ALEX TICKELL

Cherry, Neneh

b. 1964, Stockholm, Sweden

singer

Neneh Cherry joined her first group Rip, Rig and Panic in 1985 after being introduced to the rest of the band by Mark Stewart. Stewart was also responsible for introducing Nellee Hooper to **Jazzie B** and bringing the Wild Bunch to London for their first booking, so it was no surprise when Cherry chose to work with members of the Bristol collective on her debut solo album, 1995's *Raw Like Sushi*, which was a world-wide hit. When her second album *Homebrew* failed to emulate the success of her debut, executives were at a loss as to how they should recapture Cherry's original success. Unflustered, Cherry cut a track with Senegalese artist Youssou N'Dour for his album. 'Seven seconds' was released as a single in 1994 and went on to sell over 3 million records in France alone. Cherry then collaborated with **Tricky** on what was to be her third album, but only one song made it on to the finished album, 1996's *Man*, which was inspired by the death of her step-father, the jazz trumpeter Don Cherry. In 1998, Cherry began work on her fourth album with her husband and sometime producer Cameron McVey.

ANDY WOOD

Chic

Started in 1984, *Chic* was one of the first magazines (see **publishing, newspapers and magazines**) launched for black women in Britain, owned by Ratepress Ltd. Unlike its mainstream counterparts, its circulation figures did not extend into hundreds of thousands, but, unlike its counterparts, it addressed issues relevant to black women. It contained many of the departments found in mainstream magazines with the emphasis on the double discrimination or double yolk of being black and female, and the economic and social disadvantages this could bring. The traditional women's magazine elements were evident from a black perspective – lifestyle, careers, beauty and relationships. Black women finally had a magazine

from a black British perspective, similar to the US publications *Ebony* and *Essence*, which some had tended to rely upon. Discrimination and race were issues that were tackled along with politics. *Chic* was a positive magazine. Black women were able to aspire to or identify with successful women of African Caribbean origin and read about issues concerning them.

YINKA SUNMONU

children's literature

Since the 1970s, the availability of children's **literature** that actively includes a black readership has increased astonishingly, despite the reluctance of mainstream **children's publishers** to seek out black authors and illustrators, and promote fiction that portrays a multicultural society. While the rapid growth and popularity of black writing for children in North America attests to the need for picture books, folk tales, poetry and fiction across the 0–16 age range, it is only very recently that black British voices have been heard in any number, as hugely successful North American imports, such as Rosa Guy and Virginia Hamilton, have flooded the British market. Dependence on European sales has contributed to a reluctance on the part of larger British publishing companies to encourage fiction, particularly in the form of picture books, that reflects multiculturalism, as the widespread perception is that European readers prefer to see white faces.

In some ways, the marginal status of children's literature has enabled otherwise silenced black authors to publish their work, in the same way that women in the nineteenth century found it much easier to publish for children than for adults. Like Beryl **Gilroy**, women writers in particular were able to publish novels *about* their own childhoods under the guise of children's fiction, and it is still frequently the case that black writers, such as John **Agard**, Grace **Nichols**, Jackie **Kay** and Farrukh **Dhondy**, also write for children. In the shadow of the *fatwa*, it was a children's book: *Haroun and the Sea of Stories* (1991) that Salman **Rushdie** published, enabling him to seek a safe place from which to voice his wonder and mystification at the world through myth and fantasy.

While some of the books published in the 1970s, such as *My Brother Sean* (1973) written by Petronella Breinburg and illustrated by Errol **Lloyd**, are continually reissued as examples of attractive and positive images of black family life, publishing for children in the 1970s and early 1980s was subsumed by debates surrounding racial stereotyping and the need to provide black children with stories and non-fiction that reflected their own communities and histories. Farrukh Dhondy, for instance, in his collection of short stories *Come to Mecca* (1978) provides a rare opportunity to encounter the problematic lives of black British children and confront the language of racism. However, Dhondy was primarily known as a writer for adults; librarians, such as Janet Hill, recognised that despite the growth in black publishing in Britain, there was very little being written expressly for children. Her booklist, *Books for Children: the Homelands of Immigrants to Britain* (1971) attempted to attack racial bias and prejudice in existing publications and, at the same time, draw attention to the dearth of black writers for a young readership. Even by the time of the publication of *The Books for Keeps Guide to Children's Books for a Multicultural Society* by the magazine *Books for Keeps* in 1986, it was imported North American publications that had the greatest impact. W.H. Armstrong's *Sounder* (1971) or Mildred Taylor's fictional representations of racism in 1930s Mississippi, *Roll of Thunder, Hear My Cry (1976)*, provided powerful images of black children finding a positive position from which to confront racial intolerance. At the same time, Taylor's books offered positive images of black women as nurturing and strong, encouraging their children and grandchildren to embrace emancipation on many levels.

The pressure for children's literature to speak to a multicultural society encouraged white writers and illustrators to respond to the changes in British communities. While *My Mate Shofiq* (1978) by Jan Needle and novels by Peter Dickinson, Robert Leeson and others may have enabled white readers to confront their own racism, and while Shirley Hughes and other illustrators may include children of all races in their illustrations, commentators and critics of children's books have questioned the right of white writers to attempt to write from a black perspective. These debates are not resolved and, while the establishment of small publishing houses that actively publish black authors may be applauded, Jacqueline Roy, a children's writer, claims that 'books by Black writers are perceived as being irrelevant in areas other than those with high Asian or African-Caribbean populations'. The truth of this perception must be tempered by the acknowledgement that many of the developments over the last ten years have been more successful at challenging stereotypes and offering positive images of black identity. The trend, echoing the energetic growth in black children's literature in North America, is towards a much more deliberate effort on the part of children's publishers to address all readers with fictional representations of a multicultural society. The newest version of the *Books for Keeps* booklist, entitled *A Multi-cultural Guide to Children's Books 0–12* (1994) provides an encouraging picture of the growing range of texts and genres within children's literature. At the same time, it must be said that the financial restriction on library provision and the new National Curriculum reduces the amount of scope for teachers who wish to make use of the new literature available, closing off opportunities for all children to become aware of the variety of cultural heritage.

Part of the process of finding a distinctive voice has been the acknowledgement of distinct histories and folk traditions that challenge the Eurocentricity of the most familiar folk and fairy tales of German and French provenance. The publication of numerous collections of folk tales from African Caribbean cultures, such as the Anansi stories in various forms, Virginia Hamilton's collection of black US folk tales, *The People Could Fly* (1985), Trinidadian stories in Grace Hallworth's *Cric Crac* (1990) and Madhur **Jaffrey**'s *Seasons of Splendour: Tales, Myths and Legends of India* (1985) familiarise black children with their own cultural heritage, but also introduce all children to a rich vein of folklore. White picture book authors and illustrators have consciously sought to present images of Britain that included black characters since the 1970s, and have often been accused of tokenism, but it is only in the last few years that black authors have begun to find a distinctive voice, though black illustrators are still in a minority, as white illustrators are frequently called upon to provide the images. A good example is *So Much* (1994) by Trish **Cooke**, illustrated by Helen Oxenbury. The loving warmth of the book is complemented by the cadences of the language to suggest both the particularity of a strong black community and the universality of familial love. The publication of *Amazing Grace* in 1991 and other works by Mary Hoffman and Caroline Binch, including Binch's own *Hue Boy* (1993) and *Gregory Cool* (1995), have awakened publishers to the need for all children to experience emancipating texts that work on a number of levels. When Grace of the title is told that she cannot be Peter Pan in the school play because she is both female and black, her grandmother offers a universal message: not of confrontation, but of determination to accomplish one's desires against the odds.

Gregory Cool is representative of a trend to confront the tensions that cultural clashes bring. The contrasts between life in Britain and the weather, food and traditions of the parental (or grandparental) culture are frequently portrayed in children's novels of the last decade and Floella Benjamin, better known as a **television** presenter, has also published stories, such as *Coming to England* (1997), intended to familiarise the children of West Indian background with the culture of their homeland. The work of Jamila Gavin, in *The Singing Bowls* (1989) and *The Wheel of Surya* (1992), enables the author to confront the history of her Indian father, as well as her own multicultural background. James **Berry**, who won the Smarties Prize for *A Thief in the Village and Other Stories* (1987), portrays both the joys and the poverty of Caribbean life, while Beverly Naidoo, a white South African, struggles to understand the effects of apartheid through the eyes of a black child in *Journey to Jo'burg* (1987). At times, however, some of the fiction published has not been able to dispel the impression that they are merely 'problem' books, and it must be acknowledged that recent books about gender, race and disability sometimes lack the imagination and energy necessary to attract a wide readership. Some authors resist such labels, however, and Malorie Blackman, with her novel *Hacker* (1992), as well as many other titles, provides an example of an author who presents positive images of black characters within a multicultural society without comment. Recently a recipient of

an Excelle Award, the only such award for black British publishing, Blackman is part of a new generation of black children's writers published by mainstream publishers.

Organisations such as the **National Committee on Racism in Children's Books** and the **Working Group against Racism in Children's Resources** have also been active in promoting the writing of non-fiction that provides images and subject matter inclusive of black British cultural experience. If, in the 1970s, such a lack was addressed by the publication of dry and uninspiring photobooks of life in Africa, India or Pakistan, the success of North American imports supplied by Letterbox Library, Britain's main supplier of multicultural books for children, has inspired the publication of homegrown educational resource books with similar aims. Tamarind Books is currently producing a series of titles entitled Black Pioneers, written by Verna Wilkins, and there are now many examples of beautifully produced pre-readers and alphabet books, such as John Agard's *A Calypso Alphabet* (1989) or Faustin **Charles**'s *A Caribbean Counting Book* (1998). Perhaps the most energetic and inspiring trend in children's literature in the last few years has been the wealth of poetry for children by black poets. Many poets, expressing a more confrontational voice in their poetry for adults, write for children with 'a gentler voice'. According to Morag Styles:

> What began for some as a desire to educate black (and white) pupils about their cultural heritage in the Caribbean developed into a new poetry for children which took account of black experience in Britain and gave a focus for writing about West Indian life, too.

James Berry's *When I Dance* (1988) and Jackie Kay's *Two's Company* (1994) both won the prestigious *Signal* award for children's poetry and John Agard, who writes both in creole and standard English, has collaborated with Grace **Nichols**, author of *Come in to My Tropical Garden* (1990) among other titles, on numerous collections of Caribbean poetry, such as *No Hickory, no Dickory, no Dock* (1991) and *A Caribbean Dozen* (1994). The popularity of **performing poetry** and the enthusiasm with which children respond to the musical rhythms and the adventurousness of language in the dialect of this new poetry has meant that many poets, notably Benjamin **Zephaniah**, have considerable success promoting their poetry in schools and having their work anthologised in many general collections of contemporary children's poetry. It is the distinctiveness of the particularly black British voice in the most recent poetry that presents the most optimistic outlook for children's literature, responding to a rich mix of cultural reference points and offering children a way of sharing in the experience of making worlds.

Further reading

Pinsent, P. (1997) *Children's Literature and the Politics of Equality*, London: David Fulton.

Stones, R. (ed.) (1994) *A Multicultural Guide to Children's Books 0–12*, London: Books for Keeps.

Styles, M. (1998) *From the Garden to the Street*, London: Cassell.

DEBBIE THACKER

children's publishers

In the 1970s, the need to find **children's literature** for an inter-racial audience was perceived to be at the centre of anti-racist agendas. Guidelines published by the American Council on Inter-racial Books for Children, and the Bullock Report (1975) reinforced the notion that children needed to see images that challenged race stereotypes in their fiction and needed to find familiar faces and settings in the books they were given to read. The absence of black characters, or the racist portrayal in much classic children's fiction, was confronted by educationalists and librarians, yet mainstream children's publishers in Britain were slow to respond to this trend. By the 1980s, British publishers were beginning to import books by black US authors, yet there were very few black British authors writing for a young readership. Thus, while there was clearly a receptive audience for such fiction, there were few homegrown books produced. Some educational publishers chose to address the lack by producing photostory books, in order to introduce ethnic traditions of African, Caribbean, Indian and Pakistani cultures to children born in Britain. These were hardly

imaginative and although children were able to see their own ethnicity reflected in books for, perhaps, the first time, they had limited appeal.

While there has been a marked increase in the number of children's books published by mainstream publishers, a general dissatisfaction with the limitations of provision has led to the founding of a number of small independent publishing houses and book suppliers, which specialise in multicultural books, challenging the well-meaning conglomerates who have frequently been accused of having 'trivialised or pathologised the lives of families and communities through tokenism and negative stereotyping'. **Mantra Publications** was founded in 1984 by Mishti Chatterji, Robene Dutta and Sanjeevina Dutta, because they could find nothing for their own children that reflected their cultural heritage and the experience of growing up in Britain. Specialising in dual-language books, Mantra offers a wide range of picture books, both widely available 'classics' such as Carle's *A Very Hungry Caterpillar*, and multicultural folktales and myths, nursery rhymes and songs. Having recently expanded to include a range of cassettes, videos and CD-ROM formats to accompany their dual-language books, Mantra also publishes for teenage and adult markets. The belief in multicultural publishing provides a healthy challenge to many mainstream British publishers who claim the reluctance of European publishers to import picture books with black or Asian images, and Mantra actively seeks authors and illustrators who have been unable to publish due to this reluctance.

Verna Wilkins, who founded Tamarind Books in 1987, responded to the same problems in children's publishing that motivated the founders of Mantra. Her own experience upon coming to England from Grenada demonstrated the extent to which black learners were denied positive images in classroom **literature** and how these exclusions reinforce society's low expectations of black learners. The literature she was able to find for her own children seemed to provide images of black children with problems, rather than offering inspirational models, and she set out to provide them herself. Publishing books for pre-readers and her own simple illustrated stories, such as *Ben Makes a Cake* and *Mum Can Fix it*, Wilkins ensures that the children in her books set themselves goals and succeed with confidence.

Rather than seeing herself as a publisher of 'black' books, she contends that her aim is 'a seamless celebration of human potential'. She has recently extended her range to include books about disabled children and a series about influential black politicians, scientists and writers, entitled 'Black Pioneers', is in production. The positive messages she tries to provide are reinforced by her work in schools, encouraging children not merely to read but to become authors and illustrators. In 1997, Wilkins was a recipient of one of the first Excelle Awards for Lifetime Achievement. These awards, begun as an acknowledgement of excellence in black British publishing that has long gone uncelebrated, were founded in 1997 by the Write Thing, an organisation that promotes black publishing. Eric and Jessica Huntley, of **Bogle L'Ouverture**, also received a Lifetime Achievement Award and, although they do not publish children's fiction, their publications frequently address educational issues that impinge on children.

Like Tamarind, Frances Lincoln also publishes a wide range of multicultural alphabet and board books, information books about life in Africa and Asia and picture books, such as the work of Mary Hoffman and Caroline Binch. Beautifully produced and illustrated folk tales from many cultures are a speciality, with such titles as Jessica Souhami's *Rama and the Demon King*, and Fiona French's *Anansi and Mr Drybone* and *Jamil's Clever Cat, a Folktale from Bengal*. While not exclusively concerned to publish work by black authors, the production values of Frances Lincoln books are high and their promotional capability exceeds that of many smaller publishers. Magi Publications publishes a wide range of children's fiction, but specialises in the production of dual-language editions of popular picture books. Offering Bengali, Gujerati, Hindi, Punjabi and Urdu with English, Magi provides an important educational resource for multilingual families.

Finally, Letterbox Library, though not a publishing house, is a key source of multicultural books for children in Britain. Founded in 1984, Letterbox Library is a supplier of books selected by an independent panel of librarians, teachers, parents and children to provide examples of culturally diverse texts that challenge stereotypes of both race and gender. Promoting fiction through school visits and their catalogues, this organisation has been very successful in collecting titles produced by both specialist and mainstream publishers and distributing them to a wider audience.

DEBBIE THACKER

Chowdhry, Maya

dramatist

Maya Chowdhry was one of a number of black women playwrights, who include Jackie **Kay** and Jacqueline **Rudet**, to be helped by the appointment of black woman producer Frances-Anne Solomon to BBC Radio 4. It is thanks to Solomon that Chowdhry's first play *Monsoon* was broadcast as part of the BBC Young Playwrights' Festival. *Monsoon* is set in India and parallels the time of waiting for the monsoon with the experience of menstruation. Threaded throughout the piece is a poem that Chowdhry has since incorporated into other media, such as her short experimental film about menstruation. In addition to her performance poetry, Chowdhry's theatre work also includes her play *Kaahini* (1997). *Kaahini* was toured by Red Ladder and was the company's fourth Asian production in a series of plays aimed primarily at British-Asian girls. Influenced by the story of Sikhandin in the *Mahabharata*, Chowdhry's *Kaahini* examines gender roles and pressures by dramatising a narrative of gender reversal: a young Asian girl is raised by her family as a boy.

Select bibliography

Chowdhry, M. (1993) *Monsoon*, in K. George (ed.), *Six Plays by Black and Asian Women Writers*, London: Aurora Metro Press.

ELAINE ASTON

Chuhan, Jagit

b. 1955, Punjab, India

artist, curator, lecturer

Chuhan trained at the Slade School of Fine Art from 1973 to 1977. Her artwork has moved from more abstract pieces based on the natural world to self- and family portraiture. She commented that 'in Indian art – apart from Tantric art – women are always secondary to male figures' and her own work challenges this with a strong female presence. The Indian woman, often a dancer, is also central to many works. Chuhan is Reader in Eclecticism in Art at Liverpool John Moores University, where she is also chair of the Centre for Art International Research (CAIR) at Liverpool Art School. Her work is held in a number of public collections including: the Arts Council Collection; North West Arts Board; Cartwright Hall, Bradford; Arthur Andersen and Company, London; and the University of Liverpool School of Tropical Medicine. Exhibitions of her work include: 'New North' at the Tate Gallery Liverpool (1991); 'Indian Winter' at the Kapil Jariwala Gallery, London (1995); and 'In the Looking Glass' at the Usher Gallery, Lincoln (1996). With Laura Arison, her work was included in 'an intimate mosaic' at University of Liverpool Senate House in 1999. Chuhan has also co-curated 'Lines of Desire', an international drawing exhibition, which toured in 1999.

ALISON DONNELL

cinemas

Black and Asian cinemas and festivals have sought to rectify the prevailing problems of black film (see **film and cinema**) production, distribution and exhibition in the UK. In 1993, London's **Electric Cinema** in Portobello Road – the UK's oldest cinema (opened 1910) – became the first British cinema to exclusively screen black-orientated films. Other London cinemas including the Lux, **Institute of Contemporary Arts** and the Ritzy in Brixton also run diasporic and British black and Asian film programmes with supporting forums and discussions. In 1991, Marc Boothe founded Nubian Tales (see **Nubian Tales/b3 Media**) to promote, distribute and exhibit black narratives. Nubian's black films are screened at the West End's Prince Charles Cinema and the Ritzy, where guests such as Spike Lee, John Singleton and Samuel L. Jackson have led discussions about black film-making. Its offshoot, Nubian Vision, has also

offered training, marketing and screening opportunities for aspiring black film-makers.

Various annual film festivals have also focused on black and Asian 'Third' cinema strands, showing rarely screened films and discussing the difficulties of black film production and distribution with leading international black film practitioners. Since 1995, Bradford's National Museum of Photography, Film and Television has held the annual 'Bite the Mango' festival, while smaller festivals like the 'Black Screen' festival focus on the work of culturally diverse film-makers in Merseyside and the North-West. Since the 1970s, specialist Asian cinemas, including the Dominion in Southall, have existed in Asian communities throughout Britain, screening classic and recently released Hindi (or '**Bollywood**') films for expatriate Asian audiences. With Hindi films now regularly playing at multiplexes nationwide, the mainstream film industry can no longer afford to ostracise black and Asian box-office power.

SATINDER CHOHAN

Cleopatra

Zainam, b. 1980; Cleopatra, b. 1982; Yonah b. 1984

singers

Sisters Zainam, Cleopatra and Yonah Higgins make up the singing trio Cleopatra. Raised in Moss Side, Manchester, the group's name is derived from the middle sister Cleopatra, who is the lead singer. Their rise to fame started when they entered a local talent contest, which they won with a renditon of 'Hold On', an En Vogue song. As a result, Cleopatra was signed to a management contract by the competition's organisers, Errol Walters and Tony Lovell. Recognising the sisters' talent, their mother Christine nurtured it, ensuring that they were not thrust into the media spotlight like many of their contemporaries. Cleopatra then honed their craft through hard work and touring. In 1997, they secured a record deal with Warner Brothers, and, a year later, they released their debut album *Comin' Atcha*, featuring the popular song 'Cleopatra's Theme'. The album gave them three top-five hits.

Like the Jackson 5 in America, they achieved enough popularity to warrant their own cartoon programme, and it headed the **television** ratings when it aired in its weekday time slot. This was followed by 'In the House with Cleopatra' for ITV. They have become a significant group in the UK and the USA. The make-up company Covergirl uses them to advertise and they have appeared on the Queen Latifah show and CNN Showbiz Live. *Steppin' Out*, the new album released in 2000, is a collaboration with some of the best-known musical producers in R'n'B.

RAFIEL SUNMONU

Collapsed Lung

A mixed-race band, Collapsed Lung formed in Harlow in the early 1990s. They released their debut single 'Thundersley Invacar' in 1993 on Deceptive Records, the company co-founded by Radio 1 DJ Steve Lamacq. Collapsed Lung were heralded as the new saviours of British **hip hop** by some, though many critics felt that the band were too tongue-in-cheek and too close to the indie-rock scene. Despite such criticism, the band's subsequent singles were well received, as was the 1995 album *Jackpot Goalie*, which featured the band's biggest hit 'Eat My Goal'. Coca Cola chose the song as their theme for the 1996 European football championships and the band released the song on the *London Tonight* e.p. in the same year. A second album *Cooler* was released in the same year, featuring guest appearances by rapper Chris Tucker of the Killa Instinct Crew and Belinda Butcher of My Bloody Valentine. Collapsed Lung were unable to capitalise on the success of *Eat My Goal* and split up in 1997.

ANDY WOOD

Collins, Merle

b. 1950, Grenada

teacher, scholar, poet, novelist, short-story writer, activist

Raised in Grenada, Merle Collins was a member of the Grenada National Women's Organisation until she moved to Britain in 1983. As a co-editor (with Rhonda Cobham) of an early anthology, published in 1987, on black British women writers, *Watchers and Seekers*, she focused her attention on issues in British writing that had been neglected. Her poetry has appeared in many anthologies and in her collections: *Because the Dawn Breaks!* (1985) and *Rotten Pomerack* (1992) and *Lady in a Boat* (1999). She has published the novels *Angel* (1987) and *The Colour of Forgetting* (1995) and collections of short stories entitled *Rain Darling* (1990), *Jump-up-and-kiss-Me: Two Stories from Grenada* (1990) and *Inside Ant's Belly* (1994). Her novels have received less critical attention than her poetry and stories. Although often focusing on women's lives and experiences, her work is politically engaged and addresses issues of race, gender, colonisation and colonisation's consequences. *Because the Dawn Breaks!* (which is subtitled *Poems Dedicated to the Grenadian People*), for example, is concerned with the hopes and fears surrounding the Grenada Revolution in 1979, the US invasion and the murder of President Maurice Bishop in 1983. In the UK, she was a lecturer in Caribbean studies at North London Polytechnic and a commentator for the BBC. Currently, she is on the faculty at the University of Maryland, USA.

Select bibliography

Collins, M. (1995) *The Colour of Forgetting*, London: Virago.
—— (1992) *Rotten Pomerack*, London: Virago.
—— (1990) *Rain Darling*, London: the Women's Press.
—— (1987) *Angel*, London: the Women's Press.
—— (1985) *Because the Dawn Breaks!*, London: Karia Press.

TRACY J. PRINCE

comedians

The UK's first famous black comedian was Charlie Williams, a performer who glowed with warmth and charm, whose reminiscences of a disappearing working-class culture delivered in an authentic Yorkshire accent forged a strong rapport with his mainly white audience. Williams hosted the popular game show *The Golden Shot* and starred in a handful of television specials, after being shot to fame in 1971 by Granada's *The Comedians*, which also gave exposure to the Liverpudlian black comic, Jos White. Racist jokes, and particularly jokes expressing anti-immigration paranoia, were the stock-in-trade of club comedians of the era, but Williams (and White) put their own more ambiguous spin on the subject. As well as self-deprecating jokes about his race, Williams told jokes in which he bettered his white detractors. Moreover, he appeared to ridicule racism by taking on the voice of the white majority group with apparent irony, affectionately referring to Enoch Powell as 'Nocker' and complaining about the immigrants 'comin' ovver 'ere on owt they can gerron'. It would be a mistake, however, to see Williams as an anti-racist crusader: his onstage views were not too dissimilar from what he said offstage, expressing a genuine admiration for Powell, and talking about immigration 'breeding fear and unrest'. He was also happy to tell the same violent jokes about immigrants as his white contemporaries, for example talking about the Pakistani who went for a job as a conductor, so they nailed him to a chimney. His adoption of a white perspective was unsurprising given his life story. Audiences laughed when he claimed to be 'a Yorkshire lad', but that was exactly what he was, having grown up near Barnsley, worked as a miner and played professional football for Doncaster Rovers. Furthermore, a more radical line was not an option for him, having cut his teeth in solidly white venues, some of which operated a formal colour bar.

Lenny **Henry** represented a sea change in black British comedy. Henry started out with the same kind of self-deprecating approach as Williams: appearing on the television talent show *New Faces* at the age of sixteen in 1975, he started by telling the audience, 'You may have seen some of these impressions before, but not in colour'; and he spent five years as resident comedian with *The Black and White Minstrel Show*. After a brilliant and popular stint on the children's programme *Tiswas*, Henry was researching for an adult version of the show, *OTT*, when he was taken to the Comic Strip, a legendary alternative comedy venue. Influenced by the scabrous routines of Alexei Sayle, and by Dawn

French, who he went on to marry, Henry ditched the self-deprecation in favour of comedy that celebrated his blackness. His highly successful **television** work and stand-up shows are filled with characters from black culture, like Deakus (an elderly West Indian who came to the UK in the 1950s) and Theophilus P. Wildebeeste (a hip-grinding, lust-crazed **soul** singer). A vibrant, fun-packed family entertainer, Henry skilfully slips harder material into his stand-up routines, even talking about the racist thugs who defaced his front door. Having grown up in the West Midlands, one of Henry's most famous lines is, 'Me, get repatriated? To Dudley?'

Throughout the 1980s, Henry remained the UK's only high-profile black comedian. The growing alternative comedy circuit had anti-racist intentions, but, initially, most of the performers were white. By the late 1980s, this began to change, with the emergence of acts like Sheila Hyde, the Calypso Twins (a black and white double act, which featured future celebrity chef Ainsley Harriott), Salford-based comic singer Kevin Seisay, and, particularly, Felix Dexter. The real explosion in black British comedy happened in the 1990s. In late 1989, the Albany Empire set up the Black Comedy Club, quickly followed by the Hackney Empire's more successful and longer running black variety show, the 291 Club, which spawned a television series of the same name hosted by visual comedian Miles Crawford. Stars of the early black comedy scene included Llewella **Gideon**, black Muslim comic Leo X. Chester and double act Curtis and Ishmael (who would later split, Curtis Walker going on to become a successful solo act). The BBC's popular sketch and stand-up show *The Real McCoy* picked up on the emerging scene, showcasing most of the new acts alongside more established names like Felix Dexter. Starting in 1991, it ran for five series. **Channel 4** responded with *Get Up, Stand-Up*, another blend of sketches and stand-up built around the trio of Angie Le Mar, Chris Tummings and Malcolm Frederick. Meanwhile, the live circuit continued to grow, boosted by the pioneering efforts of comedian John Simmit (better known as Dipsy in *The Teletubbies*), whose Upfront organisation has run black comedy clubs all over the country. Current big names like Junior Simpson and Gina **Yashere** play both black venues and regular alternative comedy clubs, and black comics are continuing to break into television, notably Richard **Blackwood**, who has his own comedy and chat show on Channel 4.

By the mid-1990s, a specifically Asian comedy scene was also starting to emerge, with acts like Jeff Mirza and the Secret Asians. In 1996, Radio 4 aired the Asian sketch show *Goodness Gracious Me*, which ran for three series and was transferred to television in 1998 with enormous success. Starring Nina **Wadia**, Meera **Syal** (a former regular on *The Real McCoy*), Kulvinder **Ghir** and Sanjeev **Bhaskar** (of the Secret Asians), the show affectionately, but sometimes outrageously, poked fun at many aspects of Asian British culture, as well as satirising white prejudice. Perhaps most memorably, they presented a comic reversal of drunken lads on a Friday night pub and curry session in a sketch that showed a group of Indians 'going for an English' and competing over who could eat the blandest dish.

Further reading

Margolis, J. (1995) *Lenny Henry – a Biography*, London: Orion Books.
Williams, C. (1973) *Ee – I've Had Some Laughs*, London: Wolfe Publishing.

OLIVER DOUBLE

Commission for Racial Equality

The Commission for Racial Equality (CRE) is a publicly funded, non-governmental body set up under the Race Relations Act of 1976, which was introduced by the Labour government, who believed that the previous Acts of 1965 and 1968 were woefullly inadequate when it came to challenging racial discrimination. The Act, which applies to the whole of Great Britain but not Northern Ireland, makes it unlawful to discriminate against anyone because of their race, colour, nationality or national or ethnic origin. It is designed to protect everyone against racial discrimination in employment, training, housing, education and the provision of goods, facilities and services. One of the main tenets of the Act was to replace the two main bodies addressing racial issues – the Community Relations Commission and the Race Relations Board – with a single organisation to be called the Commission for Racial Equality. Section 43 of the Act defined the function of the CRE as:

> [T]o work towards the elimination of racial discrimination; to promote equality of opportunity; to influence policy, promote and encourage research in race relations; and to keep the functioning of the Act under constant review.

The CRE was therefore empowered to help individual complainants and act where persistent discrimination occurred. It was the only authority enabled to take action in cases of direct or suspected discrimination, as well as discrimination in advertising. The CRE provides information and advice to people who believe they have suffered racial discrimination or harassment. Working with both public bodies and businesses within the private sector, it attempts to promote policies and practices that will ensure equal treatment for all. The members of the Commission and the Chair are appointed by the Home Secretary. It receives an annual grant from the Home Office, but operates independently of the Government. It is entitled to enforce the law in the public interest by focusing on identifying and countering discriminatory practices by companies, industries and institutions. It may do this by issuing notices requiring unlawful practices to cease. If the discrimination continues, the CRE may apply for injunctions from the civil courts, thus laying the ground for imprisonment for contempt of court by persistent offenders. It is also authorised to allocate financial and other resources to organisations promoting harmonious race relations and equal opportunities.

The CRE was formed in June 1977. Though the Chairman and Deputy Chairman were full-time, there were also fifteen part-time Commissioners, many representing the interests of trade unions and business. From the outset, the Commission decided to adopt the bold and high-profile strategy set out in its Strategy Statement published in October 1977. During its first year it received 862 applications for help with industrial tribunals and 123 complaints of racial discrimination. By 1979, it had initiated thirty formal investigations into alleged indirect discrimination. Though they were making small gains, there were great expectations of the new regime, particularly on the part of ethnic minority (see **ethnic minorities**) organisations, and they faced a lot of criticism for a lacklustre performance. By 1981, the Thatcher government, now in their second year of office, became highly vocal in their criticism of the CRE and initiated a Home Affairs Committee Inquiry into the organisation. The inquiry focused on the body's operation efficiency, their grant-giving powers and their part in race and community relations. CRE witnesses to the enquiry were extremely critical of the government's lack of political will to promote harmonious race relations and this was a point with which the Home Affairs Committee concurred. Their report clearly stated that Whitehall had reacted unfavourably to both equal opportunities policies within the Civil Service and the CRE's draft code of practice on employment. However, the report was also highly critical of the CRE. They particularly highlighted the lack of priorities or clearly stated objectives, and blamed the dual nature of an organisation that involved itself in legal enforcement and promoting good race relations. The report suggested that the CRE had wrongly allowed promotion to dominate their agenda.

After the report, the CRE decided to reassess their priorities. They resolved to concentrate on very particular areas, including work on employment, particularly stressing the need for jobs for young black people. They massively increased project funding to groups working with black youth, including the Southall Youth Movement, the Harmbee Association and the Federation of Bangladeshi Organisations. They also began working closely with the Manpower Services Commission and Youth Training Schemes. Perhaps their biggest achievement at this time stemmed from their decision to concentrate on changes in the school curriculum to reflect the multi-cultural aspect of British society. By 1983, a quarter of the country's 115 education authorities had adopted multicultural policies. The idea of anti-racist education had taken root. To this day the CRE continues its dual role of law enforcement and promotion. They produce a whole number of publications that advise on the law, the rights of ethnic minorities and codes of practice. Many of their advertising campaigns, largely produced by advertising agency Saatchi and Saatchi, have become legendary. High-profile legal action and execution of their powers of investigation have in many cases served as the trigger for change.

Sir Herman Ousley was appointed the first black Chairman of the CRE in 1993. This former Chief Executive of Lambeth Council was viewed as highly outspoken but effective. He immediately vowed to take the Commission in a new direction; this new approach involved increasingly seeking to work with other organisations and individuals. Partnerships were forged with major employers and public bodies, as well as trade associations, the TUC and the CBI. In June 1997, they launched the Leadership Challenge and invited those people with influence, power and resources to take personal responsibility for action to end racial discrimination and inequality. Citing 'exhaustion', Sir Herman Ousley relinquished his post as CRE Chair two years prematurely in 2000. He was succeeded by former Chief Executive of Haringey Council, Gurbux Singh.

Further reading

Anon. (1987) 'Racial and ethnic relations in Britain: past present and future', *New Community* 14: 1–2.
CRE (1998) *Reform of the Race Relations Act 1976*, London: CRE.
—— (1996) *Connections, Bulletin of Racial Equality* 7 (June).
Hiro, D. (1992) *Black British, White British*, London: Paladin, HarperCollins.

ANDREA ENISUOH

Cooke, Trish

b. 1962, Bradford, England

playwright, children's author

Cooke is the daughter of Dominican immigrant parents and her plays explore issues of identity, belonging and divisions across generations and within families. *Back Street Mammy*, originally produced by Temba, is a complex exploration of adolescent sexual awakening and the dilemmas of unplanned pregnancy. In *Running Dream*, a young woman returns to her 'roots' to discover that there are both deep differences and close bonds between her and her sisters who remained in Dominica. Both plays use the device of a chorus, commenting on and entering the action, and are distinguished by their poetic quality, drawing on song and the rhythms of patois or exploring the shifting contradiction of conflicting desires. Cooke has gone on to write children's books, including *Mr Pam Pam and the Hullabazoo* (1994), the Smarties Prize-winning *So Much* (1994) and *When I Grow Bigger* (1995).

Select bibliography

Cooke, T. (1993) *Running Dream*, in K. George (ed.) *Six Plays by Black and Asian Women Writers*, London: Aurora Metro.
—— *Back Street Mammy* (1990), in K. Harwood (ed.) *First Run 2*, London: Nick Hern Books.

Further reading

Croft, S. (1993) 'Black women playwrights in Britain', in T. Griffiths and M. Llewellyn-Jones (eds) *British and Irish Women Dramatists Since 1958*, London: Open University Press, pp. 84–98.

SUSAN CROFT

Cookie Crew

A South London based female rap trio, the Cookie Crew emerged as part of a wave of British **hip hop** along with Derek B, Monie Love and the **Wee Papa Girl Rappers** in the late 1980s. While most British rap artists were seen as inferior to, or simply a pastiche of US rap, the Cookie Crew were thoroughly rooted in their South London environment. Based around the two rappers MC Remedee (Debbie Pryce) and Suzie Q (Susan Banfield), and DJ Max, the Cookie Crew's debut single 'Females' was released in 1987. The follow-up single 'Rok da house', recorded in collaboration with the Beatmasters, is often cited as the first hip hop/house

crossover and reached number five in the charts in 1988. The Cookie Crew then moved from the small Rhythm King label to FFRR/London and they were signed up by Rush Management, who managed Public Enemy. A series of chart successes followed and their debut album *Born this Way* was released in 1989. After a gap of two years, Cookie Crew released their second album *Fade To Black*, but failed to make a similar impact and the band vanished from view after 1992's *Brother like Sister* e.p.

ANDY WOOD

Cooper, Clement

b. 1965, Manchester, England

photographer

Given a camera at the age of seventeen by a teacher, Cooper began to document his local community of Moss Side and Longsight. In his first book, he concentrates on three distinct communities: that of the Robin Hood Pub, Moss Side, the Church of God, Moss Side, and various youth clubs in and around Manchester. Photographing in a simple, uncluttered black and white documentary style, Cooper took portraits of his subjects with a great sense of dignity and resilience under conditions of poverty. The series *Deep: People of Mixed Race 1994–6*, took Cooper outside of Manchester to other cities, such as Bristol, Liverpool and Cardiff. This series concentrates on single figures who look straight at the viewer, each sitter presented as utterly individual and proud of their own complex identity. Cooper's most recent project, *Primary 1997–1999*, is a series of striking portraits of primary school children. Ignoring race, Cooper photographs the entire racial spectrum of the school, again concentrating on single portraits to create an optimistic picture of a diverse community in its infancy.

Select bibliography

Cooper, C. (2000) *Primary 1997–1999*, London: Autograph.
—— (1996) *Deep: People of Mixed Race 1994–6*, London: Autograph.

—— (1988) *Presence: Photographs by Clement Cooper*, Manchester: Cornerhouse Publications.

FRANCIS SUMMERS

Cornershop

Cornershop consists of Tjinder **Singh** (vocals, guitar, scratching, dholki), Ben Ayres (tamboura, guitar, keyboards), Peter Bengry (percussion), Anthony Saffery (sitar, harmonium, keyboards) and Nick Simms (drums). They initially came to prominence in 1993, when they were asked to comment on Morrisey's Finsbury Park glorification of skinhead culture and 'British' values, and in the process became willing spokespeople for a significant debate at the time. Considered by many to be reflective of the Anglo-Asian background of the band's members (whose backgrounds range from Wolverhampton and the Punjab to Newfoundland, Canada), Cornershop are said to be evidence of the existence of a British cultural melting pot. Their **music** combines elements of Indian, Anglo and African American music styles with **hip hop**, dub samplings, rock, 1960s guitar trash with Punjabi folk music and harmonium sounds. 'Brimful of Asha', (with a Norman Cook remix), their number one hit in 1998, paid homage to Indian songstress Asha Bhosle.

Select discography

Cornershop (1997) *When I Was Born for the 7th Time*, Beggars Banquet.
—— (1995) *Woman's Gotta Have it*, Wiiija.
—— (1994) *Hold on it Hurts*, Wiiija.

SAMINA ZAHIR

cosmopolitan celebrity

The term 'cosmopolitan celebrity' was coined by the US academic Timothy Brennan in the late 1980s, to describe a particular brand of postcolonial and black literary production that was rapidly assuming a 'celebrity' status among an informed Western readership during that decade. For Brennan, the term diagnoses a dispersed, diasporic, South Asian community of intellectuals living predominantly in the US and Britain who share a preoccupation with, 'a *world* literature whose traditional national boundaries are (for them) meaningless', which privileges 'international' debates over 'internal' ones. They are, in short, 'not so much an elite *at home*, as spokespersons for a kind of perennial immigration'. Salman **Rushdie**'s work represents, for many, the epitome of this kind of cosmopolitanism. However, the term might easily be extended to include the work of a number of other black British writers, including Hanif **Kureishi**, V.S. **Naipaul** and Caryl **Phillips**. The cosmopolitan celebrity has also contributed much to **diaspora aesthetics**.

Further reading

Brennan, T. (1997) *At Home in the World: Cosmopolitanism Now*, Cambridge, MA and London: Harvard University Press.
—— (1989) 'Cosmopolitans and celebrities', *Race and Class* 31(1): 1–19.
—— (1989) *Salman Rushdie and the Third World: Myths of a Nation*, London: Macmillan.

JAMES PROCTER

Credit to the Nation

Credit to the Nation is essentially one person, Midlands-born Matty Hanson, a.k.a. MC Fusion, who was propelled to fame with the release of his debut single 'Call it what you want', in 1993. This single carried a strong anti-racist message moulded to an infectious, radio-friendly sound that took it high into the charts. The main riff of 'Call it what you want' was sampled from US band Nirvana's massive world-wide hit 'Smells like teen spirit' and Credit's audience tended to be predominantly white. This was because black audiences, particularly the **hip hop** audience, perceived him as softening rap music for mass appeal. Hanson released two further singles and an album *Take 'Dis*, all of which were minor hits, and pressure was put on Hanson to follow up the phenomenal success of his debut. Most of this success and pressure occurred while Hanson was only eighteen and, combined with several death threats from the far right and a degree of media hostility, contributed to Hanson having a nervous breakdown. After a lengthy break and change in record labels, Credit released 'Tacky love song' and an album *Daddy Wanted Me To Grow Wings* in the autumn of 1998.

ANDY WOOD

Crucial Robbie

b. Luton, England

reggae/dancehall music performer, radio DJ, record producer, club and artiste promoter, co-founder of the 'Annual People's Reggae Awards'

The ubiquitous Crucial Robbie started DJing on sound systems (see **sound system DJs**) in the 1980s and, because of his thought-provoking lyricism, soon became one of the top DJs in the country. This status was enhanced in 1989 when Robbie recorded 'Proud to be Black', arguably one of the most profound critiques of the black community's obsession with colour shadism ('if you're white you're alright, if you're brown stick around, if you're black get back'). Robbie's uncompromising approach to a problem that still represents one of the starkest reminders of the ongoing legacy of the chattel slave era was universally acclaimed, culminating in a number-one hit in the UK **reggae** charts and a number-two position in the New York reggae chart. Robbie followed up this success with a string of Top 10 hits both in Britain and abroad, and a Top 5 album, *Crucial View*, which he recorded for the **Mad Professor**'s Ariwa label. Robbie has since toured extensively throughout the UK, the rest of Europe and the USA, and has also performed in Jamaica, where he was well received. In 1989, Robbie became the presenter of the *Reggae Show* on BBC Three Counties Radio, and held this position for ten years, during which time his programme was widely regarded as one of the top British reggae shows. In fact, in 1992, Robbie was voted the 'Radio Personality of the Year' at the British reggae awards. Robbie has also voiced *Speech programmes* for

the BBC, and has presented programmes both on Radio 1 in the UK and on WNWK, New York's number-one reggae station. He is the co-owner of Jet Lag Promotions, Sovereign Roadshow 2000 (one of the most in-demand British Sound Systems), and is also the co-promoter of the 'Annual People's Reggae Awards'.

WILLIAM HENRY

cultural hybridity

Mikhail Bakhtin defines a hybrid construction 'as an utterance that belongs . . . to a single speaker, but that actually contains mixed within it two utterances, two speech manners, two styles, two "languages", two semantic and axiological belief systems' (1994: 304). According to Bakhtin, such hybridisation is a means of undoing linguistic authority, and the term has been appropriated by cultural theorists, most notably Homi K. **Bhabha**, to describe the undermining of colonial authority on the part of the colonised. For Bhabha, hybridity is the moment of the return of repressed knowledges revealing the instability and ambivalence at the heart of a colonial discourse that has attempted to establish itself as univocal and authoritative. In 'Signs taken for wonders' he describes the partialising process of hybridity, which occurs through the natives' discovery of the English book, the tool of colonisation that is turned into a site of subversion. In other words, it is the colonial moment itself that produces hybridity, breaking down the duality of colonial culture through mimicry and mockery. 'Hybridity intervenes in the exercise of authority, not merely to indicate the impossibility of its identity but to represent the unpredictability of its presence', he writes in 'Signs taken for wonders' (1994). However, Bhabha does not specify whether this insurgency comes about through the agency of the colonised, or whether it is simply the inevitable by-product of colonisation.

The concept (although not always the term) has been deployed by contemporary black cultural theorists. Stuart **Hall** uses the term ethnicity to describe this new politics of representation 'which entails an awareness of the black experience as a diaspora experience, and the consequences this carries for the process of unsettling, recombination, hybridization, "cut-and-mix" – in short the process of cultural diaspora-ization... which it implies' (Hall 1989: 447). However, Robert Young has contested the use of the term hybridity, pointing out that it is grounded in an 'implicit politics of heterosexuality' and emphasising its historical underpinnings in nineteenth-century racist discourse. 'Hybridity in particular shows the connections between the racial categories of the past and contemporary cultural discourse', he writes. It 'may be used in different ways, given different inflections and apparently discrete references, but it always reiterates and reinforces the dynamics of the same conflictual economy whose tensions and divisions it re-enacts in its own antithetical structure' (Young 1995: 27). Young warns against the ways in which we may be repeating the past rather than distancing ourselves from it by using the term 'hybridity', but Stuart Hall finds this charge 'inexplicably simplistic', marvelling at Young's conclusion that 'post-colonial critics are "complicit" with Victorian racial theory *because both sets of writers deploy the same term – hybridity – in their discourse!*' (1996: 259). Hall's exclamation reveals the contention that has built up around a term whose appropriation by twentieth-century cultural theorists can perhaps most usefully be regarded as an act of intervention of the type Bhabha describes in *The Location of Culture*. To re-deploy the term 'hybridity' may *itself* be one of 'those moments of civil disobedience', 'a sign... of spectacular resistance' whereby the words of the master become the site of hybrid insurgency (Bhabha 1994: 121).

References

Bakhtin, M. (1981) *The Dialogic Imagination*, Austin: Texas University Press.

Bhabha, H.K. (1994) 'Signs taken for wonders. Questions of ambivalence and authority under a tree outside Delhi, May 1817', in *The Location of Culture*, London: Routledge, pp. 102–22.

Hall, S. (1996) When was "the post-colonial?" Thinking at the limit', in Iain Chambers and Lidia Curti (eds) *The Postcolonial Question*, London: Routledge.

—— (1989) 'New ethnicities', in *Critical Dialogues in Cultural Studies*, London: Routledge, pp. 441–9.

Young, R. (1995) *Colonial Desire. Hybridity in Theory, Culture and Race*, London: Routledge.

SARA SALIH

D

Dabydeen, David

b. 1955, Berbice, Guyana

writer, academic

Dabydeen moved to the UK from Guyana in 1969. He was an undergraduate at Cambridge University and researched the works of the eighteenth-century visual artist (see **visual and plastic arts**) Hogarth for his Ph.D. at London University. After a Research Fellowship at Oxford University, he took a job as lecturer at the Centre for Caribbean Studies, University of Warwick, where he is now a Professor and Director of the Centre. Dabydeen has always combined his academic and writing careers, and his contribution to black British **literature** has been both creative and scholarly. His first collection of poetry *Slave Song*, which he wrote while at Cambridge and which won the Commonwealth Poetry Prize, was published in 1984, a year before the important edited study *The Black Presence in English Literature*. Two subsequent collections of poetry have been published: *Coolie Odyssey* (1988) and *Turner* (1994). Dabydeen's poetry has consistently interrogated the sexual politics of colonialism, absent voices and histories, and the power of creole to voice difference as both pain and pleasure. Dabydeen has published four novels to date: *The Intended* (1991), *Disappearance* (1993), *The Counting House* (1996) and *A Harlot's Progress* (1999). His academic scholarship in the area of black British and Caribbean literature has also been significant and his *A Reader's Guide to West Indian and Black British Literature* (1988) was followed in 1994 by the co-edited collection *Early Black Writers in Britain*. Since 1993, Dabydeen has acted as Ambassador-at-Large for Guyana and was a member of the Executive Board of UNESCO (1993–7).

Select bibliography

Dabydeen, D. (1999) *A Harlot's Progress*, London: Jonathan Cape.

—— (1994) *Turner*, London: Jonathan Cape.

—— (1991) *The Intended*, London: Secker and Warburg.

—— (1988) *A Reader's Guide to West Indian and Black British Literature*, London: Hansib.

—— (1988) *Coolie Odyssey*, London: Hansib.

—— (1985) *The Black Presence in English Literature*, Manchester: Manchester University Press.

—— (1984) *Slave Song*, Coventry: Dangaroo Press.

ALISON DONNELL

Daddy Freddy

b. 1965, Kingston, Jamaica

reggae and rap artist

As a close neighbour of the late **reggae** star Jacob Miller, Daddy Freddy (S. Frederick Small) began his recording career in Jamaica. His first song was a reggae single entitled 'Zoo Party'. After settling in Britain, Daddy Freddy shot to fame with his rapid hybrid of reggae and **hip hop** influences. His first album *Stress* was released in 1991 by Chrysalis and he has since released the long-players *Raggamuffin Solider* (Capitol, 1992) and *Old School New School* (BSI, 2000). Daddy Freddy was also featured on

US hip hop star Heavy D's *Peaceful Journey* album in 1991. Daddy Freddy was an active member of the British Anti-Apartheid movement BROTHER (British Rhyme Organization To Help Equal Rights) and also contributed to the single 'Beyond the 16th Parallel' with former MP Bernie Grant. Freddy has worked with a host of other collaborators including Asher D, Kofi and Mad Kap. After a guest appearance on Roy Castle's BBC series *Record Breakers*, in the early 1990s, Daddy Freddy set a new world record to become the fastest rapper ever.

RAYMOND ENISUOH

DADE, SUSHIL K. *see* Future Pilot AKA

D'Aguiar, Fred

b. 1960, London, England

poet, writer, academic

D'Aguiar was born in London of Guyanese parents, but left there at the age of two to live in Guyana in the care of his grandmother in a village named Airy Hall, where he stayed until twelve. Back in the UK, he was influenced by the anti-racist movement, the tensions and the poetry (such as that of Linton Kwesi **Johnson**) that came to the fore in the 1970s, but his own early works focused on Guyana and his grandmother, as well as on the more popular themes of police, politics and youth identity in London. D'Aguiar's creative work has consistently explored the themes of belonging, unbelonging and identity, and has engaged with the role of memory and sensory perceptions in relation to these issues. Since the publication of his first poetry collection *Mama Dot* in 1985, which focuses on the grandmother figure, D'Aguiar has published three further collections of poems, one verse novel, three novels and one play. His more recent work has explored the link between slavery and family bonds, as well as the political landscapes of Guyana, the UK and the USA. He has also worked for **television** and radio. His poem *1492*, about Columbus, was broadcast by the BBC in 1992 and his short film *Sweet Thames*, about black life in London, was shown on BBC 2 in the same

year. D'Aguiar has also produced scholarly work on the Caribbean writers Wilson Harris and Derek Walcott. He is currently Professor of English and Creative Writing at the University of Miami, Florida.

Select bibliography

D'Aguiar, F. (2000) *Bloodlines*, London: Chatto & Windus.
—— (1998) *Bill of Rights*, London: Chatto & Windus.
—— (1997) *Feeding the Ghosts*, London: Chatto & Windus.
—— (1996) *Dear Future*, London: Chatto & Windus.
—— (1994) *The Longest Memory*, London: Chatto & Windus.
—— (1993) *British Subjects*, Newcastle upon Tyne: Bloodaxe Books.
—— (1989) *Airy Hall*, London: Chatto & Windus.
—— (1985) *Mama Dot*, London: Chatto & Windus.

ALISON DONNELL

Dalal, Zane

b. 1965, London, England

conductor

Dala won a scholarship to Oxford University on the strength of his musical ability, most notably his organ playing. While studying at Oxford he also took on the role of choirmaster and organist at Oriel College. He then went on to win a place at the highly competitive **music** school at the University of Indiana in the USA, one of the world's largest music schools. He took the position of Assistant Conductor of their Opera Department and then moved to the University of Oklahoma as their Music Director. He has subsequently conducted internationally to great acclaim.

ALISON DONNELL

dance

In comparison to the vigorous presence of black dance in the USA since the nineteenth century, black dance forms in Britain did not flourish until the 1970s, largely due to the relatively late emergence, in the 1950s, of a substantial black British presence. The first notion of a black dance company, however, was put forward as early as 1946 by Jamaican immigrant Berto Pasuka, the co-founder, with Richie Riley, and Artistic Director of Les Ballet Negres. Classically trained in ballet, Pasuka adapted the technique and loosened its somewhat unnatural austerity to incorporate the more expressive idiosyncrasies of African and Caribbean dances. His productions explored the mythological and everyday manifestations of Jamaican culture, and sought to resolve the separation between black and white. This was the first time that these issues had been addressed in Britain within the context of movement.

After the development in the mid-1960s of contemporary dance, inspired by American dance pioneer Martha Graham, black dancers began to be employed by the mainstream contemporary dance companies, such as Rambert Dance Company and London Contemporary Dance Theatre. However, the lack of black directors and choreographers interpreting the Western technique was not directly addressed again until 1977 with the formation of a new company, MAAS Movers. Under the instruction and artistic direction of American dancer Ray Collins, MAAS staged its first production at the Oval House theatre in South London. Its fusion of classical ballet, contemporary, jazz and Afro-Caribbean dance was greeted as indubitably worthwhile by critics, though the technical standard of the dancers was imbalanced.

Their second season was choreographed by the eminent American dancer William Louther, a former leading member of Martha Graham's company. Despite its excellence, MAAS disbanded after just two years due to poor funding and, importantly, an inability to agree on a firm identity. Black dancers were often torn between the desire to parade their cultural heritage in their work (and risk being classified within the limited definition of race), and the wish to partake in the evolution of modern dance, which was seen, institutionally, as a more professional discipline. In the face of this conflict, the emergence of traditional African and Caribbean dance companies in Britain, seeking to establish the forms as viable techniques as well as to

challenge primitive stereotypes of black subjects, was inevitable. In 1976, Jamaican Barrington Anderson formed Ekome National Dance Company in Bristol. Its initial approach was to adapt traditional Ghanaian dance and music to black British experiences, though this later shifted towards the promotion of purely traditional African dance as a way of connecting black Britons to their roots.

Ekome's work conduced a host of smaller companies practising in black communities all over the UK, such as Dagarti Arts and Shikisha (the only all-women company that existed at the time), constituting a lively underground forum of black artistic expression that counteracted the denigrating effects of racism. Kokuma Dance Theatre Company and Carl Campbell Dance Company 7 were two groups that rose to national acclaim using traditional black dance forms. Kokuma was formed in Birmingham in 1978. Their technique, initially creative African dance, developed in the 1980s into a combination of African and Caribbean dances, with their first full-length production 'The Unwanted Prince', staged in 1985. In 1987 Jackie Guy from the National Dance Theatre of Jamaica was appointed Artistic Director and shifted the emphasis more towards Caribbean styles. Through collaborations with leading choreographers such as Nigerian Peter Badejo and Jamaican 'H' Patten, the company steadily grew in status, being shortlisted for the Prudential Award for Dance in 1990 and receiving the Black Award for Dance in 1993.

Previously a regular feature on the West End stage in shows such as *Hair, Jesus Christ Superstar* and *West Side Story*, Jamaican Carl Campbell founded Company 7 in London in 1978 as a contemporary Caribbean-African company. His pieces, beautiful, fluid and communicative, displayed a deep commitment to the fostering of confidence and cultural awareness in young black people, addressing such issues as identity, respect and spiritual well-being. Campbell was also concerned with de-mystifying Afro-Caribbean dance by demonstrating a clearly defined vocabulary that would be received as a performing art in its own right, with immense scope for innovation.

The first black dance company to secure fixed-term funding from the Arts Council was Adzido,

Britain's largest and most commercially impressive company specialising in traditional African dance. Formed in 1984 by Ghanaian dancer and choreographer George Dzikunu, Adzido Pan African Dance Ensemble debuted with a spectacular array of twenty-eight dancers and musicians gathered from a dozen different African countries. Their first short season at the Saddler's Wells featured a production entitled *Coming Home*, a linear narrative led by dances from Benin, Nigeria, Uganda and South Africa. The technical quality, the energy of the dancers and the flamboyance of costume and set was rewarded with an electrified response that confirmed Adzido as a mainstream national dance outfit on a par with the leading companies in ballet, jazz and contemporary dance. With continual research and development, Dzikunu delivered an infallible body of work, eventually broadening the remit in 1990 to include a fusion of dance and poetry known as 'choreopoetry' in the production *Under African Skies*. The company later spawned a smaller offshoot, Adzido 12, which meant that Adzido productions could be performed nationally and internationally virtually the whole year round.

The Caribbean focus applied by Carl Campbell and Jackie Guy expanded during the 1980s with the work of Irie! Dance Theatre, initiated by Grenadian Beverley Glean in 1984. Practising within a policy of integrated movement, which contained elements of contemporary jazz as well as Caribbean dance, Irie! drew almost exclusively on Caribbean themes. Their early productions, such as *Danse Caribbean*, which paraded an infectious contemporary and Caribbean dance fusion, were well received, encouraging the company in later works to magnify each stylistic facet to feature live **reggae**, poetry and contemporary dance techniques bordering on the balletic. Irie! were accompanied by RJC, who also fostered considerable public excitement with their contemporary and Caribbean dance fusion, often working with live DJs and incorporating drama and poetry into their repertoire.

Contemporary dance in black Britain was another area of increasing development in the 1980s. Like Adzido, Leeds based Phoenix Dance Company ranked high in the national dance arena. Formed in 1981 by Leo Hamilton, Donald Edwards and Villmore James, the company initially consisted of four male dancers, later widening to five male and five female dancers. The exquisite contemporary technique demonstrated by Phoenix won them an international audience and, although all of its members were black, Phoenix categorically rejected being classified as a black dance company. Another contemporary company, Union Dance, whose philosophy was one of multi-racial integration, also rejected such classification. South African exponent Corrine Bougaard formed Union in 1984 with the intention of freeing dance theatre from the boundaries of one culture. Within a contemporary dance framework, Bougaard drew on a variety of influences outside European mainstream dance traditions, such as street dance, martial arts and Asian dance, effectively disabling any attempts at categorisation.

This increasing diversification within 'black dance' was the predominant factor in the collapse of the Black Dance Development Trust (BDDT), an organisation that from the mid-1980s attempted to cater for African and Caribbean dance practitioners through funding, training and administration. Its main ambiguity was in whether their use of the term 'African and Caribbean dance' referred to the cultural origin of practitioners or to the styles that they were using. This lack of focus meant that the BDDT could not effectively meet the targets stated in its policy and its funding was withdrawn. In its place the Association of Dance of the African Diaspora (ADAD) emerged with a more sophisticated acknowledgement of the diversity in black British dance. The 1990s saw a substantial continuation of the ethos of Union Dance, with a host of new companies drawing from the unique cultural multiplicity of black British culture, while the older, traditionally oriented companies, such as Kokuma, applied more contemporary interpretations to their techniques.

The fusion of contemporary and African dance was first manifested in 1986 by Nigerian choreographer Bode Lawal, founder and Artistic Director of Sakoba Dance Theatre. Lawal strikingly created a blend of the traditional and the radical, drawing influences from as far as China, Cuba and Russia. His creative gall and technical brilliance won him a string of awards, including the Time Out/Dance Umbrella Award for Choreography in 1992. Lawal's desire for innovation within African dance was mirrored by Peter Badejo, who formed his own company, Badejo Arts, in 1990. His approach was distinct in its fierce, subjective tackling of the experiences of black migration to Britain. Like Lawal, Badejo opposed Adzido's portrayal of African dance as a static entity oblivious to social change, and encouraged a readiness to adapt tradition to personal experience. Badejo was also adamant that African people's dance required an infrastructure in which to further develop the genre, theoretically as well as practically. In 1993 the Bami Jo Annual International Summer School surfaced under his direction as the only intensive training ground available to African and Caribbean dance practitioners in Britain. The need for training was later further addressed by Irie!, who in 1998 initiated the first academically recognised Diploma in African and Caribbean Dance.

The spirit of innovation within African and Caribbean dance could also be seen in the work of Asian dance companies, such as Nahid Siddiqui and Co., Srishti, Chitraleka and Company, and, standing at the forefront of the genre, Shobana **Jeyasingh** Dance Company. Jeyasingh formed the company in 1989, a sisterhood of trained contemporary dancers reflecting their British/Indian experiences. Subsumed into the contemporary mode were the gestures, movements and nuances of the classical Indian dance form of Bharata Natyam, as well as jazz and street styles. Jeyasingh's choreography was both groundbreaking and thought-provoking in its exploration of social identity, winning the company three Digital Dance Awards and the prestigious Prudential Award for the Arts. The company toured internationally, as far as the USA and Singapore, and in 1995 Jeyasingh was awarded an MBE.

Black exponents of the mainstream companies were, throughout the 1990s, becoming increasingly confident in their approaches to established techniques. In 1992, Sheron Wrey, a former Rambert dancer, formed Jazzxchange Music and Dance Company. Her repertoire, based on a desire to reunite jazz dance and music, incorporated a graceful fusion of classical, contemporary, jazz and street techniques, performed to the backdrop of live jazz compositions. Wrey contradicted the notion that dancers merely obeyed choreographic instruction and laced her pieces with an atmo-

sphere of improvisation. Jazzxchange emerged against the backdrop of two other jazz companies, Bullies Ballarinas (1990) and the Jiving Lindy Hoppers (1983). The Lindy Hop was seen as a forgotten style whose roots were firmly grounded in African and European styles, and the Jiving Lindy Hoppers worked to spread awareness of the genre. Bullies Ballarinas practised a variety of jazz styles from the Charleston to tap and modern jazz, regularly training and collaborating with African dance choreographers.

Urban black culture of the 1990s found its way into the dance arena in the form of **hip hop** and street dance. MC and choreopoet Jonzi D pioneered the fusion of street culture and dance theatre with his 1995 production *Lyrikal Fearta*. His sincere and animated approach to such issues as police brutality, second-generation identity conflicts and black-on-black violence struck stylistically and theoretically at the cutting edge of performance art, and was later developed into a larger internationally toured production in 1999, *The Aeroplane Man*. These expressive adventures presented by young black dancers and choreographers in Britain, and the continuing developments that they prefigured, called for the staging of the first Black British Dance Festival in 1997. The festival showcased works spanning the broad spectrum of black dance, from contemporary African and Caribbean to street and jazz styles, thereby ensuring that the future of black dance in Britain was one of infinite stylistic possibility.

Further reading

Anon. (1994) 'Choreographers', *Revue Noire* 14 (Autumn).

Millman, A. (1987) *African People's Dance: the State of the Art*, London: AGGB.

Thorpe, E. (1989) *Black Dance*, London: Chatto & Windus.

DIANA OMO EVANS

dancehall

Dancehall represents the commercial end of the **reggae** spectrum and takes its name from the arena in which the music is popularly played, as with disco, club and rave music. Finding a mainstream club to play reggae music was, and still is, difficult, even in Jamaica. Establishments (both black and white) are mainly interested in the more Europeanised forms of black music, such as **soul** and R'n'B. Reggae promoters would provide their own spaces by hiring a venue (hall) and promote individual events (dances).

Credited with giving birth to **hip hop** and **jungle** (drum and bass), and a major influence on the rave and wider club scene, dancehall has been around since the birth of reggae music in 1968. The dancehall scene has generally been popularised by folk-hero type characters. In the late 1960s there was the rudie. This was a rebellious character who used crime to struggle against poverty and discrimination, as represented by Jimmy Cliff in the film (see **film and cinema**) *The Harder They Come*. Rudies were a strong influence on the skinhead/suedehead movements in Britain. From the mid-1970s there was the rocker, a more politically aware character inspired by **Rastafari** and Africanism. The 1970s dancehall produced heavy dance styles (steppers) and dub (music produced by dubbing tracks and sound effects together after they had been recorded). It was dub dancehall that coined the phrase 'drum and bass'. The rockers inspired another definitive reggae film, entitled *Rockers*, which was a virtual who's who of reggae artists. The **raggamuffin** appeared in the mid-1980s. This was influenced by Thatcherism and the era of Reagan, and represented a move back towards the materialism of the rudie, but with the emphasis on the enjoyment of being in a dance and dancing (as opposed to any greater enthusiasm for dancehall in general), and the cultural confidence of the rocker. It was during this era that the dancehall scene gained recognition as a distinct area within reggae. Its association with hip hop also threw dancehall into mainstream consciousness and everyone became aware of the raggamuffin and their ragga music. In Britain, dancehall is still referred to as ragga.

Dancehall has since developed its own sub-categories. The most popular is the bashment, represented by faster commercial music, which is played in a style termed '45 juggling' – playing singles (45s) in quick succession. In the UK,

dancehall did not disappear in the 1970s but instead went underground, resurfacing around the early 1990s as the dub scene. Popularised by **Jah Shaka**, one of this country's longest running and most respected Sound Systems, the dub scene has been used by others as the foundation for jungle and much of the rave scene.

Crews in the dancehall vie with one another to produce the latest dances. Most of these dances still originate in Jamaica, but each year at least one style goes international and is seen wherever dancehall is played. Some dancers have made themselves international names and a lot of money by creating new dance moves (such as Mr Bogle of the Black Roses Crew). The most popular dances include the *Bogle*, the *Butterfly* and the *Pelpa*. Artists in other areas of **music**, such as Michael Jackson and MC Hammer, have used dancehall dances and dancers. Through jungle, drum 'n' bass and UK garage, all drawing heavily on dancehall reggae, dancehall moves have infiltrated the broader club scene.

Fashion (see **fashion and design**) is an important part of dancehall and male and female dancehall turfites (hardcore patrons) take hours to prepare for an evening out. Dapper Dons rule menswear but the Dancehall Queen rules the dancehall. Popularised through Don Letts's film of the same name, she is a true diva, epitomising dancehall style, glamour and performance. Although European designer names are popular, the notion of sophistication in dancehall style is driven by African culture, with strong colours, decorative fabrics and inventive accessories. Here anyone under a size twelve is generally considered 'mauger' (skinny). As with African decoration, imagination is important and pit helmets, three pairs of sunglasses, diving gear and garments worn inside-out and back-to-front are all normal. Britain is generally more reserved than Jamaica or the USA, but even in this country the term 'theatrical display' has no meaning in the dancehall.

Sound Systems form the backbone of dancehall. Consisting of singers, selectors (DJs), operators (engineers), DJs (rappers) and box bwoy (boys) or gyal (girls) (roadies). Sounds are powerful travelling road-shows. British Sounds include Luv Injection and Asher World Movement. Originally singers and DJs worked as part of Sound Systems, but due to their increased popularity many now work solo or as part of a crew (a group of artists working together). British DJs have always had difficulties gaining international recognition for a number of reasons, but individuals such as Glamma Kid carry a great deal of international respect as well as commercial success. The selector now holds centre stage in the dancehall with Chris Goldfinger of Asher World Movement, one of this country's leading selectors, also presenting a regular dance-hall programme on BBC Radio 1. The final player here is the producer, the creator of the rhythms. True to its African roots, reggae is built around rhythm. European musicologists have often re-ferred to reggae as back-to-front music because the rhythm is placed in front of any melodies. Other forms of music, such as soul, jungle, etc., have reduced their rhythms to a simplified backbeat, while rhythm remains sacred in the dancehall. Different artists make recordings on the same rhythm and each recording carries a separate title for the rhythm. A selector will generally play records in order of their rhythms. For example, they will run the records on the 'Badda Badda' rhythm, then the records on the 'Backyard' rhythm and so on. Recording artists want to record for the producers with the hottest new rhythms. Britain has some strong producers such as Mafia and Fluxy, and Jazwad who have produced interna-tionally acclaimed rhythms.

DAVID KNIGHT A.K.A. VUSI SISWE

Dash, Paul

b. 1946, Bridge Town, Barbados

artist, lecturer

Dash came to Britain in 1957 and has lived in London since 1965. He trained at the Oxford School of Art and at Chelsea before taking an MA in Education at the University of London. He was involved in the **Caribbean Artists' Movement**. While showing and selling paintings, he taught in London schools and now lectures in art education at Goldsmiths College, where he produced a dissertation and further research on African Caribbean children in art and design education. In his practice, Dash nurtures a 'love of inspiration' and spontaneity, which he recognises as the strength of great sportsmen and musicians. His **carnival** paintings uses brightly coloured figura-tion to evoke African cultural roots and black culture's ability to provide entertainment autono-mously for itself. He also produced a large number of watercolour works plus an unexhibited series of collages, which are now coming more to the fore of his practice and which he says give him 'access to a broader range of subjects'. In 1996, following a serious illness, he produced large flower paintings for a show called 'Caribbean Connection 2: Island Pulse' and revealed his 'primary interest in formal concerns – mark-making'. Recent collages explore race and sexuality, and situate Dash as a 'black man viewing white culture'.

PAUL O'KANE

David, Craig

b. 1981, Southampton, England

singer, songwriter

Craig David began DJing in Southampton clubs at the age of fourteen, having seen DJs perform while watching his father's **reggae** band Ebony Rockers perform in venues around Southampton. David also began writing songs, and when his mother encouraged him to enter a competition to compose a song for the boy-band Damage, his entry 'Unsteady' won. David's first serious mainstream success came with his collaboration with garage producer the Artful Dodger, and their track 'Rewind (the crowd say bo-selecta)' was a massive hit in clubs and in the charts. David's debut solo single 'Fill me in' retained the distinctive two-step garage beat but had more of an R'n'B and **soul** feel to it, as does his debut album *Born to Do It*. While acknowledging the influence of the British garage scene, David has attempted to distance himself from scenes in an attempt to achieve long-term success. *Born to Do It* followed his first two singles to number one in the British charts and, in October 2000, David won three MOBO awards, for the best British newcomer, best R'n'B act and best British single for 'Fill Me In'.

ANDY WOOD

de Souza, Alan

b. 1958, Ncurobi, Kenya

artist, critic, co-editor of *Bazaar*, founder of Panchayat

De Souza migrated to England with his parents in 1965 and produced his video *The Devil's Feast*, shown at the Chelsea School of Art, in 1986. In the same year he took part in the London exhibitions 'Lifting the Veil' (**Tara Arts** Centre) and 'Un-recorded Truth' (Elbow Room). Both exhibitions showed de Souza's engagement with nationalism and power. This theme was continued in the 1989 exhibition 'Fabled Territories' in Leeds. In the 1987 'The Image Employed', at the Cornerhouse, de Souza's artwork explored the effects of AIDS and fear of homosexuality. His interest in this subject matter is apparent in the 1990 'Ecstatic Antibodies Resisting the Aids Mythology' exhibition at the Ikon Gallery. In the 1990s de Souza moved to the USA and in 1995 had an exhibition 'Fire without Gold' at the Jamaica Center Subway in New York. As well as exhibiting his own work, de Souza was an active member of arts organisations and in 1986 he joined Copyart, an arts collective and resource centre in London. This led to the founding of the Asian arts and film magazine *Bazaar* and **Panchayat**, the archive of Asian art now held at Middlesex University.

PAULINE DE SOUZA

Dehlavi, Jamil

b. India

film-maker

After studying law at Oxford University and qualifying as a barrister, Dehlavi abandoned the legal profession to study film (see **film and cinema**) at Columbia University, New York. Between New York and Pakistan, he directed his first feature *Towers of Silence* (1975), while his next *The Blood of Hussain* (1977) eerily augured General Zia's impending military *coup* in a controversial study of tyranny, revolution and martyrdom in modern-day Pakistan. It resulted in a ten-year exile from Pakistan and part relocation to London. Dehlavi shot the supernatural thriller *Born of Fire* (a.k.a. *The Master Mission*) (1986) in Turkey, pursuing his interest in Sufi mysticism and the power of religion in *Immaculate Conception* (1991) with Shabana Azmi. Set in 1980s Pakistan, the film follows a childless American-English couple who visit a fertility shrine in Karachi with devastating results. In 1994, Dehlavi directed the historical epic *Jinnah* (1998), a dramatic re-telling of the partition of India and a far from hagiographical portrayal of Mohammed Ali Jinnah, the founding father of Pakistan. The film caused further controversy in Pakistan for Dehlavi's choice of former horror actor Christopher Lee as Jinnah. Like Shekhar **Kapur**, Dehlavi represents a generation of South Asian-born film-makers working between the UK and their homelands around challenging issues of cross-cultural interest – as exemplified by Dehlavi's own liberalised films around Pakistani political and cultural identities. Based in London with Dehlavi Films, the award-winning director has also worked on various documentary projects for the BBC and **Channel 4**.

SATINDER CHOHAN

Dennis, Ferdinand

b. 1956, Kingston, Jamaica

broadcaster, journalist, educational re-searcher, novelist

Dennis is well known for his journalistic contributions to radio and **television** that explore ethnicity and identity. His BBC Radio 4 programmes include *Journey Round My People, Up, You Mighty Race: the Story of Marcus Garvey* (nominated for the 1987 Sony Radio Prize), *After Dread and Anger* and *Back to Africa*. The last programme was also made into a one-hour documentary programme for **Channel 4** Tele-vision and the New York Public Broadcast

Service and was also published in book form. In 1988, *Behind the Frontlines: Journey into Afro-Britain* won the Martin Luther King Memorial Prize. Dennis is also a novelist of some stature: *The Sleepless Summer* appeared in 1989, to be followed by *The Last Blues Dance* (1996) and *Duppy Conqueror* (1998). The first two novels take off from Sam **Selvon**'s *Lonely Londoners* and explore an older generation of Caribbean immigrants in Britain. *Duppy Conqueror* tells the story of a young boy who grows up in Jamaica, leaves his village to undo the curse put upon his family line and, on his travels in London, Africa and back to the Caribbean, takes in some of the twentieth century's key moments, themes and issues. Dennis is also co-editor, with Naseem **Khan**, of *Voices of the Crossing* (2000).

Select bibliography

Dennis, F. (1998) *Duppy Conqueror*, London: Flamingo.

—— (1996) *The Last Blues Dance*, London: HarperCollins.

—— (1992) *Back to Africa*, London: Sceptre.

—— (1989) *The Sleepless Summer*, London: Hodder & Stoughton.

—— (1988) *Behind the Frontlines: Journey into Afro-Britain*, London: Victor Gollancz.

Dennis, F. and Khan, Naseem (eds) (2000) *Voices of the Crossing*, London: Serpent's Tail.

GAIL CHING-LIANG LOW

Desai, Poulomi

b. Hackney, London, England

photographer, curator, performer, community worker

Desai works with different mediums and locations, from working with sound in prisons, with Insight Arts Trust, to working in schools with **Southall Black Sisters**, around issues of racism and religion. She was a resident performer at the Waterman's Arts Centre from 1994 to 1996, with the regular 'One Nation under a Groove' comedy nights, and had a role in the satirical farce *Papa Was*

a Bus Conductor. She has also performed with her own touring companies, the theatrical psycho-thrash metal band the Dead Jalebis, and the Sychophantic Sponge Bunch. In 2000, she created a sound installation for the Mead Gallery, and was the Creative Producer for 'Open', the Arts Council of England's international showcase of digital art by young people. She has designed for **Nation Records**, More Rockers, Durex and the Naz HIV/AIDS organisation. Her photographic work includes *from the coffee table to the kit(s)chen*, commissioned by **Autograph: the Association of Black Photographers** in 1996 and working in the Chittagong Hill Tracts.

ALISON DONNELL

Desmonds

Desmonds, a weekly black situation comedy, was first aired on **Channel 4** in 1989 and ran until December 1995. Written by Trix Worrel, the series was initially co-produced and directed by Charlie Hanson until Worrel later became director. *Desmonds* is regarded as the most successful of the ethnic situation comedies and the first **television** comedy to fully embrace the black community within a British context. *Desmonds* was based in a barber shop located in Peckham, South London, which was used as a social meeting place for a nucleus of mainly black characters from a broad spectrum of different generations. When *Desmonds* was first launched it aimed to present diverse, socially mobile characters in multi-racial Britain. The programme's setting was unique in that it was a black comedy based in a workplace, whereas the programme's predecessors had all focused on black relationships within the family home. In its attempts to challenge black stereotypes, *Desmonds* introduced black characters who were entrepreneurs, bank employees and university graduates. Actors regularly featured on the show include Norman **Beaton**, Carmen Munroe and Gyearbuor Asante. *Desmonds* concluded just weeks before its leading star Norman Beaton died.

RAYMOND ENISUOH

Dhanjal, Avtarjeet

b. 1940, Dalla, Punjab, India

visual artist

In the late 1960s, Dhanjal studied fine art at Chandigarn Art School. Here his sculptures favoured Western modernism rather than traditional Indian culture. Dhanjal taught at Nairobi University, Kenya, for two years in the early 1970s and then moved to Britain, where he has lived since, to study sculpture as a postgraduate at St Martins School of Art, London. In the late 1970s, Dhanjal created spiral aluminium sculptures, alluding to nature, for exhibitions and for a commission for Warwick University.

Striving to unite his interests in Western modernism and Eastern culture and philosophy, Dhanjal organised a Punjabi folk culture study trip in 1978 and a sculpture symposium in the Punjab in 1980. This resulted in a sculpture commission, an abstract work in stone and metal exploring the ground plan of an Indian temple, a re-occurring theme in later works. Other public commissions using abstract forms and drawing on nature followed, notably at the National Garden Festival, Stoke on Trent (1986), Wolverhampton (1986) and Birmingham (1989). Dhanjal was included in the Hayward Gallery exhibition 'The Other Story' in 1989. At the beginning of the 1990s, Dhanjal went to south India to study temple sculpture and, in 1991, started a complex commission for the Cardiff Bay Development Trust, a sculptural interpretation of *The I Ching, the Book of Changes*. In 1997, Dhajal had a major retrospective exhibition of his work at Pitshanger Manor, London, organised with the **Institute of International Visual Arts**. This included abstract works made since the 1980s in slate, a material that he finds evocative of the depth of darkness of the night in the rural Punjab. Dhanjal lives in Shropshire, where he has supported the visual arts (see **visual and plastic arts**) and encourages cultural links between Asia and Britain. He set up the Punjabi Institute exchange programme for students and teachers in the Punjab and Shropshire, and has been a trustee of the South Asian Visual Arts Festival, Sampad, and a member of West Midlands Arts Board, and has served on their visual arts panel.

Further reading

Cross, P. and Tawadros, G. (eds) (1997) *Avtarjeet Dhanjal*, London: inIVA.

JANE SILLIS

Dhingra, Leena

b. India

writer, actress, teacher

Dhingra was born in India but came to Europe with her parents after Partition in 1947. She was educated in India, England, France and Switzerland, and has studied **literature**, drama and cinematography. She has worked as an actress and teacher, as well as writing. A founding member of the Asian Women Writers' Group, Dhingra published her novel *Amritvela* with the Women's Press in 1988. The story of a woman's return to India and her family home after years in England, the novel addresses the question of living between two cultures. Her autobiographical sketch 'Breaking out of the labels' was published in *Watchers and Seekers: Creative Writing by Black Women in Britain* (1987).

Select bibliography

Dhingra, L. (1988) *Amritvela*, London: the Women's Press.

Further reading

Cobham, R. and Collins, M. (eds) (1987) *Watchers and Seekers: Creative Writing by Black Women in Britain*, London: the Women's Press.

ALISON DONNELL

Dhondy, Farrukh

b. 1944, Poona, India

teacher, political activist, playwright, novelist, short-story writer, television commissioning editor

Farrukh Dhondy left India in the mid-1960s to

study English literature at Cambridge University. In England, he became an active member of the black community and worked with the Indian Workers Association in Leicester, and, later, the Black Panther Movement in London. In the early 1970s, Dhondy joined **Race Today**. It was in this environment that he was first encouraged to write. A qualified secondary school English teacher, his writings of the late 1970s and early 1980s were primarily children's stories, broadly committed to the kinds of political agendas held by the black activist movements of that period; his collections include *East End at Your Feet* (1976), *Come to Mecca* (1978) and *Trip Trap* (1982). In 1990, he published his first adult novel, *Bombay Duck*, which displays a radical shift in form and content from his earlier works, being much closer to that associated with the **cosmopolitan celebrity**. He is the Commissioning Editor of **Channel 4**'s multicultural programming.

Select bibliography

Dhondy, F. (1990) *Bombay Duck*, London: Picador.
—— (1978) *Come to Mecca*, London: Collins/ Fontana.
—— (1976) *East End at Your Feet*, London: Macmillan.

JAMES PROCTER

diaspora aesthetics

There is (perhaps for good reason) no such thing as a unitary 'school' of cultural production that might be said to engage with 'diaspora aesthetics'. Nor is there anything like a consensual definition of the term. Indeed, given the global context of diaspora aesthetics and its conditions as a dispersed, diffuse, dislocated discourse, one of its defining characteristics might be said to be its ability to exceed the containing fixity of definitions, categories and labels. James Clifford has pointed to the 'unruly crowd of descriptive/interpretive terms' seeking to explain diaspora, citing the editor's preface to the first issue of the academic journal, *Diaspora*: 'the term that once described Jewish, Greek, and Armenian disperison now shares meanings with a larger

semantic domain that includes words like immigrant, expatriate, refugee, guest-worker, exile community, overseas community, ethnic community'.

However, despite the difficulties of the term, it is possible to talk productively about the emergence of a distinctive diaspora aesthetics within the particular context of black British culture since the mid-1980s. The key scholarly activity in this area has included work by Paul **Gilroy**, Kobena **Mercer**, Avtar **Brah**, Stuart **Hall** and Homi **Bhabha**. In very different ways, these black British intellectuals have drawn attention to the aesthetic agendas of black diasporic cultural expression (in both Britain and elsewhere) as they appear in a diversity of forms, including **music** and film (see **film and cinema**), the works of Salman **Rushdie** and Hanif **Kureishi**, as well as the cultural politics of fashion (see **fashion and design**) and style. These different modes of cultural expression, it is argued, share a preoccupation with conditions such as hybridity, syncretism, itinerancy, admixture, translation and in-betweeness. Such elements of diasporic culture have traditionally been marginalised, silenced and viewed negatively by national cultures that privilege notions of community, rootedness and the sedentary. For the above critics, however, it is the former, diasporic, categories that contain positive, celebratory, even emancipatory possibilities.

For example, Paul Gilroy, a leading commentator in this field, argues persuasively that a recognition of the diasporic conditions of black culture offers an empowering 'alternative to the different varieties of absolutism which would confine culture in "racial" ethnic or national essences'. Britain does not provide the borders of black cultural expression in this context, but must be re-conceived as the crossroads of a global web of exchanges networking South Asia, Africa, the Caribbean, the USA and Europe. It is this logic that informs Gilroy's tellingly entitled *The Black Atlantic*, arguably the most rigorous, sustained account of diaspora aesthetics to emerge from the 1980s and 1990s.

Further Reading

Bhabha, H. (1994) *The Location of Culture*, London: Routledge.

Gilroy, P. (1993) *The Black Atlantic: Modernity and Double Consciousness*, London: Verso.

Mercer, K. (1994) 'Diaspora culture and the dialogic imagination: the aesthetics of black independent film in Britain', in *Welcome to the Jungle*, London: Routledge, pp. 53–66.

JAMES PROCTER

diasporic intellectual

The notion of the diasporic intellectual encompasses a migrant figure who is unencumbered by territorial affiliation and is part of a post-national community. It is informed by the conditions of post-modernism and post-colonialism, and emphasises the movement of Third World intellectuals to the centre of the empire while also stressing the use of hybrid and syncretic practices.

Even though today the term has acquired a great figurative flexibility and refers to migrant intelligentsia who move around the globe for better education and professional status, its debt to histories of pain and alienation should not be forgotten. The term diasporic intellectual should not rob the oppressed of the vocabulary of protest and should not therefore be confused, as Kevathi Krishnaswamy warns, with the histories of refugees, exiles and migrant workers.

The original notion of diaspora refers, in fact, to a collective trauma, of the banishment and exile of Jewish communities. In a second stage the word came also to signify the dispersal and genocide of Armenians and the coercive uprooting of African people by slavery. There are also other forms of diaspora such as imperial diasporas (the indentured labour of Indian people), trade diasporas and cultural diasporas. Currently diasporas evoke globalised and transnational forces of world economy, international migrations and diasporic intellectuals who can account for multiple subject positions, such as those discussed by Homi **Bhabha** and Avtar **Brah**. Prominent examples of diasporic intellectual include Salman **Rushdie**, Edward Said, Gayatri Spivak and Stuart **Hall**.

Further reading

Brah, A. (1996) *Cartographies of Diaspora. Contesting identities*, London and New York: Routledge.

Hall, S. (1996) 'Cultural identity and diaspora', in P. Mongia (ed.) *Contemporary Postcolonial Theory*, London: Arnold, pp. 110–21.

Krishnaswamy, K. (1995) 'Mythologies of migrancy: postcolonialism, postmodernism and the politics of (dis)location', *ARIEL: a Review of International English Literature* 26(1): 125–46.

SANDRA PONZANESI

difference

The concept is fundamental to Ferdinand de Saussure's *Course in General Linguistics*, in which he argues that language is a relational system functioning through differences. 'Everything comes down to this', he writes. 'In the language itself, there are only differences ... and no positive terms' (Saussure 1998: 118). The sign is made up of signifier (that is, the word or sound pattern) and signified (that is, the idea that is being signified), and, according to Saussure, there is no natural or inevitable link between the two. Except for a number of special cases, a sound pattern has no necessary relation to what it is describing, which could just as easily be called something else. Because signifier and signified are arbitrary, they are purely relational; a language is a way of organising the world into concepts and categories, and the way it does this is through difference. If a signifier only acquires meaning through its relation to other signifiers, then meaning is never entirely self-present but must always rely on what it is not. Meaning is thus endlessly deferred from one signifier to the next, and Jacques Derrida has coined the term *différance* to describe this. In French *différance* means both difference and deferral, and it is a crucial concept in post-structuralist theory. The sign, according to Derrida, 'is deferred presence' (1998: 61), only acquiring meaning from the network of absent signifiers surrounding it. Meaning has no origin and is always marked, as it were, by the trace of its other. Derrida's conceptualisations of radical 'alterity' have obvious resonances for cultural theorists and writers concerned with issues of 'race' and difference. Homi K. **Bhabha** has been heavily influenced by Derrida and post-structuralist theory, and many of the essays in *The Location of Culture* describe the production of difference in the colonial moment, the return of the cultural repressed or other, which emerges in interstitial moments of translation or representation (see especially 'Signs taken for wonders' and 'Dissemination'). Stuart **Hall** has also written of the ways in which cultural difference disrupts the notion of a single, unified culture (see 'Cultural identity and diaspora'), and he describes 'a politics of ethnicity predicated on difference and diversity'. Difference is also crucial to African American critics and theorists such as Henry Louis Gates, where the authority of a culture that represents itself as singular and mono- is destabilised by the introduction of black difference and otherness. Gates's *The Signifying Monkey* describes 'the (political, semantic) confrontation between two parallel discursive universes: the black American linguistic circle and the white' (1988: 45), in which signifyin', as Gates coins it, is, paradoxically, a relation of difference inscribed within a relation of identity. Elsewhere, Gates emphasises the importance of 'isolat[ing] the signifying black difference through which to signify about the so-called Discourse of the Other' (1992: 69). Although in these contexts 'difference' usually denotes cultural difference, such formulations are inflected by post-structuralist theory in the ways in which they deconstruct the notion of a unitary, self-present white culture that is unmarked by the trace of its hitherto occluded raced other.

References

Derrida, J. (1998) 'Différance', in P. Kamuf (ed.) *A Derrida Reader: Between the Blinds*, Edinburgh: Edinburgh University Press.

Gates, Jnr, H.L. (1992) *Loose Canons. Notes on the Culture Wars*, New York: Oxford University Press.

—— (1988) *The Signifying Monkey. A Theory of African-American Literary Criticism,*, New York: Oxford University Press.

Hall, S. (1990) 'Cultural identity and diaspora', in J. Rutherford (ed.) *Identity, Community, Culture, Difference*, London: Lawrence & Wishart.

Saussure, F. de (1998) *Course in General Linguistics*, London: Gerald Duckworth & Co. Ltd.

Further reading

Bhabha, H.K. (1994) ''Dissemination: time, narrative and the margins of the modern nation', in *The Location of Culture*, London: Routledge, pp. 139–70.

—— (1994) 'Signs taken for wonders. Questions of ambivalence and authority under a tree outside Delhi, May 1817', in *The Location of Culture*, London: Routledge, pp. 102–22.

SARA SALIH

D-Max

In 1985 London-based photographers David A. **Bailey**, Marc Boothe, Gilbert John, Dave **Lewis**, Zak Ové and Ingrid **Pollard** began meeting to discuss and collectively develop their art. Dissatisfied with the ways in which work by black photographers had been relegated to the realm of documentary **photography**, they collaborated, thus creating opportunities to examine the shifting meanings and connotations of blackness in contemporary Britain. By working together in this strategic manner they engaged in mutual criticism and refined and strengthened their individual visions. They called themselves D-Max – a technical term that refers to the range of blacks a photographic emulsion can offer. While 'd-max' recalls the multiple shades, contours and nuances of the colour black, it also alludes to the group members' various skin tones, political affiliations and ideological stances. Members, compelled by the stereotypical and limiting perceptions of race in contemporary Britain, created work, at least in part, as a means to articulate their concerns regarding racial difference and identity. While the group was engaged in wide ethical and political concerns, members examined multiple definitions of blackness and the limitless potential of photographic practice. In 1987 D-Max mounted a touring exhibition, entitled 'D-Max', which was on view at the Ikon Gallery (Birmingham) and the Photographer's Gallery (London).

Further reading

Bailey, D. (1988) 'D-Max', *Ten.8* 27: 36–41.
Gilroy, P. (1988) *D-Max*, Birmingham: Ikon Gallery (reprinted in P. Gilroy (1993) *Small Acts: Thoughts on the Politics of Black Cultures*, New York: Serpent's Tail, pp. 115–19).

ANDREA D. BARNWELL

Dodge

b. 1968, London, England

DJ, producer

Dodge began his career during the mid-1980s in London. A strong interest in rap and the emergence of pirate radio stations in the UK had an immense influence on this embryonic stage of his career – what he describes as 'bedroom DJing'. In 1990 Dodge and IG Culture formed the rap duo Dodge City Productions. They were signed to the subsidiary of Island Records, Fourth N Broadway, and released their debut album *Stepping up and out*. Dodge made a natural transition into producing and, in 1992, launched Soul Inside Productions, delivering successful vocalist Paul Johnson, whose vocals together with Dodge's production skills made the track 'If We Lose Our Way' a huge club anthem. Dodge continues to excel as a remixer and has produced remixes for US artists such as Mary J. Blige, D'angelo, Brandy and Dru Hill, and British artists such as Kele Le Roc and Omar. Dodge has taken on new projects, working for UK artists Beverley **Knight** and Shola **Ama**. He plans to concentrate on production, DJing at clubs in London and fundraising events for charities such as Sickle Cell.

DORETH JONES

Donkor, Godfried

b. 1964, Kumasi, Ghana

artist

Donkor's work has long been informed and influenced by encounters with eighteenth-century political caricaturists, whom he regards as the pop-
artists of their day. Engravings by Hogarth and his contemporaries are re-energised by his carefully composed juxtapositions. Earlier work used sportsmen, politicians and advertising logos to examine contemporary icons in terms of a displacement of spirituality haunting omnipresent capitalism. Recent work emphasises anonymity and repetition in signs of mass production and performed sexualities – boxers and dancers become respective iconic silhouettes of 'man' and 'woman' set against *Financial Times*-pink grounds. Donkor came to London in 1973 and studied at St Martins (1985–9). He then attended a postgraduate fine art course at Escola Massana Barcelona (1990–2). He also undertook an MA in African art history at SOAS (1995–6), which first sparked his interest in comparing today's global expansionism with that of the eighteenth century. He became curator of **198 Gallery** (1996–8) and was a 1998 Dhakar Bienale prize-winner for his 'Slave to Champ' series, which describes the rise of slaves to boxing champions. He was part of the '**Transforming the Crown**' exhibition in 1997. Following an Arts Council-funded trip to the Caribbean, Donkor exhibited the work of 'The Elders (Brother Everald Brown and Stanley Greaves)' at South London Gallery, 1999. In 2000, his work was exhibitied at 'Picture This', Barbara Green Fine Arts, New York City, and at 'African Jour', Lille. He contributed to Dak'art and undertook a residency at the Horniman Museum. He is based at Gasworks Studios, London.

Further reading

Battastaaghi, S. (1994) *Artrage* (Dec.–Jan.): 32.
Brooks, F. (1994) *Third Text* 26 (spring): 97.
Garcia-Anton, K. (1998) 'Dak'art', *Third Text* 44 (autumn): 87–92.

PAUL O'KANE

Douglas Camp, Sokari

b. 1958, Buguma, Nigeria

sculptor

Sokari Douglas Camp spent her earliest years in Buguma, the principal settlement of the Kalabari people of the Eastern Niger Delta. Camp was educated at Dartington Hall School in the 1970s but returned to Nigeria regularly for the holidays, where she saw traditional rituals and celebrations taking place. She was encouraged to become an artist by her English guardian, an anthropologist, and studied at the California College of Arts and Crafts. She later gained a degree at the Central School of Art and Design and an MA degree from the Royal College of Art, London. Douglas Camp creates metal sculptures that are often automated or incorporate found objects. Her principal source of inspiration has been the masquerade, particularly the Kalabari festival in celebration of water spirits and the Yoruba Gelede Masquerade, which explores the spiritual and social roles of women in Yoruba society. Her figures of masquerades wear costumes and head-dresses rich in symbolism and have links with traditional crafts such as basket making.

Her sculpture *Sword Fish Masquerade* was installed at the Elephant and Castle near the Morley Gallery, London. Douglas Camp has had many solo exhibitions in Europe and the USA, including a major exhibition at the Museum of Mankind, London (1995–6). She has carried out public art commissions in England, Scotland and Denmark. Douglas Camp has been included in significant group exhibitions such as 'From Two Worlds' and '**Transforming the Crown**: African, Asian and Caribbean Artists in Britain, 1966–1996'. The diversity of her work is seen in commissions from Glenfield General Hospital, Leicester, Nando's Restaurant and Purelake New Homes. Douglas Camp was on the committee for the Commonwealth Memorial Gates. She received numerous prizes while studying, including a Saatchi and Saatchi Award (1982)

Further reading

Morley Gallery (2000) *Knots of the Human Art*, exhibition, London: Morley Gallery.
Museum of Mankind (1995) *Play and Display: Steel*

Masquerades from Top to Toe – Sculpture by Sokari Douglas Camp, London: Museum of Mankind.
National Museum of African Art (1998) *Echoes of the Kalabari*, Washington, DC: National Museum of African Art, Smithsonian Institution.

JANE SILLIS AND YINKA SUNMONU

Drum, the

The Drum was set up in the spring of 1995 as an independent production company. Later, in spring 1998, a new centre, based in Newtown, Birmingham, was opened. The centre has several performance and training spaces, projection facilities, meeting rooms, café and bar. The Drum is supported by Birmingham City Council, West Midlands Arts and West Midlands Probation Service. An initial grant from the Arts Council of England and the Newtown and South Aston City Challenge Company enabled the building project. Dedicated to the artistic and cultural expression of African, Asian and Caribbean people, the Drum's objectives are to support the development of contemporary black urban artistic practice, to involve people from all sections of the community in cultural activities that educate, inform and entertain, and to establish a centre of both national and international excellence. To date, the Drum has hosted a wide range and variety of activities, including multi-media events (Digital Equinox), **photography** exhibitions ('**Being Here I, II and III**', 'Deep'), performances of **music** (Jamfolk, the Well Gospel Group, the Sabri Ensemble), drama (*Lonely Londoners*, *Azadi*) and **dance** (**African Cultural Exchange**), as well as workshops and training courses reflecting a diverse range of **art forms**.

SAMINA ZAHIR

THE DUB FACTORY *see* Parvez

E

East is East

East is East (1999), the outstanding British film, was originally a play written by Ayub **Khan Din**, and produced by **Tamasha Theatre Company**. Khan Din, who at the time was better known as an actor, wrote a draft of the story while still at college. Sudha **Bhuchar**, an artistic director of Tamasha and an actor, knew of its existence and encouraged Khan Din to submit it for a new writing workshop being undertaken by her company and the Royal Court. Here it was developed with actors, director and a dramaturge. The play, directed by Kristine **Landon-Smith**, also an artistic-director of Tamasha, opened at the Birmingham Repertory Theatre in October 1996. This semi-autobiographical tale of growing up in a mixed-race, working-class family in Salford during the 1970s was immediately acclaimed by the audience and critics alike. The *Birmingham Post* said: 'It would be tempting to suggest that this play marks the real arrival of a mature contemporary British Asian theatre, but it is too good to be consigned to a ghetto. *Hamlet* is not a play about Danes but about human beings and so is this.' After the initial successful run, the play enjoyed two transfers: first, to the Theatre Royal Stratford East (February 1997), and then to the Royal Court's temporary venue in the West End. The play celebrated its hundredth performance on 9 April 1997. The impact of the play was overwhelming and Khan Din won the Writers Guild of Great Britain 'Best West End Play' and 'New Writer of the Year' awards in 1997.

It was seen by independent producer Leslee Udwin, who bought the film (see **film and cinema**) rights, and the author wrote the screenplay himself. The budget of £2.5million was financed by **Channel 4**'s FilmFour and it turned out to be the most successful film of its kind, grossing over £10 million in the UK alone. It was bought unseen by Miramax for exhibition in the USA and in France, where it was called *Fish and Chips*.

East is East, the film, was directed by a new director, Damien O'Donnell, but some of the original cast also appeared in the same roles in the film – Linda Bassett played the mother, Ella Khan, Emil Marwa was Munir or 'Gandhi' and Jimi Mistry played Tariq. The role of the father, George Khan, was played by Om **Puri**, one of India's best-known actors. The film won several awards, including the *Evening Standard* Award for 'Best Film', the BAFTA Alexander Korda award for 'Best British Film' and the Golden Spike for 'Best Film' at the Valladolid Film Festival, Spain.

The play version of *East is East* has also enjoyed several reincarnations. It was produced at the Oldham Coliseum Theatre in 1999 with Kristine Landon-Smith directing. It enjoyed a run in May 1999 in New York at the Manhattan Theater Club, directed by Scott Elliott, and in March 2001 at the Leicester Haymarket Theatre, directed by Nona Shepphard.

Select bibliography

Khan Din, Ayub (1996) *East is East London*, London: Nick Hern Books.

SUMAN BHUCHAR

Eastern Eye

From his home in London in 1989 Anwar Saheed founded this weekly newspaper (see **publishing, newspapers and magazines**), which is edited by Nayan Chohan. It is reported that it sold 30,000 copies a week nationwide in its first year. The tabloid states it is the newspaper 'for the Asian perspective'. The front-page story for its 574th issue was a show-business exclusive on the **Bollywood** Oscars. One columnist, Thufayel Ahmed, claims to be 'the Voice of Asian Britain'. The newspaper compiles and publishes Britain's Richest Asians 200 list, which appears annually. Lakshmi Mital of Ispat International, a steel-manufacturing company, emerged as the richest Asian in 2000. The youngest entry was Kashif Ahmed, who runs the fashion (see **fashion and design**) label Laundry, part of **Joe Bloggs**. Details of the list, started in 1996, receive coverage in the mainstream press. To date, *Eastern Eye* has a readership of 175,600 with a cover price of seventy pence. It contains a seven-day **television** listing of Asian entertainment on various cable channels such as Zee TV. *E mag* is a supplement to the newspaper printed with the slogan, 'It is not just a magazine. It is a way of life.' There is a regular section on Bollywood, together with a page for the Asian woman, pages on **music**, a recipe, an advice page including sexual advice and fashion and beauty features. The paper also publishes various souvenir supplements in celebration of religious and community events. *Eastern Eye* is published by the Ethnic Media Group, publishers of *Asian Times*, *New Nation* and *Caribbean Times*, incorporating *African Times* – showing the diversity of the black groups in Britain.

YINKA SUNMONU

Edge, Nina

b. 1962, England

artist, essayist

Trained as a ceramicist at Cardiff, Nina Edge has gone on to work in various media, such as batik and painting, and through gallery-specific installations, as well as for **carnival** and **theatre**. Edge has exhibited widely, her work combining both a public and private voice: in the shape of social protest, alienation and anger, as well as the personal analysis of a dual heritage. Her career has included the exhibitions 'Trophies of Empire' (Liverpool, 1992), 'Ethnic Cleansing', an installation at John Moores Gallery (Liverpool, 1994) – during which time Edge held the Henry Moore Sculpture Fellowship – and 'Mirage: Enigmas of Race and Desire' at the **Institute of Contemporary Arts** (London, 1995). In 1996 she participated in '**Transforming the Crown**', an exhibition of black British artists held in New York that offered an intensive exploration of the African and Asian presence in Europe and their contributions to late twentieth-century artistic movements in the UK. As a writer, Edge has contributed to *Third Text* (34, spring 1996) and *FAN* (4, 1992), and significantly an essay entitled 'Your name is mud' on assessing the definitional dilemmas of art/craft and the double impact of discrimination faced by black women artists and makers in *Passion: Discourses on Black Women's Creativity* (1991) edited by Maud **Sulter** (Hebden Bridge: Urban Fox Press).

DIPTI BHAGAT

Electric Cinema

Built in 1910, the Electric Cinema in Portobello Road, London, was Britain's first black cinema (see **cinemas**) and has a long history as one of the oldest serving purpose-built cinemas in Britain. It was constructed in the days when Portobello Road was a prestigious shopping area and one of the first streets in London to get electricity. Opening in

1911, around 600 people saw Sir Herbert Tree perform a silent version of *Henry VIII*. However, as the popularity of the area declined so did the cinema. It was to change hands many times and by the 1980s it had become run down. In 1992, the cinema went into voluntary receivership and sought a buyer. A year later, in July, a consortium including Choice FM and the **Voice** moved into the building. The group was said to have paid almost £1 million to get the building ready in time for the **Notting Hill Carnival** in August of that year. The aim of the owners was to promote black film (see **film and cinema**) and black directors, who often found it hard to promote their work and make black British films accessible to an appreciative audience. From an architectural viewpoint, the Electric Cinema was known for its Edwardian designs. It was also known for performances that included afternoon tea with its admission price.

YINKA SUNMONU

Emecheta, Buchi

b. 1944, Lagos, Nigeria

novelist, playwright, essayist

Buchi Emecheta migrated to London in 1962, when women writers in Africa were virtually unheard of. As well as working as a teacher, librarian and community worker, Emecheta has published more than a dozen novels and a number of works for children. She has not only succeeded in internationalising African women's writing but has become a reference point in black British writing and culture. Her works give an overview of the constituents of this dynamic culture. They offer glimpses of rural and urban Africa; the Caribbean; migration to the UK and resultant identity questions; issues of race and place, as well as cultural change. Emecheta's novels demonstrate a shift from their earlier Africa-only setting to a dual African/Caribbean-British setting. From early works like *The Bride Price* (1976) and *The Joys of Motherhood* (1979) that interrogate African culture, to later works about return and the primacy of ancestral roots, such as *Kehinde* (1994) and *Gwendolen* (1989), Emecheta's novels capture the multifaceted

nature of black British culture. The author effectively writes herself into her works, defining herself as African, a woman, black in Britain and eventually marking her position as black British. Her autobiography, *Head above Water* (1986), illustrates these marked shifts clearly. Emecheta's works have earned and received worldwide acclaim.

Select bibliography

Emecheta, B. (1994 [1989]) *Gwendolen*, Oxford: Heinemann.

—— (1994 [1986]) *Head above Water*, Oxford: Heinemann.

—— (1979) *The Joys of Motherhood*, London: Allison & Busby.

—— (1977) *Slave Girl*, London: Allison & Busby.

—— (1976) *Second Class Citizen*, London: Allison & Busby.

—— (1972) *In the Ditch*, London: Barrie & Jenkins.

Further reading

Barthelemy, A. (1989) 'Western time, African lives: time in the novels of Buchi Emecheta', *Callaloo* 12(3): 559–74.

Bruner, C. and Bruner, D. (1985) 'Buchi Emecheta and Maryse Conde: contemporary writing from Africa and the Caribbean', *World Literature Today* 59: 9–13.

PINKIE MEKGWE

EMMANUEL, DAVID *see* Smiley Culture

Empire Road

Empire Road is credited with being the first 'black' soap and ran for two series between 1978 and 1979. The show had a mixed black and Asian cast, and included storylines that were concerned with mainstream issues such as parental discipline and difficult relationships. At the time, *Empire Road* was dubbed as the 'black' *Coronation Street*, although **television** critics at the time suggested that the show was one of the few that could be watched by black people without embarrassment or anger. The show was ground-breaking in its pitch to be a 'black' soap, even though its white producer, Peter Ansorge, and the rest of the production team were keen to ensure that the show's primary purpose was to amuse and entertain rather than to provide race-related polemic. Its four principal characters comprise the Guyanese Bennett family: Everton, the 'father/godfather' (Norman **Beaton**); Hortense, Everton's wife (Corinne Skinner-Carter); Marcus, their Birmingham-born son (Wayne Laryea); and Ranjanaa Kapoor, Marcus's girlfriend (Malini Moonasar). All were, at the time at least, clear that what was unique about the series was its authenticity: it was not a white show with black faces but rather a (more) realistic account of life in 1970s Birmingham. The fact that the show had a black writer – Michael Abbensetts – was crucial in the development of realistic, credible storylines and dialogue sequences. Further, the involvement of a black director in the second series – the filmmaker Horace **Ové** – also made a significant contribution to the way in which the actors themselves developed. Despite the novelty of the show, there was none the less considerable caution about broadcasting it during prime time and on the prime channel, as evidenced by the fact that the show went out at 6.50 p.m. on BBC 2 in the Further Education slot. However, the BBC did at least recognise the worth and quality of the show from the beginning, and did not wait for the ratings to make an appearance before commissioning a further series. The second series moved from its rather marginal slot of 6.50 p.m. to the more mainstream 8 p.m.

KAREN ROSS

Eshun, Ekow

b. 1968, London, England

journalist, critic, broadcaster, writer

Between 1993 and 1996, Eshun was assistant editor of the style magazine, *The Face*. His journalistic career in style magazines (see **publishing, newspapers and magazines**) was consolidated with his appointment as editor, in 1996, of the men's magazine *Arena*, where he remained until 1999. In 1997, Eshun became a regular panellist on the BBC 2 programme *The Late Review*. He presented the four-part documentary series, *A Second Generation*, broadcast on Radio 4 in 1998. The series discussed black identity in Britain and the USA. Eshun was also the writer and co-presenter, with Jon Snow, of the **Channel 4** documentary *Living on the Line* (1999). This one-off programme traced the Greenwich Meridian Line in different directions by the two presenters, ending with their rendezvous in Timbuktu. In 1998, Eshun joined the board of the **Institute of Contemporary Arts**, London, and the London Arts Board.

CAROL TULLOCH

Essential Black Art, The

The two big survey shows of black art of 1988, 'The Essential Black Art' and '**Black Art: Plotting the Course**' demonstrated the differences between the two most important approaches to black art. 'The Essential Black Art', curated by Rasheed **Araeen**, was a foretaste of the larger show he would curate the next year, '**The Other Story**'. Araeen stressed the need to articulate a historical framework around black art, which he saw as a loose movement. Araeen argued that locating black art within contemporary art and international modernism was a more pressing issue than seeking to find what he termed 'Afro-Asian' traditions or aesthetics. Araeen also argued that recent black art practices were guilty of ignoring the earlier history of black art. The exhibition contained the work of nine artists: Araeen, Zarina **Bhimji**, Sutapa **Biswas**, Sonia **Boyce**, Eddie **Chambers**, Alan **de Souza**, Mona Hatoum, Gavin **Jantjes** and Keith **Piper**. In retrospect the list might be seen as constituting the core of black art. The catalogue contains several important essays, including a paper given by Araeen at the First National Black Convention in 1982.

Further reading

Chisenhale Gallery (1988) *The Essential Black Art,*

exhibition catalogue, London: Chisenhale Gallery.

NIRU RATNAM

essentialism

Essentialism is the belief that characteristics and qualities are innate and natural, rather than acquired and constructed, meaning that it is unnecessary or irrelevant to study identity in its social, economic or political contexts. Critics of humanism and essentialism often elide the two. Alan Sinfield argues that:

> [T]he essentialist-humanist approach to literature and sexual politics depends upon the belief that the individual is the probable, indeed necessary, source of truth and meaning. . . . But thinking of ourselves as essentially individual tends to efface processes of cultural production, and, in the same movement, leads us to imagine ourselves to be autonomous, self-determining.
>
> (1992: 37)

Indeed, cultural materialists and New Historians are precisely concerned to investigate the construction of identity categories within the contexts of history and politics. The deconstruction of gender and sexual identity has revealed some of the pernicious underpinnings of essentialism, which relies on notions of 'normality' and 'natural order' (for example, women are innately and biologically inferior to men; people who engage in homosexual acts are deviant). The category of 'race' has recently been subjected to post-structuralist readings, with critics and theorists such as Robert Young and Paul **Gilroy** placing it within its historical contexts in order to demonstrate its genesis in the eighteenth and nineteenth centuries, when it was invented. The Enlightenment obsession with categorisation and taxonomy led to the development of racial science, and, in the eighteenth century, natural historians and scientists argued that black people (specifically, Africans in this context) were innately inferior to white people and more akin to apes. It is possible to trace a line of progression from such discourses to nineteenth-century scientific racism, which eventually gave rise to anthropology and craniology, where the essential inferiority of black people was also the subject of investigation.

The African American critic, Henry Louis Gates Jnr, has been one of the key figures in the post-structuralist, non-essentialist reading of race, in which the historically and socially constructed nature of the category is investigated and documented (see, for example, *Black Literature and Literary Theory* of 1984 and *'Race', Writing and Difference* of 1986). Black British theorists and critics such as Paul Gilroy and Stuart **Hall** have also questioned essentialist formulations of race. Gilroy claims that the ontologically grounded essentialism is replaced by 'a libertarian, strategic alternative: the cultural saturnalia which attends the end of innocent notions of the essential black subject' (*The black Atlantic*: 32), although he warns against the dangers of abandoning racial essentialism only to ignore the importance of the lingering power of specifically racialised forms of power and subordination. Stuart Hall places a similar emphasis on what he calls the end of innocence 'when it comes to constructing categories of race or blackness', claiming that black identity cannot be homogenised or essentialised, and arguing for the introduction of difference into contemporary discourses concerning race. Gayatri Chakravorty Spivak has written of 'the strategic use of positivist essentialism in a scrupulously visible political interest', a practice which has been adopted by a number of post-colonial theorists and critics, even though Spivak has subsequently distanced herself from the concept. (Spivak: 205).

References

Gates, Jnr, H.L. (1992) *Loose Canons. Notes on the Culture Wars*, New York: Oxford University Press.

Sinfield, A. (1992) *Faultlines: Cultural Materialism and the Politics of Dissident Reading*, Oxford: Clarendon Press.

Spivak, G.C. (1987) 'Subaltern studies: deconstructing historiography', in *In Other Worlds. Essays in Cultural Politics*, New York: Routledge, pp. 197–221.

Further reading

Hall, S. (1990) 'Cultural identity and diaspora', in J. Rutherford (ed.) *Identity, Community, Culture, Difference*, London: Lawrence & Wishart, pp. 222–37.

Fuss, D. (1989) *Essentially Speaking. Feminism, Nature and Difference*, London: Routledge.

SARA SALIH

Eternal

Eternal formed when Kellee Brian and Louise Nurding met at the Italia Conti School in London. They were joined by sisters Easther and Vernie Bennett, releasing their debut album *Always And Forever* in 1993. As with the singles that preceded it, the album reached the Top 10 in both Britain and the USA. Prior to the release of Eternal's second album *Power Of A Woman*, in 1995, the band parted company with Louise Nurding. Although her departure appeared amicable, some sections of the British media suggested that the group had sacked Nurding, the only white member of the quartet, as part of a cynical attempt to gain success in America where **music** audiences and charts are much more sensitive to race issues. This ignored the fact that Eternal were already one of the most successful musical exports to the USA with their mix of black US styles such as R'n'B, **soul** and gospel. Both Eternal and Louise have continued to have successful careers and, in 1997, an extensive greatest hits collection was released and the year finished with Eternal winning the year's best single at the MOBO awards for 'I wanna be the only one'.

ANDY WOOD

ethnic minorities

One of the most enduring and contentious issues in post-colonial Britain has been the identity of migrants, especially non-white migrants and their children. Ethnic minorities are a social group or category of the population that, in a larger society, are set apart and bound together by common ties of race, language, nationality or culture. Often

discriminated against and disadvantaged in economic terms, many ethnic minorities believe the state and media portray them in a very different way from how they view themselves. Britain has always been a mixed society, a nation peopled by migrants. Though Britain has greatly benefited from ethnic diversity throughout its history, ethnic groups have often met with hostility and resentment. During the 1950s and 1960s, non-white ethnic and religious groups often found unity in their experience of exclusion from mainstream Britain, which is how the identity category of **black British** developed for both Asian and African diasporic subjects. However, in more recent decades, attention to the differences and specificities of ethnic communities and identities has developed. Indeed, although 'ethnic minorities' is often used as a catch-all term, it is rare for ethnic minorities to view themselves as a single group and differences of religion, language and geographical ties are often seen to be more relevant. Ethnic monitoring, the collection of statistical data on ethnic origin, initially gained currency with the Nationality Act of 1981 and, during the 1980s, the government launched 'race' checks in hospitals, dole offices and other institutions. This clearly linked the processes of differentiation with those of discrimination.

ANDREA ENISUOH

Etienne, Treva

b. 1965, London, England

actor, director, producer

Etienne's first major **television** role was in *Prospects*, at the age of nineteen. Since then, he has played lead roles on screen and stage including parts in *London's Burning*, *Macbeth* at the Royal National Theatre and Stanley Kubrick's *Eyes Wide Shut* (1999). Etienne has been involved in youth **theatre** and training since 1983, writing and directing plays for his theatre company, Afro-Sax. Projects have included a musical co-produced with the Royal Opera House. In 1980, his production company, Crown Ten, wrote and produced a drama session for the Edinburgh TV Festival and comic sketches for television including the BBC's *The Real McCoy*, with Etienne becoming its assistant director for the fifth series.

1999 was a formative year for Etienne: his short films *Driving Miss Crazy* and *A Woman Scorned* were screened on **Channel 4**'s Ba Ba Zee series. *Driving Miss Crazy* was the runner-up winner at the Acapulco Film Festival. Etienne was the only actor and black person on the Government's Film Policy Review Group Action Committee.

Select bibliography

Etienne, T. (2000) 'Colouring the face of British film and television', in C. Newland and K. Sesay (eds) *IC3: the Penguin Book of New Black Writing in Britain*, London: Penguin, pp. 207–13.

KADIJA SESAY

Evaristo, Bernardine

b. 1959, London, England

poet, novelist, playwright

Evaristo graduated from drama school and staged her first play, *Moving Through*, at the Royal Court Theatre Upstairs. She was the co-director of Spread the Word Literature Development Agency. Evaristo is now a full-time writer and has had twenty-three international tours and residencies since 1997. She is known primarily for the lyrical quality of her writing. Her debut collection of poetry, *Island of Abraham*, was published by **Peepal Tree Press** in 1994. Her first novel, *Lara*, published to critical acclaim, won the EMMA Best Novel Award in 1999. This work represents a hybrid form between poetry and prose, and between fact and fiction. It explores the family of a young mixed-race girl of Nigerian and Irish descent through a variety of disparate voices, locations and times. What *Lara* achieves is a complex and shifting sense of the different strands of cultural mythologies and histories that make up cultural identity in contemporary Britain. Evaristo won an Arts Council Writers Award in 2000 and her latest work, *The Emperor's Babe* (2001), is a novel-in-verse.

Select bibliography

Evaristo, B. (2001) *The Emperor's Babe*, London: Penguin/Hamish Hamilton.
—— (1994) *Island of Abraham*, Leeds: Peepal Tree Press.
—— (1997) *Lara*, Tunbridge Wells, Kent: Angela Royal Publishing.

GAIL CHING-LIANG LOW

F

Fani-Kayode, Rotimi

b. 1955, Nigeria; d. 1989, London, England

photographer

Fani-Kayode moved to England from Nigeria with his family in 1966, and then to the USA in 1976. He studied in Georgetown University, Washington DC, and the Pratt Institute, Brooklyn, graduating in 1983. Moving back to England that same year, Fani-Kayode became a pivotal figure in the history of British black visual art (see **visual and plastic arts**), being a founding member and chairperson of **Autograph: the Association of Black Photographers** when it formed in 1987. Making work that has often been superficially linked with the work of Robert Mapplethorpe, his photographs staged scenarios using a sexualised black male body, creating a new language of sexual **difference**, sexuality and homosexual desire, much like the work of Isaac **Julien** or Lyle Ashton Harris. His works, such as *Milk Drinker* of 1983, use simple means to generate a complex plethora of allusions. His work is also often inflected with an African tribal tradition and spirituality, referencing his Yoruba origins, such as his *Bronze Head* of 1987, or his last series of photographs produced in collaboration with Alex Hirst.

Further reading

Bailey, D.A. (1990–1) 'Photographic animateur: the photographs of Rotimi Fani-Kayode in relation to black photographic practices', *Third Text* 13 (winter): 57–63.

Sealy, M. and Pirin, J.J. (eds) (1996) *Rotimi Fani-Kayode and Alex Hirst: Photographs*, London and Paris: Autograph and Editions Revue Noire.

FRANCIS SUMMERS

fashion and design

Since the arrival of British colonial subjects following the end of the Second World War, the design and creation of objects for the body has been, in the contemporary understanding of black British culture, an area of cultural definition and personal exploration. With reference to dress, black Britain is marked with an innate sense of self-presentation and idiosyncratic styling techniques, which has come to be one of the signatory features of counter and subcultural identities.

In the use of clothes as markers of cultural difference and affiliation since the 1970s, the children of Caribbean immigrants have been the most prominent and prolific. The political radicalism of black consciousness and Black Power in the 1960s and 1970s found unique expression in the individualised dress patterns of black Britons in the form of the 'natural' or Afro hair, the wearing of Dhashikis or elaborate headties, styles that had been reconstituted into a radical parlance by African Americans. The referencing of such styles by young Black Britons was integral to the development of a diaspora aesthetic (see **diaspora aesthetics**) that compounded simultaneously the links and differences between diasporic groups, based on their particular cultural experiences. One such example was the visual rhetoric of **Rastafari**. Although a religion, during the late 1970s and early 1980s its visibility, most notably as dreadlocks, on British streets, particularly the urban spaces of inner cities such as Birmingham, Manchester, London, Bristol and Cardiff, also symbolised the cataclysmic situation of being young, black and living in Britain – the meeting of dissonance with alienation. The desire for the 'true' Rastafarian was a return to Africa in spirit, if not in reality.

The hedonism of the street styles associated with the musical genres of '**lovers' rock**' and **Soul II Soul** of the 1980s retained, respectfully, the 'ethnic' exclusivity and collective qualities of Rastafarianism. The *raison d'être* for both styles was the black experience in Britain. The urban sartorialism of lovers' rock dress and the sculptural quality of the **funky dreds** hairstyle, initially intended for the Soul II Soul sound crew, have a particular resonance in the formulation of the contemporary black British aesthetic. The impetus for their creation came from that experience, rather than adopting a style created outside of Britain, like **hip hop** from the USA, and **raggamuffin** from Jamaica. In 1990, Asian youth poignantly visualised and vocalised the maturity of their cultural identity of growing up in Britain, in the street style bhangramuffin. The dress was a fusion of hip hop and ragga clothing that was replicated in the music that blended dancehall, **reggae** and British **bhangra** and bangla music. The latter styles were the operative link to British Asian cultural self-definition.

British fashion designers were also emerging alongside the significant evolution of popular and street styles. In 1975, Bruce **Oldfield** established his couture label. To celebrate their seventy-fifth anniversary, in 1990 to 1991, *Vogue* magazine commissioned Oldfield, along with other internationally respected designers, to design and produce garments for the celebratory issue. Oldfield produced a silk jersey unitard and accompanying organza overskirt. The garments featured hand-painted designs by David Phillips. The collaboration marked the lineage of 'black British' designers.

To define a designer as 'black' or 'black British' is a contentious issue. On the one hand, to label designers in this way engenders the fear, or

perpetuation, of marginalisation. On the other, it is the desire for the validation of one's 'ethnic' identity. The transient nature of fashion requires its practitioners to be abreast of trends. For many of these designers, race is secondary, and innovation in design is primary. The work of avant-garde men's and womenswear designer and stylist Joe **Casely-Hayford** and the immaculate tailoring of Oswald **Boateng** or the innovative womenswear silhouettes created by Darla Jane Gilroy exemplify this. While the work of Derek **Lilliard** is itself cutting edge, Lilliard's original design concepts are suffused with black and urban street style references.

The exhibition 'Diverse Cultures', held at the Crafts Council in 1990, featured the work of twenty-eight makers of 'contemporary craft in all media, makers of African, Afro-Caribbean, Asian, Middle Eastern and Far Eastern origin currently living in Britain'. The venture demonstrated that, although an increasing number of designer makers may derive from a 'diversity of traditions', their work none the less goes beyond this. Julienne Dolphin Wilding recycled Thames driftwood for her giant furniture (1989). Disa Allsop, after graduating from Middlesex University in 1981, returned to Barbados where she grew up. There, like Dolphin Wilding, she made use of wood and glass washed up from the sea. She returned to Britain in 1993, first in Edinburgh, then settling in London in 1996. Her *Spaghetti Rings* (1999) were inspired by the raw material of pasta. The jewellery designer Mah **Rana** creates jewellery-based objects that explore the traditions and symbolism of the gold wedding ring. She transforms them into critiques on matrimony and relationships, not unlike the motives behind lovers' rock.

As community outreach worker at the Victoria and Albert Museum, London, Shireen Akbar invited Asian women to contribute to the Nehru Gallery National Textile Project (1993). Through the study and drawing of objects in the gallery, the women produced fourteen embroidered panels that represented feelings of hope and growth, religious and cultural harmony, or depictions of Indian and Irish women dancing together in *The Dance of Life*, from Dublin. The issue of diversity in design is summarised in the work of Lubna Chowdhary and her installation *Metropolis*, a city of 500 miniature ceramic objects. Working in this expansive format was a methodology for Chowdhary to challenge issues such as difference and origin.

In memory of the murdered black British teenager Stephen **Lawrence**, who intended to study architecture, the Architectural Association, London, established the Stephen Lawrence Scholarship following an anonymous donation in 1999. This epitaph to a life cruelly and needlessly ended so young does at least recognise the relevance of creativity and ingenuity to life that design can provide.

CAROL TULLOCH

Fashion Records

Taking its name and inspiration from 'Coxsone' Dodd's *High Fashion Dub*, Chris Lane and John MacGillivray set up Fashion Records in the basement of MacGillivray's Dub Vendor record shop in South London in 1980. Utilising the pair's extensive contacts, skills and enthusiasm for all things **reggae**, Fashion began to build up an amazing reputation both in Britain and in Jamaica. As well as being at the forefront of British reggae, having early successes with Dee Sharp and Mikey General, many Jamaican studios and producers began to send material to Lane's Class-A studio for a final mix and cutting. Fashion has always been an eclectic label and artists have included the British 'fast-talking originators' such as **Smiley Culture**, **Tippa Irie** and Pato Banton, as well as many top Jamaican artists including Horace Andy, Carlton Lewis and Junior Delgado. Over the past two decades, Fashion have covered most areas of reggae's diverse range of sounds, from dub to **dancehall** to ragga and **jungle**. Fashion and Class-A have been heralded as innovators in reggae, both for the distinctive sound of their in-house productions and for their ability to be at the forefront with new sounds.

ANDY WOOD

Federation of Worker Writers and Community Publishers

When Sam **Selvon** wrote of a kind of 'communal feeling with the Working Class and the Spades' in *The Lonely Londoners*, he claimed a fraternity that proved unreliable a decade later as London dockers joined Enoch Powell's vocal anti-immigration lobby. Nevertheless, in 1976 the seeds of that earlier sense of class-comradeship did unexpectedly unite writers in a challenge to the white, male, middle-class cultural hegemony that had controlled publishing. In that year, the National Federation of Worker Writers and Community Publishers (FWWCP), led by Chris Searle and Ken Worpole, was formed officially. The predominantly white organisation responded to complex post-war social, cultural and political developments that had increasingly threatened any notion of a cultural consensus. Nine British groups of working-class writers, including Jimmy McGovern's Liverpool writers' workshop, sought a national framework and recognition through Arts Council funding.

The FWWCP was sparked by progressive educational as well as cultural concerns. It was to create a unique environment under which black working-class writers found a safe expressive space. There were two ways in which this was achieved: the FWWCP obtained funding through new schemes to improve the standard of adult literacy, while at the same time, influenced by the radical pedagogy of Paolo Freire, it celebrated diverse voices – regional, 'foreign', ungrammatical and rebellious. Some of these groups were to provide migrant writers with opportunities to gain skills in writing and publishing at a point at which they were severed from their cultural roots and finding themselves inarticulate in their new 'Motherland'. The 1980s saw the issue of several collections by black writers including the **Peckham Publishing Project**'s *Captain Blackbeard's Beef Creole* (1981), which recorded hitherto unwritten social practices in the Caribbean through recipes and stories. The Southwark Race Equality Unit funded *So This is England* (1984), a collection of autobiographical pieces depicting the authors' experiences of coming to Britain. The second way in which the FWWCP impacted on black British expression was in the groups of creative writers who met and published local anthologies of short fiction and poetry. The democratic editorial process typically provided a safe cultural space for a second generation of disaffected black youth. In the mid-1970s, Ken Worpole remembered that Vivian Usherwood,

Hugh Boatswain and Sandra Agard were part of a group of 'very talented young black writers around Centerprise', publishing anthologies in London such as *Talking Blues* (1978). The FWWCP is barely known in academic circles but still flourishes under its original manifesto of 'working to make writing and publishing accessible to all'. Its vibrant British and international membership now includes writers' groups in Mauritius, Cape Town, Barcelona, Toronto and Melbourne.

Further reading

Federation of Worker Writers and Community Publishers (1978) *Writing*, London: Centerprise.

Morley, D. and Worpole, K. (1982) *The Republic of Letters: Working Class Writing and Local Publishing*, London: Comedia.

Shore, L. (1982) *Pure Running: a Life Story*, London: Centerprise.

SANDRA COURTMAN

feminism

Writing in the early 1990s, Patricia Hill Collins re-emphasised the constraints upon black women's intellectual culture and self-understanding: 'Because elite white men and their representatives control structures of knowledge validation ... Black women's experiences with work, family, motherhood, political activism, and sexual politics have been routinely distorted in or excluded from traditional academic discourse' (Kemp and Squires 1997: 198). Heidi Safia **Mirza** takes a similar line when she argues that 'As long as there is exclusion, both in academic discourse and in materiality, there will be a black feminism' (Mirza 1997: 21). Both critics are writing in full consciousness that feminism, too, despite its important and genuine attempts at pluralisation, 'is a largely white, Westernised construct' that can all too easily overlook the 'daily experience of race and economic hardship' (Wisker 2000: 26).

Taking on board the biases and oversights highlighted by Hill Collins and Wisker, Heidi Safia Mirza has been able to clear a space for the assessment of black British feminism through the use of a broad notion of black British feminism as a 'critical social force'. Mirza has produced a powerful 'genealogy' of black British feminist activity that she traces back to the 'activism and struggles of black women migrants' from the 1940s and 1960s'(Mirza 1997: 6). During this period, official statistics and texts elided women's involvement in the history of post-colonial migration and ignored black female work and workers. However, Mirza points us to the extant stories of black female activism during this period that have been recovered during, and since, the more confident political climate of the 1980s.

During the 1970s, black feminist activity was largely expressed through grassroots political action. Black women's involvement in the 'labour struggles that exploded in the 1970s' (Mirza 1997:7) marked a change in black, especially Asian, women's conventionally (or stereotypically) stoical response to the degrading and exploitative conditions of sweatshop and home working. Amrit **Wilson** cites the 'tremendous impact and influence of the strike at Grunwick Photoprocessing' in 1977 as an early example of immigrant Asian women's public assertion of their rights as workers and British citizens (Mirza 1997: 31).

Identity politics was the driving force of feminism in the 1980s. For black feminists, the decade enabled African, African Caribbean, and South Asian women to consciously name themselves as 'black' against – or in critical dialogue with – mainstream feminist scholarship. During this decade, academic black feminism gained an identifiable footing, largely assisted by, while also aiding, the growth and development of the new discipline of cultural studies. From within the **Centre for Contemporary Cultural Studies** at the University of Birmingham, Hazel V. **Carby** produced her ground-breaking work on differentiated models of femininity and gender, beginning with the influential essay 'White woman listen! Black feminism and the boundaries of sisterhood', first published in 1982. The feminist publishing house Virago published Bryan, Dadzie and Scafe's *The Heart of the Race: Black Women's Lives in Britain*, in 1985, and Lauretta **Ngcobo**'s important survey of black feminist writing *Let it Be Told: Black Women Writers in Britain*, in 1988. However, the central forum of black feminist debate was clearly the journal *Feminist Review*, whose 1984 special issue, 'Many Voices One Chant' provided the first, clear statement of the necessary pluralisation of the feminist project in Britain, followed by a further special issue, 'Feedback: Feminism and Racism', in 1986. In 1988, *Feminist Review* also published Chandra T. Mohanty's much anthologised essay 'Under Western eyes: feminist scholarship and colonial discourses'.

By the end of the 1980s, the concept of a (homogeneous) black critical feminism was coming under close scrutiny. Where feminism in its broadest sense was focusing in the 1990s on questions of internal difference(s), the black feminist project during this decade was similarly characterised by reflexivity, self-interrogation and an important refining of the political category 'black woman' to acknowledge the fluidity and mobility of gendered and racialised identities. Notable examples of these new versions of black feminism included *Feminist Review*'s 1993 special issue, 'Thinking through Ethnicities', and either side of this publication Helen (**charles**)'s essay 'Whiteness' (1992) and Sara Ahmed's *Differences that Matter* (1998). The end of the 1990s saw Helen (charles) among others resurrect the question of an inclusive feminist movement. While recognising the 'importance of discussing the adoption of more appropriate terminology' (charles) remains convinced that 'feminism' not only ensures a 'strategic identity' but that it is 'constructed not as a strict and impenetrable concept but one which is pervious to change' (1997: 294).

References

Carby, H.V. (1982) 'White woman listen! Black feminism and the boundaries of sisterhood', in Centre for Contemporary Cultural Studies (eds) *The Empire Strikes Back: Race and Racism in 70s Britain*, London: Hutchinson.

(charles), helen (1997) 'The language of womanism: re-thinking difference', in Heidi Safia Mirza (ed.) *Black British Feminism: A Reader*, London and New York: Routledge, pp. 278-97.

Kemp, S. and Squires, J. (1997) *Feminisms*, Oxford and New York: Oxford University Press.

Mirza, H.S. (ed.) (1997) *Black British Feminism: a Reader*. London and New York: Routledge.

Ngcobo, L. (ed.) (1987) *Let it Be Told: Essays by Black Women in Britain*, London: Virago.

Wisker, G. (2000) *Post-colonial and African American Women's Writing: a Critical Introduction*, Basingstoke: Macmillan.

Further reading

Dogson, E. (1984) *Motherlands: West Indian Women in Britain in the 1950s*, Oxford: Heinemann.

hooks, bell (1989) *Talking Back: Thinking Feminist, Thinking Black*, Boston, MA: South End Press.

Nasta, S. (ed.) (1991) *Motherlands: Black Women's Writing from Africa, the Caribbean and South Asia*, London: the Women's Press.

LYNNETTE TURNER

Figueroa, John

b. 1920, Kingston, Jamaica; d. 1999, Woburn Sand, England

poet, educator

After growing up in Jamaica and studying in the USA, Figueroa moved to England in 1946. He pursued a distinguished career in education and lectured as a professor at universities in the West Indies, Puerto Rico, Nigeria, the USA and the UK. His first collection of poetry, *Blue Mountain Peak*, appeared in 1944. Figueroa's poetry has a strong classical element that derives from his early influences by poets such as Horace, Virgil and Sappho. This is complemented, however, by his linguistic interest in Jamaican speech and Trinidadian calypsos. His Roman Catholic faith is also a recurrent theme, as are the different physical landscapes he encountered during his extensive travels. Figueroa also edited poetry anthologies, including *Caribbean Voices* (1966), an important early collection of Caribbean poetry featured in the eponymous BBC Radio programme for which he worked between 1946 and 1953. He was also a critic of West Indian **literature** and wrote about education in the West Indies.

Select bibliography

Figueroa, J. (1991) *The Chase 1941–1989*, Leeds: Peepal Tree Press.

—— (1976) *Ignoring Hurts*, Washington: Three Continents Press.

—— (ed.) (1966) *Caribbean Voices: an Anthology of West Indian Poetry*, 2 vols, London: Evans Brothers.

PAOLA MARCHIONNI

film and cinema

In 1896, the newly opened Lumière Cinématographe in Leicester Square first screened the Lumière Brothers film *Negrès dansant dans la rue* (The Wandering Negro Minstrels). An *actualité* (fifty-second film) featuring a nearby London street performance of blackfaced minstrels before an audience of white, working-class men, the *actualité* marked the baptism of black images/racial stereotypes on the British screen. The blackfaced minstrel continued to appear in British silent films such as *Dancing Niggers* (1899) and *The Lightfooted Darkey* (1899), until later films including Basil Dearden's *Pool of London* (1951) and *Sapphire* (1959) or John Boorman's *Leo the Last* (1969) sought to represent more conflicted aspects of a black British reality. As Britain's first black silent film actor, Caribbean-born Ernest Trimmingham was followed by Paul Robeson during the 1930s and Errol John and Earl Cameron during the 1940s and 1950s. Yet despite the on-screen crowning achievements of black actors, black cinema did not develop beyond stereotyped bit parts and peripheral British film industry involvement until almost seventy years after the birth of cinema itself.

The first cinematic flowerings stemmed from a growing black arts movement in 1960s Britain. The first black British drama, a twelve-minute short film *Ten Bob in Winter* by Jamaican Lloyd Reckord in 1963, conveyed alienated Afro-Caribbean migrant experiences in a contemporary London bedecked with Christmas cheer. South African actor-director Lionel Ngakane's allegorical short *Jemima and Johnny* in 1964 focused on the inter-racial friendship between a black girl and white boy in the racially hostile aftermath of the 1958 Notting Hill riots. As the official British entry at the Venice Film Festival in 1964, *Jemima and Johnny* proceeded to win the Best Short Feature Film award. Frankie Dymon Junior's short *Death May Be Your Santa Claus* (1969) wove 1960s black power, leftist politics and popular culture in a surreal narrative that followed the film's black protagonist on an imaginary course from alienation to self-empowerment, while Trinidadian Horace **Ové**'s documentary *Baldwin's Nigger* (1968) engaged with black diaspora politics. His music documentary *Reggae* (1970) demonstrated the necessary entrepreneurial skills of these self-financed film-makers and was financed by a black record producer friend. Besides financial constraints and limited distribution, a developing black British cinema was also impeded by its exclusion from white-dominated cultural debates, policies and forms of cultural production in both mainstream and independent film sectors.

In 1974, Ové's low-budget **Pressure** became the first black British feature and the first to receive funding from the **British Film Institute** (BFI). Shot in a realist style, *Pressure* deploys a classic race-relations narrative. The film explores a contradictory 1970s black British identity through the Afro-Caribbean community and black power politicisation of a disillusioned school-leaver, his shaping experiences of racism distancing him from both his white counterparts and his migrant Caribbean parents. In 1975, the BFI funded the first British Asian feature *A Private Enterprise* (directed by Peter Smith and co-written by Dilip Hiro), and then Menelik **Shabazz**'s documentary *Step Forward Youth*, which depicted socially inflected forms of British Asian experience (although black British cinema only noticeably bifurcated into British black and Asian cinema during the 1990s). These films continued the 1970s 'cinema of duty' mode of black British films. Coining the term, Cameron Bailey describes these films as being conscious of social responsibilities, engaging with social issues through a documentary realist style, aiming to retrieve forgotten narratives and histories, while altering dominant cultural stereotypes and (mis-)representations. Another 1970s 'cinema of duty' film, Anthony Simmons's *Black Joy* (1978) (co-written by Jamal Ali) depicted the street hustling tactics of the black community in Brixton from a tireless urban black male perspective. Symptomatic of early black film distribution, the film was not released until 1977 despite its completion in 1974. The 1970s BFI financed films none the less suggested a significant attitudinal shift in cultural institutions previously indifferent to black film-making.

In part, the 1981 civil disturbances and ensuing Scarman Report, which highlighted the cultural marginalisation of the UK's ethnic minorities, forced a review of funding and cultural policies towards black arts practitioners in the public sphere. In 1982, **Channel 4** was launched with a specific multicultural remit for minority audiences, further creating the framework for its subsequent support of British independent and black film-making throughout the 1980s and onwards with Film on Four. The now-defunct **Greater London Council**, other local authorities and arts organisations also initiated funding, training and development programmes for black people in the film industry. In 1983, for example, the GLC staged the 'Third Eye' film exhibition of rarely seen Third World and black films.

The Workshop Declaration of 1981, which enlisted the backing of Channel 4, the BFI, the GLC and other arts and trade organisations, supported grant-aided film and video workshops and collectives within the independent film sector. Meanwhile, independent production companies such as Kuumba Productions, Azad Productions and Social Film and Video undertook commissions in the commercially viable private sector. **Sankofa Film Collective**, **Black Audio Film Collective**, Ceddo and British Asian outfit **Retake** were among those whose theory orientated first-generation media and film school graduates produced an explosion of experimental black British creativity in the black workshop sector.

The decade had begun with Menelik Shabazz's BFI-funded ***Burning an Illusion*** (1981), which presented the prevailing identity politics of the 1980s (race, gender, class and sexuality) from a novel black female viewpoint. By the mid-1980s, the black workshops were renegotiating the aesthetic and cultural boundaries of British film-making. With the new black film aesthetic imagined, transgressed, reclaimed and envisioned, Sankofa and Black Audio produced several innovative films and directors (including many women). ***Territories*** (Isaac **Julien**, 1986), *The*

Passion of Remembrance (Maureen **Blackwood** and Isaac Julien, 1986), ***Handsworth Songs*** (John **Akomfrah**, 1986), *Looking For Langston* (Isaac Julien, 1986) and *Dreaming Rivers* (Martina **Attille**, 1988) were among those films that reacted against traditional white-centred race relation narratives and visual paradigms, energetically shifting the focus to self-reflexive personal and political experiences of blackness.

In April 1984, Sankofa's Maureen Blackwood and Martina Attille led the Black Women and Representation Seminars (funded by the GLC) to discuss black female screen stereotypes, images and access to the ownership of such representations. During the 1980s, the black workshops frequently centralised female protagonists to comment on the prevailing cultural oppressions of the period. In 1984, the Retake Film and Video Collective produced the first British Asian workshop feature – *Majdhar* – which sought to depict the politicised self-discovery of a young Pakistani woman abandoned by her husband in Britain. East-End Bengali filmmaker Ruhul **Amin** also began incorporating pronounced Bengali female perspectives in neo-realist-tinged films such as the feature *A Kind of English* (1986) and a later short film *Rhythms* (1994).

1985 witnessed the release of the Hanif **Kureishi** scripted ***My Beautiful Laundrette*** (directed by Stephen Frears). Critically acclaimed (though heavily criticised in more conservative Asian quarters) and an unexpected commercial hit financed by Channel 4, the film narrated a homosexual love story between a young Asian businessman and an ex-National Front member in a damning indictment of Thatcher's Britain. Displaying a searing anarchic edge, *My Beautiful Laundrette* proved the viability of (British) Asian 'issues' in the commercial sphere. The film also launched Kureishi as a screenwriter, writing *Sammy and Rosie Get Laid* (1987), his critically panned directorial debut *London Kills Me* (1991) and his sharp return to screenwriting form in Udayan **Prasad**'s ***My Son the Fanatic*** (1997).

In contrast to the politically incisive *My Beautiful Laundrette*, Ové's *Playing Away* (1986) and the Trix Worrell-scripted *For Queen and Country* (1988) offered contrasting appraisals of 1980s Britain. The light-hearted *Playing Away* represented the relationship between black people and Middle England through the colonial export of cricket and a friendly match between teams from Brixton, South London and Suffolk. *For Queen and Country* portrayed a disillusioned black Falklands war hero returning to a South London council estate to encounter further instances of class and race warfare. Demonstrating the struggle for black actors to secure roles, the film created controversy when black British actor Gary McDonald was replaced by a more bankable American 'star' Denzel Washington to raise the film's £4 million budget.

The handful of 1980s films foregrounded critiques of black British identity, as illustrated by the 1988 'Black Film, British Cinema' symposium at London's **Institute of Contemporary Arts** – an ensuing period that also witnessed directorial debuts and reconfigurations of race, gender, class and sexuality in British history from black female film-makers Martina Attille with *Dreaming Rivers* (1988), Maureen Blackwood with *A Perfect Image?*, Ngozi **Onwurah**'s student film *Coffee-Coloured Children* (1988), Gurinder **Chadha**'s *I'm British but...* and continuing work from documentary film-maker Pratibha **Parmar**.

The Thatcherite 1980s had inaugurated a period of rampant commercialism and eventually witnessed the abolition of the GLC, as well as hostility to both the politically correct brigade and the public sector. The political climate led to the erosion of many public-sector funding channels for black film-makers and by 1990 the virtual end of the black workshops. Yet the 1990s release of debut features from ex-black workshop directors represented a hybridised, populist and varied black opus during an increasingly individualistic decade: Julien's alternative 1977 *Young Soul Rebels* (1991); Akomfrah's *Who Needs a Heart* (1991); Chadha's dramedy, the Meera **Syal**-scripted *Bhaji on the Beach* (1993), the first British feature directed by a black woman; Onwurah's political action movie *Welcome II the Terrordome* (1994); Suri Krishnamma's *A Man of no Importance* (1994); Prasad's *Brothers in Trouble* (1995); Don Letts's *Dancehall Queen* (1997), the most profitable black British film of the 1990s; and Julian **Henriques**'s *Babymother* (1998).

Yet the problems of commerce and funding have remained. Film on Four (and especially former head David Aukin) have supported a number of projects including *Bhaji on the Beach*, *Babymother* and

black-themed *The Crying Game* (1992). In recent years, lottery-funding consortia have offered other potential sources of public finance but were reluctant to invest in risky 'black-themed', 'black-directed' or 'black-starred' films. Potential public and private investors have shied away from black cinema in a highly competitive industry that exhibits scant understanding of the multi-ethnic film market and its heterogeneous audiences. *My Beautiful Laundrette*, *Bhaji on the Beach*, *Dancehall Queen* and the Ayub **Khan Din**-scripted *East is East* (1999) are the unparalleled critical and commercial successes of recent decades, crossing over from a black/Asian niche into the mainstream British and international market. The technological arrival of cable and satellite television, DVD and the Internet suggests wider production and distribution outlets for black film-makers, who like the 1960s film-makers must otherwise rely on restricted channels of funding and distribution.

Native South Asian directors such as Shekhar **Kapur** have directed big-budget productions in the UK, while British Asian audiences have asserted their box-office clout with the resurgence of Hindi films at the multiplexes (and several top-ten UK box-office **Bollywood** hits). Chadha opened the Sundance Film Festival 2000 with *What's Cooking*, while *East is East* grossed over $14 million in the UK alone. Producers such as Nadine **Marsh-Edwards** and Parminder **Vir**, actors including Adrian **Lester** and Thandie **Newton**, and cinematographers like Remi **Adefarasin** (*Elizabeth*) have exerted their influences in the mainstream television and film industries. For these reasons, black cinema has cause to remain optimistic, rather than fearful, of the future.

A new generation of film-makers includes Shani **Grewal** (*Guru in Seven*), Newton Aduaka (*Rage*), Menhaj Huda (*Jump Boy*), Alrick Riley (*The Concrete Garden*), Stella Nwime (who won a Cannes Palme D'Or for her first short film *Is it the Design on the Wrapper?*) and Treva **Etienne** (*Driving Miss Crazy* and *A Woman Scorned*). This suggests that the necessary screen talent is manifesting itself in a previously uninterested industry. Yet the fact that Paul Robeson remains the most successful black British actor to date and an Oscar-nominated actress such as Marianne **Jean-Baptiste** (for Mike Leigh's *Secrets and Lies*, 1995) has difficulty finding worthy screen roles indicates the obstacles on, as well as behind, the big screen. Organisations such as Marc Boothe's Nubian Tales (see **Nubian Tales/b3 Media**), established in 1991 for the promotion and distribution of black diasporic cinema, training schemes and initiatives such as Black Coral Training and various independently established production companies are maintaining the momentum of black film-making in the UK.

Further reading

Bailey, C. (1990–1) 'Cinema of duty', *CineAction* 28: 38–47.

Bourne, S. (1998) *Black in the British Frame*, London: Cassell.

Malik, S. (1996) 'Beyond the cinema of duty?', in A. Higson (ed.) *Dissolving Views: Key Writings on British Cinema*, London: Cassell.

Mercer, K. (1986) 'Recoding narratives of race and nation', in K. Mercer and I. Julien (eds) *Black Film, British Cinema*, ICA Documents 7, London: ICA.

Young, L. (1996) *Fear of the Dark: 'Race', Gender and Sexuality in the Cinema*, London: Routledge.

SATINDER CHOHAN

Flava

A black **music television** programme by Brighter Pictures productions, *Flava* is now on its fifth series with **Channel 4**. The series offers a mix of videos, entertainment news, studio guests and live studio performances, as well as video diaries of artists. The programme has had several significant 'specials', including an Asian *Flava* special, which was the first terrestrial Asian music show, and a half-hour documentary featuring an exclusive interview with Mel G, the married **Mel B**. With associated radio and club events, the *Flava* brand has been successful in bringing black music and entertainment to prime-time television and to the wider British cultural scene.

ALISON DONNELL

Forrester, Denzil

b. 1956, Grenada

visual artist

Forrester studied at the Central School of Art and the Royal College of Art (RCA), having come to the UK in 1967. After leaving the RCA, Forrester drew inspiration from the blues clubs he was visiting and started to sketch while he was there. Later, he used these to paint large-scale works on canvas set in clubs. He was influenced by the anti-racist struggles going on in the UK at the start of the 1980s and started to depict important political moments and confrontations, for example *Funeral of Winston Rose*. Forrester's iconography, whether dealing with black cultural life or the anti-racist struggle, is broadly expressionistic, recalling the German Expressionists with his flattened picture plane, and vivid, nocturnal colours. These are seen to best effect in his many works set in clubs, which thematically recall works by Aaron Douglas and others of the Harlem Renaissance. His works are deliberately large-scale and, in tandem with his vivid colours, this results in bold, strong statements about black creativity and resistance.

Further Reading

Harris Museum and Art Gallery, Preston (1990) *Dub Transition: Denzil Forrester: a Decade of Paintings*, exhibition catalogue.

Whitechapel Gallery, London (1986) *From Two Worlds*, exhibition catalogue.

NIRU RATNAM

Fowokan

b. 1943, Kingston, Jamaica

sculptor, jeweller, essayist, poet

George Kelly, Fowokan, arrived in England in 1957 and lived in Brixton, South London. One of his teachers at secondary school was Stuart **Hall**. It was on a visit to Nigeria, in the ancient city of Benin, that George was inspired to become an artist. Taking the Yoruba name 'Fowokan', meaning 'one who creates with the hand', Fowokan began practising as a sculptor in 1980. He is mainly self-taught and his work is deeply informed by African thought and concepts. His essays have been published in magazines and books. Fowokan has worked with educationists in schools and universities on a range of social studies, history and arts projects, which involved taking African art into schools across England.

Fowokan is best known for his sculptures of African figurative forms made of modern materials such as fibreglass. Since 1983 he has received commissions to produce works for the South Bank Spring Festival, Marcus Garvey Centenary celebrations, the African People's Historical Monument Foundation, and portraits and one-off pieces for private individuals. He has exhibited at the Studio Museum, Harlem and the Royal Academy, London. His sculptures are in collections such as the W.E.B. Du Bois Institute at Harvard University, the University of the West Indies, Unilever and Marcus Garvey Park, as well as in private collections in various parts of the world.

MARGARET T. ANDREWS

Francis, Armet

b. 1945, Jamaica

photographer

Francis came to Britain aged eight and became a professional photographer in the late 1960s, working in advertising, fashion (see **fashion and design**) and photo-journalism. His work has been widely published and internationally exhibited; however, it is most readily available now via *Children of the Black Triangle* (1985), which contains a representative collection of Francis's compassionate photographs of his people re-tracing the routes of the Atlantic slave trade covering the UK, USA, Africa and the Caribbean. The images are interspersed with examples of his poetry. *In situ* portraiture and a reportage style (often black and white) captures evocative and humane imagery constantly in search of 'innocence but not naivety'; thus, children, interesting to Francis for their 'basic

energy', regularly appear. Francis's publications also thoughtfully provide comprehensive yet succinct black history sections, demonstrating his thorough and conscientious approach to his art and providing a good example of an artist's role in the community. He has exhibited at: the Photographer's Gallery (1983); 'The Colours of Black' (1986), County Hall, London; the Fotogallery, Cardiff (1987) and '**Transforming the Crown**' (1997), Royal Festival Hall.

Further reading

Autograph (1997) *Party-Line – Black British Photography*, CD-ROM.

Francis, A. (1985) *Children of the Black Triangle*, Seed Publications.

Owusu, K. (ed.) (1988) 'Interview by Kwesi Owusu', in *Storms of the Heart*, London: Camden Press, pp. 181–90.

(1986) 'Interview with Anna Arnone', *City Limits* (February): 78–9.

PAUL O'KANE

Francis, Joy

b. 1965, London, England

journalist, the Creative Collective founding director

Francis is the former editor of **Pride** magazine. She began her career on the award-winning *Community Care* magazine in 1992, where she rose to the position of deputy features editor. Her varied career includes lecturing, devising media training for voluntary organisations, work for national radio and writing articles for a diverse range of national newspapers and magazines (see **publishing, newspapers and magazines**). In 1998, she created and was launch editor of *Public Sector*, a weekly newspaper supplement for African Caribbean and Asian public-sector professionals. In 2000, it was shortlisted by, and commended in, the **Commission for Racial Equality** Race in the Media Awards for Best Specialist Publication. The Creative Collective acts as a conduit between the mainstream media, policy makers and black community groups. It is spearheading a media internship pilot targeted at ethnic minority media students in partnership with the Freedom Forum, an international media foundation, and the London College of Printing's media school. With backing from broadcaster Jon Snow (Channel 4 News) and Jonathan P. Hicks, political correspondent on the *New York Times*, the pilot will offer three African, Caribbean and Asian media students paid placements for three months on national and regional publications. The *Nottingham Evening Post* and *The Big Issue* have agreed to take part as part of a long-term diversity strategy. The Collective has just launched a quarterly glossy magazine called *Mediavibe* and is working with Black Britain On-line to develop a CD-ROM and website to facilitate more racially inclusive programmes on **television** and stories in the print press.

Select bibliography

Wilson, M. and Francis, J. (1997) *Raised Voices*, Mind Publications.

YINKA SUNMONU

FRASER, NEIL *see* Mad Professor

Fraser-Munro, Ronald

b. 1963, Cheshire, England

writer, director, producer, performer, graphics–video artist

Ronald Fraser-Munro's multi-media and cross-platform work encompasses text, theatre, audio, **photography**, movement, video and the digital arts. Since 1985, his unique work has been distributed throughout Britain, mainland Europe and the USA. Fraser-Munro is concerned with new models for contemporary arts practice, individual empowerment and the political aspects of creativity. He has collaborated with artists and non-artists to create a series of independent and challenging art productions and projects. The focus of his work is the scrutiny and evaluation of man-made devices that control human society, culture and the

environment. A continuing theme is the role of Church, State and the military in shaping our existences and the exploration of the packaging, visual modification, costume and external dressing of the human form to convey societal, cultural or political messages. Recent works have involved an engagement with the media (in its widest sense) as a tool or additional canvas to express and distribute ideas. Fraser-Munro employs the attitude of 'By Any Media Necessary' in creating his work and believes that the artist and the individual have a duty to question, observe, explore and comment upon the human condition, development and demise. Ronald Fraser-Munro is CEO of K3 Media (Contemporary Art, Culture and Media Production). He works extensively with individuals and artists through the K3 CDE Workshops to encourage expression and creativity through art. His key works include: *Hey Up Oswald!* (1993); *Vague – the Naked Shroud* (1995); *Quack F-M!* (1994); *LSD TV!* (1996); and his forthcoming *Millennium Trilogy* (*Manwoe, Nerodamus Rex* and *Anatomy of a Schwartze*).

CATHERINE UGWU

From Negative Stereotype to Positive Image

'From Negative Stereotype to Positive Image' (1993) was one of the first exhibitions to explore recent debates about **photography**, anthropology and the representation of race. Originated by Birmingham Central Library, the exhibition was developed as a response to questions raised by the presence of large numbers of negative, pre-conceived or primitivist 'ethnographic' images and a general absence of positive, contemporary images of people of African Caribbean origin in the Library's massive photographic collections. It presented the work of four Birmingham photographers, Sir Benjamin Stone (1838–1914), Ernest Dyche (1887–1973), Vanley **Burke** (1951–) and Claudette **Holmes** (1962–). Each produced images of people of African Caribbean origin at different moments in time in response to a range of social and economic, personal and political forces. Their images were displayed alongside books, periodicals and other contextual material. In addition to co-curating the project, Holmes was also commissioned to produce a new body of work for the exhibition. The exhibition, first shown in Birmingham Central Library, then toured to venues in the UK and USA. An archive of material relating to it is held at Birmingham Central Library.

Further reading

Edwards, E. (1996) 'From Negative Stereotype to Positive Image', *Photography Quarterly* 68: 16–20.

Goodhall, P. (ed.) (1996) 'Re-thinking representation: photography, visual anthropology and the diaspora', Conference Papers, Watershed, Bristol.

James, P. (1997) 'Ethnographic images in Birmingham Central Library', *History of Photography* 21(1) (spring): 81 (special issue on 'Anthropology and Colonial Endeavour', ed. Elizabeth Edwards).

Morris, A. (1993) 'From Negative Stereotype to Positive Image', *Autograph* 94: 2–3.

PETER JAMES

From Two Worlds

'From Two Worlds' was one of the first exhibitions of black British **visual artists** to attempt to articulate a specific theme, rather than merely be a survey show. The theme chosen by the curators, three from the Whitechapel and three black artists, was that of cultural synthesis. They argued that the artists on show synthesised their original and their host cultures. The artists exhibiting included Rasheed **Araeen**, Sonia **Boyce**, Lubaina **Himid**, Gavin **Jantjes** and Keith **Piper**. Despite the fact that 'From Two Worlds' set a precedent for themed rather than 'visibility' shows, the actual theme it chose was criticised heavily at the time. Many of the artists made no reference in their work to an imagined or real originary culture. Additionally, the presence of the core of black artists suggested that this was another survey show with a hastily added theme. Furthermore, the concept of synthesis, which was popularly used to analyse the works of black and Asian artists in the 1950s and 1960s, was

coming to be seen as simplistic and soon would be replaced by concepts such as hybridity.

Further reading

Whitechapel Art Gallery (1986) *From Two Worlds*, exhibition catalogue.

NIRU RATNAM

Fun-da-mental

Fun-da-mental were formed in 1991 by Bradford-born Aki Nawaz, co-founder of **Nation Records**. They combined a strong image with lyrics that sought to put across strong political messages without resorting to simplistic sloganeering. Fun-da-mental have received praise and criticism in almost equal amounts from the British media. Singles such as 'Wrath of the black man' and 'Dog tribe' have sought to promote unity between Afro-Caribbeans and Asians, exploring the similar experiences and shared goals of both in combatting racism, and the group's line-up reflects this ideal. Their debut album *Seize the Time*, released in 1994, mixed the directness and intensity of rap with **Bollywood** soundtracks, and began to highlight Fun-da-mental's ability to link local struggles with global events, both musically and lyrically. Fun-da-mental's second album was a collection of instrumental remixes of *Seize the Time* and, in 1998, they released *Erotic Terrorism*, which was poorly received by both the media and any potential audiences, who found it easier to dismiss the band rather than engaging with the issues raised by them. Fun-da-mental's importance in opening the door for acts such as **Asian Dub Foundation** and **Black Star Liner** is hugely important, as is the innovative nature of their **music** and lyrics.

ANDY WOOD

funky dreds

The collective **Soul II Soul** consisted of a sound system, DJs, designers, dancers and singers. Originally known as Jah Rico, the North London 'sound' was managed by Master B and Papa

Harvey. The partners eventually changed their street names to **Jazzie B** and Daddae Harvey, respectively. In an attempt to establish an identity for the Soul II Soul DJ crew, Jazzie B and another member of the collective, Aitch, created the Funky Dred hairstyle of dreadlocks on the crown of the head and shaved back and sides for its crew members. They believed it symbolised the roots of **reggae** culture and the urban **dance** scene. It was adopted by black British men, and some women, across the country and internationally. In March 1986, graphic designer Derek Yates was commissioned by Jazzie B and Daddae Harvey to create a T-shirt for the Soul II Soul crew featuring 'the funky dred head'. The graphic detail became the figurehead of the Soul II Soul ideology. The symbol comprised a black male head with a funky dred hairstyle and goatee beard, round sunglasses and earphones, apparently a portrait of Harvey. In 1987, the first Soul II Soul outlet opened at 142 Camden High Street, London. The collective established its own range of clothing designed by Nicolai Bean (Jennifer Lewis) and accessory merchandise. The funky dred head was featured on badges, T-shirts, hats, bags and knitted jumpers. In 1989, a second shop was launched at 147 Tottenham Court Road.

CAROL TULLOCH

Future Pilot AKA

b. Glasgow

musician

Future Pilot AKA is the pseudonym chosen by Glaswegian Sushil K. Dade. Dade was originally the bassist in the Soup Dragons, who released their first single in 1986. The Soup Dragons were at the fore of a new generation of young independent guitar bands being championed by the **music** press and Dade, as an Asian British musician, was one of only a handful of non-white faces involved in the scene. The Soup Dragons initially utilised a fast, punk-pop sound but evolved into a more dance-orientated outfit in the early 1990s. The Soup Dragons split up in the mid-1990s and Dade began recording and producing as Future Pilot AKA. The singles took on the concept of 1970s dub soundclashes with titles such as 'Future Pilot AKA versus the Revolutionary Corps of Teenage Jesus', and, although they were only released as limited pressings, Future Pilot AKA received enthusiastic reviews and the singles quickly became collectors' items. A lengthy list of the cool and credible lined up to work with Dade, including **Cornershop**'s Tjinder **Singh**, who appears on Future Pilot AKA's debut album released in 1999. His second album, *Tiny Waves Mighty Sea*, was released in 2001.

ANDY WOOD

G

Gabrielle

b. 1970, London, England

singer, songwriter

Gabrielle, born Louise Gabrielle Bobb, started singing for free in West End nightclubs, while temping during the day to make a living. She had always dreamed of becoming a singer. Her first song 'Dreams' was released as a demo but failed to make the Top 100. It was later re-released in 1993 and was entered in the *Guinness Book of Hit Singles* as the highest ever chart entry for a debut female act. It eventually reached number one. Through 1993 to 1994, Gabrielle wore an eye patch over her right eye to hide a squint. It became her trademark look, although the squint was eventually corrected through surgery. She is credited with releasing nine singles – five of which were Top 10 hits – and two albums in three years. In 1994, she won the Brit Award for the best newcomer, and, in 1997, this was followed by another Brit Award, this time for best female artist. Her third album *Rise* became her first number one album in the UK and spawned three Top 10 hits. It also won Best UK album at the MOBO Awards 2000 and the title track from the album became her second number one. Many of her songs are autobiographical, conveying emotions of determination and hope. Gabrielle is influenced by artists like Marvin Gaye, Michael Jackson, Diana Ross, Duran Duran and Lisa Stansfield. Her liking of such a diverse range of music is present in her own recordings, which appeal to both R'n'B and pop fans. In 2001

Gabrielle released 'Out of Reach' for the popular film (see **film and cinema**) *Bridget Jones's Diary*.

Select discography

Gabrielle (2000) *Rise*.
—— (1996) *Gabrielle*.
—— (1993) *Find Your Way*.

RAFIEL SUNMONU

Gavin, Jamila

b. 1941, India

writer, musician

Gavin wrote her first children's book entitled *The Magic Orange Tree and Other Stories* (1979) at the age of thirty-eight. Raised in India and Britain, she was aware of being excluded from stories and writes stories for children that are inclusive and reflect the multicultural society in which we live. Some of her titles – *The Mango Tree* (1998), *Out of India* (1997) and *Grandpa Chatterji* (1994) – highlight cultural diversity. One of her most loved books is *Digital Dan* (1984). In 2000, she published *Coram Boy*, a saga set in eighteenth-century England, which is aimed at children aged twelve plus. Gavin trained as a musician and attended Trinity College of Music as a junior exhibitor. She went on to become a piano scholar there. She worked in radio as a studio manager with BBC Radio and went on to become Production Assistant/Director for Music and Arts at BBC TV. The author of over nineteen books, she has been shortlisted for many major book awards, including the *Guardian* Award for Children's Fiction.

Selected bibliography

Gavin, J. (2000) *Coram Boy*, London: Mammoth.
—— (1994) *The Wheel of Surya*, Oxford: Heinemann New Windmills.
—— (1986) *Stories from the Hindu World*, London: Macdonald.
—— (1984) *Digital Dan*, London: Methuen Children's Books.
—— (1983) *Kamla and Kate*, London: Methuen Children's Books.
—— (1982) *Double Dare and Other Stories*, London: Methuen Children's Books.
—— (1979) *The Magic Orange Tree and Other Stories*, London: Methuen.

YINKA SUNMONU

Gayle, Mike

b. 1970, Birmingham, England

writer, journalist

Educated at Lordswood Boys' School, Birmingham, Gayle had a range of careers on his mind when he started thinking about what to do with his life, but writing books was not one of them. He thought about social work and teaching before deciding on **music** journalism. His first foray into writing was for the university magazine (see **publishing, newspapers and magazines**). He then went on edit a music fanzine and joined a Birmingham listings magazine. Gayle moved to London and embarked on a postgraduate diploma in journalism. While freelancing, he started to write for the recently launched *Bliss*; they needed an agony uncle and Gayle got the job. *My Legendary Girlfriend* (1998), his first novel, was started because he thought he had a story to tell that people would like, saying that the universality of getting dumped – the wallowing in self-pity, the pining, the lack of dignity – had too much comic potential not to write. Gayle's work thus far is characterised by the way he uses relationships, which gives his novels a popular feel. One critic called him a romantic novelist and Gayle has been dubbed in the media as the male Helen Fielding.

As a freelance journalist he has contributed to the *Sunday Times*, the *Guardian*, *The Times*, the *Express*, *FHM*, *Cosmopolitan*, *More*, *B*, *Just Seventeen*, *Bliss*, the *Scotsman* and *Top of the Pops* magazine. Gayle's subsequent novels *Mr Commitment* (1999) and *Turning Thirty* (2000) have also achieved notable success. His work has been published in Europe, Australia and North America.

Select bibliography

Gayle, M. (2000) *Turning Thirty*, London: Flame.
—— (1999) *Mr Commitment*, London: Flame.
—— (1998) *My Legendary Girlfriend*, London: Flame.

YINKA SUNMONU

Ghir, Kulvinder

actor, comedian

Ghir has worked in **theatre**, film (see **film and cinema**) and **television**, playing roles as diverse as Aslam in the 1986 film *Rita, Sue and Bob too*, Terry Singh in the television series *Body and Soul* and a part in Brecht's *Caucasian Chalk Circle* with the Théâtre de Complicité. Although he has appeared in *The Real McCoy* and the popular television medical drama *Holby City*, as well as making a guest appearance in *The Bill*, since 1998 Ghir has become best known as part of the enormously popular ***Goodness Gracious Me*** comedy team, along with Meera **Syal**, Nina **Wadia** and Sanjeev **Bhaskar**. He played the role of Ali's servant in the television production of *Arabian Nights* (2000).

ALISON DONNELL

Ghosh, Amitav

b. 1956, Calcutta, India

novelist, journalist

Ghosh grew up in East Pakistan, Sri Lanka, Iran and India, and after graduating from the

University of Delhi he went to Oxford where he obtained his D.Phil. in Social Anthropology in 1982. This was based on field work completed in Egypt, and *In an Antique Land* (1992), a work of non-fiction, is based on this research. He is the author of three novels, *The Circle of Reason* (1986), *The Shadow Lines* (1988), and *The Calcutta Chromosome* (1996). Like other contemporary Indian novelists, (Sara Suleiri, Amit **Chaudhuri**), Ghosh's texts move between continents and time zones. *The Shadow Lines* describes the relationship between the narrator's family in Calcutta and Dhaka, and an English family in London. It is concerned with the presentation of history and the forces of nationalism and it represents the arbitrariness and potential violence of the 'shadow line' that is drawn between people and nations. *The Calcutta Chromosome* also crosses continents, taking place in Calcutta and New York. It combines science fiction and high Victorian melodrama, and weaves between past, present and future. Ghosh lives in New York and teaches at Columbia University.

Select bibliography

Ghosh, A. (1996) *The Calcutta Chromosome: a Novel of Fevers, Delirium and Discovery,* London: Picador.
—— (1992) *In an Antique Land*, London: Granta.
—— (1988) *The Shadow Lines*, London: Bloomsbury.
—— (1986) *The Circle of Reason*, London: Granta.

SARA SALIH

Gideon, Llewella

b.1967, London, England

comedian

Comedy is a difficult entertainment genre to break into at the best of times and to be a black British female aiming for national recognition poses its own particular challenges. There is a school of thought that suggests that black British comedy (see **comedians**), however that may be defined, cannot break into the mainstream due to difficulties in trying to understand the language and innuendo. Gideon challenges what can be seen as this stereotypical attitude. Significantly, she featured in the first radio programme in Britain featuring an all black cast. *The Airport*, broadcast in 1995 and 1996 on Radio 4, was a comedy sketch programme based on the goings on at the airport. It featured fellow comedians Felix Dexter, Roger Griffiths, Robbie Gee, Josephine Melville and Jo Martin, several of whom also contributed to the scriptwriting. Gideon has also toured with her one-woman-show, *The Little Big Woman*, where she entertained the audience with sketches and jokes around relationships, politics, love and the office bitch. A four-part series (with Lynn Peters) entitled *The Little Big Woman Radio Show* was broadcast on Radio 4 in 2001. Along with Gina **Yashere**, Angie Le Mar and Angie Greaves, she is carving out her own brand of comedy that has led to recognition within the black community and work with 'The Write Thing' in many of their shows. She has appeared in the cult comedy **television** show *Absolutely Fabulous* as Nurse Orla Brady, and in the Spice Girls films *Spice World* (1997) and *Different for Girls* (1996). Gideon, who has worked for the **Voice** newspaper, is a director of Jewel Impact Productions.

Select bibliography

Gideon, L. (1999) *The Little Big Woman Book*, London: Desert Hearts.

YINKA SUNMONU

Gifford, Zerbanoo

b. 1950, Calcutta, India

writer, campaigner

Zerbanoo Gifford came to England from India with her parents at the age of three. She was educated at Roedean, Watford College of Technology, the London School of Journalism and the Open University. Gifford's first book, *The Golden Thread* (1990), documented the achievements of Asian women, in particular their contribution to British society, and featured women such as Meera **Syal**, Madhur **Jaffrey** and Naseem **Khan**. She has since published several educational books that draw attention to the positive presence of Asians in Britain, including *Asian Presence in Europe* (1995) and *Dadabhai Naoroji on the first Asian MP in 1892*, which were both published by **Mantra Publications**. She has always been very active in the charitable sector and has been a Director of the Charities Aid Foundation India, as well as of Anti-Slavery International.

In addition to her extensive charity work and writing, Gifford has worked in politics. She was the first Asian woman councillor for the Liberal Party, has three times contested parliamentary seats and, in 1986, was asked to chair the Liberal Commission looking into ethnic minority involvement in British life. In 1989, she was awarded the Nehru Centenary Award for her work in international politics. In 1991, she was nominated for the Women of Europe Award. She is Founder and Honorary Director of the Asha Foundation, dedicated to the representation, support and enablement of all minority communities within Britain.

Select bibliography

Gifford, Z. (1995) *Asian Presence in Europe*, London: Mantra Publishing.
—— (1990) *The Golden Thread*, London: Pandora Press.
—— (1996) *Thomas Clarkson*, London: Anti-Slavery International.

ALISON DONNELL

Gift, Roland

singer, actor

Gift joined Andy Cox and David Steele in 1983 to form one of the most popular pop bands of the 1980s, Fine Young Cannibals. Their two albums, *Fine Young Cannibals* (1986) and *The Raw and the Cooked* (1988), were chart successes. Both 'She Drives Me Crazy' and 'Good Thing' were number one successes from the acclaimed second album. During this period, Gift received critical acclaim for his music and was on the cover of *Rolling Stone* magazine. The band recorded a 1980s cover of the Buzzcocks' 'Ever Fallen in Love?' for the film *Something Wild* and were subsequently approached by director Barry Levinson to compose the soundtrack for his *Tin Men* (1987). Gift also took to film (see **film and cinema**), appearing in *Absolute Beginners* (1986) and Hanif **Kureishi**'s *Sammy and*

Rosie Get Laid (1987), and was more or less out of public view until his appearance at the Edinburgh Festival in 1999 where the *Observer* commented on 'the lasting purity of his voice'. His solo album, *Long Day's Journey into Night*, was released in 2001.

ALISON DONNELL

Gilroy, Beryl

b. 1924, Springlands, Guyana; d. 2001, London, England

teacher, educationalist, writer, ethno-psychologist

Beryl Gilroy left home for London University in 1951, already a well-respected teacher in pre-independent British Guiana. In the UK institutional racism denied her professional opportunities and she was forced to find work as a ladies' maid and a washer-up at Joe Lyons Café. Her eventual employment as a young teacher in a multicultural school in London, where she battled against the system, was to fuel a sense of anger in her. This resulted in her ground-breaking, but nevertheless good humoured, autobiography *Black Teacher* (1976). Her continued services to education were marked by an honorary doctorate from the University of North London in 1995.

Gilroy was one of the Caribbean writers who took direct action to oust racist materials from the classroom by publishing over sixteen books for children in the 1960s and 1970s. The 1980s saw the release of her adult fiction and she began to attract critical attention as a writer, especially for *Frangipani House* (1986) and *Boy Sandwich* (1989). She writes contemporary and historical fiction, and has published *Sunlight on Sweet Water* (1994) – an evocative memoir of Afro-Guyanese village life. She wrote a novel of migration *In Praise of Love and Children* in the 1960s, but it was rejected by publishers (only finally being published by **Peepal Tree Press** in 1995). Gilroy received recognition as a creative writer, this time in the USA with an award presented at Florida International University in 1996. Her creative work reveals a lifelong exploration of cultural dislocation, which has been matched by an academic interest: a Ph.D.

in ethno-psychology was conferred by Century University in 1987.

Select bibliography

Gilroy, B. (1996) *Gather the Faces*, Leeds: Peepal Tree.

—— (1996) *Inkle and Yarico*, Leeds: Peepal Tree.

—— (1994) *Black Teacher*, London: Bogle L'Ouverture (first published 1976, Cassell).

—— (1994) *Sunlight on Sweet Water*, Leeds: Peepal Tree.

Further reading

Anim-Addo, J. (1996) *Framing the Word: Gender and Genre in Caribbean Women's Writing*, London: Whiting and Birch.

SANDRA COURTMAN

Gilroy, Paul

b. 1956, Bethnal Green, London

academic

Formerly a DJ, writer, musician and Professor of Sociology at Goldsmiths College, University of London, Gilroy is now Professor of Sociology and African American Studies at Yale University. While in Britain, Gilroy established a reputation as the leading analyst of the cultural politics of 'race'. His first major publication *'There Ain't no Black in the Union Jack'* – which takes its title from the popular expression of British racist, anti-immigration sentiment – was arguably the first study to locate and historicise the presence of black people in British cultural life. Gilroy's first book addresses the concern that black British subjects are largely seen as either problems or victims, and argues for the necessity of 'representing a black presence outside these categories'. 'Racism' Gilroy argues, 'rests on the ability to contain blacks in the present, to repress and deny the past' (1987b: 12). Gilroy's characteristic mode of cultural analysis, which gained international recognition and acclaim with the publication of **The Black Atlantic**, is clearly evident in *'There Ain't no Black in the Union Jack'*. By

focusing 'on how "race" and racism articulate various forms of action, some of which are not usually dignified by the labels of formal politics' (1987b: 13), Gilroy is able to scrutinise the processes and operations of various forms of anti-racist *cultural* politics, while additionally enabling critical analysis of the expressive culture of black Britain. A key aspect of Gilroy's study, and one that has subsequently necessitated a more complex theorisation of cultural **difference** and cultural identity, is his compelling (anti-essentialist) assessment that black expressive culture in Britain 'shows that culture does not develop along ethnically absolute lines but in complex, dynamic patterns of syncretism in which new definitions of what it means to be black emerge from raw materials provided by black populations elsewhere in the diaspora' (1987b: 13). Gilroy's own use of the critical and theoretical language of prominent African American intellectuals, such as James Baldwin, Ralph Ellison and W.E.B. Du Bois (through use of concepts such as 'double consciousness', the 'colour line'), establishes precisely the global affiliations and connections that form the basis of his most influential work, *The Black Atlantic: Modernity and Double Consciousness*. Highly regarded as the most rigorous account of **diaspora aesthetics**, and winner of the Before Columbus Foundation's American Book Award in 1994, *The Black Atlantic* develops and refines Gilroy's analysis of the syncretic dimensions of black vernacular cultures. The book also provides a ground-breaking re-assessment of modernity, in which the observations of black thinkers are shown to offer 'other bases for ethics and aesthetics than those which appear immanent within the versions of modernity' that 'myopically Eurocentric theories construct' (1993a: 45). *Small Acts*, published in the same year, anthologises a number of Gilroy's shorter essays (including interviews with Toni Morrison and bell hooks, and articles on Spike Lee and the black British boxer Frank Bruno) and maintains his commitment to 'interpreting black cultural forms politically without reducing them to politics alone' (1993b: 15). Gilroy's most recent book, *Between Camps: Nations, Cultures and the Allure of Race* (published in the US under the title *Against Race: Imagining Political Culture beyond the Color Line*) extends analysis of race and 'race-thinking' through consideration of fascist and neo-fascist cultures. Perplexed by the specularisation and commodification of blackness, Gilroy attempts to advance democratic political culture beyond its preoccupations with skin colour, racial purity, and problematic concepts of national identity.

Select bibliography

Gilroy, P. (2000) *Against Race: Imagining Political Culture beyond the Color Line*, Cambridge, MA: Harvard University Press.

—— (2000) *Between Camps: Nations, Cultures and the Allure of Race*, Harmondsworth: Penguin.

—— (1997) *Between Camps: Race and Culture in Postmodernity*, London: Goldsmiths, University of London.

—— (1995) *The Status of Difference: from Epidermalisation to Nano-politics*, London: Goldsmiths, University of London.

—— (1993a) *Small Acts: Thoughts on the Politics of Black Cultures*, London: Serpent's Tail.

—— (1993b) *The Black Atlantic: Modernity and Double Consciousness*, London: Verso.

—— (1987a) *Problems in Anti-racist Strategy*, London: Runnymede Trust.

—— (1987b) *'There Ain't no Black in the Union Jack': the Cultural Politics of Race and Nation*, London: Hutchinson.

LYNNETTE TURNER

Givanni, June Ingrid

b. Georgetown, Guyana

programming consultant

June Givanni was born in Guyana and educated in the UK. She has two social sciences degrees and has also studied French, but her passion has been to highlight the contribution of African, Caribbean and Asian film-makers to world cinema. To this end, she has worked as a writer, consultant programmer and curator for **television** and film festivals (see **film and cinema**). Givanni's career in media began when she joined the **Greater London Council** in 1983 and co-ordinated the Third Eye Film Festival, curating the Anti-Racist Film Programme that

brought the work of black and Third World film-makers into greater focus. She has undertaken many studies and argued for the creation of specialist distribution circuits for such products during the 1980s. Her article *In Circulation*, part of ICA Documents, discussed this further. Givanni worked at the **British Film Institute**, where she created and managed the African Caribbean Unit. She compiled the first comprehensive directory of black and Asian films in the UK (1987, revised 1992), and set up the specialist journal ***Black Film Bulletin***. Givanni also organised the film and television section of the nationwide AFRICA 95 festival, which focused on the work of African artists. She has been a guest curator for several international festivals, including: 'Images Caraibes', Martinique (1988–92); Creteil Film Festival, Paris (1989); 'Africa at the Pictures', London (1990); São Paulo Short Film Festival, Brazil (1997) and Kerala International Film Festival, India (1998).

In 1998, she joined the programming team of the Toronto International Film Festival and programmed its *Planet Africa* section for three years. She has been involved in film development and has worked closely with the director Euzhan Palcy. Givanni has lectured at several UK universities and has published numerous articles on cinema and television. She is currently a programme officer at the Independent Television Commission.

Select bibliography

Givanni, J. (ed.) (2000) *Symbolic Narrative/African Cinema*, London: BFI.

—— (1998) *Black Cinema from Europe*, London: Channel 4.

—— (1995) *Remote Control: Black Participation in British TV*, London: BFI.

SUMAN BHUCHAR

Glynn, Martin

b. 1957, UK

writer, poet, theatre director, arts development consultant, cultural activist

Martin Glynn is a celebrated poet and writer. He

has produced and directed performance works, written plays for **theatre** and radio, and developed texts for live performance and the screen. Glynn is an established Arts Development Consultant and workshop facilitator. He has initiated and implemented development schemes and creative-writing programmes for arts institutions, schools, prisons and libraries. Working with young people, special needs groups and culturally diverse constituents, his work addresses issues of empowerment. He has worked in Britain, mainland Europe, North America and the Caribbean. Glynn is the founder and Director of BLAK (UK) (Being Liberated and Knowledgeable), an organisation that aims to use the arts as a tool for personal transformation. Forming partnerships with a range of national and international institutions, BLAK (UK) develops programmes and provides work and training opportunities for writers and artists.

CATHERINE UGWU

Goldie

b. 1966, Walsall, England

performer, producer, DJ, entrepreneur

Since the release of *Timeless* in 1995, Goldie has often been referred to as the first 'superstar' of **jungle**. Goldie was one of the first producers of this music to gain a major recording contract at a time when breakbeat/jungle was still very much an underground phenomenon. Midlands-born Goldie, who spent most of his childhood in a series of care institutions and foster homes, originally had a background in the early **hip hop** and graffiti tagging scene. In 1990, he became involved in the growing jungle scene and recorded several singles for the Reinforced label under the name Rufige Cru. Discovered by **Grooverider**, one of Goldie's original inspirations, Goldie began to make a name for himself, collaborating with **A Guy Called Gerald**, Rob Playford and, on his second album *Saturnz Return* (1998), rapper KRS-1. Goldie also runs the Metalheadz club and record label, which has released singles by Alex Reece, Lemon D and Doc Scott among others. In 1998, the **Black Audio Film Collective** made a film about

Goldie's life, *When Saturn Returnz*, which was premièred on Channel 4 the same year.

ANDY WOOD

Goodness Gracious Me

Goodness Gracious Me began in July 1996 on Radio 4 but, due to its popularity, moved to **television** and, although initially screened on BBC 2 at 11.15 p.m., was later aired at peak time. The *Goodness Gracious Me* team toured the country in the spring of 1999, comprising Kulvinder **Ghir**, Meera **Syal**, Nina **Wadia** and Sanjeev **Bhaskar**, with producer Anil Gupta. They are considered by some to have created a 'British/Asian Comedy' genre. Attracting both praise and criticism, the programme has won awards from the **Commission for Racial Equality** alongside commendation and criticism from the UK's Asian communities. While for some it shows the increasing self confidence of British-Asians, for others it allows the white English yet another opportunity to laugh at the UK's Asian communities. Yet the show often relies on Asian and English jokes being turned around, such as in the case of one of the programme's best-known sketches 'Going out for an English'. The series also highlights the amount of racism experienced by many Asian performers due to the apparent need to be accepted by a 'white majority' audience. When the audience majority was thought to comprise Asians, *Goodness Gracious Me* was considered an 'Asian comedy', yet when found to be 80 per cent white it became 'mainstream'.

SAMINA ZAHIR

Grant, Eddy

b. 1948, Plaisance, Guyana

musician, songwriter, producer

Edmond Montague Grant was born in Guyana and moved to London with his family in 1960. Trained as a pianist, guitar player and trumpeter, Grant's musical aspirations peaked during the 1960s when he, along with four friends, formed the mildly successful band The Equals. After releasing several singles that did not fare well, the group finally found success with the release of 'Baby Come Back'. In 1971, Grant became ill and left the band. Several years later, Grant changed his image from a bleached blonde punkster to a dreadlocked pop icon and established Coach House Studios and his own record label Ice Records. Grant also began songwriting and producing and his **music** is best described as an eclectic blend of rock, soca, and funk. In 1977 Grant made his solo debut with *Message Man* and his first hit, 'Living On The Front Line', reached number 11 in the British charts. In 1982 Grant released his biggest hit 'I Don't Wanna Dance', succeeded by 'Electric Avenue' which was successful both in Britain and America. Another of Grant's more memorable songs, 'Romancing The Stone', was written for the film (see **film and cinema**) of the same title. Six years later, Grant released 'Gimme Hope Jo'anna', a song which expressed a strong anti-apartheid sentiment. In 1993 Grant returned to the charts with 'Soca Baptism' from the album of the same name, and in 2000 he presented fans with his *Greatest Hits Collection*. Grant's love of music goes beyond songwriting and producing; he is also a collector of music and is reported to have amassed one of the world's largest collections of calypso music.

TRACEY L. WALTERS

Greater London Authority

The Greater London Authority (GLA) may be defined as a strategic city government established to serve the interest of Londoners. It was set up in April 2000 when an interim team was put in place to prepare the foundations for the new government. Ken Livingstone became the first Mayor of London when he was elected on 4 May 2000 and one of the things the mayor is committed to is raising the artistic and cultural profile of London. The capital is steeped in a rich history that includes **theatre**, fashion (see **fashion and design**), museums, **literature**, design and heritage. The contribution of ethnic minority (see **ethnic**

minorities) groups to this cultural profile in London is gradually being recognised and the Mayor is aiming to promote this. Indeed, the GLA, through its Cultural Strategy arm, not only aims to represent London's cultural interests on a regional, national and international level but to raise the profile of ethnic minority arts and culture. The priority is to ensure that the cultural diversity of London is represented. In October 2000, the GLA launched Black History Month London 2000, with readings from poet Benjamin **Zephaniah** and a specially commissioned website. September 2000 saw the announcement of a review to safeguard the future of the **Notting Hill Carnival** following the deaths of Abdul Bhatti and Greg Watson. The report, while examining aspects of public safety in great depth, also highlights the educational and cultural aspects of **carnival**, its growth as an international attraction and its contribution to **black British** culture. Further work by the GLA will include project development and promoting opportunities in the arts and cultural industries. Training is another topic on the agenda and the GLA will support a number of arts and cultural centres across London, namely: the Rich Mix Centre, Tower Hamlets; the Stephen **Lawrence** Technocentre, Deptford; the Bernie Grant Centre for performing arts, Tottenham; and the **Talawa Theatre Company**.

Further reading

GLA (2000) *Without Prejudice? Exploring Ethnic Differences in London*, London: GLA.

YINKA SUNMONU

Greater London Council

The Greater London Council (GLC) was established by the London Government Act of 1963. During the first seventeen years, power regularly shuttled between Labour and Conservative administrations, and although black people loyally supported Labour at election times, they were rarely active in party politics themselves. However, when the Labour Party began to adopt more proactive policies on racism, more black people became politically active. In the May 1974 local elections, the number of Labour councillors from **ethnic minorities** rose from nil to ten, and the Conservatives trailed with two. The next year the Trinidadian David (later Lord) Pitt became the first black chairman of the GLC. In 1981, Labour radical Ken Livingstone became leader of the GLC. Developing his administration on a left-wing platform he courted much controversy. He introduced the Fares Fair policy (cutting London transport fares) and an ethnic minorities committee. The administration also massively increased arts spending for ethnic arts programmes from £10,000 in 1981 to £2.5 million by 1985. Margaret Thatcher's government appeared determined to abolish the GLC and a bill for abolition eventually went through Parliament. Abolition was timetabled for midnight 31 March 1986. The last year of the GLC was largely dominated by attempts to find jobs for its 22,000 strong staff and, after abolition, most of its services were transferred to government-appointed bodies.

Further reading

Forrester, A., Lansley, S. and Pauley, R. (1985) *Beyond our Ken: a Guide to the Battle for London*, London: Fourth Estate.
Livingstone, K. (1986) *If Voting Changed Anything They'd Abolish it*, London: Collins.

ANDREA ENISUOH

Greensleeves

Greensleeves began as a record shop in 1975, with the record label being founded in 1977. Greensleeves specialised in releasing **reggae** and, with early releases including albums by Augustus Pablo and Barington Levy, rapidly attained a reputation for being a quality reggae label. As the 1980s progressed, Greensleeves diversified its sound to take on board developments within reggae, working with producers from the **dancehall** scene such as Linval Thompson. Other Greensleeves artists included Scientist, Black Uhuru, Burning Spear and Yellowman, and Greensleeves had a number of hits throughout the 1980s including **Tippa**

Irie's 'Hello darling' in 1986. As well as releasing records, Greensleeves has also distributed and licensed a number of other reggae labels. The label has continued to expand and thrive with releases including Sizzla, **Jah Shaka**, Alpha and Omega, and Beenie Man, who reached the UK Top 10 in 1998 with his song 'Who am I?' Greensleeves has consistently achieved crossover chart hits while maintaining a high-quality artist roster and catalogue, including its range of mid-priced samplers and compilations, which have helped bring reggae in all its diverse forms to a wider audience in the UK.

ANDY WOOD

Gregory, Joy

b. 1959, Bicester, Oxfordshire, England

photographer

Gregory studied at Manchester Polytechnic, completing her BA in communication, art and design in 1986. Her contribution to the Cameraworks exhibition 'Autoportraits' (1990) abandoned the soft layering that had characterised her work, for a direct approach to the exploration of the black face. Her later series *Objects of Beauty* (1995) deals with objects of femininity such as stockings and combs, shown against tape measures. This work examines the fact that no object exists free of a cultural context, and that beauty is a subjective, not universal, concept. Her most recent project *Memory and Skin* (1998), completed for 'Photo 98' in Huddersfield, is a multi-media mapping of the slave trade and the black diaspora. It presents photographs from Nantes, Rotterdam, the Caribbean and Haiti, with interviews and conversations with groups from Europe and the Caribbean, the project acts as a narrative, or passage through history.

Further reading

Sand, M. and McNeill, A. (eds) (1998) *Continental Drift: Europe Approaching*, New York and Munich: Prestel-Verlag.

Gupta, S. (1995) *Joy Gregory: Monograph*, London: Autograph.

FRANCIS SUMMERS

Grewal, Shani

b. 1958, Punjab, India

film director

Shani Grewal came to the UK as a child and grew up in West London. He graduated from Harrow College with a degree in film (see **film and cinema**) and **television** studies in 1982. His short film *Vengeance* (1984), made for 20th Century Fox, was shortlisted for Best Short Oscar in 1986. Grewal then worked as a studio director for a magazine show *Sunday East* on **Channel 4**, which was produced by H.O. **Nazareth**. As an independent film-maker, Grewal wrote and directed his debut feature *After Midnight* (1989), which starred Saeed **Jaffrey**, Hayley Mills and Ian Dury. The film, set in a Dublin hotel over the course of one night, tells of an old caretaker showing a new, younger one the ropes. As head of production for String of Pearls PLC, he produced, wrote and directed *Double X: the Name of the Game* (1992), featuring Norman Wisdom. His last film, *Guru in 7* (1998), was dubbed the 'Asian Alfie'. It created a stir as it depicted the leading man, Sanjay, bedding seven different women in seven days after he has been ditched by his girlfriend. Grewal has recently directed *Watching the Detectives* (2000), written by Meera **Syal** for Carlton Television, as part of the Single Voices series. He is working on a new thriller, *Crime of the Century*, and has a film script, *Paradise*, in development with the Yorkshire Media Production Agency.

SUMAN BHUCHAR

Griffiths, Derek

actor, presenter

Derek Griffiths first came to the attention of the **television**-viewing public as the presenter of the classic children's programme *Play School* in the 1960s. Griffiths continued this line with *Play Away* in the early 1970s, although by then he was also acting in the comedies *Up the Chastity Belt* and *Up Pompeii*, both screened in 1971. He later played Rex in *The Alf Garnett Saga* (1972), Johnny in *Don't Just Lie There Say Something* (1973) and Alex in *Rising Damp* (1980). After almost a twenty-year break, Griffiths returned in 1997 to play the role of Barry Ungulates in *Fierce Creatures*.

ALISON DONNELL

Griffiths, Donna

b. mid-1970s, England

live artist/performer, writer, researcher

Griffiths began making performances featuring herself and her mannequin Louise in larger than life, comic-book styles in 1995. In October 1996, Griffiths was chosen to be an **Institute of Contemporary Arts** (ICA) **Live Art** Attached Artist, culminating in an outside performance of *Donna and Louise's Grand Day Out in London* at the ICA, July 1997.

Griffiths's work covers historical, social and racial representations questioning contemporary black identity. Her performances explore fairy-tale narratives and stereotypical labelling of black people, using **television** soaps, **music** and other forms of contemporary culture as a resource. She has produced intervention performances within museums questioning the origins of ethnographic exhibits. In *Le Nouvelle Collection*, Nottingham Castle Museum and Art Gallery, April 1997, Griffiths appeared as a mystical Princess on a catwalk, aligning herself with ethnographic exhibits on display. *Princess Donna's Magical Kingdom* in Nottingham, October 1998, continued such explorations.

Griffiths writes for *Live Art Magazine* and *Artist's Newsletter*. She has worked independently with **Black Mime Theatre Company** in 1994 and 1995, Nottingham Playhouse on a hip hopera production in 1996 and has collaborated with other practitioners in community-based productions.

DONNA GRIFFITHS

Grooverider

DJ, producer, artist

Grooverider is best known for his skill as a DJ in the British **jungle** scene and has been intrinsic in discovering performers such as **Goldie** and **LTJ Bukem**, and giving them their first major forum through club nights such as Rage in the early to mid-1990s. Grooverider set up his own label, Prototype, and released an array of innovative and inventive singles by new artists who were being ignored by major record labels, traditionally wary of taking risks. Grooverider then licensed Prototype through Sony, releasing a compilation entitled *The Prototype Years*, which featured a mixture of new-comers and also established underground artists such as Dillinja and Lemon D along with two of his own tracks, recorded under the pseudonym Codename John. Grooverider has mainly concentrated on his DJing, presenting shows on Radio 1 and Kiss FM, and has held several residencies at Metalheadz. In 1998, however, Grooverider released his debut single as Grooverider, 'Rainbow of colour', and an album, *Mysteries Of Funk*, later in the same year.

ANDY WOOD

Gupta, Sneh

b. Kenya

actress

One of five children, Gupta travelled as a child in order to follow her father's teaching career, but she left home at seventeen to gain independence and study nursing. After winning Miss Anglia TV, Gupta worked on the popular **television** programme *Sale of the Century*. She later acted in the television series *Angels* and, most memorably, took the role of Princess Sushila in the film (see **film and cinema**) *The Far Pavilions*. Gupta also started her own production company.

ALISON DONNELL

Gupta, Sunetra

b. 1965, Calcutta, India

novelist, scientist

Sunetra Gupta divides her time between writing and researching infectious diseases at Oxford University. After spending her childhood in various African countries, she graduated from Princeton University in biology, and completed her Ph.D. in mathematical biology at Imperial College, London, in 1992. Her creative writing style – fluid, musical and rich in metaphors and literary allusions – as well as the elaborate plot structures, which she has been developing since her first novel, are among the elements that differentiate her writing from that of other South Asian writers in Britain. Her novels reflect both her Bengali family culture and her international background. *Memories of Rain* (1992), winner of the 1996 Sahitya Akademi Award, tells the story of a failed relationship between an Englishman and his Indian wife. In *The Glassblower's Breath* (1993), which narrates the wanderings of an Indian woman in London, Gupta's writing has been compared to Virginia Woolf's. An accidental scientific discovery in *Moonlight into Marzipan* (1995) gives the author the opportunity to explore issues of creation, love, death and betrayal.

Select bibliography

Gupta, S. (1995) *Moonlight into Marzipan*, London: Orion.
—— (1993) *The Glassblower's Breath*, London: Orion.
—— (1992) *Memories of Rain*, London: Phoenix House.

PAOLA MARCHIONNI

Gupta, Sunil

b. 1953, New Delhi, India

artist, curator, writer

In 1983 Sunil Gupta settled in London, pursued his career in **photography** and exhibited in the 'New Contemporaries'. Throughout the 1980s he was involved in various exhibitions promoting Asian photography, including 'Darshan' (1986), an exhibition of ten Asian photographers funded by the **Greater London Council** and held at Camerawork. In 1992 Gupta became a secretary at the Organisation of Visual Arts, which provided him with more opportunities to curate exhibitions. 'Disrupted Borders' (1993), which explored resistance to Eurocentric notions of culture, was his first visual project with **Institute of International Visual Arts** and their first exhibition. He represented Britain in the 'Havana Bienal' (1994) in Cuba and was exhibited in '**Transforming the Crown**' (1997). Gupta's second major undertaking was to explore issues of homosexuality and the attitudes of society. He was part of a curatorial team, which included **Panchayat**, for the exhibition 'Extreme Unction: HIV Aids, Ethnicity and Race' held at the Ikon Gallery in 1994. The show explored the Asian community's reaction towards AIDS and reflected the ideas that Gupta had written about earlier in two articles 'The hidden India' in *Gay Times* (1984) and 'Closetted by caste and class' in *Inside Asia* (1985).

PAULINE DE SOUZA

Gurnah, Abdulrazak

b. 1948, Zanzibar, Tanzania

novelist, essayist, lecturer

From the yarns of identity, sexuality, religion, migration and racism, novelist Abdulrazak Gurnah beautifully spins dark worlds that are as inspiring as they are unsettling. From the coast of East Africa to Britain, Gurnah's fictional worlds resonate with a plurality and fluidity characteristic of black British culture. *Memory of Departure* (1987) tells of a young

boy's ambition to leave home. Home bespeaks tormenting memories of a brother's death by fire, moral debasement, corrupt leadership and general disillusionment. Departure becomes freedom into a different kind of bondage. Schisms abound – between African, Arab and Indian, and between the 'haves' the 'have-nots' – impeding true love, friendship and self-realisation. The outlet becomes a self-charted journey, away from traditional kinship ties. Set in Kent, *Pilgrims Way* (1988) focuses on a mixed-race relationship. *Dottie* (1990) addresses notions of history in migration: identity effacement; displacement; rejection, dejection and decay; and their transposition onto younger generations. *Paradise* (1994), shortlisted for the 1994 **Booker Prize** and Whitbread Prize, lays bare power machinations by exploring meanings of family, honour, loyalty and servitude, while *Admiring Silence* (1996) plots a Zanzibar–London–Zanzibar journey, exposing the paradoxical meanings of 'home'. His latest novel, *By the Sea* (2001), tells the story of two men who leave Zanzibar and meet in an English seaside town. Gurnah was also editor of Heinemann's African Writers Series and has edited two collections of essays on African writing. He has worked as an academic throughout his writing career and is a Senior Lecturer in English at the University of Kent.

Select bibliography

Gurnah, A. (2001) *By the Sea*, London: Bloomsbury.
—— (1996) *Admiring Silence*, Middlesex: Penguin Books.
—— (1994) *Paradise*, Middlesex: Penguin Books.
—— (1990) *Dottie*, London: Jonathan Cape.
—— (1988) *Pilgrims Way*, London: Jonathan Cape.

PINKIE MEKGWE

H

hairdressing

The adage that a woman's hair is her crowning glory is apt for black women. Traditionally, the way a woman wore her hair in Africa was a mark of social and marital status, age and identity. The condition of one's hair for people of African origin is associated with the politics of race. Light-coloured skin equates to straight hair, dark skin to tight curls or 'nappy' hair, as the phrase is known.

Plaiting is the most traditional hairstyle used by black women. There are hundreds of styles and innumerable names for plaits including: silky dreads, Konkobi, braids, twists, Senegalese twists, cane row, French plaits, the equivalent of a basket weave and flat twist bun. Christine Allu of Hair by Alrems specialises in plaiting hair and creating new designs. Like many women before her who have embraced the art of hair plaiting, she was taught by elders as part of the African tradition while growing up. For the young, hair plaiting is a form of bonding between mother and child. The scent of hair pomade and resting between a mother's knees while she parts the scalp and plaits is not only a lived reality but an important subject in black literary fiction. It is a time when stories can be related and passed down, therefore also feeding the oral tradition. The existence of plaiting as an art form is increasingly being recognised and *BH* (Black Hair) and *Black Hair and Beauty* magazines have acknowledged this through special features on braids and an award for braiders in the BBH/Wahl awards. Men are also conscious about the styling of their hair, from the bald look sported by DJ Trevor Nelson to the Bantu knots favoured by singer Craig

David. An interesting history of the male hairstyle is related in *Men of Color – Fashion, History, Fundamentals*, by Lloyd Boston, published by Artisan. Although it is from an American perspective, it offers an insight into the importance of the barber shop in society, parallels hair trends that are familiar in Britain and provides a history of the methods used for straightening or texturising hair.

As well as hairdressing salons being viable businesses in black communities, hairdressers or barbers also fulfil a community function. People build up a rapport as they talk about the issues of the day and just chat. Their status as places for exchange and trust can be observed through the fact that some of the questionnaires for the *Voice* adoption survey were left at hairdressers for interested clients to fill in. In the early 1980s, Roots, an upmarket salon opened in Victoria in the Ecclestone Road area. They produced a glossy magazine of the same name. Other fashionable hairdressers, Splinters and Ebony of Mayfair, were in direct competition with each other on Maddox Street. This brand of salons produced high-quality hairdressing where professionalism was the key. St Clairs, one of the earlier black hairdressers, which opened on Bryanston Street W1, created its own range of hair care products that were sold in the salon and in markets. Winston Issacs, who had links with Splinters, is a pioneer in the black hairdressing field and has done much to promote the profession. Over the years, black hairdressing stars have emerged – Terry Jacques, Frank Bisson, Desmond Murray. Critics argue that Errol Douglas, who has been nominated for British Hairdresser of the Year at the British Hairdressing

Awards several times, is taking hairdressing and the concept of the black hairdressers into a new era. His salon based in Belgravia, his concept and his professionalism have made him successful in the mainstream.

The long-running Afro Hair and Beauty Show, which is held annually at the Alexandra Palace, provides an opportunity for the public to view the latest trends for black hair in the USA and Britain. They introduced a natural hair care section as part of the hair village. Arlene Scott of From the Root Salon is one of the pioneers of natural hair care and a return to traditional roots in Britain. Allu explains that African Caribbeans have traditionally cared for their hair using clay, coconut oil, shea butter and aloe vera. Henna has been used to colour hair. Many of these items have also found popularity in the West for their soothing and healing properties. The use of headwraps is an alternative to hair styling. African women have made the tying of these scarves a fine art, creating what can only be described as magnificent sculptures. It is an African tradition that is being embraced by black British women. The popularity is such that **X Press** has produced a headwrap calendar and they have become a fashion (see **fashion and design**) statement. Carmona, based in South London, is a company specialising in African style and silky wraps.

The subject of black hair may always be a contentious issue and one that is debated from the street to the academy. African American writer Alice Walker discusses the significance of hairstyles in her essay 'Oppressed hair puts a ceiling on the brain' (1988), while cultural theorist bell hooks takes up the issue in 'Straightening our hair' (1998). Within the British context, Kobena **Mercer**'s essay, 'Black hair/style politics', foregrounds the need to acknowledge hairstyling as a specific cultural activity whose practices change within particular historical and social contexts. Moreover, Mercer argues for hairstyling to be 'evaluated as a popular art form articulating a variety of aesthetic "solutions" to a range of "problems" created by ideologies of race and racism' (1994: 100). However there is a need to open up more discourse from a black British perspective on many of these issues relating to cultural, gender identities and the politics of hairstyling.

It is certainly important to trace the ways in which hairstyles have moved in step with the political climate. The most powerful example that can be traced to colonial times is the introduction of the straightening comb and chemicals for straightening hair, so that black women could mirror the styles of Europeans. The psychology of straightening hair can be such that some women hardly see the natural texture of their hair as they continue with the regular maintenance of retouching the roots. However, in the 1960s, the time of the Black Power movement and James Brown's 'Say it loud, I'm black and proud' anthem, the Afro became popular. In the 1970s, the jherri curl or wet look, which used a different chemical process to create loose curls similar to ringlets, became a trend that was fashionable for both sexes. Braids became popular with extensions and beads (traditionally cowrie), or ribbons and thread, attached to them. Yet, cultural critics who point to a link between black hairstyles and employment progression demonstrate that braids and dreadlocks did not find favour with some employers and there have been cases of discrimination brought against employers on this basis. There is a general argument that black women with straight hair have more opportunities in the workplace than those with other hairstyles. However, when Bo Derek stepped out of the water in the 1979 film (see **film and cinema**) *10* sporting braids with beads on the end, it was a catalyst for change. The late 1980s saw the emergence of the weave-on, where false hair could be attached to one's own. At first, hair wedges were attached with hairclips but the process has become very sophisticated now, with sewing on, plaiting and bonding. Xtension Masters, established by Tai Arogundade in 1992, is the leading weave salon in the country. A broader range of styles appeared in the 1990s. Women started to experiment with colour such as red and blonde. Relaxers remained popular throughout with manufacturers introducing brands that were not as harsh on the hair and contained herbal components. With some women realising the damaging effects perming could have on their hair, the natural look returned, not necessarily in the form of an Afro but as dreadlocks, twists and corkscrews. However, wearing natural hair is still seen by some as radical or brave instead of an expression of one's self, although there is a growing acceptance of the Afrocentric look that started to come back in the 1990s.

An examination of hairdressing among Asian Britain women requires a comparison between the styles and techniques applied in the East and West. Traditionally, Indian women were characterised by their long hair, which could stretch down to their waists and was either plaited or tied into a bun. Variations on this theme included tying part of the hair up and allowing wisps to drop freely. In some cases, the hair was adorned with flowers to enhance the style and make it aromatic. Perfumed oils and herbs were often created especially for one's coiffure to provide it with sheen, keep it healthy and add delicate smells. The use of camphire as a conditioner served to highlight and colour the hair. Asian British women, while wearing some of the styles mentioned above, have embraced the full range of hairstyles available in Britain from hair lengths that are short, medium and long. For the Sikh community the hair is of symbolic importance and men's hair is never cut but worn in a turban.

References

hooks, bell (1998) 'Straightening our hair', in J.D. Lester (ed.) *Diverse Identities: Classic Multicultural Essays*, Lincolnwood, IL: NTC Publishing.

Mercer, K. (1994) 'Black hair/style politics', in *Welcome to the Jungle: New Positions in Black Cultural Studies*, London: Routledge.

Walker, A. (1988) 'Oppressed hair puts a ceiling on the brain', in *Living by the Word: Selected Writings 1973–1987*, London: the Women's Press.

Further reading

Banks, I. (2000) *Hair Matters: Beauty, Power and Black Women's Consciousness*, New York: New York University Press.

Byrd, A. and Tharps, L.A. (2001) *Hairstory: Untangling the Roots of Black Hair in America*, New York: St Martins Press.

Johnson, P. and Harris, J. (2001) *Tenderheaded*, Pocket Books.

Little, B. (1996) *Good Hair*, New York: Simon & Schuster.

Sieber, R. and Herreman, F. (eds) (2000) *Hair in African Art and Culture*, New York: Prestel Publishing Ltd.

Walker, A. (1987) 'Dreads', in *Anything We Love Can Be Saved*, London: the Women's Press.

YINKA SUNMONU

Hall, Ian

b. Guyana

organist, singer, composer, conductor, teacher

Hall was educated at Archbishop Tenison's School in London and later at Keble College, Oxford, where he was Oxford University's first black **music** graduate. He taught for many years in comprehensive schools in England and was an ILEA adviser in multi-ethnic studies from 1977. In Ghana he taught at several educational institutions, including at the Institute of African Studies at the University of Ghana. He has been organist in four London churches and his Bloomsbury Mass was televised live. His other most popular compositions include the London Mass and Pslam 47, which is dedicated to Martin Luther King. As well as performing and officiating at many musical events, Hall is President of the Bloomsbury International Society, which he founded in 1970 and which aims to promote international, inter-ethnic understanding.

ALISON DONNELL

Hall, Stuart

b. 1932, Jamaica

sociologist, cultural critic

Stuart Hall's work has been central to the formation and development of cultural studies as an international discipline. Hall was educated in Jamaica and the UK, attending Oxford from 1951 to 1957 as a Rhodes scholar. In his early years in the UK he was involved with expatriate West Indian politics. With friends from the Communist Party and the Labour Club, Hall became part of what was known as the New Left, becoming a founder editor for the journal *Universities and Left Review*, later *New Left Review*, while also teaching in South London. Hall described the New Left as a 'social movement' rather than a proto-political party. It involved the Labour Party, trade unions, the anti-nuclear movement, students and intellectuals.

Hall left the *Review* in 1961 to teach 'complementary studies' at Chelsea College, London, and was invited by Richard Hoggart to join him at the **Centre for Contemporary Cultural Studies** (CCCS), Birmingham University, in 1964. Hall's work with others at the CCCS inaugurated a radical shift in cultural criticism in the academy. His work on **television**, popular culture, newspapers and magazines (see **publishing, newspapers and magazines**) offered key critical foundations and reference points in the rapidly developing field of cultural studies. Papers such as 'Encoding and decoding in the media discourse' (1973) and texts like *Policing the Crisis, 'Mugging', the State and Law and Order* (1978) have been recognised as landmarks in cultural studies. His analysis of Thatcherism formed a significant amount of his work, such as *The Hard Road to Renewal: Thatcherism and the Crisis of the Left* (1973), and numerous articles in *Marxism Today*. In 1979, Hall left Birmingham for a post at the Open University, where he remained until retirement as a Professor of Sociology in 1998. Much of his later work came to focus on race, ethnicity and diaspora, including 'Minimal selves' (1989) and 'Cultural identity and diaspora' (1990), which have become central to theories and debates around questions of cultural identity, contemporary British politics and post-coloniality.

Select bibliography

Hall, S. (1988) 'New ethnicities', in K. Mercer (ed.) *Black Film, British Cinema*, ICA Documents 7, London: BFI/ICA, pp. 27–31.

—— (1988) *The Hard Road to Renewal: Thatcherism and the Crisis of the Left*, London: Verso.

—— (1976) *Resistance through Rituals: Youth Subcultures in Post-war Britain*, London: Hutchinson.

—— (with C. Critcher, T. Jefferson, J. Clarke and B. Roberts) (1978) *Policing the Crisis: 'Mugging', the State, and Law and Order*, London: Macmillan.

—— (with D. Hobson, A. Lowe and P. Willis) (1980) *Culture, Media, Languages: Working Papers in Cultural Studies (1972–1979)*, London: Hutchinson/CCCS.

Further reading

Morley, D. and Chen, K.-H. (1996) *Stuart Hall: Critical Dialogues in Cultural Studies*, London and New York: Routledge.

ELEANOR BYRNE

Handsworth Songs

Directed by John **Akomfrah** and made by **Black Audio Film Collective** (BAFC), *Handsworth Songs* (1987) is a critical black film (see **film and cinema**) of the 1980s, moving between documentary, historiography and political narrative, focusing on the civil disobedience that erupted in reaction to repressive policing of black communities in London and Birmingham in the early 1980s. Although produced on the independent cinema circuit, it received widespread critical and media interest, particularly with regard to issues of race and ethnicity, both in terms of representation on **television** and in film, and the racial politics of 1980s Britain. According to another member of the BAFC, Reece **Auguiste**, this involved trying to 'find a structure and form which would allow us the space to deconstruct the hegemonic voices of British television newsreels.'

The film had a contradictory reception: it received critical acclaim and won many prizes including the Grierson Award from the **British Film Institute**; in contrast, negative receptions followed from a review in the *Voice*, exclaiming 'Oh no, not another riot documentary'. Salman **Rushdie** notably wrote an article in the *Guardian*, '*Songs* doesn't know the score', where he took issue with the film-makers' claims to 'tell other stories' and accused the film of reproducing mainstream media images of black rioters looting shops. Rushdie's argument was taken up by Stuart **Hall** and Darcus **Howe**, who both disagreed with the complaint that the film reproduced racial stereotypes of black people. For the film-makers, the film was an attempt to 'excavate the hidden ruptures and agonies of "race"', by looking at the riots as 'a political field coloured by the trajectories of industrial decline and structural crisis'. For the BAFC, the archive constituted a privileged terrain of knowledge and their practice of mixing documentary footage with archival material on black migration (for instance the calypso singer Lord Kitchener singing 'London is the place for me' for the British news reporter) was an attempt to retrieve new meanings and identities from historical sources.

Further reading

Auguiste, R. (1988) '*Handsworth Songs*: Some background notes', *Framework*, 35: 6.

Gilroy, P. and Pines, J. (1988) '*Handsworth Songs*: audiences/aesthetics/independence', interview with Black Audio Film Collective, *Framework* 35: 11.

ELEANOR BYRNE

Hansib Publishing

Hansib Publishing is said to be the biggest black and Asian publishers in Britain. It is owned by magazine and newspaper (see **publishing, newspapers and magazines**) publisher Arif **Ali**. Unlike **X Press**, which specialises in fiction, Hansib publishes a diverse range of books from travel, to politics to children's novels. Academic and prize-winning author David **Dabydeen** published his second collection of poetry, *Coolie Odyssey*, with Hansib, as well as his co-written book, *A Reader's Guide to West Indian and Black British Literature*, which has a chapter on **carnival** and calypso. Readers seeking works on politics, slavery, **music**, Caribbean travel and **literature** are likely to find something on the Hansib list. The company has received national media attention for some of their publications. With Hounslow Council, Hansib published a survey revealing that black councillors face racial abuse from other councillors

and that, despite the existence of black mayors, black councillors rarely reached senior positions.

YINKA SUNMONU

Harkishin, Jimmi

b. 1965, Paris, France

actor

Born in France to an Italian mother and an Indian father, Harkishin is now probably best known as Dev Alahan, the manager of the local shop in the long-running Manchester soap opera *Coronation Street*. Harkishin has enjoyed roles in some of the most important Asian films (see **film and cinema**) of the 1990s, including Ranjit in *Bhaji on the Beach* (1993) and Iyaaz Ali Khan in *East is East* (1999), as well as starring in the popular **television** series *Medics* as Dr Jay Rahman.

ALISON DONNELL

Harris, Wilson

b. 1921, New Amsterdam, Guyana

novelist, poet, critic, cultural philosopher

One of the father figures of Caribbean **literature**, Harris settled in Britain in 1959 where his first novel, *Palace of the Peacock*, was published the following year. This immediately established him as a writer of great visionary power; his imagination delves deeply into the South American hinterland of myth and ritual. (He had worked professionally in South America in the 1950s as a surveyor.) Allusive, metaphorical and with a range of references, from Amerindian symbolism to European literature, all his fiction draws on this experience and offers profound allegories for contemporary cross-cultural society.

Besides producing more than twenty novels and some poetry, Harris has lectured internationally and received prestigious academic honours for his critical work. His creative influence extends over many black British writers such as David **Dabydeen**, Fred **D'Aguiar** and Pauline Melville.

Select bibliography

Harris, W. (1999) *Selected Essays of Wilson Harris*, ed. A. Bundy, London: Routledge.
—— (1996) *Jonestown*, London: Faber.
—— (1993) *The Carnival Trilogy (Carnival, The Infinite Rehearsal, The Four Banks of the River of Space)*, London: Faber.
—— (1985) *The Guyana Quartet*, London: Faber.

Further reading

Maes-Jelinek, H. (ed.) (1991) *Wilson Harris. The Uncompromising Imagination*, Sydney: Dangaroo.

TOBIAS DÖRING

Headley, Victor

b. Jamaica

novelist

Victor Headley grew up in London. His controversial debut novel *Yardie* rapidly gained cult status and became a bestseller. The first in a trilogy that includes *Excess* (1993) and *Yush!* (1994), *Yardie* heralded a new wave of black British pulp fiction that has been fostered by the publishing company **X Press**. Dealing with topics such as crime, drugs culture and gang war, the books have been criticised by some for the 'hard' masculinities they glamorise and the negative stereotypes they pander to.

Select bibliography

Headley, V. (1994) *Yush!* London: the X Press Ltd.
—— (1993) *Excess*, London: the X Press Ltd.
—— (1992) *Yardie*, London: the X Press Ltd.

JAMES PROCTER

Heath, Roy

b. Guyana

writer

Heath came to the UK at the age of twenty-four to read modern languages at London University. He was called to the English Bar in 1964 and to the Guyana Bar in 1973. He taught French in a London comprehensive school for many years. Heath had published essays and short fiction while in Guyana. His first novel *A Man Come Home* was published in 1974 and, in 1978, his second novel *The Murderer* won the *Guardian* Fiction Prize. These were followed by a triology on the Armstrong family: *From the Heat of the Day* (1979); *One Generation* (1981) and *Genetha* (1981). Heath subsequently published *Kwaku* (1982), *Orealla* (1984) and *Shadow-bride* (1988).

ALISON DONNELL

Henriques, Julian

b. 1951

film-maker, director

Henriques is the son of renowned sociologist Fernando Henriques. He was a **television** researcher before moving on to produce and direct music and arts documentaries for the BBC. Under the **music** and art series *Made in Latin America*, he produced and directed two films – *States of Exiles* and *Dictating Terms*, as well as the documentary *Derek Walcott: the Poet of the Island*, before embarking on executive producing for his company, Formation Films (founded 1987). His move into directing drama led to the production of *Exit no Exit*, a **dance** drama for **Channel 4** and the Arts Council, which told the Orpheus myth against the setting of the London Underground. *We the Ragamuffin*, for Channel 4, won the Best Musical and Best Independent Production prizes at the National Black Programming Consortium. Henriques made his mark in the black British movie industry with the debut film ***Babymother***, his first foray into screenwriting. Filmed in Harlesden, London, with a strong cast including Shakespearean actor Wil Johnson, the film is a **reggae** musical based on **dancehall** culture. It depicts black British working-class culture and explores the popular theme of babymothers.

Henriques, who lectures on film at universities, is working on a new script with the knowledge that nobody who has produced a black film in Britain has gone on to produce a second one. Formation Films, now in its thirteenth year, produces documentaries, television series and feature films. Henriques is married to television producer Parminder **Vir**.

YINKA SUNMONU

HENRY, ANTHONY *see* Tippa Irie

Henry, Lenny

b. 1958, Dudley, England

comedian

Born Lenworth George Henry, Lenny Henry left school at sixteen to become an electrical engineer in a welding factory. He had his first show-business break soon after when he won the **television** talent show *New Faces*. He went on to perform in *The Minstrel Show* until 1979, when he left due to constant criticism from Britain's black communities. He later commented that he could no longer tolerate playing such a part. Henry became one of an extremely small band of black entertainers on television, being a regular on *Tiswas* and also acting in the television sitcom *The Fosters*. In 1981, *Three of a Kind* was first aired and consequently established him as a television personality, a position consolidated by his own show in 1984, featuring characters such as Theophilus P. Wildebeeste and Delbert Wilkins. Henry frequently received criticism from the black community, who saw him as having 'sold out', first for performing on *The Minstrel Show* and later for the characters he chose to portray in his own show, such as the aforementioned Theophilus P Wildebeeste, whom they felt played up to damaging racial stereotypes. In 1998, Lenny Henry received a CBE in the New Year's Honours List, partly for his work with Comic Relief. He is married to comedienne Dawn French.

SAMINA ZAHIR

Himid, Lubaina

b. 1954, Zanzibar, Tanzania

curator, painter, Reader in Contemporary Art

Himid studied **theatre** design at the Wimbledon School of Art, and attended the Royal College of Art (1982–4) and the University of East Anglia in 1984, where she gained an MA in cultural history. She is currently a Reader in Contemporary Art at the University of Central Lancashire. Himid was a key figure in the development of black artists in Britain in the 1980s, both as a curator and an artist. She established a gallery in London in 1983 and curated numerous exhibitions, including the groundbreaking 'Five Black Women' (1983), at the Africa Centre. Her work has appeared in group shows such as '**The Thin Black Line**' (1985), at the **Institute of Contemporary Arts**, and '**The Other Story**' (1989), at the Hayward Gallery. Her work is marked by a preoccupation with satire of white culture and European cultural orthodoxies, and also by celebratory representations of creative black women and of black people's strategies to resist cultural imperialism and neo-colonialism. In the early 1990s, Himid collaborated with writer and artist Maud **Sulter** on projects examining the history of black women artists, both in the West and in post-colonial Africa. In 1994, she exhibited at the Fifth Havana Bienal, Cuba, and, in 1995, she held a solo exhibition in New York, 'Lubaina Himid: Cultural Links', at Peg Alston Fine Arts. Her more recent work includes 'Venetian Maps', a touring exhibition and 'Plan B', an exhibition reflecting her residency at the Tate Gallery, St Ives (1999–2000). Her work is held in public collections including the Tate Gallery, London, the Victoria and Albert Museum, London, and New Hall, Cambridge.

Further reading

Sulter, M. (ed.) (1990) *Passion: Discourses on Black Women's Creativity*, Hebden Bridge: Urban Fox Press.

ELEANOR BYRNE

hip hop

Hip hop culture and rap **music** are largely portrayed as a global phenomenon with distinctive African American origins, located specifically within a time and a place – the mid- to late 1970s in the South Bronx. While it is fair to say that many of the most successful artists and producers on the international stage have predominantly been African American, this view of hip hop and rap is problematic in that it both ignores other influences and actors within the style's birth and growth, and the fact that without the mainstream charts, or 'official' histories of hip hop/rap, distinctive, indigenous scenes exist apart from the USA with their own distinctive influences, styles and lyrical concerns.

In Britain, hip hop/rap fans originally relied upon access to a small number of import records from the USA or hybrid variants of rap such as Art Of Noise's *Beat Box*, but with the release of the *Streetsounds* series of electro compilations, rare and hard to come by cuts became easily available in Britain, much as the budget **reggae** compilations had promoted reggae two decades previously. Among the volumes of Stateside sounds was 1984's *UK-Electro*, which showcased the fledgling British scene. Morgan Khan's *Streetsounds* compilations were also mixed by British DJs, although whether this was to promote the scene or for economic reasons it is not clear. Manifestations of the hip hop style, including breakdancing, scratch mixing, body popping, graffiti and fashion (see **fashion and design**), became even more popular in Britain with the release of *Wild Style*, the seminal documentary of the New York hip hop scene, which was also released in 1984. The hip hop scene was not limited to London, but flourished in most cities in Britain. Although electro and rap were often portrayed as inauthentic, childish and un-musical, it was a popular form that encouraged participation in many forms, not merely passive consumption.

With the emergence of US acts such as Run DMC, LL Cool J, the Beastie Boys and Public Enemy in the British charts, hip hop and rap began to enter a new phase. While the British scene was still in thrall to the USA, the number of British artists encouraged to release records began to grow, although many of these releases were often criticised as being parodies or poorer versions of an original form. The case of Derek B is one that highlights the schisms between the mainstream and the more underground hip hop community. Derek Borland was an A&R man for the rap label Music For Life, which had been set up to license and issue records from the States. Financial problems and the changing nature of the hip hop scene left Music For Life unable to continue releasing US productions and to fill a gap in release schedules Borland recorded a single, 'Rock the beat'. Released in 1986 as Derek B, the single is one of the first homegrown British rap records. Two further singles were released on Music For Life, one of which, 'Good groove', reached number sixteen in the charts and Derek B became the first British rapper to appear on Top Of The Pops. Derek B was then signed to the prestigious Rush Management and signed a major record deal. Despite Derek B's prior involvement in the hip hop scene, many fans and critics felt that he was too Americanised, not 'real' enough or, worse still, simply a parody of a superior form.

Other British artists who achieved success but often gained the ire of the hip hop community included the **Cookie Crew**. Cookie Crew achieved a great deal of success with a form of hip hop/rap that was informed equally by their experiences of growing up in South London as it was by the music being produced in the USA. Their debut album, 1989's *Born this Way* was recorded in New York and was co-produced by Stetsasonic's Daddy-O and DBC, along with one track 'Bad girls (rock the spot)' that was produced by Derek B. She-Rockers, Monie Love and **Wee Papa Girl Rappers** all had varying degrees of success, though only Monie Love (Simone Johnson) was able to translate her late 1980s success into a long-term career by relocating to New York, where she worked with seminal artists such as Queen Latifah, Jungle Brothers and De La Soul.

Although this period is often reflected upon in a rather disparaging fashion, the success of several of these artists inspired British acts to find their own voice and style. Groups and rappers such as Three Wize Men, Overlord X and Silver Bullet released records that were distinctively British, both musically and in their lyrical concerns. Silver Bullet's fast-style rapping owed as much to reggae as it did to hip hop on singles such as the fierce and furious 'Ruff karnage' and '20 seconds to comply' with their film samples, punchy bass lines and ferocious, breakneck vocal delivery. Three Wize Men presented their unglamorous, street-influenced raps in undisguised East London accents to minimal backing, while Overlord X described the reality of life in London on tracks such as 'Rough In Hackney'. In contrast to the large number of novelty rap records being released in Britain by Stateside acts such as the Fat Boys, these records offered a refreshing and innovative take on hip hop. The media, radio and **television** had also begun to make serious attempts to promote British hip hop and rap by the end of the decade.

However, the major breakthrough predicted for British hip hop/rap at the dawn of the 1990s never happened, although several individual acts such as Definition Of Sound prospered. There have been several reasons given for this. First, many producers, MCs and fans moved on to other genres. Second, the release of NWA's debut album, 1988's *Straight Outta Compton*, had a massive impact and influence upon rap, both in the USA and in Britain, and gangsta rap began to outsell all other genres. In contrast to tales of ghetto life in south LA, whether real or imagined, combined with a clipped, funky production, British hip hop somehow sounded less threatening, less in your face. Also, it was easier to deal with questions of race and racism when they came from the other side of the Atlantic.

Away from the mainstream, hip hop and rap continued to mutate and develop as an underground form. Groups such as Katch 22, Gunshot and the Brotherhood developed their own distinctive takes on hip hop, while Asian British artists such as **Apache Indian**, **Kaliphz**, **Fun-damental**, **Asian Dub Foundation** and **Hustlers HC** all brought new voices and influences to a scene that had previously marginalised their involvement. While the British hip hop scene has always been racially mixed, prior to the early 1990s there were few Asians visibly involved as DJs, producers or MCs, with the exception of Morgan Khan, despite the large numbers of Asian British youths who were heavily into hip hop culture. **Credit to the Nation** and Kaliphz charted but faltered, as did the majority of the aforementioned acts, although Asian Dub Foundation and Gunshot

had released three full-length albums by 2001 despite earlier problems with record labels.

On an underground level, artists such as Blade, Katch 22 and Mark B were heavily influential as they circumvented bigger labels to define their own scene. Katch 22 released three albums, including the epic *Dark Tales from Two Cities*, which featured contributions from the Cookie Crew and traversed a diverse range of sounds. Although Katch 22 split up in 1994, they influenced many current acts and co-founder Andrew Ward records for Son Records as Huntkillberry Finn. Although the scene remained underground for the remainder of the decade, the music has developed and early in 2001 a number of artists emerged at the forefront of another renaissance year for British hip hop. While many of those involved in the contemporary scene are well known within the hip hop community the level of success they have achieved is new. Mark B and Blade's single 'The unknown' became the first wholly British hip hop single to be playlisted by Radio 1 since 1996's 'One shot' by the Brotherhood. Ty, who has worked with MC Mell'O and the Nextmen, released his debut album *Awkward* and Speeka, Blak Twang and Roots Manuva have all released well-received debut albums and, importantly, have been backed by radio play and media coverage. Influential US label Def Jam opened their British imprint in 2001 and labels such as Ronin, Big Dada, Hombre and Son are thriving along with clubs such as Scratch, Lyrical Lounge and Counter Culture. The new artists have also begun to experience success in the US; while UK hip hop producer Skitz produced Roni Size and Reprazent's (see **Size, Roni and Reprazent**) 'Dirty beats' single, Reprazent's MC Dynamite returned the favour by contributing raps to two tracks on Skitz's debut album *Countryman*, acknowledging the current influence of hip hop upon contemporary **dance** music genres.

ANDY WOOD

Hodges, Jo

b. 1959, Leicester, England

screenwriter, author

Almost in the same vein as Zadie **Smith** and

Diran **Adebayo** in terms of instant critical acclaim, Hodges's **film** *The Girl with Brains in Her Feet*, from Alliance Communications and Lexington Films, was placed on general release in 1998. That same year, it was published as a novel by Virago enabling her to join the roll call of honours of the few black British writers to have achieved a film/novel tie simultaneously. Hodges's life reads almost like a screenplay. She is an example of a bright child who decided to aim for popularity in school and was consequently expelled. Yet despite the initial setback she was accepted at art college. A few years later she moved to London, where she went into advertising, achieving notable success. Hodges realised that despite the financial rewards it was not what she wanted and she applied for a writers course from the back of the *Guardian* newspaper. A screenplay was sent to Carlton Television and it won her a place on their highly coveted writer's course, where she won a competition to have a twenty-minute screenplay filmed for **television**. Determined to nurture her craft, Hodges applied to the National Film and Television School. She had to write a 'treatment' before being considered for a place and started the script *The Girl with Brains in Her Feet*. It has been shown on cable television and is now available on video. She has also written short films.

YINKA SUNMONU

Holiday, Amanda

b. 1964, Sierra Leone

painter, video director

Holiday studied fine art at Wimbledon College. Her work consists of large-scale, figurative, mixed-media drawings, such as *The Hum of History*, 'a cyclic story about hope in the 80s' in charcoal and chalk. In 1989, Holiday made an Arts Council video on contemporary radical black **visual artists**, titled '*Employing the Image*', which featured Sonia **Boyce**, Simone Alexander, Zarina **Bhimji**, Keith **Piper** and Alan **de Souza**. In 1990, she made three further films (see **film and cinema**) for an Arts Council/**Channel 4** collaboration: *Umbrage, Manu Tupapau* and *Miss Queencake*. Her

work has been shown at many of the major black exhibitions of the 1980s, including: 'Creation for Liberation', 'Some of us arc Brave', '**Black Art: Plotting the Course**' and '**Black Perspectives**'.

Further reading

(1992) *Women's Art Magazine* 44 (Jan.–Feb.): 17.
(1991) *Feminist Art News* 3(8): 28.

PAUL O'KANE

Holmes, Claudette May

b. 1962, Birmingham, England

photographic artist

Claudette Holmes is among a number of black British women photographers whose work has made an important contribution to challenging stereotypical representations of black people. Following a period working in Birmingham's community arts sector in the early 1980s, Holmes established herself as a freelance photographer and began developing the techniques of montage and hand-colouring that became the distinctive hallmarks of her work. Her images have been exhibited in group, solo and survey exhibitions in Britain, continental Europe and the USA. Her exhibitions include: 'Womaness' (1990) (with Roshini **Kempadoo**), Wolverhampton Art Gallery; 'Manipulated Images' (1992), Picture House, Leicester; 'Sharp Voices, Still Lives' (1990), Birmingham Museum and Art Gallery; 'The Critical Decade' (1993), Museum of Modern Art, Oxford; and 'Black Britsh Photographers' (1992), Houston FotoFestival, Texas. In 1993, Holmes was commissioned to co-curate and produce new work for the innovative exhibition '**From Negative Stereotype to Positive Image**'. She won the Chrissie Bailey Photography and Education Award in 1996 for a project linked to the exhibition 'Self Evident', shown at Birmingham's Ikon Gallery. Holmes's work has been published in journals and magazines in the UK and the USA. Her work is held in both private and public collections.

Further reading

Bailey, D.A. and Hall, S. (eds) (1992) 'Critical decade: black British photography in the 80s', special issue, *Ten.8* 2(3).

Edwards, E. (1997) 'Beyond the boundary; a consideration of the expressive in photography and anthropology', in M. Banks and H. Morphy (eds) *Rethinking Visual Anthropology*, London: Yale University Press.

Gilligan, C. (1992) 'Manipulated Images', *Autograph* (February): 2–4.

PETER JAMES

Horizon Gallery

In 1985, the London-based organisation the Indian Arts Council in the UK proposed to establish a gallery space devoted to the work of artists from ethnic minority (see **ethnic minorities**) communities. Subsequently, the Horizon Gallery was set up, but as a space specifically devoted to artists from India and the Indian diaspora. The most important exhibition of the short-lived gallery was 'In Focus', held in 1990 as a response to **The Other Story**. The Horizon Gallery felt that 'The Other Story' ignored a number of artists who had come to the UK in the 1960s and who formed the Indian Artists United Kingdom collective in 1964. The gallery and the collective behind it were important in offering an alternative to the predominant mode of black or Afro-Asian art during the 1980s articulated by Eddie **Chambers** and Rasheed **Araeen** respectively. Their viewpoint was one based on an older notion of multiculturalism rather than anti-racism or cultural diversity. Arguably this strand of thinking and curating has been written out of contemporary accounts of black **visual arts**.

Further reading

Horizon Gallery (1990) *In Focus*, exhibition catalogue.

NIRU RATNAM

Hosain, Attia

b. 1913, Lucknow, India

writer, actress

Hosain came from an aristocratic landowning family; her father was one of the first Asians to study at Cambridge and the Middle Temple. She was educated at La Martiniere and Isabella Thoburn College in Lucknow, and also received lessons in Urdu, Arabic and Persian at home. She was the first woman in her family to be awarded a degree. Hosain was inspired to follow a career in writing by her contact with the Progressive Writers Group in India and the wider nationalist movement of the 1930s. She worked as a journalist and broadcaster, as well as writing short stories. She came to the UK before Independence in 1947 and worked for the BBC Eastern Service, presenting programmes for women in Urdu. She also acted in radio plays and later on the West End stage and **television**. Hosain's collection of short stories, *Phoenix Fled*, was first published in 1953 and her novel, *Sunlight on a Broken Column*, in 1961. Both publications explore pre-Independence and pre-Partition India in the process of major political change. Her work was later republished by Virago, and collected in their volume *The Inner Courtyard: Stories by Indian Women*, edited by Lakshmi Holstrom.

Select bibliography

Hosain, A. (1988 [1961]) *Sunlight on a Broken Column*, London: Virago.

ALISON DONNELL

Howe, Darcus

b. 1944, Trinidad

political activist, writer, broadcaster

Howe arrived in Britain in 1961 and worked in Notting Hill at the Mangrove Restaurant, where he was one of the Mangrove Nine (see **Mangrove Trials**) arrested in a police raid, whose trials became a *cause célèbre* at the end of the decade. A former Black Panther and a political activist since the 1960s, Howe was editor of **Race Today** and in the 1980s organised the New Cross march to protest about the circumstances surrounding the deaths of black children in a fire there in 1981. Howe first achieved media presence as the presenter of the **Channel 4** chat show *Devil's Advocate*, which ran for several years and was consciously controversial. Howe provoked debate between a studio audience and a usually contentious guest on often highly charged issues – one programme debated the repatriation of African Caribbeans in Britain. In 1998, when Channel 4 showed a documentary in the *Dispatches* series suggesting that young blacks are responsible for 80 per cent of sex crimes/rape, Howe chaired a round-table discussion immediately afterwards with black guests to debate the topic. This **television** discussion was important for bringing forward the debate on race, crime, disadvantage and the lack of role models for black males. In 2000, Howe presented *White Tribes* for Channel 4, which involved him travelling around Britain interviewing people to discover the meaning and concept of Britishness. Other programmes include *Trouble in Paradise* and *England my England*, which also interrogate the notions of nationalism, belonging and race.

Howe is well respected in the black community for taking a stance on black issues on a local and national level, although it would be wrong to suggest that political activism is his main contribution to black British culture. He studied law, has taught children Shakespeare at GCSE level and he reads the classics, books on Marx included. Howe writes for national newspapers (see **publishing, newspapers and magazines**) including the *Guardian* and the *Sunday Times*, and was a columnist on *The New Statesman*. His writing has covered many subjects including the Jamaican football team, cricket and the **Notting Hill Carnival**. He has also acted in the film (see **film and cinema**) *The Stonemaker*, which premièred at the Munich Film Festival.

YINKA SUNMONU

HUDSON, MATTY *see* Credit to the Nation

Hunningale, Peter

b. 1962, England

reggae singer, songwriter, producer, musician, record label owner

Lovers' rock has long been the UK's biggest selling branch of **reggae music** on the underground market, and, since the mid-1980s, Peter Hunningale has been, arguably, its greatest exponent. Nicknamed Mr Honey Vibes, Hunningale has been a constant force in the UK reggae charts with such number ones as 'Be My Lady' in 1987, 'Raggamuffin Girl' with **Tippa Irie** in 1989 and 'Baby Please' and 'Perfect Lady' both in 1995. From 1987 to 1997, Hunningale released seven albums including: *The New Decade* on Mango/ Island in 1991; *Mr Vibes* featuring Tippa Irie on his own Street Vibes label in 1992; *Done Cook & Currie* on Rebel MC's Tribal Base imprint, also in 1992; and the politically conscious *Mr Government* in 1994 on **Mad Professor**'s Ariwa imprint. A talented singer, songwriter, producer and musician, Hunningale has collaborated with such artists as the late Dennis Brown and Janet Lee Davis. Commercial success has continued to elude Hunningale. However, he had his biggest commercial hit in 1996 alongside Mafia and Fluxy, Glamma Kid and Nerious Joseph (under the banner PASSION) with the national Top 75 single 'Share Your Love'.

Further reading

Larkin, C. (1998) *The Virgin Encyclopedia of Reggae*, London: Virgin

DEREK A. BARDOWELL

Hunt, Marsha

b. 1946, Philadelphia, USA

actor, singer, novelist

Marsha Hunt arrived in Europe in 1966, launching her music career in London by singing with the blues bands of Alexis Korner and Long John Baldry, before making her name on London's West End stage in the musical *Hair*. She appeared later on screen and **television**. Her solo career began with Track Records, the same label as the Who and Jimi Hendrix, where she produced two hit singles. In 1972, she became a radio broadcaster with the newly launched Capital Radio, hosting a chat show and black **music** show. Her literary career started in 1985 when she was commissioned to write her autobiography, *Real Life*. In 1994, she conceived and created the **Saga Prize**, the first prize in Britain for aspiring black British writers with the aim to have four new black British writers signed to mainstream publishers by the year 2000. The last winner was a controversial novel about police culture, *Canteen Culture* by Iyke Eze Anyika.

Select bibliography

Hunt, M. (1998) *Like Venus Fading*, London: Flamingo.
—— (1995) *Repossessing Ernestine*, London: Flamingo.
—— (1993) *Free*, London: Hamish Hamilton.
—— (1990) *Joy*, London: Virago.
—— (1985) *Real Life*, London: Chatto & Windus.

KADIJA SESAY

Huntley, Accabre

b. 1967, London, England

poet

Accabre Huntley is of Guyanese parentage, the daughter of Jessica and Eric Huntley who founded **Bogle L'Ouverture** Press. She has been reading and writing poetry since childhood, appearing nationally and internationally on both radio and **television**, and with Keith Waithe and the Macusi Players. Her work also appears in several anthologies, including the ground-breaking *News from Babylon* (1984), edited by James **Berry**, and children's anthologies such as Grace **Nichols**'s *Black Poetry* (1988). She leads poetry workshops in primary and secondary schools, and is a member of the Poetry Society's Poets in Schools scheme, as well as the Poetry Society's Examinations Department Advisory Group.

Select bibliography

Bacon, S. (ed) (1992) *Chasing the Sun*, London: Simon & Schuster Young Books.
Berry, J. (ed.) (1984) *News from Babylon*, London: Chatto & Windus.
Huntley, A. (1983) *Easter Monday Blues*, London: Bogle L'Ouverture Publications.
—— (1977) *At School Today*, London: Bogle L'Ouverture Publications.
Nichols, G. (ed.) (1988) *Black Poetry*, London: Blackie.

KADIJA SESAY

Hussein, Waris

b. 1939, India

director

Hussein came to England at the age of eight with his father and mother, Attia **Hosain**. He was exposed to the hard edge of English culture at Clifton College boarding school, and then graduated from Cambridge. He studied at the Slade School of Art and then joined the BBC as a **television** director. Hussein helped to create *Doctor Who* and directed its first episode. Later he directed dramas, including *A Passage to India* and *Edward and Mrs Simpson*. He now works mainly in Hollywood.

ALISON DONNELL

Hustlers HC

Hustlers HC were a West London based **hip hop** trio who had evolved out of running sound systems. They were also responsible for the founding and running of the influential club night Bombay Jungle, which mixed up Asian styles such as **bhangra** with hip hop and other contemporary dance forms. Bombay Jungle would in turn inspire clubs such as **Anokha** and **Outcaste**. Hustlers HC signed to **Nation Records** in 1993 and released their debut single 'Big trouble in little Asia' in 1994. A melodic, laid-back hip hop track, lyrically 'Big trouble in little Asia' was an articulate rap dealing with the issues and problems facing Asian British youths and the questions of identity, culture and belonging that arose out of their position in Britain. These were issues that Hustlers HC were particularly aware of as the only visible Sikh hip hop act involved in the UK scene. A second single 'Vigilante' was released the same year. Despite the positive reception and impact of both these singles Hustlers HC have largely been inactive and were presumed to have split up around 1996.

ANDY WOOD

Hylton, Richard

b. 1960, England

artist, critic, curator

Hylton began his career making art that dealt with issues around race and class, such as in his photo-work *Untitled* of 1989, where symbols of economic power were used. Hylton's primary interest was in the construction of a national identity in terms of a more pluralistic approach. His collaboration with Bashir Makhoul, *Yo-Yo, Yo-Yo* of 1996 used found film footage to look at symbolic exchange and alienated communication between cultures. His first major curatorial project was 'Imagined Communities', a National Touring Exhibition in 1995, which featured such artists as Yinka **Shonibare**, Gary Simmons and Sophie Calle. Using the theme of fragmented and multiple communities, the exhibition questioned the assumptions of a notion of community that was fixed and located in history or tradition. As a reviewer, he has shown resistance to multi-cultural narratives being imposed upon artists, especially where it labelled them doubly as 'ethnic'. For example, he was extremely critical of the exhibition 'Cities on the Move', curated by Hans Ulrich Obrist in 1999, for presenting non-Western art works as artifacts rather than cogent artworks.

Further reading

Hylton, R. (ed.) (1995) *Imagined Communities*, London: South Bank Centre.
(1996) *Third Text* 11(36) (Autumn).

FRANCIS SUMMERS

IC3: the Penguin Book of New Black Writing

IC3: the Penguin Book of New Black Writing is an anthology of commissioned work from writers of African descent based in Britain. Edited by Courttia **Newland** and Kadija **Sesay**, and published in April 2000, this book is considered by many to be a landmark collection of almost exclusively new work from across the writing community. The controversial title of the collection is taken from the police identity code for black people (Identity Code 3), and is believed by the editors to be the only collective term that relates to people of African descent living in Britain. Divided into three sections reflecting first, second and third generations, the book focuses on four genres of writing: poetry, short fiction, essays and memoirs. *IC3* features work from close to one hundred writers, including many established names such as David **Dabydeen**, Bernardine **Evaristo**, Jackie **Kay** and Benjamin **Zephaniah**. The collection also features many writers whose work was unknown at the time of publication.

ANDREA ENISUOH

identity politics

Identity politics is an idea with wide currency, especially among gay and lesbian theorists, as well as those writing about race. Diana Fuss has defined identity politics as 'the tendency to base one's politics on a sense of personal identity – as gay, as Jewish, as Black, as female' (1989: 97). Identity politics is predicated on the existence of a stable identity or an essence that provides a stable political platform, and as such it invests the private and the personal with macro-political significance. As Fuss points out, the basic assumptions of identity politics give rise to a set of unanswered (and perhaps unanswerable) questions about the relationship of politics to identity: the nature of identity as 'a natural, political, historical, psychical or linguistic construct' (1989: 97) and the political implications of an assumed ontological stability. These questions link up with issues surrounding **essentialism**, and many theorists (including some queer theorists) accept that identity politics and essentialism both have their political uses. In particular, a number of African American critics recognise that the post-structuralist attempt to deconstruct identity may overlook or even elide its socio-political and economic 'reality' for the subject. '[I]t's important to remember that "race" is only a socio-political category, nothing more', writes Gates in *Loose Canons*, but at the same time he acknowledges its practical performative force 'as a reality rather than a metaphor' (1992: 37–8). The post-colonial critic Gayatri Chakravorty Spivak has written of 'the *strategic* use of positive essentialism in a scrupulously visible political interest', a practice that has been adopted by a number of other theorists and critics, even though Spivak later distanced herself from the concept (1988: 205).

The issue has been taken up by black British theorists, including Stuart **Hall** and Paul **Gilroy**. In his essay, 'Cultural identity and diaspora', Hall acknowledges the importance of the 'act of imaginative rediscovery which [the] conception of a rediscovered, essential identity entails', but he stresses the impossibility of generalizing about cultural identity. According to Hall, 'cultural identities are contingent, historically local and constructed, and like everything which is historical, they undergo constant transformation' rather than being eternally fixed in an essentialized past. His essay '**New ethnicities**' also emphasises the constructed, relational nature of black identity 'which cannot be grounded in a set of fixed trans-cultural or transcendental racial categories, and which therefore has no guarantees in nature'.

References

Fuss, D. (1989) *Essentially Speaking. Feminism, Nature and Difference*, London: Routledge.

Gates, Jnr, H.L. (1992) *Loose Canons. Notes on the Culture Wars*, New York: Oxford University Press.

Hall, S. (1990) 'Cultural identity and diaspora', in J. Rutherford (ed.) *Identity, Community, Culture, Difference*, London: Lawrence & Wishart, pp. 222–37.

—— (1989) 'New ethnicities', in *Critical Dialogues in Cultural Studies*, London: Routledge, pp. 441–9.

Spivak, G.C. (1988) 'Subaltern studies: deconstructing historiography', in *In Other Worlds. Essays in Cultural Politics*, New York: Routledge, pp. 197–221.

Further reading

Lott, T. (1999) *The Invention of Race. Black Culture and the Politics of Representation*, Oxford: Blackwell.

SARA SALIH

Imaani

singer

Imaani came into the **music** business after a chance encounter on a train with a producer when she had left college and moved to London. She had her first major break as lead vocals on Incognito's 1996 album *Beneath the Surface*. In 1998, she struck a recording deal with EMI/Crysalis Records and also became the first ever black entrant to represent the UK at the Eurovision Song Contest. She came second with the song 'Where Are You?', which went on to be a Top 20 hit in the UK charts. She subsequently released a cover of Adina Howard's 'Freak In Me' and has had a successful career in Europe.

ALISON DONNELL

Institute of Contemporary Arts

The Institute of Contemporary Arts (ICA) was founded in 1947 as a cultural centre dedicated to avant-garde exhibitions and films. Its support of black culture started in 1972. After forming the Arts Liberation Front, an international organisation that challenged the political and cultural restrictions that artists were subjected to, David **Medalla** and John Dugger constructed 'People Weave a House' (1972). This was an installation where visitors were invited to contribute designs. In 1985 '**The Thin Black Line**', curated by Lubaina **Himid**, took place at the ICA. The exhibition showed works by Sonia **Boyce**, Sutapa **Biswas**, Maud **Sulter**, Ingrid **Pollard** and Chila Kumari **Burman**. It was the first black feminist exhibition to be shown in a major art institution. In 1986, after the publication of the report *Art on the South Bank*, the ICA invited the authors Balraj Khanna, Richard Cork and Shirley Reed to organise a seminar that discussed the level of support for black artists. In 1995 David A. **Bailey** curated 'Mirage', a multi-media exhibition. This was followed by a conference in which Stuart **Hall**, Paul **Gilroy** and Henry Lewis Gates jun. discussed issues raised by the exhibition. In 1998 Steve **McQueen** had his solo exhibition, which was followed by a conference entitled 'Steve McQueen: Me Political?'. The conference explored his interest in film (see **film and cinema**) and the way that he and other artists were moving away from the legacy of black art.

Further reading

ICA Documents 1972–1998, London.

PAULINE DE SOUZA

Institute of International Visual Arts

The foundation of the Institute of International Visual Arts (inIVA) was the result of a series of consultations by the Arts Council from 1990 onwards on the possibility of a visual arts (see **visual and plastic arts**) organisation that dealt with cultural diversity. It was founded as a limited company in 1993, and acquired permanent premises in 1995, with Stuart **Hall** as its chairman and Gilane Tawadros as its director. Its initial aims were to produce exhibitions, organise lectures and discussions, and initiate educational programmes in a field loosely demarcated by the term 'New Internationalism'. Despite initial hostility from other Arts Council clients, wary of an institute that specifically addressed cultural diversity, and members of the black visual art world who were uneasy with the concept of New Internationalism, the Institute has developed and consolidated its position as a major international arts organisation. Recent projects include solo retrospective exhibitions of artists such as Keith **Piper**, books ranging from international film (see **film and cinema**) to monographs and lecture series. As well as continuing to commission work and collaborate on ventures, the Institute also has a special interest in new technologies. Its library is one of the few places in the UK devoted to contemporary international art.

NIRU RATNAM

intellectual life

Unlike the USA, where a discernable African American intellectual tradition has existed throughout the century, black intellectual activity in Britain cannot be so easily defined in terms of a tradition or lineage. 'Black' (as a political articulation) is a more inclusive umbrella term in Britain, and nothing as distinctive as the long march of the US civil rights movement has publicly galvanised and defined black political and intellectual activity this side of the Atlantic. Yet, since the post-war period of large-scale migration to Britain (1953–4), black intellectual life has taken shape around two determinate strands: on the one hand, academic research, politics and policy-making; on the other, various forms of cultural-intellectual activity, which are distinct from strictly academic or publicly political forms of intellectual inquiry.

As in the USA, 'race relations' has been a primary focus of black intellectual intervention and debate. 'Race relations' became a dominant social issue in the late 1950s and 1960s, largely because of the weight of party-political consensus around the idea that putting a quota on the number of black people in Britain would enable better cross-racial social relations. In anticipation of the institutionalisation and legitimisation of racism – most notably exercised through the 1962 Commonwealth Immigrants Bill, which 'restricted the admission of Commonwealth settlers to those who had been issued with employment vouchers' (Fryer 1984: 381) – the Institute of Race Relations (IRR) was established in 1958 as an independent educational charity to 'promote the study of race relations and make suggestions for their improvement'. In 1972, the IRR began to respond more concertedly to the specific needs of black people in Britain. Its status as a 'think-tank', alongside its commitment to recognise and publicise the 'contribution that black people have made to this country's history in the struggle against racism', re-establishes links (if not an intellectual lineage) with intellectual forums such as the Pan-African Conference of 1900, which provided the 'first occasion upon which black men would assemble in England to speak for themselves and endeavour to influence public opinion' (Fryer 1984: 282).

Despite the pre-eminence of the 'black presence' as a catalyst for intellectual intervention, black intellectual endeavour in Britain has never been restricted to overtly political forms of engagement. Significant contributions to intellectual life include the work of novelist and writer Salman **Rushdie**, whose work has significantly advanced notions of hybridity and mongrelisation, the film-maker Isaac **Julien**, who uses both film (see **film and cinema**) and performance to interrogate the links between 'territory and identity, territory and control, [and] the spatial politics of surveillance' (Gilroy 1993: 167) and the painter Sonia **Boyce**, whose work distinctively examines the visual symbolism of ethnicity and national identities.

Intellectual life is, none the less, predicated on circularity: the intellectual is required to speak the language of intellectuals and needs to participate in those debates fuelled by intellectual inquiry. If intellectuality – or the condition of being an intellectual – is dependent on the need to reproduce or sustain oneself as an intellectual, then historically one of the most significant obstacles for the realisation of black intellectuals has been the forms of overt and institutionalised racism that have hindered their access to visible vehicles of intellectual legitimation: grants, fellowships, university chairs, publication, broadcast media, government committees, and other networks of knowledge that otherwise maintain Eurocentric theories of the political and aesthetic. Minority status produces a clear effect on the ideal of 'freedom' so commonly associated with the intellectual process. It also affects the public perception of the black intellectual. As Homi K. **Bhabha** points out in 'Black and white and read all over':

> It is commonly held that the authenticity of the intellectual, whether conservative or radical, is founded on the possibility of free and unfettered choice among competing ideas and interests.... By this logic, minority intellectuals lack the ethical autonomy to be properly representative because they lack the conditions of freedom: they are, so to speak, parti pris.
>
> (Bhabha 1999: 35)

In addition, the 'popular binarism between theory and politics, the intellectual and activist' has not assisted the broader understanding of black intellectual projects. As Bhabha cautions, 'there are many forms of political writing whose different effects are obscured when they are divided between the "theoretical" and the "activist"' (1999: 11). Paul **Gilroy**, whose writing has persistently interrogated the formal differences of black political and intellectual activity from the European mainstream, is 'fascinated with how successive generations of black intellectuals' have understood their interconnectedness with the 'intellectual heritage of the West since the Enlightenment'. Gilroy has consistently scrutinised this connection and analysed how black subjects have 'projected it in their writing and speaking, in pursuit of freedom,

citizenship, and social and political autonomy' (Gilroy 1993: 2).

As Gilroy is also acutely conscious, the 'problem of weighing claims of national identity against other contrasting varieties of subjectivity and identification has a special place in the intellectual history of blacks in the West' (1993: 30). This particular situation is touched on by Bhabha when he describes the predicament of the black intellectual who 'arises from behind the black mask to address a range of publics': 'there is a palpable anxiety,' Bhabha notes, 'about his or her "representative" status' (1999: 35). Stuart **Hall** is similarly – and more candidly – articulate about the burden of representativity surrounding the black intellectual. As a migrant, Hall feels it inappropriate to behave within Britain in line with the distinctive 'tradition in the Caribbean of what public intellectuals like me are supposed to do'. He is also extremely conscious that his social class and educational background has meant that he is 'deeply and profoundly... privileged in relation to the majority experience of blacks' (Drew 1999: 217). While Hall takes seriously his responsibility to voice the experiences of black British peoples, he emphasises that his expression of the majority experience will always be an 'interpretation':

> Intellectuals sometimes come on as if what they want to do is divest themselves of their intellectual responsibility and just be guys in the hood – and they're not. If they *can* make a connection, superb; but that in itself is a politics. It means learning from people you don't know; it means trying to understand experience; it means constructing alliances across differences that are ineradicable.
>
> (Drew 1999: 217)

For Hall, the intellectual is a highly visible, public figure. Although he resists unmediated and under-analysed notions of leadership, 'responsibility' and connectedness are major components of Hall's definition of the intellectual. Yet, if the high public profile of the intellectual creates difficulties and problems for black male intellectuals, then it is understandable that public assumptions surrounding the intellectual, or calls for community leadership, do not fit automatically or easily with black female intellectual activity.

Like Stuart Hall, the scholar bell hooks has spoken openly about her own social position, emphasising the 'great gulf' that is 'going to exist' between the underclass black woman and the 'experience of a black woman like myself whose position is very much in a bourgeois context' (Gilroy 1993: 222). None the less, hooks has lectured extensively on the troubling 'denial of gender as a problematic' that is evident in black political and intellectual activity, particularly in neo-black nationalism and Afrocentrism. For hooks, this act of denial 'creates a fiction of our social reality that is so dangerous because it can't really see what's happening with black women'. Noting that 75 per cent of the black poor in the USA are black women and children, hooks has argued persuasively that this statistic underscores similarities between the 'underclass black woman in Africa somewhere in an urban context and the underclass women in the United States' (Gilroy 1993: 222). This blindness to the situation of women has, hooks argues, 'made it difficult for us to create a group of dissident, insurgent black intellectuals who are moving in new ways on a different ground' (Gilroy 1993: 232). The very specific nexus of gender and blackness has been explored in a highly visible manner by philosopher Helen **(charles)**, whose name draws immediate attention to the problematics of the surname. (charles) not only foregrounds the otherwise naturalised patriarchal assumptions embedded in the conventional surname, but notes through her act of reinscription the fact that the family names of many African Caribbean people derive from slave-owning patronymics.

(charles)'s characteristic interrogation of the intersections and borders between personal experience and intellectual practice is shared also with cultural critic Gargi Bhattacharyya and cultural theorist Sara Ahmed. Each has provided intensely personalised and situated accounts of the interplay of colour, gender, politics and theory in black female identity within British post-imperial society. Heidi Safia **Mirza** has similarly noted the important connections between political and personal identity that characterise the work of many black women intellectuals. In her introduction to the seminal shaping anthology, *Black British Feminism: a Reader*, Mirza resists advancing a 'naïve essentialist universal notion of a homogeneous black womanhood' but points out that black British feminists are engaged in a subtle project to 'invoke some measure of critical race/gender reflexivity into mainstream academic thinking. In telling our different story, in exposing our personal pains and pleasures, Black British feminists reveal *other ways of knowing* that challenge the normative discourse' (Mirza 1997: 5). Mirza closes her introduction on an admonitory note: 'As long as there is exclusion, both in academic discourse and in materiality, there will be a black **feminism**' (Mirza 1997: 21).

The recognition of exclusionary practices alongside the need to keep visible the struggle for equality characterises the aims of the key journals of black intellectual debate. ***Race and Class***, founded in 1959 (and first published under the title *Race*), has long promoted black political writing and provided a forum for the voices of black radical intellectuals. During the 1970s, *Race Today*, launched by a collective of black activists, importantly recorded the activities of, and discrimination suffered by, black political groups. The international visual-studies journal ***Third Text*** was established in the mid-1980s to provide 'Third World perspectives on art and culture'. The late 1990s saw the launch of the interdisciplinary journal *Interventions*, with the explicit aim of providing both a forum for an international range of participants and a platform for the 'different and distinctive priorities, histories, and agendas' of 'postcolonial intellectuals'. With its references to post-colonial intellectuals and its intention to examine the documents that define the global post-colonial struggle, the launch of this journal documents the changing shape of black intellectual forums, critical theory and the nature of black intellectual debate within the academy at the turn of the century.

References

Bhabha, H.K. (1999) 'Black and white and read all over', in G.A. Olson and L. Worsham *Race, Rhetoric, and the Postcolonial*, New York: State University Press.

Drew, J. (1999) 'Cultural Composition: Stuart Hall on ethnicity and the discursive turn', in G.A. Olson and L. Worsham *Race, Rhetoric, and the*

Postcolonial, New York: State University Press, pp. 205–39.

Fryer, P. (1984) *Staying Power: the History of Black People in Britain*, London: Pluto.

Gilroy, P. (1993) *Small Acts: Thoughts on the Politics of Black Cultures*, London and New York: Serpent's Tail.

Mirza, H.S. (ed.) (1997) 'Introduction', in *Black British Feminism: a Reader*, London and New York: Routledge.

Further reading

Ahmed, S. (1998), *Differences that Matter*, Cambridge: Cambridge University Press.

(charles), H. (1992), 'Whiteness – the relevance of politically colouring the "non"', in H. Hinds *et al.* (eds) *Working Out: New Directions for Women's Studies*, Falmer: University of Brighton Press.

Cruse, H. (1967) *The Crisis of the Negro Intellectual*, New York: William Morrow.

Watts, J.G. (1994) *Heroism and the Black Intellectual: Ralph Ellison, Politics, and Afro-American Intellectual Life*, Chapel Hill and London: University of North Carolina Press.

LYNNETTE TURNER

International Book Fair of Radical Black and Third World Books

Organised by **Bogle L'Ouverture** Publications, **New Beacon Books** and **Race Today** Publications, the First International Book Fair of Radical Black and Third World Books was held in Islington, London, in April 1982. Largely the brainchild of poet, publisher and Book Fair Director John **La Rose**, it immediately became a prestigious annual event. Leading black artists and anti-racists including Suresh Grover, Gus John and Linton Kwesi **Johnson** sat on the Organising Committee. The ethos of the Book Fair was to mark the new and expanding phase in the growth of radical ideas and concepts, and their expression in **literature**, politics, **music**, art and social life. The Book Fair would host concerts, lectures, readings, conferences and forums on literature, arts, racism and racist attacks. Participants included artists and activists from Africa, the Caribbean and the USA. Actor Norman **Beaton**, poet (Edward) Kamau Brathwaite, playwright Biyi **Bandele** and actress and theatre director Yvonne **Brewster** are among the many that have participated. Though the main Book Fair remained London based, associated Book Fairs were also organised in Leeds, Bradford and Glasgow. Though in 1991 the organising Committee decided the Book Fair should be held every two years, the last was held in 1993.

ANDREA ENISUOH

J

Jaffrey, Madhur

b. Delhi, India

actor, cookery writer

Jaffrey grew up in Delhi and met her future husband, the actor Saeed **Jaffrey**, at Unity, an English **theatre** company in the city. She first came to the UK in the late 1950s as a drama student at the Royal Academy of Dramatic Arts, but the Jaffreys then moved to the USA, where she still lives and has remarried. She has worked in both radio and **television** drama, as well as acting in several Ismail Merchant films, including *Heat and Dust* (1982), *Shakespeare Wallah* (1965) and *Cotton Mary* (1999). She has acted on Broadway and in 1999 took a role in Ayub **Khan Din**'s *Last dance at Dum Dum* in London. In 1999, she also played the part of the traditional mother in the film (see **film and cinema**) *Chutney Popcorn* (1999) about an inter-racial, lesbian, parenting couple. However, she is best known in the UK as a cookery writer; she has published almost a dozen books on Indian cookery and also made an accompanying television series. In this way, Jaffrey has played a major part in making Indian food accessible to British cooks. She has her own line of Indian food products in association with Tilda.

ALISON DONNELL

Jaffrey, Saeed

b. 1929, East Punjab, India

actor

Saeed Jaffrey began his acting career in India, after forming Unity, an English **theatre** company in Delhi, where he met Madhur Bahadur, who later became his wife. He worked as a radio broadcaster with All India Radio and went to the USA on a Fulbright Scholarship, studying drama in Washington. The Jaffreys lived in the USA until the couple separated in 1964, when he came to work in the UK. The film (see **film and cinema**) that established him internationally was *The Man Who Would Be King* (1975), by John Huston, where he played the Gurka, Billy Fish. Other credits include *My Beautiful Laundrette* (1985) and *After Midnight* (1989). His Indian break came with Satyajit Ray's film *The Chess Players* (1977), where he played the aristocratic Meer (for which he won the Filmfare Award). This led to his being spotted by **Bollywood** where his first film was *Chashmé Buddoor* (1981), directed by Sai Paranjpe. To date he has appeared in over a hundred Bollywood films, including *Masoom* (1982), *Ram Teri Ganga Maili* (1985) and *Ram Lakhan* (1989), and he is noted in the *Guinness Book of Records Millennium Edition* as being the person with 'most appearances in international films'. He played three roles in *Masala*

Jamal, Ahmed 155

(1990), a film by the Canadian director Srinivas Krishna, for which he received a nomination as 'best actor' in 1991 for a Genie, the Canadian Academy Award. He is a well-known face on British television and was the dapper Jimmy Sharma, who ran the Jewel in the Crown restaurant in the **Channel 4** sitcom *Tandoori Nights*. He joined the UK's longest running soap *Coronation Street* for eight months, playing the international business tycoon Ravi Desai. A retrospective of Jaffrey's work was held at the Birmingham International Film and Television Festival in 1995, where he was given the Norman **Beaton** Award for his contribution to 'multi-cultural film and television'. More recently, he appeared on the British stage in *Staying On* (1997) and as Colonel Pickering in *My Fair Lady* (1998). He is an excellent mimic and performed all eighty-six characters and the narrator for a BBC world service radio version of Vikram Seth's *A Suitable Boy* (1997). In 1995, he was awarded an OBE for services to drama.

Select bibliography

Jaffrey, S. (1998) *Saeed: An Actor's Journey*, London: Constable.

SUMAN BHUCHAR

Jah Shaka

b. Clarendon, Jamaica

Rastafarian cultural activist, musician, performer, percussionist, record producer/promoter, reggae sound system owner/selector/operator

Heralded as one of the true pioneers of black **music** in Britain, since the mid-1970s the name Jah Shaka has become synonymous with Rastafarian (see **Rastafari**) roots music, dubwise and Marcus Garvey's black consciousness. After learning the business on a local sound system (see **sound system DJs**), 'Freddie Cloudburst', during the early 1970s, Shaka left to create his own sound, which has now acquired legendary status. Shaka's live events are renowned for their spiritually uplifting nature, and are described as having 'a cleansing effect on the soul'. Shaka, who named himself after the Afrikan warrior Shaka Zulu, is widely regarded as King David's warrior and is a true exponent of what the US rapper KRS-1 dubs 'edutainment'. This is the power to educate and entertain the masses on a humanitarian level, through positive messages from an Afrocentric musical perspective. Shaka is also a recording artist in his own right, as well as a proficient record producer for his own Jah Shaka label, which has featured many leading recording artists from the UK, Africa and the Caribbean. What is in many ways unique about Shaka is the fact that his message is universal and therefore his live performances attract a largely cosmopolitan audience, without any hint of compromising his Rastafarian perspective. From his London base, Shaka is involved in many educational, cultural and health projects that demonstrate his commitment to the global black struggle. The Jah Shaka Foundation exemplifies this commitment, as it provides assistance to various projects in Jamaica, Ghana and Ethiopia. The Foundation has managed to distribute medical supplies, wheelchairs, books, various tools and even transportation to some of the clinics and schools in these areas, as well as making other significant contributions to their local communities. In the words of the man himself: 'Music must have two essential qualities, it must be spiritually uplifting and educational. . . . Music to me is like a part of life, like my Rastafarian faith, and as long as I continue living I'll continue loving God and playing music.'

WILLIAM HENRY

Jamal, Ahmed

b. 1951, Lucknow, India

director, producer

Ahmed Jamal was born and brought up in the Indian subcontinent. He comes from a distinguished family of Muslim scholars in Lucknow. He studied in Bangladesh and worked as a copywriter for an advertising agency in Pakistan. He came to Britain in 1973 and was originally involved with Bite Theatre, a group that produced non-naturalistic political **theatre**. In 1982, he went to study film at the London International Film School. After graduation, together with his brother Mahmood **Jamal** he set up the first fully franchised Asian workshop, **Retake Film and Video Collective**. Here, he directed the first British Independent Asian feature film (see **film and cinema**), *Majdhar* (1984). Jamal, set up an independent company, First Take Limited, in 1989, specialising in factual current affairs documentaries about the Middle East and Asian communities of the UK. He produced and directed many pioneering observational documentaries for BBC and **Channel 4**, including: *A Suitable Girl* (1995), on the arranged marriage system among the British Asian community; *The Bounty Hunter* (1992), about a man who brings back runaway girls; *Dancing Girls of Lahore* (1991), on the dancing girls based at the Diamond Market of Lahore; and *The Fundamental Question* (1994), a seminal work focusing on how the West encouraged Islamic radicalism in the Middle East. His 1994 *Beach Boys of Sri Lanka* for BBC 2 won the One World Broadcasting Trust Award for network **television**. In 1999, he directed, *Dead Man Talking*, a ground-breaking murder investigation using forensics for Channel 4. It was nominated for the BBC TV's Asia Awards. Jamal has directed *Mad Dogs* (2000), an independently financed retro sci-fi feature-length comedy set in London. It stars Jonathan Pryce, Paul Barber, Saaed **Jaffrey**, Iain Fraser and Indira Varma.

SUMAN BHUCHAR

Jamal, Mahmood

b. 1948, Lucknow, India

poet, writer, producer

Mahmood Jamal, who comes from a distinguished family of Muslim religious scholars in Lucknow, came to the UK in 1967. Jamal has been involved with the political and cultural life of Britain. He was a regular participant in *Black Voices*, a forum for Third World writers, which he co-edited (with Rasheed **Araeen**), and *Black Phoenix*, a serious

magazine looking at contemporary art from a Third World perspective.

During the 1970s and 1980s, Jamal was writing and performing poetry at the Trubador Café and with Poetry Olympics. His poems appeared in the *London Magazine, Poetry Round* and were heard on Radio 3. Together with his brother, Ahmed **Jamal**, he set up **Retake Film and Video Collective** in 1983 to engage in film (see **film and cinema**) production. Jamal produced documentaries with Retake and in 1989 set up his own company, Epic Flow Films, which has produced many **television** series, such as *The Peacock Screen* (1991), on Indian cinema, and *Islamic Conversations* (1993), on Islam and modernism. He was the lead writer for *Family Pride*, the first Asian soap made by **Channel 4** and Central Television. In 1997, he wrote and produced *Turning World*, a three-part drama for Channel 4 about the closure of a mental asylum, starring Roshan Seth and Art Malik, and directed by David Blair. Jamal is active in the Producers Alliance for Cinema and Television, where he talks about equal representation of Blacks and Asians in the television world.

Select bibliography

Jamal, M. (ed. and trans.) (1986) *The Penguin Book of Modern Urdu Poetry*, London: Penguin.
—— (1992) *Grandchildren of Albion*, London: New Departures [cassette/CD version, 1994].

SUMAN BHUCHAR

James, C.L.R.

b. 1901, Tunapuna, Trinidad; d. 1989, Brixton, England

historian, novelist, political analyst, cultural critic, journalist, activist

Cyril Lionel Robert James is an iconic figure in the culture of the Caribbean diaspora as a result of his lifetime of anti-establishment agitation, his faith in ordinary people and his celebration of culture. Following the division made by Paul **Gilroy** in the **black**

Atlantic, James seems to belong firmly on the side of 'routes' – travel, movement – rather than 'roots' – belonging and stable identification. James came to Britain from the Caribbean in 1932, lived in the USA from 1939 to 1953, spent much of the 1960s and 1970s travelling in Africa, Europe and America, and in 1981 'settled' in Brixton, London, where he died in 1989. James's intellectual journeying is even more extensive and impressive than his physical travels, so much so that only part of it can be mentioned here. During his early years in Britain, James wrote on cricket for the *Manchester Guardian*, which eventually led to one of his best-known books *Beyond a Boundary* (1963), generally still regarded as one of the classic studies of cricket, but also a remarkable demonstration of the way in which sport – for which many still blindly continue to claim apolitical status – is enmeshed in politics, ideology and more. In the case of cricket, this consisted of a particularly powerful combination of colonialism and capitalism, race and class. James's radically different and challenging perspective on cricket is typical of his intellectual approach, and even in relatively early works like *The Black Jacobins* and *A History of Negro Revolt*, both published in 1938, he was tackling subjects that were unpopular or, in the case of the latter, almost unheard of. In the former, James offers a fundamental re-evaluation of the history of the San Domingo slave rebellion, challenging the interpretations of specific events as well as more widely held perceptions of the roles of the black slaves and the Western nations.

Among key ideas from these books to which James remained loyal were the ability of the masses to think and act for themselves, the complex interaction of race and class, and the connections and continuities between resistant or revolutionary struggles, even those that appear to be geographically or historically separated. James was far more than an intellectual analyst of race and class resistance, however. During his early years in Britain he was a member of the Independent Labour Party, while his time in the USA saw him involved with Trotskyist groups. He had a long-held belief in Pan-Africanism, and was involved in the epoch-making Fifth Pan-African Congress in Manchester in 1945, which included so many leaders of African and Caribbean independence.

The fact that so many of these leaders, epitomised by James's one-time friend Kwame Nkrumah in Ghana, allowed the promise of independence to be betrayed did little to dent James's remarkable life-long faith in the potential of ordinary people.

Select bibliography

James, C.L.R. (1980) *Spheres of Existence*, London: Allison & Busby.
—— (1971) *Minty Alley*, London: New Beacon Books.
—— (1963) *Beyond a Boundary*, London: Hutchinson.
—— (1938) *The Black Jacobins: Toussaint L'Ouverture and the San Domingo Revolution*.

PATRICK WILLIAMS

Jantjes, Gavin

b. 1948, Cape Town, South Africa

artist, writer, curator, arts administrator

Jantjes studied in South Africa and, later, in Hamburg. There he explored screen-printing techniques and much of his early work was politically charged graphic work. He came to the UK in 1982 and became involved within the circle of black art through conference papers, articles and his own artwork. Jantjes exhibited in the major group shows, 'Into the Open', **'The Essential Black Art'** and **'The Other Story'**. He also co-curated and exhibited in **'From Two Worlds'**. Jantjes's work traced the history of the diaspora, among other themes. Jantjes was a council member of the Arts Council of Great Britain, and was responsible for the Arts Council's policy on Cultural Diversity. With the disbanding of the **Greater London Council** in 1986, which had been the most important funder of black culture, this was a crucial spell for the Arts Council. Jantjes was the Arts Council consultant during the creation of the **Institute of International Visual Arts**, the institution born from the legacy of 1980s black visual art practices. Jantjes is currently Artistic Director of the Henie Onstad Kunstsenter in Oslo, Norway.

Select bibliography

Jantjes, G. (1998) *A Fruitful Incoherence*, London: inIVA.

NIRU RATNAM

Jazzie B

b. 1963, England

entrepreneur, songwriter, producer, artist, DJ, founder of Soul II Soul

Born Romeo Beresford, Jazzie B was the catalyst in taking underground black British culture and integrating it into the mainstream through his company **Soul II Soul**. Founded in 1982 by Jazzie B and Phillip 'Daddae' Harvey, Soul II Soul was initially a sound system, but it became an empire. Jazzie B signed Soul II Soul, the recording group and label, to Virgin Records and enjoyed massive club success with the single 'Fairplay' featuring Rose Windross in 1987. Soul II Soul's profile increased with the success of their two clothing stores and Jazzie B's profile as a club and pirate DJ. Jazzie B used a plethora of talented singers, musicians and producers, and helped fuse the most influential sounds of young black Britain (**reggae**, lovers, jazz and rare grooves) and transpose them into Afrocentric UK street soul. Soul II Soul went on to win two Grammy Awards for 'Back To Life' and 'African Dance'. Their 1989 debut album, *Club Classics Volume One* became, arguably, the definitive UK **soul** album of the 1980s and, perhaps, the 1990s too. Since 1987, they have sold almost 30 million records world-wide. In 1996, Jazzie B, still the foundation of Soul II Soul, won a special award for his contribution to **music** at the inaugural MOBO awards. He has also built a recording studio in Antigua.

DEREK A. BARDOWELL

Jean-Baptiste, Marianne

b. 1969, London, England

actress, singer

Jean-Baptiste trained at the Royal Academy of Dramatic Art. She made her film (see **film and cinema**) debut in the 1991 film, *London Kills Me*. Her performance as Hortense in the award-winning *Secrets and Lies* won her an Oscar nomination (1997) for Best Supporting Actress. It was this film that sealed her importance as a black actor in the British film industry, for she became the first black British person to receive a nomination. This is also significant in terms of gender and the roles open to black British actresses. Nominations for a Bafta Award and Golden Globe Award as Best Performance by an Actress in a Supporting Role were received for the same film. The year 1997 became a turning point for Jean-Baptiste. Critical of the discrimination within the British film industry and voicing her disappointment at being omitted from a group of actors invited to celebrate the fiftieth anniversary of the Cannes Film Festival, she sought work in the USA. Her subsequent credits include *28 Days* (2000) with Sandra Bullock and *The Cell* (2000) with Jennifer Lopez. Jean-Baptiste has worked in **television**, and on stage at the National Theatre in *The Way of the World* and Shakespeare's *Measure for Measure*. She is a classically trained singer who has recorded a blues album and co-written **music** for the film *Career Girls* (1997). Her latest film, *Women in 2001*, is a comedy drama. Jean-Baptiste is married to ballet dancer Evan Williams and has a daughter.

YINKA SUNMONU

Jegede, Emmanuel Taiwo

b. 1943, Nigeria

sculptor, poet, story writer, book illustrator

Jegede came to England in 1963, having completed a sculpture apprenticeship in Lagos. He set up a studio and foundry at Riverside, London, in 1970 and, through work with the Africa Centre, Keskidee Centre, Commonwealth Institute and Westbourne Gallery became known for his carved and bronze-cast sculpture, and also for his 'spiritual and allegorical' paintings. His work adheres to Yoruba tradition, expressively relaying folk tales and operating as metaphorical symbols of hope, despair, fortitude and inequality. He was a member of the panel for Festac 1977 – the Second World Black and African Festival of Arts – and returned to Nigeria in 1982 to make sculpture for a year at the invitation of the government. Jegede purposefully shunned assimilation by European influence to speak in a language common to the people of his homeland. As a result, his work's position within British culture rather insistently asserts the African foundations of European modernism. 'The vitality of the sculptures and paintings...speak clearly of the creative energy that has gone into reconciling two dauntingly different cultures' (*City Limits* 1984: 25–31). He wrote the lyrics for a musical – *The Father and Child Reunion* – and is known internationally as a poet, story writer and book illustrator, which are all means by which he broadcasts his interest in stories. In the early 1980s he worked as an artist/designer for Haringey Council and has throughout his career made numerous works for public spaces. In 1986, he made *Prayer of Peace* for Islington Council, installed in Elthorne Park. Another example is *Endless Omen* in Nene Park, Peterborough. His exhibitions include 'New Horizons' (1985), 'The Colours of Black' (1986) and 'Joy of a Living Race' (1994).

Further reading

Fox, G. (1986) *Arts Review* (14 December): 686.
Garlake, M. (1986) *Art Monthly* 96 (May): 13.
Hodge, A. (1986) *Meshack Asare: Emmanuel Taiwo Jegede – Paintings, Ceramics, and Poems.*
Lee, D. (1986) *Arts Review* (31 January): 42.

PAUL O'KANE

Jeyasingh, Shobana

b. 1957, Madras, India

artistic director

Shobana Jeyasingh established the Shobana Jeyasingh Dance Company in 1989, as an all-female British Indian company. In 1993 they won the Prudential Awards for the Arts. Shobana Jeyasingh was awarded an MBE in 1995. The **dance** company specialise in producing new works along-side live **music**, educational outreach, residencies and choreographic commissions. Company policy is to create work that is Asian in technique and British in context. Hence, Jeyasingh fuses the classical Indian dance technique of *Bharat Natayam*, in which all of the company's dancers are trained, with contemporary British influences alongside dance styles that draw, for instance, on martial arts from north-east India. Pieces such as *Intimacies of the Third Order* offer, feels Jeyasingh, a third order, something other than the 'norm'. The third space is, for her, a space where that other than binaries can grow, a space that gives power to the edges. Jeyasingh's 1999 piece *Configurations* reflected her own situation as a classically trained Indian dancer living in London, while *Fine Frenzy* (1999) is equally inspired by the shifting cultural mix she experiences in London.

SAMINA ZAHIR

Joe Bloggs

A mass-market fashion (see **fashion and design**) company established in 1986, the Joe Bloggs brand is the brainchild of flamboyant entrepreneur Shami Ahmed (b. 1962, Pakistan), who came to Britain in 1964. Most famous for the extra-wide, low-slung, flared jeans that were popular among Manchester ravers in the early 1990s, the style is brash basics: baggy denims and T-shirts emblazoned with the Joe Bloggs name. The company's success in the hugely competitive jeans market was partly due to keeping most of the production in Britain, enabling new styles to be supplied to shops more quickly. Ahmed first worked on his father's market stall in Lancashire, before persuading him to set up the Legendary Joe Bloggs Inc. Co., combining both his knack for self-promotion and his desire for a distinctively British-sounding company in its name.

Bloggs is now just part of a portfolio of clothing businesses run by Ahmed, including Gabicci and Elizabeth Emanuel, as Ahmed has branched out into purchasing and turning around ailing companies. His continued presence in the *Sunday Times* 'Rich List' is a marker of his financial acumen and he continues to expand his fashion and property interests.

Further reading

Davies, Hunter (1994) 'Not any old Joe Bloggs', *The Independent 2*, 15 November.

REBECCA ARNOLD

Johnson, Amryl

b. 1960, Tunapuna, Trinidad; d. 2001, England

novelist, essayist, poet

Born in Tunapuna, Trinidad, Amryl Johnson immigrated to England at the age of eleven. She majored in African and Caribbean studies at the University of Kent. The experience of being a transplant in British society continuously informs her work – in her first book of poetry, published in 1982, *Long Road to Nowhere* and in later works, *Tread Carefully in Paradise* (1991), *Blood and Wine* (1991) *Gorgons* (1992) and *Calling* (2000). For her, the daily facts of life in Britain are that 'Black women in white-dominated Britain...are having to deal with as much racism as ever' (*New Internationalist*, January 1992) Her book, *Sequins for a Ragged Hem* (1987), is the story of her return to the Caribbean as a native but also a stranger/outsider. Immersed back into her birth culture, national and cultural identities become confusing: 'Again and again, these seven words stabbed at my brain: Where do you stand in all this?...The question of identity was a very powerful and disturbing one.' Johnson gave poetry readings, participated in writers' workshops and was often a writer-in-residence in the British school system.

Select bibliography

Johnson, A. (1987) *Sequins for a Ragged Hem*, London: Virago.
—— (1982) *Long Road to Nowhere*, London: Sable Publications.

TRACY J. PRINCE

Johnson, Linton Kwesi

b. 1952, Jamaica

poet, musician, political activist

Linton Kwesi Johnson came to live in London in 1963. He went to school in Brixton and did a degree in sociology at Goldsmiths College, University of London. At school, Johnson was active in the Black Panthers, later becoming a founding member of the **Race Today** Collective. His poetry is characterised by its commitment to black politics, and many of his poems were first performed at significant demonstrations in the 1970s and early 1980s. Johnson's earliest work was published in the Collective's journal *Race Today*. His second collection *Dread Beat and Blood* appeared both in print and on vinyl, marking the beginning of his experimentation with dub poetry (poetry which draws on the rhythms of **reggae music** and Rastafarian speech). In 1980, he formed his own record label, LKJ, and subsequently released a number of albums. Johnson received a C. Day Lewis Fellowship in 1977 and was also awarded at the thirteenth Premo Internazionale Ultimo Novecento for his achievements in poetry and music. His work continues to challenge generic conventions and presents a highly charged fusion of political, lyrical and performative elements.

Select bibliography

Johnson, L.K. (1991) *Tings and Times: Selected Poems*, Newcastle upon Tyne: Bloodaxe Books.
—— (1980) *Inglan is a Bitch*, London: Race Today Publications.
—— (1975) *Dread Beat and Blood*, London: Bogle L'Ouverture.

JAMES PROCTER

Joi

Joi came into being as Joi Bangla, an East London organisation dedicated to promoting aspects of Bengali and South Asian cultures in the mid-1980s. Out of this came the Joi Bangla sound system formed by the London-born brothers Farook and Haroon Shamsher. In 1988, the pair released a white label single 'Taj Mahal' and began introducing their own material into Joi Bangla sets. As Joi they released their debut single 'Desert storm' in 1992 and set up the Joi club night in London a year later. In 1996, they released the *Bangladesh* e.p. on **Nation Records** and performed at that year's **WOMAD** festival. This led to them signing to Real World, for whom they recorded their debut album *One and One Is One*, which was released in 1998. Sadly, in 1999, Haroon died of a heart attack aged thirty-three. Just prior to his untimely death he had visited Bangladesh and made a series of field recordings, which Farook used as the basis for Joi's second album *We Are Three*, which was released in 2000. Despite having only released a handful of records in a long career, Joi remain at the forefront of an innovative Asian British **music** scene.

ANDY WOOD

Jones, Adebayo

b. 1964, Nigeria

fashion designer

Adebayo Jones established his name as a trading name to enable him to carry out commissions for private clients. A Bachelors degree holder in history and sociology, Jones turned to fashion (see **fashion and design**) to fulfil a lifelong passion, enrolling at the Central School of Fashion (1998–9), where he enhanced his skills in design, pattern cutting and garment construction. He later found work with Talala Couture, Katherine Hamnett and Isabell Kristensen Couture in their well-established fashion houses. The focus of Jones's work is on ladies' daywear, occasion/evening and bridal wear. He creates spectacular gowns with elaborate techniques that show off his expertise. His history and background are influential in his work, which is drawn from an interest in art, travel and archival research. Jones's trademarks are period corsetry and boned bodices, plus fine tailoring together with the use of classic lines and luxurious fabrics. He also uses damask and lace, which hints at his African origin. He exhibits at trade shows all over

the world, at fashion shows in London and Switzerland, on the BBC's *Clothes Show* and at the London Fashion Café. Jones's clients include supermodels, and celebrities from stage, screen and the media. Features have appeared in *OK*, *Inside Soap* and ***Pride*** magazine. He has appeared at a private showing at the Queen's Boardroom on Epsom Ladies Day.

YINKA SUNMONU

Jones, Fae

b. 1972, Oxford, England

vocalist, performer

In Oxford, during the mid-1980s, Fae Jones became a member of the internationally acclaimed Pegasus Theatre and African/Caribbean performance artists Foundations. She built on this early activity, performing at various venues of the underground rave phenomenon that swept through Britain in the late 1980s and early 1990s. In 1990 she became lead vocalist in a Bristol-based group Sublove, with co-member DJ Die. Later on that year she worked with both DJ Die and Roni Size (see **Size, Roni/Reprazent**).

Jones relocated to London in 1993 where she joined an all-girl R'n'B group, Infiniti. The following year Infiniti signed to Warner Brothers/Chapell Recordings and released their debut single 'Tonite'. The group toured nationally and internationally, and worked with both British and US producers, including Michael Nerada Walden. In 1995, they signed to Arista Records and released their second single 'Will you be my baby', which entered the Top 40 pop charts. Infiniti appeared on many **television** programmes and performed at community events like AraFest (Anti-Racist Alliance Festival). In 1998, a year after launching her solo career, Jones was nominated for a MOBO (Music Of Black Origin) Award and became involved with various projects working with producers both in Britain and the USA.

DORETH JONES

Jordan, Diane Louise

b. 1962, London, England

presenter, actress

In 1990, Diane Louise Jordan became the first black presenter on *Blue Peter*, one of the BBC's flagship children's **television** programmes. Her career path could have been different if she had opted to go to Manchester University to read English, instead of taking up a dare to apply to the Rose Bruford drama school in Kent, the former college of Bernardine **Evaristo**. Jordan spent six years on *Blue Peter* and, when she left in February 1996, a show was devoted to her participation over the years and a potted history. Work in adult television beckoned. She presented *Songs of Praise* and co presented *The London Marathon*. There were additional credits – *Bright Sparks*, *Out and About* and *All that Matters* for BBC 1, *Animal Times* (a programme about a wildlife hospital) and *Dream Ticket* for LWT. Jordan has participated in Children in Need and, patron of many charities, she supports NCH National Action for Children and has helped to launch National Adoption Week, the yearly adoption awareness campaign organised by the British Agencies for Adoption and Fostering for potential adopters and foster carers. She is also the patron of the British Dental Health Foundation. Jordan presented the special broadcast of *Diana, One Year On*, marking the anniversary of the death of the Princess of Wales and was the only celebrity invited to sit on the high-profile Diana, Princess of Wales Memorial Committee by Chancellor Gordon Brown. As an actress she had a small part in Mike Leigh's 1988 film (see **film and cinema**) *High Hopes* and appears in pantomime. Her success, along with Andi **Peters**'s, has paved the way for more black presenters such as Josie D'Arby and Angelica Bell.

YINKA SUNMONU

Joseph, Tam

b. 1947, Dominica

artist

Joseph exhibited in a number of black art exhibitions, including 'Into the Open' and '**From Two Worlds**', and was an important member of the circle of practitioners and theorists engaged in debates about what black art might constitute. Joseph came to the UK aged eight and studied at the Central School of Art and, briefly, the Slade. Like many, he was deeply influenced in the 1970s by the US Civil Rights movement, and developed a direct but always witty style. Joseph's works range from ironic tableaux of social ills through to simplified, quasi-naïve works that reference media and popular depictions of British blacks. During the mid-1980s, Joseph's work was characterised by simple, caricatured figures bringing humour into the field of anti-racism, and prefiguring later uses of irony by 1990s artists. Joseph's iconography might owe something to his background as a graphic designer but it ought not to be overlooked that he has experimented widely with materials, for instance using sand to good effect in a number of works.

Further reading

Chambers, E. (1999) 'Tam Joseph: learning to walk', in V. Clarke and G. Tawadros *Run through the Jungle: Selected Writings by Eddie Chambers*, London: inIVA.

NIRU RATNAM

Julien, Isaac

b. 1960, London

film-maker

Born in London's East End, Julien came to prominence in the 1980s as a founder member of **Sankofa Film Collective**. He studied film at St Martins, where he made the short documentary *Who Killed Colin Roach?* in 1983. The theme of this film was the death in custody in mysterious circumstances of the black youth, Colin Roach, in Stoke Newington police station. The film focuses on the black community's struggle for recognition of the fact that there were questions for the police to answer and that continued brutality was no response. Already we can see the outline of the themes that Julien has continued to explore in work for both film and **television**.

Sankofa, along with **Black Audio Film Collective**, pioneered new forms of film-making that explored the black presence in Britain in a variety of innovative ways. Eschewing the tools of documentary, they attempted to incorporate not just a black consciousness but also a historical subconscious, reaching back into the multiple routes of memory to understand the position of the black Briton in the 1980s. A perfect example is Sankofa's 1986 production *The Passion of Remembrance*, directed by Julien and Maureen **Blackwood**, which interweaves a variety of themes and narratives to achieve an almost dreamlike quality. Also notable is the introduction and incorporation of a detailed set of questions concerning gender and sexuality, and their role in black struggle. In the hands of Julien the very category of black is deconstructed and shown to be multiple. Black identity is not simply an essentialised given but, rather, in line with the formulations of theoreticians such as Stuart **Hall**, it is a process of being in the world that can take innumerable shapes. These concerns inform Julien's filmic tribute to the African American poet Langston Hughes, *Looking for Langston*. Released in 1989, this was a great critical success, even if some were less than pleased about Julien's treatment of the poet's sexuality.

The attention that such work attracted led the **British Film Institute** to back a feature production that eventually had a budget of £1.2 million, which was a significant deal for a British independent. The film, *Black Soul Rebels*, was released in 1991. It incorporated all the ideas that Julien had been working with over the previous decade. Taking the watershed year of 1977, it examined the British **soul** scene of the time. In doing so it deliberately left the terrain of certain political narratives of the time that played up the alliance of punk and **reggae** under the sign of the Anti-Nazi League. By doing so Julien produced a complex examination of the legacy of empire in a post-colonial country. While the film attracted a great deal of attention, generating the funds for further feature length projects has proved difficult.

A programme produced originally for television went on general cinema release in 1996. In this film, *Frantz Fanon: Black Skin, White Mask*, the techniques Julien used in *Looking* were employed to treat the life of Frantz Fanon, but the effect was not as stunning, perhaps because, although fierce in his revolutionary resolve, Fanon was austere in his sexuality. None the less, some of Julien's other work for television deserves mention. The two-part *Black and White in Colour*, which was broadcast in 1992, was a magnificent survey of the black image on television. The 1994 programme he made for *Arena*, 'The Darker Side of Black', explored the homophobic cultures of **hip hop** and Jamaican **dancehall**, and ended on the uncomfortable thought, enunciated by the programme's narrator, theorist Paul **Gilroy**, that the violence inherent in these subcultures might itself be a legacy of slavery. This link-up with academics has been one of the strengths of Julien's *œuvre* (academics have found his movies attractive too: Gilroy had a cameo role in *Rebels* and Stuart Hall appeared in Julien's 1993 short *The Attendant*), which has constantly challenged the easy answers and struggled to find comfort in complexity.

GARETH STANTON

jungle

Between 1992 and 1994, jungle emerged from the British hardcore scene, which in itself was a mutation of the predominant house/rave scene. Unlike hardcore, with its emphasis on speed and stripped down sounds and cartoonish samples, jungle has been a more hybrid sound, equally as influenced by **hip hop** and dub **reggae** as it is by house and techno. Simon Reynolds suggested that 'Jungle is where all of the different musics of the African American/Afro-Caribbean diaspora reconverge.' The site of this reconvergence was in Britain, particularly London, and jungle was seen as an indigenous British musical form. Fiercely underground, jungle relied upon a small but rapidly expanding network of small record labels, pirate radio stations and clubs. The 12" single and dub-plate were the main currency of jungle as opposed to albums and compact discs, reviving a tradition that had dominated the reggae sound systems both in Jamaica and in Britain.

When the jungle scene was given media exposure it was portrayed as being a dark, dangerous scene, which excluded non-blacks, despite the fact that crowds at raves were mixed, as were the producers of the music. Many artists did cultivate outlaw images to display their status as outsiders, which came to the fore in releases such as **A Guy Called Gerald**'s *28 Gun Bad Boy* and Shy FX's 'Gangsta kid'. However, jungle was a broad church and less dark records such as 4 Hero's 'Journey into the light' and **LTJ Bukem**'s 'Atlantis' showed different facets to Jungle. The year 1994 saw jungle begin to break into the mainstream scene with General Levy and M Beat's 'Incredible' reaching the Top 40. This simultaneously brought jungle to a wider audience and highlighted schisms within the scene. Many people within the jungle community dismissed the record as a novelty. Essentially a reworking of a ragga track originally released by Levy entitled 'Incredible general', the record was a lightweight jungle track. Other artists such as **Goldie**, 4 Hero, LTJ Bukem and **Grooverider** were to take a once derided form even further into the mainstream. Goldie's 1995 album *Timeless* was heralded as the first jungle album, although its release was preceded by A Guy Called Gerald's *Black Secret Technology* and 4 Hero's *Parallel Universe*.

However, the success of *Timeless* was unprecedented and saw jungle become accepted by, and absorbed into, the mainstream. Many artists shied away from the major label and media co-option of a once derided scene and musical form. Jungle broke off into two main camps: the ambient, jazz-influenced drum and bass of artists such as Bukem and the more experimental underground sounds of Johnny L, Ed Rush and Dilinja. Radio 1 once again stepped in where the pirates had once innovated and began the highly successful *One in the Jungle* programme. Jungle remixes are almost compulsory additions to most mainstream artists' releases and Goldie is almost a household name, although many of the scene's original movers and much of the music have been marginalised.

ANDY WOOD

K

Kaliphz

Rochdale MCs Kaliphz released their debut single 'Vibe da joint', in 1994. Their songs were constructed around the mixing, scratching and ragged instrumentation of the Funk Regulators with the five MCs rapping at breakneck speed. At a time when British **hip hop** was largely derided by audiences as being inferior to US imports, Kaliphz were one of only a few Asian British acts, along with Hustlers HC, on the scene, which made their success and impact all the more significant. Kaliphz' first few singles were largely devoid of political content or references to the band's background, although Kaliphz were quick to point out that, as Asians in the hip hop world, by simply performing and recording they were involved in a political act, and Kaliphz' third single 'Hang 'em high' was an open attack on organised racism. In 1996, Kaliphz released their debut album *Seven Deadly Sins* and a collaboration with the boxer Prince Nasseem, 'Walk like a champion', which was the band's first Top 30 hit. Despite the success of the single, Kaliphz have not recorded or performed since 1997.

ANDY WOOD

Kapoor, Anish

b. 1954, Bombay, India.

artist, sculptor

Kapoor attended Hornsey College of Art (1973–7)

and Chelsea School of Art (1977–8). He showed his early work in group shows such as 'Object and Sculpture' (1981), at the **Institute of Contemporary Arts**, and in solo shows, including the Lisson Gallery in 1982. His early sculptures included his well known, striking rounded organic forms in pigmented powder. In 1983, he exhibited in the group show at the Hayward Gallery 'The Sculpture Show', and showed at the 'XVII Bienale de São Paulo', Brazil, in the same year. His work has been represented and shown by the Lisson Gallery since 1982. In 1989, his exhibition 'Anish Kapoor: Drawings' appeared at the Tate Gallery. He won the Turner Prize in 1991 and has acquired an international reputation. Kapoor's work now focuses on huge monumental pieces using materials such as limestone, fibreglass and polished steel to create excavations of space. These works reveal a preoccupation with voids and cavities, playing with presence and absence, as in 'Adam' (1988–9) and 'Ghost' (1997). He held a very successful major installation in 1998 at the Hayward Gallery, including a series of polished steel concave and convex structures embedded into the structures of the gallery floor and walls requiring structural alterations to the gallery itself.

Further reading

Bhabha, H.K. (1998) 'Anish Kapoor: making emptiness', in *Anish Kapoor*, Berkeley and London: Hayward Gallery, University of California Press, pp. 11–41.

ELEANOR BYRNE

Kapur, Shekhar

b. 1945, India

film-maker

Born into an Indian film (see **film and cinema**) dynasty, Kapur graduated from the Hindi film industry as an actor, in films such as *Ishq Ishq Ishq* (1974) and *Bhula Na Dena* (1980), and as a director/producer. His Hindi directorial debut *Masoom* (1982) was followed by the curry western *Joshilay* (1985), from which he resigned before completion, and then *Mr India* (1987), an invisible man story. A qualified chartered accountant, Kapur also worked as a fashion (see **fashion and design**) model, advertising and **television** director, and presenter on the provocative **Channel 4** discussion programme *On the Other Hand*, before directing *Bandit Queen* in 1994. Kapur's controversial film about the life of the low-caste folk heroine Phoolan Devi incurred the wrath of censors, politicians, and Devi herself on charges of defamation. None the less, *Bandit Queen* was critically acclaimed as a powerful portrayal of caste and female oppression. In 1998, Kapur directed the Oscar-nominated historical epic *Elizabeth* in another study of personal and political female transformation, depicting Elizabeth's accession as Queen against the religious conflicts and violence of seventeenth-century England. Successfully bridging the Hindi and British film industries, Kapur is currently collaborating with Andrew Lloyd Webber on both the tentatively titled **Bollywood** stage musical *Bombay Dreams* and a screen adaptation of Webber's *The Phantom of the Opera*. In addition to his Indian Starlight Television company, Kapur has also launched plans for the broadband Web channel IndiaGeek.com with Farrukh **Dhondy** to stream innovative short films, dramas, animation and documentaries for the Indian diaspora.

SATINDER CHOHAN

KAPUR, STEVE *see* Apache Indian

Kaur, Parm

poet, playwright, performer, live art producer and director

Parm Kaur has written, performed, directed and produced several **live art** works. For the 10th Anniversary Celebrations of the **Asian Women Writers' Collective** in 1994, she performed in *Head Heart Affairs*, which brought together **dance**, poetry, flute and saxophone. In 1995, she wrote and produced *And You Ask Me Why Are You Angry?*. A solo piece with elements of text, movement and electro-acoustic music, it was a commission for the Asian Women Writers' Collective and was performed at the Oval House, London. Another commission, this time from the Junction in Cambridge, followed in 1996 for a Transhalles European Conference. In the same year, Kaur was invited to join a series of playwrighting workshops with 'Spread the Word', and working with Winsome **Pinnock** led to a workshop and reading of Kaur's play *One Day My Prince Will Come* at the Oval House. *The Story of the Moon*, combining Kathak dance, *tabla*, prose and poetry, was first performed at the Battersea Arts Centre in 1996 and at the Pegasus Theatre, Oxford. In 1997, her play *Relatively Sane* was workshopped and read at the Oval House as a result of playwrighting workshops with the Kali Theatre Company. Kaur was the Southern Arts/BBC Thames Valley FM Writer in Residence in 1997. In 1998, Future Perceptions commissioned two monologues: *Relatively Sane*, based on the play of that name was performed by Nina **Wadia** and directed by Carol Russell, and staged at the Brix Theatre, Brixton; and *And You Ask Me Why Are You Angry?*, a reworking of the mixed-media piece of that name, with the actress Siddique Aktar. Her 2000 touring production 'Jibbering into the Mirror', which incorporates movement, video and text, and electro-acoustic music, was supported by the London Arts Board. Her poetry has been broadcast on *Woman's Hour*, Radio 4, Greater London Radio and BBC Thames Valley FM. Her work has been anthologised in *The Fire People* (1998), edited by Lemn **Sissay**, and *Bittersweet: an Anthology of Black Women Poets* (1998), edited by Karen McCarthy.

ALISON DONNELL

Kaur, Perminder

b. 1965, Nottingham, England

artist

One of a new generation of 'British Asian' artists, Perminder Kaur has exhibited both as a solo artist and in group exhibitions. Kaur grew up in an Asian family but surrounded by an English environment, and at art school found that the aesthetic forms and ideas of her Sikh family culture were relatively unfamiliar to her. This led to her striving to assimilate the diverse cultural backgrounds with which she found herself faced. This sense of attempting to bring 'together' is an element frequently reflected in her work, often from a quite personal shifting between cultural contexts, such as in her piece titled *Innocence* (1995). In 1997, she exhibited as part of 'Krishna: the Divine Lover', National Touring Exhibitions, Whitechapel Art Gallery, UK and, in 1998, in 'Where I Am' (Galeria Da Mitra, Lisbon) as part of Caminho do Oriente, Expo '98. Kaur was one of a number of artists involved in 'Independent Thoughts', an exhibition held as part of the commemoration of the fifty-year partition of India and Pakistan. Her 1999 exhibition 'Out of Breath' drew on two broad elements, war and play, while acknowledging previous interests and influences.

SAMINA ZAHIR

Kay, Jackie

b. 1961, Edinburgh, Scotland

dramatist, poet

Kay's first play, *Chiaroscuro* (Theatre of Black Women, 1986), was influenced by Ntozake Shange's *For Coloured Girls*. *Chiaroscuro* stages an exploration of lesbian and black identity that remains central to Kay's poetic and dramatic work, as evidenced in her second play, *Twice Over* (Gay Sweatshop, 1988). Her subsequent **theatre** work also stresses the oppression of women, and includes *Every Bit of It* (Sphinx, 1992–3), which draws on the life and **music** of Bessie Smith, and the poetry text for the workshopped music-theatre

production of *Twice Through the Heart* (1997), originally a poetry documentary for BBC 2 **television**. Kay's poetry is widely anthologised and critically acclaimed. In addition to writing poetry for children, Kay has published two major collections: *The Adoption Papers* (also broadcast on BBC Radio 3) and *Other Lovers* (winner of the Somerset Maugham award). In 1999, Kay published her debut novel *Trumpet* and received high critical praise. The novel is the story of Joss Moody, a mixed-race jazz trumpeter, who on his death is revealed to be a woman, and again powerfully addresses questions of how race and gender define our lives and identities, this time in narrative form.

Select bibliography

Kay, J. (1999) *Trumpet*, London: Picador.
—— (1993) *Other Lovers*, Newcastle upon Tyne: Bloodaxe Books.
—— (1991) *The Adoption Papers*, Newcastle upon Tyne: Bloodaxe Books.
—— (1989) *Twice Over*, in P. Osment (ed.) *Gay Sweatshop: Four Plays and a Company*, London: Methuen.
—— (1987) *Chiaroscuro*, in J. Davis (ed.) *Lesbian Plays*, London: Methuen.
Kay, J., Collins, M. and Nichols, G. (1996) *Penguin Modern Poets: Volume 8*, Harmondsworth: Penguin.

ELAINE ASTON

Keegan, Rita

b. 1949, New York City, USA

artist, lecturer, archivist

Born in the USA of Caribbean and Canadian parentage, the work of Rita Keegan (née Morrison) came to public prominence within the 1980s Black British Arts movement. Her work has explored memory, history, dress and adornment, often through the use of her extensive personal family archive – a photographic record of a black middle-class Canadian family dating from the 1890s to the present day. Between 1969 and 1972 she studied Fine Art at the San Francisco Art Institute. In 1979, Keegan came to the UK and, in 1982, in the aftermath of the 1981 Brixton uprisings, she was one of the founder members of the Brixton Art Gallery. She was the co-founder in 1984 of Copy Art, a resource and education space for community groups and artists working with the emerging reproductive technologies of computers, scanners and photocopiers. From 1985 to 1990 Keegan was a staff member of the Women Artists Slide Library (WASL), where she established the Women Artists of Colour Index. In the early 1990s Keegan was the Director of the **African and Asian Visual Arts Archive** (AAVAA). She was also responsible for the establishment of a digital-media under-graduate course in the Historical and Cultural Studies department at Goldsmiths College, University of London. Keegan has been at the forefront of black women artists working with digital media. Her work has been exhibited at many venues, and these exhibitions include: '**Transforming the Crown**', New York, 1997; 'Trophies of Empire', Bristol, 1992; 'Family Histories: Eating with Our Memory, Sleeping with the Ancestors', 198 Gallery, London, 1998.

Further reading

Chambers, E. (1992–3) 'Trophies of empire', *Art Monthly* (December/January): 13–14.
Cheddie, J. (1999) 'Documents of memory', *Third Text* 45 (April): 88–9.
Rendell, C. (1987) 'Actual lives of women artists', *WASL Journal* (October/November): 10–11.

JANICE CHEDDIE

KELLY, GEORGE *see* Fowokan

Kempadoo, Roshini

b. 1959, Crawley, Sussex, England

photographer

Kempadoo studied at the West Midlands College of Higher Education and at Derbyshire College of Higher Education, finishing her studies in 1989. Appropriating advertising techniques of photographic construction, her work acts as a polemic against

oppression and repression of dis-empowered communities. Her work is a visually articulate dissection of the issues of race, politics and economics. For example, her *Changing Spaces* series of 1991 looks at tourism and its ideologies of cultural innocence, while *ECU: European Currency Unfolds* of 1992 is a critique of the domination of Third World countries by European economic powers. Kempadoo's work has been defined by her use of new technology. This is most evident in her Internet project *Sweetness and Light* of 1996, which juxtaposes country estates with images of computers and keyboards, implying that the Internet replicates the age-old hierarchies of the colonial experience. Her most recent project, a Photographers Gallery commission, *Lapping it up* (1997), returns to the theme of tourism, self-portraiture and memory, commenting on attempts at racial assimilation with an image of white lotion being rubbed into black skin.

Further reading

Robinson, D. (1991) *Confrontations*, Walsall: Walsall Museum and Art Gallery.
Willis, D. (1997) *Roshini Kempadoo*, London: Autograph.

FRANCIS SUMMERS

Khan, Addela

b. 1970, Ilford, England

photographer

Khan studied for a degree in visual arts at University College Wales, Aberystwyth, and stayed on for an MA in studio studies and art history, where she researched the representation of the Indian courtesan dancer. In 1989, she was awarded the University College of Wales Francis Williams Art Prize. In 1994, she was awarded a London Arts Board Individual Artists Award and she has a solo exhibition at the Contact Gallery, Norwich. As in other of Khan's one-person shows, a video screening accompanied the exhibition. She was also commissioned by **Autograph: the Association of Black Photographers** to produce new work in 1994 and took part in 'Recent Issue', a survey exhibition of recent British **photography** shown in London. In 1995, Kahn participated in 'The World's Women On Line' project based at Arizona State University.

Further reading

Deepwell, K. (ed.) (1995) *New Feminist Art Criticism*, Manchester: Manchester University Press.

ALISON DONNELL

Khan, Keith

b. 1968, Wimbledon, England

artist, designer, performance artist

Khan was born in Wimbledon of Trinidadian parents and studied Fine Art at Middlesex University and Wimbledon School of Art. He began work in **carnival**, organising large events that involved lots of people, while also working in performance and **live art**. He took a piece called *Images from Purdah* to night-clubs in New York. Khan's career has been eclectic, engaging with diverse audiences and practices. He consistently uses the energy of popular culture in his visual art, live work and carnival. Eight years producing costumes for **Notting Hill Carnival** and Trinidad Carnivals led to numerous commissions from companies such as the Welsh National Opera, the Royal Court, the Royal Albert Hall and the Science Museum. Forming the arts organisation **Moti Roti** with Ali **Zaidi**, together they have created a body of work that includes the **Institute of Contemporary Arts** commission *Wigs of Wonderment. Flying Costumes, Floating Tombs* and *Moti Roti, Puttli Chunni* have both won *Time Out* dance and performance awards. Khan is working towards an online presentation of *Wigs of Wonderment* with the University of East London. In 2000 he created the piece *Coming of Age*, designed to use the architecture of the Royal Festival Hall to its fullest with eighty Indian dancers and a specially created score by Shri – who is part of the Asian underground **music** circuit. This project won a BBC Asia Achievement Award in the Arts. He has also completed some design projects for IBM, Coca Cola, and Ericsson.

Khan's latest commission was by the DFEE, a project that involved the participation of 1,300 young people, and which was unveiled in the Turbine Hall of the Tate Modern in March 2001. In 1999 he worked as the production designer for the opening ceremony for the Millennium Dome, as well as the costume and 3-D designer for the central show, collaborating very closely with Mark Fisher, Micha Bergese and Peter Gabriel. His input involved the celebration of new British design, including contemporary fashion (see **fashion and design**); he also storyboarded the entire post-midnight segment, second by second, to maximise and profile the work of other carnival artists. With the central show, Khan developed many new technological pieces such as the plant stilts and costumes seen in most of the publicity images for the Dome. He was also the colourist for the entire central show. Khan is on the board of London Arts, responsible for the support and development for the arts in London. At the beginning of 2000 Khan was racially and viciously attacked, and as a consequence has become more determined to act towards combating entrenched racism within the arts and society. His work is both internationally profiled and critically acclaimed.

ALISON DONNELL

Khan, Naseem

b. 1939, Birmingham, England

journalist, arts critic

A pioneering advocate of cultural diversity and the significance of black British arts, Khan attended Roedean school and then graduated from Oxford with a degree in English. After teaching in Finland and working in journalism, Khan moved into a career in arts policy development. Her 1976 report, *The Arts Britain Ignores*, was the first study of minority arts commissioned by the Arts Council, Gulbenkian Foundation and Community Relations Commission. The report, and the regional inter-ethnic conferences that supported its launch, initiated debate on the issue of cultural support and resulted in the formation of **Minorities' Arts Advisory Service**, which Khan initially directed. Her second publication, *Ocean of Milk*, was a continuation of her interest in classical Indian **dance**; she had attended the first Indian dance school in London in the 1960s. In 1984, Khan organised the 'Festival of India in Britain', which promoted the Asian arts within the UK and also flew across artists from the Festival of India. Khan has continued her work in the arts and journalism, and in 1999 she was awarded an OBE for her services to cultural diversity. In 2000 she co-edited *Voices of the Crossing* with Ferdinand Dennis (London: Serpent's Tail).

ALISON DONNELL

Khan, Shaheen

b. 1960, Moshi, Tanzania

actor, writer

Shaheen Khan, a sociology graduate from Kingston Polytechnic (now University) began her acting career as a teenager with *Parosi*, the Asian neighbours' series on BBC in 1976–7. She joined **Tara Arts** in 1979, appearing initially in the community productions and later in their professional plays. These included *Meet Me, Chilli in Your Eyes* and *The Little Clay Cart*. Other stage credits include *Kirti Sona* and *Ba* (see Jyoti **Patel**), *House of the Sun* and *A Tainted Dawn* (see **Tamasha Theatre Company**).

She has worked extensively in **television** including *London's Burning, Boon, Medics, Casualty* and *Grange Hill*. Khan has appeared in many films, such as Tanika Gupta's *Flight* (1998, directed by Alex Pillai); and *My Sister Wife* (directed by Leslie Manning). In the much acclaimed ***Bhaji on the Beach*** (1993), directed by Gurinder **Chadha**, she played Simi, the feisty refuge worker who takes the women on the seaside trip to Blackpool. This character has become a gay icon in the USA. Most recently Khan appeared in a short film (see **film and cinema**), *The Dancer*, by Satinder Sohal. She began writing jointly with Sudha **Bhuchar**, and they have written many plays for Radio 4, including three series of *Girlies*, about the travails

of four thirty-something Asian women. Their debut stage play *Balti Kings* was produced by Tamasha Theatre Company in 1999–2000. A six-part radio series *Balti Kings* followed in 2001.

Select bibliography

Khan, S. and Bhuchar, S. (1998) *Dancing Girls of Lahore* (unpublished radio play).

SUMAN BHUCHAR

Khan, Shamshad

b. 1964, Leeds, England

poet, author, workshop facilitator, editor, literary adviser

Shamshad Khan has played a significant role in the promotion of black **women's writing** and experimental performance poetry in Britain. Her poetry is both lyrical and political, and has been widely anthologised, most notably in *Bittersweet* (1999) and *The Fire People* (1998), two of the most important contemporary collections of black poetry published in Britain. She has recited her work on local and national radio, including Woman's Hour on Radio 4, and performs regularly in English and Urdu, often using soundtracks and collaborating with contemporary dancers. Her short story, 'The Woman and the Chair' was published to critical acclaim in 1994. Khan co-edited the anthology of northern black women writers, *Healing Strategies for Women at War* (1999), and runs creative writing workshops for school children and adults. She is treasurer of the Commonword literature development project, and has worked for the Greater Manchester Low Pay Unit. She is Literature Adviser to the North West Arts Board

Select bibliography

Khan, S. (1994) 'The Woman and the Chair', in R. Ahmad and R. Gupta (eds) *Flaming Spirits*, London: Virago Press.

Khan, S., Guise Williams, M. and Lin, T. (eds) (1999) *Healing Strategies for Women at War*, Manchester: Crocus.

Further reading

Khan, S. (1999) 'Heart (W)rap' and 'A Day Out', in K. McCarthy (ed.) *Bittersweet: Contemporary Black Women's Poetry*, London: the Women's Press.

DIANA OMO EVANS

Khan Din, Ayub

b. 1967, Salford, England

actor, scriptwriter

Khan Din began his career as an actor, appearing in both *My Beautiful Laundrette* and *Sammy and Rosie Get Laid*. However, he found himself increasingly limited by the few roles available to Asian or minority ethnic actors. Hence, he began to write scripts that called for a diverse range of character portrayals. His first play *East is East* (1997) originated as a partnership with the Royal Court Theatre; the play toured to sell-out houses and went on to become an enormously successful film in 1999 (see **film and cinema**). *East is East* was a semi-autobiographical view of his childhood in Salford, growing up as the son of an English mother and a Pakistani father. Both as a play and a film *East is East* received very mixed reviews, varying from critical acclaim to condemnation from, for example, the Asian community. Of his work Khan Din has commented 'I don't write to please any particular part of the community – I write to please myself.' Khan Din's second play *Last Dance at Dum Dum* was not as well received as *East is East*, although it also covered mixed-race relations. The play is about a section of the Anglo-Indian community in 1980s Calcutta living in a crumbling bungalow known as Dum Dum.

SAMINA ZAHIR

King of the Ghetto

Never a stranger to controversy, Farrukh **Dhondy**'s **television** drama serial, *King of the Ghetto*, produced sharply divided reactions both within and between the two principal communities featured in the serial – white English and migrant Bangladeshis. The drama, which was broadcast during the mid-1980s, was produced in the aftermath of widespread civil/racial unrest (the 1981 'race' riots) and during a period of significant community-building in the wake of the Scarman Enquiry. Ironically, the Race Relations Act (1976) prevented the production team from advertising for 'Bengali' actors, so careful wording asked for individuals who could 'act Bengali'. However, despite the producer Stephen Gilbert's insistence that the serial reflected absolutely the conditions of real life for the characters it portrayed, one of the main things the serial will be remembered for was the demonstration outside the BBC's TV Centre by 200 members of Brick Lane's Bangladeshi community, protesting against the inappropriate portrayal of themselves and their community. Of particular concern was the casting of a white actor (Tim Roth) as the activist who eventually leads the Bangladeshi squatters' movement: for many people, not only the casting of a white man but also the characterisation of that activist as a skinhead was deeply offensive. The development of a new stereotype in the serial, that of the well-educated Bengali businessman who exploits the alleged 'stupidity' of his fellow community members for his own nefarious ends was also criticised, not only for its potential to pander to the racists, but also because it denied the more positive contributions that many Bengali and other Asian communities were making both to their own micro-societies and to the UK more generally.

KAREN ROSS

Knight, Beverly

b. 1974, Wolverhampton, England

R'n'B singer and songwriter

Encouraged to sing by her cousin, artist and producer Don E, a 21-year-old undergraduate called Beverly Knight would burst on to the UK R'n'B scene with her debut single 'Flava of the Old School' in 1995. The success of that single, originally released in March of that year, catapulted Knight to the forefront of the UK R'n'B scene. While only grazing the national Top 40 with

'Flava', her debut album *The B-Funk* finally quashed the common conception that British R'n'B was only a poor imitation of US R'n'B. Knight soon severed ties with the label Dome Records, which put her recording career on hold for two years. She returned in 1998 with a new label, Parlophone, and with the aptly titled come-back single 'Made it Back', which featured the US rapper Redman, and the album *Prodigal Sista*. She won a MOBO award for Best UK R'n'B Artist for her comeback efforts. It took a full-year promotional assault to properly re-establish Knight within the popular market, and a remixed version of 'Made it Back' and the follow-up single 'Greatest Day' were released in 1999. Both cracked the UK national Top 20 and pushed her into national prominence.

DEREK A. BARDOWELL

Kureishi, Hanif

b. 1954, Kent, England

novelist, playwright, film-maker, director

Hanif Kureishi took a degree in philosophy at King's College, London. He won the George Devine Award for his play *Outskirts* in 1981, and a year later became Writer in Residence at the Royal Court Theatre. In 1984, he wrote *My Beautiful Laundrette*, which received an Oscar nomination for Best Screenplay. His first novel *The Buddha of Suburbia* won the Whitbread Prize for Best First Novel. His writing is pioneering for the way in which it has complicated and destabilised dominant representations of black subjectivity in the 1980s and 1990s, making him a key practitioner of what Stuart **Hall** calls the new ethnicity (see **new ethnicities**). In the late 1990s, Kureishi's writing has displayed a preoccupation with youth subcultures, particularly **dance**/drug culture, and in 1995 he co-edited *The Faber Book of Pop*.

Kureishi's films (see **film and cinema**) depict the changed and changing lives of first- and second-generation Pakistani immigrants in London, but, for Kureishi, race, like class and sexuality, is not a subject matter as much as it is an illuminating perspective by which the familiar grows unfamiliar, estranged from habitual and sedimented forms of being. *My Beautiful Laundrette* (1985) focuses on the love affair between two young men, a Pakistani (Omar) and a cockney (Johnny), as they try to make a go of Omar's uncle's laundrette. Inter/intra-racial, social and sexual tensions fuse and contradict, producing a powerful commentary on Britain's marginalised classes. *Sammy and Rosie Get Laid* (1987) also explores an inter-racial relationship, overlaid with a harsh criticism of Tory politics and a refusal to sentimentalise the 'homeland' (Sammy's father Rafi is a corrupt politician fleeing from an equally corrupt Pakistan). The subculture of youth and drugs in London is unevenly navigated in *London Kills Me* (1991). **My Son the Fanatic** (1998) charts the downward-spiralling relationship between a father, Parves (Om **Puri**), and a son, Farid (Akbar Kurtha), as the former turns to a prostitute for love and the latter to Islamic fundamentalism for cultural identity.

Select bibliography

Kureishi, H. (1997) *Love in a Blue Time*, London: Faber.
—— (1990) *The Buddha of Suburbia*, London: Faber.
—— (1984) *My Beautiful Laundrette*, London: Faber.

Selected filmography

Kureishi, H. (1998) *My Son the Fanatic* (dir. Udayan Prasad), Miramax.
—— (1987) *Sammy and Rosie Get Laid* (dir. Stephen Frears), Cinecom Entertainment Group.
—— (1985) *My Beautiful Laundrette* (dir. Stephen Frears), Orion Classics.

JAMES PROCTER AND ALPANA SHARMA

L

La Rose, John

b. 1927, Trinidad

publisher, poet, essayist, film-maker, book
fair director

In Trinidad in the 1940s and 1950s, La Rose
became involved in workers' rights movements,
becoming General Secretary of the West Indian
Independence Party. Having settled in London in
1961, La Rose was an active member of Britain's
black community in the early 1960s, founding
New Beacon Books in 1966 and co-founding,
with Edward Kamau Brathwaite and Andrew
Salkey, the **Caribbean Artists' Movement**
later the same year. His debut volume of poetry
Foundations (1966) was the first book published by
New Beacon; he has since published another
volume and worked on several critical books, as
well as editing the *New Beacon Review*. He also
worked on the first academic study of calypso with
Raymond Quevedo (Calypsonian Attilla the Hun).
La Rose was Chairman of the Institute of Race
Relations in the period 1972–3, and of Towards
Racial Injustice, the campaign journal of which
was *Race Today*. He has taken an active role in
the establishment of the Black Parents Movement
(1975) and European Action for Racial Equality
and Social Justice (1990) and in 1991 became
Chairperson for the Board of Trustees of the New
Beacon Educational Trust. He is the Director of
the **International Book Fair of Radical Black
and Third World Books**.

Select bibliography

La Rose, J. (1991) *Eyelets of Truth within Me*, London:
New Beacon Books.
—— (1966) *Foundations*, London: New Beacon
Books.
La Rose, J. and Quevedo, R. (1983) *Attila's Kaiso*,
London: New Beacon Books.

ALISON DONNELL

Laird, Trevor

actor

Laird has had an eclectic career, playing the boy
under the car in *The Long Good Friday* in 1980, and
making a guest appearance in an episode of *Doctor
Who* in 1986, as well as appearing in the black
British film (see **film and cinema**) *Burning an
Illusion* (1981), produced and directed by Menelik **Shabazz**. Since his role as Hortense's brother
in the award-winning Mike Leigh film *Secrets and
Lies* (1996), Laird has established a higher profile,
playing Wesley Carter in the **television** series
Undercover Heart (1998) and Trevor in the British
gangster film *Love, Honour and Obey* (2000).

ALISON DONNELL

Lamba, Juginder

b. 1948, Kenya

visual artist

Lamba emerged through the first survey exhibition of black art, 'Into the Open', but his involvement with black art was tangential, and he was never part of the core group of subsequent shows. This was despite co-writing the first booklet attempting to present black art as a movement, *The Artpack: a History of Black Artists in Britain* (1985). Lamba's text in the booklet highlighted the role of primitivism in modern art. Lamba's work is concerned with the legacy of 'primitive' art, his wooden carvings deliberately inviting primitivist readings. His use of weathered timbers, scarred by age, is suggestive of the passing of history, as well as of the history of **the black Atlantic**. Lamba's attempt to articulate a position within these conflicting histories is perhaps a legacy of his own experience as an East African Asian. With a background in philosophy, Lamba's work is both clever and questioning, and draws on a range of references from modernism through to Greek mythology.

Further reading

Chambers, E., Lamba, J. and Joseph, T. (1985) *The Artpack: a History of Black Artists in Britain*, London: Haringey Arts Council.

NIRU RATNAM

Lamming, George

b. 1927, Barbados

novelist

Lamming first left Barbados for Trinidad in 1946, where he taught until he migrated to London in 1950, travelling on the same boat as Samuel **Selvon**. Lamming worked as a broadcaster for the BBC in order to support his early writing career. His first novel *In the Castle of My Skin* (1953) remains a classic of Caribbean **literature**. In terms of black British

cultural production, his two most important works are his experimental second novel *The Emigrants* (1954) and a non-fictional account of his move to the metropolitan centre: *The Pleasures of Exile* (1960). Written in the 1950s, these two texts have since come to occupy a central place within the literary tradition of post-war black British writing, and need to be taken into account in any appreciation of contemporary black British culture. His one other work to be set in England was the 1971 novel *Water With Berries*, which, like *The Pleasures of Exile*, writes back to Shakespeare's *The Tempest* and the relationship between Prospero and Caliban. Lamming went on to write more novels and worked as a lecturer and academic for many years. He has received the Somerset Maugham Award for Literature, a Guggenheim Fellowship and an Honorary Doctorate from the University of the West Indies.

Select bibliography

Lamming, G. (1972) *Water with Berries*, London: Longman.
—— (1960) *The Pleasures of Exile*, London: Michael Joseph.
—— (1954) *The Emigrants*, London: Michael Joseph.

JAMES PROCTER

Landon-Smith, Kristine

b. 1958, London, England

actor, director, artistic director

Kristine Landon-Smith is of mixed Australian and Indian parentage. She was born in London but grew up in Sydney, returning to the UK in 1978 to train at the Royal Scottish Academy of Music and Drama. After graduation, she worked as an actress for many years. In 1985, she co-founded the Inner Circle Theatre Company, where she produced and acted in *Spring Awakening* at the Young Vic Studio. In 1989, she was offered a short placement as a director/teacher at the National School of Drama, Delhi. Here, she adapted and directed Mulk Raj Anand's novel *Untouchable* for the second-year students. Once back in the UK, she teamed up with her friend, Sudha **Bhuchar** to produce the same play here. They founded the **Tamasha Theatre Company**, and its first play, *Untouchable*, was performed in Hindi and English. The success of this production led Landon-Smith and Bhuchar to continue to progress Tamasha as a **theatre** company, and also gave impetus for Landon-Smith to develop as a director – she has since directed all of Tamasha's plays. Her varied career also includes stints as guest director at Rose Bruford College of Speech and Drama and Bristol Old Vic Company, as well as work with BBC Radio Drama. Landon-Smith has directed several radio plays; some have been adaptations of Tamasha stage productions, including *Women of the Dust*, which won the **Commission for Racial Equality**'s Race in the Media Award for Best Radio Drama. Her other radio drama credits include: *Capricornia* (about the 'stolen generation' of Aboriginal children); *The Good Person of Ajmer*, *Dancing Girls of Lahore* and *Calcutta Kosher*. In 1999, she was invited to direct the stage production of ***East is East*** at the Coliseum Theatre, Oldham, and *The Orchestra* for Southwark Playhouse. In 2001, she directed the Agatha Christie Festival season at the Palace Theatre, Westcliff.

SUMAN BHUCHAR

LAWRENCE, SANDRA *see* Wee Papa Girl Rappers

Lawrence, Stephen

b. 1975, London, England; d. 1993, London, England

student

One of the most haunting and shocking stories of the 1990s was the murder of Stephen Lawrence, an 18-year-old student who wanted to become an architect. Lawrence was killed at a bus stop in Eltham on 22 April 1993, in an attack by five white youths. A week later, an inquest opened into his death and was adjourned. Although the men accused of his murder, Neil and Jamie Acourt, Gary Dobson, Luke Knight and David Norris, were arrested at different stages in May 1993, the Crown Prosecution Service dropped the murder charges. On 15 August, Scotland Yard announced an internal review of the investigation. Four months later, on 21 December, the inquest was reopened and adjourned after the Metropolitan Police said that it had received new evidence. Stephen's parents, Neville and Doreen, announced that if action was not taken on the new leads they would mount a private prosecution. Their determination for justice and the activities of their solicitor, Imran Khan, led to newspaper investigations and community involvement. The Anti Racist Alliance called on Bexley Council to close the British National Party headquarters in Welling and there were marches. What the Lawrences did not realise at this time was that the case would continue for more than six years with claims by police of insufficient evidence and testimony ruled inadmissible. Indeed, the head of the investigation, Detective Superintendent Brian Weeden, said in 1998, following the public inquiry into Lawrence's death, that he was unaware of the law that would permit him to arrest suspects on suspicion, an admission widely criticised in the media. Lawrence's death also raised issues of how the police approached such cases and most importantly how they reacted when they reached the scene. Police Constable Linda Bethel was one of the first officers on the scene and she admitted that she had not realised the seriousness of Lawrence's wound and that her first aid kit was left in the patrol car. Also, Doreen Lawrence, in a statement read to the public inquiry into the handling of the case, said that the police had not informed her about the investigation's process. It was also alleged that a police officer had screwed up a piece of paper with the names of Lawrence's suspected killers on it.

On 15 April 1994, almost a year after Lawrence's death, the Crown Prosecution Service refused for the second time to prosecute because of insufficient evidence. Four months later, the police launched another investigation under a new investigating officer. The Lawrence family started a private prosecution on the second anniversary of their son's death, applying to Greenwich magistrates for arrest warrants. In August 1995, a committal hearing began at Belmarsh magistrates court. The charges against Jamie Acourt and David

Norris were dropped due to lack of evidence. Dobson, however, was charged with murder on 29 August and the following month Knight and Neil Acourt were sent to trial. The trial started at the Old Bailey on April 1996, almost three years after the murder. Four days later, it collapsed after it was considered that the evidence provided by Duwayne Brooks was inadmissible. Brooks was the young man and friend of Lawrence who announced in August 1999 that he was to sue the Metropolitan Police for negligence. Despite this disappointment, the Lawrences continued with their fight for justice. The inquest re-opened on 10 February 1997 at Southwark Coroner's Court. Three days later, the jury returned a verdict of unlawful killing.

The full weight of the media attention and the significance of the continuing interest in the case was demonstrated when the *Daily Mail*, on 14 August, published the front page with the headline 'Murderers' and a photograph of the suspects. Objections were raised from the Lawrence family and others when it was reported in April 1999 that the five suspects were to be interviewed on the ITV *Tonight* programme. Previously, their mothers had given an interview to the BBC Radio 4 *Today* programme claiming their sons' innocence and political conspiracy.

It took five years for the Metropolitan Police to offer a full apology to the Lawrence family and this was given at the public inquiry in June 1998 when Metropolitan Police Assistant Commissioner Ian Johnston made a statement. The Stationery Office published the MacPherson report on 24 February 1999. It pointed to the failings of the Metropolitan Police investigation, police discrimination and racial stereotyping. The report gave seventy recommendations covering accountability; defining racial incidents; prosecution of race crimes; family and victim treatment; racial awareness training; stop and search practices; handling of complaints; police recruitment; national curriculum; and anti racist practices. It illustrated that institutional racism existed not only within the police service but in schools, local government and other public institutions. The report led to further allegations and criticism of the mishandling of evidence and calls for the resignation of Metropolitan Police Commissioner Sir Paul Condon, who is also linked

to the **Notting Hill Carnival**. Doreen Lawrence, responding to the report, stated that:

> We have spent years telling those in authority how we perceived what has happened. When one of your children has been brutally murdered you are looking for those with power to do something about it. My son was stabbed and left to bleed to death on the night of 22 April 1993 while police officers looked on. They treated the affair as a gang war and from that moment on acted in a manner that can only be described as white masters during slavery.

Certainly, the issue of race and of the practices of racism have been central to both the case itself and its reception. Writing in the *Guardian*, **New Nation** editor Michael Eboda and journalist Kamal Ahmed asked, 'Who owns Stephen Lawrence', pointing out that, in media terms, the story had been covered in the black press by the **Voice** journalist Paul Macey since the start of the inquest. Yet it was only following the *Daily Mail*

> front-page splash just after the inquest into Stephen's death that the national media started to realise this was a story that deserved some space. Until then, although it had appeared as a second or third lead in a few broadsheets, the press as a whole had shown little or no interest.
> (*Guardian*, 22 February 1999)

In a written answer in the Commons in July 1999, Home Secretary Jack Straw reported that the costs for the investigation into the murder of Stephen Lawrence reached £4,199,000. In December 1999, the Metropolitan Police agreed an *ex gratia* settlement of £320,000 with the Lawrences for its failure to investigate Stephen's death, but it would not admit negligence. The Stephen Lawrence Trust was officially registered as a charity and its website declares, 'Stephen Lawrence a life worth remembering.' The trust is working on the final stages of an educational and arts building in Lewisham, South East London, to be called the Stephen Lawrence Technocentre. The centre will provide training for students, particularly black and disadvantaged young people who want to pursue further education in architecture and related subjects. Lewisham College and Greenwich University are expected to work in partnership to provide Foundation Degrees there and the initiative was mentioned in a press pack produced by the **Greater London Authority** and has its support.

Stephen Lawrence's death and the campaign around it have highlighted the spectrum of disadvantage in fields such as housing and education. There have been some changes, even though observers are critical of the time it has taken, and is taking, to implement recommendations from the MacPherson report. The Qualifications and Curriculum Authority has announced that the names and schools of candidates will be removed from examination papers before marking to avoid any bias. The Metropolitan Police Racial and Violent Crime Task Force compiled a database of confirmed or suspected racists under the Operation Delton initiative to help police make connections with possible racist incidents. The Greater London Authority launched the Black Londoners Forum (2000) to tackle discrimination and inequality in the capital, applying the recommendations of the report. Newham Council became the first in the country to set up a Lawrence Inquiry Sub-committee to examine race relations in the borough. The Metropolitan Police is to introduce a Policing Diversity training programme for officers by 2001 that will include training in cultural awareness. However, 1990 Trust Director Lee Jasper pointed out that black people are individuals and that the training should be careful of not perpetuating stereotypes.

Stephen Lawrence attended Eglington Primary School, Plumstead Blackheath Bluecoats Church of England School and he liked **hip hop**, sport and fried chicken and rice. The life of Stephen Lawrence has been kept alive in the broadcast media. **Black Britain** made an award-winning documentary on Stephen Lawrence, Marianne **Jean-Baptiste** starred in a television programme and there has been a play, as well as the memoir 'Living to be me: teenage reflections', in **IC3: the Penguin Book of New Black Writing**, reflecting on what it can mean to be black and British. The name Stephen Lawrence is an instant reminder of racial discrimination and race relations in Britain; it is a name instilled in the national consciousness as both personal tragedy and cultural wrong. Additionally, the name Stephen Lawrence evokes the strength and commitment that Neville and Doreen Lawrence showed in pursuing their fight for justice, which eventually achieved national and international significance and effected a re-examination of race relations in Britain. For Britain, the death of Stephen Lawrence presents an occasion to remember the cost of racism and the urgent need for change; and for parents, it is an emotional reminder of what their children mean to them and the fear of loss, plus the suffering and pain of the Lawrence family, as Joan **Anim-Addo** writes:

> That night, roused, I checked mentally
> my young manchild was in bed. He was.
> But it wasn't so for you Doreen.
> It wasn't so for you.
> And so history moves; an underground river
> deep in sores hearts. My son; our sons.

Further reading

Anim-Addo, J. (1998) *Haunted by History*, London: Mango Publishing.

(2000) *Racial Harassment: Action on the Ground*, Joseph Rowntree Foundation.

(2000) *Stephen Lawrence Inquiry: Home Secretary's Action Plan – First Annual Report on Progress*, Home Office: London.

(2000) *The Power of Language*, Manchester: Greater Manchester Police Appropriate Language Working Party.

(2000) *Winning the Race – Embracing Diversity.*

(1999) *A Culture of Denial*, Leicester: De Montfort University and 1990 Trust.

The Stephen Lawrence Inquiry: Report of an Inquiry by Sir William MacPherson of Cluny (Cm 4262–1).

YINKA SUNMONU

LAWRENCE, TIMMIE *see* Wee Papa Girl Rappers

Lester, Adrian

b. 1970, Birmingham, England

actor

Lester has played supporting roles in Kenneth Branagh's musical version of *Love's Labours Lost*

(1999) and in Ben Elton's *Maybe Baby* (2000), and also starred as a presidential aide opposite John Travolta and Emma Thompson in *Primary Colours* (1998). He has also worked in **television**, taking the part of Orpheus in the 2000 production of *Jason and the Argonauts* and that of Danny in *Storm Damage*. Lester won the Olivier Award in 1996 for *Company*. Like Marianne **Jean-Baptiste**, Lester has now based his career in the USA because of the lack of good roles for black actors in the UK, although he came back to the UK to play Hamlet.

ALISON DONNELL

Levy, Andrea

b. 1956, England

novelist

Andrea Levy's three novels have appeared in quick succession, and they collectively deal with growing up as a black person in a racist society and with the cultural conflicts between migrant parents and their British-born children. In *Fruit of the Lemon*, protagonist Faith Jackson visits Jamaica, the land of birth of her parents, when disillusioned with Britain. Ultimately such a return is revealed to be no option for the generation Levy writes about: they are bent on making it in the land of their birth. As Levy herself asserts: 'If Englishness doesn't define me, then redefine Englishness' (Jaggi 1996). Like Levy's own father, Angie's parents in *Every Light in the House Burnin'* arrived on the *Empire* **Windrush**; despite assertions not to rise 'above her station', Angie aims at a career in the arts and refuses to live out her parents' immigrant dream. She is aided by her light complexion, as the concept of 'racial passing' is thematised in this text. In her second novel, *Never far from Nowhere*, Levy deals with so-called mixed relationships; Olive has a white partner, which poses problems among peers and family.

References

Jaggi, Maya (1996) 'Redefining Englishness', *Waterstone's Magazine* 6: 62–9.

Select bibliography

Levy, A. (1999) *Fruit of the Lemon*, London: Headline Review.
—— (1996) *Never far from Nowhere*, London: Headline Review.
—— (1994) *Every Light in the House Burnin'*, London: Headline Review.

MARK STEIN

Lewis, Dave

photographer

Lewis studied film and photographic arts at the Polytechnic of Central London. Since graduating in 1985, he has produced photographic series dealing with issues of personal experience and public institutions, such as *Black Youth and Mental Health: Part 1*, in 1991, and *European Stories*, in 1994. Placing black individuals in contrast to larger structures of power, such as the Church or the law courts, in his *Who's in...?* series of 1995, Lewis highlighted the lack of black representation in these sites of power. As his contribution to the 'Impossible Science of Being' exhibition at the Photographers Gallery, Lewis made work in response to the ethnographic collections in such institutions as the Royal Anthropological Institute and the Pitt Rivers Museum, Oxford. Using a wide-angle lens and multiple exposures, his **photography** highlighted that these collections were only one subjective view of a entire people. More recently, he has photographed black ex-servicemen against a backdrop of Second World War propaganda posters, pointing out that British history and contemporary British national identity is not exclusively white.

Further reading

Charity, R., Pinney, C., Poignant, R. and Wright, C. (eds) (1995) *The Impossible Science of Being*, London: Photographers Gallery.
Iles, C. and Roberts, R. (eds) (1997) *In Visible Light*, Oxford: Museum of Modern Art.

Malik. R. (1998) *Dave Lewis: Monograph*, London: Autograph.

FRANCIS SUMMERS

Lewis, Shaznay

b. 1975, London, England

singer

Before forming the all-girl band All Saints in 1994, Shaznay Lewis was a backing singer working in various studios and clubs. Along with band co-founder Melanie Blatt she was briefly signed to ZTT Records and the duo released one single 'If you want to party', which sank without trace before the pair were released from their contract. The pair continued to write and record, and were signed to London Records as a four-piece on the strength of a demo tape in 1995. As the main songwriter in All Saints, Lewis brings an R'n'B and **hip hop** sensibility to All Saints' **music**, which gives the band an edge of street credibility that many of their contemporaries lack. The All Saints' debut album was co-produced by Neneh **Cherry**'s (one of Lewis's heroines) husband and producer Cameron McVey. Their second single, 'Never ever', released in late 1997, was one of the biggest selling singles of the year and along with their self-titled album made All Saints one of the most successful British bands of the 1990s. All Saints released *Saints and Sinners* in 2000 and the band split in 2001.

ANDY WOOD

Lilliard, Derek Alvin

b. 1963, London, England

menswear designer, stylist

Lilliard graduated from Epsom School of Art and Design with a Higher National Diploma in fashion (see **fashion and design**) and textile design in 1983. Between 1983 and 1985, he worked for Louis Daniel in London, and as a freelance designer in Paris. Lilliard established his label D.A. Lilliard in 1985, with the sale of an entire collection to the London-based retailers Jones for their Greenwich Village outlet. Lilliard's designs attracted international clients selling to Italian retailers such as Corner Shop, Ora, Academy, Woolf and Bazaar, and to Nieman Marcus in New York between 1986 and 1988. Lilliard expanded his design range to include made-to-measure clothing aimed directly at high-profile celebrities in the **music** industry, including styling commissions from **Jazzie B** of **Soul II Soul** and the Pasadenas. In 1993, Lilliard launched his first menswear shop, D.A. Lilliard, on 44 Monmouth Street, Covent Garden, London. An understanding of his West Indian heritage and tailoring ability earned him the commission, in 1994, from the Victoria and Albert Museum of two men's suits for the Caribbean Style section of the exhibition, 'Streetstyle: from Sidewalk to Catwalk, 1940 to Tomorrow'. Three years later, Lilliard held his first catwalk show in London. In 1999, the designer extended his portfolio to include an accessory range, the diffusion line Casino and D.A., Lilliard's urban sportswear label.

CAROL TULLOCH

literature

Although debates on black British literature tend to be confined to the post-war period, its history dates back at least as far as the 1700s. The earliest writings, such as Briton Hammon's *A Narrative of the Uncommon Sufferings and Surprising Deliverance of Briton Hammon*, published in 1760, and Ukawsaw Gronniosaw's *A Narrative of the Remarkable Particulars in the Life of James Albert Ukawsaw Gronniosaw, an African Prince, related by Himself* (1770) were oral narratives, recorded by white amanuenses. Followed later by writers like Ignatius Sancho, Olaudah Equiano and Mary Seacole, there was, by the end of the nineteenth century, a range of (largely African, polemical and autobiographical) writing in print.

It was not until the middle of the twentieth century, however, and in the aftermath of the Nationality Act of 1948 (designed to encourage immigration from Britain's colonies and former colonies), that a genuinely substantial body of black British literature began to emerge. During the

1950s and 1960s, this literature was dominated by male Caribbean writers who had come to settle in and regard London as a literary capital. The major figures of this period include George **Lamming**, Sam **Selvon**, Wilson **Harris**, Andrew **Salkey**, V.S. **Naipaul**, Kamau Brathwaite and James **Berry**. The pioneering novels by this generation of writers – such as *The Emigrants*, *The Lonely Londoners* and *The Mimic Men* – depict transient lifestyles structured around temporary accommodations (basements, hostels, bedsits), while at the same time offering a sustained re-invention of the metropolitan centre that remains influential within contemporary black British writing.

Although the work of these early writers was initially met with acclaim, finding itself fostered by publishing houses and Henry Swanzy's *Caribbean Voices* BBC radio programme, it was felt by practitioners like Kamau Brathwaite that by the mid-1960s interest was beginning to decline. In response to this, Brathwaite, Andrew Salkey and John **La Rose** came together to form the **Caribbean Artists' Movement** (CAM), which was active between 1966 and 1972. CAM provided an important forum for artistic debate, while also encouraging the sense of a 'community' of West Indian artists in Britain. Although a primarily 'artistic' project, the rise of black consciousness in the late 1960s and early 1970s soon impacted on CAM, which became increasingly politicised. Linton Kwesi **Johnson**, one the best-known black polemical artists/activists in Britain, was present at many of the CAM sessions, and has spoken of its influence on his own development as a writer.

In many ways, the work of Linton Kwesi Johnson was characteristic of a new phase of black British writing that would dominate the 1970s and early 1980s. Politically committed and linguistically self-conscious, experimenting with creole and musical forms (what Johnson terms 'dub poetry'), and largely poetry-based, it included work by John **Agard**, E.A. **Markham**, John **Figueroa**, Grace **Nichols** and Fred **D'Aguiar**. The writings of these and other poets were collected in important early anthologies edited by James Berry: *The Bluefoot Traveller*, published in 1976, and *News for Babylon*, published in 1984.

Although the 1970s and early 1980s tends to be dominated by African Caribbean writers, impor-

tant work by South Asian artists did begin to emerge in this decade, including novels and short stories by Farrukh **Dhondy** and Tariq **Mehmood**. These writings share the strong political commitment of other black British writings of the time. Similarly, if the literatures of that period tend to quote from the aggressively male, masculinist vocabularies of the Black Power movement, then this was also the period in which a significant body of women's writing began to appear, including work by Grace Nichols, Beryl Gilroy, Buchi Emecheta and Valerie Bloom.

What tends to characterise these very different literatures of the 1970s and early 1980s is their shared adoption of realist modes of narrative depiction. Consider, for example, the social documentary style of Beryl Gilroy's *Black Teacher*, Emecheta's *In the Ditch*, Mehmood's *Hand on the Sun*, Dhondy's *Seige in Babylon*, or even Johnson's of these texts seek to narrate 'actual' events: from the autobiographical structure of Gilroy and Emecheta's novels, to the documentation of black historical events in the work of Dhondy, Mehmood and Johnson. The realist emphases of these writings can be largely explained in terms of their authors' political commitment to confronting and trying to break down certain racist mythologies of the black community at a particularly vulnerable moment in its history. In a sense, it was part of an attempt to take control of representations of black Britishness at a time when they were becoming increasingly unsavory within the national media. It was about a refusal to be spoken for and a desire to speak for, or delegate on behalf of, the larger black community. This put a pressure on the black artist to try and describe things 'they way they really were'.

The polemical literary project of the 1970s and early 1980s was increasingly problematised in the late 1980s and 1990s. A particular area of concern was the way in which those realist writings tended to essentialise black British experience, suggesting that certain versions of blackness were somehow more accurate, authentic and more 'real' than others. Similarly, it carried with it the problem of constructing a black subject that was necessarily always and only positive. Stuart **Hall** takes issue with this phase of cultural representation in his important work on '**new ethnicities**', suggesting that:

> What is at issue here is the recognition of the extraordinary diversity of subjective positions, social experiences and cultural identities which compose the category 'black'; that is, the recognition that 'black' is essentially a politically and culturally *constructed* category, which cannot be grounded in a set of fixed trans-cultural or transcendental racial categories and which therefore has no guarantees in Nature.
>
> (Hall 1988: 28)

This diversity of subjective positions has certainly become increasingly apparent within the literatures of the 1980s and 1990s. The work of writers like Hanif **Kureishi**, Salman **Rushdie**, Ben **Okri**, Caryl **Phillips**, Rukshana **Ahmad**, Meera **Syal** and Jackie **Kay** has all played a part in opening up and re-inventing 'blackness' within contemporary cultural production. Many of these writers have drawn attention to the cultural hybridity of racial identities in their work in a way that productively pollutes 'blackness', making its boundaries less fixed and more fluid and its contents more multiple and shifting.

Karim Amir, Hanif Kureshi's first-person narrator in *The Buddha of Suburbia*, is instructive in this context. Karim's inability to 'handle' drink and drugs, his refusal to fight, his effeminacy and homosexuality all interestingly compromise the kinds of rigid masculinity produced and perpetuated through the 1970s and early 1980s. (However, his refusal to take *any* political stand by the end of the novel is certainly not unproblematic.) Similarly, Karim's unstable sense of racial identity, as the son of a Pakistani father and white English mother, a narrator more familiar with suburban England/ Englishness than with the streets and rhetoric of the black inner city, raises important, complex questions about the boundaries and authenticity of 'blackness'. When does 'black' stop and 'white' begin? It is this kind of coming to terms with the *in-betweeness* of black cultural identities that has energised and informed the dominant literatures and cultural criticism (see, for example, the work of Homi **Bhabha**, Paul **Gilroy**, Stuart Hall, Kobena **Mercer**) of the late twentieth century.

The de-stabilisation of 'blackness' in the 1990s has not just taken place within 'high' literary discourse either, but can also be traced within contemporary black popular writing, such as the detective fictions of Mike **Phillips**: *Blood Rights* and *The Late Candidate*. Black popular fiction has come of age in the 1990s, with commercial bookshops like W.H. Smith and Waterstones dedicating whole sections of their shelves to this genre. The success of black popular fiction was confirmed with the publication of Victor **Headley**'s *Yardie* in 1992. Published by **X Press** (one of the most successful black presses of the 1990s), *Yardie*, it has been argued, was the first novel to gain a genuinely popular 'cult' status among black Britons. *Yardie*'s popularity has been controversial, however. If the text contributes to the unsettling of earlier, 1970s constructions of the black subject, refusing to present 'black' as always and only 'positive', 'good' or 'right on', then its portrayal of women as merely the adjuncts of an irresistible male hypersexuality has earned it a good deal of criticism.

The cultural contribution of post-war black British literature was remembered at the ***Windrush*** anniversary celebrations in 1998, which organised a number of readings and performances by leading writers and poets, as well as 'literary walks' around black London. These events paid testimony to the cultural importance of black British literature over the post-war period and its continued significance as a cultural form within the contemporary period.

Further reading

Berry, J. (ed.) (1984) *News for Babylon*, London: Chatto & Windus.

—— (ed.) (1976) *Bluefoot Traveller – an Anthology of West Indian Poets in Britain*, London: Limestone Publications.

Dabydeen, D. and Wilson-Tagoe, N. (1987) *A Reader's Guide to West Indian and Black British Literature*, Coventry: Rutherford Press/Dangeroo Press.

Gilroy, P. (1987) *'There Ain't no Black in the Union Jack': the Cultural Politics of Race and Nation*, London: Routledge.

JAMES PROCTER

live art

Live art is the generic term given to work that embodies a live, physical presence, with an issue or concept at its core directing the development of the artistic form. It is a site for works of contemporary black artists exploring black identity in a way that cannot be defined or presented as one main discipline, with process, context and site being uppermost in the artist's mind.

Formulated post-1960s in response to the search for non-gallery spaces in which artists could produce work that would not be instantly consumed and sold as the latest commodity, live art developed from happenings, which planned and improvised theatrical activity, manipulating found materials with some degree of audience interaction. During the 1970's and 1980's, artists such as Bobby Baker and Rose English created works that focused on everyday actions, routines and rituals, which were heightened or dislocated within a presented piece. Baker produced a series of performances that satirised and represented the life of a housewife with the rituals of cleaning the kitchen or baking a cake. This work came to be known as *performance art*, as work closely linked to the performing arts was presented as an ephemeral event before an audience.

Black British communities, meanwhile, were creating subversive acts of their own. The year 1965 saw the first ever **Notting Hill Carnival**; a politically resistant multiple art form that subverted and ridiculed the 'white massa'. In representing themselves and their culture in their own terms, **carnival** asserted black people's presence in post-war Britain in such a strikingly visual and theatrical way that it could no longer be ignored. It affirmed their new identity as black people, with a specific cultural heritage, now living, moving and breathing in Britain.

In contemporary 'multicultural' Britain, live art is a burgeoning form of black cultural expression; an amoebic form that is constantly developing and resisting permanent definition; a site and context in which black artists are asking relevant and interrogating questions regarding contemporary black British identity, which could not be shown in any other way. Live art does not homogenise or romanticise an essentialist black culture. That which was previously marginalised becomes main-stage; giving voice to cultural difference in all of its diversity. The personal and political freedoms that were fought for and historically given voice to in carnival are now communicated through dislocated narratives, reworked notions of history, mixed media and new technologies. As society and means of communication have advanced, so has the desire of black contemporary artists to convey their realities in forms that are accessible and understood by wide audiences, but most importantly ensuring that they are not excluded from the contemporary arts forum. The desire to be and to be seen converge in the creation of works that advance the definition of black arts and culture, and live art becomes a relevant, poignant way of looking at the human condition.

Live art has an immediacy and power to touch the audience, whether physically or emotionally: 'the only evidence following the event existing in the memories and imaginations of both artists and audience' (Ugwu, 1995). Live art reflects contemporary reality with a blurring of disciplines and the fusing of current events; be it a glimpse of a bomb blast, a **television** show, a theme tune, a trip to Cyberspace and beyond. Live art is very much a contemporary form, addressing real, dominating issues as cultural boundaries break down and the global village becomes an Internet-aided reality. The established notions of 'British' heritage, nationality and history are fading and live art, as a hybrid form, articulates a fragmented and hybrid identity.

It is within this changeable framework of contemporary realities that many black artists have chosen to express their conflicting realities and shifting identities. The artists include Susan Lewis, **SuAndi** and Ronald **Fraser-Munro**, who have performed nationally and internationally. Susan Lewis's performance *Ladies Falling* in 1996 used movement, slides and text to explore black female identity. Appearing as an eighteenth-century English lady dressed in a crinoline, drinking tea with sugar, the obvious references to the products of slavery place the viewer within her framing and position of reference. A projected film (see **film and cinema**) showing black and white family photos remind the viewer of the histories and extended narrative relevant to migrated black peoples. Discarding the traditional linear theatrical narrative for a dislocated one, Lewis's character threatens to fall into the audience or off the stage, creating the re-negotiation of not only the theatrical space but of black female identity itself.

Ronald Fraser-Munro has created a mythical representation of black male identity using poetry and new technologies. In his 1996 performance of *Cesare Cappucinno*, Fraser-Munro performed in a blond wig and briefs, and held a horse whip. He directly questioned audience members as he walked through the auditorium; re-negotiating the space and breaking the traditional rule of the fourth wall and the demarcations of space normally observed in traditional theatrical performances. Fraser-Munro used a computer during the performance to activate spoken text, thus blurring real time and performance time. Such mechanisms take Fraser-Munro's work beyond traditional theatre and create a fusion of techniques that is live art.

References

Ugwu, C. (ed.) (1995) 'Let's get it on – the politics of black performance', London: Institute of Contemporary Arts.

DONNA GRIFFITHS

Live Art Development Agency

An organisation responding to new artists, practices and ideas in London, the Live Art Development Agency offers a portfolio of services for the support of the live art sector in London. It is primarily concerned with supporting and developing emerging artists, culturally diverse artists and artists involved with high-risk work.

Live art is now widely recognised as a practice that reflects and disrupts the shifts that have taken place in visual art (see **visual and plastic arts**), performance art, **theatre**, **dance**, new writing, digital media and the moving image, and which responds to the hybridity and sophistication of our cultural experiences and expectations in the modern world. Live art challenges what art can be and what art can do and say, and has proved itself to be a potent and exciting forum for artists

and audiences. Being so fluid, live art has no fixed paths or signposts – its exploratory processes and broad-based practices demand different approaches to ideas of art, artist, programme, audience and critical development. The Live Art Development Agency is a new model that aims both to meet these growing needs and to raise the awareness and appreciation of live art in London and beyond. The Live Art Development Agency offers a range of initiatives specifically for London-based artists and organisations working with live art and new performance practices, such as information, bursary schemes, access to video and publication archives, debate and general advice. It also offers advice to national and international organisations and individuals interested in engaging with London-based live art practitioners.

CATHERINE UGWU

Lloyd, Errol

b. 1943, Jamaica

artist, art critic

Errol Lloyd travelled to London in 1963 to study law but eventually studied art. In 1967 he produced a bust of C.L.R. **James** and joined the **Caribbean Artists' Movement** (CAM), where he participated in CAM's art exhibition at the University of Kent. He was establishing a reputation as a sculptor and became deeply involved with CAM in 1968. He participated with Ronald **Moody** and Karl 'Jerry' Craig in 'The Artists in the Caribbean' symposium at CAM's conference. Earlier in the year he participated in another symposium with Aubrey **Williams**. By October 1968 he was a member of CAM's committee and resigned in 1971. Lloyd's paintings in 1968 were bold and naturalistic. He specialised in figurative imagery in works such as *Marcus Garvey* (1968) and *The Lesson* (1972). In the early 1980s Lloyd established close contacts with GLC organisations that promoted black art. Between 1980 and 1985 he was a member of the **Minorities' Arts Advisory Service** and joined the editorial board of *Artrage* in 1982. In the same year he sat on the Bhownagree Gallery Committee at the

Commonwealth Institute. He left *Artrage* and the gallery committee in 1985.

PAULINE DE SOUZA

Locke, Donald

b. 1930, Stewartville, Guyana

artist

Locke studied painting, sculpture and ceramics at the Bath Academy of Art in Corsham in 1954. He arrived in London in 1971 where he continued working in all three areas while teaching ceramics at Chester College of Further Education. He established a reputation as a ceramic artist and exhibited at the 1972 'International Exhibition of Ceramics' at the Victoria and Albert Museum. His 'Two Sculptures from a Ritual Fertility Suite' were included in the 1975 'International Biennale of Sculpture' in Hungary. In the following year he had an independent show at the Round House and later in 1977 displayed work at the 'FESTAC Exhibition' in Nigeria. In 1978 his work 'Trophies of Empire' was displayed at the Afro-Caribbean Art Exhibition, and was also shown in '**The Other Story**' exhibition in 1989. In sculpture and ceramics alike, Locke develops works from his own memory into more abstract shapes. Locke moved to the USA in 1980 where he stopped painting and sculpting to concentrate on ceramics.

Further reading

Araeen, R. (1989) *The Other Story*, London: Hayward Gallery.

PAULINE DE SOUZA

Looking for Langston

Looking for Langston (**Sankofa Film Collective**, 1989) is a film written and directed by London-based film-maker Isaac **Julien**. It is a meditation on Langston Hughes (1902–1967) and the Harlem Renaissance, and in it Julien explores the interconnected relationship between race, male homosexuality, fantasy and desire. Starring Ben Ellison,

Mathew Baidoo and John Wilson, *Looking for Langston* is a sophisticated compendium of archival images of important black figures (such as Countee Cullen, Palmer Hayden and Richmond Barthé), footage from 1920s Harlem, music by Blackberri and poetry by Essex Hamphill and Bruce Nugent. It is set primarily in a dimly lit, dream-like speakeasy where men, dressed in fashionable tuxedoes, dance and drink champagne, despite the disapproval of a hostile and violent outside world. This film addresses issues of voyeurism, racial and sexual difference, the black male body and visual fetishisation. By exploring these interconnected themes, Julien examines topics that have historically been examined under the guise of homophobia, been deemed ambiguous and, therefore, omitted from sources on black art and culture in the 1920s and 1930s. While it does not claim to discover an authentic voice or sexual identity for this important twentieth-century literary figure, *Looking for Langston* provides a contemporary reflection and gives urgency and new impetus to Hughes's question, 'What happens to a dream deferred?'

Further reading

Mercer, K. (1994) 'Dark and lovely: black gay image-making', in *Welcome to the Jungle: New Positions in Black Cultural Studies*, New York: Routledge, pp. 221–31
—— (1994) 'Reading racial fetishism: the photographs of Robert Mapplethorpe', in *Welcome to the Jungle: New Positions in Black Cultural Studies*, New York: Routledge, pp. 171–219.

ANDREA D. BARNWELL

Loose Ends

In 1980 Steve Nichol, a keyboard and trumpet player, Jane Eugene, a student at the London College of Fashion, and Carl McIntosh, a jazz-bass player, formed the influential group Loose End. In 1981 they signed a contract with Virgin (UK). In 1983 the trio changed their name to Loose Ends and in 1984 they signed with MCA in America. In 1985 the single 'Hanging on a String

(Contemplating)' topped the R 'n' B charts. The following year, 'Slow Down', from their second album *Zagora*, was equally popular. In 1988 'Watching You', from the album *The Real Chuckeeboo*, reached number two. Despite the widespread appeal of this British **dance** and urban contemporary group in the 1980s, the original trio broke up in 1990. McIntosh, joined later that year by Linda Carriere, Sunay Suleyman and Christine and Trisha Lewin, released *Look How Long*. Despite the talent that the reformulated group demonstrated, Loose Ends never regained its initial popularity. McIntosh continued to produce several musicians, most notably Caron Wheeler, a former member of the group **Soul II Soul**.

ANDREA D. BARNWELL

lovers' rock

The name 'lovers' rock' was coined from the name of a South East London record label during the early 1970s. From his Dip Studio, Dennis Harris, along with musicians like Fish Salmon, Jah Bunny, John Kypie and Matumbi's Dennis Bovell, began to produce a sound that mirrored their relationship with Jamaican roots and US soul **music**, while being influenced by coping with life in 1970s Britain. Their unique style soon became more popular than many of the Jamaican **reggae** imports and in many ways overcame the bias for non-British reggae music, which was largely deemed inauthentic. Lovers' rock provided an alternative to the male-dominated roots rock reggae scene and made singers like Louisa Marks, Carol Thompson, Sandra Cross and Janet Kay household names. Lovers' rock did still deal with the harsh realities of the black British experience, and artistes like Sister Audrey commented on what it meant to be black and British in her hit song 'English Gal', on the Ariwa label. The passion for lovers' rock soon spread throughout Britain, producing acts like the Investigators, Cool Notes, Natural Mystic, the In Crowd and a host of other bands and solo artists.

Lovers' rock was soon to influence the Jamaican music scene, as exemplified by Sugar Minnott's cover version of Michael Jackson's *Good Thing Going*

and his tribute song, *This Is Lovers Rock*. Many of the biggest names in Jamaican reggae – Beres Hammond, Gregory Issacs, Freddie Mcgregor and Sanchez D – are regarded as lovers' rock artistes. However, during the 1980s, the mass appeal of **dancehall** reggae and its reliance on live DJing, coupled with a serious lack of media and record company interest, meant that lovers' rock went through a decline. The late 1980s and early 1990s saw a revival in the fortunes of lovers' rock and Janet Kay's successes in the Japanese market paved the way for other reggae performers to subsequently tour there. In Britain, the Heywood brothers and Mafia and Fluxy began working on their own productions with artists like Sylvia Tella, Vivian Jones and Peter **Hunningale**. As well as being among the most sought after British reggae musicians and producers, the brothers have worked with nearly every top Jamaican and British reggae producer. They also often work in conjunction with that old stalwart the **Mad Professor** and are well featured on his Ariwa label. This has ensured that lovers' rock continues to be heard and new producers like Mykey (Mad) Simpson and his MCS label are successfully promoting new artistes like Dawna Lee, who is widely regarded as one of the UK's best singer/songwriters. Lovers' rock is currently undergoing a revival, which means that the pioneers of the movement are now performing throughout the UK with a new wave of artistes. Ironically, just as in its seminal phase, the genre provides a welcome alternative with regard to the black music scene in Britain.

WILLIAM HENRY

lovers' rock style

Lovers' rock, the fusion of **soul** and **reggae**, was created by the 'sound' master Lloyd Coxsone and the producer Dennis Bovell in the mid-1970s, marked by the song they jointly produced 'Caught in a lie', which featured Louisa Mark on vocals. Bovell went on to produce a number of female singers in the genre. This resulted in a high percentage of black British female artists (the 1980 Black Echoes Top 40 featured thirteen female lovers' rock records), DJs and producers (Carroll

Thompson's label C&B was established in 1981) in the genre. Though lovers' rock focused on the dynamics of relationships, some female contributors exploited their strong position to discuss issues of gender and race as in 'Liberated women' by Ranking Ann and the DJ Sister Audrey's 'English girl'. The clothing and accessories favoured by followers of lovers' rock were marked by sartorial elegance. Menswear included three-piece, single breasted suits with double vents, Gabbici cardigans, Farah trousers, silk or rayon plain or self-stripe shirts and long leather or camel single breasted coats. Accessories could include beaver or bowler hats and berets, gold rings and chains; loafers, long scarves and Italian-style shoes in pastel shades. Hairstyles were either dreadlocks or a 1"-high haircut. During the late 1970s, womenswear retained the disco ethos of platform shoes, 'boob tube' and harem trousers, and an afro or corn row hairstyle. From the early 1980s, a streamlined image emerged of knife-pleated knee-length skirts, silk or rayon blouses, camel coats, flat or court patent Bally shoes and short gold necklaces.

CAROL TULLOCH

LTJ Bukem

b. 1967, London, England

DJ, artist, record label owner

LTJ Bukem began DJing in the 1980s, mixing a variety of different aspects of black **music** together. It was this awareness of the history of the music he listened to that made Speed, the club he set up with Fabio in 1994, an important catalyst in introducing wider influences to the hardcore sound of **jungle**. Bukem made the move from DJ in 1995, releasing *Logical Progressions* and setting up his own record label, Good Looking. Bukem and Good Looking have both been credited with bringing drum and bass to a wider audience and accused of watering the music down, but the label has continued to thrive while remaining independent. Good Looking had, by the beginning of 1999, released four compilation albums: *Logical Progression* volumes one and two, which concentrate on the drum and bass core of the label, and *Earth* volumes

one and two, which allow Good Looking artists to release more experimental tracks, mixing in **hip hop**, **soul**, dub, latin and jazz influences with drum and bass. In 1998, LTJ Bukem featured in an episode of BBC 2's *Modern Times*, 'DJ', which showed Good Looking's attempts to break the music to global audiences.

ANDY WOOD

Lyons, John

b. 1933, Port of Spain, Trinidad

painter, poet, journalist, lecturer

Lyons came to England in the early 1960s and studied at Goldsmiths College and Newcastle. Lyons's neo-expressive figuration is evident in a painting entitled *The Photographer* (1986). This can also be seen in *Two Girls* (1986), where he reveals a constructive process beneath his stylised depictions of daily life. Meanwhile, working in oil pastels and gouaches, *My Mother Earth is Black Like Me* (1986) demonstrates his ability to voice the collective weight of oppressive history and the challenge to establish the culture of a migrant community. Lyons provided a contextualising essay for Denzil **Forrester**'s *Dub Translation* (1990) and in *Self-Portrait with Jumbi Bird* (1990) demonstrated a more fantastic form of figuration. One series of his work concerns itself with devils, demons and supernatural characters appearing in Trinidad's **carnival**. He thus continues an African storytelling tradition via the modern means of expressive painting. Lyons now runs the Hourglass Studio Gallery at Hebden Bridge, near Halifax, and his work is held in national collections. He has won several literary prizes and worked as a **theatre** designer, exhibition adviser and as a teacher of both visual art (see **visual and plastic arts**) and writing. His later paintings use an increasingly vivid, at times fluorescent, palette in an allegorical approach to visual art that complements and embellishes his literary interests. His exhibitions include: '**Black Art: Plotting the Course**' (1987); '**The Other Story**' (1989–90); 'Let the Canvas Come to Life with Dark Faces' (1990); 'Behind the Carnival' (1992–4), Huddersfield Art

Gallery; and 'Vibrant Energies' (1995), paintings and poetry, Chinese Arts Centre.

Further reading

Chambers, E, Lamba, J. and Joseph, T. (1985) *The*

Artpack: a History of Black Artists in Britain, London: Haringey Arts Council.

PAUL O'KANE

M

McDonald, Trevor

b. 1939, Trinidad

broadcaster, journalist

Trevor McDonald had the dubious claim to fame of being one of the few prominent black figures in British cultural life to be featured in the satirical puppet show *Spitting Image*. Appearing alongside the popular sporting figure Frank Bruno, such prominence might suggest that the image of McDonald is offered up as another comforting stereotype. In this version of events McDonald's high profile as anchorman for ITN's flagship *News at Ten* programme simply functions to conceal the very absence of black faces on British **television**, certainly in such symbolically charged roles as that of newscaster. With his own public support to campaigns for proper English and his love of cricket it would be easy to see that the white establishment should cling to such a figure. This, however, would be to ignore McDonald's own roots in the Caribbean and the way in which a certain style of education was valued and cricket was seen as a vehicle of dissent and national pride. On these grounds one might wish to place him in the same camp as the Trinidadian intellectual and political historian C.L.R. **James**, but the comparison only goes to illustrate what James knew so well, that history is a complex process. McDonald's own account of these issues can be found in his 1993 autobiography, *Fortunate Circumstances*.

GARETH STANTON

McLeod, Jenny

b. 1964, Nottingham, England

playwright, novelist, screenwriter

Jenny McLeod began writing at twenty-three, when she entered a playwriting competition organised by Nottingham and Derby Playhouse. She won first prize with *Cricket at Camp David*. She has since had six plays commissioned and produced. Her second play *The Wake*, in 1991, won a national competition run by BBC TV to find new writers. *Raising Fires* won first prize in the LWT Plays on Stages Award in 1993 and was performed at the Bush Theatre a year later. McLeod was the Writer in Residence at the Nottingham Playhouse in 1991 and at the Tricycle Theatre Company in 1995, for which she staged *It's You*, a youth play, and *Victor and the Ladies*. McLeod published her first novel, *Stuck up a Tree*, in 1998 and received a London Arts Board bursary to work on her second novel in 2000. Her success as a staged and published playwright has led to her being commissioned as a screenwriter to develop a project for Lenny **Henry**'s Crucial Film Company.

Select bibliography

McLeod, J. (1998) *Island Life*, London: Nick Hern Books.
—— (1998) *Stuck up a Tree*, London: Flamingo.
—— (1991) *The Wake*, London: BBC Books.

KADIJA SESAY

McMillan, Michael

b. 1962, High Wycombe, England

playwright, essayist

Mcmillan's first play *The School Leaver* was selected for the Royal Court Theatre Young Writer's Festival in 1978, as was *Hard Time Pressure* (1980). In 1981, *Day of Action*, based on the black community's response to the New Cross Fire Massacre, toured London with the Brent Black Peoples' Theatre. *On Duty*, based on the real experiences of NHS worker Rita Maxim, was made into a drama documentary for **Channel 4** in 1984. Between 1990 and 1992, he experimented with site-specific **live art** works, such as *Portrait of a Shopping Centre as a Cathedral*, devised with artist Keith **Piper** and performed in Dalston Shopping Centre in 1990. In 1993, *Invisible* toured with Double Edge Theatre Co.; in 1996, again in collaboration with Keith Piper, he wrote and produced *I Hope it's not a Black Man*. In 1998, the much acclaimed *Brother to Brother* played at the Lyric Studio Hammersmith. Also in 1998, McMillan wrote *The Diaries*, a radio play of dramatic monologues, for NOW fm and *After Windrush*, which was produced by Oval House.

Select bibliography

McMillan, M. (1992) *Living Proof: Views of a World Living with HIV and AIDS – Photography and Writings*, London: Artists' Agency.
—— (1989) *On Duty*, London: Akira Press.

SUZANNE SCAFE

McQueen, Steve

b. 1969 London, England

visual artist, film-maker

McQueen's work marks a departure in the debate around representation of the black body. From his first film (see **film and cinema**) *Bear* through to his most ambitious piece *Drumroll*, the work focuses on the artist's own ambiguous presence, which is neither the object nor returner of the gaze. His films, nearly all shot in black and white, are resistant to straightforward interpretation, instead relying on lingering camerawork and subtle editing to evoke a mood that is neither welcoming nor didactic. McQueen is one of a new generation of artists rejecting the label 'black', although he first came to prominence in the group exhibition 'Mirage', which focused on the legacy of Frantz Fanon. He is sometimes regarded as part of the young British art phenomenon, but this too is a category that he does not fit into easily. Lauded remarkably soon after his graduation, McQueen has enjoyed critically acclaimed solo exhibitions both in New York and at London's **Institute of Contemporary Arts**. McQueen won the 1999 Turner Prize, having turned down a nomination once before.

Further reading

Haye C. (1998) 'Motion pictures' *frieze* 28: 39–43, Institute of Contemporary Arts Steve McQueen exhibition catalogue.

NIRU RATNAM

Macka 'B'

b. Wolverhampton, England

Rastafarian cultural activist, musician, poet, performer

Macka 'B' is widely regarded as the most 'conscious' [conscious as in an Afrocentric, **Rastafari** stance to speak about the reality of black oppression without fear of reprisal] and lyrically consistent of all the British DJs, evidenced in the fact that he has been releasing thought-provoking singles and albums for over fifteen years. His 1986 debut release for **Mad Professor**'s Ariwa label, *Sign Of the Times*, went straight to the number one slot in the British **reggae** album chart and at the time was acclaimed as the most militant album released by a British reggae artist. Macca 'B' began DJing at the age of sixteen on a local sound system (see **sound system DJs**) called Exodus and soon gained a reputation for his lyrical dexterity and infectious witticism. In 1984, he featured on a black-orientated **television** programme called *Ebony*, where every week he would deliver a live topical social commentary in front of a studio audience. It was while performing on this programme that he was noticed by the Mad Professor, who invited him to travel to London and record an album. Around the same time he was approached by **Fashion Records**, who had recently released **Smiley Culture**'s 'Police Officer', which was a national pop chart success. Macka 'B' subsequently recorded three singles for Fashion; however, his pro-black Rastafarian (see **Rastafari**) perspective was too much for the commercially oriented outfit. Thus, when he approached them with a song entitled 'Apartheid Must Be Destroyed' in 1984, he was informed that it was too controversial as they believed Mandela would be released the following year. Macka 'B' has recorded twelve albums for the Ariwa label and has performed in Botswana, Hawaii, Japan, the USA, Canada, Australia, New Zealand and right across Europe. One of his most memorable performances was alongside the Twinkle Brothers, one of Jamaica's leading reggae bands, at the 'Solidarity' concert held in Poland in 1990. Macka 'B' states that his **music** is designed to promote a positive notion of blackness and that is why he refuses to compromise his messages because 'sometimes you have to do what is right, no matter bout the consequences, cos people don't care what they do to us'.

WILLIAM HENRY

Mad Professor

b. Guyana

record company owner, musician, producer, engineer, mixer, re-mixer, performer

The Mad Professor (a.k.a. Neil Fraser) is arguably the most successful independent black record producer in Britain. His Ariwa record label, which has been in business for over twenty years, has over two hundred releases, both singles and albums, many of which have reached the number one spot in various countries world-wide. He has also established himself as the owner of Britain's largest

black recording studio, has worked with many of the top performing artists on the global **reggae** scene and his Ariwa crew are constantly touring world-wide.

Mad Professor received his pseudonym as a child in Guyana: unlike other children he was not interested in playing games or sports, and he much preferred to play with old wires and transistors and actually built his first transistor radio when he was ten years old. After arriving in England with his family a few years later, he started working for an electronics firm. However, he soon noticed that he was often overlooked and, realising that it was not his ability he was being judged by, he left and founded his first recording studio, which he built in his front room in 1979. It is this attitude that has maintained his position as one of the only black record producers in the UK who refuses to promote negativity in his music. Prof. only associates himself with spiritually uplifting music and therefore does not shy away from 'controversial' pro-black perspectives. Since the Mad Professor released his first album *Dub Me Crazy*, he has established himself as a master of the 'dub concept album' epitomised in his *Black Liberation Dub*, which Prof. suggests is designed 'to take the listener into a militant mood'. Due to his reputation for venturing into musically uncharted waters, Prof. has worked with many luminaries in the music business, right across the musical spectrum, including Lee 'Scratch' Perry, **Sade**, U Roy and **Massive Attack**. Prof. is also a performer in his own right. When his Ariwa crew are touring, Prof. uniquely re-mixes live dub tracks, as he refuses to play recorded releases at live events.

WILLIAM HENRY

Man Mela Theatre Company

The Man Mela Theatre Company was set up in 1993 in order to celebrate the British Asian experience through dramatic productions and workshops inspired by the poetry and prose of the Indian subcontinent. Man Mela's Artistic Director is Dominic Rai and the administrator is Caroline Goffin. Based at the Albany Theatre, Deptford, and working in partnership with the Arts

Council, the British Council and the Nehru Centre, the **theatre** company has organised a number of national productions since its inception. These have included *Asian Voices*, which explored the experiences of the British Asian community in the twentieth century, and three productions that toured nationally; *Azadi: the Story of Freedom*, which addressed the Partition of India in 1947, *Across the Black Waters* and *The Untouchable Century*, both of which were adapted from novels by Mulk Raj Anand.

In 2000–2001, Man Mela plan to stage a triple bill entitled *The Cornershop*, and a dramatic interpretation of Saadat Hasan Manto's famous story of Partition, *Toba Tek Singh*, adapted by Amarjit Chandan as *The Exchange of Lunatics*. The company actively encourages new writing talent from all ethnic backgrounds through its *Write Now!* workshops, and also organises workshops and residencies on contemporary British Asian **literature**.

ALEX TICKELL

Mango Publishing

Mango Publishing is a new small press founded in 1995 by Joan **Anim-Addo**. Based in London, Mango specialises in the Caribbean voice, with a particular focus on Caribbean **women's writing**. Mango publishes both new and established writers, whether domiciled in the UK, the Caribbean or in the diaspora. The press publishes poetry, fiction, essays and history works, and has published works by established writers such as Beryl **Gilroy**, Velma Pollard and Jacob **Ross**, as well as works by newer and lesser known writers and scholars.

Mango's 2000 programme includes the launch of a new series of texts in translation, sometimes published as dual-language editions. The first titles in this series aim to bring the writing of women in Cuba, where they have literary stature, to a wider readership. Mango Publishing was established to fill the publishing lacuna that has existed for Caribbean writers, particularly women.

JOAN ANIM-ADDO

Mangrove Trials

In the early 1970s, as relations between the British police and black youths rapidly deteriorated, a number of significant group arrests were made in close succession that would leave a deep imprint on the cultural consciousness of the black British community. Those arrested included the Mangrove Nine (arrested August 1971), the Metro Four (arrested May 1971), the Oval Four (arrested March 1972), the Brockwell Park Three (arrested June 1973), the Swan Disco Seven (arrested September 1974), the Cricklewood Twelve and the Stockwell Ten (both arrested March 1974). However, it was the Mangrove Nine – the first of these groups – who would come to symbolise most poignantly the struggles of the black community against increasingly invasive, racialised policing strategies. The Mangrove restaurant, on All Saints Road, Notting Hill, was repeatedly raided in a series of unsuccessful drug raids by the police in 1970. In August that year, its Trinidadian owner Frank Critchlow and a number of customers and supporters organised a protest march against the disruptive policing of the restaurant. The event was the source of much anxiety, as police and the media interpreted the march as a foreboding early expression of the Black Power movement as it had already been expressed on the other side of the Atlantic. During the protest march, disturbances broke out between the police and protestors, and a number of black men and women were arrested, including the future *Race Today* editor Darcus **Howe**. These protestors were named by the black community as the 'Mangrove Nine'. This name entered local folklore when, at the Mangrove trial, the protestors – some representing themselves – won their court case against the police. Photographs of the protest taken by Horace **Ové** (who later became one of Britain's leading black filmmakers) were used in evidence at the trial. The event came to represent a pioneering example of politicised resistance and of official recognition of institutionalised racism within the police force.

JAMES PROCTER

MANN, JASMINDER *see* Babylon Zoo

Mannafest

Mannafest, founded in 1995, are a performance company that grew from the demise of the Urban Poets Society. The company works under artistic directors Vanessa Richards and Khefri Riley (a.k.a. KA'frique) and, using poetry as a foundation, creates multi-media events combining various art forms such as **music**, DJ culture, visual art (see **visual and plastic arts**) and multi-media technology, in alternative spaces. Their aim is to contribute to the world-wide resurgence of African diasporic urban culture. Based on this principle, they provide Arts in Education Programmes and create Public Art Commissions, collaborating with international artists to produce and direct multi-media events such as *Trans-Metaphoria* (1995) and *Mango Lick* (1997–8).

Select bibliography

Richards, V. (2000) 'Stakis Hotel, Maybelline Ruby Ice', in C. Newland, and K. Sesay (eds) *IC3: the Penguin Book of New Black Writing in Britain*, London: Penguin.
—— (1998) 'Post Caribbean reds', in K. McCarthy (ed.) *Bittersweet*, London: the Women's Press.
—— (1998) 'Tupac came to me in a dream . . .', 'Icarus', 'He lays on his back', in L. Sissay (ed.) *The Fire People*, Edinburgh: Payback Press.
Riley, K. (1998) 'Love in La-La Land', in K. McCarthy (ed.) *Bittersweet*, London: the Women's Press.
—— (1998) 'thru', 'Icarus', in L. Sissay (ed.) *The Fire People*, Edinburgh: Payback Press.

Selected discography

Mannafest (1999) *kissultimate*, London: Monumental Records.

KADIJA SESAY

Mantra Publications

Established in 1984, Mantra Publications specialises in Asian books by Asian writers for young readers, as well as multicultural titles. Their first book, *Tales from India*, was five mythological and folktales in English accompanied by an audio cassette, available in either English, Gujarati or Punjabi. Mantra are the only publishing (see **publishing, books**) company in Britain specialising in dual-language books, reflecting the growing multiculturalism of Britain. Their books are now all published in English alongside one of twenty-five other Asian, African or European languages. Other school materials, such as multilingual posters, are also produced. Their fiction and non-fiction youth titles reflect the life of young Asians in Britain and issues that affect them, incorporating traditional as well as 'streetwise' life. Topics include street gangs and cultural border crossings. Two of their novelists, Sailesh Ramakrishnan and Ravi **Randhawa** have written award-winning books. Mantra's intentions are to promote global understanding and increased awareness of the diversity of cultures by producing books that represent people of various **ethnic minorities**, rather than being dominated by a single culture (see **children's publishers**).

KADIJA SESAY

Markandaya, Kamala

b. 1924, Karnatak region, India

novelist

One of the most important Indian novelists writing in English, Markandaya was born to an upper middle-class Brahmin family and came to England in the 1940s. Her prolific writing career started with the successful novel *Nectar in a Sieve* (1954), which focuses on Indian peasant life. Most of Markandaya's works are set in India and cover a wide range of characters, settings and experiences. The East–West encounter and its clash of cultural values is at the heart of many of her novels and dominates what is considered her most stylistically accomplished work, *A Silence of Desire* (1960). The painful immigrant experience of an Indian family in Britain, a sense of loss and nostalgia, and questions of identity are explored in *The Nowhere Man* (1972).

Select bibliography

Markandaya, K. (1982) *Pleasure City*, London: Chatto & Windus.

—— (1977) *The Golden Honeycomb*, London: Chatto & Windus.

—— (1972) *The Nowhere Man*, New York: Day.

—— (1969) *The Coffer Dams*, London: Hamish Hamilton.

—— (1960) *A Silence of Desire*, London: Putnam.

—— (1954) *Nectar in a Sieve*, London: Putnam.

PAOLA MARCHIONNI

Markham, E.A.

b. 1939, Montserrat

poet, writer, dramatist, editor, critic

Markham moved to the UK from Monserrat in 1956. He grew up in London and read English and philosophy at university. He worked in the West Indies in the early 1970s as a director with the Caribbean Theatre Workshop. As a writer he is probably best known for his poetry, of which there are now six collections. The 1993 collection, *Letter From Ulster & The Hugo Poems*, yokes together the north-east province of Ireland and the Caribbean island of Montserrat, and raises the historical connection between these two lands. A similar journeying across a geographical and historical terrain, this time in the form of a travelogue, can be seen in *A Papua New Guinea Sojourn: More Pleasures In Exile* (1998), which documents his life as a media co-ordinator in New Guinea in the 1980s. He has also published two collections of short stories and, in 1999, **Peepal Tree Press** published *Marking Time*, a campus novel. He has had an editorial role with ***Artrage*** and *Ambit*, and currently edits *Sheffield Thursday* magazine. He has edited *The Penguin Book of Caribbean Short Stories* (1996) and the useful collection of Caribbean poetry *Hinterland* (1989). Markham also organises the annual, international *Sheffield Thursday* poetry and short-fiction competition, and the biennial Hallam Festival of Literature. He is a Professor in the Department of English at Sheffield Hallam University. In 1997, he was awarded a Certificate of Honour by the Government of Montserrat.

Select bibliography

Markham, E.A. (1999) *Marking Time*, Leeds: Peepal Tree Press.

—— (1998) *A Papua New Guinea Sojourn: More Pleasures in Exile*, Manchester: Carcarnet Press.

—— (ed.) (1996) *The Penguin Book of Caribbean Short Stories*, London: Penguin Books.

—— (1993) *Letter From Ulster & the Hugo Poems*, Lancs: Littlewood Arc.

—— (ed.) (1989) *Hinterland*, Newcastle upon Tyne: Bloodaxe Books.

—— (1984) *Human Rites*, Canada: Anvil Poetry Press.

ALISON DONNELL

Marsh-Edwards, Nadine

b. 1960, England

producer

A co-founder of **Sankofa Film Collective** in 1984, Marsh-Edwards has been a pivotal force in developing a black British cinema from the workshops through to the international sphere. Working variously as an editor, production manager, producer and executive producer on classic films such as ***Territories***, *The Passion of Remembrance* (1986), *Dreaming Rivers* (1988), ***Looking for Langston*** and *Home away from Home* (1993) and ***Young Soul Rebels*** (1992), Marsh-Edwards's collaborations with emerging black directors have cemented her role as a leading black female producer in the UK. She worked with Ngozi **Onwurah** on *Flight of the Swan* (1992), Isaac **Julien** on his feature debut *Young Soul Rebels* and Gurinder **Chadha** on the short *A Nice Arrangement* (1991) and Bafta-nominated ***Bhaji on the Beach*** (1994). In 1994, Marsh-Edwards established Xenos Pictures, her own London- and South-African based production company, executive-producing Debbie Isitt's feature film *Nasty Neighbours* in 1999. She is also a partner in Xencat Productions, which produced Les Blair's *Jump the Gun* (1996). As well as her involvement in the creative dimensions of black film-making, Marsh-Edwards has been extensively involved with various organisations promoting the British film (see **film and cinema**) industry. A founder member of the London Film and Video Development Agency directorate (1992), she was also a panellist on the British Screen National Development Fund (1994–5) and a member of the **British Film Institute** Production Board (1995–7). In 1999, Marsh-Edwards was appointed the Development Producer at BBC Drama Scotland but continues to develop her own projects through Xenos.

SATINDER CHOHAN

Martin, S.I.

b. 1959, Bedford, England

novelist, music promoter, journalist

Martin's debut novel *Incomparable World* is a historical thriller informed by thorough historical research. Its central character Buckram is a former slave who gained his freedom by fighting for the British in America's War of Independence and gained a passage to Britain. In this eighteenth-century world of crime, press gangs and fear of re-enslavement, Buckram is barred from working within any London guild. As the novel unfolds, Buckram meets the high and low of black British culture, including Olaudah Equiano and Ottobah Cugoano. However, the novel not only mischievously invokes the beginnings of black British literature; Buckram envisages a future London in which generations 'of his kinfolk, freedmen, English-born and bred [are] transforming this wet, cold island with African worship and celebration' (p. 40). S.I. Martin is currently working on a science fiction novel.

Select bibliography

Martin, S.I. (1996) *Incomparable World*, London: Quartet Books.

MARK STEIN

Martin, Taslim

b. 1962, London, England

ceramicist

While studying at the Royal College of Art (1996–8), Martin won the Eduardo Paolozzi Travel Scholarship. In Nigeria he undertook a series of interviews with artists and educators at the Universities of Benin, Lagos and Obafemi Awolowo in Ife. Printmaker and painter Dr Bruce Onobrakpeya also discussed with Martin the question of Nigerian national identity in the arts. Martin's work ranges from expressive sculptural pieces, such as *Tenderly* (1999), a female nude in terracotta cast in bronze, to more design-oriented work. Martin's ceramic seating explores the uses and forms of clay as a material suitable for furniture. Citing the technical and formal beauty of modern sanitary ware, Martin's work brings together the legacy of Duchamp's urinal *Fountain* (1912) as art and quotidian ceramic design object. His work has been shown in numerous exhibitions, including the Sotheby Contemporary Decorative Arts Show, London; The Scottish Gallery, Edinburgh; Mission 45, London; and the South Hill Park Arts Centre, Bracknell, Berkshire, where Martin has been artist-in-residence since 1999.

Further reading

Martin, T. (1999) 'Artist's eye', *Art Review*, February, p. 49.

LINDA SANDINO

MARY SEACOLE HOUSE *see* Brixton Black Women's Group

Mason-John, Valerie

b. 1962, Cambridge, England

reporter, essayist, editor, film and television presenter, mime and performance artist, poet, actor, playwright

Valerie Mason-John, a.k.a. Queenie, was raised in several white foster homes, and placed in Barnados between the ages of five and eleven. Trans-racial fostering has been only one of the many political and social issues she has engaged with. From 1988 to 1989, she worked in Australia, documenting the land rights struggle. Mason-John has worked for the *Guardian*, the **Voice**, *City Limits*, the *Pink Paper*, *Everywoman* and *Spare Rib*, among others, and has covered the issues of race, **feminism** and sexuality as part of her journalistic writing. In 1993, she co-wrote the first ever study of the British black lesbian community, *Lesbians Talk Making Black Waves*, and, in 1995, she edited the anthology *Talking Black: Lesbians of African and Asian Descent Speak Out*. When she co-hosted on the main stage of the 1996 Lesbian, Gay, Bisexual and Trans-gender Pride Festival, the *Voice* described her as 'a black gay icon'. In 1997, her sell-out play *Sin Dykes* broached the controversial topics of relationships between black and white women and S. & M. sex in the black lesbian community. Mason-John's compère and performance persona, Queenie, has worked as a **television** presenter, hosted poetry events, club nights and the Lesbian Beauty Contest, and wrote and appeared in the one-woman show *Brown Girl in the Ring*. In 1998, Mason-John published a collection of her plays, prose and poems, also under this title.

Select bibliography

Mason-John, V. (1999) *Brown Girl in the Ring*, London: Get a Grip.
—— (ed.) (1995) *Talking Black: Lesbians of African and Asian Descent Speak Out*, London: Cassell.
Mason-John, V. and Khambatta, A. (1993) *Lesbians Talk Making Black Waves*, London: Scarlet Press.

ANITA NAOKO PILGRIM

Massey, Jamila

b. 1934, Simla, India

actress

Jamila Massey is possibly the most senior established Asian actress in the UK; she has been in the business for fifty-three years. She came to the UK in 1946, and acted in plays for the BBC World Service as a child. She went to school in Wembley and read English and Latin at King's College, London. Although she continued acting, the pickings were small and the parts derisory. Her big break came with a BBC film (see **film and cinema**), *A Touch of Eastern Promise* (1972), part of Second City Firsts, where she played an Indian actress who comes on a tour of England and encounters a besotted fan. She has had a prolific career in radio, **theatre** and film, and has appeared in most **television** soaps, including *Parosi*, *Brookside*, *Albion Market* and *Angels*. Her latest role is as Mrs Parvez in *The Cappuccino Years* and she is familiar as Auntie Satya in *The Archers*. Massey's major role was in the ITV comedy, *Mind Your Language*, where as Jamila Ranjha she spoke her own invented language. In addition to her acting career, Massey chaired and sat on Equity's Afro-Asian committee for many years. She and her husband Reginald **Massey** have written several books together.

Select bibliography

Massey, R. and Massey, J. (1989) *The Dances of India*, London: Tri-colour.
—— (1976) *The Music of India*, London: Kahn and Averill.

SUMAN BHUCHAR

Massey, Reginald

b. 1932, Lahore, India

writer, poet, director

Massey grew up in Lahore, but moved to India when Lahore became the capital of Pakistan upon independence and studied in Simla and later at St

John's University, Agra. He was awarded a scholarship to read journalism at Lille University, France, and following that came to the UK in 1962. Massey got an opening writing arts reviews for *The Times*, where he specialised in Indian **dance** and **music**. Together with his wife, Jamila **Massey**, he wrote several books, including an entertaining novel, *The Immigrants* (1973), about a first-generation working-class man who comes to settle in the UK.

Massey has been a champion for Asian artistic expression in Britain, particularly Indian dance, and his first book: *Indian Dances – Their History and Growth*, co-authored with Rina Singha, is still regarded as a standard work on the subject. Massey now writes for the specialist magazine *The Dancing Times*, and the University of Surrey published his writings on dance in 1996. He also worked in film, and his seminal piece was the feature documentary, *Bangladesh: I Love You* (1982), which he wrote, produced and directed; Massey persuaded boxer Mohammed Ali to tour the country and documented his response. He is also a published poet.

Select bibliography

Massey, R. (1999) *India's Kathak Dance – Past, Present and Future*. New Delhi: Abhinav Publications.
—— (1996) *Lament of a Lost Hero*, Calcutta: Writers Workshop.
Massey, R. and Singha, R. (1967) *Indian Dances – Their History and Growth*, London: Faber.

SUMAN BHUCHAR

Massive Attack

Originally members of Bristol's Wild Bunch, whose name still adorns their records, the trio took their inspiration from both the **hip hop** crews and **reggae** sound systems that had also inspired the anarchic Wild Bunch. Utilising a range of guest vocalists and collaborators, including reggae legend Horace Andy, **Tricky** and Shara **Nelson**, they released their debut album *Blue Lines* in 1991. At a time when **dance** music was largely upbeat, single based and instrumental, *Blue Lines* was song based

and timeless, as much influenced by Jamaica's Studio One as by rap and contemporary dance **music**. A second album *Protection* followed in 1994, co-produced by Nellee Hooper, and a year later *No Protection*, an album of dub versions by the **Mad Professor**. Guests on *Protection* included Tracey Thorne and Nicolette, who went on to produce her own debut album *Let No-one Live Rent Free In Your Head*. In 1998, Massive Attack released the hugely anticipated *Mezzanine* album, which won a Brit Award for best album, and worked with Madonna in the same year. Massive Attack have also set up their own record label, Melankolic, and have released material by Horace Andy among others.

ANDY WOOD

Matura, Mustapha

b. 1939, Port of Spain, Trinidad

dramatist

Noel Matura, a Trinidadian of Indian descent, arrived in England in 1961. Having worked as a hospital porter, and spent time in Italy, he returned to England in 1963, married and took a job in a factory. Inspired by the 1960s wave of black consciousness, he changed his first name to the less European Mustapha and wrote four short plays. In 1970, director Roland Rees persuaded Ed Berman of the Ambiance Theatre to add these *Black Pieces* to his 'Black and White Power Season' of black US plays. Here, Matura introduced the authentic voice of the West Indies, which has subsequently characterised his plays. This production led the producer Michael White to commission *As Time Goes By* (1971), which explored the problems experienced by the immigrant confronted with British culture. In *Welcome Home Jacko* (1979), probably his most popular play, Matura portrayed the quest for identity of second-generation black youth. In other plays, such as *Play Mas* (1974), *Independence* (1979), *Meetings* (1982) and *The Coup* (1991), Matura has looked back to his homeland. In 1990, the National Theatre produced *The Coup*, the first play commissioned from a black British writer.

Select bibliography

Matura, M. (1992) *Mustapha Matura: Six Plays*, London: Methuen.

D. KEITH PEACOCK

Mau/Earthling/Cuba

Earthling were formed in Bristol by rapper Mau and T. Saul, and their location, combined with their laid-back, **hip hop**-influenced sound, saw the media label them as being part of an emerging 'Bristol sound' centred around bands such as **Massive Attack**, Portishead and **Tricky** – artists whose music was lazily labelled 'trip hop'. Earthling collaborated with Portishead's Geoff Barrow on several songs but were largely ignored in favour of their better known predecessors. After releasing their only album *Radar* in 1995, along with several singles including 'Blood music' in 1996, Earthling split up. *Radar*, however, showed that Earthling were more than just opportunists with its sparse instrumentation, strong beats and Mau's sly, endearing vocals. These vocals are particularly notable on the song '1st Transmission', with pop-cultural references and an attempt to place the experiences of black British musicians firmly in the centre, and not the margins, with its chorus: 'I know who I am/I'm not who you think I am'. In 1998, Mau returned as guest vocalist on Cuba's critically acclaimed debut single 'Cross the line' and the follow-up 'Havana'. Mau has also appeared regularly as part of Cuba's live line-up.

ANDY WOOD

Maya

Relatively new on the market (launched in 2000), *Maya* has already earned its place in the Asian British consciousness by becoming the first international glossy magazine (see **publishing, newspapers and magazines**) to be published in this country aimed predominantly at Asian readers. There has been a void in high-gloss magazines for Asian British women, who will be able to find the most fashionable Western clothes and *shalwarkameez*

in this publication. Although Maya is a girl's name, it translates as 'illusion' in Sanskrit. The quarterly magazine, published by the Dolphin Media Group, is being hailed as an up-market publication equivalent to *Harpers & Queen*. Aimed at second- and third-generation Asian women, it will bridge the gap between East and West, and promote Asian heritage and culture. Beauty will feature strongly and Asian influences are already felt with *bindis*, Ayurvedic skin treatments and henna painting. In terms of fashion (see **fashion and design**), saris are emerging as a serious mainstream fashion item and they have been worn by Olympic gold medallist Denise Lewis, singer and former *Eastenders* actress Michelle Gayle and Cherie Blair among others. There will also be celebrity interviews that will include **Bollywood** stars. *Maya* has a target circulation of 45,000, which, if met, will surpass that of *Pride* magazine, aimed at women of African Caribbean descent in Britain, which sells around 24,000 copies.

YINKA SUNMONU

Medalla, David

b. 1942, Manila, Philippines

visual artist, editor, gallerist

Medalla has been involved in a number of projects and galleries. He was co-director of the Signals Art Gallery, which specialised in kinetic art and art from Latin America, and edited the periodical *Signals*. He was also involved with the performance group the Exploding Gallery. Becoming politicised after a period of travel, Medalla's work became more confrontational. Along with friends, he founded the group Artists for Democracy, which foregrounded the links between art and international politics, and produced work that addressed anti-imperialist struggles and ethnography. During these activities, Medalla also produced experimental performances and more conventional artworks that were both witty and moving. Medalla's signature works, the bubble machines, which were made soon after his arrival in London in the early 1960s, took the form of transparent gateways filled with a constant stream of foam. The works were kinetic and pushed the parameters of sculpture; as the bubbles filled the sculpture they would overflow and fall around the piece, their gentle growth suggesting an organic process.

Further reading

Brett, G. (1995) *Exploding Galleries: the Art of David Medalla*, London: Kala Press.

NIRU RATNAM

Mehmood, Tariq

b. Pakistan

novelist, activist

Mehmood came to live in Bradford, England, in the early 1960s, where he became involved in a number of radical political groups. In 1981, he was arrested as one of the 'Bradford 12', a group of Asian youths who were caught in possession of petrol bombs. Arguing that they were intended as a defence to the growing threat of racial violence in the city, Mehmood and the others were acquitted eleven months later. His novel *Hand on the Sun* is set in Bradford and describes the politicisation of the South Asian community in the late 1970s/early 1980s.

Select bibliography

Mehmood, T. (1983) *Hand on the Sun*, London: Penguin Books.

JAMES PROCTER

Mel B

b. 1975, Leeds, England

singer

Prior to her successful audition for the Spice Girls, Yorkshire-born Melanie Brown had begun a career as an actress, having had a number of small parts on shows such as *The Bill* and *Coronation Street*. The world-wide success of the Spice Girls made her a household name as Mel B or 'Scary Spice', as the band released a string of hit singles, albums and a film *Spice World* (1997). The Spice Girls have largely been portrayed as a manufactured pop gimmick but their music has continually adapted influences such as rap and R'n'B, and the band have continued to maintain their phenomenal success. Mel B released her debut solo single, a collaboration with the American R'n'B star Missy 'Misdemeanour' Elliott, as Melanie B in 1998. 'I want you back' was a number one hit despite being harder sounding than the Spice Girls more pop-orientated output, and Mel B began recording her debut solo album with US producer Nas and collaborators including the rapper Timbaland, with whom she recorded a version of Cameo's 'Word up', Missy Elliott and Mary J. Blige. Mel B was a guest presenter at 1998's MOBO (Music Of Black Origin) awards. As Melanie B, she released her second solo album, *Hot*, in 2000.

ANDY WOOD

MENSON, MICHAEL *see* Rebel MC

Merali, Shaheen

b. 1959, Tanzania

visual artist, curator, arts administrator

Merali emerged as a batik artist, before turning in the late 1980s to sculpture and installations exploring colonialism and consumerism. Early pieces included critiques of the British consumption of tea, highlighting the drink as a product of empire. Merali's best known installation, *Going Native*, typifies the artist's use of multiple themes and approaches encompassing installation, video projection, artefacts, sound and slides. Much of Merali's artistic output has an undercurrent of sensuality, such as the slides of sunseekers on Goa's beaches, suggestive of the role that desire plays in colonial relations. Merali's work has shifted in its approach. Early student work used materials such as mud, hemp and stone, and was influenced by Tantra, while later work looks to the wider field of post-colonial theory. This may be seen as symptomatic of a wider shift in the work of black artists in

Britain at the end of the 1980s. Merali has also worked as a curator, co-curating the international exhibition 'Slow Release' (London, 1999) among other shows. Merali also founded the arts organisation **Panchayat**.

Further reading

Cubitt, S. 'Going native: Columbus, Liverpool, identity and memory', *Third Text* 21: 107–20.

NIRU RATNAM

Mercer, Kobena

b. 1960

literary and cultural critic

A leading scholar in the field of black British cultural studies, Kobena Mercer is also a prominent theorist of diasporic cultural practices and an important critic of the contemporary visual arts (see **visual and plastic arts**). It is indeed to the points where visual culture, black British social, cultural and political history, and the cultural forms of the black diaspora intersect, inform and complicate one another that Mercer has devoted much of his attention.

His first book, *Welcome to the Jungle: New Positions in Black Cultural Studies* (1994), demonstrates that breadth and convergence of his interests. A collection of essays written over a period from the mid-1980s onward, *Welcome to the Jungle* includes analyses of black independent film (see **film and cinema**) in Britain, the metaphors of monstrosity in Michael Jackson's 'Thriller' video, the photographs of Robert Mapplethorpe, constructions of black masculinity in, through and against constructions of queer identity and desire, and the very notion of 'identity' as an organising category of what Mercer calls the 'post-consensual' cultural politics of the late twentieth century. Mercer's thoroughgoing critique, in this text, of fixed models of 'identity' (a critique, that is, of the desire to counteract the bewilderments of a 'post-consensual' cultural dispensation by naming, asserting or defining a stable racial, cultural or sexual identity) accords both with his later elaboration of the

concept of 'identification' (which demands a close historicising attention to the ways in which identities are formed, reformed and subvert their formalisation) and his consistent exploration of the relations between identity, desire and identification.

The turn to desire is crucial, also, to Mercer's examination of the inter-articulation of black and queer modes of identification in a range of visual forms. His important writings in this regard include not only his work on Mapplethorpe but his *Eros and Diaspora: Rotimi Fani-Kayode and Alex Hirst* (1996) and 'True confessions: a discourse on images of black male sexuality', written with Isaac **Julien** (with whom Mercer regularly collaborates) for the Open University's Reader on Identity and Diversity: *Gender and the Experience of Education* (1995). In addition to these texts, frequent contributions to film, literary and visual culture journals, numerous catalogue contributions for exhibitions of twentieth-century artists and a full monograph on the work of the multi-media artist Keith **Piper**, Mercer is a regular lecturer and teacher at universities throughout Britain and the USA.

Select bibliography

Mercer, K. (1994) *Welcome to the Jungle: New Positions in Black Cultural Studies*, New York and London: Routledge.

IAN BAUCOM

Mercury, Freddie

b. 1946, Zanzibar, Tanzania; d. 1991, Kensington, London, England

musician

Mercury, the lead singer of the rock group, Queen, was in fact born Farok Bulsara to Zoroastrian Gujerati parents living in Zanzibar. He spent his childhood there, before moving back to where he was educated in Bombay. Bulsara's first band, the Hectics, was formed while he lived in India. Bulsara and his family moved to the UK in 1964, and the young musician changed his name to Freddie Mercury. The group he made his name with, Queen, became one of the most famous acts of rock history. Despite Queen being the first band to play stadiums in South America, they never toured South Asia. With his pale Parsee skin, few questioned the cultural origins of Mercury when he was alive. While Mercury admitted to his Zoroastrian religious heritage, he never publicly admitted to his Indian ethnicity, at a time when there were no well-known South Asians in the British popular **music** industry. Mercury's deception is a poignant reflection on cultural prejudices of the 1970s and 1980s, when it was not thought that Asians could be popular music stars.

Further reading

Ratnam, N. (1997) 'A colouring book', *frieze* 33: 39–40.

NIRU RATNAM

métis(se)/mixed race

The key writings on 'mixed-race' identity largely focus on the experiences of those women (and interest has been expressed almost exclusively by women) whose mixed-race identity involves relations between white Europeans and black diasporic Africans. Yet, the driving force of such interrogations is to point out the problems in essentialist definitions of blackness (and indeed whiteness) or what Paul **Gilroy** has spoken of in a different context as 'ethnic absolutism'. Through her pioneering ethnographic work in Bristol between 1990 and 1992, anthropologist Jayne Ifekwunigwe proposed that those who are defined as neither black nor white occupy a different discursive position to those who more comfortably situate themselves (or are located) in black or white categories of identification. Ifekwunigwe uses the French-African term *métis(se)* (*métis* – masculine, *métisse* – feminine) both to describe informants who have British mothers and African or African Caribbean fathers, and more critically to re-name those who have been described as 'mixed race'. She argues that by 'virtue of lineage', *métisse* women 'situate themselves within at least two specific and yet over-lapping historical narratives'. Ifekwunigwe

stresses that these women's 'experiences of multiple identities, which are necessarily contradictory, socio-culturally constructed and essentialized, demand new paradigms for looking at citizenship and belonging' (Ifekwunigwe 1997: 127).

References

Ifekwunigwe, J.O. (1997) 'Diaspora's daughters, Africa's orphans? On lineage, authenticity and "mixed race" identity', in H.S. Mirza (ed.) *Black British Feminism: a Reader*, London and New York: Routledge, pp. 127–52.

Further reading

Alibhai-Brown, Y. and Montague, A. (eds) (1992) *The Colour of Love: Mixed Race Relationships*, London: Virago.
Anzaldúa, G. (1987) *Borderlands/La Frontera: the New Mestiza*, San Francisco: Aunt Lute Books.
Kay, J. (1991) *The Adoption Papers*, Newcastle: Bloodaxe Books.
Young, R.J.C. (1995) *Colonial Desire: Hybridity in Theory, Culture and Race*, London and New York: Routledge.

LYNNETTE TURNER

Ming, Bill

b. 1944, Bermuda

artist

Ming studied art at Mansfield (1975–6) and sculpture with creative writing at Maidstone (1979). Once described as the work of a global-village storyteller, his work draws on traditional wood carving but incorporates unusual colouring and gluing to fuse a 'medley' or 'jigsaw' of eclectic references in objects capable of transmitting ancient, industrial or contemporary imagery. Ming worked with Arts Education for a Multicultural Society (AEMS) in Cheshire, in 1989, and has had several one-person shows. He has often worked in schools via a series of residencies and workshops, and acted as an adviser to the Arts Council. Ming won a John Moores fellowship in 1992 and exhibited at Liverpool's Bluecoat Gallery the following year ('Two Rock Passage to Liverpool', 1993). Found objects sometimes find their way into his work, which is grounded in two-dimensional collages. Ming sees art as an 'act of healing' and once described his goal as providing 'symbols of solidarity' evoking 'journey, growth and creativity', as well as 'exploring the balance between physical and spiritual worlds'. Other exhibitions include: Mappin Gallery Sheffield (1989), City Art Gallery Derby (1994) and '**Transforming the Crown**' (1997), RFH.

Further reading

Sidey, T. (1987) *Arts Review* (11 September): 613.

PAUL O'KANE

Minorities' Arts Advisory Service

The Minorities' Arts Advisory Service (MAAS) was formed in 1976 as a result of the *Ethnic Minority Arts Report* written by Naseem **Khan** and commissioned by the Arts Council, Gulbenkian Foundation and the Community Relations Committee. The aims of MAAS are to promote ethnic identity and preserve cultural traditions. It published the first issue of *Echo* in May 1976, then later re-titled it *Artrage* in 1982. In the same year MAAS founded the *Black Arts in London* magazine in association with the Arts Media Group to complement their *London Register of Artists and Performance*, first published in 1978. In 1979 MAAS supported the development of other ethnic art organisations, such as the West Midland Ethnic Minority Arts Service, North-West MAAS in Manchester and the South Wales Ethnic Arts Team in Cardiff. After 1983 the service organised national conferences to analyse the development of black art. The first of these, 'Critical Perspectives for the Development of Non Western Arts', chaired by Errol **Lloyd**, examined issues of creativity, artistic direction and funding. Earlier, in 1976, MAAS held open conferences in Leicester, Manchester and the Keskidee Arts Centre in London, all to enable people to discuss various issues.

Further reading

Araeen, R. (1987) *The Essential Black Art*, London: Chisenhale Gallery.

PAULINE DE SOUZA

Mirza, Heidi Safia

b. 1958, London, England

academic, community activist, writer

Professor Heidi Safia Mirza is the first person to hold the Chair of Racial Equality Studies at Middlesex University, London, where she is also head of the Centre for Racial Equality Studies. Mirza was involved in black women's community activism in the 1980s as **Greater London Council** Black Women's Representative and chair of Lambeth Women's Community Network. In 1997, she was appointed by the Secretary of State for Education and Employment to the Government-led Schools Standards Task Force; she is also a member of the Metropolitan Police Racial and Violent Crime Advisory Task Force – a body established in response to the Stephen **Lawrence** Inquiry. She has written numerous articles on black women in higher education, and on the educational strategies of the black community in the UK and South Africa. In 1997, she edited a collection of essays that provides an overview of black **feminism** in Britain: *Black British Feminism*.

Select bibliography

Mirza, H.S. (ed.) (1997) *Black British Feminism*, London, New York: Routledge.
—— (1992) *Young Female and Black*, London, New York: Routledge.

SUZANNE SCAFE

Mishra, Jyoti

b. 1966, Rourkela, India

musician, producer

Jyoti Mishra moved to England in 1969. He was

strongly influenced by the work of groups from the indie scene, such as the Pixies and the Wedding Present, and was involved with a number of bands before forming his own group. Mishra formed **White Town** as a guitar band and began releasing singles on his own label, Satya Records. As well as developing his own musical style, he regularly produced other bands and DJ'd in indie clubs. White Town initially released a number of limited-edition singles, but by the time the debut album was launched the majority of the group had moved on, leaving just Mishra. His number one hit 'Your Woman' came from nowhere and was an eclectic fusion of **dance** beats and sampled 1930s jazz trumpets with a synthesised voice-over. The lyrics on the track were deliberately enigmatic, with a man's voice proclaiming 'I could never be your woman.'

SAMINA ZAHIR

Mistry, Dhruva

b. 1957, Kanjari, India

visual artist

Before deciding to return to India, Mistry was on his way to becoming one of the most successful black British artists. The youngest ever member of the Royal Academy, Mistry had exhibited in a number of shows as well as receiving commissions for large-scale pieces of public art. He received many positive reviews for his dramatic pieces at the entry to the 1985 'Hayward Annual'. Mistry was never part of the black art movement and his success, along with Anish **Kapoor**, is significant in view of this. Mistry's iconography initially appears to be deeply influenced by his Indian cultural heritage, for example *Sitting Bull* (1984), made for the Liverpool International Garden Festival. Yet his style is more eclectic than this, drawing on Egypt as well as India, with the sculpture room in the British Museum being a particularly rich source. Mistry leaves himself open to charges of pandering to Orientalism but on closer inspection it would be fair to say that Mistry's animals and humans are a strange collection of hybrids that undercut any attempt to pin them down culturally.

Further reading

Kettle's Yard Gallery (1985) *Dhruva Mistry: Sculptures and Drawings*, exhibition catalogue, Cambridge: Kettle's Yard Gallery.

NIRU RATNAM

Misty in Roots

Misty in Roots first formed in 1975 as the backing band for the late Jamaican performer Nicky Thomas. The London-based band began to attract attention as they emerged at the forefront of a British **reggae** scene along with bands including **Aswad** and Steel Pulse. Misty in Roots' burgeoning reputation as a fantastic live band and their lyrical dissatisfaction with mainstream British politics made them popular not only with reggae audiences but also with sections of the punk audience, and Misty in Roots played at dozens of **Rock against Racism** concerts throughout Britain. However, it was not until 1979 that they were to release their debut album, a live set recorded in Belgium, called *Live at the Counter Eurovision*. Misty in Roots released their second album *Wise And Foolish* in 1982, followed by *Earth* a year later. *Earth* was heavily influenced by a nine-month period in which the band lived in Zimbabwe and Zambia, as was 1985's *Musi O Tunya*. *Forward*, in 1989, was one of the most successful Misty in Roots records in terms of sales and a 'best of' album, *Chronicles*, was released in 1994.

ANDY WOOD

Moody, Ronald

b. 1890, Jamaica; d. 1984, London, UK

sculptor, writer

Moody arrived in London in 1923 to study dentistry but, upon seeing the Egyptian figures at the British Museum in 1928, discovered his true vocation was sculpture. Self-taught, he rapidly became adept and his solo shows in Paris (1937) and Amsterdam (1938) received critical acclaim. He promptly abandoned dentistry and settled in Paris, but was forced to flee when France fell to the

Germans in 1940. Devastated by this and the atom-bombing of Japan, Moody's subsequent work concerned man's dual potential: self-destruction or spiritual evolution. Following his 1946 London solo show, Moody contracted tuberculosis and, unable to work, spent three years scripting broadcasts and writing short stories, emerging in 1950 with a solo show in London. Thereafter, Moody sculpted and exhibited until 1983, using a variety of materials, while also participating in the activities of the Society of Portrait Sculptors (1953–70), Société Africaine de Culture, Paris (1954–9), **Caribbean Artists' Movement** (1967–73) and Festac '77. In 1977 Moody was awarded the Musgrave Gold Medal, Jamaica's most prestigious cultural award, and his mythological bird *Savacou* stands on the UWI campus in Kingston. Since his death there has been growing interest in Moody's work, which is now in many prestigious collections, including those of the National Portrait Gallery and the Tate.

Further reading

Moody, C. (1999) 'Midonz', *Transition 77*, USA: Duke University Press.

Myrone, M. (2000) *Representing Britain 1500–2000: 100 works from the Tate Collections*, London: Tate Publishing.

CYNTHIA MOODY

Mosaic

Based in Brighton, East Sussex, Mosaic is a community organisation of black and mixed-parentage families and individuals. It was set up in 1990 to offer support to youth and parents through regular contact and sharing activities, representation and consultation, as well as campaigning on local committees and forums on subjects ranging from racism and racial harassment to education and religion. Mosaic recognises the multicultural backgrounds of black and mixed-parentage youth. The organisation strives to support their different ancestral needs in various ways. One such way has been the establishment of the Mosaic Library. It provides resources that represent over fifty cultural heritages, thus provid-

ing images that foster positive identity. Mosaic also fosters black British visibility through cultural celebrations, arts work and exhibitions. Mosaic's major cultural performance highlight has been the celebration of the yearly Black History Month, often involving **music**, poetry and a wide range of indigenous foods. Other festivals celebrated are the Chinese New Year and Islamic events. Members meet monthly and the community is kept informed through a monthly newsletter.

PINKIE MEKGWE

Motherland Project

The Motherland Project was based at Vauxhall Manor School, South London. Its aim was to use drama as way of representing and memorialising the history of black women. The project relied heavily on oral testimony. The first play *Slave Girl* was staged at the Oval House Theatre in 1979 and focused on women slaves in nineteenth-century USA. *Wicked Women* (1980) looked at the plight of women in medieval Europe. Their third, and best known production, *Motherland* (1982), was more heavily autobiographical and was structured around accounts by local West Indian women who came to live in England in the 1950s. The play is set in the period between the Queen's Coronation in 1953 and the Notting Hill riots of 1958.

Further reading

'Motherland' (1982), Caribbean special issue, *Ambit 91*.

JAMES PROCTER

Moti Roti

Set up in 1991 by Keith **Khan** and Ali **Zaidi**, Moti Roti is an award-winning artist-led organisation that celebrates individuality and diversity through art. It produces, presents and tours an eclectic mix of work from innovative **theatre** to installations, increasingly informed by new technologies and digital media. The company's work has been influenced by a long-standing involvement with **carnival**, and it continues to work with a diverse range of people on projects, such as Fresh Masaala and Chameleon. The scale of many of its projects, such as *Flying Costumes, Floating Tombs*, is epic and visionary, while others, such as *Wigs of Wonderment*, are small scale, intimate and crafted for the individual. Moti Roti's work has been presented in a number of theatres and galleries, from the Royal Albert Hall to the New Art Gallery, Walsall; the company have also created site-specific works for locations such as Brick Lane in the East End of London. All of the company's work is culturally eclectic, visually seductive, sensitive to space, participatory and transformative. The company has taken work to Pakistan, Denmark and the USA. They have been a recipient of the *Time Out* London Dance and Performance Award. Keith Khan was one of the artists involved in the design of the Dome (see **live art**).

CATHERINE UGWU

music

In order to offer some type of an overview as to what can be expected in a section entitled 'black music', we must first establish, for the sake of clarity, some notion of what black music is:

> [B]lack music is that which is recognized and accepted by its creators, performers and hearers...encompassing the music of those who see themselves as black, and whose musics have unifying characteristics which justify their recognition as specific genres.
>
> (Oliver 1990: 8)

What is fascinating about this notion of black music is that it allows us to recognise a black musical presence in Britain, long before the *Empire **Windrush*** era of the late 1940s and early 1950s. In fact, there were many African soldiers and servants, including musicians, who arrived on these shores in 54 BCE as part of the invading Roman armies, and this black presence is dotted throughout British history. For instance, in 1505, James IV of Scotland employed a black drummer, while during the same period a black trumpeter, John Blanke, performed for both Henry VII and Henry VIII of Engand. In 1596, when Elizabeth I unsuccessfully ordered the expulsion of the black itinerants, who she suggested were threatening the economic stability of the white population, many of them were deemed to be musicians and entertainers. Curiously, her own troupe of Ethiopian drummers who entertained the royal court was never thought to be in any danger. By the eighteenth century, there were 15,000 to 20,000 blacks living in England who were said to have kept many black-only functions, such as elegant balls in the centre of London.

The major impact of black musicians on British culture has arguably taken place since the arrival of the *Empire Windrush* in 1948, as the growing black population brought with them their various styles of music-making from across the African and Asian diasporas. A good example of this was the impact that the Nigerian guitarist Ambrose Campbell and his percussion-orientated band, the West African Brothers, had on the 1950s British jazz scene as they demonstrated the genre's African origins in their captivating live performances. Add to this the vibrant mixtures the calypsonians from the Caribbean brought with them and we can see a precedent for our contemporary, multicultural music scene. For instance, the record label Melodisc, which generally specialised in releasing 'race' (black) recordings from 'various sources' throughout the African diaspora, began to release calypso records here in 1951. Melodisc also 'signed the celebrated troubadour, Lord Kitchener, who had been living in England since 1948' (Gilroy 1987: 163). More importantly, the blacks who were now residing in England began to create their own outlets for their own types of music. One luminary of this period was Daddy Peckings, who from his Studio One record shop in Shepherd's Bush, West London, was the first person to sell Jamaican popular music like bluebeat, **ska**, rocksteady and their world-renowned successor, **reggae**.

In the context of black British musical culture, a common-sense notion would arguably suggest a type or style of music that expresses the experiences of non-white people in a racist society. This type of expression is arguably only fully appreciated through an understanding of music as politics; not in a narrow politically reactionary manner, which suggests that non-white people only truly express themselves out of the context of victimhood. On the contrary, the suggestion here is that black music creates that space in which alternative notions of being black, both positive and negative, can be discussed and debated across the urban landscape. One of the most visible and highly influential sites for the promotion of this alternative black perspective was the reggae sound system (see **sound system DJs**). These sound systems transcend any notion of just being 'large mobile discos', as they represent a 'powerful medium within the black communities' (Gutzmore 1993). They are in essence one of the main outlets for contemporary black musical styles ranging from roots reggae to drum and bass. Their impact on influencing and maintaining alternative notions of black British identity has been immense, as witnessed during the blues **dance** era of the late 1960s and early 1970s. Blues dances or *shubeens* (which means to shove-in) were improvised night-clubs, which were held in any available venue, ranging from one single room to a whole house. It has been suggested that these dances were a reaction to black exclusion from white-owned clubs and dancehalls, prevalent during this period. This is not to suggest that there were not any night-clubs that played black music. On the contrary, there were clubs scattered across London like the Roaring 20s, in Carnaby Street, West End; Four Aces in Dalston, North London; Q Club in Praed Street, Paddington; and Bouncing Ball in Peckham, South East London, to name a few. However, what was really significant about this era was that British musicians began to produce their own styles of music, of which **lovers' rock** was one of the most influential. This genre was dominated by female singers and was geared towards providing an intimate space for couples to dance with one another, in direct contrast to the harder edged, rebellious roots music that was being imported from Jamaica. Singers like Louisa Mark were to introduce a melodic mix of soul and reggae, and her cover version of Robert Parker's R'n'B hit 'Caught You in a Lie', along with Janet Kay's 'Silly Games', was probably the most famous hit from this era.

One of the most respected and influential musicians to emerge during this period was Dennis Bovell, who also had his own highly successful reggae band, Matumbi, and engineered and produced for many lovers' rock singers. In fact, the name lovers' rock was taken from his South London-based record label. What is crucial about Bovell's influence on black British musical culture was that he played a major role in breaking the bias that was levelled against home-produced music, which was often regarded as less than authentic when compared to Jamaican reggae. Bovell, along with other local producers, began to release his records on a white label, as this was the format that the majority of Jamaican forty-fives or pre-releases would take. Furthermore, because of his successes, he was recruited by major record labels like Island Records and Radar Records, who utilised his services for their emergent white punk rock bands, who identified with reggae in much the same way as the mods did with ska in the 1960s.

Another significant factor in the history of black British music, which began in the 1970s and still resonates in the contemporary black music scene, is the appropriation of black music's anti-establishment stance by racially diverse audiences. This arguably began with the incorporation of black music's political voice and its alternative views on the significance of cultural expression, as exemplified by the punk rock movement. In fact, Bob Marley in his song 'Punky Reggae Party' acknowledged the presence of the punk rockers. However, punk rock was paradoxical by nature as the white supremacist group the National Front, argued that punk was totally white music. They embraced the Stranglers' 'I Feel Like a Wog' and the Clash's 'White Man in the Hammersmith Palais', 'as they sought to make a connection between the position of dispossessed whites and the experience of racism' (Gilroy 1987: 124). Ironically, it was the punk movement that opened the doors of many white clubs to black music and pop concerts began to feature various black bands, such as **Aswad**, **Misty in Roots** and, probably the most acclaimed of all British reggae bands, Steel Pulse. Aswad were in fact renowned for mixing a jazz/funk style with a heavy reggae bassline and rhythm section, which was appealing to both black and white audiences. Moreover, it has been suggested that they were almost like two bands in one as they could play a different set for a predominantly white audience. Crucially, this outlook has been trans-ferred to many black musicians who display this mentality when providing softer 'crossover' remixes to hardcore tunes. This viewpoint becomes crucial when we consider notions of inclusion and exclusion for the generations of blacks who were born in Britain, and whose very presence challenges notions of Britishness as an exclusively white domain. This is because unlike many of their family members, peers or contemporaries, who hail from beyond these shores, many of these blacks feel a rootedness to the land of their birth. This is a rootedness that often manifests as hybridised types of 'underground' music that are both 'us' and 'other', as they confront such hegemonic notions as 'Brit pop' and 'cool Britannia'.

The group **Soul II Soul** was probably one of the best examples of how the 'underground' surfaced and rearranged the dance music scene as they encouraged clubbers to mix across class- and racialised boundaries; 'people checked us as a form of rebelling' (**Jazzie B** 1987). Taking their eclectic musical backgrounds from the clubs into the recording studio, they redefined what it meant to be black in Britain in the late 1980s and 1990s. Dr Vibes, of the sound system Street Life Unlimited, and Winner Roadshow's Chris Sweeney suggest that this vibe was born out of an appreciation of all types of black music from across the diaspora that could be played side by side in one location. Therefore, it was not unusual to hear a live ragga DJ (Jamaican-style rapper) chatting over a soft **soul**, rare groove or **hip hop** tune, or to hear a hip hop rapper live on a hardcore reggae/**dancehall** tune.

These forms of hybridised experimentation led to the birth of **jungle** music. Even the naming of this highly influential genre of black British creativity is contested. Many suggest that this reggae-inspired music was named after a place called Arnett Garden in Kingston, Jamaica, which is commonly known as 'jungle', or that it was because it represented the diverse cultural mix in the urban jungles of British society. Others suggest that it was because white society generally brands all black music as 'jungle' music as it is 'too black' – a load of old 'mumbo-jumbo'. It is this idea of music being too black that often creates a problem for the white mainstream consumer because, according to the *Encarta Africana*:

> As the [jungle] scene grew it remained racially diverse, but, especially in the larger London venues, there was often a distinct black/white split on the dance floor. The reggae/techno hybrid meant that more blacks were attending raves, sparking a media panic in which jungle events were stigmatized by racist stereotypes of crack usage and violence. 'Drum & bass' came to describe a cleaner strain catering to a white audience with music stripped of Caribbean influences.
>
> (Clayton 1999)

The argument is that once the radically subversive origins of the musical forms that are used in the mainstream multicultural scene are exposed, they are often rejected by the mainstream consumer. Jungle music is nice to dance to, as long as you take the jungle out of it! Therefore, the fact that blacks often choose to utilise black music to express their heartfelt opinions, in and of itself, challenges the visage of a settled, multicultural British society. An insight into this cultural perspective is provided by Back, who suggests that:

> The modes of expression that are produced possess a kind of triple consciousness that is simultaneously the child of Africa, Asia and Europe. In the language of black vernacular cultures, the music has gone *outernational*, simultaneously inside and beyond the nations through which it passes.
>
> (Back 1996: 185)

It is the lived experiences of blacks in Britain that are often reflected in the music, as for many it is the only avenue they have to freely express an alternative notion of Britishness, which does not have to be compromised for mainstream acceptance. This is a crucial aspect of contemporary cultural resistance when one considers British black music as a political voice for the oppressed. What then happens to the voice once it has been sanitised for mainstream acceptance, without this type of recognition? Can we all 'forget our troubles and dance' as Bob Marley suggested? Many would have us believe that this is the case as post-modern subjects in an ever decreasing world, in which black music is accepted as long as it replaces 'roots' for 'routes'. For instance, the organisers of the spuriously entitled Music Of Black Origins (MOBO) Awards always emphasise the fact that their awards are nothing to do with skin colour, but are based on promoting those artistes whose contributions to black music generally go unrecognised. This position is supposedly justified in our post-industrial context by the massive amounts of press coverage and media exposure bestowed upon the ceremony itself. However, when placed in the context of exactly what music of black origins is, or more importantly is not, and which artistes are recognised, the difference between this ceremony and other music ceremonies remains uncertain. In fact, in the lyrics of a song by the white pop group *Five*, 'Everybody Get up', they suggest that they are 'keeping it real'. Does this then mean that self-confessed wiggers ('white wannabe niggers') should receive a MOBO Award as they acknowledge a style of rap that for them is identifiably black? If this is not the case, why do we not have a Music Of White Origins Awards ceremony, which recognises the contributions of groups like the Reggae Philharmonic Orchestra?

Black music stripped of its origins arguably fulfils and perpetuates the historically constructed, un-challenging and acceptable role that reduces it to that which is acceptable to white people: minstrelised, hedonistic, posturing. This is because to mention origins in the context of British society and then disregard the reasons as to why black Britons deemed it necessary to develop their own types of music is insulting, to say the least. Not recognising the role skin colour plays within the British music industry is an affront to those pioneers who utilised music as an alternative space, within which to voice their disapproval at a system that persecuted them for this very same reason.

WILLIAM HENRY

When employing the term 'Asian British music' within the context of a black British music overview it is important to make the point that the use of such a term is not to set the music and performances of British musicians of South Asian descent in opposition to musicians of African descent, or to suggest that the term black British music is redundant. Nor am I trying to suggest that the term 'black music' can simply be replaced by terms such as 'Afro-Asian'

(Oliver 1990). Instead, I feel that it is important to acknowledge that while British music of Afro-Caribbean origin has been of huge influence and has been actively consumed by many Asian British musicians, performers and audiences (along with white audiences as well), the subsuming of such a diverse array of music and cultures into the overarching term 'black' has often left Asian British musical and cultural productions marginalised and invisible. Rupa Huq makes the point that while, until recently, Asian youths were often stereotyped and portrayed as passive victims, trapped between 'two-cultures' and 'un-cool', black music and 'Black iconography in popular culture contrastingly has always been seen as cool and hard by youth culture at large' (Huq 1996: 63). These cultural stereotypes even continue to hold strong in the face of a growing awareness of, and popularity for, the cultural and musical output of Asian British musicians along with clubs, record labels, designers, *et al*. The media friendly tags and banners such as 'the new Asian cool', which operate in opposition to clumsy, exclusionary tags such as 'cool Britannia', reinforce the myth that prior to this recent legitimisation by a media and industry ravenous for new ideas, images and sounds, Asian youths were simply and irrevocably un-cool. This point was reiterated in an article in *The Times*, when **Outcaste** co-founder 'Shabs' made the point that his label and club were actively distanced from the influence of **bhangra** as 'It was never cool to be an Asian then.' The new music and styles being promoted in clubs such as Outcaste were promoted to give Asian British culture 'a predominant street style, credibility' in a way that had been seen as an essential feature of 'black models of popular culture' (Sharma *et al.* 1996: 76).

Yet for all the hype and excitement generated by contemporary artists and labels as diverse as **Apache Indian**, Nitin **Sawhney**, **Cornershop**, **Asian Dub Foundation**, Bally **Sagoo**, Outcaste and **Anokha** – to name but a few prominent Asian British purveyors of a diverse range of influences, sounds and approaches – this explosion in music has been a long time coming, at least in terms of academic and media coverage. Asian British music and musicians have received scant and often inaccurate coverage at other times. Beginning with the British mainstream media's belated 'discovery' of an already flourishing bhangra scene in the late

1980s, the media tended to focus not on the music but on the audiences, especially at the popular daytime bhangra events, which featured live bhangra bands and sound systems, and which were attended by huge audiences of Asian British youths from a diverse range of backgrounds. The media represented such events as being odd and 'exotic', portraying homogenous crowds of 'othered' Asians and largely ignoring the fact that a number of bands, including Southall's Alaap, had been performing live since the late 1970s or that the bhangra daytime events had evolved out of the popular daytime events that had mainly played hip hop, electro, soul and funk records in clubs and venues to the same audiences. From the daytimers, which were largely operated as hobbies or sidelines by enthusiasts, emerged established London club nights such as Bombay Jungle and Hot 'n' Spicy, and bhangra acts ranging from the traditional to those infusing their sound with electro, disco and **reggae**, who enjoyed a great deal of success, though largely outwith the mainstream. Alongside the popularity of live bhangra came new bands and record labels, and even the first Asian British music paper *Ghazal and Beat*, which covered the scene nationally. It is worth noting that despite the large crowds attending a number of bhangra events, these nights were only held on weekday nights rather than prime weekend slots, as club owners often feared they would lose business by catering for a predominantly Asian audience.

Outwith the bhangra scene and prior to the **post-bhangra** bands that emerged parallel to (and in some cases from) the bhangra scene in the 1990s, other forms of music existed such as Quwwali, a Sufi devotional music that is performed within many Muslim communities in Britain, and Ghazal, a poetic form set to music ranging from traditional folk to pop and film (see **film and cinema**) music. The best known Ghazal album released in Britain was Najma Akhtar's 1988 album of westernised Ghazal: *Qareed*. Much was made of **Babylon Zoo** reaching number one in the British charts with 'Spaceman', citing singer Jas Mann as the first Asian to reach the top of the charts. This oft repeated assertion ignored the fact that Glaswegian Sushil Dade (**Future Pilot AKA**) had already spent several weeks at the height of the charts, appearing more than once live on *Top of the Pops*, as a member of the Soup Dragons with their

dance–pop–ragga crossover version of the Rolling Stones' 'I'm free'. Sheila Chandra also made the charts in 1982 with her collaborative work with Monsoon before going on to have a reasonably successful solo career, although 'So lonely' has often been written off as a quasi-Indian flavoured novelty record (Sharma *et al.* 1996: 79). Echobelly, fronted by Sonya Aurora-Madden, enjoyed fleeting success in the mid-1990s and with their guitar-led pop–rock were adopted as members of the Britpop 'movement', while **Cornershop** and the Voodoo Queens began as guitar bands loosely affiliated to the riot grrrl/independent scene and played to predominantly white audiences. **White Town** have been a fixture of the British underground scene for over a decade prior to having a massive hit with 'Your woman'. Aki Nawaz of **Fun-da-Mental** and co-founder of **Nation Records** began his musical life drumming for the gothic-punk band Southern Death Cult as one of only two Asian punks in Bradford, and, most famously, Freddie **Mercury** enjoyed immense success both as a member of Queen and as a solo artist, although his Asian background was rarely commented upon.

So Asian British music and musicians are an integral part of popular culture and not a peripheral one. The fact that the post-bhangra acts have had the most mainstream success in a period of sustained media interest with Cornershop arriving at number one with 'Brimful of Asha', a playful tribute to the **Bollywood** actress and playback singer Asha Bosle, Talvin **Singh**'s *OK* album winning the 1999 Mercury Prize, and Nitin Sawhney's fourth album charting. The all-girl band Trickbaby had a surprise hit with 'Eena meena dicka' in 1996, an impressive update of an old Hindi film song, and the KK Kings had success with their 'Holidays in the united KK Kingdom', which was featured in the soundtrack to Gurinder **Chadha**'s film *Bhaji on the Beach*. Bally **Sagoo** and Apache Indian have both achieved international success and Outcaste and Anokha club nights have consistently been voted as best club nights in Britain. Both Outcaste and Anokha have been the focus of much of the media attention, being featured in newspaper supplements, style magazines and music publications, as have many of the new generation of Asian British artists, although sales have not always been commensurate with critical praise. Many of the artists have achieved only short-term success, though this is not a unique feature of Asian British music, and many other artists have achieved considerable longevity and growing appeal with a sound that destroys essentialist concepts of what 'Asian' music should sound like. One commentator suggests that 'Young Asians are much more interested these days in breaking into the mainstream market by producing a sound that appeals outside the Asian community without altogether abandoning their Asian identity' (Anwar, quoted in Sharma *et al.* 1996: 78); and this seems to be echoed by Asian Dub Foundation member Chandrasonic, stating in an interview that 'We don't want to be allied to any Asian underground. It ghettoises us....Being Asian is our starting point, not the end.'

The movement of Asian British music(s) from the periphery into the mainstream has been a long and as yet uncompleted move and brings with it risks, but it also makes a highly visible and audible assault upon stereotypes that have largely been left unchallenged within the same mainstream that seeks to embrace 'new' musical forms. Sanjay Sharma suggests that the importance of the new groups, particularly a group such as Asian Dub Foundation, is that they pose a threat to essentialist theories of identity formation, and that their music, lyrics, performances and interviews mark the possibility of a transcendence in the normative representation of both 'blackness' and 'Asianness' as well as 'Britishness'. This, indeed, is one of the many important aspects of the Asian British bands, both past and present.

ANDY WOOD

Further reading

Clayton, J. (1999) *Encarta Africana*, Microsoft.
Gilroy, P. (1987) *'There Ain't no Black in the Union Jack'*, London: Hutchinson.
Gutzmore (1993) in Winston James and Clive Harris (eds) *Inside Babylon*, London: Verso.
James, W. and Harris, C. (1993) *Inside Babylon*, London: Verso.
Mitchell, T. (1996) *Popular Music and Local Identity. Rock, Pop and Rap in Europe and Oceania*, London: Leicester University Press.
Oliver, P. (ed.) (1990) *Black Music in Britain. Essays on the Afro-Asian Contribution to Popular Music*, Buckingham: Open University Press.
Sharma, S., Hutnyk, J. and Sharma, A. (eds) (1996) *Disorienting Rhythms: the Politics of the New Asian Dance Music*, London: Zed Books.

Mwelwa, Hilary

b. Zambia

singer, songwriter

Mwelwa moved to England at the age of six and developed interests in **literature** and poetry at her boarding school in Surrey. She began singing in the early 1990s while studying for her biomedical degree and took a year out to produce her first demo record in 1994 as Hill St Soul. Her own singing style is influenced by Aretha Franklin and the **soul**, gospel and African **music** that she grew up with. She has co-written songs with Maysa Leak of Incognito. In 1999, her debut track 'Strictly a Vibe Thing' gained support from urban radio, as did 'Soul Organic' from her first album, released with Dome Records. She won the *Blues and Soul* magazine (see **publishing, newspapers and magazines**) Best Newcomer award in 1999.

ALISON DONNELL

My Beautiful Laundrette

The screenplay for *My Beautiful Laundrette* (1985) was written by Hanif **Kureishi** and it was directed by Stephen Frears. A low-budget independent production, partly funded by **Channel 4**, it took the film (see **film and cinema**) world somewhat by surprise and gained substantial critical and mainstream attention. The film was shot in only six weeks and was first screened at the Edinburgh Film Festival in autumn 1985, then appeared at the London Film Festival before going on nationwide release. Both its subject matter and its form caused a considerable amount of controversy, as Kobena **Mercer** admits, 'few would have anticipated that a gay romance between a British-born Asian and an ex-National Front supporter, set against the backdrop of Thatcherite enterprise culture, would be the stuff of which box office successes are made'.

The film's action takes place around inner-city London, evoking both the bleakness of Thatcherite Britain in the mid-1980s through its focus on unemployment, squatters and political activism, and the emerging enterprise culture among Asian communities. Johnny, played by Daniel Day Lewis, and Omar, played by Gordon Warnecke, find their childhood friendship is rekindled by a chance meeting, but they are now on either side of a racial and cultural divide. Through the relationship that develops between its two lead characters, Johnny and Omar, the film explores questions of desire, racism, homosexuality, class and cultural politics. The film received an Oscar nomination in 1985, and it was welcomed in many quarters as signalling a radical shift in representations of race and its avoidance of stereotypes, but equally received hostile criticism accusing it of exactly the opposite practice.

Further reading

Kureishi, H. (1996) *My Beautiful Laundrette and other Writings*, London: Faber & Faber.

ELEANOR BYRNE

My Son the Fanatic

Written by Hanif **Kureishi** and directed by Udayan **Prasad**, the film *My Son the Fanatic* (1997), developed from Kureishi's short story of the same name, explores a range of dilemmas facing first- and second-generation British Asians in a cultural landscape whose contours have been fundamentally altered by the radicalisation of Islamicist politics in Britain in the wake of the **Rushdie Affair**. To that extent, it takes up issues broached in Kureishi's 1995 novel *The Black Album*, such as the incommensurability or otherwise of value systems labelled 'liberal' and 'fundamentalist', and the desirability of cultural separation versus the likelihood of cultural mixing, construed either as potentially positive syncretism or dangerously degenerative 'muddle'. The film follows Anglophile taxi driver Pervez as he (especially in the eyes of others) transgresses cultural, racial, moral and professional boundaries, and pays the price in terms of the loss of his son, his wife and his best friend. This is contrasted with what could be seen as the son's transgressions, particularly his espousal of militant Islam (the 'fanaticism' of the title), which leads him to take part in increasingly violent attacks on local prostitutes, especially one befriended by his father. At one level, the film is structured like a philosophical debate: 'liberalism' versus Islam, or (easy) materialism versus (difficult) religious ideals. At the same time, it is firmly rooted in contemporary social problems: the tensions created by generational shifts in aspirations and behaviour patterns in diasporic communities, for example, or the ability of local communities to determine particular forms of public behaviour (here, clearing prostitutes off the streets of the neighbourhood). As well as being a study of transgressive behaviour, *My Son the Fanatic* has been received as another of Kureishi's transgressive texts, managing to offend the sensibilities of a number of constituencies within the United Kingdom. As Kureishi remarked of an earlier work, 'They [the Asian community] think I'm perpetually throwing shit at them.'

PATRICK WILLIAMS

N

Naidu, Vayu

b. 1957, Delhi, India

storyteller, performer, writer

Naidu has achieved international recognition for her transcultural storytelling skills, both as a writer and a performer. Her productions include *The Word is Out* (1995) and *Kathasuniascea* (1996–7). *Kathasuniascea* works through music and movement to retell stories from India, Nigeria and Ireland. With composer Judith Weir she created *Parting Company* (1997), a celebration of European and Indian mythologies following fifty years of India's independence. As a storyteller she has toured **literature** and **music** festivals in Greece, Portugal, Sweden, France, Ireland, Germany and Italy. She has performed in a range of venues including concert halls, schools, prisons and shelters. Naidu is founder and artistic director of the intercultural storytelling company Brumhalata. She writes stories for children (published by HarperCollins), which have been taken up in the **Channel 4** animation film *Biswas*, and a volume of her retelling of Indian folk tales is published by Tulika, Madras. Naidu is also storytelling consultant for Channel 4 World Faith films, and is artistic producer for Natak, a cultural initiative designed to promote and to celebrate Asian arts at the Haymarket Theatre, Leicester. In 1994, the University of Leeds awarded Naidu Europe's first Ph.D. in oral tradition as performance. 'The Vayu Naidu Company' is dedicated to performance storytelling and methods, apprenticeships, corporate visions and communities in asylum. During 2000 Naidu worked as writer and performer on *Future Perfect* with Judith Weir for the Birmingham Contemporary Music Group. Naidu moved to Canterbury in 2000 and was awarded an AHRB fellowship in the creative and performing arts based at the University of Kent for her project *The Presence of Absences: Exploring Technique and Manifestation in the Contemporary Performance Storyteller.*

Select bibliography

Naidu, V. (2000) *The Empty Vessel: Storytelling and the Healing Arc of Narrative*, London: Jessica Kingsley Publishers.
—— (2000) *Stories from India*, Hove: Wayland-Macdonald Books.

ELAINE ASTON

Naipaul, Shiva

b. 1945, Port-of-Spain, Trinidad; d. 1985, London, England

writer, journalist

Shivadhar Srivinasa Naipaul graduated with a degree in Chinese from University College, Oxford, and took up a career in journalism. He published two novels, *Fireflies* in 1970, which won the John Llewelyn Rhys Memorial Prize for Literature, and *The Chip-Chip Gatherers* in 1973, which won the Whitbread Prize for fiction. He then turned his literary attentions mainly to travel writing. Although his career as a novelist has always been overshadowed by that of his brother, V.S. **Naipaul**, he was a respected travel writer, publishing mainly in the *Spectator*. He travelled widely and spent a year as a Guggenheim Fellow in the USA. His works included *North and South: An African Journey* (1978), *Black and White* (1980) and *Beyond the Dragon's Mouth* (1984). He published his final novel, *A Hot Country*, in 1983. When he died suddenly of a heart attack, the *Spectator* established the Shiva Naipaul Prize, awarded annually for the best travel essay by a writer under thirty-five.

Select bibliography

Naipaul, S. (1983) *A Hot Country*, London: Hamish Hamilton.
—— (1980) *Black and White*, London: Hamish Hamilton.
—— (1973) *The Chip-Chip Gatherers*, London: Longman.
—— (1970) *Fireflies*, London: Longman.

ALISON DONNELL

Naipaul, V.S.

b. 1932, Chaguanas, Trinidad

novelist, travel writer

Sir Vidia Surajprasad Naipaul is one of the most successful, if controversial, literary figures in the history of post-war black British writing (see **literature**). Regularly nominated for the Nobel Prize, he was knighted in 1990, by which time he had written and published some thirteen books. His work has been widely acclaimed by the Western literary establishment, and his many prizes and awards include the John Llewelyn Rhys Memorial Prize, the Somerset Maugham Award, the Hawthornden Prize, the W.H. Smith Prize and the Booker Prize, awarded for *In a Free State*, published in 1971. Born into a Brahmin family, and the son of a journalist, Naipaul came to settle in England after winning a Trinidadian government scholarship. Naipaul studied English between 1950 and 1953 at University College, Oxford, and, in 1954, he began work as a writer and editor for Henry Swanzy's *Caribbean Voices* radio programme.

His first three books were: the novel *The Mystic Masseur* (1957); the novel *The Suffrage of Elvira* (1958); and the short-story collection *Miguel Street* (1959). They focus predominantly on political subjects within Hindu West Indian communities, and are characterised by a humour that is notably absent in his later work. Though regarded primarily as a novelist, Naipaul is also an important essayist (see, for example, the articles collected in *The Overcrowded Barracoon*, published in 1972). A regular reviewer for the *New Statesman* in the late 1950s and early 1960s, the vast majority of his work since the 1970s has been non-fictional. After the publication of what many regard as his major novel *A House for Mr Biswas* (1961), Naipaul wrote *The Middle Passage* (1962): the first of a series of travel books that would include *An Area of Darkness* (1964), *Finding the Centre* (1984) and *A Turn in the South* (1989). These writings document the author's travels in India, the Caribbean, Africa and the southern USA. It was in these travel writings that many of his most negative and controversial opinions on India and the Caribbean were to appear, earning him the nickname (coined by Derek Walcott's well-known pun on *An Area of Darkness*) 'V.S. Nightfall'.

Naipaul's British-based fictions include *Mr Stone and the Knights Companion*, *The Mimic Men* (1967) and, perhaps most substantially, his semi-autobiographical novel *The Enigma of Arrival* (1987). The last is set in rural Wiltshire, providing an intriguing alternative to the dominant urban setting of contemporary black British writing. Naipaul's personal sense of detachment from England, of being a perpetual refugee, a diasporic nomad, comes through strongly in these works.

Select bibliography

Naipaul, V.S. (1987) *The Enigma of Arrival*, Harmondsworth: Penguin.
—— (1967) *The Mimic Men*, London: Andre Deutsch.
—— (1964) *An Area of Darkness*, London: Andre Deutsch.
—— (1961) *A House for Mr Biswas*, London: Andre Deutsch.

JAMES PROCTER

Namjoshi, Suniti

b. 1941, Bombay, India

writer

After relocating from India to Canada, Suniti Namjoshi now lives and writes with Gillian Hanscombe in Devon, England. Namjoshi mixes lesbian and feminist issues with a whimsical style. Her stories introduce readers to a delightful cast of animal characters like the Blue Donkey and the One-Eyed Monkey, who frequently represent their creator's views. Namjoshi's poems and fables often re-write fairy tales, folklore and mythology from India and the West in order to expose the patriarchal and racist ideologies that inform them. This theme of subversion is continued in longer fiction like *The Conversations of Cow*, which describes the travels of Suniti, an expatriate Indian lesbian, and Bhadravati, a Brahmin lesbian cow, and the *The Mothers of Maya Diip*, which narrates the adventures of the Blue Donkey in a matriarchal state. Namjoshi's adept use of fantasy and humour to tell old stories in new ways, and to create new and different ones, makes her a unique and delightful voice in the field of black British writing.

Select bibliography

Namjoshi, S. (1995) *Feminist Fables and Saint Suniti and the Dragon*, New Delhi: Penguin.
—— (1989) *Because of India*, London: Onlywomen Press.

ASHA SEN

Nasta, Susheila

b. 1953, Wallington, Surrey, England

academic

Susheila Nasta is Senior Lecturer in English at the Open University. She has previously taught at Homerton College, Cambridge, and at Queen Mary and Westfield College at the University of London. She is founder-editor of **Wasafiri**, a journal that publishes critical and creative writing from Africa, the Caribbean and South Asia. She has published extensively on Caribbean **literature**, in particular on the work of Samuel **Selvon**, on whom she has edited *Critical Perspectives on Sam Selvon* and also *Foreday Morning: Selected Prose 1946–1986/Sam Selvon* in collaboration with Kenneth Ramchand. Nasta is perhaps best known for her edited project *Motherlands: Black Women's Writing from Africa, the Caribbean and South Asia*, a popular critical anthology that forwards a transnational reading of black women's writings in their affiliation and difference. By focusing on the concept of motherhood as part of a long-standing feminist tradition, the contributors re-visit and appropriate this subject and trope within the context of post-colonial literature. Related issues such as motherlands and mother tongues are explored in the work of writers such as Jean Rhys, Ama Ato Aidoo and Anita Desai, among others, in a thought-provoking and compassionate manner. Nasta is currently working on early black British writings.

Select bibliography

Nasta, S. (1992) *Select Bibliography on African, Caribbean and South Asian Fiction in English*, London: British Council.
—— (1991) *Motherlands: Black Women's Writing from Africa, the Caribbean and South Asia*, London: the Women's Press.
—— (ed.) (1988) *Critical Perspectives on Sam Selvon*, Washington, DC: Three Continents Press.
Nasta, S. and Ramchand, K. (1989) *Foreday Morning: Selected Prose 1946–1986/Sam Selvon*, London: Longman.

SANDRA PONZANESI

Nation Records

Nation was co-founded by Katherine Canoville and Aki Nawaz of **Fun-da-mental**, who relocated to London from Bradford with the concept of putting together a record company to promote acts who were fusing together diverse musics, particularly world musics with Western styles. After failing on several occasions to convince established record companies of the validity of their idea, the pair formed Nation as an independent concern. The first release from Nation was a compilation, *Fuse*, which featured Natacha Atlas as a member of !Loca and Talvin **Singh**, recording as Mahatma T. **Transglobal Underground**'s 'Templehead' became a cult hit and releases followed from Fun-damental, Loop Guru, **Hustlers HC** and the black South African group Prophets of Da City. In 1994, **Asian Dub Foundation** released their debut single 'Conscious' followed by an album in 1995. In an attempt to undermine the control the larger mainstream record companies held over the **music** industry, Nation tried to distribute their music through the network of Asian shops but this was largely a failure. Nation continued to release a constant catalogue of diverse and innovative records, although since the release of Fun-damental's *Erotic Terrorism* in the autumn of 1998 Nation has been inactive.

ANDY WOOD

NATIONAL COMMITTEE ON RACISM IN CHILDREN'S BOOKS *see* Working Group against Racism in Children's Resources

Natt, Sarbjit

b. 1962, India

silk painter

The subcontinent's tradition of almost consummate excellence in textiles is echoed in Natt's delicate and vivid fabrics of hand-painted *phulkari* and *bagh* style motifs, which emulate the characteristic folk embroidery of the Punjab. Britain's colonial history inevitably initiated intimate contact with other countries, many of which have had a significant impact on the craft practice of the centre itself. To British-educated Sarbjit Natt, the Punjabi motifs are both new and familiar, the traditional shapes utilised in textiles allowing her to express her specific inherited cultural position within contemporary British craft practice. Her silk accessories employ her own technique of resist painting, and her colours are reminiscent of those subcontinental textiles. Natt entered into the craft establishment through the 'Diverse Cultures' exhibition at the Crafts Council (1990), held in

celebration of the increasing visibility of black craft makers and artists in Britain, and the travelling 'Colour into Cloth' exhibition (1994). Her textiles are also held in the **Bradford art galleries and museums** transcultural collections.

DIPTI BHAGAT

Nazareth, H.O.

b. 1944, Bombay, India

writer, producer

H.O. Nazareth is a writer and producer who is always known as 'Naz'. He came to Britain in 1965 and went on to read philosophy and politics at the University of Kent. During the early years, he also wrote and recited poetry in London. Naz wrote articles for the radical left magazine, the *Leveller*, and also *Time Out*, and later was part of the group that created *City Limits*.

When he interviewed director Horace **Ové** for the *Leveller*, Ové talked about a script he was developing and asked Naz to co-write it with him. This script became the **television** film *The Garland* (1981), and led to the creation of Penumbra, an independent production company, whose first production was a series of six films of lectures given by the radical Marxist, C.L.R. **James** in 1982. This was at the advent of **Channel 4** and Penumbra's output found a home on this channel. Naz also produced the *Sunday East* magazine programme for Channel 4.

In 1984, Naz, together with independent director Faris Kermani, formed Azad Productions. The impetus here was to focus on programmes for people originating in the Indian subcontinent. The company closed in 1989, but made many television documentaries, including, *A Fearful Silence* (1986), about domestic violence within the Asian community, and *A Corner of a Foreign Field* (1986), directed by Udayan **Prasad**, about the lives of Pakistanis in Britain. When Ové went on to pursue an independent film career, Naz continued with Penumbra. He has always resisted the idea of being pigeon-holed into an ethnic slot, and has made many cutting edge documentaries and won several prizes. The company's credits include: *Suffer* *the Children* (1988), on the torture and detention of children living under apartheid in South Africa; *Bombay and Jazz* (1992), about the music of Bombay and its relationship to jazz musicians; *China Rocks: the Long March of Cui Jian*, on the top Chinese Rock star; *Doctors and Torture*, about medical involvement in torture in Latin America; and *Stories My Country Told Me*, about nationalism and culture. Penumbra has also produced work for radio and is now developing feature films (see **film and cinema**).

Select bibliography

Nazareth, H.O. (1984) *Lobo*, Bombay: Clearing House, London: Penumbra Productions.

SUMAN BHUCHAR

Nehru Gallery

The Nehru Gallery at the Victoria and Albert Museum opened in November 1990, confirming the authority of the Victoria and Albert in Indian art outside the subcontinent. The museum is still criticised for its brevity of representation, selecting merely 500 objects from its vast Indian collection to illustrate the history of major developments in Indian cultural, political and social life between 1550 and 1900, and the effect of European rule on Indian art. Yet in 1990, the gallery was hailed as a fulfilment of the need to display the collections of nineteenth-century Orientalists, bringing these objects to the attention of British aesthetic concerns and the British public. In its post-imperial context, the Nehru Gallery has attempted outreach projects with a significant portion of its intended audience: Indian and South-east Asian Britons, a community with whom the Gallery shares a common ancestor, the British Raj. In this sense the Nehru Gallery addresses a very specific colonial history and post-colonial diaspora. Thus the collection must be viewed critically in the context of a design museum founded on nineteenth-century exclusivities of design and ethnographic material, which defined and separated Asian from other non-Western material cultures.

DIPTI BHAGAT

Nelson, Shara

singer

Although Shara Nelson is best known for her work with **Massive Attack** on their debut album *Blue Lines*, particularly as the haunting voice on the singles 'Unfinished sympathy' and 'Safe from harm', Nelson has had a successful solo career. Her debut album *What Silence Knows* and its follow-up *Friendly Fire* featured contributions from US rappers P.M. Dawn and the British band Saint Etienne, and *What Silence Knows* was nominated for the 1995 Mercury Music Prize for Best Album. Shara Nelson has also been nominated for Brit Awards on at least three occasions. Despite glowing reviews, the sales of *Friendly Fire* were disappointing and a planned third album was put on hold. Nelson began a series of collaborations, including working with producer and arranger David Arnold on a new version of the James Bond theme 'Moonraker'. She also began working as part of the Presence project and in late 1998 released the single 'Sense of danger', which was hailed as an 'Unfinished Sympathy' for the end of the decade. Presence released the acclaimed *All Systems Gone* in early 1999.

ANDY WOOD

Nelson, Trevor

b. 1964, East London, England

DJ, A&R consultant, presenter, broadcaster

In the early 1980s, Trevor Nelson entered the realm of dance **music** by importing and distributing for underground **dance** record label GM Records. By the mid-1980s, he began DJing for the pirate radio station Kiss FM and for Madhatter's sound system. Then, during the 1990s, Nelson took an active role in the development of black/club culture. His contributions to community events like the **Notting Hill Carnival** have had an extensive impact in promoting dance music: high life, **hip hop**, R'n'B, **reggae**, rare groove, soca and **soul**. MOBO (Music of Black Origin) Award-winning Nelson has successfully managed to diversify his skills by becoming A&R consultant for Cooltempo/EMI records, and by promoting Lynden David Hall and Mica Paris. He has also interviewed artists such as D'angelo, Whitney Houston and Gangstarr, among others. In 1996, Nelson became a broadcaster for the BBC Radio 1 *R&B Chart Show* and *Rhythm Nation*; he also presents MTV's *The Lick Chart Show* and *The Late Lick*.

DORETH JONES

Network East

Britain's diverse 'Asian' communities have been catered for as a discrete audience segment since at least 1953, when the BBC began broadcasting *Asian Club*, and both the public-sector broadcaster and the various companies comprising the independent sector have a long history of targetted programmes for minority ethnic audiences. *Network East* replaced the long-standing *Asian Magazine* in 1987 and made a highly significant break with much previous 'ethnic' programming for Asian audiences, which had been broadcast in community languages. The BBC's traditional response to catering to the needs of its 'Asian' audiences was to imagine either that many people preferred programmes in one of the majority languages such as Hindustani or else that migrant communities were not fluent in English. By taking the decision to axe *Asian Magazine* and replace it with a livelier magazine/lifestyle series in the form of *Network East*, the BBC made a decision that was to have a significant impact on Asian audiences. For example, members of Asian audiences in Scotland made national news when they protested about the format and language preference of the new show, demanding that *Asian Magazine* be reinstated or else they would withhold their licence fee. It wasn't and they didn't. *Network East* has evolved over the past thirteen years and, under its new producer Gurdip Bhangoo, the 2000 schedule has included a variety of content including quiz shows, celebrity interviews, live music, food, and location reports from all over the world focusing on popular Asian culture. The strand has also spawned a documentary off-shoot, *East*, a peak-time BBC 2 broadcast series comprising eight 30-minute programmes covering a wide variety of topics.

KAREN ROSS

New Beacon Books

Founded in 1966 by John **La Rose**, New Beacon Books has become one of the UK's best-known and most influential **publishing houses** to specialise in works by black British, Caribbean and African writers, academics and critics. Named after the politically and culturally radical Trinidadian magazine of the 1930s, *The Beacon*, New Beacon Books initially operated as the first specialist publisher of Caribbean materials in the UK. New Beacon has retained a commitment to the validation of those cultures, writings and histories that have been denigrated and denied with the Western contexts of colonialism and diaspora. By responding to the increasing demand for publications about Caribbean, African and black British cultures during the contemporary period, New Beacon Books has developed a strong and diverse list covering political, economic and educational theory, sociology, children's books, school texts, creative writings, criticism and journals. It has also retained an important outlet for publications in these fields since it took on a bookselling role in its connection with the **International Book Fair of Radical Black and Third World Books**; New Beacon Books has played a central role in the establishment of a network of specialist publishers.

The publishing house has helped to make several literary reputations, such as those of James **Berry**, a black British, Jamaican-born poet, and Erna Brodber, a Jamaican novelist. However, it has also launched lesser known novelists such as Ruel White and Norman Smith, and reprinted several early seminal works such as C.L.R. **James**'s *Minty Alley*, the first Caribbean novel to be published in the UK (1936; first reprinted 1971). Furthermore, New Beacon has provided a publisher for texts on specific events significant to Britain's black population, such as Anne Walmsley's *The History of the Caribbean Artists' Movement* (1991) and a distributor for reports such as *Murder in the Playground* and *Police Carnival* (1989).

In 1991, the New Beacon Educational Trust was founded. The Trust's stated aim is: 'The advancement of the public in matters relating to the political, social and cultural history of persons in the United Kingdom of Caribbean, African and Asian descent.' Its main objectives are the establishment of a research centre and the provision of facilities for research activity, and the study and practice of performance works. The immediate aim of the trust was to open the George Padmore Institute in North London. Named after the late Trinidadian-born activist, writer and intellectual, the institute serves as a resource centre with books, magazines, newspapers (see **publishing, newspapers and magazines**), journals, photographs, tapes, letters and other materials relating to organisations and events (such as the **Caribbean Artists' Movement**, the **Carnival** Movement and the Black Youth Movement), and to many other issues relevant to the black population in the UK. With the establishment of this educational foundation, New Beacon has consolidated its role in resourcing and promoting black culture in the UK.

ALISON DONNELL

new ethnicities

'New ethnicities' was a term coined by Stuart **Hall** in his influential essay of the same name, first published in 1987. The essay was written partly in response to a wider ongoing debate at this time over two black British films: the **Black Audio Film Collective**'s *Handsworth Songs* and **Sankofa Film Collective**'s *The Passion of Remembrance*, released in 1987 and 1986 respectively. This debate was centred on the cultural politics of black representation, and it is to this issue that Hall turns in 'New ethnicities'.

'Black', he argues in this essay, is not a given, or natural formation, but a discursively constructed category that demands careful interrogation. Hall goes on to articulate a shift in the modes of representation within black British discourse during the mid-1980s. The 1970s and early 1980s had witnessed the appropriation of 'black' as a political category bringing together what were in fact very different cultural communities: African, Carib-

bean, South Asian. The mid-1980s, however, saw 'the end of the innocent notion of the essential black subject' (Hall 1988: 28). 'Black', in this context, became a pluri-signifying category that is crossed and complicated by gender, class and ethnicity. For Hall, 'ethnicity' needs to be dissociated from the shallow rhetoric of 'multiculturalism' to become a term that gestures towards the constructedness of the 'black' subject.

The rise of a new politics of black representation since the mid-1980s, he suggests, has been made possible by a recognition of the black British community as a diasporic community that is at once hybrid, unsettled and radically impure. Hall identifies these conditions in a range of contemporary black British films, from Sankofa's *Territories* and *The Passion of Remembrance* to Hanif **Kureishi**'s *Sammy and Rosie Get Laid* and *My Beautiful Laundrette*.

Although Hall coined the term, he is certainly not the only cultural commentator responsible for putting the issues of ethnicity on the agenda. Paul **Gilroy**, and more recently Kobena **Mercer**, have also played a key role in the interrogation of black subjectivity and the politics of representation in the 1980s and 1990s: analysing everything from **reggae music** to black hairstyles.

Further reading

Gilroy, P. (1989) 'Cruciality and the frog's perspective: an agenda of difficulties for the black arts movement in Britain', *Third Text* 5: 33–44.

Hall, S. (1988) 'New ethnicities', in K. Mercer (ed.) *Black Film, British Cinema*, London: ICA, pp. 27–31.

Julien, I. and Mercer, K. (1988) 'Introduction: de margin and de centre', *Screen* 29(4): 2–11.

JAMES PROCTER

New Nation

The *New Nation* newspaper (see **publishing, newspapers and magazines**) was launched in November 1996, by husband and wife team Elkin Pianim and Elisabeth Murdoch, daughter of broadcaster and newspaper owner Rupert

Murdoch. A weekly paper, its cover price was twenty-five pence for the first two editions and fifty-five pence thereafter. The sixty four-page tabloid newspaper, aimed at the black community, covered sport, **literature**, **music**, news and current affairs.

The intention was to present a positive image of black British life and culture. The emphasis was on style, content and good-quality writing. The arrival of the *New Nation* had an impact on its competitors, the *Voice* and the *Weekly Journal*. The former eventually changed its publication day from a Monday to a Tuesday, while the *Weekly Journal* changed its style. Significantly, a number of *Voice* journalists left the newspaper to join *New Nation*, including *Weekly Journal* editor *Richard Adeshiyan*, who went on the edit the new paper. *New Nation* was characterized by the use of numerous columnists and the way it was neatly divided into departmental sections including a section specifically for women. Pianim and Murdoch eventually sold the *New Nation* to the Ethnic Media Group, which publishes **Eastern Eye** and **Asian Times**.

YINKA SUNMONU

New Playwrights Trust

Formed in 1986, the New Playwrights Trust (NPT) was set up as a national support organisation for new writers for performance with a brief including developing work by writers from groups under-represented in the **theatre**. Among projects designed to support the work of black and Asian playwrights in Britain, Blackwright, jointly produced with **Black Audio Film Collective**, attempted to log black and Asian writing for performance, a project subsequently developed by the **Theatre Museum Archive**. NPT also ran programmes of workshops and seminars, and produced a number of articles in its newsletters, and more extensive reports such as *Two Tongues*, which examined bilingualism in theatre. *Two Tongues* focused especially on the Half Moon Young People's Theatre's Bengali/English production *Kola Pata Bhut* (The Hopscotch Ghost). NPT has also produced guides to the market for black and Asian writers. Further, both the discussion of **Moti Roti**'s

Maa in the NPT-commissioned *Writing Live* (like Michael **McMillan**'s *Live Writing*) and *Going Black under the Skin* explore the possibilities of developing new approaches to dramaturgy and playmaking to reflect black experience. In 1999, NPT was relaunched as Writernet, offering its services as an on-line resource and aiming to link writers with potential producers via its website.

Further reading

Black Writing: a Guide for Black Writers, introduction by Michael McMillan, London: NPT.

SUSAN CROFT

new racism

The term 'new racism' was coined by Martin Barker in his book *The New Racism: Conservatives and the Ideology of the Tribe* (1981). New racism emerged in the late 1960s, and has been particularly associated with individuals like Enoch Powell, and, more recently, the controversial Bradford headmaster Ray Honeyford. Unlike imperial racism, which tends to construct and cite racial **difference** in terms of so-called 'biological' differences (for example in skin colour, smell or brain size), the new racism discriminates in terms of cultural differences that are delineated by national boundaries and which incur a division between 'insiders' and 'outsiders'.

Select bibliography

Barker, M. (1981) *The New Racism: Conservatives and the Ideology of the Tribe*, London: Junction Books.
Smith, A.M. (1994) *New Right Discourse on Race and Sexuality: Britain, 1968–1990*, Cambridge: Cambridge University Press

JAMES PROCTER

Newham Asian Women's Project

Founded in 1987 and based in East London, Newham Asian Women's Project (NAWP) was set up to provide help and advice to women and children experiencing domestic violence. It first opened as a hostel to provide emergency accommodation to women in this position. Over time, NAWP has expanded so that it has three additional sites, a resource centre, refuge and second-stage hostel. Information and advice is available on mental health issues, as well as counselling and befriending services. The counselling service for girls and women aged twelve to fifty-five was established in 1997. Sessions are conducted in the five major languages – Gujerati, Urdu, Hindi, Punjabi and Bengali. NAWP conducted an analysis of the women attending its mental health and counselling support groups and found that three out of five of its clients attempted self-harm. A young women's support group is now in existence, along with a mentoring scheme and mental health project. The organisation provides a service for women who may feel isolated by their problems in the local community and responds to user needs. It is committed to promoting and celebrating the lives of Asian women and their children in Britain. Actress and writer Meera **Syal** is its patron.

Select bibliography

Newham Asian Women's Project *Growing Up Young, Asian and Female in Britain*, London: Newham Asian Women's Project, Newham Innercity Multifund.

YINKA SUNMONU

Newland, Courttia

b. 1973, London, England

novelist, playwright

Newland's novels embody London's young black urban experience, but he explores more diverse themes in his shorts stories and plays. He wrote his first play in 1998, *Estates of Mind*, and his second, an adaption of Euripides' *The Women of Troy*, was acclaimed at the 1999 Edinburgh Festival. His third play was *The Far Side* (2000). **Television** writing credits include an episode of *Portobello Road* for BBC 2. Both novels are dramatised for the screen.

Select bibliography

Newland, C. (2000) 'His healing hands', in L. Hollis (ed.) *Rites of Spring*, London: Fourth Estate.
—— (2000) 'Suicide note', in N. Royle (ed.) *The Time Out London Book of Short Stories*, vol. 2, London: Penguin.
—— (1999) 'Complexion doesn't make the black man', in T. Fischer and N. Norfolk (eds) *Vintage: New Writers (8)*, London: Vintage.
—— (1999) *Society Within*, London: Abacus.
—— (1999) 'The great white hate', in P. Antoine (ed.) *Afrobeat*, London: Pulp Faction.
—— (1997) *The Scholar*, London: Abacus.
Newland, C. and Sesay, K. (eds) (2000) *IC3: the Penguin Book of New Black Writing in Britain*, London: Penguin.

KADIJA SESAY

Newton, Thandie

b. 1972, Zimbabwe

actress

Born to a Zimbabwean mother and British father, political unrest led to Newton moving at the age of four from Zimbabwe to Cornwall. At eleven, she enrolled at the Art Education School, London, where she studied modern **dance**. An injury at sixteen destroyed her hopes of becoming a dancer. Newton, who wanted to pursue the performing arts, started to audition for film (see **film and cinema**) roles. She was cast in the film *Flirting* (1990), along with Nicole Kidman. Although she accepted a place to read anthropology at Cambridge University, she combined acting with studying, obtaining parts in *Interview with the Vampire* (1994), *The Journey of August King* (1995) and *Jefferson in Paris* (1995). The name Thandie means 'beloved' and it is apt that she starred in Oprah Winfrey's long awaited film *Beloved*. The magazine (see **publishing, newspapers and magazines**) *Vanity Fair* featured Newton as part of its Class of 1999 – an annual review of a selection of young actors and actresses predicted to become Hollywood stars. She won the role of the leading lady in the blockbuster *Mission: Impossible II* (2000) with Tom Cruise and was sought after as an angel for the film *Charlie's Angels* (2000), based on the classic **television** series. However, Newton was unable to take the role due to scheduling commitments. Her importance in black British film history cannot be over-stated. She has broken through the ranks in Hollywood to obtain parts traditionally given to white actresses. She is married to director and screenwriter Oliver Parker. In September 2000, she gave birth to a daughter.

YINKA SUNMONU

Ngcobo, Lauretta

b. 1932, Cabazi, South Africa

teacher, novelist, critic

Born in Cabazi, South Africa, Lauretta Ngcobo was the firstborn in a family of four. When her father died (when she was eight), her mother struggled to provide for the family yet was determined to have all of her children educated, regardless of gender. It was in school that Lauretta began to see the collisions between the cultures of apartheid South Africa and began to understand the disapproval felt for her barefoot, rural black culture, which was grounded in an oral tradition. Living in the UK since 1963, she went into exile after the political turmoil in Sharpeville (1960). In London, she works as a teacher and a writer. She often focuses on the divisions between rural and urban South Africans – with the men forced by economics and apartheid laws to leave their wives and children behind for months and years while earning a living in the city. Her novels, *And They Didn't Die* (1990) and *Cross of Gold* (1981), are concerned with the lives of rural women – focusing on the women's rebellions of the late 1950s and 1960s. In 1987, she edited *Let it Be Told: Essays by Black Women Writers in Britain* and in 1993 published *Fiki Learns Like Other People*.

Select bibliography

Ngcobo, L. (1987) *Let it Be Told: Essays by Black Women Writers in Britain*, London: Virago.

TRACY J. PRINCE

Nia Centre for African and Caribbean Culture

The Nia Centre, on the borders of inner city Moss Side and Hulme in Manchester, opened its doors on 26 April 1991. This unique development at its time was the result of £1.3m investment and 20 years of community activity. Nia is a Ki-Swahili word meaning 'purpose' and is one of a set of words which, taken together, form a set of seven principles known as 'Nguso Saba'. These expound the virtues of purpose, unity, self-determination, work and responsibility, economics, faith and creativity. This is the ethos that underpinned this ambitious development. Nia had hoped to offer an array of **art forms** utilising versatile performance space. Not only would it host traditional theatre, but also cabaret-style seating, gigs, as well as conference facilities. The launch offered an array of artists with a wide appeal to a variety of audiences. However, like most black arts organisations, it was doomed to a series of crisis situations due to the project growing faster than the development of the board of directors and professional staff at its disposal. The Nia Centre suffered from the negative propaganda of the media about the Moss Side and Hulme areas of Manchester, experiencing recruitment, programming and funding problems. Nia closed its doors in the winter of 1997.

Further reading

Khan, K. (1997) *The Landscape of Fact*, London: the Arts Council of England.

Khan, N. (1976) *The Arts Britain Ignores*, London: Commission for Racial Equality and the Arts Council of Great Britain.

Owusu, K. (1986) *The Struggle for Black Arts in Britain*, London: Comedia.

PAWLET WARNER

Nichols, Grace

b. 1950, Guyana

poet, writer, editor

Nichols grew up in Guyana and worked there first

as a teacher and then as a reporter for the *Chronicle*, finally taking a job with Government Information Services before moving to the UK in 1977. Her first poetry publication, *i is a long memoried woman*, a striking poem cycle that narrates and re/members the experiences of black women from slavery onwards, was awarded the Commonwealth Poetry Prize in 1983. However, Nichols is possibly best known for her 1984 collection *The Fat Black Woman's Poems*, which also explores the gendering of black identity and the racial dimensions of women's lives, but this time in irreverent and iconoclastic poems. Her poetry is critically acclaimed and widely anthologised. Her novel *Whole of a Morning Sky* (1986) focuses on a Guyanese childhood unfolding against the backdrop of political unrest. Nichols has also published works for children, including *Can I Buy a Slice of Sky?* (1993) and *Asana and the Animals* (1997). Together with her husband John **Agard** she has edited the children's poetry anthologies *No Hickory, no Dickory, no Dock* (1991) and *A Caribbean Dozen* (1994), a collection of poems by thirteen Caribbean poets including Valerie **Bloom**, Faustin **Charles** and James **Berry**. Nichols published *The Poet Cat* in 2001.

Select bibliography

Nichols, G. (1998) *Lazy Thoughts of A Lazy Woman* London: Virago.
—— (1984) *The Fat Black Woman's Poems* London: Virago.
—— (1983) *i is a long memoried woman* London: Karnak House.

ALISON DONNELL

Nimarkoh, Virginia

b. 1967, London, England

artist

Nimarkoh studied at Goldsmiths from 1986 to 1989. Using found photographs, her work questions identity in relation to history as recorded through snapshots. Concentrating on the disparity between memory and **photography**, she presents half-formed narratives in an ambiguous manner. In an untitled work of 1992, two photographs were shown together, one of a white baby held in the arms of black women, the other of a black baby held in the arms of white women: juxtaposing images that confuse assumptions and suggest multiple readings. Nimarkoh's work encourages a personal reconstruction of events, both intimate and historical. Her contribution to the 'New Histories' exhibition of 1996 was to request photographs of the staff and directors of the Boston ICA as babies, and then to show these photographs in their respective places on an organisational chart. Abandoning the re-presentation of photographs in her latest project, she asked street artists to execute drawn portraits of her likeness, gathering the results into her 1999 book *Nubian Queen*, staging the perception or experience of her 'self' through the 'other'.

Select bibliography

Nimarkoh, V. (1999) *Nubian Queen*, London: the Camberwell Press.

Further reading

Bate, D. and Leperlier, F. (1994) *Mise en Scène*, London: ICA.
Gangitano, L. and Nelson, S. (eds) (1996) *New Histories*, Boston, ICA.

FRANCIS SUMMERS

NITRO *see* Black Theatre Co-operative

Notting Hill Carnival

London's Notting Hill Carnival, which takes place annually at the end of August, is a direct outcome of the post-Second World War movement of Caribbean people to Britain and the cultural adaptation of Caribbean communities locally. Although it has its origins in the Trinidad **carnival**, it has changed over time to reflect the experiences of African Caribbean people in Britain. It started in the early 1960s as the Notting

Hill Festival, a form of creative expression in the wake of the racism, deprivation and riots in Notting Hill in 1958. Despite a hostile response to early attempts at establishing the festival, an estimated 1 million revellers were attending the event by the mid-1980s. The growth of interest in carnival is further indicated in the increasing cross-cultural involvement it attracts and conservative figures suggest that 1.5 million revellers attended Notting Hill Carnival during the year 2000. From its community beginnings, London's Notting Hill Carnival has become Europe's largest street event and a celebrated international event that attracts tourists from all over the world.

The event has an official motto, 'Every spectator is a participant – carnival is for all who dare to participate.' More than eighty floats and mobile sound systems were found on the route on Bank Holiday Monday. Carnival consists of the traditional processional route and the children's day route, which happens on Sunday. There are a number of competitions including a costume gala. People are not only presented with the sights and sounds of carnival but with African Caribbean food. Over the years, a number of other minority ethnic groups have started to become involved in the festival and produce a range of multicultural dishes. Carnival is seen by many as spontaneous and artistic, and the street is the showcase in which to enjoy that colourful experience. In fact, the preparation for carnival begins months before the event and involves different agencies headed by the Notting Hill Carnival Trust. The making of costumes and choices of **music** and **dance** also takes place long before the event.

There are five disciplines that make up carnival – calypsonians, masquerades and costume bands, mobile sound systems, static sound systems and steelbands. Musically, soca is said to be the heartbeat of carnival, but increasingly popular attractions have included the static sound systems where major stars from the USA have flown over to perform. However, the spirit of carnival *per se* would be lost without the bands, music and spectacle. Sounds of soca, salsa and steeldrums ring out on the circular route that stretches for approximately three and a half miles encompassing Ladbroke Grove, Arundel Gardens, Westbourne Park Grove, Kensington Park Gardens, Chepstow Road, Great Western Road, Westbourne Park Road, Elkstone Road, Golborne Road and Kensal Road. Jour Ouvert marks the official start of carnival.

Yet carnival has not been without controversy and riots over the years. Carnival 2000 was marred by the deaths of two men – Abdul Bhatti and Greg Watson. As a result, Mayor of London, Ken Livingstone, called for a review into the safety of the carnival. For years, people have voiced a number of concerns about public safety and anti-social behaviour, among other things. The review group looked at how the situation could be improved so that carnival could be made safer and remain in Notting Hill. Critics have also mentioned links between violence and so-called gangsta or rap music, but more research needs to be done in this area.

Although large numbers of schools now take part in the annual carnival programme, which is found in cities such as Bristol and Liverpool, as well as in London, carnival as an art form and educational resource has received scant attention or scholarly interest. The creation and design of costumes cannot be underestimated. An exhibition of carnival costumes was shown for a few months at the Victorian and Albert Museum. Carnival is beginning to be taught in higher education. There are courses at Middlesex University, and the Centre for Caribbean Studies at Goldsmiths College, London, has looked at carnival in **literature** and held a panel on carnival during one of its conferences. Theses on carnival are beginning to appear and what is needed is a body of academic work that can attend to the cultural complexity and the strong performance dimension, as well as the social context of this event.

Further reading

Arts Council (1986) *Masquerading, the Art of Notting Hill Carnival*, Arts Council.

Knobil, M. (1996) *Images of the Carnival*, Creative and Commercial Publications.

Owusu, K. (2000) *Black British Culture and Society: a Text Reader*, London: Routledge.

Owusu, K. and Ross, J. (eds) (1988) *Behind the*

Masquerade, the Story of the Notting Hill Carnival, London: Arts Media Group.

YINKA SUNMONU AND JOAN ANIM-ADDO

Nubian Tales/b3 Media

Marc Boothe established Nubian Tales in 1992 with the intention of manifesting a commercially viable cultural forum for the exhibition, promotion and distribution of black film (see **film and cinema**). It has since become one of Britain's leading specialists in the genre, raising the profile of the work of black film-makers and actors on an international scale. Part of its expansion has been the creation of a Film Club, a weekly film column in *New Nation* and a daily 'Videoscope' slot for London's Choice FM. An annual film season works to encourage audience discussion of black films with its critically acclaimed MasterClass Series,

facilitating workshops around the films screened during the programme. In accordance with the 1990s emergence of new media, Nubian Tales branched out to form Digital Diaspora, a cultural networking event featuring interactive media. A successful outset eventually led to the production of '40 Acres and a Microchip', Europe's first major conference on urban culture and new media. As a result of the diversity and wealth of cultural information that became accessible because of its work, Nubian Tales then spawned the alternative lifestyle website, 23–59, covering **literature**, clubs, **theatre** and visual art (see **visual and plastic arts**) as well as film. The expanded remit necessitated a new title for this pioneering organisation, which has contributed hugely to the sophistication of black British culture – b3 Media, meaning 'Beats, Bytes and the Big Screen'.

DIANA OMO EVANS

O

Ocean, Billy

b. 1950, Trinidad

singer

Billy Ocean emigrated from Trinidad to the UK as a child. In 1976, after years of working as a tailor and pursuing a side-career in **music**, Ocean's Motown-flavored song 'Love Really Hurts without You' climbed to number three in the British charts. Already popular in his adopted home throughout the late 1970s, Ocean earned significant acclaim in the USA in 1981 for his **dance** hit 'Nights (Feel like Getting Down)'. In 1984 *Suddenly*, an album that peaked at number nine and featured Ocean's number-one hit 'Caribbean Queen (No More Love on the Run)', thrust him into international stardom. In 1986 Ocean released *Love Zone*, the singer's most successful album that went multi-platinum, which included the pop hits 'Love is Forever' and 'There'll be Sad Songs'. 'When the Going Gets Tough, the Tough Get Going', also from *Love Zone*, became the theme song for the movie *Jewel of the Nile*. In the late 1980s several singles such as 'The Colour of Love' and 'Get Outta My Dreams and into My Car', which were featured on *Tear Down These Walls*, were also successful on the pop, R 'n' B and Contemporary Urban charts. Following a three-year recording hiatus in the early 1990s, Ocean recorded *Time to Move On*. While it was not as popular as his earlier recordings, it featured Ocean's signature ballads and several dance tracks. Several remixes and greatest hits recordings by Ocean are currently available on Jive, RCA/Columbia Music Vision Video and Epic.

ANDREA D. BARNWELL

Odonkor, Mowbray

b. 1962, London, England

artist

Odonkor, who lives and works in London, studied fine art at Wimbledon and is known for paintings and drawings depicting self-portraits that concern judgement, hybridity and undefinable nationalities. She has described her work as 'opening out for discussion some of the ideas, beliefs, histories that make up the fabric of our existence', while contributing to 'the stories of our people'. In Odonkor's imagery we find the second generation familiarising themselves with British culture while processing the legacy of slavery, imperialism, colonialism and apartheid. Her exhibitions include: 'Creation for Liberation' (1985), 'Young, Black and Here' (1986), 'The Image Employed' (1987), 'Black Perspectives' (1987) and 'History and Identity – Seven Painters'(1991).

Further reading

Hall, C. (1992) 'History and identity', *Arts Review* (March).

PAUL O'KANE

Ofili, Chris

b. 1968, Manchester, England

visual artist

The winner of the 1998 Turner Prize, Ofili rose to prominence as part of the young British art movement. As a student he went on a scholarship to Zimbabwe, and, on his return, started incorporating both elephant dung and dots in his paintings – the latter inspired by Matapos cave paintings. Subsequently, Ofili developed a signature iconography that mixes caricatured black figures, magazine cut-outs and religious imagery. Collected by Charles Saatchi, Ofili exhibited in the infamous 'Sensation' exhibition. This was followed by a successful solo exhibition at the Serpentine in 1998. With his ironic, playful imagery, Ofili marks a clear break with the previous generation of black visual artists (see **visual and plastic arts**). His work rarely addresses political or social situations, but his style can be seen as corresponding to recent post-colonial theory around hybridity. Ofili's commercial worth is also a great deal higher than his predecessors – as well as being part of the Saatchi collection, he is represented in the UK by the well-known dealer Victoria Miro and in New York by Gavin Brown.

Further reading

Ratnam, N. 'Chris Ofili and the limits of hybridity', *New Left Review* 235: 153–9.

Serpentine Gallery (1998) *Chris Ofili*, exhibition catalogue, London: Serpentine Gallery.

NIRU RATNAM

Okri, Ben

b. 1959, Nigeria

novelist, poet

Okri was educated in Nigeria and England, where he took a degree in comparative literature at Essex University. Between 1981 and 1987, he was poetry editor for the journal *West Africa*, and, in 1984, became a broadcaster for the BBC World Service.

He is currently a full-time writer and occasional reviewer.

Published in 1980, Okri's first novel *Flowers and Shadows* presents a conventional narrative structure that was subsequently abandoned in the explicit experimentalism of his later work. His two short-story collections *Incidents at the Shrine* (winner of the Commonwealth Writers' Prize for Africa, and the *Paris Review* Aga Khan Prize for Fiction) and *Stars of the New Curfew*, published in 1986 and 1989 respectively, as well as his **Booker Prize**-winning novel *The Famished Road* (1991), are exemplary of this kind of experimentation. Blending modernist/postmodernist narrative strategies with postcolonial politics, these texts display a diaspora aesthetic (see **diaspora aesthetics**) of in-betweenness and hybridity evident elsewhere in contemporary black British writing. Abandoning linear chronology, and borrowing the fluid, cyclical time patterns of Yoruba myth, Okri conjoins worlds, realities and visions within spiritual, stylised dream sequences in a manner not dissimilar to the magic realist techniques of writers like Salman **Rushdie**. Okri has pursued these techniques in sequels like *Astonishing Gods* (1995), *Dangerous Love* (1996) and *Infinite Riches* (1998). In 1999, he published *Mental Fight*, an epic poem that is structured around the millennium celebrations of 2000.

Select bibliography

Okri, B. (1999) *Mental Fight*, London: Weidenfeld & Nicolson General.

—— (1998) *Infinite Riches*, London: Weidenfeld & Nicolson General.

—— (1991) *The Famished Road*, London: Vintage.

—— (1980) *Flowers and Shadows*, London: Longman.

JAMES PROCTER

Oldfield, Bruce

b. 1950, London

fashion designer

Bruce Oldfield studied fashion (see **fashion and design**) at St Martin's School of Art and began to work on a freelance basis immediately after leaving college in 1973, designing for several high-profile companies such as Yves Saint Laurent, Liberty and Henri Bendel. The son of a Jamaican boxer and a white Londoner, his childhood was spent in a number of locations including Harrogate, County Durham and a Dr Barnardo's children's home in London. In 1975, he received a grant from the home that enabled him to set up his own London-based fashion house, Bruce Oldfield Ltd. Oldfield has always been attracted to the high standards and technical workmanship found in couture. He recognised that there was a market for understated, flattering clothes and aimed for a 'classic' timeless look. Oldfield is probably best known for his couture and 'ready to wear' evening dresses, with high-profile clients such as the late Princess of Wales, Joan Collins and Anjelica Huston. In 1990 he was awarded an OBE and made an honorary fellow of both the Royal College of Art and Durham University.

Select bibliography

Oldfield, B. and Howell, G. (1987) *Bruce Oldfield's Season*, London: Pan.

SAMINA ZAHIR

Olton, Munirah

b. 1959, Middlesex, England

ceramicist

Olton has always shown some form of artistic talent. As a teenager, she used to make her own clothes and was able to cut and design intuitively. Olton moved from Hertfordshire to London in 1991, where she enrolled on an adult education class in ceramics. Six years later she started a degree in arts for community at the University of Surrey, Roehampton School of Art. Olton is now excelling in a field where black ceramists are few and black British women ceramists even fewer. Her work has been featured in *Untold* magazine and she exhibits on a regular basis, including at Brixton Art Gallery, which promotes black British art. Afrocentricity is reflected in her work with a modern feel, in pieces such as vases with cowrie shells in the

middle. The message is to ensure that black people do not lose their symbols but rather understand what they mean and incorporate them, where possible, into everyday living. For Olton, art is part of a historical cycle that can be created and re-created. She is currently working on an art project for Charing Cross Hospital, London, which is one of her most challenging pieces to date, consisting of a stylised sweep of fish cast on waves. She is the founder member of Falongo Arts.

YINKA SUNMONU

Onwurah, Ngozi

b. 1963, England

film-maker

As the daughter of a Nigerian father and British mother, Onwurah's short film (see **film and cinema**) *Coffee-Coloured Children* (1988) is a raw semi-autobiographical study of two mixed race children in Newcastle. Her next short *The Body Beautiful* (1991) dramatically examined the profound effects of female body image, beauty and sexuality through the maternal bond between a white mother, undergoing a mastectomy, and her black daughter, embarking on a modelling career. Inspired by Maya Angelou's same-titled poem, Onwurah deconstructs stereotypical images of black women and their sexuality in *And Still I Rise* (1993), seaming together interviews, archival images and live action in an emblematic blend of spirited narrative and striking visual image. *Monday's Girls* (1993) forcefully explores the iria women's initiation ceremony in Nigeria from the viewpoint of two young Waikiriki girls, pitting modern individualism against community tradition. In 1994, Onwurah became the first black British woman to direct a feature. A political action thriller based on an old tribal legend, *Welcome II the Terrordome* explored black and white relations in a violent British dystopia but disappointed commercially and critically. Onwurah continued to direct and produce (with her brother Simon under their company Non-Aligned Communications) a number of documentaries and dramas including *Behind The Mask* (1996) and *I Bring You Frankincense* (1996).

Onwurah established herself as a leading 1990s black British female independent film-maker, analysing race, race representations and traditions in an imaginative yet fiercely politically conscious Anglo-Nigerian style.

SATINDER CHOHAN

OPESAN, OLA *see* Agbenugba, Gbenga

Organisation of Women of Asian and African Descent

The Organisation of Women of Asian and African Descent (OWAAD), which existed between 1978 and 1983, was the first national black women's organisation in the UK. Its founder members included Stella Dadzie, Olive Morris and Sylvia Erike, and its aims were to provide an organised, co-ordinated response to political and social injustice, to issues of racism and sexism. It also aimed to heighten public awareness of the presence and contribution of black women in Britain and to bring a women's perspective to black politics of the late 1970s and 1980s. The first OWAAD conference, held in Brixton, London, in March 1979, was attended by 300 women from all over Britain; conference papers were published in 1979 and included an overview of the historical position of black women in Britain, as well as articles on education, housing and aspects of British law. *FOWAAD*, a bi monthly newsletter, provided a network for newly emerging and more established black women's groups and included the publication of cultural items such as poetry, and reviews of **literature**, film (see **film and cinema**) and **theatre**.

Further reading

Bryan, B., Dadzie, S. and Scafe, S. (1985) *The Heart of the Race: Black Women's Lives in Britain*, London: Virago.

Sudbury, J. (1998) *Other Kinds of Dreams*, London: Routledge.

SUZANNE SCAFE

Oriental Star Agencies

Set up in 1966, Oriental Star Agencies (OSA) are a recording label and management company based in Birmingham. Starting from a very small transistor radio shop, they addressed the demand for entertainment from the Asian diaspora. After approaching EMI in London, they began importing Indian and Pakistani records; the response was overwhelming and led to Oriental Star Agencies becoming the wholesale specialists for the UK. For many Asian artists they represent one of the few management/PR companies accessible both to Asian artists and to their current audiences. Subsequent demand for live performers and entertainers encouraged OSA to set up Star, their own recording label. The first bands signed were Anari Sangeet Party and Bhujangy Party. 'Bhabiye Akh Law Gayee', the first release in the 1970s by Bhujangy Party, was considered by many to be the first song that mixed modern Western musical instruments with traditional Asian **music** and sounds. OSA have names such as Bally **Sagoo**, Stereo Nation and Ustad Nusrat Fateh Ali Khan on their books. Ali Khan, who recorded all of his music with OSA until his death in 1997, was arguably one of the greatest musicians from the Indian subcontinent.

SAMINA ZAHIR

Other Story, The

'The Other Story', an exhibition of works by Asian, African and Caribbean visual artists (see **visual and plastic arts**) in the UK, was held at the Haywood Gallery, Southbank Centre, London, from November 1989 until February 1990. Curated by Rasheed **Araeen** and featuring the work of twenty-four artists, this exhibition is now widely regarded as a crucial event of black art in Britain as it brought the work of black British artists to public and critical attention. It is also acknowledged to be an event that sparked much controversy and debate concerning black British art as a cultural category. The installations spanned forty years of post-war Britain and gave a historical perspective to this neglected tradition. The oldest artist included was Ronald **Moody** and the youngest Sonia **Boyce**.

When the exhibition was staged, it aimed to offer a 'new perspective on art' and, as its title announces, to represent the 'other', then relatively unknown, story of black British experience and artistic expression. In its project to explore the complex cultural identity of black Britain, the exhibition gave expression to the increasingly politicised and committed works of the 1970s and 1980s. In its inclusion of artists from Asia, Africa and the Caribbean, 'The Other Story' emphasised both the multi-ethnic identity of black British culture and also the sense of a shared, although plural, cultural experience in relation to the visual arts. The show was strongly shaped by Araeen's curatorial vision and gave representation to those artists he regarded as having been unfairly neglected despite being modernists of note. Artists whose work was shown include Rasheed Araeen, Eddie **Chambers**, Keith **Piper** and Lubaina **Himid**. A special double issue of *Third Text*, a journal founded by Rasheed Araeen and dedicated to 'Third World Perspectives on Contemporary Art and Culture', supplemented the exhibition catalogue and consolidated the cultural significance of this exhibition with a series of critical and scholarly pieces by Geeta Kapur, Iqbal Geoffrey, Gilane Tawadros and others.

Further reading

Araeen, R. (ed.) (1993) *The Other Story*, Manchester: Southbank Centre, Cornerhouse Publications.
(1989) *Third Text* 2, 8 and 9 (autumn, winter).

ALISON DONNELL

Outcaste

Outcaste was originally formed by 'Shabs' Jobanputra and Paul Franklin in 1994 as an offshoot of their successful Media Village PR company to promote Asian British musicians. The Outcaste club night became immensely popular as a focal point for the Asian British **music** scene, while the label has developed from being one that predominantly released singles for the club market to releasing fully realised and critically acclaimed albums by artists including Nitin **Sawhney**, **Badmarsh** and **Shri**, as well as the *Outcaste Untouchable Beats* compilations. The compilations, the first of which was released in 1997, were highly successful, mixing together the music of a previous generation of pioneers including Ananda Shankar alongside Outcaste stalwarts and new artists such as Niraj Chaq and Pressure Drop. Although Outcaste is still a reasonably small label, it has built up a network of distribution deals in other countries including France and India, and Nitin Sawhney's third album for the label *Beyond Skin* charted in Britain. The US **hip hop** giant Tommy Boy distributed the Outcaste compilations in the USA. Several compilations were released in late 2000, including *Outcaste – the First Five Years* and *New Breed*.

ANDY WOOD

Ové, Horace

b. 1939, Trinidad

film-maker

Horace Ové travelled to Europe in 1960 and, after a period spent in Italy, he went to London to study film-making. In his wide and varied career subsequently, he has worked in both film (see **film and cinema**) and **television**, producing critical work that has continuously confounded the expectations of its audiences. In 1968, he shot *Baldwin's Nigger*, a film of the US author James Baldwin discussing what it meant to be black in Britain at that time, with a largely black audience. This programme remains a crucial document for researchers of Britain's black presence. Long before the **music** had entered the mainstream of film interest, Ové made *Reggae* (1970), which sought to give an account of the social history of what was to become a global phenomenon. In an effort to counter the negative visions of the black presence served up by the newspapers (see **publishing, newspapers and magazines**), he collaborated with writer Sam **Selvon** to make *Pressure* (1975), a feature film that attempted to understand the worlds of young black people growing up in a world which was hostile to them.

Black faces on British television had been a rarity in the post-war period. One notable exception, however, was Michael Abbensett's ***Empire Road*** (1978–9), which was an authentic soap opera of black British life, starring the actor Norman **Beaton**. Only two series of the programme were made, much to the consternation of all those involved in its production. Ové directed three episodes of the second series, causing some upset with his hands-on approach to directing. His mission to escape the facile depictions of black lives served up by the British press continued with his 1979 film for the BBC's Play for Today slot. *A Hole in Babylon* dramatises the 1975 siege of a Spaghetti House restaurant in London. The film seeks to understand the motivations of the characters involved in the incident that, ultimately, would cost them their freedom. In the mid-1980s, Ové was to pick up some lighter themes. In collaboration with the writer Caryl **Phillips**, he made *Playing Away* (1986), which pitted a black cricket team from Brixton against a white village side. Against this essentially comic backdrop, Ové weaves a beguiling series of narratives that set out the diversity of the black experience in Britain. Although, at its inception, Ové was hopeful about the support **Channel 4** might afford black filmmakers, he soon expressed disillusionment (although Channel 4 did screen his complex and distressing work *When Love Dies*, in 1990). As a result, Britain's hold on Ové weakened and more recently his critical voice has roamed a wider stage, even though his concerns have remained constantly focused on the black experience of modernity.

GARETH STANTON

Owusu, Kwesi

b. Sekondi, Ghana

writer, editor, director

Kwesi Owusu was educated at Adisadel College and the London School of Economics, and lectured at the University of London. He has a distinguished ancestry as the grandson of Daniel Essoum Gwira, a major figure of the Ghana legal profession and a relative of Kobina Sekyi, one of the first black playwrights to be published. In the 1980s, Owusu founded African Dawn with Sheikh Gueye and Wanjiku Kiarie. This **music** and poetry group, which was later joined by Wala Danga, Vico Mensah and Merle **Collins**, released four albums and worked with Ngugi Wa' Thiongo on the British **theatre** production of *The Trial of Dedan Kimathi* in 1984. In 1986, he published *The Struggle for Black Arts in Britain*, followed by *Behind the Masquerade* (1987) with Jacob **Ross** on the **Notting Hill Carnival**. He has edited two important collections: *Storms of the Heart: an Anthology of Black Arts and Culture* (1988), with over forty contributors, and *Black British Culture and Society: a Text Reader* (2000). Owusu has also had a successful career in film (see **film and cinema**) since the 1980s, when he took the position of apprentice producer and director with Cinema Action, a **Channel 4** Television-franchised workshop. With Kwate Nee Owoo he made *Ouaga* (1988), a documentary on African cinema and, in 1992, their feature, *Ama*, a joint Channel 4/Artificial Eye production broke box office records in Accra, Ghana, and was also screened in London's West End, at Cannes and at other international film festivals. He has subsequently co-directed *Segrin Africa* (1993), and the first part of a trilogy on African World **cinema**, as well as working on pop videos. Kwesi was a member of the consortium that bought the **Electric Cinema**; he has also been an editorial board member of ***Artrage*** and a Research Associate of the African Studies Centre at the University of Cambridge, and works with the portal Griot World.

Selected bibliography

Owusu, K. (2000) *Black British Culture and Society: a Text Reader*, London: Routledge.
—— (1988) *Storms of the Heart: an Anthology of Black Arts and Culture*, London: Camden Press.
—— (1987) *Behind the Masquerade*, London: Arts Media Group.
—— (1986) *The Struggle for Black Arts in Britain*, Comedia.

ALISON DONNELL

Oyekan, Lawson

b. 1961, London, UK

ceramicist

Oyekan's ceramics explore a range of themes – the human body, ideas of social interaction and cohesion, and the 'dimension of light' in enclosed spaces. His work is mostly hand-built, which makes it possible for him to produce large-scale pieces, but he is also an expert thrower, a technique he generally reserves for work in porcelain, a medium he explored during his research as the Darwin Scholar at the Royal College of Art (1988–90). In 1986, a trip to Nigeria enabled him to study ant-hills and beehives, which inspired a series of symbolic works in terracotta and crank (rough clay) with dry slip markings and pierced holes, some inscribed with Yoruba text, 'like tattoos on the human body'. This work was exhibited after his residency at Loughborough College of Art and Design (1994–5) for the one-person show at the City Art Gallery in Leicester (1995). He is an elected Fellow of the Craft Potters Association. His work is held in public collections by the Los Angeles County Museum of Art, Los Angeles; Stedelijk Museum, Amsterdam and the Victoria and Albert Museum, London.

Further reading

Britton, A. (1995) 'The human presence in clay', *Ceramic Review* 156: 10–13.

Talbot, H. (1995) 'Lawson Oyekan', *Studio Pottery* 15: 15–17.

LINDA SANDINO

P

Palmer, Eugene

b. 1955, Kingston, Jamaica

artist

Palmer came to England with his parents in the
mid-1960s. He studied at Wimbledon School of
Art and received an MA from Goldsmiths College
in the early 1980s. His early, abstract works are
marked by strident colours, which spread across
the canvas and retain suggestions of spiritual
fantasies. His abstract paintings were shown at
the Waterloo Gallery (Jamaica, 1981). In 1983
'The Flag' marked his transition from abstract to
figurative painting. A cropped, loosely painted
black figure floating on a red background highlighted his interest in black culture. Palmer
exhibited regularly in the 1980s, especially in
'Artists Against Apartheid' (1985) and 'Caribbean
Expressions in Britain' (1987). His success was
established by a different style of painting. In 'Our
Restless Hearts' (1991), he brought a personal
poetry into the classical tradition as family snapshots and the work of black photographer William
Roberts became important sources.

Further reading

Chambers, E. and Morris, L. (1993) *Eugene Palmer*,
Norwich: Norwich Gallery, Norfolk Institute of
Art and Design.

PAULINE DE SOUZA

Panchal, Shanti

b. 1951, Gujarat, India

visual artist

Panchal studied in Bombay and participated in a
number of exhibitions in India before moving to
the UK. Panchal was one of the four Indian artists
invited by the India High Commission to undertake major restoration work to damaged murals.
He also participated in a number of group
exhibitions, before becoming involved with the
black art movement in the UK in the mid-1980s.
Panchal's most significant involvement with black
art came with the **Greater London Council**'s
Anti-Racist mural project of 1985. The Council
was supportive of black art, which it termed 'ethnic
arts' and, during its Anti-Racist year in 1984,
decided to commission four murals in sites that
were linked to Britain's black and Asian populations. Panchal, along with the young artist Dushka
Ahmad, was given what was earmarked as a
permanent site in the East End of London, but
their idea was rejected as being too inflammatory
after consultation with the local community. The
mural was subsequently modified to meet local
concerns. It is a key example of the increasing
problems that the anti-racism movement was
experiencing at that time.

Further reading

Cartwright Hall (1988) *Earthen Shades: Paintings by*

Shanti Panchal, exhibition catalogue, Bradford: Cartwright Hall.

NIRU RATNAM

Panchayat

Founded in 1988, arts organisation Panchayat took its name from the basic foundation of Indian democracy – the council of village elders. The organisation was initially set up by Shaheen **Merali**, Bhajan Hunjan, Symrath Patti, Alan **de Souza** and Shanti Thomas. Its initial aim was to be an education and resource project promoting South Asian artists in Britain through access to its archive, publications and educational projects. As well as dealing with ethnicity, the organisation was also committed to issues around class, gender and disability from the outset. Subsequently the Panchayat archive moved to the University of Westminster, where it is currently housed. As the critical climate changed, Panchayat's objectives have developed in order to deal with a wide set of post-colonial issues. In particular, issues around identity have been the focus of much of its recent work; it also aims to promote Internationalism. The organisation is now involved in conferences, exhibitions, workshops, publishing and graduate and postgraduate degree courses. Recent projects include the international exhibition 'Slow Release', the exhibition 'Unbound Geographies/Fused Histories' (both London, 1999) and the conference 'Ex-centric'. Panchayat's current co-ordinator is Shaheen Merali.

NIRU RATNAM

Paris, Mica

b. 1969, London, England

R 'n' B singer, songwriter

Born Michelle Wallen, Mica Paris is probably UK R'n'B's most respected female vocalist. Despite struggling to find a market to fit her raspy but classically soulful voice, Paris has been a major musical force since releasing her debut single 'My One Temptation' in 1988. Paris's talents garnered comparisons with her R'n'B contemporary Whitney Houston after the success of Paris's 1989 debut album *So Good*. Future albums, however, followed a frustrating trend as her then-label, 4th & Broadway, tried desperately to sell this prodigious talent to the USA. Her sophomore album *Contribution* tried to cash in on the popular early 1990s **hip hop/soul** market, while her third effort *Whisper a Prayer* was an attempt to sell her as an English Whitney Houston. Nevertheless, Paris's talents attracted some legendary artists, producers and songwriters, such as Prince, Nile Rodgers (formerly of the group Chic), Rakim and Curtis Mantronik. She also released one of the true classics of British R'n'B, 'Should've Known Better' with Omar in 1990. Paris found musical liberation in 1998 and assumed more creative control on her fourth effort *Black Angel*. Despite attracting as much attention for her skimpy attire at industry functions as for her **music**, *Black Angel* is the greatest illustration of Paris's innovative talent.

DEREK A. BARDOWELL

Parmar, Pratibha

b. 1955, Nairobi, Kenya

film-maker

Pratibha Parmar is an internationally acclaimed film-maker whose signature mark is a bold treatment of unconventional themes. Born in Nairobi, Kenya, she moved with her Indian family to England in 1967, studying at Bradford University and at the **Centre for Contemporary Cultural Studies** at Birmingham University. Starting out as a social worker in the British Asian community, Parmar travelled to India in 1975, where among other activities she worked with Mother Teresa. Parmar also worked in the feminist publishing collective, Sheba Feminist Press, where she edited and published writings by women of colour, including the British publication of *The Cancer Journals* (1980) by Audre Lorde. She was active in the anti-racist movement in the UK in the 1970s, in OWAAD (**Organisation of Women of Asian and African Descent**) in the early 1980s, and continues to speak on issues of racism, sexism and homophobia around the world.

To a large extent, all of Parmar's films reflect her engagement with these same issues. Her social and political agenda, often leavened with a hefty dose of erotic playfulness, was already evident in her early documentaries for **Channel 4** Television: *Memory Pictures* (1986); *Sari Red* (1988); and *Flesh and Paper* (1990). *A Place of Rage* (1992), featuring such African American feminist activists as Angela Davis, Audre Lorde, June Jordan and Alice Walker, won the Prized Pieces competition for best historical documentary at the National Black Programming Consortium in the USA. *Warrior Marks* (1993) was made in collaboration with Pulitzer Prize-winning novelist, Alice Walker, author of *The Color Purple*. The film (see **film and cinema**) and the ensuing book about its making, co-authored by Parmar and Walker, earned international fame while establishing that Parmar was not afraid to tackle head-on the culturally sensitive subject of female circumcision in Africa. In June 1995, Parmar completed *Jodie*, a documentary film celebrating Hollywood actress Jodie Foster for the Channel 4 series, 'Celluloid Icons'. *The Righteous Babies*, an hour-long documentary about popular culture, **feminism** and rock **music**, and *A Brimful of Asia*, a half-hour documentary about the explosion of second-generation Asian talent in the UK, were both completed in July 1998 for Channel 4 Television. In addition to her documentary films, Parmar has made two short feature films, *Memsahib Rita* (1994) and *Wavelengths* (1997). She is also the co-author and editor of several published books. She lectures regularly at universities and colleges in the USA and the UK and resides in London.

Select bibliography

Parmar, P. (1991) 'Perverse politics', *Feminist Review* 34(1).

Parmar, P. and Walker, A. (1993) *Warrior Masks: Female Genital Mutilation and the Sexual Blinding of Women*, London: Jonathan Cape.

Parmar, P., Gever, M. and Greyson, J. (eds) (1993) *Queer Looks: An Anthology of Writing About Lesbian and Gay Media*, London: Routledge.

Further reading

Foster, G.A. (1997) 'Pratibha Parmar: an assault on racism, sexism and homophobia', in *Women Filmmakers of the African and Asian Diaspora: Decolonizing the Gaze, Locating Subjectivity*, Carbondale and Edwardsville: Southern Illinois University Press, pp. 73–94.

Knippling, A.S. (1996) 'Self (en)gendered in ideology: Pratibha Parmar's *Bhangra Jig* and *Sari Red*', *Journal for the Psychoanalysis of Culture and Society*, 1(2): 119–24.

ALPANA SHARMA

Parvez

reggae artist, record producer

b. Birmingham, England

Of Pakistani parentage, Parvez grew up in Birmingham listening to **reggae** music and following local sound systems, and after a brief spell in a rock band he formed Aduwa, a reggae group. In 1994, Parvez created a home studio and launched the Dub Factory with his 12" 'The World Nowadays/Poetry in Motion' and received positive attention. Moving to the Blue Studio, he released his first album *Voyage into Dub – the First Journey* in 1995, which met with success and has since featured on a number of compilation works. In 1996, this was followed by a second album, *Various Dub Dance Tracks*, and a move into touring with his long-term vocal collaborators Rita Pereira and Echo Ranks. Parvez's success on tour led to a phone call from Bally **Sagoo**'s Ishq Records label and a record deal that resulted in the album *Revolution* in 2000. In his latest work the ethnic complexity of being an Asian reggae artist is more stated, and the creative possibilities of this cross-cultural interaction are more fully realised with the stylised vocals of one of India's leading singers, Ram Shankar.

ALISON DONNELL

Pascall, Alex

b. Grenada

broadcaster, writer, carnival arts educator, oral historian

Born in Grenada, Pascall came to Britain in 1959,

having represented his country as a musician the previous year in the *Bee Wee Ballet Dance Troupe* at the inauguration of the Federation of the West Indies. In 1974, he was invited to join the BBC for his knowledge in African and Caribbean cultures. His work developing ***Black Londoners*** on BBC Radio London is said to have established a black presence in the British media. The programme, originally planned as a test series of six programmes, became the first black daily radio show in British history. From 1984 to 1989, Pascall was chairman of the **Notting Hill Carnival** Arts Committee. His drive to internationalise Caribbean cultural developments in Britain helped the formation of the Foundation for European Carnival Cities in 1985, with whom he served as a founder Vice-President. In 1986, he was appointed national co-ordinator of 'Caribbean Focus '86' and worked on 'Caribbean Express '86', the only known cultural exhibition train in Britain, which travelled to eighteen cities in twenty-one days, running educational workshops. His work for the BBC has continued and in the 1990s Pascall has researched and produced documentaries for BBC Radios 2 and 3, including *A Different Rhythm*, *Caribbean Folk Music* and *World War Calypso*. Pascall is pioneering a school community programme *Roots to Torfaen* to encourage pupils, parents and community members to explore their roots, celebrate cultural diversity in their area and discover global links. With a comprehensive personal archive on Caribbean folk arts, Pascall aims to build a Caribbean Heritage Centre. In 1996, he was awarded an OBE for services to community relations.

YINKA SUNMONU

Patel, Jyoti

b. 1970, Eldoret, Kenya

playwright

Jyoti Patel grew up in Leicester and began writing at thirteen. She initially wanted to be an actress and was part of the Leicestershire Youth Theatre, which performed at the Haymarket Theatre. Here she met schoolteacher Jez Simons and they began a long writing collaboration. Their first piece, *Awaaz* ('Voices') (1983), was written for the Youth Theatre.

It was about a schizophrenic Asian girl who hears Western and Asian voices giving her contradictory messages. This began her career writing for **theatre**, later **television** and now script editing. Patel and Simons formed a company, Hathi Productions. Her strong point was to write bilingual English–Gujarati scripts, arguing that this was how many young Asians spoke at home. *Prem* (1987) was a teenage love story between a Gujarati girl and a Muslim boy. *Kirti, Sona & Ba* (1988) was the story of three generations of Gujarati women. While writing for theatre, the pair were head-hunted for the BBC soap *Eastenders* (1989). Patel has since developed an independent career in television drama. She was series editor for *Casualty* and *Grange Hill*, developed *Family Affairs*, the Channel 5 soap, and *Holby City* for the BBC. The writing partnership ended after the play *Moonlight Serenade* in 1997.

SUMAN BHUCHAR

Peckham Publishing Project

The Peckham Publishing Project, a non-profit organisation, was part of the Bookplace on Peckham High Street, a community bookshop for people living in Southwark. It was anti-racist, multicultural and promoted ethnic minority literatures (see **literature**). Local people were given the opportunity to write and publish, and **children's literature** was an important part of the project: an Asian children's story was translated into English, another examined how children would react to a little boy with dreadlocks and there was a children's storyboard book about the daily lives of black children. Publications were widespread, from education titles to histories about the local area, to titles about the community, women, reminiscence work and literacy. A series of books were published for adults learning to read. Some of the publications, such as *So this Is London*, were funded with help from the London Borough of Southwark Race Equality Unit, the **Greater London Council**, Community Arts Committee and the Greater London Arts Committee. Women produced a collection of poems entitled *I Want to Write it Down – Writing by Women in Peckham* and there was a publication on Jamaican social life and customs. *So this Is London* focuses on the experiences of immigrants coming to the capital and their reactions to housing, school and life in general, as well as their expectations. One author remarked, 'I've been longing to go back to a land where to be black was natural, not a disgrace.' The importance of the Peckham Publishing Project is that it gave a voice to people who did not readily have one in terms of access to mainstream publishing (see **publishing, books**). It also allowed and encouraged events and experiences to be documented and circulated, and was important to issues around self-development.

Select bibliography

Simeone, L. (1984) *Marcellus*, London: Peckham Publishing Project.

Peckham Publishing Project (1984) *So this Is England*, London: Peckham Publishing Project.

—— (1983) *Golfers: Stories from a Bermondsey Childhood*, London: Peckham Publishing Project.

—— (1981) *Captain Blackbeard's Beef Creole and Other Caribbean Recipes*, London: Peckham Publishing Project.

—— (1980) *I Want to Write it Down – Writing by Women in Peckham*, London: Peckham Publishing Project.

YINKA SUNMONU

Peepal Tree Press

Based in Leeds and founded by Jeremy Poynting, the publishing house Peepal Tree Press began humbly in a back bedroom in 1986. It has now established itself as a specialist publisher focusing on the Caribbean, South Asia, Africa and diasporic homelands. With over a hundred titles in its list, Peepal Tree publishes quality literary paperback titles, both fiction and poetry, as well as critical, cultural and historical studies. The press is committed to publishing writings that explore multi-ethnic and multicultural societies and their pasts, and also has a strong commitment to publishing new writers. Their list contains work by established authors and academics such as

Kamau Brathwaite, Beryl **Gilroy**, Ismith Khan and David **Dabydeen**, but has also pioneered important new voices such Lakshami Persaud – the first Indian Trinidadian woman novelist.

ALISON DONNELL

Perera, Shyama

b. 1958, Moscow, Russia

journalist, presenter

Perera came to the UK with her parents in 1963; her father had been working for the Sri Lankan Embassy in Moscow. She began her career as a reporter with a news agency and eventually worked on the *Guardian*. She was later noticed by the Head of Features at London Weekend Television, who had remembered her distinctive pink hair, and asked her present their Asian programme *Eastern Eye*. She also worked on LWT's *Six O'clock Show* as 'the prat'. Tired of this role, she set up a PR company and later returned to the *Guardian* as a reporter, also presenting the BBC's ***Network East***. Perera works as a writer and broadcaster and in 1999 she published a novel, *Haven't Stopped Dancing Yet* (London: Sceptre), about four girls growing up in London.

ALISON DONNELL

performing poets

The 1970s saw the emergence of a performing-poetry scene in Britain with the Liverpool Poets (Adrian Henri, Roger McGough and Brian Pattern) and others such as Joolz and John Cooper Clarke bringing together elements of **music**, comedy and poetry, often in order to articulate the urban politics of the time. In this decade of police hostility and race riots, these politics usually had everything to do with race, and one of the most significant cultural developments of this era was that of black British performance poetry. Linton Kwesi **Johnson**, who called his practice dub poetry to signal its **reggae** rhythms and his allegiance to Jamaican performing poets such as Mikey Smith and Mutabaruka, was a catalyst for a new scene. Johnson's own style of performance and his willingness to speak directly of racist attacks and police brutality set a new mode, which was clearly more to do with articulations of a politics of resistance than the works of earlier performing poets, such as James **Berry**, who had drawn on Jamaican speech rhythms in order to perform poems of cultural difference more than of opposition. Much of the early work of black performing poets in the UK came directly out of this highly charged context and was aggressively political and often confrontational. However, increasingly there was a sense that these polemical forms were limited and limiting, and poets began to explore more widely for both form and content.

In the 1980s, it was the women poets who took over the mantle of strong political work, needing to voice not only race politics but also issues around gender. Following on from Jean 'Binta' **Breeze** and Merle **Collins**, the next generation of performing women poets emerged as both more firmly identifying as black and British, and more strident in their message. Performers such as Dorothea **Smartt**, performance artist Bernardine **Evaristo** and poet and musician Akure **Wall** networked through organisations such as Spread the Word and the **Centerprise Women's Café** in what was a fairly separate women's scene. In the 1990s, the campaigns of voicing and visibility were less needed and performing poets again re-fashioned their work to cater for more aware and diverse audiences, and there was less separation between male and female, and black and white performers. More women performers, such as Patience **Agbabi**, Shirley Mitchell (Cuban Redd), Melissa Reid (Mad Melissa) and **SuAndi**, produced interesting individual work and also established clubs and alliances to provide wider support. The emphasis upon communal involvement and an engagement with grassroots activities has remained an important part of the scene and, in the 1990s, Lemn **Sissay** has promoted both Asian and black performing poets through workshops, community publishing and school-based work.

Oration, dramatic arts and poetry have always been mutually informing art forms, especially in Caribbean and African cultures, and performing poets are situated along an active and creative continuum between intense dramatic styles and lively readings. While much has been made about the page versus the stage, now that nation language or creole has a literary status, most performers publish those works that act as performance scripts, and they are widely acknowledged to have value in their published form. Indeed, many poets such as John **Agard**, Grace **Nichols** and Jackie **Kay** are now known mainly for their single-volume works, although performative elements remain significant to their poetry. From the margins of British culture, black performing poets are now a popular cultural presence and the nomination of one of the UK's best-known performers, Benjamin **Zephaniah**, for the professorship in poetry at Cambridge University (albeit unsuccessfully) is an indication of the prestige that this cultural practice has now rightly attained.

Further reading

Brown, S., Morris, M. and Rohlehr, G. (eds) (1989) *Voiceprint – an Anthology of Oral and Related Poetry from the Caribbean*, Harlow: Longman

Markham, E.A. (ed.) (1989) *Hinterland*, Newcastle upon Tyne: Bloodaxe Books

ALISON DONNELL

Peters, Andi

b. 1971, London, England

presenter

Peters's first job in television came at the age of seventeen as a presenter with Thames Television. However, national recognition was achieved as the anchor of the popular children's **television** programme *Live and Kicking*, which he presented with Emma Forbes in the prime-time Saturday morning slot. He is also to be remembered for his appearances on Children's BBC television with Ed the Duck and the Broom Cupboard. Moving on from children's television, Peters took a senior position at LWT before joining **Channel 4** in 1998 as commissioning editor for youth and children's programmes, and programming editor of T4, covering the Sunday morning slot, 9 a.m. to 1 p.m. He has also presented adult shows such as *The Travel Quiz*, a general knowledge programme,

Celebrity!, a celebrity gossip programme, and *Andi Peters meets...*, a programme where he interviewed celebrities, including Mariah Carey. Successful behind the scenes as well as at the forefront, he produced *The O-Zone* for BBC and *The Noise* for ITV. His show *Shipwrecked*, a teenage docu-soap, is Channel 4's highest rated show. Peters has made it to Hollywood in *Toy Story 2* as the voice of Baggage Handler Number Two. The professionalism of Peters, along with that of Diane Louise **Jordan**, has surely helped to pave the way for a new set of black BBC presenters such as Josie D'Arby and Angelica Bell.

YINKA SUNMONU

Phillips, Caryl

b. 1958, Basseterre, St Kitts

novelist, scriptwriter, editor

Born in the Caribbean, Caryl Phillips was brought up in England and read English at Queen's College, Oxford. Although recognised primarily as a novelist, he has also produced work for **theatre**, **television**, radio and film (see **film and cinema**). His first novel *The Final Passage* was published in 1985 and returns to fictionalise that pioneering phase of migration from the Caribbean to Britain in the 1950s. The female protagonist, Leila, opens up a number of important feminist concerns that have generally been neglected within this male-domi-nated period of settlement. Phillips's later works, such as *A State of Independence, Higher Ground, Cambridge, Crossing the River* (1993) and *The Nature of Blood* continue with, and embellish upon, the kind of diasporic framework produced in *The Final Passage*. Moving between dispersed locations, histories and cultures, Phillips's novels produce a hybrid (see **cultural hybridity**) poetics of migration not dissimilar to Paul **Gilroy**'s notion of the **black Atlantic**. Like other cosmopolitan celebrities (see **cosmopolitan celebrity**), his work has been met with a good deal of acclaim in both Britain and the USA. *Crossing the River* was shortlisted for the **Booker Prize** and won a James Tait Black Memorial Prize, while Phillips himself has been awarded the Martin Luther King Memorial Prize

and a Guggenheim Fellowship. Phillips has also published a work of non-fiction, *The European Tribe*, and an autobiographical travel narrative, *The Atlantic Sound* (2000). He has edited an anthology of British migrant writing, *Extravagant Strangers: a Literature of Belonging* (1997) and is also series editor for the Faber Caribbean Series launched in 1998. Phillips is Professor of English at Amherst College, USA.

Select bibliography

Phillips, C. (2000) *The Atlantic Sound*, London: Faber & Faber.
—— (1997) *Extravagant Strangers: a Literature of Belonging*, London: Faber & Faber.
—— (1993) *Crossing the River*, London: Bloomsbury Publishing Ltd.
—— (1985) *The Final Passage*, London: Faber & Faber.

JAMES PROCTER

Phillips, Mike

b. 1952, Guyana

writer

Mike Phillips arrived in London from Guyana with his family in 1956. As an academic, Phillips taught at the University of Westminster for eleven years, leaving to pursue a full-time writing career. Phillips has won a number of awards for both books and screen plays and was a previous Writer in Residence at the Royal Festival Hall; he has also been Writer in Residence at the South Bank Centre. Phillips's work is undoubtedly multifaceted: *The Dancing Face* (1997), for example, examined some of the finer details around citizenship, including the role played by 'racial' coding and skin colour. Known as an exceptional crime writer, Phillips is one of many practitioners who prefer not to have their work defined as that of a 'black' artist, although he frequently explores black identity in contemporary British society. In 1998, he compiled *Windrush: the Irresistible Rise of Multi-racial Britain* with his brother Trevor **Phillips**, as a companion to the **television** documentaries and as part of the

Windrush season. Phillips is currently the Arts Foundation Fellow for thriller writing.

Select bibliography

Phillips, M. (1997) *The Dancing Face*, London: HarperCollins.

—— (1996) *An Image to Die For*, London: Harper-Collins.

Phillips, M. and Phillips, T. (1998) *Windrush: the Irresistible Rise of Multi-racial Britain*, London: HarperCollins.

SAMINA ZAHIR

Phillips, Trevor

b. 1953, London, England

television producer, journalist

Phillips's parents had migrated to the UK from Guyana, and he was educated there at Queen's College, Georgetown, before taking a degree in chemistry at Imperial College, London. A leading presence in broadcast journalism, Phillips has worked as a presenter on *The London Programme* (LWT), *Crosstalk* (LNN) and *In Living Colour* (BBC Radio 4). He is also an experienced producer (the documentary *Diana: Portrait of a Princess* is one of his credits) with his own production company. He is an Executive Producer for factual programmes for London Weekend Television and an ITV executive. Phillips also writes a weekly column for the *Independent* and often writes for the *Guardian* and *Prospect*. In 1998, he produced four documentaries tracing the influence of black Britons of Caribbean descent as part of the ***Windrush*** season and, with his brother Mike **Phillips**, published a companion to the series, *Windrush. The Irresistible Rise of Multi-Racial Britain* (1998), which contains interviews, letters and excerpts from newspaper articles, as well as commentary. Phillips is active in the voluntary sector too and is Chairman of the Runnymede Trust, the Board of Hampstead Theatre and the London Arts Board. He is also a member of the Arts Council and the management board of The Prince of Wales' Trust.

Select Bibliography

Phillips, M. and Phillips, T. (1998) *Windrush. The Irresistible Rise of Multi-racial Britain*, London: HarperCollins

ALISON DONNELL

photography

Photography is an art form (see **art forms**) that occupies a unique position within the arena of black visual arts (see **visual and plastic arts**). In the 1970s, the use of a documentary form by many black photographers has to be seen within a wider political framework, as part of an attempt to reposition the guaranteed centres of knowledge seemingly presented by realism and the classic realist text. Examples include the photographic imagery of carnival as a diasporic phenomenon by Horace **Ové**, the portrait of a growing community in Handsworth, Birmingham, by Vanley **Burke** and the imagery by Armet **Francis** in the Black Triangle project. This was a struggle to contest negative images with positive ones.

By the 1980s, the campaign to contest negative images had moved on to an enquiry into the politics of the image itself. The question of authorship, **essentialism** and cultural nationalism was critiqued in relation to photographic images of black people. In the sphere of mass media there were popular images of race produced by the famous Benetton campaign. However, within the photography sector there were images of black males by Robert Mapplethorpe, photographs of the black community in Handsworth by Derek Bishton and John Reardon, as well as images of black artists and the black community in London since the 1950s by Val Wilmer, which opened up debates about whites imaging blacks. It was here that the black photography movement produced its most innovative and exciting work, exploring complex debates around fine art practices, gender, sexuality and being black and British. Artists such as Ingrid **Pollard**, Joy **Gregory**, David **Lewis**, Samena **Rana**, Clement **Cooper**, Faisal **Abdu'Allah**, Chila **Burman** and Franklyn Rodgers all engaged with these issues, and there is the use of new technology by Roshini **Kempadoo**.

The links with the diaspora made by Sunil **Gupta**, Maud **Sulter**, Sutapa **Biswas**, Mumtaz Karimjee and Armet Francis, and the installation work of Zarina **Bhimji**, Virginia **Nimarkoh**, Richard **Hylton** and Sonia **Boyce** all pushed the boundaries of a lens-based art form. Black photographic work has also been one of the key sites for critical debate on areas of sexuality. One can consider the work of Rotimi **Fani-Kayode**'s 'Technique of Ecstasy' series and **Ajamu**'s 'Black Bodyscapes' as important interventions in debates on sexuality. The process of image making has also been under scrutiny, as seen in the Watershed show '**From Negative Image To Positive Stereotype**' and the growth of the artist/curator/publicist, as seen in the careers of Armet Francis, Sunil Gupta, Mark **Sealy**, Maud Sulter, Jenny Mackenzie and David A. **Bailey**. This was also the period when groups began to form in order to strengthen the representation and activity of black photographers in Britain. **Autograph: the Association of Black Photographers** (1988), **D-Max** (1987) and Polareyes (1987) are all examples of successful collaborative ventures.

The 1980s saw a growth in black exhibitions at the Photographers Gallery, Camerawork, Battersea Arts Centre, Cave Arts Centre, Brixton Art Gallery, Cornerhouse Group, the Cockpit Gallery and the Pavilion. These shows tended to be either ones that were curated on a gender basis, such as 'Intimate Distance' (1989) or 'Testimony' (1986); along cultural groupings, such as 'Fabled Territories' (1989), 'Aurat Shakti' (1986) or 'Darshan' (1986); or as general survey projects such as 'Reflections of the Black Experience' and 'Black Edge' (both in 1986). There were also shows that linked the specifics of black British photography to British photography, such as the Spectrum women's photography festival and the Newcastle Commissioning Agency, Projects UK. Other shows linked black British photography to a wider diasporic community such as US/UK Photography Exchange (1989) and the Commonwealth exhibition 'Pictures of Everyday Life' (1987). Alongside these exhibitions came the publication of several key monographs. These were: the independently produced *The Black Triangle* by Armet Francis (1985); *Black Male/White Male*, the first publication to launch the work by Rotimi Fani-Kayode (1988);

and *Presence*, which explored the work of Clement Cooper (1988). *Polareyes*, the first independent black women's photography journal, was launched in 1987, and there were other journals like *Camerawork*, *Feminist Review*, *Bazaar*, *Aperture* ('Towards a bigger issue', 1988), *Creative Camera* ('The drum issue', 1984), *Revue Noire* and *Ten.8* ('Black image', 1984; 'Black experiences', 1986) that all ran key texts on black photographic image making, and in some cases produced special issues on black photography.

The 1990s began with a series of powerful exhibitions, which established the agenda for the rest of the decade. 'Ecstatic Antibodies' (1990) explored the myths surrounding the AIDS virus and representation, and 'Autoportraits' (1990) became the first exhibition curated by Autograph to de-construct the black body and self-portraiture. 'An Economy Of Signs' (1990), 'Disputed Identities' (1990), 'The Empire's New Clothes' (1990) and 'Disrupted Borders' (1993) explored black photography in Indian, US and European diasporas. 'Photovideo' (1991) looked at the advances photography made in new technologies, while 'Photogenetic' (1995) explored the relationship between photography, visual art and film (see **film and cinema**). In this sense, the 1990s saw the blurring of the old oppositions of black/white, good/bad and documentary/avant-garde with the questioning of access to the means of representation and the relationship of black photographers to institutions. Visibility and exclusion remained important issues. What becomes most apparent in the 1990s is the historic role photography has played in the exploitation of racial difference. This becomes the major focus for many artists, as demonstrated in the exhibitions 'Fine Material For A Dream' (1992), a re-examination of Orientalism; 'The Impossible Science Of Being' (1995), a contemporary exhibition commissioning photographers to examine the early use of photography in anthropology, medicine and criminology; and 'In Visible Light: Photography and Classification in Art, Science and the Everyday' (Museum of Modern Art, Oxford, 1997). A culmination of this interest and perspective was shown in the Barbican show 'Africa by Africa' in 1999, which examined the last 100 years of photographic history through the eyes of African-born photographers.

Further reading

Bailey, D.A. and Hall, S. (eds) (1992) 'Critical decade: black British photography in the 80s', special issue, *Ten.8* 2(3).

Young, L. (1993) 'Identity, realism and black photography', in M. Sealy (ed.) *Vanley Burke: a Retrospective*, London: Lawrence & Wishart

DAVID A. BAILEY

Pine, Courtney

b. 1966, London, England

saxophonist, composer

Courtney Fitzgerald Pine taught himself to play the tenor saxophone at the age of fourteen. He left school at sixteen to join a **reggae** band and in the early 1980s set up his own seminal band the Jazz Warriors, which also launched the careers of a new generation of British jazz talent, including Julian Joseph, Cleveland Watkiss, Steve Williamson and Gary Crosby. In 1987, aged twenty-one, Pine signed to Island Records and released his debut album *Journey to the Urge Within*, which sold 100,000 copies, and he became the first jazz artist to crack the British Top 40 record charts. He is also renowned for incorporating Jamaican sounds into a heretofore purist art form. Since the mid-1990s, Pine has been signed to Universal/Polygram in the USA where his records sell a respectable 60,000 copies. During this period Pine became regarded as a British musical innovator incorporating the sounds of **hip hop** and drum and bass into jazz. He has also performed and recorded with major artists including Art Blakely, Elton John and Mick Jagger. Pine was the subject of an ITV *South Bank Show* documentary.

RAYMOND ENISUOH

Pinnock, Winsome

b. 1961, Islington, London, England

playwright, screenwriter

Daughter of Jamaican parents, Pinnock studied at Goldsmiths College before joining the Royal Court Young Writers' Group. Her plays address the experience of her parents' generation as immigrants, the economic pressures and dreams of the Mother Country that lay behind their migration (*A Hero's Welcome*) as well as the betrayal of their aspirations and forging of strategies for survival (*The Wind of Change* and *A Rock in Water*; the latter about the life of Claudia Jones). In *Leave Taking*, she explores the conflict between her parents' generation and her own, rejecting constricting definitions of achievement – academic and financial success – to struggle towards a new hybrid sense of black British identity that refuses victimisation.

Select bibliography

Pinnock, W. (1996) *Mules*, London: Royal Court Theatre/Clean Break.

—— (1990) *A Hero's Welcome*, in K. George (ed.) *Six Plays by Black and Asian Women Writers*, London: Aurora Metro.

—— (1989) *A Rock in Water*, in Y. Brewster (ed.) *Black Plays 2*, London: Methuen.

—— (1988) *Leave Taking*, in K. Harwood (ed.) *First Run 2*, London: Nick Hern Books.

Further reading

Croft, S. (1993) 'Black women playwrights in Britain', in T. Griffiths and M. Llewellyn-Jones (eds) *British and Irish Women Dramatists Since 1958*, London: Open University Press, pp. 84–98.

SUSAN CROFT

Piper, Keith

b. 1960, Birmingham, England

visual artist

As a student Piper met Eddie **Chambers**, who was already attempting to formulate black art. Subsequently, Piper helped Chambers organise the exhibition 'Black Art an' Done', the first exhibition to articulate Chambers's notion of black art. Piper, Chambers and other young black artists then exhibited under the name, the Pan-Afrikan Connection, and later as the **Black Art Group**. Piper went on to exhibit in almost all of the major black group exhibitions of the decade, and was arguably the best-known proponent of black art. Piper's use of text echoed earlier political art, but this was only one of many approaches and materials in his *œuvre*. His thematic concerns expanded in the 1990s to encompass black masculinity, the role of the Church in black culture and, most significantly, the implications of new technologies for black culture, a theme that still preoccupies the artist. His most recent body of work 'Relocating the Remains' has taken both real and virtual forms, with many of his pieces addressing the freedoms and constraints of new technologies for black subjectivity.

Further reading

inIVA (1997) *Keith Piper: Relocating the Remains*, exhibition catalogue.

NIRU RATNAM

Pitshanger Manor and Gallery

Founded in 1996, the Pitshanger Gallery is recognised as a co-operative arts complex that offers a variety of arts and crafts activities, as well as an extended cultural programme. The gallery has collaborated with important institutions, such as the **Institute of International Visual Arts**, with which it held the 'Avtarjeet Dhanjal Works 1970–1996' exhibition (1997). The show contained a collection of sculpture and drawings covering three decades. In the same year while working with the Organisation for Visual Arts it showed 'Facades: Views of Indian Architecture' to celebrate 50 years of Indian independence. The exhibition consisted of nineteenth-century photographs owned by the Canadian Center for Architecture as well as commissioned works by contemporary Indian artists Abul Azad, Dinesh Khanna and Ram Rahman. Furthermore, with **Autograph: the Association of Black Photographers**, under the heading 'Prejudice and Pride' it celebrated and commemorated **Windrush** in 1998. The exhibition '*Empire Windrush* Revisited 1948–1998', was mounted as part of the

BBC's *Windrush* initiative and reflected the experience and contribution of the Jamaican people in Britain. It also aimed to highlight the social and cultural contribution of all African-Caribbean people living in Britain. In the following year the exhibition 'Empire and I' was shown, in which nine contemporary artists assessed contemporary ideas of race and nation.

PAULINE DE SOUZA

Pollard, Ingrid

b. 1953, Georgetown, Guyana

photographer

Pollard gained a BA at the London College of Printing and then joined the groundswell of black women artists whose work rose to prominence in the early 1980s. Her early group exhibitions were as part of '**Black Woman Time Now**' (1983), Battersea, and 'Celebration of Black Women' (1984), Southall. She was a member of the influential **D-Max photography** group exhibiting in Birmingham's Ikon Gallery in 1987, where she exhibited her Lake District series, 'Pastoral Interlude'. In the late 1980s and 1990s, she has shown in both group and solo exhibitions in the UK, Europe and the USA, including the group show 'Interrogating Identity' (1991), Grey Art Gallery, New York, and the solo show 'Oceans Apart', Art-in-General, New York. Her work has consistently explored questions of nation, race and identity, for example, featuring photographs of black and Asian people in rural English landscapes, provoking questions about assumptions of space and belonging, and their relation to narratives of nation.

Further reading

Fraser, J. and Boffin, T. (eds) (1991) *Stolen Glances: Lesbians Taking Photographs*, London: Pandora Press.

ELEANOR BYRNE

post-bhangra

Post-bhangra is a catch-all term for the diverse range of Asian British **music** and performers who rose to prominence in the 1990s in the wake of the 1980s **bhangra** explosion. While the term post-bhangra may not be a definitive tag covering a set genre of music, it does highlight the importance of bhangra as a catalyst for a new generation of Asian British performers moving beyond the largely underground (in terms of mainstream culture) bhangra scene who were either influenced by bhangra or actively rejecting its influence. Media interest in Asian British popular culture, particularly music, in the second half of the 1990s has grown as audiences and critics became aware of the diverse range, not only of the Asian British community but of its youth cultures and art forms, after initially portraying the Asian community as being homogenous. This media portrayal of the musics of the Asian diaspora within Britain began to take the form of a rejection of bhangra, with the focus firmly upon the idea of the 'new Asian cool' and its implication that in the past Asians were both uncool and invisible, and that somehow the importance of the new generation of Asian British musicians, performers, DJs and producers lies in their distancing themselves from bhangra, or, at the very least, distancing themselves from an essentialised media view of bhangra. A number of influential post-bhangra movers such as **Outcaste**'s director Shabs Jobanputra have taken this route, telling *The Times* in August 1993 that 'It was never cool to be an Asian then.'

While it is true that the musical output of many of the post-bhangra acts has no roots or influence in bhangra music, it is equally true that much of the output does retain some influences from bhangra and many performers initially emerged from the bhangra scene. The diversity of the new music produced by Asian British artists, however, is limitless, going far beyond the experiments in fusing bhangra to modern musical styles such as techno, ragga and rap. Where bhangra is retained as an influence it becomes no more or less important than the other influences, which range from diverse sources such as punk, **Bollywood** film (see **film and cinema**) music, electro, ragga, **hip hop**, drum and bass, and classical Indian

music as well as bhangra to emphasise a depth of influences and creativity.

At the beginning of the 1990s, a new breed of Asian British performers began to create a wave of interest in their music, though for many bands their similarity lay only with their perceived ethnicity and their intent to provoke debate and to shatter illusions as to what kind of music critics and audiences expected Asians to make. Musically the bands were immensely disparate, with bands like **Cornershop**, Voodoo Queens and Echobelly being guitar based and performing to largely white audiences, while acts such as **Fun-da-mental**, KK Kings, Loop Guru and **Hustlers HC**, who encompassed a number of influences including hip hop and sampling in their sound, or others such as **Apache Indian**, **Babylon Zoo** and **White Town**, were firmly located within the mainstream of music, albeit briefly in the case of the last two. Fun-da-mental were perhaps the most overtly political of this new wave of Asian British bands using their music and interviews as a forum for the exploration of a range of local and global issues, and to take a strong stance against racism. Other acts emerged, often on the **Nation Records** label, who would espouse a political view similar to Fun-da-mental, including **Asian Dub Foundation**, while other performers preferred to be less overtly political in their lyrics and music, while simultaneously acknowledging that it was a political act to be an Asian British performer in a music scene not used to such an event. **Kaliphz**, an Asian British hip hop group, maintained a sense of their own identity in a scene dominated by artists trying to mimic African American idioms and styles, stating in the music weekly *Melody Maker* in December 1994 that '...you don't have to be like another race to be involved with hip hop....keep your own identity and bring your own flavour to the scene'.

As the 1990s progressed, the terms post-bhangra and 'new Asian cool' have lost a great deal of their potency though interest in Asian British cultures remains strong. Clubs such as **Anokha**, Outcaste and Sitar Funk have helped bring the music to the fore along with acts such as Cornershop who reached number one in the British charts in 1998 with 'Brimful of Asha', which was a playful tribute to the Indian singer Asha Boslie. Outcaste has also existed successfully as a record company dedicated to promoting Asian acts, including contemporary artists such as Nitin **Sawhney**, **Badmarsh** and **Shri**, and older artists including Ananda Shankar, who has been recording and performing since the early 1970s. The compilations *Untouchable Outcaste Beats* have played an important role in highlighting the important influence of Asian performers both past and present, along with Talvin **Singh**'s *Anokha – Soundz Of The Asian Underground* collection. The last years of the decade have seen bands such as Asian Dub Foundation and **Black Star Liner** becoming influential along with Cornershop, Talvin Singh and **Anjali**, while new artists such as Amar and the all-girl bands India, Spellbound and Trickbaby have been signed to major labels. These acts follow in the footsteps of Bally **Sagoo** and Apache Indian, two artists who have achieved worldwide success having emerged from the Asian British music scene. Bally Sagoo's roots incidentally lie firmly in the bhangra scene of the late 1980s and early 1990s, but it is the limitless influences that he brings to his best work which highlights the infinite possibilities of Asian British music post-bhangra.

Further reading

Huq, R. 'Asian kool? Bhangra and beyond', in S. Sharma, J. Hutnyk and A. Sharma (eds) *Disorienting Rhythms: the Politics of the New Asian Dance Music*, London: Zed Books, pp. 61–80.

ANDY WOOD

post-colonial space

The notion of post-colonial space refers to a set of discursive practices that aims at subverting previous colonial hierarchies. By enacting different ways of writing and reading, the post-colonial space forwards a politics of representation in which the former 'colonial-peripheral' subject can 'speak back' and offer alternative viewpoints on their situation and condition. The concept can be dated back to Edward Said's foundational text *Orientalism*, in which he explores how the West has represented, possessed and manipulated the Orient as 'other' in order to construct a positive image of the Western self.

Said's Foucauldian analysis of imperial discourse has been followed by an avalanche of further studies; among the most prominent are Homi **Bhabha** and Gayatri C. Spivak, who have concentrated on the representation of the post-colonial space as a re-articulation of the hegemonic relationship between dominant and subaltern groups. This binary opposition is visible within the world-wide relocations of cultures with the friction between processes of rapid globalisation, which foster assimilation, and countering phenomena of particularism, which safeguard local values and alternative identities. The result is the production of a heterogenous and diffused space that is not devoid of internal contradictions. The academic Anne McClintock finds the term 'post-colonialism' too suspicious because it is too prematurely celebratory of the so-called end of 'colonialism'. Furthermore, she fears that the term recentres global history around the single rubric of European time when used in its singularity. On the other hand, the Indian Marxist critic Aijaz **Ahmad** accuses McClintock of inflating the term to such an extent as to make it politically useless. The squabble around the nature and breadth of post-colonial space is symptomatic of the complexities of the colonial legacy, and of the difficulties of coming to terms with it in a language that does not reproduce dominant discourses. It is therefore essential to refer to post-colonial space while keeping in mind its internal differences and geopolitical discrepancies.

Further reading

Ashcroft, B., Griffith, G. and Tiffin, H. (eds) (1985) *The Post-colonial Studies Reader*, London and New York: Routledge.
Blunt, A. and Rose, G. (1994) *Writing Women and Space. Colonial and Postcolonial Geographies*, New York and London: the Guildford Press.
Loomba, Ania (1998) *Colonialism / Postcolonialism*, London and New York: Routledge.

SANDRA PONZANESI

Prasad, Udayan

b. 1953, Sevagram, Maharashtra, India

film director

Udayan Prasad grew up in an ashram in India and came to Britain when he was nine. He originally applied to read archaeology at Birmingham University but left to take a place at Leeds Polytechnic to study graphic design. He spent all of his time in the film department enjoying the excitement of cinema (see **film and cinema**). After graduation, he worked as a film technician and then went on to study at the National Film and Television School, Beaconsfield. Prasad's professional career began in documentaries and his credits include: *Arena: Invisible Ink* (1987), about Indian writers writing about the UK; and *A Corner of a Foreign Field* (1986), about lives of early Pakistani immigrants in Britain. However, he was frustrated that people began to see him as a director only capable of making Asian subjects and so he took a drama director's course at the BBC and moved into making **television** films, which he describes as 'eccentric English pieces'. He argues that there is no reason why he cannot make films about the English as he has lived in the UK and imbibed much of English values. His television films include: *Here is the News* (1989), starring Richard E. Grant as an investigative journalist; *Running Late* (1992), about the mad world of a television personality portrayed by Peter Bowles; and *102 Boulevard Haussmann*, about Proust. Prasad directed the feature *Brothers in Trouble* (1995), set in the 1960s, about eighteen Pakistani illegal immigrants struggling to survive in Bradford. He also directed ***My Son the Fanatic*** (1997), written by Hanif **Kureishi**. This film has been much commended in the British film industry as a sensitive portrait of human emotion and one with perfect comic timing. Prasad's most recent work is *Gabriel and Me* (2001), a comic fantasy about a little boy coming to terms with the impending death of a parent.

SUMAN BHUCHAR

Prescod, Colin

b. 1945, Port-of-Spain, Trinidad and Tobago

film-maker, academic, broadcaster

Prescod moved to the UK in 1958. He began his career in further education and was Senior Lecturer from 1969 until 1989 at the Polytechnic of North London, where he continues to lecture periodically. Prescod joined the BBC in 1989, and while there he moved from being producer to commissioning editor and then to Head of the African Caribbean Unit. As Head, he actively encouraged the production of a range of documentary, magazine and talk show programmes. Prescod is presently Co-project Director of the European Multi-cultural Media Agency (AMMA), an initiative that aims to give documentary awards to young Europeans. He also works as an independent film (see **film and cinema**) and **television** producer and consultant. He is chair of a number of committees including the Institute of Race Relations (London) and Board Director of the Association for the Cultural Advancement of Visual Arts (ACAVA).

Select bibliography

Prescod, C. (1997) 'Dealing with difference beyond ethnicity', in D. Lavrijsen (ed.) *Intercultural Arts Education and Municipal Policy*, Netherlands: Royal Tropical Institute.

SAMINA ZAHIR

Pressure

The film *Pressure* was directed by Horace **Ové** and co-written with novelist Sam **Selvon**. Made in 1974, it was the first black-produced feature film (see **film and cinema**) about black British experience, and the first to be funded by the **British Film Institute**. The film tells the story of Tony, a British-born black teenager, and his growing disillusionment with the racism of the society in which he finds himself. He drifts steadily into petty crime before getting involved with a Black Power organisation. The film works to articulate the politicisation of black British identity in the 1970s. *Pressure*'s documentary realism has been seen by a number of critics as exemplifying the dominant modes of black representation in that decade.

JAMES PROCTER

Pride

Pride magazine celebrates its tenth anniversary in 2001. It was launched as a quarterly magazine (see **publishing, newspapers and magazines**) to address the needs of black British women aged between twenty-five and thirty-four. Although it did not have the same glossiness as its US counterparts *Ebony* and *Essence*, it filled a void for black women in this country. *Pride* was once part of the Voice Communications enterprise, and Deidre Forbes, who moved from the **Voice** newspaper to editing the magazine, is credited with pioneering the magazine and developing its image. It featured the typical departments of fashion (see **fashion and design**), beauty and features, but from a black British perspective that made black women in this country visible. To date, it is the only black British women's 'glossy' of its kind and is now published monthly. The magazine's image was radically transformed when former *Voice* arts editor Dionne St Hill took over. She branded it with her own style and started the shift to making it glossier, and, soon, *Pride* did not look out of place beside its mainstream competitors. During the brief editorship of Joy **Francis**, it became more informative, investigative and could be compared with *Marie Claire*. Francis beat the nationals to exclusives with film-maker Guy Ritchie, and on the legalisation of prostitution in the Netherlands. She also convinced celebrity designer Wale Adeyemi to design special T-shirts, and Kanya King, MOBO's CEO, to sponsor them to raise awareness of, and money for,

breast cancer in the black community. Over twenty celebrities, including Richard **Blackwood**, attended a special photoshoot to model the T-shirts.

YINKA SUNMONU

Priest, Maxi

b. 1962, London, England

singer, songwriter

Born Max Elliot, Maxi Priest began his musical career singing live with the Saxon Sound System at **reggae** sessions. In 1984, he co-produced Philip Levi's groundbreaking 'Mi God mi King', the first British reggae recording to reach the top of the Jamaican charts, reversing the trend of Jamaican records dominating the British reggae charts. Maxi Priest's debut album showcased his talents as a vocalist and a songwriter, but it was with more pop-orientated albums such as 1987's Sly and Robbie-produced *Maxi* that he made his breakthrough. On subsequent albums, including *Man With the Fun*, Maxi Priest has deftly employed influences from reggae, **soul** and R'n'B. As well as collaborating with Sly and Robbie, Maxi Priest has worked with Shaggy, **Apache Indian**, **Soul II Soul** and Dennis Brown, and has set up his own label Dugout in order to promote new British acts. Maxi Priest's records have consistently charted around the world as well as in Britain and his songs have appeared on the soundtracks of films, including *How Stella Got Her Groove Back*. Maxi Priest also appeared in the film (see **film and cinema**) *Scam* along with the actor Christopher Walken.

ANDY WOOD

projects supporting black media talent

That the portrayal of black people in film (see **film and cinema**) and **television** continues to be seen as problematic is evidenced by the number of research studies, conferences, seminars and media-generated initiatives that have aimed to both identify the nature of the 'problem' and also offer some partial ameliorative strategies. The 1990s in particular have seen black representation on and in television taken up as an issue not just for individual nation states, but across Europe and beyond. Public broadcasting organisations have begun, slowly, to consider what they can do to halt the perpetuation of stereotypical portraits of black people. In 1992, for example, a conference was held in the Netherlands that looked specifically at public broadcasting for a multicultural Europe (PBME), with the express objective of developing a programme of action. Twelve countries sent delegates and, as a result of the conference, a number of pan-European collaborative projects were set up and a resolution put to the European Commission (EC) to take a number of actions, including funding a European Co-ordination Point to facilitate positive actions against racism and xenophobia in radio and television. One very visible outcome of the conference has been the publication of *Spectrum* magazine by PBME, intended to 'present a voice of reason and a campaigning voice in a continent increasingly afflicted by racial violence and intolerance of cultural difference' (*Spectrum* 1, 1993: editorial). The magazine (see **publishing, newspapers and magazines**) is distributed by the BBC TV Equal Opportunities Department and, by the summer of 1994, was already collecting material on European broadcast initiatives for inclusion in the third issue. *Spectrum* is produced with the help of a grant to PBME from the EC's EUROFORM Programme and the EC also funded, through its Horizon Programme, the Black European Media Project, which aimed to create employment and training opportunities for young black people in the European media industry. This one-year project (1992–3) was jointly supported by the Scottish Office. In 1995, PBME held a second conference to assess what the initiative had achieved over the past two years and what still needed to be done in the future.

Also in 1992, the **British Film Institute** (BFI) made two documentaries for the BBC, as part of the BBC's Black and White in Colour season, on the contribution that black people have made to British television. In November 1992, a conference

on the same topic – 'Black and White in Colour Conference: Prospects for Black Intervention in Television' – took place and explored specific issues such as multicultural programming, black international production and the disjunction between black comedy's success and the neglect of black drama. The following year, the International Broadcasting Trust and the Centre for Multicultural Education (Institute of Education) organised a conference, 'Can We Get it Right?', which explored representation issues in programmes and reports made about the developing world. As **Hall** points out, what the media 'produce' are representations and images of the social world, and frameworks within which to understand that world, and among the definitions offered by the media is one about 'race' (Hall, 1981). No matter how well-meaning and empathic a production team is towards the developing world or other issues that foreground blackness, it seems almost inevitable that it is 'race' that is seen as the problem rather than racism.

Parts of the television industry itself have developed a number of initiatives aimed at enabling black media practitioners and/or aspirants to place their feet on the bottom rungs of the professional ladder. The BBC, for example, set up the Television Training Trust (TTT) in 1990 (under Section 37 of the Race Relations Act) as a means by which people from black and 'ethnic minority' (see **ethnic minorities**) communities could be offered 'a chance to gain television production skills and pursue a career in programme-making' (BBC publicity material). This scheme has since been renamed the Television Production Trainee Scheme and is a general scheme for all-comers but with half the places (five) reserved for black candidates. This change has been prompted by the fact that within the BBC and by trainees themselves, the TTT scheme was seen as being of a lower standard/value than the mainstream training programme. The BBC has also offered the Technical Operations Bursary Scheme to enable black entrants to gain technical skills and twelve bursaries are made available each year. In January 1998, the BBC launched a mentoring scheme for black media professionals already working in the Corporation, in an effort to improve their poor staff retention record for black employees.

The BFI recently established an African Caribbean Film Unit within the Institute, which launched a new quarterly journal in 1993 – **Black Film Bulletin**. The *Bulletin* aims to keep readers up to date with the latest developments, projects and people involved in black film production, and features notice-board items as well as more reflective pieces. During the summer of the launch year, the *Bulletin* organised a summer screen celebration that highlighted the range of new work produced by black British film-makers, including film school and independent productions, television previews and trailers for new British and US commercial films. With more than 400 people attending the screening, it is clear that there is interest in black-originated work but, as Adepegba argues, the appetite (and, more importantly, the funding interest) is for commercial films that are popular and profitable. 'I'm not talking here about your avant-garde experimentalist Black film co-op types. Just mention their names and the investors are gone and the audience know enough not to show up'.

Although this is not an exhaustive list of positive action strategies, it does provide a few examples of the kinds of strategies developed to enhance the opportunities for talented black individuals to access the industry. This is not about special pleading but about equality of opportunity.

KAREN ROSS

publishing, books

The establishment of black publishers in Britain, unlike that of mainstream publishers, has not been a predominantly male domain. Some of the most ground-breaking works, and most commercially successful black publishing ventures in Britain, have taken place with women at the helm. In the 1960s, two of the forerunners were Jessica Huntley of **Bogle L'Ouverture** Press and Margaret **Busby**, co-founder of Allison & Busby. They made significant strides within the arena of book publishing, with the additional work of regularly hosting readings and events for black writers from the

USA, the Caribbean and Africa. Nor were their companies borne of any 'women's movement', as were women's presses run by non-black women in Britain at that time. Margaret Busby set up Allison & Busby with Clive Allison, soon after they graduated from London University in 1967. They published authors such as Chester Himes, George **Lamming** and Buchi **Emecheta**. Jessica Huntley approached her publishing career from a different stance. Radical and community publishing was popular when she started in 1969 and her writers were culturally and politically ground-breaking. Bogle L'Ouverture published dub poet Linton Kwesi **Johnson**'s acclaimed collection *Dread Beat and Blood*, in 1975, and were the first publishers to recognise the talents of the Mancunian/Ethiopian poet Lemn **Sissay**, publishing his second collection *Tender Fingers in a Clenched Fist*, in 1988. Other books such as Walter Rodney's *How Europe Underdeveloped Africa* (1972) and Andrew **Salkey**'s *Anancy's Score* (1973) made a strong impact on black **literature** internationally. Both of these women and their successes exemplified the possibilities for small and independent presses.

New Beacon Books was established in 1966, started publishing in 1967 and, like Bogle L'Ouverture in West London, established a bookshop in North London in 1973. This remains the premier black bookshop in Britain, run by John **La Rose** and Sarah White, and it is still seen as an institution and focus for black publishing and culture in Britain. Karnak House was started in 1979 to publish a wide variety of black writings. Their first publication in 1979 was *New Planet: Anthology of Modern Caribbean Writing of Poetry and Prose*. Other titles were award winners, including Grace **Nichols**'s *i is a long memoried woman*. Their titles explore African world communities in various disciplines, specialising in African science and philosophy. Other small publishers that emerged in this decade but which no longer publish include Karia Press, which published Caribbean authors based in the islands or Britain, such as Grenadian writers Jacob **Ross** and and Elean Thomas, supporting collections of poetry and prose, as opposed to novels.

Community presses flourished during this time too. An important outlet for black writers was a community centre, Centerprise, started by Glenn

Thompson, who eventually started Writers and Readers in New York. Centerprise Publications began in 1973, documenting the lives of individuals and community groups of black people in the East End of London. They published such books as *Word Up from the Women's Café*, and *Living and Winning* by Pauline Wiltshire. One community publishing house that remains in existence is Crocus Books, borne out of Britain's first literature development project, Commonword, in Manchester in 1986. Crocus Books launched two years later, mainly publishing anthologies and has scored success with such books as *Healing Strategies for Women at War*, works from seven Mancunian women poets such as **SuAndi**, Shamshad **Khan** and Maya **Chowdhry**, and *Kiss*, an anthology of love poetry. Pete Kalu, the Literature Development Project Worker who has overseen these titles, has since started his own small company, Mongrel Press.

Small publishers went through difficult times in the mid-1990s, finding it difficult to compete with the discounting of books, which occurred when the Publishers' Association decided not to uphold the Net Book Agreement in 1996. Large publishers began to buy up small presses and women's presses with strong backlists and integrated them as imprints. These included Little Brown's purchase in 1997 of Virago, Maya Angelou's UK publisher, who also published a landmark collection of writing by the **Asian Women's Writers Collective**, *Flaming Spirit* (1994), which included writing by Meera **Syal** and Rukhsana **Ahmad**. Despite these factors, other specialised publishers began to emerge as there was little material being published that reflected the lives and experiences of Britain's black population. For similar reasons, Nigerian novelist Buchi Emecheta also set up her publishing company, Ogwugwu Afo – the Great Survival – with her sons. They published her autobiography, *Head Above Water*, and one of her novels, *Double Yoke*, distributing the books themselves with great success. Emecheta strongly believes that black women must own their own presses and this is one reason why she signed over the rights of her children's books to SAKS Publications. One favourable change was that producing books became easier with the advance of technology, particularly desktop publishing. The hurdles that small presses still have difficulty in overcoming,

though, are obtaining reviews in the mainstream press and effective distribution of their books.

On their departure from the *Voice* newspaper, in 1991, Dotun **Adebayo** and Steve Pope set up the populist **X Press** publishers and scored an instant success with their first publication, *Yardie* by Victor **Headley**. Unlike some of the other small publishers, they successfully held on to their author and sold the rights to Pan. They used their journalistic experience and contacts to create publicity around themselves and, as a result, as Adebayo stated, the publishing house itself became better known than its books and authors, and therefore diversification into other areas was deemed necessary for their more 'literary' as opposed to populist authors. X Press have three other imprints: XPress Black Classics, which includes titles such as Ralph Ellison's *Invisible Man*; 20/20 for speculative fiction, not solely by black authors; and Nia, for their literary authors such as African American J. California Cooper. The Classics are an important source of revenue, since all the books are now out of copyright and therefore no royalties have to be paid to authors.

Throughout the 1990s, black women remained at the forefront of the publishing arena with the doyenne Jessica Huntley still publishing, albeit on a smaller scale. Verna Annette Wilkins started Tamarind, a multicultural children's books publisher in 1987. She began by writing and publishing the books herself, as she did not see enough representation of black figures in books for her children. Since then, Tamarind has won two awards and has expanded its remit to include representation of children with disabilities. Wilkins has also produced a series of books for BBC Television's *Science Challenge* series and expanded her product base to include puzzles and posters.

One of the most promising ventures was Angela Royal Publishing. Royal was an editor with Penguin for fifteen years before branching out on her own in 1994, with the intention to 'publish writers and books from around the world which challenge the cultural climate'. Her first book, *La Giraffe*, by French author Marie Nimier, was a finalist for the Prix Goncourt, France's biggest literary prize. ARP joined forces with literature promoters, the Write Thing, but the partnership folded within six months. Although not a 'women's press', her next two writers, Bernardine **Evaristo** and Leone **Ross** have become acclaimed black women writers in Britain. Their backlist includes a personal development book by Susan L. Taylor, editor in-chief of *Essence*, America's biggest selling black women's magazine, but the press has been dormant since the late 1990s.

Mango Publishing, founded in 1995, specialises in Caribbean texts with a particular focus on Caribbean women's writing, publishing both new and established writers. Their list includes a new series of texts in translation, some published as dual-language editions. They also publish the *Mango Season Journal* out of the **Caribbean Women Writers' Alliance**. Rosemary Hudson decided to specialise in black writers with her company, BlackAmber, launching her first title *One Bright Child* by Patricia Cumper early in 1998. Hudson's aim in starting BlackAmber was to add another dimension in different accents to the recorded British experience. The second author she published, Alex Wheatle, has since been taken up by a mainstream publisher, Fourth Estate.

Like Tamarind, SAKS Publications has specialised, steering away from novels to concentrate on exposing new writers through anthologies since 1996. Kadija (George) **Sesay** – who co-edited the ground-breaking *IC3: the Penguin Book of New Black Writing* with novelist Courttia **Newland** for Penguin – Saffi George and Stella Oni first published, *Burning Words, Flaming Images*, consisting of poetry and short stories by writers of African descent. Their second anthology, published in 1999, *Playing Sidney Poitier and Other Stories*, included both published and new writers, and this a trend they intend to continue, in-between showcasing writers with a litmag called *SABLE*.

Asian publishing houses such as Soma emerged alongside the better-known black ones, but Soma now only distribute and wholesale books. Indeed, **Mantra Publications** was the only independent Asian publishing house, including a wide selection of literature for Asian teenagers, until Aark Arts started publishing in the late 1990s. Aark Arts is a small literary publishing house for contemporary writing and multi-media arts. The award-winning poet, editor and literary columnist Sudeep **Sen** is the director and managing editor of the publishing house, which has a panel of editors and advisers who include practising writers, editors, critics, academics and artists. Sen gained his publishing experience in New York as an editor of a corporate consultancy firm, then as an assistant editor of a leading literary journal, *Boulevard*. Aark Arts was started to promote poetry and arts from across the world, especially younger and neglected writers. Sen has embraced the new and specialised targets for distribution without going through traditional distributors to be stocked in bookshops. This is a strategy that also eliminates the problem of returned books from retailers which are damaged and cannot be resold, which can be a significant financial loss for small publishers.

A significant number of these small publishers have been supported at some stage with funding for individual texts from London Arts (previously London Arts Board). **Peepal Tree Press** also received funding to set up their own printing press in Leeds. Like Karia before them, they publish Caribbean authors, most of whom still live in the islands or the USA, but, as yet, few black British-based authors except for the already established Beryl **Gilroy** and Evaristo's first poetry collection. The difficulties that small publishers face are primarily to do with the control of marketing and distribution. This problem grows alongside the advent of book chains and mega-bookstores, which do not provide the facility to deal with small publishers in terms of space, point of sale material and stock. These publishers are combating this through more innovative forms of publishing, utilising the Internet to overcome their other primary difficulties of marketing and distribution. SAKS publications, for example, were still able to secure funding from London Arts, even though they did not include a traditional distributor in their marketing mix. This has been necessary since the specialised distributors began to consolidate their network in the mid-1990s and were no longer willing to distribute books by publishers who produced only one or two titles a year that they considered had a short shelf life.

Small and independent publishers have suffered too, with the depletion of small bookshops, many of which have gone out of business. Small publishers, like large ones, have re-examined the aspect of printing in bulk and often prefer to reprint on a regular basis rather than stockpiling. The Internet has proven to be an excellent advanced information tool for small publishers. It provides a means of control over distributing books and information, not only for publishers but also for authors. Many have created interactive websites to stay in touch with their readership – maintaining a loyalty with current readers and targeting new ones. The Internet will be an increasingly important tool for small black publishers in marketing and distributing their books, and it is highly valuable to small and independent specialisation that is the trademark of the black publisher in Britain.

KADIJA SESAY

publishing, newspapers and magazines

Although newspapers and journals for Britain's black community emerged in the early twentieth century, and multiplied in the 1960s, they were not generally available nationally on news-stands until the early 1970s. However, the 1980s was a decade of expansion for black publishing (see **publishing, books**) in Britain, and general and specialised publications in business, news, women's and cultural politics, as well as glossy magazines, all emerged with an increasing slant towards consumerism rather than intellectualism. However, by the mid-1990s, it became apparent that the market that these publications were aimed at was not large enough, and not economically viable enough to support sales for so many publications. Many magazines were being produced by people who had little or no experience in journalism and misconceived beliefs that obtaining advertising revenue was easy. Although they would reduce costs by producing black and white magazines with colour covers or with eight colour page sections, without secure and adequate financial backing, and often with virtually no marketing budget, they were short lived and many hardly survived beyond their launch issues. The mid- to late 1990s was a time of consolidation, with a few publishing houses owning the most market-effective publications. With more trained black journalists, both through study and

opportunities, magazines and newspapers were produced more regularly and looked more professional.

Improved quality since the 1970s has also meant that it has become increasingly easy for journalists who wanted to use the black press as a stepping-stone into mainstream and broadcast journalism and writing careers. Nevertheless, the arena has been dominated by three groups: **Hansib Publishing**, Voice Communications and the Ethnic Media Group.

Guyanese-born Arif **Ali** is widely credited with establishing black and Asian publishing in Britain on a national basis when he launched the magazine *West Indian Digest* in May 1971 and relaunched the weekly newspaper, *West Indian World* in May 1973, which had been founded in June 1971 by Aubrey Barnes, and which survived under different ownerships until 1985 with little competition. In 1979, Ali launched another monthly magazine, the *Asian Digest*, and in the next decade, two newspapers, *Caribbean Times* and **Asian Times** in 1981. These papers effectively catered for two of Britain's largest minority communities and were complemented in the mid-1980s with the publication of *African Times*. Ali was the first publisher to train young black men and women at a time when mainstream press in Britain covertly avoided training or employing black journalists. Hansib provided black communities with their strongest media voice to date, which in effect also forced the mainstream press to include more black British content. Hansib sold its two newspapers in 1996 but continues to publish books and journals.

Ethnic Media Group's foundation was the **Eastern Eye** newspaper, started in 1989 by Sarwar Ahmed. A strong competitor to *Asian Times*, aimed more at a younger, Anglo-Asian market, they also bought **New Nation** newspaper in 1997. *New Nation* was started by Ghanaian businessman Elkin Pianim, son-in-law of media magnate Rupert Murdoch. With solid financial backing, it was considered to be the most viable competition to the *Voice* newspaper. Some of the most experienced new breed of black journalists were recruited to work on *New Nation*, enticing away some of the best *Voice* journalists and those from its sister paper, *The Weekly Journal*, which had been launched as a broadsheet in 1992 for Britain's growing black business and professional community, who rejected the *Voice* as a tabloid. *New Nation* was seated somewhere in-between, and was launched with much publicity and ceremony, yet lasted for just eleven months. Earlier in the last decade, another newspaper presented itself as a more up-market alternative to the *Voice*. *Black Briton* was launched by ex-deputy editor of the *Voice*, Joseph Harker, and was published from August 1991 to June 1992, ironically closing just two months after the *Voice* launched the *Weekly Journal*.

The largest selling black newspaper, the *Voice*, was launched in 1982 by Vee Tee Ay Publishing's four founders: Val McCalla, Viv Broughton, Alex **Pascall** and Robert Govender. The latter two departed very shortly after the paper started. Their objective in maintaining the *Voice*'s dominant market position has meant that during its life the publishing group has never shied away from using its resources to undermine other publications that were viewed as possible threats. This has included launching new publications, undercutting advertising rates, using similar visual and audio adverts and changing its publication day. It has maintained its position and is one of the few black British publications that can claim to be ABC audited, which has helped it to secure consistent major advertisers. Diversifying into other areas, the company became Voice Communications when it instigated and purchased various other magazines and supplements: *Chic*, *Now*, *Black Beat International*, *VS* and *Pride*. Yet by the end of 2000, Voice Communications retains only one product, the *Voice*, with falling sales, and, with claims of financial irregularities within the company, it had to cancel its annual community award ceremony.

The first black British lifestyle magazine was *Root*. Patrick Berry, Neil Kenlock, Godfrey Hope and Wayne Wilson published the first issue in October 1979. They recognised a gap in the market and collectively felt that the black community had a need for a sophisticated colour magazine. It worked and copy-cats began to flood the market. **Chic** was one of those that undercut *Root*'s advertising rates and, with its additional advantage of being distributed with an established and booming newspaper, it became increasingly hard for *Root* to compete. The largest area of revenue from black consumer products with an advertising budget came from African American hair-care products, and, with new publications on the market, they began to spread their revenue across the magazines. *Root* was sold to Hansib in 1987 and Patrick Berry and Neil Kenlock (who had been a photographer with the original *West Indian World*), eventually moved into broadcast media as the directors of Choice FM Radio.

Black Beauty and Hair is the longest running glossy magazine. Pat Petker and Robert Hawker bought it in the early 1980s from IPC Magazines and started publishing it under Hawker Publications in 1982. They also own the largest black trade and consumer exhibition, the Afro Hair and Beauty Show, which they took over from Pianim's Westminster Publications when he sold *New Nation* in 1998. Irene Shelley, its editor since 1987, has seen the black hair market expand and contract at various times, and, with it, advertising revenue. Therefore, *Black Beauty and Hair* has not only had to become increasingly professional to stave off competition from magazines such as *Pride* and *Black Hair*, but it has had to change format and include more fashion and some general features.

Pride magazine was initially launched by the four business minds of Peter Murray, William Ansong, Lee Morgan and Fay Williamson as a quarterly magazine in 1990, under the premise that, as they were 'Joe Public', they knew what Joe Public wanted. None of them were journalists but they had their own financial backing to produce a colour/black and white magazine on a quarterly basis and use freelance journalists. Controversial articles earned them a profile, yet, despite their well-meaning start, their *naïveté* and inexperience in journalism became more obvious, and affected sales. They eventually sold it to Voice Communications three years later, who changed it from a lifestyle to a women's magazine. Voice Communications only retained *Pride* for a few years, with their ex-arts editor Deirdre Forbes at its helm, successfully increasing its readership. When they decided to sell it, she attempted to organise a consortium to buy it out, but it was eventually bought by C.J. Cushnie.

Although the first black women's magazine, *Candice* from the outset was more concerned with women's self-improvement and cultural roots; the idea for it came from an educational magazine, *Wadada*, in the early 1980s. In 1989, its publisher, Rasheda Ashanti was ready to launch her women's magazine and was given a grant from the Department of Environment for her launch issue. Consecutive issues were sporadic as she received assistance from her local Hammersmith Economic Development Unit and Black Business Development Association. *Candice*, which then became *Candace*, was published until 1996, during which time Ashanti received several takeover offers (including one from EMG, which, if successful, would have given them a complement to their other ethnic publications).

Surwarh Ahmed's new company, Smart Asian Media, has also moved into the women's magazine market with his *Asian Woman*, a glossy magazine. Launched in June 2000 as a quarterly, Ahmed saw it as the most viable tool to market various products to its target market. Yet, despite consistent attempts to produce a British-based lifestyle and/or women's magazine, African American publications have remained more popular, particularly *Ebony* (lifestyle), *Essence* (for women) and *Ebony Man*. Britain's first black male magazine, *Untold*, came into being in 1998. Although much criticism is given to British magazines for having too much African American content, this is to be expected, because African Americanism is a pervasive presence in other areas of black British culture and the mainstream press.

Another trend in magazines was the more conscious and authoritative, community and cultural political magazines. The first of these was *Staunch*, started by Don Kinch in 1979 and published into the early 1980s. As it was the only publication of its kind, initially securing advertising from companies like Carlsberg did not prove a problem, but *Staunch* was soon overtaken by the increased number of magazines and newspapers on the market. The most successful and consistent was *The Alarm*, published by Alarm Promotions, from 1993, ceasing publication in 2000. Pascoe Sawyer and his partner Hazel Alexander also organised the monthly African Market Fair in North West London for almost the same period of time. Since *The Alarm*, *BLU Magazine*, a news-zine from New York, stepped in to fill that gap from a Brighton base.

Many of these magazines were run by editors who had other jobs and who relied on payments from advertising before the next issue could be published. The recession that hit Britain in the late 1980s and early 1990s affected their cashflow and therefore their regularity, which in turn prevented further major advertisers from considering them. Therefore, even those publications run on a commercial basis have had very difficult times and have sometimes successfully fostered other activities, such as book and directory publishing, award ceremonies, **music** management and broadcasting. Again, Hansib was the forerunner when, in July 1993, it published the *Ethnic Minority Directory*, with its comprehensive listing of all types of organisations and businesses in the community. In 1975, Hansib pioneered the first community awards, which spurred future organisations to hold awards that became fixtures in black Britain's social calendar.

Little known by the public, however, is the dominant presence that the Mirror Group have in Britain's black press. In the 1940s, they purchased *West Africa*, the oldest magazine, which had been started in 1917. They sold their interests in it in 1979 to the *Daily Times* in Nigeria, the state-owned and largest press organisation, who bought when their current editor, David Williams, made it known to Obasanjo's government that there was an imminent takeover bid by the apartheid South African regime, who wanted to utilise it as a propaganda tool. Now, they are the owners of South News, who also own Ethnic Media Group. As the ethnic population approximates a fifth of London's population (in East London, where EMG are based, they constitute approximately two-thirds of the population), the group see the multicultural market as a central area of expansion in readership. The largest and state-owned printing press in Ghana, the Graphic Corporation, bought *West Africa* in 1999 after it was put into liquidation. For the first time in its history, this politics and news magazine for English-speaking West Africans has an editor from a French-speaking African country, Senegalese Adama Gueye. To retain and attract a broader readership, *West Africa* has expanded to include more pages of entertainment and sports to attract a wider market base.

West Africa's longevity reveals the importance in Britain of those publications that have indigenous readers, quite often with significant readerships. With a large West African, particularly Nigerian, population in Britain, they have spawned their own news magazines, newspapers and magazines, too. Some, like Concorde Press, owned by the late president elect, M.K. Abiola, have a UK subsidiary office. Similarly, the Asian community have several own-language publications such as *Garavi Gujarat*, which have remained important for the older, migrant Asian population.

The new century saw the launch of on-line publications, most notably the black women's PreciousOnline and, for black music, darkerthanblue. com. With financial backing from Chrysalis, their expansion into broadcast media is just a matter of time.

Further reading

Benjamin, I. (ed.) (1995) *The Black Press in Britain*, Stoke-on-Trent: Trentham Books Ltd.

Hansib (eds) (1986) 'Arif Ali', *Third World Impact*, London: Hansib Publishing.

KADIJA SESAY

Puri, Om

b. 1950, India

actor

Om Puri is a character actor who has become an unlikely star in the West. His craggy pock-marked face and deep, penetrating eyes have turned him into a leading man for many of the new-wave English-language Asian films currently on the international circuit. Puri trained at the National School of Drama, Delhi, and at the Film and Television Institute, Pune. He started work in **theatre** and his film (see **film and cinema**) career began within the 'art movie' sector of Indian cinema. Two early outstanding performances were in Govind Nihalani's films: first, as the silent tribal accused of murdering his wife in *Aakrosh* (1980); and, second, as the frustrated policeman who cannot control his temper in *Ardh-Satya* (1983), for which he won the National Award for Best Actor. In 1989 Puri was given the Padma Shri (India's highest honour) by the president of India for his 'outstanding contribution to Value Based Cinema'. He has appeared in over fifty Indian films, including *Mirch Masala* (1985), *Mrityu Dand* (1997), *Chachi 420* (1998) and *Kunwara* (2000), and until the 1980s was a strong supporter of art cinema, refusing to star in **Bollywood** films.

Puri has also worked extensively in international cinema and his first international role was a cameo as the angry slum dweller in *Gandhi* (1982). Other credits include Hussain Shah in *Brothers in Trouble* (1996); Parvez, the taxi driver in **My Son the Fanatic** (1997), directed by Udayan **Prasad**; and the doctor in *Sam & Me* (1991), by Deepa Mehta. He played Ghulam in *Such a Long Journey* (1998) and also the tyrannical father, George Khan in **East is East** (1999), for which he received the Best Actor nomination by BAFTA and London Film Critics. In 2001, he finished a film in Wales entitled *Happy Now.*

SUMAN BHUCHAR

Q

Quarshie, Hugh

b. Ghana

actor

Quarshie came to England as a young child and read politics, philosophy and economics at Oxford University. He was also president of the Oxford Union African Society and the co-director of the Oxford and Cambridge Shakespeare Company. He took up journalism after graduating and went on to be sub-editor of the *West Africa Magazine*. He has since enjoyed a successful acting career in **theatre**, **television** and film (see **film and cinema**). On stage he has acted in *Julius Caesar*, *Faust* and *Macbeth*, among a list of many for the Royal Shakespeare Company, and has also played for the Oxford Playhouse, the Savoy Theatre and the Royal National Theatre. His television credits include *Medics*, *Rumpole of the Bailey* and *Surgical Spirit*, as well as two BBC Shakespeare productions *Titus Andronicus* and *A Midsummer Night's Dream*. He has appeared in *Nightbreed* (1990), *The Church* (1988), *Highlander* (1986) and *The Dogs of War* (1980), but is perhaps best known for his film role as Captain Panaka in *Star Wars: Episode I – The Phantom Menace*. As well as acting, Quarshie has co-directed *Othello* at the Greenwich Theatre and written a play, *The Prisoner of Hendon*.

Select bibliography

Quarshie, Hugh (2000) 'Conventional folly: a discussion of English classical theatre', in K. Owusu (ed.) *Black British Culture and Society: a Text Reader*, London: Routledge.

ALISON DONNELL

Quaye, Finley

b. 1974, Edinburgh, Scotland

singer

Of Ghanaian lineage, Quaye hails from a musical family: his father Cab Quaye was a jazz composer, and his brother Caleb Quaye played guitar with artists such as Elton John and Hall and Oates. His musical career began with a one-take voice track for **A Guy Called Gerald**, which inspired his interest in dub **music**. Other musical influences included the rather unorthodox New Yorker, John Zorn, alongside recognised greats such as Jimi Hendrix, Charles Mingus and Bob Marley. Quaye recorded his first solo outing on a four-track tape, for which he sang and played drums, bass and guitar. It was in June 1997 that he released the single 'Sunday Shining', which proved to be his first UK chart hit. The name acknowledged Marley's influence, taken from his track 'Sun is Shining'. Quaye's debut album, *Maverick a Strike* (Epic, 1997) offered a blend of **reggae**, dub, ambient, jazz and indie. The album charted well into the forties and featured a number of hit singles such as 'It's Great when We're Together', 'Your Love Gets Sweeter' and 'Even after All'. He was voted Best Male Singer at the 1998 Brit Awards.

His second album *Vanguard* was released with Sony in 2000 but did not achieve the same success.

SAMINA ZAHIR

queer theory

The most notable theorists in this branch of theory, dealing with gender, sexuality and the body, include Judith Butler (*Gender Trouble, Bodies That Matter*), Eve Kosofsky Sedgwick (*Between Men*; *The Epistemology of the Closet*), Jonathan Dollimore (*Sexual Dissidence*) and Alan Sinfield (*Cultural Politics – Queer Reading*; *The Wilde Century*). Eve Kosofsky Sedgwick describes queer as 'a continuing moment, movement, motive – recurrent, eddying, troublant', pointing out that 'the word "queer" itself means *across* – it comes from the Indo-Latin root *torquere* (to twist), English *athwart*'. As a practice it represents the 'gaps, overlaps, dissonances and resonances, lapses and excesses of meaning when the constituent elements of anyone's gender, of anyone's sexuality aren't made (or can't be made to signify monolithically' (Kosofsky Sedgewick 1994: 8). Broadly speaking, queer could be defined as a way of deconstructing identity categories (particularly those relating to gender) in order to render them unstable. Queer theorists set out to upset oppositions between gay and straight, homo/heterosexual, essence and construct, dominant and subordinate – a collapsing of binaries that Jonathan Dollimore calls 'sexual dissidence', or Judith Butler's 'gender trouble'. As a practice, queer is pre-eminently textual; it is akin to a deconstructive mode of reading and interpretation, and it is a refusal to signify monolithically. Queer is, as Sedgwick notes, a fraught term as well as a term that is freighted with meaning, an unstable subject position referring to a range of ontological and textual possibilities. It is important not to confuse queer theory with **identity politics**: while queer theory is certainly concerned with identity categories, it is concerned to unravel and destabilise them. Identity politics presupposes an essential,

stable identity, whereas in queer theory the subject is constructed, riven, fissured and contradictory.

Although queer theory has maintained its connections with **feminism**, there has been an increasing interest in 'race matters' in this field. Judith Butler's *Bodies That Matter* (1993) includes a chapter on passing and queering in the African American novelist Nella Larsen, while *Excitable Speech* (1997) draws out the parallels between race hate and homophobia in the legal profession and the army in the USA. Since queer theory subjects both ontological and biological **essentialism** to scrutiny, it has obvious relevance for theorists working on race and identity. In *Essentially Speaking* (1989), Diana Fuss's chapter, entitled '"Race" under erasure?' discusses the implications of essentialism for post-structuralist African American literary theory, pointing out that the deconstruction of 'race' has been one of the most contentious issues in the field in recent years and noting the predominance of materialism in African American literary theory. She urges the development of alternative and different theories in order to reassess the predominant ethnocentrism in this field.

References

Fuss, D. (1989) *Essentially Speaking: Feminism, Nature and Difference*, London: Routledge.

Kosofsky Sedgwick, E. (1994) *Tendencies*, London: Routledge.

Further reading

Butler, J. (1990) *Gender Trouble. Feminism and the Subversion of Identity*, New York and London: Routledge.

Kosofsky Sedgwick, E. (1994) *Epistemology of the Closet*, London: Penguin.

—— (1994) *Tendencies*, London: Routledge.

SARA SALIH

R

Race and Class

Formerly titled *Race*, this journal was first published in November 1959. Its new title, *Race and Class*, adopted from October 1974, reflected a change in emphasis towards issues of racism, Third World struggles and imperialism. Published on behalf of the Institute of Race Relations by Sage publications, *Race and Class: a Journal for Black and Third World Liberation* is a long-running quarterly journal dedicated to intellectual and political work around the issues of race, class and identity politics. The journal is edited by A **Sivanandan** and Hazel Waters, both of the Institute of Race Relations, London. It is both international and multidisciplinary in its scope, covering topics such as racism, legacies of empire, popular culture, globalisation and migration. The journal has recently focused on the issue of racism in Europe as well as the issues of refugees and asylum seekers.

ALISON DONNELL

Race Today

A vital publishing outlet and support network for many of the prominent black British writers, intellectuals, activists and performers of the 1970s and 1980s, *Race Today* was a key political and arts journal for the dissemination of black culture within the UK. The book press Race Today Publications published single-volume works by Linton Kwesi **Johnson**, Jean 'Binta' **Breeze** and Farrukh **Dhondy**, as well as political titles by Darcus **Howe**, John **La Rose** and others. The collective was a joint organiser of the Radical Black and Third World Book Fair and established the C.L.R. **James** Institute. The journal ceased publication in 1990 with a statement that 'This has been determined by the changes in the community and the changes in the world.' On the death of C.L.R. James, who had lived above their London offices, in 1989, they decided to concentrate on the publications of this great intellectual's works and the book list was changed from Race Today Publications to Black Jacobins Publications.

ALISON DONNELL

Radical Alliance of Poets and Players

Radical Alliance of Poets and Players (RAPP) was a 1970s Black Nationalist artists' collective of musicians, poets, and actors who recognised the inherent relationship between **music** and poetry and drew upon both art forms to compose their musico-poetic-dramatic performance pieces. Leading members of the organization include coordinator and director Shango Baku, bass guitarist, drummer and percussionist; Archie Poole, treasurer, tenor saxophonist, drummer, flute player and clarinetist; Judith Prescod, secretary, drummer, and percussionist and Winston Speede, organizer and flute player. Each member of RAPP combined their musical, poetic, and thespian skills with their ability to carry out various administrative duties for the group. RAPP was heavily influenced by the tenets of **Rastafari**, which were incorporated into their work. Underscoring the **Caribbean Artists' Movement**'s (CAM) black arts mantra of merging artistic creativity with political consciousness, RAPP created art which functioned as a tool for entertaining and educating the black masses within their local community and abroad. In 1977 the members of RAPP travelled to Nigeria where they participated in FESTAC. RAPP is most recognised for the publication *Dem A Come* (1978). Shango Baku also published *Writings from the Dread Level* (1976) and *3 Plays of Our Time* (1984).

TRACEY L. WALTERS

radio comedy

Although black comic performers first broadcast on the infant BBC during the mid-1920s, the profile of self-representative black radio comedy in Britain has been historically minimal to non-existent. 'Blackface' comedy, however, enjoyed a lengthy residency on both BBC radio and television, only disappearing from the airwaves in 1973 with the demise of BBC Television's *Black and White Minstrel Show*. Its popular radio comedy predecessor (running from 1933 to 1950) was *The Kentucky Minstrels*, which, while largely using 'blacked-up' performers, also featured the genuinely black American cross-talk double act of Harry Scott and Eddie Whaley. Although never maliciously racist, such early variety formats rooted in 'stage' minstrelsy traditions relied heavily upon obsolete and damaging stereotypes for their comedic effects.

Similarly negative and inaccurate representations of black characters retained a minimal presence within radio comedy for some decades. Tropical 'natives' such as Bigga Banga in *ITMA* (1939–49), for instance, added an element of 'harmless' exoticism to the regular cast of characters, and, as late as the 1950s, *The Goon Show* (1951–60) featured periodical appearances from singer Ray Ellington in roles that would now be considered unacceptably reliant upon colonial caricature. Even during the 1970s and 1980s, when black performers were beginning to make a

significant impact upon British television comedy, scant progress was made in the sphere of radio. Black comedy was the victim of a narrowcasting policy within the BBC, whereby the only dedicated outlet for speech-based entertainment was the culturally conservative Radio 4, which preferred to concentrate on its staple fare of white, male, middle-class sketch formats and sitcoms.

The breakthrough show for black radio comedy in Britain only came in 1995, when *The Airport* was broadcast on Radio 4. The impetus for creating the sketch-show-cum-sitcom came initially from within BBC Light Entertainment Radio, largely due to departmental embarrassment at having hitherto failing to innovate within the field of black comedy. The series' writing and performing team featured the talents of Jo Martin, Felix Dexter, Roger Griffiths, Eddie Nestor, Josephine Melville and Llewella **Gideon**, who played the disgruntled employees of the world's worst airport. Two series of four episodes were recorded at the Theatre Royal, Stratford East, to the evident approval of the show's live audience. However, the Radio 4 listenership offered a less enthusiastic response, finding *The Airport*'s robust and occasionally scatological humour too much to bear in a teatime slot. Essentially, the show failed to find its audience, producer Gareth Edwards later observing that the overlap between the show's live fans and the pre-existent Radio 4 listenership had been regretably small.

Furthermore, while *The Airport* generated favourable press coverage for both the BBC and the show's participants at its time of broadcast, its long-term influence within British radio was limited. Certain personnel from *The Airport* have continued to contribute to BBC output. Roger Griffiths and Eddie Nestor were among cast members who subsequently appeared in Martin **Glynn**'s 1997 basketball sitcom *Double Dribble*, while Llewella Gideon starred in Lisselle Kayla's 1998 media-based sitcom *The Emerald Green Show*. In 2001, Radio 4 broadcast a four-part series by Llewella Gideon (with Lynn Peters) called *The Little Big Woman Show*. In common with much emergent comedic talent, however, young black performers are more frequently approaching an increasingly de-regulated and accessible television industry rather than serving a 'traditional' apprenticeship in radio.

HUW BUCKNELL

raggamuffin

This subculture originated in Jamaica in the late 1980s in response to the island's plummeting socio-economic climate. Though the philosophy professes to be a non-violent 'creative system within the system', the acceleration of gun and gang culture associated with raggamuffin has overshadowed this position. This is reiterated by clothing and accessories worn by raggamuffins: 'gun-shot' or bullet hole jeans worn, by men and women, attained iconographic status when worn by the ragga artist Shabba Ranks. In Britain the subculture augmented the continued disaffection among black people, particularly the youth of Caribbean, African and Asian descent. The ragga dress style is marked by the clear demarcation between the sexes, using dress to heighten the visibility of their sexuality. The dress for men was click suits, shredded or patchwork jeans, long velvet shirt with matching baggy trousers, leather parka, linen trouser suits with contrast-coloured panels, lycra vests, linen suits with lace back panels, argyle socks with diamond studs, gold-cap teeth, baseball caps with Rastafarian (see **Rastafari**) colours and gun pouches. Female counterparts accessorised with giant 'Kiss Me' gold ear-rings, body-conscious lycra clothing with slashes or tears, bra tops, suits in viscose or denim with numerous rows of fringing, brightly coloured fishnet tights, PVC clothing and 'batty riders' and severely cropped shorts. Also popular were intricate hairstyles or wigs and hair-pieces, festooned with hair decorations, ringlets and finger perming – with a particular fixation on coloured hair. Items shared by men and women were meshed and slashed T-shirts or vests, large and extensive amounts of gold jewellery, face piercings, gold-capped teeth and bandanas tied around the head.

CAROL TULLOCH

Rana, Mah

b. 1964, London, England

jeweller

Mah Rana graduated from the Royal College of Art in 1989, after completing her first degree at Buckinghamshire College. In 1995 she was a finalist in the Jerwood Prize for Jewellery. Her jewellery and art pieces have been exhibited continuously in Britain, the rest of Europe and the USA. Her work encompasses production ranges sold through major department stores, fashion and couture commissions, as well as installation pieces in which Rana explores the symbolic meanings of jewellery. Her installation work is particularly telling in her transformation of second-hand wedding rings. The 'ready-made' gold with its evocative resonances is fabricated into a variety of narrative objects (halo, thorny twig, toothless comb), which are then placed within three-dimensional tableaux. The title of each work conjures up a particular aspect of experience, such as 'Have you ever dreamt your teeth have fallen out?' (1998) or 'I never promised you a rose garden' (1996). In 1997, Rana was a co-founder of the BRICK Arts Organisation, funded by the Arts Council of England and the London Arts Board, to promote artists and art projects using specially designed cube boxes as exhibition sites. Her work is held by several major public collections, including: the Crafts Council, London; the National Museum of Scotland, Edinburgh; the Birmingham Museum and Art Gallery; and the Nottingham Castle Museum.

LINDA SANDINO

Rana, Samena

b. 1955, Pakistan; d. 1992,
    Buckinghamshire, England

artist, curator

Samena Rana came to England at the age of twelve for treatment at the Stoke Mandeville Hospital after an accident. The accident was to leave Samena permanently (dis)abled and throughout her life she dedicated part of her infamous energy to challenging attitudes towards (dis)ability and helping to create access for artists with (dis)abilities. Her tireless campaigning helped contribute to the policy shifts at the **Institute of Contemporary Arts** (London), the Camerawork Darkroom and at the University of Westminster. During the later part of her life, Samena created a seminal piece of work, cast out of memory that sought to defy and challenge. 'The Flow of Waters' was a vast documentation and recantation about (dis)ability, as a movement, as a convention of representation and an articulation of difference and beauty. The exhibition was initially curated by Sunil **Gupta** for the 'Disrupted Borders' (1994) exhibition at the Photographers Gallery, London, and then by Shaheen **Merali** and Alan **de Souza** for 'Crossing Black Waters', at the City Gallery, Leicester, and a tour. Her work has been shown in several exhibitions, including: 'Darshan' (1985), Camerawork; 'Keepin' it Together' (1992), the Pavillion, Leeds; 'Out of India' (1997), Queen Museum of Art, New York City; 'Crown Jewels' (2000), Kampnagel, Hamburg, and NGBK, Berlin. The Samena Rana Archive is held in part of the **Panchayat** Archive, University of Westminster.

SHAHEEN MERALI

Randhawa, Ravinder

b. 1952, India

writer, activist

Ravinder Randhawa is the founder member of the **Asian Women Writers' Collective**. Her first novel, *A Wicked Old Woman* (1987), follows Kulwant Singh's escapades as she challenges the Orientalist fantasies of ex-boyfriends and Labour Party comrades, and attacks the complacency of 'yuppie' sons and race-relations officers. Kulwant finally finds community in a group of women who overcome differences as they fight against popular misrepresentations of their South Asian British identities. Randhawa's second novel *Hari-Jan* (1992) provides a comic look at life through the teenage eyes of a British Asian girl, Harjinder Singh, as she tries to outwit her conniving mother,

her 'boyfriend', the maddeningly attractive Suresh and the dastardly duo, V.T. and Shakuntala. Both novels confront issues of race, class and gender, and celebrate inter-racial friendship and romance. Randhawa has also been published in anthologies like *A Girl's Best Friend* (1988). All Randhawa's fiction mixes colloquial English with smatterings of Hindi slang and references to Anglo-American popular culture, which helps to represent the hybrid identities she celebrates.

Select bibliography

Randhawa, R. (1992) *Hari-Jan*, London: Mantra.
—— (1987) *A Wicked Old Woman*, London: Women's Press.

ASHA SEN

Raphael, Alistair

b. 1966, Kent, England

artist, arts adviser

Raphael studied at Canterbury, Falmouth and Chelsea art colleges. He now lives and works in London, where he acts as senior programmer for the Whitechapel Gallery. Born of Indian parents, Raphael uses photographic processes and diverse materials to respond to, and form a dialogue with, specific sites and contexts. Information 'about' the body and information 'in' the body, the passage of time and a preoccupation with the coded procedures of science, medicine and technology are recognisable features of his work. Raphael has referred to AIDS, architecture, homosexuality and immigration-as-pestilence while speaking of 'mapping biology onto buildings' and 'the institution as diseased'. Dismissing the habitual subject–object relation of the standard art-encounter he often attempts to surround or implicate the viewer, and it seems therefore appropriate that a parallel career as an arts adviser and educator has elevated him towards responsibility for the workings of the institution as a whole. His exhibitions include: 'Four by Four Post-Morality' (1990), Cambridge Darkroom; 'Hygiene' (1997), IKON Gallery; 'You Don't Know Me but . . .' (1998), Pitshanger

Manor; 'Maps Elsewhere' (1998), **Institute of International Visual Arts**/Beaconsfield; 'To Be Continued...' (1999), New Art Gallery, Walsall; and 'Cities on The Move' (1999), Hayward Gallery.

Further reading

(1992) 'Interview with Sonali Fernando', *Bazaar* (autumn).

Raney, K. (ed.) (2000) *Show and Tell: Visual Literacy and the Art Curriculum*, London: Middlesex University/Routledge.

Raphael, A. (ed.) (1999) *Artists In Research*, London: inIVA.

PAUL O'KANE

Rastafari

Edward Said has defined Rastafarianism as 'an interpretive community' to accommodate its various categorisations: a cult or a sect, a religion or political organisation, a subculture or a streetstyle. Ostensibly, it is a religion that emerged in Jamaica in the early 1930s out of the teachings of Leonard Percival Howell, Archibald Dunkley and Joseph Hibbert. Howell, for example, wanted Jamaicans to turn their allegiance to Haile Selassie I who had been crowned Emperor of Ethiopia on 2 November 1930. The political references of the movement derive from their associations with the views of anti-colonialists such as the Jamaican publisher Dr Robert Love, who in 1901 advocated in his newspaper *The Jamaica Advocate*, 'Africa for the Africans'. The movement is not a homogeneous entity, but comprises four tribes: the Nyabinghi Order; the Ethiopian Orthodox Church, established in Jamaica in 1969 with branches in London at the same time; the Ethiopian National Congress; and the Twelve Tribes of Israel established in Trench Town, Jamaica, in 1968. The essential belief of Rastafari is that: Haile Selassie I is the Head of their family; Africa is the homeland of all black people; and Marcus Garvey was a living prophet. Among the Twelve Tribes of Israel, repatriation to Africa is fundamental belief. During the 1970s, Rastafarianism attained international

recognition through the evocative and political overtones based on the above, communicated by **reggae** artists associated with the movement, such as Bob Marley and the Wailers, Big Youth, Burning Spear, and by the Rastafarian aesthetic, which augmented the Black Consciousness and Black Power movements of previous decades. This combination of elements was attractive to black men and women in Britain, who found a vehicle to reclaim their 'blackness' in the face of the racism and alienation they experienced.

Dress styles varied enormously, but there was strong emphasis on the wearing and eating of natural goods. During the late 1970s and early 1980s, the mainstay of the Rasta uniform for a 'King' and a 'Queen' was army surplus garments: berets, khaki army shirts, trousers and jackets. In addition, more orthodox clothing such as denim shirts and jeans, leather bomber jackets, track-suits and trainers were worn. The cultivation of dreadlocks, though not essential to define an individual as a Rasta, was none the less a symbolic icon of Rastafarianism. The Rasta 'Queen' wore cotton 'African' fabrics with, perhaps, a matching headwrap or crocheted hat. The Rastafarian colours of red, for the one and only true church – the Church Triumphant; gold, for 'the wealth of the land'; and green, for 'the rich luxuriant land that is Africa' were ubiquitous around the body in knitted or crocheted 'tams', wrist-bands, scarves, plaited or knitted waist ties, jumpers, braces, T-shirts, epaulettes or badges. The colour black is sometimes added to the trilogy to signify the people of the African diaspora.

CAROL TULLOCH

Rebel MC

b. 1965, London, England; d. 1997, London, England

MC, DJ, performer, producer

Rebel MC (Michael Menson) was co-founder of the **reggae** sound system Beat Freak before joining Double Trouble, who had a hit with the pop/**ska** crossover single 'Street tuff', and then embarking upon a solo career. Despite initially being marketed to pop audiences as the UK's answer to the risible MC Hammer, Rebel MC's **music** was less smooth, with his reggae roots and influences coming to the fore with a mix of ragga, fast-style, rap and roots reggae. Typical Rebel MC lyrical concerns included poverty, oppression and social injustice, as highlighted on the single 'Rich and getting richer'. Rebel MC's debut solo album *Black Meaning Good* was released in 1991 and featured contributions and collaborations from reggae artists such as Dennis Brown and Barrington Levy. A second album *Word, Sound And Prayer* came out in 1992. Rebel MC worked with publications such as *The Face* to promote anti-racism and was actively involved in the Musicians against the War campaign during the Gulf War. Rebel MC had also set up his own record label and production company, Tribal Bass.

Michael Menson died in February 1997 in North London, two weeks after being covered with petrol and set alight in the street. Police initially treated his death as suicide but began a murder investigation following pressure from his family and an inquest verdict. Two men were later convicted and deputy assistant commissioner John Grieve – head of the newly formed Racial and Violent Crimes Taskforce – described his killing as 'an unprovoked racist murder'.

ANDY WOOD

reggae

While it is universally acknowledged that reggae is an immensely popular musical form that origi-nated in Jamaica, it is important to remember that its popularity, impact and influence in Britain has, over the past four decades, been more than that of producer–consumer. British producers and artists have at various points achieved success in Jamaica as well as in Britain and further afield, while often pioneering new strands in the music that could not have happened anywhere else. Even today, reggae's influence can be heard in musical forms such as **jungle**, as well as in more traditional forms.

The first sound systems (see **sound system DJs**) started in Britain in the early to mid-1950s. As with the Jamaican sound systems, they predominantly played US R'n'B imports and it was not until the 1960s that British sound systems began to play Jamaican imports, as the records became more readily available. As with the Jamaican scene, certain sound systems would link up with studios or producers to gain exclusive access to their records. Duke Vin's sound system, one of the first British sound systems in the 1950s, linked up with Sir Coxsone Dodd's Jamaican Studio One. With the growth of sound systems playing **ska** and roots reggae came a new and often mixed audience. Many Jamaican producers, always keen to find new markets for their **music**, began to record tracks aimed specifically at the British audiences with singles such as 1969's single 'Skinhead moonstomp' by Symrapip, which was particularly popular among the predominantly white skinhead culture. While the reggae scene centred around the sound systems, specialist shops and labels such as **Trojan Records** and Pama were thriving. However, the mainstream market, media and radio largely ignored the reggae scene despite the success of records such as Desmond Dekker's 'Israelites', which topped the charts in 1969. Many reggae records sold incredibly well but were often ignored or were poorly represented in the charts as their sales were largely outwith the main chart return shops.

In the early 1970s, there was a growth in the number of UK-produced reggae releases and groups, along with a proliferation in independent record labels. While many of the established sound systems chose to ignore these indigenous produc-tions, often rejecting them as poor imitations of the original Jamaican sound, groups such as Matumbi, **Aswad** and Black Slate had recorded several popular and credible records by the mid-1970s. Matumbi, led by Dennis Bovell, were particularly influential. Having started out playing live at a variety of sound system nights, Bovell then set up his own Sufferers HiFi sound system, at which Matumbi would also perform live. Matumbi had begun recording for Trojan but had departed the label shortly after the company insisted on issuing the band's cover of Hot Chocolates' 'Brother Louie', which Bovell claims was recorded as a joke. Trojan chose to release a cover version rather than one of Matumbi's own compositions in order to market the band to a pop audience. Matumbi departed Trojan to pursue their own vision of reggae. Trojan, which had failed to build upon its earlier successes catering to a by-now diminishing market for crossover reggae/pop, folded in 1975, largely through its failure to evolve.

Despite some resistance to UK productions, many of the newer sound systems played predominantly British reggae; some through choice, others through necessity as new Jamaican releases became harder to find. The British scene began to differ dramatically from the Jamaican scene in a number of ways. Many of the bands embraced the live performance as an integral part of their ethos, whereas the majority of the Jamaican bands were still show bands, largely playing **soul** and pop covers. As the decade progressed, the lyrical concerns of British reggae performers became concerned with issues and events relevant to their lives in Britain along with questions of culture and identity. Finally, the album began to eclipse the single as UK reggae's medium.

Contemporaneous with the growth of a more militant, roots strand of UK reggae was the growth in popularity of **lovers' rock**, a more melodic and polished form of reggae that re-introduced American soul influences to the music. Lloyd Coxsone had been introducing soul records during sets with his sound system Sir Coxsone International and enlisted Dennis Bovell to record a version of 'Caught in a lie'. Using British-born musicians in preference to established Jamaican stalwarts, Bovell began to develop a new strain of reggae that would, in time, become a recognisably original British style. Louisa Marks had a huge hit with the track and others would follow. The term 'lovers' rock' was coined later, after Bovell used it as the name for one of his labels. Lovers' rock was perceived as being a purely female form, although many male performers recorded lovers' tracks. However, at one stage in 1980 alone, there were thirteen female lovers' rock records in the reggae Top 40. Parallel to the rise of lovers' rock was the continued growth in popularity of the more rootsy groups such as Steel Pulse, **Misty in Roots**, Aswad and Matumbi. These bands were to achieve success during the punk era as live audiences took them to their hearts. It is often argued that their success came through their acceptance by punk audiences and association with events such as the **Rock against Racism** concerts but, by the 1976 to 1978 period, many of these bands were already well-established. Matumbi had sold well in excess of 100,000 copies of *Man in Me*, while Steel Pulse's debut album *Handsworth Revolution* was fast on its way to becoming one of the most successful reggae albums released. Still, exposure to new audiences did not harm the bands and the influence of reggae upon punk was far more pronounced. The Clash covered Junior Murvin's 'Police and thieves' on their debut album before decamping to Jamaica to record with Lee Perry, Dennis Bovell produced the debut album *Cut* for the all-female group the Slits, while the Ruts recorded an album *Rhythm Collision Dub* in collaboration with the **Mad Professor**. Outwith lovers' rock, reggae was still a largely male-dominated form, though female artists began to emerge towards the end of the 1970s. Ranking Ann, Lorna Gee and Olive Ranking all tasted success in the male-dominated roots arena while Culcha Posse rose to prominence as the first female-ran sound system. Dub poets such as Jean 'Binta' **Breeze** emerged, who were in turn influenced by Linton Kwesi **Johnson**, who recorded a series of influential albums, largely with Dennis Bovell's Dub Band, and remains a popular live performer in Europe.

As the music scene changed, many reggae bands struggled into the 1980s, though by changing their style or touring outside Britain some remained successful. Aswad began to embrace a more pop approach, though they still released the *Aswad In Dub* album recorded with the legendary dub producer and sound system operator **Jah Shaka**. Dub, with its reliance on the studio, continued to thrive with releases from Mad Professor, Jah Shaka and Twinkle Brothers, among many. The reliance upon the studio and its associated technology would set the agenda for British reggae's next change. With the influence of **hip hop** and street culture came the 'fast-talking originators' such as **Smiley Culture** and **Tippa Irie**. Emerging from the sound system culture, these MCs developed new lyrical approaches that had more in common with the involved, often humorous message raps of US artists such as Grandmaster Flash. These lyrics came with a particularly British slant as highlighted on tracks such as Smiley Culture's 'Cockney translation' and Tippa Irie's 'Complain neighbour'. Fast-talking had much in common with Jamaican **dancehall**, which relied less upon musicianship and more on studio trickery and the prominence of the MC. The fast-talking era was short lived but spawned a number of hits and successes, and again was seen as an almost uniquely British genre.

From the mid-1980s British reggae became less influential and Jamaican artists and styles have re-asserted their dominance. Small labels and inde-pendent producers such as Neil (Mad Professor) Fraser's Ariwa Sounds, **Greensleeves**, **Fashion Records** and On-U-Sound have thrived, with Greensleeves in particular embracing the ragga scene. The rise of the rave scene has thrown up a number of acts who are as influenced by reggae as they are by techno, acts such as Zion Train and Dreadzone, while the Mad Professor has remixed the likes of **Massive Attack**. Strands of reggae can be heard in jungle, in the music of **Tricky**, **Asian Dub Foundation** and even in the music of white bands such as the Boo Radleys, who employed Augustus Pablo to remix tracks. There are still numerous thriving sound systems operating throughout Britain, while organisations such as Culture Promotions run the Dub Club in London and have promoted reggae performances at main-stream music festivals around Britain and further afield. Labels such as Pressure Sounds, Trojan and Blood and Fire have been responsible for re-issuing many classic reggae albums to a growing audience. While British reggae's influence in the charts may be negligible, its influence upon the music scene has been immeasurable.

Further Reading

Bradley, L. (2000) *Bass Culture. When Reggae Was King*, London: Penguin.

Hebdige, D. (1990) *Cut 'n' Mix. Culture, Identity and Caribbean Music*, London: Comedia/Routledge.

ANDY WOOD

Reneau, Francis

b. 1953, Belize

concert pianist, composer, teacher

Reneau was born in Belize, and learnt to speak Spanish and Russian alongside English. He began his musical education in 1971 when, having won the Swiss Foundation Scholarship to the Guildhall, he undertook a course of **music** there. During his time at the Guildhall (1971–6), Reneau distin-guished himself by winning a number of major prizes. His talent was also recognised in national competitions during this period. In 1974, he won a Gold Medal at the Royal Overseas League Competition. He won a British Council Scholar-ship in 1997, enabling him to attend the Moscow Conservatoire, where he completed his musical education and training. Reneau subsequently undertook a teaching career in various institutions. From 1991 he practised as a Professor of Piano both at Colchester Institute and at Watford School of Music. He was also a Professor of Piano at Trinity College of Music and returned to the roots of his musical training when he worked as a Professor of Piano at the Guildhall School of Music. As a concert pianist, Reneau has performed in a wide variety of venues nationally and internationally, including the Wigmore Hall and La Scala Recital Hall, Milan. Reneau's contribu-tion to inner-city community life in Britain is impressive. Since the 1970s, he has been involved in the musical life of local schools in Brixton and he is to be found most Sundays playing the organ in a local church. He has also written several composi-tions: *Mass in Blues* (1971), *A Mass for the Church of England* (1974) and *Celebration* (1997). Reneau has been nominated for an MBE for his contribution to music.

AN'YAA ANIM-ADDO

Retake Film and Video Collective

Retake Film and Video Collective was set up in 1982 by Ahmed and Mahmood **Jamal**, as an ACTT-franchised workshop. It was the only Asian franchised workshop with a remit to provide a contemporary focus for Asian culture through the media of film (see **film and cinema**) and video. The workshop made productions, was a facilities resource and undertook training and exhibition work. Retake was based in Camden and some of its documentaries dealt with issues specific to the borough. The first, *Living in Danger* (1984), highlighted racial harassment of tenants on a local housing estate, while *An Environment of Dignity* (1985) examined the provision for ethnic elderly people in Camden. Retake made the feature film *Majdhar* in 1984, written and directed by Ahmed Jamal. The story dealt with a young Asian woman, Fauzia, played by Rita **Wolf**, who is abandoned by her husband after her recent arrival from Pakistan. This separation frees her from the more repressive aspects of Asian culture and the film focuses on the relationships she forms across social and cultural barriers that shape her personality. The film was shown at many festivals and was arguably the first film to represent modern British Asian identity.

During its seventeen-year history, Retake produced many campaigning videos on social and welfare rights issues, ran courses on Indian and Iranian cinema, and offered practical technical training for Asians wanting to enter the media. Other ground-breaking programmes were *Sanctuary Challenge* (1985), made with Theatro-Technis, documenting the struggle of two Cypriot refugees fighting a deportation order, and *Hotel London* (1987). This drama dealt with the effects of the housing crisis in the capital and was shot in bed and breakfast accommodation used by councils after months of research with homeless families. It starred Jonathan Pryce, Alpana Sen Gupta and Aftak Suchak. *Who Will Cast the First Stone?* (1988) dealt with the issue of the Zina ordinances of Pakistan, which affected women adversely, and received the Golden Gate Award at the 33rd San Francisco International Film Festival for the Best of Category (broadcast television sociology). In 1988, Retake won the **British Film Institute** Award for Independent Film and Video.

SUMAN BHUCHAR

Richards, Derek

b. 1963, UK

artist, musician, multimedia producer, founder and director of HyperJAM

Derek Richards has emerged as a key cultural player in the arts and digital media arena. While facilitating several art and training projects for Artec, Richards developed the critically acclaimed CD-ROM piece 'Permanent Revolution Part 1', which has been exhibited nationally and internationally. Richards co-founded Digital Diaspora in 1994, an organisation established to stage projects and events that address issues of race within the development of 'new media'. In 1995, Digital Diaspora staged 'Digital Slam', an event linking the Kitchen in New York with the ICA in London by ISDN for a series of real-time collaborations. It was acclaimed by the media as the 'world's first transatlantic jam session'. In 1996, Richards collaborated with a number of artists to form Displaced Data, and this organisation curated 'Translocations', an exhibition of digitally produced and interactive work by artists of colour for the Photographers Gallery, London. For this exhibition, Richards collaborated with Keith **Piper** to create 'Permanent Revolution Part II', a walk-through environmental installation. Richards founded HyperJAM in October 1997, bringing his experience and expertise to the staging of unique events and the provision of multimedia-content production services (see **live art**).

CATHERINE UGWU

Riley, Joan

b. 1958, St Mary, Jamaica

writer

Riley left Jamaica for Britain as a young woman and gained a BA from the University of Sussex in 1979, and an MA from London University in 1984. As well as writing powerful socially engaged works, Riley has always been active in community work and has worked in drugs advice and on women's issues. Her novels – *The Unbelonging* (1985), *Waiting in the Twilight* (1987) and *Romance* (1988) – all focus on the lives of women of Caribbean descent in Britain. *The Unbelonging* documents the difficult and painful transition that Hyacinth must make in settling in Britain with her father and narrates her encounters with racial and sexual oppression, abuse and mental illness. *Waiting in the Twilight* takes the perspective of an elderly woman looking back on her life and her struggles against a racist culture. *Romance* looks across the generations in a more positive way as the two maturing female protagonists reflect on the strong cultural heritage that they have been given by their grandmothers. Riley has commented that her works are meant to represent black people as 'neither all good nor bad but a very real part of thinking, feeling, uncertain humanity'. In 1992, Riley was awarded the *Voice* Award for Literary Excellence and Literary Figure of the Decade, and, in 1993, she won the MIND Book of the Year Prize for *A Kindness to Children*.

Select bibliography

Riley, J. (1992) *A Kindness to Children*, London: the Women's Press.
—— (1988) *Romance*, London: the Women's Press.
—— (1987) *Waiting in the Twilight*, London: the Women's Press.
—— (1985) *The Unbelonging*, London: the Women's Press.

ALISON DONNELL

Rock against Racism

Rock against Racism (RAR) was formed, using the growing popularity of punk and its perceived links with **reggae** music as outsider or 'rebel' cultures, as an active response to the growing popularity of the National Front from the mid-1970s. Under the slogan 'Love music, hate racism', RAR promoted a series of concerts or 'carnivals' (see **carnival**) throughout Britain. featuring bills of punk and reggae bands including the Clash, **Misty in Roots**, X-Ray Spex and **Aswad**. RAR also published a magazine *Temporary Hoarding*, which was based upon the format of punk fanzines. Although ostensibly a celebration of multiculturalism, the predominantly white punk acts generally headlined the events and the reggae bands included on such bills were often marginalised, despite the adoption of reggae into the sound of acts such as the Slits and the Clash. The 'carnivals' were successful in terms of the size of audience and

the press coverage they received. RAR has, over the decades been adopted in other countries although its influence waned in Britain. In 1986, one of RAR's founders, David Widgery, published a history of the organisation entitled *Beating Time*, the only volume to fully cover RAR's impact.

ANDY WOOD

Rodney, Donald

b. 1961, Birmingham, England; d. 1998

visual artist

Donald Rodney was a key artist in the development of black art at the start of the 1980s. Having met Keith **Piper** as a student at Trent Polytechnic, Rodney exhibited as part of the collective, the Pan-Afrikan Connection. His work was central to the development of black art as a movement, ranging from didactic pieces, which have come to characterise the movement, to more reflective, open-ended pieces. Rodney used a wide range of materials but is perhaps best known for his haunting use of X-rays towards the end of the decade, when his condition of sickle-cell anaemia started to worsen. Rodney's X-ray works can be read on a number of levels, from the intensely personal to more general observations on black cultural politics. This width of possible readings prefigured later, more open-ended approaches to ethnicity. Despite having to work increasingly from the hospital bed, Rodney's final solo show in 1997 was widely acclaimed, in particular a tiny house constructed from Rodney's own skin removed during an operation. Rodney died in March 1998.

Further reading

Chambers, E. 'His catechism: the art of Donald Rodney', *Third Text* 44: 43–54.

NIRU RATNAM

Ross, Jacob

b. 1956, Grenada

poet, playwright, journalist, novelist,
   creative-writing tutor

Jacob Ross studied at the University of Grenoble,
France, and has lived in Britain since 1984. He was
formerly an editor of **Artrage**, Britain's leading
intercultural arts magazine. Ross's first collection of
short stories *Song for Simone* (1986, Karia Press) was
described as 'The most powerful crystallisation of
Caribbean childhood since George Lamming's *In
the Castle of My Skin*'. He is currently a freelance
tutor of creative writing and teaches part-time at
Goldsmiths College, University of London. He has
co-authored *Behind the Masquerade: the Story of
Nottinghill Carnival* (1986) with Kwesi **Owusu** and
co-edited *Voice, Memory Ashes* (1998) with Joan
Anim-Addo. His most recent collection of short
stories is *A Way to Catch the Dust and Other Stories*
(1999).

Select bibliography

Ross, J. (1999) *A Way to Catch the Dust and Other
   Stories*, London: Mango Publishing.
Ross, J. and Anim-Addo, J. (eds) (1998) *Voice,
   Memory Ashes*, London: Mango Publishing.
Ross, J. and Owusu, K. (1986) *Behind the Masquerade:
   the Story of Nottinghill Carnival*, Arts Council of
   England.

JOAN ANIM-ADDO

Ross, Leone

b. 1969, Coventry, England

novelist

During her childhood Ross lived both in Jamaica
and England. She received a first-class honours
degree in **literature** and social science from the
University of the West Indies and a Masters in
international journalism from City University,
England. She has worked as a freelance journalist
for numerous national publications, specialising in
entertainment and the politics of race, gender and

sexuality. Her first novel *All the Blood is Red* (1996)
was nominated for the 1997 Orange Prize, and
both this title and her much acclaimed second
novel *Orange Laughter* (1999) have been translated
into French.

Select bibliography

Ross, L. (2000) 'Black Narcissus', in C. Newland
   and K. Sesay (eds) *IC3: the Penguin Book of New
   Black Writing in Britain*, London: Penguin, pp.
   409–13.
—— (1999) *Orange Laughter*, London: ARP.
—— (1998) 'Facade' and 'Phone call to a rape crisis
   centre', in K. Sesay (ed.) *Burning Words, Flaming
   Images*, London: SAKS Publications, pp. 95–102
   and 34.
—— (1996) *All the Blood is Red*, London: ARP.

KADIJA SESAY

Roy, Chinwe

b. Eastern Nigeria

artist

Chinwe Roy came to Britain in 1975, shortly after
the Biafran war, because in Nigeria at that time
there were very limited opportunities for women to
study art. She began her studies at East Ham
College and gained a degree in graphic design at
Hornsey College of Art. Although she set up a
graphic design company with a friend, Roy
remained interested in fine art and took up portrait
painting on a full-time basis in 1988. She is
probably best known for her *African Diaspora* series
of five paintings, which were commissioned by
Kriss Akabussi. These works, which depict the
African slave trade, have received wide media
attention and recognition. As Roy has commented:
'I am greatly inspired by people; but especially by
the survival spirit and tenacity of the people of
Africa. It is not surprising therefore that my
portraiture has developed in the area of figurative
historical paintings.' Her most recent exhibition
'Africa – Past, Present and Future' was shown at
the Royal Commonwealth Society in 1999. Roy
has had several major commissions, including

Commonwealth Secretary-General, Chief Emeka Anyaoku, and she is working on a commission for Her Majesty the Queen.

ALISON DONNELL

Rubasingham, Indhu

b. 1970, Sheffield, England

theatre director

Rubasingham studied drama at Hull University and was awarded an Arts Council Bursary as trainee director at the Theatre Royal Stratford East in 1993. She then received the Karabe award to be an associate director at the Gate Theatre, Notting Hill, where she directed *Shankuntala* and *Sugar Dollies*. Rubasingham is among the new breed of **theatre** directors, who work across a range of subjects that focus on expressions of being British from a multi-ethnic perspective. Her approach is characterised by using all the space available in the auditorium and by her interest in the dynamics between the audience and the performers; she invites the spectators to become part of the action. To date, she has directed seventeen plays, ranging from comedy to epic to contemporary drama. Her credits include: *Party Girls*; *The 'No Boys' Cricket Club*; *Lift Off*, and *Starstruck*. The Royal National Theatre co-produced her play *A River Sutra* (adapted by Tanika Gupta from Gita Mehta's novel) and later invited her to direct *The Waiting Room*, also by Gupta. She was an associate director with the Birmingham Repertory Theatre, where she directed *The Ramayana* (2000), which is transferring to the Royal National Theatre (April 2001). Rubasingham is currently serving on panels for the Arts Council and London Arts.

SUMAN BHUCHAR

Rudet, Jacqueline

b. 1962, London

dramatist

In 1983 Rudet founded the **theatre** company Imani-Faith 'for and by black women'. She is one of just a few black women playwrights to achieve success on the contemporary stage. Her first professionally performed play, *Money to Live* (1986), was staged at the Royal Court Upstairs by the **Black Theatre Co-operative**. The play treats the subject of women who take up stripping because of economic hardship. Despite Rudet's concern that the male direction of her drama objectified the women to the detriment of her social commentary, the play was a success. Two more plays followed at the Royal Court: *God's Second in Command* (1985) and *Basin* (1987). *God's Second in Command* describes how a Caribbean family comes to terms with a gay son, and the play was later produced on BBC radio (1990). Like Jackie **Kay**'s *Chiaroscuro*, Rudet's *Basin* examines friendships and relations between women. The play developed as a response to an earlier piece of writing, *With Friends Like You*, and a trip to Dominica to visit relatives. Written on her return to England, *Basin* was Rudet's means of giving expression to her rediscovery of the love of black women.

Select bibliography

Rudet, J. (1987) *Basin*, London: Methuen.
—— (1986) *Money to Live*, London: Methuen.

ELAINE ASTON

Rushdie Affair, the

The Rushdie Affair was prompted by the publication of Salman **Rushdie**'s controversial novel *The Satanic Verses* on 25 September 1988. The novel was banned in Pakistan in October, and, early in the following year, separate protests in India, Pakistan and Bradford were backed up with Ayatollah Khomeini's infamous *fatwa*, pronounced on 14 February 1989. The latter drove Salman Rushdie into hiding for almost a decade. Khomeini's *fatwa* was followed by further Muslim demonstrations, the banning of Penguin books in forty-five Islamic countries, the fire-bombing of bookshops and public burnings of *The Satanic Verses*, as well as the killing of a Belgian imam, his assistant and a Japanese translator of Rushdie's work. It is these events that are generally regarded as constituting 'the Rushdie Affair'.

Discussions of the offence caused by *The Satanic Verses* have tended to focus on Rushdie's re-naming of the prophet Muhammad as 'Mahound' (or false prophet), the name used by early Christian detractors of Islam. The section in which the whores of Jahilia take the names of the prophet's wife gave further offence. Rushdie, however, has staunchly defended these accusations, by drawing attention to the 'fictionality' of the novel. For example, he has emphasised the fact that the offending passages of the novel all take place within the hallucinating, schizophrenic imagination of Gibreel Farishta, one of the novel's central characters. Rushdie has also defended *The Satanic Verses* in his allegorical children's novel *Haroun and the Sea of Stories* (1990).

The *fatwa* against Rushdie was rescinded by the Iranian foreign minister in September 1998.

Further reading

Appignanesi, L. and Maitland, S. (ed.) (1989) *The Rushdie File*, London: Fourth Estate.

'Beyond the Rushdie Affair: Special Issue' (1990) *Third Text* 11.

Rushdie, S. (1990) *Haroun and the Sea of Stories*, London: Granta.

—— (1988) *The Satanic Verses*, London: Viking/ Penguin.

Ruthven, M. (1990) *A Satanic Affair: Salman Rushdie and the Rage of Islam*, London: Chatto & Windus.

JAMES PROCTER

Rushdie, Salman

b. 1947, Bombay, India

novelist, essayist

Born into a wealthy Muslim family, Rushdie was sent to school at Rugby, England, in 1961, and later went on to take a degree in history at King's College, Cambridge. For much of the 1970s, he worked in advertising (a career demanding the kind of linguistic inventiveness that would later re-emerge in his fiction), while trying to establish himself as a writer. During this decade he wrote an unpublished novel, *The Book of The Pir*, and *Grimus*, published in 1975.

Despite the negative critical reception of *Grimus*, Rushdie began work on what would become his first major novel, *Midnight's Children*, which won (among other awards) the **Booker Prize** in 1981, and was later nominated 'the Booker of Bookers'. Re-writing the history of India's independence through the flawed memory of Saleem Sinai, *Midnight's Children* employs a range of narrative techniques – magic realism, intertextuality, meta-fictionality, hybridity (see **cultural hybridity**) – that have since become trade-marks of Rushdie's fiction. Translated into over a dozen languages, *Midnight's Children* brought Rushdie international acclaim, making him the epitome of what Timothy Brennan terms the **cosmopolitan celebrity**. This success continued with his 1983 Pakistan-based novel, *Shame*, which was shortlisted for the Booker Prize and won France's Prix du Meilleur Livre Etranger.

However, Rushdie's remarkable literary achievements in the West in the early and mid-1980s were tainted towards the end of that decade, with the tragic events surrounding the publication of his controversial novel, *The Satanic Verses*, in 1988. In that year, the novel was shortlisted for the Booker Prize and won the Whitbread Prize for Best Novel, while finding itself banned in both India and South Africa. The '**Rushdie Affair**' was subsequently fuelled by the *fatwa* placed on the novel's author by the Iranian religious leader Ayatollah Khomeini. The ground-breaking **diaspora aesthetics** of cultural intermingling and hybridity practised within Rushdie's fiction was turned upside down by *The Satanic Verses*, which inspired inter-racial antagonisms and hatred during the late 1980s and early 1990s.

Rushdie's next novel, *Haroun and the Sea of Stories* (1990), won the Writer's Guild Award; marketed as a children's fantasy story, the text also offers a complex allegorical defence of *The Satanic Verses*. *East, West* (1994), a collection of short stories, and his two novels *The Moor's Last Sigh* (1995) and *The Ground beneath her Feet* (1999) represent other major fictional contributions by Rushdie over the 1990s. Also a highly talented essayist and non-fiction writer, books like *The Jaguar Smile* (1987), *Imaginary*

Homelands (1991) and *The Wizard of Oz: a Short Text about Magic* (1992) offer illuminating insights into the political and creative projects of the writer. Rushdie is a Fellow of the Royal Society of Literature and Commandeur des Arts et des Lettres.

Select bibliography

Rushdie, S. (1999) *The Ground beneath Her Feet*, London: Jonathan Cape.
—— (1990) *Imaginary Homelands: Essays and Criticism 1981–1991*, London: Granta.
—— (1988) *The Satanic Verses*, London: Viking/ Penguin.
—— (1981) *Midnight's Children*, London: Picador.

JAMES PROCTER

Ryan, Veronica

b. 1956, Plymouth, Montserrat

sculptor

Ryan studied extensively from 1974 until 1984 at various institutions, including the Slade School of Art and the School of Oriental and African Studies. Using a sculptural vocabulary of embryonic protective forms, her *Earthbound* of 1983 is an un-ethereal shape, refuting the modernist aesthetic of sublime beauty. Although her work used images and forms derived from organic sources, the work addresses a broad range of issues. Most significantly her interest in boundaries, and their implicit opposition of inclusion and exclusion, imbues her subtle work with an unsettling air. She has also used repetition to give a sense of internal rhythm that both continues and ruptures, as in her *Pierced Repetitions* of 1988. Most recently, she has made work that deals with containment, cellular progression and visceral interiority, such as in her *Empty Compartments Full of Dust* of 1993. In this work the contents of a vacuum cleaner were placed inside the sculpture, making reference to the shedding of human skin, and to the trace of the body.

Further reading

Maharaj, S. and Bettinger, B. (1988) *Veronica Ryan*, Cambridge: University of Cambridge and Kettle's Yard.
Martin, R. and Ryan, V. (1987) *Veronica Ryan*, Bristol: Arnolfini Gallery.
Santacatterina, S. and Ryan, V. (1995) *Veronica Ryan*, London: Camden Arts Centre.

FRANCIS SUMMERS

S

Sade

b. 1959, Ibadan, Nigeria

singer, songwriter

Helen Folsade Adu moved to Essex from Nigeria at the age of four; she came with her English mother after her parents divorced. She studied fashion (see **fashion and design**) at St Martin's College and began her vocal career singing with the band Pride, while also was working as a fashion designer and model. She then moved on to lead the group Sade and have a series of hits with singles like 'Your Love is King' and 'Smooth Operator'. The debut album, *Diamond Life* (1984), won her the Grammy award for the Best New Artist. Two further albums in the 1980s, *Promise* (1985) and *Stronger than Pride* (1988), made her an icon of the decade and she is one of the few recording artists to appear on the cover of *Time* magazine. She released *Love Deluxe* in 1992 and a compilation album *The Best of Sade* in 1994. After an eight-year break, Sade returned in 2000 with the album *Lover's Rock* that went straight into the British charts at number three. She was nominated for Best British Female Solo Artist at the 2001 Brit Awards.

Further reading

Bengo, M. (1986) *Sade*, Paperjacks.

ALISON DONNELL

Saga Prize

The Saga Prize was set up by Marsha **Hunt** in 1995 to further black British writing. It ran for four years. Entrants needed a black African ancestor and a birthplace in the UK or the Republic of Ireland when submitting their unpublished first novel. The winner received prize money of £3,000 and a book contract. While being set up, the prize quickly became controversial due to its 'afrocentric' nature and the restrictive definition of blackness. The **Commission for Racial Equality** was opposed to the insistence on certain geo- and bio-data bars. The debate over this prize confirms the unsettled nature as to what constitutes black British **literature**. However, the fact that a Folkestone-based travel firm catering for the aged sponsored the prize reveals the wide interest now directed towards black British literature. The four winners of the Prize were (to 1998): Diran **Adebayo**, *Some Kind of Black* (1995); Joanna **Traynor**, *Sister Josephine* (1996); Judith Bryan Edwards, *Bernard and the Cloth Monkey* (1997); and Ike Eze-Anyika, *Canteen Culture* (1998).

MARK STEIN

Saghal, Gita

b. India

presenter, producer

Saghal was educated in both India and Britain, and

made her first major career break as a presenter and researcher for **Channel 4**'s current affairs programme *Bandung File*. She later moved into producing both **television** and film (see **film and cinema**), and continued to work as a researcher. Saghal has been an active member of the black women's movement in Britain, particularly in connection to the **Southall Black Sisters**.

ALISON DONNELL

Sagoo, Bally

b. India

artist, producer, remixer, DJ

Birmingham-based Bally Sagoo has had a varied and prolific career since emerging from the **bhangra** scene, both as a DJ and the producer of the popular single 'Hey Jamalo' in 1990. Sagoo has been integral not only in bringing bhangra to a wider audience but for his willingness to mix bhangra with other styles of **music** utilising his skill as a remixer. Sagoo has also experimented with remixing Indian film (see **film and cinema**) songs, leading to the release of an album *Bollywood Flashback*, and in turn Sagoo has had several of his own compositions featured in the film *Kartoos*. Sagoo has presented his own show on MTV India and has been involved in producing original film scores in the wake of *Kartoos*'s success. Bally Sagoo also recorded an album, *Magic Touch*, with the late Nusrat Fateh Ali Khan and had a hit UK album with *Rising from the East*, which was largely made up of Hindi and Punjabi compositions. In addition to this, Sagoo has also released the R'n'B/**hip hop**-influenced *Dil Cheez* and the *Star Crazy* series of bhangra albums, as well as setting up his own label, Ishq.

ANDY WOOD

Salkey, Andrew

b. 1928, Panama; d. 1995, USA

novelist, poet, anthologist, broadcaster, teacher

Salkey was educated in Jamaica and at London University, living in England between 1952 and 1976. His novels about black British experience include *Escape to an Autumn Pavement* (1960), *The Adventures of Catullus Kelly* (1969) and *Come Home, Malcolm Heartland* (1976). Perhaps Salkey's most important contributions to contemporary black British **literature**, however, have been as an organiser and anthologist of black cultural production more generally. Along with Kamau Brathwaite and John **La Rose**, Salkey was a founding member of the **Caribbean Artists' Movement**, as well as editing numerous collections of poetry and prose by West Indian and black British writers during the 1960s and 1970s.

Select bibliography

Salkey, A. (1969) *The Adventures of Catullus Kelly*, London: Hutchinson.
—— (1960) *West Indian Stories – an Anthology*, London: Faber.
—— (1960) *Escape to an Autumn Pavement*, London: Hutchinson.

JAMES PROCTER

Sam, Agnes

b. Port Elizabeth, Eastern Cape, South Africa

writer

Before embarking on her writing career, Sam read zoology and psychology in Lesotho, trained as a teacher in Zimbabwe and worked in Zambia for ten years, where she taught pre-colonial African history. She later read English at York University, England, and completed her experimental novel *What Passing Bells* at the same time. Her collection *'Jesus is Indian' and Other Stories* focuses on Indian immigrants to South Africa and, although it often looks at the experiences of women, it is written around Sam's researches into the history of her great-grandfather, an indentured labourer who arrived in South Africa in 1860 and achieved his freedom in 1913. Her poetry and short stories have been published in the journal *Kunapipi* and *Charting the Journey: Writings by Black and Third World Women*

(1988). Sam has written about the experience of being a black South African woman writing to earn a living in England in *Let it be Told* (1987).

Select bibliography

Sam, A. (1994) *'Jesus Is Indian' and Other Stories*, Oxford: Heinemann.

Further reading

Grewal, S., Kay, J., Landor, L., Lewis, G. and Parmar, P. (eds) (1988) *Charting the Journey: Writings by Black and Third World Women*, London: Sheba.

Ngcobo, L. (ed.) (1987) *Let it Be Told: Black Women Writers in Britain*, London: Virago.

ALISON DONNELL

Sanderson, Lesley

b. 1962, Malaysia

visual artist

Sanderson's work addresses identity, and in particular the raced and sexed subject, and the role of the stereotype. She first came to attention in the exhibition '**Black Art: Plotting the Course**', and the lack of didacticism in her work is indicative of the shift going on within the parameters of black art. Sanderson's work has used the self-portrait to question an ethnicised subjectivity, and, in doing this, she builds on a tradition of work that encompasses artists such as Rasheed **Araeen** and, in the USA, Adrian Piper. Like many younger black British artists, Sanderson's work can be interpreted in conjunction with recent theory. Sanderson's work invites Orientalist readings, not only by using herself as subject matter, but also by the use of Chinese letters and calligraphy. Simultaneously, the works undermine such readings through the non-inviting expressions of the subject and the use of the Western technique of cross-hatching. The fragmentary nature of identity – a key concept in recent post-colonial theory – is explored in many of Sanderson's works.

Further reading

Wrexham Library Arts Centre (1994) *These Colours Run: Lesley Sanderson*, exhibition catalogue.

NIRU RATNAM

Sankofa Film Collective

Sankofa were one of a number of black independent film (see **film and cinema**) collectives and workshops that emerged in the UK in the 1980s and whose existence was interwoven with the cultural politics of **arts funding** in this decade, from bodies like the **Greater London Council** and notably from **Channel 4**. Martina **Attille**, Maureen **Blackwood**, Nadine **Marsh-Edwards** and Isaac **Julien** were the collective's members. The collective offered particular perspectives distinct both from mainstream cinema and from independent cinema, while none the less drawing influence from film theory and independent European cinematic practices. Sarita Malik has commented that:

> [T]he dynamic of personal and political equipped the film and video workshops of the 1980s with creativity and commitment to tell the types of stories which the mainstream British media had to date largely ignored. There was a commitment to new forms of representation, new ways of seeing black people.
>
> (Malik, 1996: 203)

Their first film *Who Killed Colin Roach?*, directed by Isaac Julien, appeared in 1983. It was made through work with the Roach family support committee and concerned the death of a young black British man in the foyer of Stoke Newington police station. Their subsequent film *Territories* (1984/5), also directed by Julien, built upon the group's desire to produce a follow-up programme that put the subject of the earlier film into a broader political and cultural context. It focused on the ways in which black cultures were being contained. They are perhaps best known for their 1986 production *The Passion of Remembrance*, directed by Maureen Blackwood and Isaac Julien. This had at its centre a concern with ideas of reconstructing the historical past, offering a critique of historical moments in black people's struggle. Nadine Marsh-Edwards and Isaac Julien suggest that the film arose through the need to create a dialogue with those from the previous generation whose struggles they had always admired, a need to work out how to move on from their positions to envisage change. Martina Attille states, 'we see the film as an enquiry into how a political activist was defined in the past, and maybe how in the future we could construct ourselves in relation to class, race and sexuality' (Pines, 1988: 55). The film deployed a fragmented mosaic type of narrative, exploring public and private spaces, and deploying multiple perspectives in order to problematise the notion of a single event or single truth. Their subsequent film *Dreaming Rivers*, directed by Martina Attille, appeared in 1988, exploring black women's identities and desires, and was followed in 1989 by **Looking for Langston**, directed by Isaac Julien, a film devoted to remembering and re-visiting the work of the gay black Harlem Renaissance writer, Langston Hughes.

Further reading

Malik, S. (1996) 'Beyond "the cinema of duty"? The pleasures of hybridity: black British film of the 1980s and 1990s', in A. Higson (ed.) *Dissolving Views. Key Writings on British Cinema*, London and New York: Cassell.

Pines, J. (1988) 'Interview with Sankofa Film Collective', in K. Mercer (ed.) *Black Film, British Cinema*, ICA Documents 7, London: ICA/BFI, pp. 55–7.

ELEANOR BYRNE

Savacou

Savacou, named after the bird in Carib mythology, was the Journal of the **Caribbean Artists' Movement**, and was started by Kamau Brathwaite and Ken Ramchand at the University of Jamaica. Andrew **Salkey** and John **La Rose**, in the UK, were on the editorial board, with Salkey as general editor. The journal marked the beginning of independent black publishing. Its purpose was to 'bring together the work of creative writers, academics, and theoretical thinkers, and to provide a forum for artistic expression and thought in the Caribbean today'. *Savacou* provided a platform for new creative writing for young urban blacks. It was viewed as revolutionary, yet it reflected the creative change that gradually took place in Jamaica. It was to be published three times a year, but lack of funds meant that this was irregular. Two issues were produced in 1970, two in 1971 and then only one each year up to 1979 (none in 1976 or 1978). Between 1979 and the last issue, there was a nine year gap. *Savacou* 16, published in 1989, was edited by Brathwaite.

Further reading

Walmsley, A. (ed.) (1992) *The Caribbean Artists' Movement, 1966–1972: a Literary and Cultural History*, London: New Beacon.

KADIJA SESAY

Sawhney, Nitin

musician

Originally a member of a band along with Talvin **Singh**, Nitin Sawhney released his debut album *Spirit Dance* in 1993 on the World Circuit world-**music** label. In the wake of his debut with its complex mix of Indian and Western music, Sawhney toured Britain, Europe and Canada before signing to the **Outcaste** label, releasing his second album *Migration* in 1995. *Migration* featured the vocals of Natacha Atlas and gained a great deal of critical acclaim. Sawhney has since released *Displacing the Priest* (1996) and *Beyond Skin* (1999), which were as well, if not more positively and enthusiastically, received. In addition to composing and performing his own records, Sawhney has written and recorded soundtracks for a number of **television** programmes and films (see **film and cinema**) including *Split Wide Open* and *The Dance of the Shiva*, a film about the role of Indian soldiers during the First World War. He is also an accomplished radio and television writer, and has both written for and appeared in *Goodness Gracious Me*, *Network East* and *Eastern*

Eye. Sawhney has recorded a lecture on his approach to making music for the Open University and has held numerous workshops around the UK.

ANDY WOOD

Seal

b. 1963, London, England

singer, songwriter

Sealhenry Olumide Samuel was born in London of Nigerian and Brazilian parentage. Before taking his musical career seriously, he explored electrical engineering and designing leather clothes. Seal first toured with bands in Thailand and Japan, and launched his own pop career back in the UK. Success came with his first album, *Seal*, released in 1991, for which he won the Brit Awards for Best Album, Best Male Artist and Best Video. His second album, also entitled *Seal*, was released in 1994 and continued his success. At the 1995 Grammy Awards he won Record of the Year, Song of the Year (for 'Kiss from a Rose') and Best Male Pop Vocal Performance. Seal currently lives in Los Angeles, USA.

ALISON DONNELL

Sealy, Mark

b. 1960, London, England

curator, director

Mark Sealy studied at Goldsmiths College, London University, and then worked in Fleet Street for a major national newspaper. He subsequently worked for three years with Network Photographers in development of reportage features, syndication and sales, before moving on in 1991 to become Director of **Autograph: the Association of Black Photographers**. In his role at Autograph he has initiated the production and publication of several exhibitions, publications and artists' commissions. Sealy has curated several major international **photography** exhibitions, including an audiovisual programme for Rencontres d'Arles in 1993, and initiating retrospectives on

the photographic works of Gordon Parks and James Van Der Zee in London. He has edited books on the works of Vanley **Burke** and Rotimi **Fani-Kayode**. In 1998 he co-curated 'Revealing Views: Images on Ireland' at the Royal Festival Hall in London and he is currently working on a book project with Stuart **Hall** on photography and identity. Sealy lectures extensively throughout the UK and abroad, and was, for several years, a member of the Arts Council of England's Photography Advisory Structure. In 1995, he acted as the photography coordinator for the prestigious AFRICA 95 season and, in February 1996, he was a member of the jury for the World Press Photography Competition in the Netherlands. He has also been a jury member for the 1997 Nikon–UNESCO awards in Paris. Sealy is the Vice Chair for the recently founded National Museum and Archive of Black History and Culture.

ALISON DONNELL

Selvon, Sam

b. 1923, Trinidad; d. 1994, Trinidad

novelist, journalist, poet, essayist, short-story writer

Sam Selvon, an Indian Caribbean writer, began writing poetry and fiction while serving in the Royal Navy reserve during the Second World War. He then took up a post as fiction editor of the *Trinidad Guardian*'s literary magazine until he came to Britain, on the same ship as George **Lamming**, in 1950. Selvon has poetry and short stories published in a number of newspapers (see **publishing, newspapers and magazines**) including the *London Magazine* and *New Statesman*. He also worked for the BBC during the 1960s and 1970s, producing two **television** scripts: *Anansi the Spiderman* and *Home Sweet India*. In 1974 he co-wrote the script for *Pressure*, the first black-produced feature film (see **film and cinema**) on black Britain, with Horace **Ové** who directed the film. His so-called 'London' novels span more than twenty years, starting with *The Lonely Londoners* in 1956 and ending with *Moses Migrating* in 1983. Along with Lamming, Selvon's work is the most acclaimed of the early post-war period, and his writing has been highly influential in terms of subsequent black British literature and criticism. Of particular note here are Selvon's foundational experimentations with language and modified forms of Caribbean dialect, which have since been emulated by black British writers across the post-war period. Selvon was awarded Trinidad's Hummingbird Medal of Literature in 1969 and two Guggenheim Fellowships.

Select bibliography

Selvon, S. (1975) *Moses Ascending*, London: Davis-Poynter.
—— (1957) *Ways of Sunlight*, London: MacGibbon & Kee.
—— (1956) *The Lonely Londoners*, London: Allan Wingate.

JAMES PROCTER

—— (1995) *Dali's Twisted Hands*, Leeds: White Swan Books/Peepal Tree Books.
—— (1994) *Mount Vesuvius in Eight Frames*, Leeds: White Swan Books/Peepal Tree Books.
—— (1993) *New York Times*, London: the Many Press.
—— (1992) *Kali in Ottawa*, Rima and London: Paramount.
—— (1990) *The Lunar Visitations*, New York: White Swan Books.
—— (1996 [1983]) *Leaning against the Lamp-Post*, South Carolina: University of South Carolina Press.

Further reading

Dawes, K. (ed.) (1996) *Sudeep Sen: a Bio-Biographical Critical Sourcebook*, South Carolina: University of South Carolina.

KADIJA SESAY

Sen, Sudeep

b. 1964, Delhi, India

poet, editor, publisher, critic

Sudeep Sen gained his Masters degrees in English **literature** and journalism in the USA, before returning to New Delhi as a journalist and documentary film-maker (see **film and cinema**). He has received several grants and awards, including the Hawthornden Fellowship, a Bread Loaf Writers Conference Scholarship and the Faber & Faber poetry grant (Arvon Foundation). His works have appeared in national and international publications, and have been broadcast on radio. From 1992 to 1993, he was the international poet-in-residence at the Scottish Poetry Library in Edinburgh, and, in 1995, he was a Visiting Scholar at Harvard. In the same year he edited an issue of **Wasafiri** on Asian writing and set up a publishing company, Aark Arts, for poets.

Select bibliography

Sen, S. 1997) *Postmarked India: New and Selected Poems*, New Delhi: HarperCollins.

Sesay, Kadija

b. 1962, London, England

journalist, writer, publisher

Kadija Sesay is a literary activist, of Sierra Leonean descent. She organises the Writers' HotSpot, which organises trips for writers to the Gambia, New York and Cuba. She created Calabash for the Centerprise Literature Development Project and, with two other women, set up SAKS Publications. She is a freelance journalist, and her poetry and short stories have been published and broadcast. Her work has appeared in anthologies including *The Fire People* and **Afrobeat**, and as part of the 'On the Buses' programme for the 1997 Stoke Newington Festival. It has also been broadcast on the BBC World Service and BBC's London Live radio. She has read her work at various festivals in the UK and in Washington DC, Palestine and the Gambia. She runs and teaches poetry and fiction 'Sable Creative Writing' courses, and is managing editor of *SABLE LitMag*. Her work in creative arts has earned her various awards and nominations: Cosmopolitan Woman of Achievement (1994); Candace Woman of Achievement (1996); the *Voice*

Community Award in Literature (1999); and Millennium Woman of the Year (2000). Sesay is a George Bell Fellow and the General Secretary for African Writers Abroad (PEN). She is very involved in creative writing work and journalism training with young people, including work for: the Victoria and Albert Museum; National Year of Reading; the **Commission for Racial Equality**; TS2K; and Westminster Summer University. She is also a writer in residence for the Youth Quest programme in the USA. In 2000, her co-edited collection *IC3: the Penguin Book of New Black Writing in Britain* was published and is already recognised as a significant contribution to the archive of black writing in Britain.

Select bibliography

Sesay, K. (ed.) (1998) *Burning Words, Flaming Images*, London: SAKS Publications.
—— (ed.) (1993) *Six Plays by Black and Asian Women Writers*, London: Aurora Metro.
Sesay, K. and Newland, C. (eds) (2000) *IC3: the Penguin Book of New Black Writing in Britain*, London: Penguin.

ALISON DONNELL

Seth, Roshan

b. 1942, Patna, Bihar, India

actor

Roshan Seth is an internationally known actor. He grew up in India and was educated at the Doon School, one of India's best-known public schools. He came to Britain and trained at the London Academy of Music and Dramatic Art (LAMDA) in 1965 and began working in **television** and repertory **theatre** in the early years. He was chosen for the RSC's world tour of *A Midsummer Night's Dream*, directed by Peter Brook, and had also worked in a film in 1974, *Juggernaut*, directed by Richard Lester. However, getting good parts was difficult in the UK, so he returned to India disillusioned in 1977. Seth stopped acting for five years and took a job as editor of the quarterly journal published by the India International

Centre, Delhi. During this period, he was asked to play Nehru in Attenborough's, *Gandhi* (1982) and he took leave from his job to do that. He later got the BAFTA nomination for his part.

The turning point came in 1982 when writer David Hare met him in Delhi and offered him the part of Victor Mehta in his *A Map of the World*. Seth resigned from his job and returned to acting. *A Map of the World* opened at the Adelaide Theatre Festival, played at the Sydney Opera House, Royal National Theatre, London and Public Theatre, New York, where Seth received a Drama Desk nomination. He went on to play the Fool in Hare's production of *King Lear* at the National, and has starred alongside some big stars. He appeared as the Doctor with Racquel Welch in Shaw's *The Millionairess* and he played the husband, Jay, opposite Sharmila Tagore, in Mira Nair's *Mississippi Masala*. Seth's recent film credits include: *Vertical Limit* (2000); *Bombay Boys* (1998); *Wings of Hope* (2000) and *Such a Long Journey* (1998), where his sensitive portrayal of Gustad Noble won him a Genie for 'Best Actor' at the Vancouver Film Festival, 1998. On television he played the title role of Haroon Amir in Hanif **Kureishi**'s *Buddha of Suburbia*, earning the Royal Television Society's nomination for 'Best Male Performer'. He has appeared in much radio drama and was the narrator of Salman **Rushdie**'s *Midnight's Children* for Radio 4's *Book at Bedtime*.

SUMAN BHUCHAR

Sewell, Tony

b. London, England

author, journalist, researcher

Tony Sewell was born and educated in London, and after completing a degree in English he migrated to Jamaica and achieved some prominence as a teacher. After returning to Britain he continued his teaching career in London before turning to journalism and becoming Arts Editor and, later, a controversial columnist for the *Voice* newspaper. Sewell is best known for his work in both print and broadcasting, tackling black male underachievement in the British education system and consulting on Jamaican history. He is also well known for his often politically charged essays in the black press. His critically acclaimed biography of the Jamaican-born black-rights leader Marcus Garvey, *Garvey's Children* (1990), was followed by the sensationalist novel *Jamaica Inc.* (1993), a fictional account of crime and corruption in the Jamaican government. Sewell later obtained his Ph.D. and lectured at Kingston University and other educational institutions.

Select bibliography

Sewell, T. (1993) *Jamaica Inc.*, London: X Press.
—— (1990) *Garvey's Children*, Basingstoke: Macmillan Press.
—— (1988) *Keep on Moving*, London: Voice.

RAYMOND ENISUOH

Shabazz, Menelik

b. Barbados

film-maker

Menelik Shabazz is one of Britain's few pioneering black film-makers. His documentary *Step Forward Youth* in 1977 was one of the first to receive funding from the **British Film Institute**. He is also editor of the journal *Black Filmmaker*. His first film, which he both directed and wrote, was ***Burning an Illusion*** and remains his sole feature film (see **film and cinema**) to date. Of Barbadian origin, Shabazz drew upon both his Barbadian heritage and a sense of being in the UK when writing and directing films. Barbadian culture is reflected in *Burning an Illusion*, with the importance attached to books as Barbados has the highest literacy rate in the West Indies. In 1999, Shabazz was Festival Director for the Pan-African Film Festival, showing forty feature films, documentaries and shorts at the **Institute of Contemporary Arts** in London.

Select filmography

Shabazz, M. (1995) *Catch a Fire*.
—— (1988) *Time and Judgement*.

—— (1981) *Burning an Illusion*.

SAMINA ZAHIR

Shah, Fahmida

b. England

silk painter

Fahmida Shah paints directly onto silk, making wearable textiles and hangings, using colour and motifs, often in unexpected conjunctions, which reveal a clear subcontinental influence. Shah has also worked as project co-ordinator for the Bedford Asian Women's Textile Project and has exhibited in several solo and group exhibitions. She was one of three craft makers at the Foyle Gallery showing how makers use craft as a vehicle of cultural transition in a Festival of South Asian Visual Arts (1994) throughout the West Midlands, an event celebrating the work of contemporary British artists of Southeast Asian descent. Shah also became active in East London's contribution to the **Nehru Gallery**'s National Textile Project (1993), an outreach project involving Asian women's groups from around the UK making embroidered panels for display in the Victoria and Albert Museum. The project aimed at initiating dialogue between the prestigious, imperial institution and the untrained skills of immigrant minorities. Shah's textiles are included in **Bradford art galleries and museums**' transcultural collections, with the work of other textile artists working in the UK, as individual explorations of dual heritage in a broad material arts collection related to the Indo-Pakistan subcontinent.

DIPTI BHAGAT

Sheikh, Farhana

b. Lahore, Punjab, Pakistan

writer, teacher

A teacher and writer, Farhana Sheikh published her only novel, *The Red Box*, in 1991. It is an interesting, and in some ways quite ambitious, first novel, where form and content strive to work together in a way not often attempted in this kind of work. The main character Raisa is a young British Pakistani woman researching the lives of other Pakistani women in Britain for her MA dissertation. Although popular images would project the idea of 'women talk' as a significant component of Asian and diasporic communities, *The Red Box* dramatises some of the difficulties and tensions involved in women speaking across the divides of generation, class or education, even within their own community. That difficult process also involves Raisa learning how to speak to her interviewees, and her explanation of what she is trying to do often clarifies things for her, too:

> I mean . . . unless we understand who we are – how we live, what we suffer, what we admire, what we hate, what we put up with, what we fight for – and how we have become who we are . . . unless we understand all that, how will we ever change the things that hold us down?
>
> (Sheikh 1991: 155)

The awareness of a range of differences within the all-too-readily homogenised or singularised community is important, and the novel works hard to embody that in the variety of women's voices, especially in Raisa's interviews with her principal informants, the schoolgirls Tahira and Nasreen. Above all, the connection between 'understand[ing] who we are' and 'chang[ing] the things that hold us down' is seen to hold true, not in any Utopian manner, but in the credible way in which differently empowered individuals can manage to have some impact on the circumstances of their lives.

Select bibliography

Sheikh, F. (1991) *The Red Box*, London: the Women's Press.

PATRICK WILLIAMS

Shinebourne, Janice

b. 1947, Guyana

writer, editor, critic

Shinebourne, of Chinese and Indian ancestry, began writing at an early age, and in her adult creative work she drew on both these early writings and on her time in Guyana. She has lived in London since 1970, when she studied for a BA. She has since taught in colleges and gained an MA in contemporary English studies from the University of London. Shinebourne's first novel *Timepiece* won the Guyana Prize in 1987 and tells of Sandra and her transition from rural to urban life in Guyana. Her second novel *The Last English Plantation* (1988) focuses on two crucial weeks in the life of an adolescent girl, as she makes a personal transition to the high school against the backdrop of Guyana's political upheavals. Shinebourne's short stories are widely anthologised and her work has been broadcast on the BBC World Service. In 1997, she was Visiting Fellow at New York University.

Select bibliography

Shinebourne, J. (1988) *The Last English Plantation*, Leeds: Peepal Tree Press.
—— (1987) *Timepiece*, Leeds: Peepal Tree Press.

ALISON DONNELL

SHOBANA JEYASINGH DANCE COMPANY *see* Jeyasingh, Shobana

Shonibare, Yinka

b. 1962, London, England

visual artist

Along with Chris **Ofili**, Shonibare's emergence has signalled a new approach to black cultural identity in the visual arts (see **visual and plastic arts**). Shonibare's work is playful, ironic and witty, referring to ethnicity in unexpected ways. Most typical is his use of 'African' textiles. Shonibare has made a number of installations that feature brightly coloured and patterned textiles. Despite their 'exotic' appearance, the fabrics are in fact manufactured in places such as Manchester. Shonibare's interrogation of the signifiers of ethnicity works to bring out the hidden presence of colonialism within history, and his recent work has begun to address this more directly – works such as *Diary of a Victorian*

Dandy critique received accounts of British history and art history. His work addresses both the post-colonial and the post-modern, and it is unsurprising that Shonibare, like Ofili, **Kaur** and **McQueen**, has not emerged as part of a black movement, but instead within the structures of young British art. Collected by Charles Saatchi, Shonibare exhibited in 'Sensation', and is represented in the UK by the dealer Stephen Friedman.

Further reading

Ikon Gallery (1999) *Yinka Shonibare: Dressing Down*, exhibition catalogue, Birmingham: Ikon Gallery.

NIRU RATNAM

Shri

b. Bombay, India

Shrikanth Sirian is a classically trained *tabla* player, who relocated to London after a period playing bass guitar in an Indian rock band. Signed to **Outcaste**, Shri released his debut album *Drum the Bass* in 1997. Produced by Nitin **Sawhney** and featuring vocals from Meera **Syal** and the rapper JC001, *Drum the Bass* is a beautiful album that mixes together disparate influences in ways that sound unforced and natural. In 1998, along with **Badmarsh**, the pair released the album *Dancing Drums*, which was hailed as the definitive Outcaste release. While being a more dance-floor friendly album than Shri's debut solo release, *Dancing Drums* is still an inventive and powerful record, ranging from the duos' reinvention of Ananda Shankar's 1970s track 'Dancing drums' to the playful theme music to an imagined **Bollywood** film '*The Asian Detective*', on which Shri plays bass guitar and mixes. A second album *Tribal*, written and recorded with Badmarsh. was released early on in 2001 on Outcaste. As with *Drum the Bass* and *Dancing Drums*, Shri plays the majority of the live instruments. The duo performed material from *Tribal* at the London Jazz Festival in 2000 with the rapper UK Apache.

ANDY WOOD

Siffre, Labi

b. 1945, London, England

poet, songwriter, singer, playwright

The writer and performer of the hit song '(Something Inside) So Strong', Labi Siffre has written and recorded eight albums of songs and an album of poetry. Two of his works for **theatre** have been performed: the stage adaptation *Tail Spin*, produced at the Wilde Theatre, Bracknell, and the play *DeathWrite*, produced at the Sherman Theatre, Cardiff, and later televised by HTV. Three volumes of his poetry have been published: *Nigger* (1993), *Blood on the Page* (1995) and *Monument* (1997, also available on CD). '(Something Inside) So Strong', which won the Ivor Novello Award for Best Song Musically and Lyrically in 1987, was written, in the first instance, for the black community of apartheid South Africa, and has since become an anthem for the marginalised and dispossessed all over the world. Throughout his career, Labi Siffre has spoken out against racism, homophobia, rape, the abuse of children and all forms of power abuse. His work dramatically evokes the damage caused by much of what we accept as normal in Western cultures. His essay 'Choosing the stick they beat you with' appears in ***IC3: the Penguin Book of New Black Writing in Britain*** (2000).

Select bibliography

Siffre, L. (1998) *The Last Songs*, Xavier Music Ltd.
—— (1997) *Monument*, Xavier Books.
—— (1993) *Nigger*, Xavier Books.
—— (1988) *So Strong*, China Records Ltd.

ANITA NAOKO PILGRIM

Sikand, Gurminder

b. 1960, Jamshedpur, India

visual artist

Gurminder Sikand came to Britain from India when she was ten. She studied fine art, gaining a degree from Birmingham Polytechnic in 1983, and then moved to Nottingham. Sikand works on paper, on a small scale, using watercolour, ink and gouache. Her work focuses on themes and iconography that recur in Western and Indian societies. She relates the fusion of imagery in her paintings to her own life experience of a childhood in India and adolescence and adulthood spent in Britain. Many of Sikand's images relate to the symbolism of birth, death and rebirth. Hindu beliefs and mythology directly influence her work, for example the multi-headed and many-armed beings in her paintings recall the gods, goddesses and demons of Hindu mythology. She has powerfully explored the relationship of women with the environment in a series of works inspired by the Chipka Movement in nineteenth-century India, in which women embraced trees to stop them being destroyed. Sikand's work is often highly decorative and contained within a border, a style borrowed from the women artists of the Mithila region of southern Indian, whose floor and wall paintings are filled with pattern within a decorative border. Sikand's paintings have been included in landmark exhibitions of work by black contemporary British artists such as: '**Black Art: Plotting the Course**', which toured from Oldham Art Gallery during 1988 and 1989; 'Let the Canvas Come to Life with Dark Faces' at the Herbert Art Gallery, Coventry in 1990; and '**Transforming the Crown**: African, Asian and Caribbean Artists in Britain, 1966–1996, in New York in 1996. She has had may solo exhibitions of her work, in particular at the University of Notttingham in 1994 and at Walsall Museum and Art Gallery in 1995. Sikand has undertaken numerous artist's residencies since the 1980s, hosted by education, community and cultural organisations.

Further reading

Beauchamp-Byrd, M.J. (1997) *Transforming the Crown: African, Asian and Caribbean Artists in Britain 1966–1996*, New York.

Chambers, E. (1988) *Black Art: Plotting the Course*, Oldham: Oldham Art Gallery.

Day, P. and Chambers, E. (1990) *Let the Canvas Come to Life*, Coventry: Herbert Art Gallery.

Lucas, P. (1995) 'Eyes on the body', *Women's Art Magazine* 62 (January/February): 31.

JANE SILLIS

Simon, Josette

b. 1960, Leicester, UK

actress

Simon has had a distinguished career as the first leading black actress with the Royal Shakespeare Company (RSC) and has played in fifteen of their productions, including *Golden Girls*, for which she received a 'Plays and Players' Best Actress nomination. In 2000, she played the Queen in the RSC's *Don Carlos* and Titania in their *A Midsummer Night's Dream*. She has also worked in film (see **film and cinema**), most notably in the 1987 *Cry Freedom* and the 1989 *Milk and Honey*, for which she won the award for Best Actress at the Atlantic Film Festival, Canada and the Paris Film Festival. Her most popular **television** role was as Dayna Mellanby in the cult science fiction television series *Blake's 7*, which she played from 1980 to 1981, when the series ended. She has continued to work in television and has made guest appearances in episodes of *Silent Witness*, *Kavanagh QC* and *Dalziel and Pascoe*. In 2000, she was nominated for the Prix Futura Award, Berlin, for her radio performance in *Dictator Gal*.

ALISON DONNELL

Singh, Talvin

b. 1970, London, England

musician, producer, remixer

Talvin Singh is a classically trained musician, who studied for several years as a teenager in India before returning to his native London. He has played *tablas* with a diverse range of bands and musicians, from **Massive Attack** to Bjork, whom he has also remixed. Prior to the release of his debut album in 1998, Singh was best known for his involvement in **Anokha** and the discovery of the 17-year-old singer Amar, whose debut album Singh co-produced. His debut solo album *OK* reflects Singh's immersion in a diverse range of **music**, which Singh asserts is not simply the fusion of elements but the result of his real-life experience of music. The title was chosen because it was the most universal term Singh could think of in an attempt to reject the notion that Asians in Britain are marginal to mainstream culture. *OK* has been remixed by artists such as Underworld and 4Hero and Singh has in turn remixed Madonna. In 1998, the style magazine (see **publishing, newspapers and magazines**) *ID* predicted in its eighteenth-birthday edition that Talvin Singh would be one of the most influential creative people of the next eighteen years. He released *Ha* in 2001.

ANDY WOOD

Singh, Tjinder

b. 1968, Wolverhampton, England

singer, activist

In addition to fronting the highly successful band **Cornershop**, Tjinder Singh has been involved in a number of other musically related activities outwith Cornershop. As a student activist he gave lectures on the relationship between, and the role of, popular **music** and politics at both Cambridge and London universities, and in March 1994 he addressed the Socialist Forum Youth Conference on the subject of youth and cultures of resistance, highlighting the danger of pop music only dabbling in fashionable politics and diluting its ability to provoke debate and change. Singh, along with Cornershop's Ben Ayres, formed an offshoot band, Clinton, in order to diversify and experiment with more technology and home-recording techniques. Clinton have released two singles to date, 'Jam jar' in 1994 and 'Superloose' in 1995, which was remixed and re-issued in 1997. Clinton released their debut album in 1999, *Disco and the Halfway to Discontent*, and contributers include Noel Gallagher of Oasis. Tjinder Singh has also sung on tracks by

Slacker who are signed to XL, home of the Prodigy, and has worked with **Future Pilot AKA**.

ANDY WOOD

SIRIAN, SHRIKANTH *see* Shri

Sissay, Lemn

b. 1967

poet

A well-known performance poet, Sissay's first successful publication was *Tender Fingers in a Clenched Fist* (L'Overture, 1988) at the age of twenty. His verse can be lyrical, thought provoking and dramatic; his use of words pulsating and captivating. His poems have been published on a central London Bus route, laid into the streets of Manchester and painted on the side of a public house in the same region.

Born to Ethiopian parents, part of his life story was portrayed in *Internal Flight*, a documentary broadcast by the BBC in 1995. His work has appeared in wide-ranging publications such as the *Times Literary Supplement*, the *Independent* and *The Face*. He has been published in numerous anthologies and edited *The Fire People* (Payback Press, 1998), a ground-breaking anthology of new black British poets. His musical talent is shown in his work on the Leftfield album *Leftism*, where he penned '21st century poem'. The album went double platinum. He is working on an album to be released in Germany.

Sissay used his literary talent in a children's literacy programme for BBC 1 and is currently working on a children's book for Bloomsbury. His work is innovative, as shown in work screened at the **Institute of Contemporary Arts** theatre, and he travels all over the world to perform.

Select bibliography

Sissay, L. (2000) *Rebel without Applause*, Edinburgh: Payback Press.
——(1999) *Morning Breaks in the Elevator*, Edinburgh: Payback Press.

(2000) *Gone with Petrouchka*, featuring work from Lemn Sissay, performance at the Institute of Contemporary Art.

(1998) *Jazz606*, television series, BBC 2.

YINKA SUNMONU

Sivanandan, A.

b. 1923, Sri Lanka

political activist

Ambalavaner Sivanandan came to live in Britain in 1958, in the aftermath of the Notting Hill riots. Most of his political writings have first appeared in **Race and Class**, which is produced by the Institute of Race Relations (founded and directed by Sivanandan). Sivanandan has written on a wide range of black issues in Britain, Sri Lanka, the USA and South Africa. His collected essays, *A Different Hunger* (1982) and *Communities of Resistance* (1990), represent key documents in the historicisation of black British politics. As Stuart **Hall** states in his introduction to *A Different Hunger*, '[Sivanandan] is one of a handful of key black intellectuals who has actively sustained the black struggle in Britain over more than two decades' (Hall 1982: ix).

Select bibliography

Sivanandan, A. (1990) *Communities of Resistance: Writings on Black Struggles for Socialism*, London: Verso.

—— (1982) *A Different Hunger: Writings on Black Resistance*, London: Pluto Press.

JAMES PROCTER

Size, Roni/Reprazent

b. Bristol

musician

When Roni Size and Reprazent won the 1998 Mercury Music Award for their album *New Forms* it created a great stir through the media. More than any other act, Reprazent have closed the gap between studio technology and live musicianship, consistently producing records that are as much a part of the subculture of **dance** music as they are of the mainstream. Roni Size honed his musical skills at the Basement Project in his home town of Bristol and it was to the Basement Project that he pledged the bulk of the £25,000 Mercury Prize money. Reprazent are a true collective but are also involved in their own projects. DJ Krust is a renowned producer and artist in his own right, and Onallee, vocalist for much of *New Forms*, signed a solo deal with EMI in 1998. Although the **music** of Roni Size and Reprazent has a very tangible jazz feel to its drum and bass core, Size sees their synthesis of live and programmed sounds as having its roots in funk, which was highlighted in the hit single 'Brown paper bag', which, in Size's own words, was 'more James [Brown] than jazz'. *In the Mode* (2000) on the Talkin' Loud label is a 'harder edged' follow-up album.

ANDY WOOD

ska

Ska originated in Jamaica and has its roots in the popularity of the US R'n'B of the early 1950s and 1960s there. When the US imports began to dry up, Jamaican producers and sound system operators such as Coxsone Dodd and Prince Buster began producing local versions of R'n'B. Initially, many of the records produced were imitations of the R'n'B sound as imported from the USA, but local musicians began to add their own influences to the **music**. Prince Buster made the brave move of promoting this home-grown form of music through his sound system over other forms of music. The competitive nature of sound systems meant a constant need for new sounds and within the ska scene there emerged a diverse range of acts for different moods and occasions. The predominance of recordings over live performances meant that the ska scene was easily transported to Britain, where singles such as Prince Buster's 'Madness' and Desmond Dekker's 'Israelites' rapidly gained cult status despite radio's reluctance to play ska or **reggae**. Ska quickly adapted to the requirements of the British scene with special deals being set up between sound system operators in Britain and producers in Jamaica to license exclusive versions of songs and records, such as 1969's 'Skinhead moonstomp', which was recorded and released specifically with a mixed British audience in mind. Although Millie had reached number one in 1964 with the novelty ska–pop crossover single 'My boy lollipop', ska's impact on the national charts was minimal and less so still after the development of rock steady, a more lyrical, streetwise and political variant of ska. In the late 1970s, ska enjoyed a revival as a major influence on the Coventry-based band the Specials, who set up their own label Two-Tone to release their debut single 'Gangsters'. Other acts, including the Selecter and Madness (who took their name from the Prince Buster single), signed to the label and the Specials were joined by Rico Rodriguez, a founder member of 'Sir' Coxsone Dodd's legendary ska band the Skatalites. However, despite the Two-Tone ethos of promoting positive multiculturalism and the Specials' implicit anti-racism in songs such as 'Concrete jungle', the bands often attracted a far-right element in their audience. The Two-Tone label enjoyed considerable success in its short life-span, though by the end of the label in 1981 the majority of the bands had departed. The Specials split in the same year after releasing their finest single 'Ghost Town', which stayed at number one in the British charts for a number of weeks. Ska has remained popular in Britain, with numerous brief revivals occurring from time to time, although they seem more rooted in nostalgia than a serious attempt to reinvent the music. The Selecter and Madness still tour. Ska has also had an influence on US mainstream acts such as Rancid and No Doubt, who borrow from the music of ska and Two-Tone, though in a far less political or imaginative form.

ANDY WOOD

Small, Heather

b. London, England

singer

After growing up in West London's Ladbroke Grove, the diminutive Heather Small first rose to fame as the lead singer for the highly successful group M People. Since the band formed in 1991 they have risen from playing the circuit in local Manchester night-clubs to becoming one of the most successful bands of the 1990s, selling over 10 million records world-wide and playing to international audiences in their tens of thousands. The focal point of M People's music is Small's distinctive voice. She is widely regarded as one of the finest black voices in the international **music** industry. In 2000, Small launched her own solo career with her single and album, both titled 'Proud'. Inspired by 1970s gospel, **reggae** and **soul**, she is regarded as one of the most eclectic female vocalists in Britain. However, M People are still intact and Small is currently recording and performing music with this successful band.

RAYMOND ENISUOH

Smartt, Dorothea

b. 1963, London, England

poet

Dorothea Smartt is a poet, writer and live artist. She was the first Black Literature Development Worker at Centerprise Community Centre, and since then has worked as a Poet-in-Residence for Brixton Market and as an Attached Live Artist at London's **Institute of Contemporary Arts**. She has also received several commissions and bursaries. She writes within a tradition of artists working and re-working diasporic connections and about black women's hair. Her work has been broadcast on **television** and radio, and appears in ground-breaking anthologies, including *IC3: the Penguin Book of New Black Writing* and *The Fire People*, and journals, including *Kunapipi*, and *Wasafiri*.

Select bibliography

Halpin, B. and Smartt, D. (eds) (1993) *Word Up: Words from the Women's Cafe*, London: Centerprise Publications.

Smartt, D. (2001) *Connecting Medium*, Leeds: Peepal Tree Press.

—— (2000) 'Medusa? Medusa black!', in L. Goodman (ed.) *Mythic Women/Real Women*, London: Faber & Faber.

—— (1998) 'The passion of remembrance', in G. Spraggs (ed.) *Love Shook my Senses*, London: the Women's Press.

—— (1987) 'My mother's hands', in D. Choong, G. Pearse, O. Cole-Wilson and B. Evaristo (eds) *Black Women Talk Poetry*, London: BlackWoman Talk.

KADIJA SESAY

Smiley Culture

b. 1963, London, England

reggae artist

In the early to mid-1980s, Smiley Culture (David Emmanuel) was one of a number of MCs operating with the Saxon International Sound System. Alongside the likes of **Tippa Irie** and Phillip 'Papa' Levy, they were known as 'fast talking originators' for their role in encouraging and promoting a form of **reggae** called fast-style. Fast-style brought a **hip hop**/rap influence to reggae as MCs began to work stories, everyday experiences and multiple perspectives into their lyrics and vocals. In 1984, Smiley Culture released his debut single 'Cockney translation' on the **Fashion Records** label. Musically and lyrically, 'Cockney translation' seemed to catch on with its slick, breathy production and a lyrical rap questioning notions of identity and belonging, contrasting Jamaican patois and Cockney rhyming slang while demolishing several stereotypes. The single charted and was followed up by 'Police officer'. Both singles were number one in the UK reggae charts and charted nationally, with 'Police officer' reaching number twelve despite the fact that its groundbreaking video cost only a fraction of the budget of the average pop promo. 'Police officer' was reissued in 2000 as part of the Fashion retrospective compilation *Essential Dancehall Reggae*.

ANDY WOOD

Smith, Marlene

b. 1964, Birmingham, England

artist

Smith studied art from 1983 to 1987 at Bradford College. Having set aside an initial burst of angry, violent images, her mature work describes a collective intimacy using memorabilia such as old photographs in collaged paintings and mixed-media installations to examine ways in which history is created. In the catalogue for 'Along the Lines of Resistance' (1988) she says: 'The real concern is with what has *not* been recorded or photographed.' Smith wrote the introduction to 'The Image Employed' catalogue (Cornerhouse, 1987) – a show she co-curated with Keith **Piper** – and stated in her text for '**The Thin Black Line**' exhibition that she '[seeks] to contribute to the building of a material culture that might have been denied'. The loyalty and directness of her aims are perhaps summed up in her statement: 'my audience is the people in the work'. Those people are often women who 'go about ... what they see as their duty, to survive, to struggle on'. Smith has worked with West Midlands Minority Arts Service and as Director of the **Black Art Gallery**, London. She acted as a member of the **Live Art** and Cultural Diversity Steering Group at the Arts Council (1990–3) and now works freelance – currently assembling the 'Digital Folders' archive project for the **African and Asian Visual Arts Archive**. Other exhibitions include: 'Heart in Exile' (1983); 'Radical Black Art' (1984); 'The Thin Black Line' (1985); and 'Some of Us Are Brave' (1986).

Further reading

Alexander, S. (1986) 'The Black Art Group', *Artrage* 14 (autumn): 30.

PAUL O'KANE

Smith, Zadie

b. 1975, London

writer

It is true to say that nobody could have foreseen the attention that would surround Zadie Smith's first novel *White Teeth* (2000). It catapulted her from a hopeful first-time novelist to a literary heavyweight. The novel won the *Guardian* First Book Award, the Whitbread First Novel Award and the International E Book Award. Success has been fast for Smith, who studied at King's College, Cambridge, and wrote the novel in her senior year. The manuscript was eventually auctioned by her agent under a lucrative deal and described by Salman **Rushdie** as 'an astonishingly assured debut'. Despite the publication of just one book, Smith has received critical acclaim in the literary field and the fact that she is young and can develop her craft even further has led to great expectations. She won a prize at the Ethnic Media Awards and was shortlisted for the **Booker Prize**, Orange Prize and Whitbread Book of the Year. An excerpt from *White Teeth* also appeared in the US magazine *Essence*, along with the work of other notable young writers. Like Courttia **Newland** and Diran **Adebayo**, she is showing a generation of young black Britons that they can succeed in the world of **literature**.

YINKA SUNMONU

soul

Soul, as a form of **music**, is difficult to describe. There is a danger of merely accepting the reified view of soul music as being a historically fixed genre, as a marker of authenticity in the way that blues music has become a museum piece. Many soul *aficionados* in Britain portray soul as being a specifically African American sound, which only really existed in a fixed period from, say, the early 1960s to, at a push, 1975. The active consumption of the records of this era by white audiences in Britain and nostalgia for the northern soul era tend to confirm this state of affairs. A quick survey of soul on the Internet confirms this viewpoint, with the majority of British soul sites being given over to content relating to northern soul, Wigan Casino and the reminiscences and memories of that era. Recently, several scholarly books have been published about the links between 1960s soul music and the US Civil Rights Movement, which, while being well written and researched, confirm the view of soul as a music from another era and another place. However, soul, as a form and an influence, has a resonance in many forms of music being produced in Britain, both as a source of samples and inspiration and also as a form with its own distinctive genealogy. Even prior to 1965, Ben E. King asked 'What is soul?', while Public Enemy may well have been criticising this revisionist or limited view of the music when they asked 'Who stole the soul?'

Although the music of the black USA was popular in Britain, particularly the 1960s sounds of Motown, Stax and Atlantic, the enjoyment of soul music was not limited to white, working-class audiences or the mod youth subculture. From the 1950s onwards, clubs catering for black audiences played imports of American R'n'B and, later, soul, and no self-respecting sound system was without its share of R'n'B and soul tunes. Soul was a major influence upon the strand of **reggae** known as **lovers' rock**, which was a peculiarly British form of reggae. Like the reggae scene, the soul scene largely depended upon the recorded rather than the live medium, with rare imports being particularly sought after prizes.

By the beginning of the 1970s, soul had fallen out of favour with the mainstream, although outwith London it remained popular. With the resurgence of black US musical forms in the form of disco and Philly soul, it made a comeback, with its lush, expansive productions and use of studio technology. In the 1970s, soul even spawned several British variants including Carl Douglas's rather kitsch 'Kung fu fighting'. By the 1980s, soul/funk hybrids such as Junior Giscombe, Linx and Imagination were enjoying hits but the soul scene remained largely underground. Artists such as Omar enjoyed popularity in London with acclaimed singles such as 'There's nothing like this' and 'I don't mind waiting' on the tiny Kongo label. However, outside of London few people had heard of Omar until he signed to Talkin' Loud, and then

RCA, in the early 1990s. Pirate stations such as Horizon, JFM and Kiss rose to prominence in the 1980s while Capital Radio and Radio London had shows dedicated to soul, jazz, funk and fusion. Manchester had a strong soul scene to rival the capital in the late 1980s and although very few of the artists made it out of the region, radio shows such as *Souled Out* regularly attracted massive audiences.

The late 1980s success of **Soul II Soul** spawned a revival of sorts with labels such as Acid Jazz and Talkin' Loud taking on board acts such as Omar and Incognito, whose Jean Paul Manuick had previously played in a soul band and had written songs for Maxi **Priest**. Talkin' Loud was co-run by the London based 'rare-groove' DJ Norman Jay, who had previously ran the critically and commercially under-rated Global Village label for Phonogram. The Young Disciples Femi debut album for Talkin' Loud, 1991's *Road To Freedom*, was praised as a landmark British soul album and Young Disciples Femi, along with Brand New Heavies, Galliano, Incognito, Diane Brown, former Soul II Soul vocalist Caron Wheeler, Shara **Nelson** and Omar enjoyed varying degrees of success, both in Britain and in the USA, where they were marketed as an antidote to the relentless onslaught of swingbeat and R'n'B under the tag 'the new British Soul rebels'. Many of these acts only had a marginal impact and several were dropped by their labels. In the second half of the 1990s, many British soul and R'n'B acts were dropped, including Noel McKoy and First Class; many of them before they had even released a record. Omar signed to RCA and reached the Top 40 with several singles, although his album *This Is Not a Love Song* failed to chart and Omar was dropped in 1998. British labels have found it difficult to deal effectively with and promote British soul and R'n'B acts, and seem to prefer more pop crossover acts such as All Saints, or American acts. Although there is a thriving underground scene, as with the **hip hop** scene of a few years earlier, it is run with minimal exposure and finances, and has yet to develop an alternative structure to work within.

Despite much pessimism there are still outlets for British productions and Norman Jay and the Young Disciples Femi are prolific and popular club DJs, while Jay released his first mix album in 2000.

Although many labels are only in a position to release limited cuts of singles, labels such as Dome have released several compilations, including the *Delicious* album in 1998.

ANDY WOOD

Soul II Soul

Founded in 1982 by **Jazzie B** and Phillip 'Daddae' Harvey, Soul II Soul began as a sound system and quickly became a black British musical and cultural institution. With the philosophy of 'A Happy Face, a Thumpin' Bass, for a Lovin' Race', Soul II Soul is a company that has incorporated a recording group, a label and studio, a production company, a website and two clothing stores. However, it was as a recording group that they were most influential. Signing to Virgin Records in 1986, and with Jazzie B, 'Daddae' and Nellee Hooper behind the production boards, they enjoyed international success in 1989 with 'Keep on Movin'' and 'Back to Life', both featuring singer Caron Wheeler, from the definitive UK soul album of the 1980s and 1990s *Club Classics Volume One*. Soul II Soul's sound, a reflection of young black Britain, soon broke in the USA. Soul II Soul won Grammy Awards for 'Back to Life' and 'African Dance', and three Soul Train Awards for 'Keep on Movin''. They also nurtured and worked with some of the UK's finest talents, including vocalists Caron Wheeler and Charlotte, and producers Hooper (**Massive Attack**, Madonna, Bjork) and Howie B (U2). Since *Club Classics Volume One*, Soul II Soul has released five more albums and sold over 6.8 million albums and 20 million singles world-wide.

DEREK A. BARDOWELL

sound system DJs

The art of DJing is probably best understood as the Jamaican counterpart to African American rap. However, from the outset it is necessary to state that DJing, or 'toasting', as it was formerly known, is the forerunner of rap and played a seminal role in the creation of the **hip hop** movement, which came out of the South Bronx in the 1970s. The history of toasting is linked to the development of sound system culture, which emerged in Jamaican dance-halls in the 1940s and 1950s. According to Clarke, the DJ or toaster would 'scat' while R'n'B was being played 'in an effort to urge the dancer on to greater emotional frenzy and also to inject more feeling into the music'. This soon led to the DJs becoming recognised as performers and, once the reliance on African American **music** subsided, local produc-tions would invariably feature a DJ version. This type of community-based expression is closely linked to the traditional West African *Griot*. *Griots* are social commentators who can be hired to sing about various issues or even individuals, and they have a large repertoire of songs, which DJs would eventually term 'nuff lyrics'.

During the early 1950s, the subsequent migra-tion of Jamaicans to Britain and their numerical dominance soon established sound system culture as a 'core institution' within these shores. Conse-quently, there was a reliance on imported Jamaican music and this reliance was maintained until the 1970s. However, during the late 1970s, there was a significant shift in the social perception of the sound system in Britain, as the DJ who would generally introduce records and ad lib during musical changes began to offer a topical social commentary. Initially, these social commentaries were influenced by the lyrics of the Jamaican DJs who dominated **reggae** music, which during this period was heavily reliant on imported Jamaican music, in the format of live audio cassettes, 'yard tapes' and recorded releases. This situation was soon to change as many of the British-born DJs began to address the socio-cultural problems they faced, confronted with racial exclusion in the land of their birth. Moreover, Radio DJs like Tony Williams, on the now defunct Radio London's *Rockers FM*, would constantly feature live DJing on his shows. This was to have a major influence on what we now readily recognise as freedom (pirate) radio stations, who adopted the sound system ethos to great effect.

By the 1980s, the British DJs were achieving global recognition and sound systems like Saxon, Coxone, Frontline, Wasifa, Ghetto-tone, King Tubby's, Jamdown Rockers, Java High Power, Unity and a host of others became household names within the black community. In 1984,

Saxon, from South East London, became the first British sound system to tour New York with a full complement of DJs, including **Tippa Irie**, Papa Levi, Daddy Colonel and Rusty. Moreover, record companies who aimed to capitalise on the vibrancy of this phenomenon sought many of the DJs who were associated with these sound systems. Many of the DJs who were signed up during this period, such as Papa Levi, Tippa Irie, Aser Senator, Peterkin, **Smiley Culture**, Lana G and Ranking Anne, achieved high-profile successes. In fact, black British musicians like Maxi **Priest**, **Daddy Freddie**, Tenor Fly and **Jazzie B** of **Soul II Soul** began their careers on sound systems. However, once the DJs had outlived their commercial usefulness they were subsequently discarded by the predominantly white-owned record companies, who did not generally recognise the validity of this type of expression from a black perspective. One exception has been the **Mad Professor**'s Ariwa label, which has continued to promote pro-black reggae music for over twenty years. Prof. is behind the continuing exposure of DJs like Macka 'B', Pato Banton, Chucky Star and Starkey Banton. This has inspired companies like Joe Grine, Nine Lives and MCS Records to follow this lead and promote black British DJ music by new and old artists alike. MCS has released tracks from a host of British DJs, including Prento Youth, Ultimate Warrior, Simeon, Leslie Lyrix and Demolition Man.

WILLIAM HENRY

Southall Black Sisters

In 1979, Asian women at risk from domestic violence were able to seek help from Southall Black Sisters (SBS). The organisation tackles topics that were previously taboo in the Asian community such as mental illness, arranged marriages and cultural/generational conflicts. Women also contact the centre for help on health, sexual abuse, immigration and harassment and racism. When it first started, meetings were conducting in women's homes but a **Greater London Council** (GLC) grant helped to change that. They now receive some funding from Ealing Council. There are currently four full time workers (three of whom receive funding from Ealing Council and the fourth from charities). Up to a thousand women a year seek help. SBS helps vulnerable women by providing case-workers who work in an advisory capacity. There is also interaction with support groups.

SBS has mounted many campaigns nationwide. Justice for Women, launched in 1989, fought for the release of eight women who were imprisoned for killing their violent partners. Kiranjit Ahluwalia, jailed for life in that year for killing her husband, was released on appeal three years later. In June 2000, Hannana Siddiqui, of SBS, resigned from the Home Office working party on forced marriage, chaired by Lady Uddin and Lord Ahmed, in protest at its support on mediation, as this would still place women at risk from abuse. The advice centre won the Martin Ennals Civil Liberties Award for human rights activities in 1992.

YINKA SUNMONU

Souza, Francis Newton

b. 1924, Goa, India

painter

Souza was the first Asian or black artist in the UK to enjoy widespread critical acclaim and public exposure. He left India in 1949, complaining about the censorship of his work for alleged obscenity, having been a key member of the Progressive Artists Group there. Between 1949 and 1955, Souza's work received little attention, until he was noticed by Stephen Spender and the young gallerist Victor Musgrave. Souza showed with growing success with Musgrave's gallery and Gallery One, every year between 1955 and 1962. According to gallery estimates 6,000 people saw his 1961 solo exhibition. After Gallery One closed, Souza exhibited with the Grosvenor Gallery before leaving the UK for New York in 1967, where he still lives in comparative obscurity.

Souza's expressionistic style and references to Byzantine and Roman Catholic imagery make him an important model for later post-colonial theories that stress the similarities rather than incommensurability of coloniser and colonised. His work was widely written about during his time at Gallery One, with a monograph being produced in 1962. Although he subsequently faded from public view, recent exhibitions in London suggest he is gradually being rediscovered.

Further reading

Mullins, E. (1962) *F.N. Souza*, London: Blond

NIRU RATNAM

Staying Power

First published in 1984 and written by Peter Fryer, *Staying Power: The History of Black People in Britain* is now recognised as one of the definitive works on this subject. As a journalist in 1948, Fryer was sent to report on the arrival of Jamaican workers at Tilbury on the *SS Empire Windrush*, and his interest in the history of black people began. The Preface to *Staying Power* acknowledges the possible anomaly of a white writer giving an account of black British history, while affirming the belief that it is possible for him/her to 'think black' – that is, to grasp imaginatively as well as intellectually the essence of the black historical experience. The book is wide-ranging in its scope, beginning with the division of Moors stationed in Carlisle in the third century AD, and ending with the acts of resistance and rebellion that took place in the 1980s in London, Liverpool and Bristol, the very cities that, as Fryer points out, were once Britain's chief slave ports. Throughout the book, emphasis is placed on the retrieval of hitherto lost or occluded histories and personalities, and these are juxtaposed with a chronicle of white attitudes towards race and the black community.

SARA SALIH

Stuart, Moira

newscaster

Stuart was one of the first black women newscasters on **television** and, as a newscaster, is one of the most recognisable faces on television by virtue of her professionalism over fifteen years. She joined BBC Television News in 1981. Stuart started at the BBC as a production assistant in the Radio's Talks and Documentaries Department. She then became a Radio 4 announcer and newsreader, and a programme presenter on Radio 2. For over six years she presented *News After Noon*, *The 5.40 News*, *The Nine O'clock News* and *The Six O'clock News*. During the 1980s, Stuart was one of the few black newscasters on television along with Trevor **McDonald** and Zenab **Badawi**, who built up a profile several years later. Over the years, Stuart has presented several radio and television programmes including *Best of Jazz*, *The Quincy Jones Story*, *Open Forum*, *The Holiday Programme* and *BBC Talent 2000*, the new talent-search programme. She has also made regular appearances on *Call my Bluff*. The TV and Radio Industries Club Awards voted her Best Newscaster in 1988 and she won the 1989 Television Personality in the Women of Achievement Awards. Five years later, this was followed by an award for Best Female Personality by the Black Journalists Association (1994) and Best Media Personality by the *Voice* newspaper (1997). In 1999, the BBC announced that Stuart was to return to daily mainstream newsreading on the new *Breakfast Show*.

YINKA SUNMONU

SuAndi

b. 1951, Manchester, UK

poet, writer, performer, activist, Cultural Director of Black Arts Alliance

Born of Nigerian and British heritage, SuAndi is a Manchester-based poet, performer and cultural activist. Since 1985, she has performed her poetry at national and international venues and festivals. Recently introducing a visual language to her work, she has developed several highly structured **performance works**, which are a heightened form of writing, a form that enables her to combine linear narrative with the ability to concurrently expose successive layers of fact and symbol. Her live works include *This Is All I've Got to Say* (1993)

and *The Story of M* (1994), an ICA Live Arts Commission.

SuAndi regularly leads educational workshops and community-based initiatives. She has commissioned programmes of live work, curated visual art (see **visual and plastic arts**) exhibitions, completed a number of consultancies and organised conferences. Her poetry has been published in anthologies, publications and journals. Books include *There Will Be no Tears*, *Nearly Forty* and *Style*. *I Love the Blackness of My People* is her fourth collection of work. She recently received a Mary Seacole opera commission and wrote the libretto for Britain's first black production. SuAndi is the Cultural Director of **Black Arts Alliance**, an organisation dedicated to promoting black artistic and cultural practice. She is a member of many boards including North West Arts Board. She has attended numerous conferences nationally and internationally as a speaker and performer. She is recognised for her innovative work within the Disability Arts Sector. Her work was recognised with an OBE in the Queen's 1999 New Year Honour's List, following her Winston Churchill Fellowship in 1996. The Arts Council of England, North West Arts Board and Calouste Gulbenkian New Horizons Fund have all supported her work.

CATHERINE UGWU

Sule, Gloria Ojulari

b. 1950, London, England

artist

Sule was born to a British mother and Nigerian father. Having spent her early life in a children's home, much of Sule's work explores identity, and in particular the issues facing mixed-race people in Britain and what it means to be stripped of family or heritage. Much of her work is influenced by the Yoruba traditions of her father's culture, as well as masquerade and festivals. She received a BA (Hons) degree in Fine Art Painting as a mature student at Norwich School of Art and Design in 1996. She also holds a City and Guilds Certificate of Further Adult Education Teaching. Sule works hard to promote art in her local community, and this is reflected in her participation in community arts, adult education and early-years education. She has conducted workshops in schools with children of all ages and works closely with Bath and Somerset Council. Painting and textiles are among her specialisms. Her mural, covering seven metres on a side of a building as part of the Renewal Scheme in St Paul's, Bristol, is well known and easily recognisable. Other commissions include shop signs, again as part of the 1999 Renewal Scheme, murals in Brighton Street and fascia, St Agnes, Bristol. She exhibits across the country and has formed Gloarts, a company specialising in posters and cards. Sule is committed to promoting positive images of black people. Her work has been featured in a special supplement of the *Voice* newspaper.

YINKA SUNMONU

Sulter, Maud

b. 1960, Glasgow, Scotland

poet, journalist, visual artist

Winner of the Vera Belle Prize in 1984 with 'As a Blackwoman', Sulter's writing has consistently explored and re-defined the conceptual map of black femininity. Sulter's poems engage directly with female sexuality, motherhood, desire and belonging. Her treatment of these topics frequently teases out the psychological and physiological dimensions in relation to the informing context of the history of the transatlantic slave trade upon women of the African diaspora. In 'As a Black-woman' Sulter writes that the 'bearing of my child is a political act', and her second collection, *Zabat: Poetics of a Family Tree*, extends her analysis of the complex politics of black women's agency and creativity through poems that engage with rape and violation, but most strikingly through the speakers' varied and various relations to, and imaginings of, Africa and African identity. Sulter's poetry is published by the small independent press, Urban Fox, but has also been anthologised in *Watchers and Seekers* and *Dancing the Tightrope*.

Select Bibliography

Sulter, M. (1991) *Echo: Works by Women Artists 1850–1940* (Selected and introduced by Maud Sulter), Liverpool: Tate Gallery.
—— (1990) *Passion: Discourses on Blackwomen's Creativity*, Hebden Bridge: Urban Fox.
—— (1989) *Zabat: Poetics of a Family Tree*, Hebden Bridge: Urban Fox.
—— (1985) *As a Blackwoman: Poems 1982–85*, London: Akira.

Further reading

Burford, B., MacRae, L. and Paskin, S. (eds) (1987) *Dancing the Tightrope: New Love Poems by Women*, London: the Women's Press.
Cobham, R. and Collins, M. (eds) (1987) *Watchers and Seekers: Creative Writing by Black Women in Britain*, London: the Women's Press.
Ngcobo, L. (ed.) (1987) *Let it Be Told: Essays by Black Women in Britain*, London: the Women's Press.

LYNNETTE TURNER

Sunmonu, Yinka

b. 1962, London

writer, journalist

Sunmonu is a spokesperson on adoption and fostering in the black community. Her work on fostering and adoption was featured in the **Channel 4** *Adoption on Trial* series and a paper on her adoption survey for the *Voice* newspaper (the first of its kind on black attitudes towards adoption) appeared on the Channel 4 website. She continues to produce the *Voice*'s colour supplements on education and adoption issues. Sunmonu was also the First Social Secretary of 'Women in Publishing', where she organised the successful 'three cooks and their books' dinner. She was the first cookery columnist to create original recipes for *Woman to Woman* (the *Voice* colour supplement), and in 1999 she became Food Editor for the online portal 'Black Britain Online'. She runs her own business, Yinka's Pantry, which supplies cakes to the Forum Hotel and the Jamaica Blue Coffee Shop in London. Her articles have been carried by *Aspire Magazine, West Africa, Community Care, Woman to Woman,* the *Voice, Foster Care* and *Adoption and Fostering Journal.* She has been seconded to work on the **Notting Hill Carnival** review as an Information and Research Officer. She has a BA (Hons) in English, African and Caribbean studies and an MA in creative and life writing from Goldsmiths College. She has contributed to the short-story collection **Afrobeat** (1999, Pulp) and her first novel is under offer.

ALISON DONNELL

Sutherland, Luke

b. Orkney, Scotland

musician, novelist

Luke Sutherland was brought up in Orkney and in the Perthshire town of Blairgowrie. He formed the band Long Fin Killie while at Glasgow University and, in 1994, they signed to the independent label Too Pure, for whom they recorded three albums, *Houdini* (1995), *Valentino* (1996) and *Amelia* (1998). Despite positive critical acclaim and constant touring, the experimental nature of much of Long Fin Killie's output meant that they never broke out of their status as a cult band. While recuperating from an illness after the demise of Long Fin Killie, Luke Sutherland wrote his debut novel *Jelly Roll* which was published in 1998 and nominated for the Whitbread book prize in the same year. Sutherland's current project, Bows, released their debut album *Blush* in 1999 and followed its release with a second album *Britannica* in 2000. A second novel *Sweet Meat* was published later in 2000 while *Jelly Roll* is being filmed for **Channel 4**. Luke Sutherland also plays violin for the band Mogwai and appeared live with them at the Reading and Glastonbury festivals, as well as on their acclaimed album *Cody.*

ANDY WOOD

Syal, Meera

b. 1963, Essington, nr Wolverhampton, England

novelist, actress

After taking a strong interest in drama and acting at school, Meera Syal went on to read English and drama at Manchester University. In her final year she co-wrote and acted in the one-woman play *One of Us*, which tells the story of Nishi, an Indian teenager who has left Birmingham to become an actress. The play won the National Student Drama Award and Syal took it to the Edinburgh Festival where she was spotted by a London **theatre** director and she spent seven years at the Royal Court Theatre. Syal moved on to write the screenplay for Gurinder **Chadha**'s **Channel 4** film **Bhaji on the Beach** (1993), which tells the story of a Birmingham-based South Asian women's collective, and their day-trip to Blackpool. Syal has since pursued a successful acting career in theatre, **television**, radio and film (see **film and cinema**). A member of the **Goodness Gracious Me** team (a successful radio and television comedy programme), Syal also wrote the first Asian radio sitcom *Masala FM*, and has subsequently achieved some success as a writer, and was also a member of the **Asian Women Writers' Collective**. Her first novel, *Anita and Me* (1996), is a semi-autobiographical account of Meena's childhood in a declining mining village near Birmingham. Her second novel *Life isn't All Ha Ha Hee Hee* (1999) focuses on the lives and loves of three Asian women who share schoolgirl pasts and complex emotional futures. Characterising all of Syal's work is an attention to the destabilisation of the essentialised, always 'right on' black subject. Syal has been awarded the MBE for her services to drama.

Select bibliography

Syal, M. (1999) *Life isn't All Ha Ha Hee Hee*, London: Doubleday.
—— (1996) *Anita and Me*, London: Flamingo/ HarperCollins.

—— (1990) 'Finding my voice', in M. Sulter (ed.) *Passion: Discourses on Blackwomen's Creativity*, Hebden Bridge: Urban Fox Press, pp. 57–61.

Syal, M. and Chadha, G. (1994) *Bhaji on the Beach*, London: Umbi.

JAMES PROCTER

T

Talawa Theatre Company

Talawa is a Jamaican word, derived from Old Ashanti or Tiwi, meaning 'small but stalwart' or 'strong, female and powerful'. The **theatre** company bearing that name was founded in 1985 by Yvonne **Brewster**, Carmen Munroe, Mona Hammond and Inigo Espejel. Its director is Yvonne Brewster, who co-founded the Barn Theatre in Jamaica in 1965 with Trevor Rhone, but has worked in Britain since 1974. Initially, the company was concerned with the portrayal of black women. After seven years, it had, however, produced only one play by a woman – Ntozake Shange's *The Love Space Demands*. Brewster proposed that the company should adopt the wider aim of informing, enriching and enlightening British theatrical and dramatic discourse by employing in the production process ancient African ritual and black political experience. Talawa also set out to introduce the British public to the work of black playwrights and to imbue the classics with a new cultural perspective by casting them solely with black actors. Unlike most black theatre companies, Talawa has had its own building – the Cochrane Theatre in central London – since 1991.

Further reading

Goodman, L. (1993) *Contemporary Feminist Theatres*, London: Routledge.
(1991) 'Drawing the black and white line/defining black women's theatre: an interview with Yvonne Brewster', *New Theatre Quarterly* 7(28) (November): 361–8.

D. KEITH PEACOCK

Tamasha Theatre Company

Tamasha Theatre Company was formed in 1989 by Kristine **Landon-Smith** and Sudha **Bhuchar** in order to adapt *Untouchable*, a classic Indian novel by Mulk Raj Anand. *Tamasha* is an Indian word, meaning 'spectacle', and the company brought a fresh look to the Asian **theatre** scene in the UK. *Untouchable*, which was performed in Hindi and English, created a large Indian village at London's Riverside Studios with the action being played in the round. The success of the first production demonstrated that there was an appetite for contemporary Asian drama and so the team continued to develop more work. Their second play, *House of the Sun*, was adapted from Meira Chand's novel, and it was a sort of Asian take on the Australian soap opera *Neighbours*, dealing with families in a block of flats in modern-day Bombay. Tamasha has a unique approach to producing drama. All the material for the plays is researched to the minute detail in order to create an authentic depiction of life. However, apart from *Untouchable*, all the productions have been rendered in English.

The work of Tamasha drew large Asian audiences to the theatre, at a time when the prevailing view was that Asians did not attend theatre. This showed that the company's unique approach of naturalism and its use of humour to raise social concerns struck a chord with audiences. The look was also very visual. *House of the Sun* depicted a large block of flats complete with a working lift on stage, while, for *Women of the Dust*, a huge construction site with a cement mixer symbolised the cycle of toil of the itinerant Rajasthani women labourers building palatial edifices for the Indian elite. *A Shaft of Sunlight*, about communal tension in India, and *A Yearning*, a Punjabi adaptation of Lorca's *Yerma*, followed. For six years, the company toured one production a year across the UK, predominantly to small-scale venues (see **theatre venues**). It was the success of ***East is East*** in 1996–7 that confirmed Tamasha's reputation as a leading theatre company on the national touring circuit. The following year, the company was invited to the Edinburgh International Festival with their production *A Tainted Dawn*, which dealt with the effects of the partition of India on ordinary people. In 1998, Tamasha caused a sensation with their musical, *Fourteen Songs, Two Weddings and a Funeral*, based on a blockbuster **Bollywood** film (see **film and cinema**), *Hum Aapke Hain Koun* (1994). This was a unique experiment that combined all the ingredients of Bollywood movies, such as song, **dance**, romance, tragedy and melodrama, with the techniques of a West End musical. The show won Tamasha the BBC Asia Award for Achievement in the Arts in 1998, and the TMA/Barclays Theatre Award for Best Musical in 1999. The show was remounted in 2001 for the middle-scale touring circuit. It was with their 1999–2000 production, *Balti Kings*, a 'slice of life' comedy set in a kitchen of a Balti restaurant that the company moved to performing to middle-scale venues on the national circuit.

SUMAN BHUCHAR

Tara Arts

Tara Arts is the oldest Asian **theatre** company in the UK. It was founded by three students: Jatinder **Verma**, Ovais Kadri and Sunil Saggar, who were all affected by the death of Gurdip Singh Chaggar in Southall in July 1976. As young Asians they wanted to express their response to this tragedy and found theatre to be the best medium. Their first play, *Sacrifice*, an adaptation of Rabindranath Tagore's work, was used as a metaphor to talk about Asian life in contemporary Britain. It was performed in 1977 at the Battersea Arts Centre and set the tone for Tara's future work and their next production, *Fuse*, which looked at an Indian student at a British school. Then came *Playing the Flame*, about sexual relationships between young Asians. Tara developed at a time when there was no contemporary theatre work being undertaken by Asians in Britain and it met with a favourable audience response. It soon became apparent that Jatinder Verma was the driving force behind Tara, and the company launched into play after play critically examining contemporary British society, as well as the legacy of its colonial relationship with India. It was with *Lion's Raj* in 1982, that the company acquired Equity status and changed from being an ethnic arts organisation to a professional theatre company.

As Tara developed as a theatre company, it had two key priorities. One was to respond to the politics of the time and the second was to explore what was Asian about its theatre. These led them to adapt Indian classics and *The Little Clay Cart*, by Sudraka, was the first in 1984 (remounted in 1986). This investigation showed that an Asian company based in Britain could not replicate ancient Sanskrit theatre, but rather had to apply the principles of Indian theatre in a comfortable way in order to discourse with a theatre-going audience familiar with Western conventions. For Tara, it is an ongoing search to find a theatrical language and style of performance drawn from its cultural antecedents that can also be successfully transposed to theatre today. After focusing on Indian classics, the next step was to take Western classics and render them 'Indian'. This was partly a strategy to get the establishment to take note of how non-whites have been informed by their English **literature** and also partly a riposte to the avant-garde of Europe, which revived its own sense of theatre through Eastern and African theatrical styles. The first play in this vein was *The Government Inspector*, and this was followed by *Roundheads and Peakheads* and *Danton's Death*. In 1990, Jatinder Verma was invited to direct a play at the Royal National Theatre and he chose to do *Tartuffe*.

Although it was not a Tara production, he selected Tara actors and used the Tara performance style.

To date, the company has staged over seventy-five plays and their major project was a three-year work, *Journey to the West*. This was a trilogy – *Exodus* (1998) by Neil Biswas and Jatinder Verma, *Genesis* (1999) by Jatinder Verma and *Revelations* (2000) by Jatinder Verma – dealing with the experience of the migration of Indians to East Africa, and then from there to the UK. Tara has had a company of regular actors, and many notable British Asian actors such as Paul **Bhattacharjee**, Ayub **Khan Din**, Sudha **Bhuchar** and Shaheen **Khan** have passed through its stable.

SUMAN BHUCHAR

Taylor, Robert

b. 1958, England

photographer, writer, barrister

Taylor was called to the Bar (Gray's Inn, London) in 1983 after a career in air traffic control with the Royal Navy. His photographic career took off in the late 1980s while he was also working in educational publishing. His two 1994 solo shows, 'Black Who' and 'Imagining Intimacy', set down his strong interest in questions of identity and sexuality. Solo shows, 'White Noise' in 1995 (a photo installation) and 'Black on Black and White', Oxford LGC in 1996, continued the development of these themes, and in 1996 he took part in the 'Graphic Responses to AIDS' exhibition at the Victoria and Albert Museum, London. His work is featured on the **Autograph: the Association of Black Photographers** *Party-Line* CD-ROM and has been widely reviewed, with major feature articles in the gay and arts press. He has illustrated two **Institute of Contemporary Arts** publications and states that: 'My main photographic preoccupations are pleasure and personal politics. I am particularly interested in difference and the possibility that the distinctions that can be drawn between people are as exciting as they are threatening.' While **photography** remains his main interest, he is also actively involved in projects such as the co-production of a **Channel 4** comic

documentary about *Black Divas* and their queer fans, broadcast in September 1996, and writing. His work is held in the collections of the National Portrait Gallery and the Victoria and Albert Museum.

Select bibliography

Taylor, R. (2000) *Gay Planet*, London: Quarto.
—— (2000) *Portrait Party*, London: Chronos.
—— (1995) *Let's Get it on*, London: ICA.
—— (1994) *Safer Sexy*, London: Cassell.

ALISON DONNELL

Tegala, Simon

b. 1973, UK

artist, lecturer, stage designer

Simon Tegala is a critically acclaimed visual artist. His practice encompasses a variety of media from drawing, **photography**, sculpture, video installation, performance, Internet and digital art. Since graduating in 1995 from Goldsmiths College, his work has been shown in twenty-five exhibitions in ten different countries. He is currently represented by the Laure Genillard Gallery, London. His work has been exhibited in a number of major institutions including the National Gallery of Denmark, the Whitechapel Art Gallery, **Institute of Contemporary Arts**, A-Space (Toronto), the Hayward Gallery and the Museum of Contemporary Art, Gothenberg (2000). In 1998, he completed a major project, *Anabiosis*, which was produced by the **Institute of International Visual Arts** (inIVA). *Anabiosis* was a major success and was shortlisted for the Cap Gemini Digital Art Prize (1998). He was shortlisted for the Paul Hamlyn Award for Sculpture in 1996 and for the MOMART Fellowship at the Tate Liverpool. He has lectured and tutored at Central St Martins School of Art. Tegala has designed for stage and created live slide and video projections for concerts. He is currently working on *Anabiosis World*, which will exist on electronic signs in ten different countries and live on the Internet, simultaneously.

CATHERINE UGWU

television

As we arrive at the new millennium and the Internet is being touted extensively as the communications medium of choice, why should we be bothering to talk about television and, moreover, to be doing so via the written word? Well, the answer is pretty straightforward. In many parts of the world, the real challenge is to find safe drinking water; it is not about surfing the Web. If you take a clipboard and stand outside your local supermarket asking shoppers what they think about the information superhighway, you are as likely to get a strange look as a meaningful answer. If, on the other hand, you ask about the latest plotline in a country's most popular soap opera, most people will be able to offer a view. *That* is why television is important: it is universal (well, almost); it is popular; it is accessible; and, most importantly, 99.9 per cent of homes (in the Western world at least) have one. If we are interested in exploring persuasive modes of communication, television remains the medium *par excellence*.

So, in a *Companion to Contemporary Black British Culture*, what can we say about black people's contribution to the development of British television culture? More specifically, how can we relate the impact of television's portrayal of black communities to the bigger picture of Britain's social and cultural life? The first myth to explode, perhaps, is that black people on British television is a recent phenomenon: it is not. In fact when the BBC began broadcasting in November 1936, its first few faltering frames were full of a black comedy double act called 'Buck and Bubbles'. Admittedly, the pair were not British entertainers but, from those first fledgling television broadcasts, black people were going to be an intrinsic part of British television. What this very brief introductory essay will attempt to do, therefore, is to provide a thumbnail sketch of the relationship of black people and issues of 'race' to British television, charting watershed programmes and events, and exploring the contribution that black media professionals have made to changing the landscape of British television.

The post-war years saw Britain attempting to re-establish itself as a major power in the world and to bolster the confidence of the British public. These dual concerns were reflected in television's pre-occupation with all things colonial. In the early to mid-1950s, much of the programming that dealt with black issues was concerned with looking at black communities as they existed outside the British context, often as the exoticised 'other'. The comparative expense involved in television production meant that a number of programmes went out on to the streets to canvass opinion about social issues of the day – the vox pop approach – and this innovative form of programme-making coincided with the recruitment of a number of media practitioners who were interested in making 'socially responsible' programmes such as *Does Britain Have a Colour Bar?* (1955) and *People in Trouble: Mixed Marriages* (1958).

By the 1960s, the race-relations problematic had taken a solid hold in Britain, both providing an explanatory framework within which to analyse 'society' and identifying race as a social rather than political problem requiring social solutions (Ali, 1993). It was arguably Powell's 'rivers of blood' speech in 1968 that proved the turning point for both press and broadcasting in the UK, at last opening up the public debate on race that had been raging beneath the surface of polite society. The reality of white racism had to be finally acknowledged and, for the news media at least, blackness became inextricably linked with an internal conflict that needed to be contained (Tulloch, 1990). This equation of 'black equals problem' continues to be an abiding theme in both fictional and factual programming in contemporary media.

One of the first and perhaps most popular British programmes to discuss race themes was *Till Death Us Do Part*, which was originally broadcast from 1966 to 1974 on BBC 1. As well as constant repeats since the mid-1970s, the programme's main character, Alf Garnett saw a 1980s revival with a follow-up series, *In Sickness and in Health*. Although Alf's creator, Johnny Speight, argued at the time of the original broadcasts and since that his intention was to expose racist bigotry through the exaggerated utterances of Alf, such an intention has back-fired for many commentators. The enormous popularity of the show signified that there was something about it that appealed to a significant proportion of the viewing public.

Three notorious British comedy series of the 1970s to feature black characters were *Love Thy Neighbour* (Thames Television, 1972–5), *Mind Your Language* (BBC 1, 1976) and *It Ain't Half Hot Mum* (BBC 1, 1973–81). All three utilised standard sitcom formulas such as *double entendre*, quarrels, underdog cleverness and so on, and all were seen at the time as harmless fun. However, these shows that incorporated a specific 'race' theme were seldom able to transcend the limitations of the genre, and, although bolder than the previous generation, they none the less peddled the same stilted range of character types (Ross, 1996). In 1976, London Weekend Television launched *The Fosters*, the first comedy series to feature an all-black cast; the show ran for a second season in 1977. *The Fosters* was the first series to describe an 'ordinary' black family and their life without constantly privileging their problematic blackness, and was a British re-working of the very popular American show *Good Times*. Following quickly on the heels of *The Fosters* came *Empire Road*, the first black soap, which ran for two seasons between 1978 and 1979. The series had a predominance of African Caribbean and Asian characters, and included storylines that were concerned with mainstream issues such as parental discipline and difficult relationships.

A review of British programming broadcast during the 1950s–70s period would not be complete without reference to the notorious *The Black and White Minstrel Show*, one of the BBC's most popular series, which ran for twenty-one years, between 1958 and 1978. In today's more enlightened social climate, it would be unthinkable to broadcast such blatant caricatures, but even in the show's infancy dissenting voices were heard. However, the show was extremely popular, regularly attracting audiences of 12 million and sometimes as high as 18 million viewers. Woffinden (1988) suggests that part of its appeal lay in its vitality, since the minstrels mimed to pre-recorded tapes and were therefore free to indulge in dynamic and energetic **dance** sequences that gave the shows a lively and fresh appearance. If portraits of black communities suffered from narrowcasting during the early years of British television, the initiation of a fourth channel in 1981 (**Channel 4**) was heralded as the breaking of a new dawn: here

was a channel set up specifically to cater to minority interests, which would also have a positive knock-on effect on the other television companies. At the very least, Channel 4 has expanded independent television production and encouraged more black practitioners into the industry (Mercer, 1990), but the real and enduring changes in black images have been slow in coming.

By the 1980s, other types of 'black' humour were being broadcast, such as *No Problem!* (London Weekend Television, 1983–5), *Tandoori Nights* (Channel 4, 1985 and 1987) and **Desmonds** (Channel 4, 1988–94). As shows like *No Problem!* traded on making gentle fun of aspects of African Caribbean life, Asian communities have been exposed to similar ridicule in so-called comedy series like *Tandoori Nights*. This latter series was written by Farrukh **Dhondy**, who was also co-writer on *No Problem!*, and centred on the goings-on at a local Indian restaurant, The Jewel in the Crown, and its rival establishment, The Far Pavilions. This is ethnicity as farce. However, one of the few British comedy series to have received almost universal acclaim has been *Desmonds*, which completed a fourth series at the end of 1994. The show won the Best Channel 4 Sitcom award in 1992 and the series producer Humphrey Barclay attributed its success to the warm and friendly atmosphere of the family (cited in the **Voice**, 15 December 1992).

Where humour has been particularly successful in challenging stereotypical images has been in the area of British-based alternative comedy with personalities such as Lenny **Henry**, Ben Elton, Harry Enfield and black troupes such as the Bibi Crew, They Wouldn't and the Posse all performing counter-cultural routines. Shows such as *Spitting Image, Saturday Night Live, The Comedy Store, The Real McCoy* and *Get Up, Stand-Up* have done much to highlight and explore issues of racism and sexism. The most popular genre (in terms of viewing figures) is arguably the soap opera and every week ratings are dominated by soaps. However, despite the 'realist' philosophy that underpins soaps, very few have introduced significant black characters into their main narratives (Bourne, 1998). While it is true that most soaps, including now defunct examples such as *Crossroads*, have regularly introduced black characters into storylines, they have mostly been fleeting and specific to particular situations. It is also the case that the same actors stay on the soap circuit, being reinvented as the standard stern Asian father, the dutiful Asian mother, the rebellious black teenager and so on in a never-ending cycle of typecasting. *EastEnders'* producer Julia Smith reports having made a conscious decision that, when the new soap was launched, it would be a working-class series that would reflect the cultural diversity of the real East End. Smith claimed that the series would deal with controversial topics and would be 'drama which could encompass stories about homosexuals, rape, unemployment, racial prejudice, etc. in a believable context...we had a Bengali shop owner, a Jewish doctor and Caribbean father and son, a Turkish Cypriot cafe-owner married to an English girl' (Smith quoted in Buckingham 1987: 16) Five years later, all of the original black and minority characters had left the series, some in the glare of publicity.

In June 1991, the first British Asian soap *Family Pride* was broadcast, directed by David Vaughan-Thomas and produced by Central TV for Channel 4. The serial, originally conceived as a 26-parter to be broadcast twice a week, centred on the rivalry between two successful Asian families, the Bedis and Rizvis, and was devised as an antidote to the stereotypical portraits of Asian life found in most other popular programmes. 'Our characters are mostly achievers...they are successful and relatively affluent, now they're looking at how best to provide for their children in a society which has come to accept the Asian input' (Zia Mohyeddin cited in Smurthwaite, 1991: 23). If this is a rather optimistic assessment of white Britain's response to Asian communities, the fact that an Asian soap was made at all is still noteworthy. The soap returned for a second run in December 1992 with the introduction of two new families, the Doshis and the Alis. The newcomers were less affluent than the original characters and presented a balance to counter the criticisms that Asian family life had been portrayed as unrealistically wealthy in the first run.

Overall, the 1990s saw some 'improvement' in the volume of black actors now seen on screen, but, sadly, there have been very few leading roles for, or series that have revolved around, a black character in British drama so far this decade, although the Channel 4 series *Little Napoleons* was a particular exception. As with film (see **film and cinema**), the most common way in which television includes black actors (outside comedy) is through the crime genre. However, it should also be said that black media professionals are beginning to obtain a slightly more visible presence outside the restrictions of the crime genre. For example, hospital-based dramas and comedies have usually recruited at least one black actor as a health-care professional (see for example *Casualty*, *Surgical Spirit* and *Cardiac Arrest*). Similarly, a number of current affairs and news programmes have become less self-conscious about recruiting black media personnel and now regularly feature black newscasters and presenters: Zenab **Badawi** on *Channel 4 News*; Carmen Pryce on *Tomorrow's World* (BBC 1); Sankha Guha on *Here and Now* (BBC 1); and, of course, veteran news presenters such as Trevor **McDonald** and Moira **Stuart**. Slowly the landscape of mainstream television is changing and audiences are seeing more realistic representations of contemporary British society, but, for many people, the more satisfactory option is either to turn towards specifically targeted strands such as those that emerge from the multicultural units at the BBC or Channel 4, or else subscribe to one of the burgeoning stations that are now available on satellite or cable.

References

Ali, Y. (1993) 'Address to the 9th Birmingham Film and Television Festival', 15 October.

Bourne, S. (1998) *Black in the British Frame: Black People in British Film and Television 1896–1996*, London: Cassell and the Arts Council of England.

Buckingham, D. (1987) *Public Secrets: EastEnders and Its Audience*, London: British Film Institute.

Mercer, K. (1990) 'Black people in British television', *Artrage* 27: 5–8.

Ross, K. (1996) *Black and White Media: Black Images in Popular Film and Television*, Oxford: Polity Press.

Smurthwaite, N. (1991) 'Talking about a revolution', *Television Today* 5750: 23.

Tulloch, J. (1990) 'Television and black Britons', in A Goodwin and G Whannel (eds) *Understanding Television*, London: Routledge, pp. 141–52.

Woffinden, B. (1988) 'Blacking up, backing down', *The Listener*, 30 June.

KAREN ROSS

television prizes

In addition to television network strategies, the Arts Council initiated the Black Arts Video Project Scheme in the late 1980s to support new directors in the production of imaginative arts documentaries on black cultural issues. There were ten winners in the 1992–3 competition, including five newcomers and five more established practitioners. Building on the success of this initiative, in 1992 independent Carlton Television and the Arts Council ran a competition to offer commissions for the production of original, five-minute films (see **film and cinema**) on any aspect of black arts, **music** or culture. The budget ceiling for each film was £10,000. In the literature accompanying the competition, the Arts Council reported that one of the objectives of the competition – subsequently marketed as Synchro – was to stimulate the production of videos about black arts and cultural subjects by new video-makers. It was hoped that, as a result, professionalism would be encouraged and a contribution would be made towards greater professional opportunities in the future. In the end, eight films were commissioned and these were subsequently screened as two thirty-minute compilations on Carlton TV in early 1994. Alongside this initiative, the Arts Council and Carlton TV are also aiming to establish a training programme to help encourage an understanding of the commissioning process and television production skills. In 1993, the BBC ran a script-writing competition – Black Screen – to develop new black writing talent, and twelve writers subsequently began working with BBC script-editors, although ultimately only six scripts actually resulted in broadcast dramas. The competition was repeated in 1994, with a similar outcome.

The **Commission for Racial Equality** (CRE) has also added its weight to the debate, and in 1992 launched its Race in the Media Awards to 'encourage more informed coverage of race relations issues' (RIMA publicity literature). In 1994, its second year, the keynote speaker at the awards presentation was Peter Brooke, the Heritage Secretary, who emphasised that responsible reporting and fair presentation of the issues were of crucial social importance. He added that the Race in the Media Awards, by recognising good practice in the treatment of race and ethnic issues, made an important contribution towards 'better journalism and...helped create a climate in which sensitive reporting of race issues becomes a matter of course'. (CRE Press Release, 12 June 1994)

At the European level, two major prizes are now available for individuals producing media works that conrtribute to the promotion of understanding and 'tolerance' between different ethnic groups. The Prix Iris Media Award for Equality and Tolerance celebrated its third series of awards in 1999, in conjunction with the annual meeting of the Intercultural Programme Group of the European Broadcasting Union (EBU), making awards for media productions in the categories 'TV fiction and non-fiction which are of outstanding quality in contributing to a better mutual understanding between ethnic and cultural groups' (Prix Iris publicity, 1999). Prix Iris is a co-production of the Dutch Anti Discrimination Council (ADO) and NPS Television, and is supported by the European Commission, the Secretary-General of the Council of Europe, the European Cultural Foundation, the EBU, the Dutch Ministry of Health, Welfare and Sport (VWS) and the Dutch Broadcasting Corporation NOS. In 1997, out of the European Communities Year Against Racism, the EMMA (European Multicultural Media Agency) initiative was born to support the work of new young filmmakers across Europe to develop a twenty-five-minute documentary. The competition resulted in four films being made, which were broadcast across Europe during 1999.

KAREN ROSS

Ten.8

During the 1980s and 1990s, Ten.8, an organisation based in Birmingham in the West Midlands, was responsible for showcasing and producing some of the key works and debates around the contested arena of black **photography**. Ten.8 was a fusion of developments in writing from the Birmingham **Centre for Contemporary Cultural Studies** along with a rising wealth of black and white photographers and writers within the area, such as Vanley **Burke** and Maxine **Walker**, as well as Derek Bishton (one of the founding members), who had an interest in black subjects in his writing and photographic work. The organization, which was managed by a small editorial group, curated and toured photographic shows locally, nationally and internationally. However, the organisation will always be remembered for its journal, *Ten.8*, which took as its title the largest negative size in **photography** (10 × 8 inches) with which one could obtain maximum quality. In 1984, in collaboration with the Photographers Gallery, the organisation produced the landmark issue 'Black image', which included writings from Stuart **Hall**, C.L.R. **James**, Pratibha **Parmar** and many others. In 1986 the organisation began to invite practitioners to edit special editions, which included 'Black experiences', edited by David A. **Bailey** (then Chair of the group), in 1986; 'Evidence', edited by Val Wilmer, in 1986–7; and 'Homosexualities Part Two', edited by Sunil **Gupta**, in 1989. By the 1990s the journal developed into a photo-paperback and the organisation invested all of their resources in the last issue, 'The critical decade', edited by Stuart Hall and David A. Bailey, in 1992. This was a seminal publication that looked at the last ten years of black art activities and the role black photography played in shaping those activities and the attendant debates.

DAVID A. BAILEY

Territories

The film *Territories* was produced in 1984 by **Sankofa Film Collective**. Directed by Isaac **Julien**, *Territories* is structured around the **Notting Hill Carnival** and its representation within televisual discourse (particularly BBC documentaries). The film is divided into two parts: the first draws together documentary footage of the **carnival**; the second shows two black film-makers analysing and deconstructing that footage. Stylistically, the film (see **film and cinema**) is itself carnivalesque, superimposing and juxtaposing different images, voices and coverage in a way that signals the limits of documentary realism and its ability to 'represent' the Notting Hill Carnival. Cultural critics like Kobena **Mercer** and Stuart **Hall** see *Territories* as central to the shift in black cultural production, away from the realist aesthetics of the 1970s and early 1980s, and towards the more self-conscious, experimental aesthetics of the late 1980s and 1990s.

Further reading

Diawara, M. (1990) 'Black British cinema: spectatorship and identity formation in *Territories*', *Public Culture* 3(1): 121–50.

JAMES PROCTER

theatre

In 1956, the English Stage Company at the Royal Court Theatre initiated what was to be a new era in British theatre with John Osborne's *Look Back in Anger*. In December 1958, it also produced Errol John's *Moon on a Rainbow Shawl*, which had won first prize in the *Observer* play competition of 1957. The play, like many immigrant plays to follow, was set in the West Indies, in this case Trinidad. The Royal Court also gave a main house production to Barry Reckord's *Flesh to a Tiger* in 1958, and Sunday night productions without décor to Wole Soyinka's *The Invention* in November 1959, Derek Walcott's *Sea at Dauphin* and *Six in the Rain* in 1960, and Barry Reckord's *You in Your Small Corner* in October of the same year. Reckord's *Skyvers* (1963) was, significantly, produced with an all-white cast because the Royal Court claimed that they could not find any black actors. In 1966, the company also gave a main house production to Wole Soyinka's *The Lion and the Jewel*, and a Sunday night performance to Partap Sharma's *A Touch of Brightness*. Although black drama did, therefore, have some presence in the early New British Theatre it was indeed sparse and did not, considering the significance of immigration from the West Indies and other

British ex-colonies since 1948, reflect that theatre's declared concern with life in contemporary Britain.

It was not until 1970 that the first seeds of a black British theatre were sown with Ed Berman's proposal for a '**Black and White Power Season**' of black American plays at the Ambiance Theatre in London. The white director Roland Rees, who later founded the Foco Novo theatre company, persuaded Berman to include black British writing and, through various black friends, made contact with a Trinidadian writer, Mustapha **Matura**, who had lived in Britain since 1961. Matura contributed four short plays, subsequently entitled *Black Pieces*, which he had written some time before without hope of production. Here, for the first time, Matura reproduced the authentic voice of the working-class, black West Indians who were attempting to settle in Britain. Two of the black actors in these plays, T-Bone **Wilson** and Alfred Fagon, were prompted by this experience to write plays themselves. The production had, therefore, resulted in three notable achievements. It had 'discovered' a black writer, encouraged others to begin writing and exhibited the availability of black actors. The plays proved to be a great success and led to a commission from the influential producer Michael White, which resulted in Matura's next play, *As Time Goes By*, which was produced by the Traverse Theatre, Edinburgh. in 1971.

It was, however, during the early 1970s, at a time when touring theatre groups were concerned with women's and gay issues, 'ethnic arts' had become a subject for consideration by funding bodies and black awareness had crossed the Atlantic, that a discrete black theatre began to emerge in Britain. The primary aims of this new theatre were to produce new plays by black writers on subjects of interest to black audiences, and to employ black actors and black technicians. The four best-known and enduring examples of such companies formed in Britain during the 1970s and 1980s, each with a clear perception of its theatrical and dramatic discourse, were Temba, **Talawa Theatre Company**, the **Black Theatre Co-operative** and **Tara Arts**.

Temba, the first British black theatre company, founded by actors Alton Kumalo and Oscar James, took its name from the Zulu word for 'hope'. While appearing at Stratford in 1972, Kumalo and James had become aware that black actors were caught in the catch-22 situation of being undercast because of lack of experience. One aim of the company was, therefore, to offer such experience. Temba's work was initially issue-based and placed particular emphasis upon racism. However, after the Arts Council's 'Glory of the Garden' review threatened the company with closure, in 1984 the director Alby James (son of Jamaican immigrants and brought up in North London) became the company's artistic director. James had already worked for the Royal Shakespeare Company and the Royal Court, and applied this experience to re-constituting the company. He expanded Temba's African-orientated programme to include material from the USA and the Caribbean. Like other small theatre companies during the 1980s, he also set up co-productions with theatres in Leicester and Birmingham, which could offer a potential audience from their large immigrant communities. James considered that the focus on racism, which now appeared to be the theme most favoured for black theatre by funding bodies, particularly in the aftermath of the riots of the early 1980s and in the light of the Tory policy on urban regeneration, represented a form of discrimination. He set out to replace this with 'a drama of celebration', which embraced both black and European cultures, and would offer a sense of dignity and self-worth to the black community. This constituted, therefore, a policy of accepting the black community's minority status while at the same time establishing a naturalised presence for black performers and writers within British culture by performing plays with black casts by both black and white dramatists. Unfortunately, the company was finally terminated in 1992.

In 1979, the absence of a forum for black playwriting led Mustapha Matura and the white director Charlie Hanson to set up the Black Theatre Co-operative (BTC) Having collaborated on the lunch-time production of two of Matura's plays, *More* and *Another Tuesday*, at the **Institute of Contemporary Arts**, they tried to interest theatres in Matura's new play, *Welcome Home Jacko*. Unable to find a venue, they set up their own company and presented the play at the 'Factory' in Paddington in May 1979. This company formed the nucleus for the BTC. Unlike Temba's attempt under Alby to incorporate both black and white culture, the aim of the BTC was to offer opportunities for black British writers, performers, technicians and directors; in other words, to open up areas of the theatre that had been hitherto predominantly occupied by whites. This policy, as was intended, was to some extent successful in gaining admission for black writing and black practitioners into mainstream, white British theatre and television. This showcasing generally necessitated performance in the type of realistic, well-made plays, which would provide the kind of substantive roles found in the mainstream theatre. Nevertheless, it must be acknowledged that the company truthfully portrayed, to the acclaim of the black community, the singular experience of black British youth in plays such as Matura's *Welcome Home Jacko*.

The Talawa Theatre Company, whose name is a Jamaican word, derived from Old Ashanti or Tiwi, meaning 'small but stalwart' or 'strong, female and powerful'', was founded in 1985 by four women, Yvonne **Brewster**, Carmen Munroe, Mona Hammond and Inigo Espejel. It is directed primarily by Yvonne Brewster, who co-founded the Barn Theatre in Jamaica with Trevor Rhone in 1965 but who, since 1974, has worked in Britain. Initially, the company was particularly concerned with the portrayal of black women, but Brewster's wider aim was, however, to inform, enrich and enlighten British theatrical and dramatic discourse through reference in her productions to African ritual and black political experience. Like Temba, the company also aimed to place the classics of European theatre in a fresh cultural perspective by casting black actors and to introduce the British public, both black and white, to the work of black playwrights. Since 1991, the company, unusually for black theatre, has had its own building, the Cochrane Theatre in central London.

A similar cultural fusion has also been seen in the work of the Asian company, **Tara Arts**. Jatinder **Verma**, its founding director, came to England with his parents from Kenya at the age of fourteen as result of the Idi Amin's expulsion of Asians. Like Alby James, Verma was university educated, but studied neither **literature** nor theatre. Tara Arts is the only Asian company with

revenue funding from the Arts Council. It was formed, in 1976, in response to violent attacks on Asians in London's Southall and was, in part, an attempt to assert an Asian presence. The company was fortunate to be provided with a somewhat ramshackle base by the **Greater London Council** (GLC). Verma soon became aware that Tara Arts was, however, in danger of being marginalised under the category of 'ethnic arts' and, therefore, although it initially employed agitprop to portray the Asian experience in Britain, the company gradually began to develop a discourse that linked Western classical theatre with the non-naturalistic elements of Asian dance, music and the visual arts. It also utilised a theatrical discourse drawn from Indian cinema and from Bhavai, an Indian popular theatrical form similar to the *commedia dell'arte*. This intertextuality was intended by Verma not only to break from naturalism but also to create a distinctive voice that reflected the cultural diversity of immigrant experience.

The Tara Arts intertextual approach has been applied to plays including Gogol's *The Government Inspector*, Buchner's *Danton's Death* and Molière's *Tartuffe*. The last was performed at the National Theatre, an occasion which Verma saw as an acknowledgement of the Asian presence in the British national cultural landscape. In 1992, Tara Arts also produced the first classical Asian play to be performed at the National Theatre, *The Little Clay Cart*. In part owing to the Tory government's attempt to ameliorate racial tension and regenerate the inner cities in the wake of the riots that had erupted at the beginning of the decade, the 1980s saw the emergence of other black theatre companies such the British-Asian Theatre Company, Hounslow Arts Co-operative, the Asian Theatre Co-operative, Double-Edged Theatre, Carib Theatre and Tamasha. In common with the companies described above, their aims were: to be free of white control; to adopt an oppositional to British mainstream theatre, which was perceived as white and inherently racist; to present work by black writers that dealt either with contemporary black experience or with the effects of Britain's colonial heritage; and to assert a right to public funding equivalent to that of white constituency theatre. On a more practical level, the formation of such companies was intended to provide work and training for black actors and technicians. As might be expected, black theatre was largely confined to those areas of the country with the largest immigrant and second-generation populations. Chief among these was London, whose GLC became the leading funding agency for black arts. After the abolition of the GLC by the Thatcher government, the responsibility for funding in London was transferred to the Greater London Arts Association. Although the black theatre movement, despite various Arts Council bursaries, has achieved only limited access to the mainstream theatre for black directors, administrators and technicians, and has largely left unresolved questions of nomenclature, separatism, integrationism or multiculturalism, and the viability of a black theatrical and dramatic discourse, it has nevertheless encouraged the appearance of more black performers in the institutional theatre and on television. It has also resulted in more racially integrated casting, has publicly explored racism and has to some extent brought black experience to the attention of the white majority.

Further reading

Gilroy, P. (1987) *'There Ain't no Black in the Union Jack'*, London: Hutchinson.

Khan, N. (1976) *The Arts Britain Ignores*, London: Commision for Racial Equality.

Owusu, K. (1986) *The Struggle for Black Arts in Britain*, London: Comedia.

Philips, M. (1981) 'Black theatre in Britain', *Platform* 3: 3–6.

Tompsett, R. (1996) 'Black theatre in Britain', *Performing Arts International* 1(2).

D. KEITH PEACOCK

Theatre Museum Archive

The Theatre Museum in London's Covent Garden holds a range of material relating to black **theatre** in both its core and special collections, and is developing, through its education departments and its contemporary collecting policy, a number of projects to continue to build a Black Theatre Archive. The Museum's core collections contain playbills, programmes and reviews, and are the largest of their kind in the world. These collections document British, especially London, theatre and, in some cases, date back to the eighteenth century. The Museum continues to collect this material on a daily basis. The Museum also holds extensive additional collections including photographs, posters, costumes, paintings, scripts, stage designs, files of material on companies and individuals, and the National Video Archive of Performance. Among material related to black theatre are programmes for the hugely popular 1903 musical *In Dahomey* and for the black theatre seasons at the Arts Theatre in the 1980s, as well as playbills, portraits and engravings for the appearances in London of the great nineteenth-century black Shakespearean actor, Ira Aldridge, and much other material awaiting discovery. Videos include the Blackgrounds oral history interviews and live recordings of productions such as **Talawa Theatre Company**'s *King Lear*, Biyi **Bandele**'s *Oroonoko* at the RSC, Tamasha's Ayub **Kahn Din**'s *East is East* and Roy Williams's *Lift Off* for the Royal Court Theatre.

Additionally, the Museum holds a number of special collections and archives, including: the Temba Theatre collection, which includes reviews, scripts and other material relating to this important black theatre company and others; the archive of the **Black Mime Theatre Company**, including photographs, business records, audio and video, marketing and other material; the unpublished scripts of playwright Alfred Fagon; and both archival material and costumes and head-dresses from the South East Asian Dance School, Akademi. Black theatre is represented in other special collections like the Unity Theatre Archive, which includes material relating to Paul Robeson and his appearance with this workers' theatre company. The Museum has also developed projects building on archive material, including, in conjunction with Positive Steps company, a residency (2000) by surviving members of the first black British **dance** company Ballets Negres (founded 1946) to recreate their first ballet, *Market Day*, with contemporary young people; a Black Theatre History Trail for young people, to mark Black History Month 1999; and a log of plays by black writers produced in Britain. It is developing a number of joint projects with Black Theatre Forum and Middlesex University to preserve material relating to Black Theatre History and make teaching resources on this topic available on the Internet. The Museum actively seeks to supplement and fill gaps in its holdings, recognising that black theatre has often been poorly represented in the collections, and is keen to build contacts with, and ensure the preservation of material relating to, companies, organisations and individuals in black theatre. The Museum makes material available in gallery displays, for individual research through its study rooms and for educational use through workshops and group sessions.

SUSAN CROFT

Theatre of Black Women

A black feminist **theatre** company established in 1982 by Bernardine **Evaristo**, Patricia Hilaire and Paulette Randall, who met at Rose Bruford College through their collaboration on final projects and collective involvement with the Royal Court's Writers' Workshops (together with the Young Peoples' Theatre, the starting-point for many contemporary black playwrights). The four formed a company primarily to re-stage their one-woman shows for a wider audience: *Chameleon* (1983, Randall), *Hey Brown Girl* (1983, Hilaire) and *Tiger, Teeth Clenched not to Bite* (1983, Evaristo). Randall withdrew from the company and has gone on to write for radio and to direct extensively in black theatre, including with Temba and Nitro/**Black Theatre Co-operative**, while Evaristo and Hilaire devised the first of two shows: *Silhouette* (1984) and *Pyeyucca* (1985), exploring self-image and history. *Silhouette* addresses mixed-race identity and black women's internalisation of white racist values as self-hatred. Part of an upsurge of black theatre in the supportive climate of the **Greater London Council** under Ken Livingstone, they were the first company devoted to exploring the experience of black women and one of the first black companies to eschew realism or the theatre of political persuasion in favour of a poetic aesthetic that would allow a deeper and more inward exploration of black female identity and its contra-

dictions and complexities, a style strongly influence by US writers Ntozake Shange, Adrienne Kennedy and Alice Walker. Evaristo and Hilaire went on to establish workshops in directing, design and other theatre skills, and, themselves both poets, to commission external writers, especially poets, to develop work for performance. Notable collaborations include those with Jackie **Kay** whose *Chiaroscuro* (1986), together with Jacqueline **Rudet**'s *Basin* (1985), was one of the first British plays to focus on black lesbian experience, and Gabriela and Jean Pearse whose children's play *Miss Quarshie and the Tiger's Tale* (1986) draws on the African-Caribbean folk-tales of Anansi the spider. Like the earlier devised plays, *Chiaroscuro* uses ritual, storytelling, stylised movement, symbolism and poetic language to explore its theme, but intersperses these with naturalistic scenes focusing on four contemporary women. Ruth Harris wrote the company's final shows: *The Children* (1987), and the harrowing monologue *The Cripple* (1986), based on the life of Pauline Wiltshire, recounting her experience of disability and social rejection, rape, abandonment and single parenthood. The company's scripts are largely unpublished. Evaristo has gone on to develop her career as a writer of poetry and fiction.

Further reading

Croft, S. (1993) 'Black women playwrights in Britain', in T. Griffiths and M. Llewellyn-Jones (eds) *British and Irish Women Dramatists since 1958*, London: Open University Press, pp. 84–98.
—— (1985) 'Interview', *The Plot* 2 (autumn).
Kay, J. (1987) *Chiaroscuro*, in J. Davis (ed.) *Lesbian Plays*, London: Methuen.
Sulter, M. (ed.) (1990) extracts from *Pyeyucca* (with Hilaire, Theatre of Black Women, 1985) *Passion: Discourses on Blackwomen's Creativity*, Hebden Bridge: Urban Fox.

SUSAN CROFT

theatre venues

Even though black **theatre** remains marginalised in British culture, there are theatres that have dedicated themselves to presenting black productions; some spaces mount in-house productions, while others receive touring shows. Each type of venue has been instrumental in ensuring a forum for black performance in Britain. Black theatre productions are usually seen in community arts venues or fringe theatres; it is rare for a black production to open in the West End, although some (usually musicals) have made successful West End transfers. The Theatre Royal, Stratford East, and the Tricycle Theatre are perhaps the two most prominent places for the production of black theatre in London in the late twentieth century.

The Theatre Royal, Stratford East, has developed from staging the occasional black show to having ethnic theatre central to its programme. Reflecting the racial mix in Newham, the theatre has been crucial in developing a popular ethnic theatre in the East End. Comedy revue nights during the 1990s regularly showcased black and Asian talent such as the Posse, the Bibi Crew and Asian comedy groups. The theatre's commitment to producing ethnic arts has increased markedly since **Black Theatre Co-operative**'s production of Mustapha **Matura**'s *Welcome Home Jacko*, which was produced there in 1979. Other notable productions include Tunde Ikoli's *Scrape off the Black*, Femi Elufowoju Jnr's *Tickets and Ties* and Clarke Peter's *Five Guys Named Moe*, which transferred to the West End. While the Theatre Royal, Stratford East, has primarily invested in black British talents, the Tricycle Theatre has foregrounded African American plays. Black Theatre Co-operative presented Lorraine Hansberry's *A Raisin in the Sun* (1985), and Carib Theatre Company's production of James Baldwin's *The Amen Corner* (1987) was the first play to transfer to the West End. Subsequent West End transfers include the musicals *Ain't Misbehavin'* and *Kat and the Kings*. The Tricycle has housed the British premières of: Howard Sackler's *The Great White Hope*, August Wilson's *Joe Turner's Come and Gone*, *The Piano Lesson* and *Two Trains Running*; and Alice Childress's *Trouble in Mind*; as well as working in collaboration with leading black theatre companies.

Of Britain's mainstream theatres, the Royal Court Theatre has a long history of providing space for black theatre productions. In 1958, Errol John's award-winning *Moon on a Rainbow Shawl*, was

seen there and forty years later, in 1998, **Tamasha Theatre Company** produced Ayub **Khan Din**'s *East is East*. A new writing theatre, the Royal Court is regarded as a 'rite of passage' space for budding young British playwrights. As a writer in residence, Winsome **Pinnock** produced *Talking in Tongues* for the upstairs theatre and *A Rock in Water* for the Young People's theatre. Her play *Mules*, for the Clean Break Theatre Company, also premièred in the upstairs theatre. Other playwrights seen at the Royal Court include Biyi **Bandele**, Wole Soyinka and Chinua Achebe.

Other venues that have played an instrumental role in providing spaces for the production of black theatre are the Lyric Theatre Studio, in Hammersmith, which has shown plays by Winsome Pinnock and **Talawa Theatre Company**, and the nearby Riverside Studios, which programmes British and visiting black theatre productions. The Warehouse Theatre, Croydon, has collaborated with Black Theatre Co-operative and produced plays by Jacqueline **Rudet**; the Bloomsbury Theatre and the Lewisham Theatre both stage popular Jamaican comedies, and the experimental **Institute of Contemporary Arts** has embraced the talents of artists such as Dorothea **Smartt** and Susan Lewis. The Albany, Deptford, Chat's Palace, the Cockpit Theatre, Hoxton Hall and Jackson's Lane remain crucial community arts venues that mount theatre-in-education and other community arts shows, as does the Oval House Theatre, which regularly features performances by black writers. Indeed, the Oval House Theatre offered a platform to up-and-coming black directors and playwrights, as well as companies such as the British West African company Teata Fahodzi. Diverse in their programming, they are active in providing a much needed space for black gay and lesbian theatre; Queenie, a.k.a. Valerie **Mason-John**, produced two sell-out shows, *Sin Dykes*, and *Brown Girl in the Ring*, and Steven Luckie directed *Boy with Beer* and *Talking about Men*. As a community arts venue, the Oval house is also home to a carnival Mas band, The South Connections.

In the late 1980s, black theatre seasons were paramount to raising the profile of black theatre in Britain. Each season staged three plays that served as a showcase for black playwrights, directors and performers. The Arts Theatre hosted the 1987 run, and the 1989 season played at the Euston Shaw. Black theatre practitioners have long bemoaned the absence of a building base for black theatre in Britain. In 1991, Talawa Theatre Company successfully secured the funds to obtain a three-year lease on the Cochrane Theatre; this meant that they were able to produce at least three shows each year. Shows included Wole Soyinka's *The Road*, Ntozake Shange's *The Love Space Demands*, Biyi Bandele's *Resurrections* and a black production of *King Lear*. Umoja Theatre Company also managed their own small theatre, the Base, which accommodated various black theatre productions as well as cabaret and comedy nights. Comedy and cabaret is a regular feature at the Hackney Empire, a theatre that also houses plays, musicals and talent contests, including the televised *291 Club*.

Although there is a certain London bias, many black companies toured to regional arts and community venues throughout England. The West Yorkshire Playhouse, Bristol Old Vic Studio and the **Nia Centre for African and Caribbean Culture** in Manchester are just some of the theatres that received touring shows. The Nottingham Playhouse, the Birmingham Repertory theatre and the Liverpool Everyman mounted co-productions with established black theatre companies, while the Contact theatre in Manchester and the Nuffield, Southampton, co-produced black theatre with the Tricycle Theatre.

Further reading

Hedley, P. (1993) 'Black theatre development at Theatre Royal, Stratford East', in R.A. Thompsett (ed.) *Black Theatre in Britain*, Amsterdam: Harwood Academic Press, pp. 23–34.

—— (1998) 'A theatre director's journey to the obvious', in T. Ikoli (ed.) *Scrape off the Black*, London: Oberon Books, pp. 7–25.

LYNETTE GODDARD

Thin Black Line, The

The Black Women group both exhibited and critiqued the nascent black art movement and white **feminism**. Their seminal exhibition was 'The Thin Black Line' at London's **Institute of Contemporary Arts** (ICA) in 1985, curated by Lubaina **Himid**. Himid noted in the catalogue that the approaches by the participants differed; some work was direct and confrontational, other work by artists such as Sonia **Boyce**, Ingrid **Pollard** and Veronica **Ryan** took a more contemplative approach. Serious problems with the ICA's handling of the exhibition were voiced at a seminar held during the exhibition run. The exhibition was physically marginalised by being held in the corridor and upstairs gallery rather than the main gallery, ironically repeating the social marginalisation that much of the work addressed. Exhibitors' names were mis-spelled in the catalogue and the request to list them alphabetically ignored. The exhibition can now be seen as not only the most important Black Women exhibition but also one of the most glaring attempts by a mainstream institution to gain credibility through a token show of black British artists without changing institutional politics.

Further reading

ICA (1985) *The Thin Black Line*, exhibition catalogue, London: ICA.

NIRU RATNAM

Third Text

Rasheed **Araeen** edited the short-lived periodical *Black Phoenix* at the end of the 1970s. The magazine (see **publishing, newspapers and magazines**) lasted three issues before underfunding led to its demise. *Third Text*, the first issue of which came out in autumn 1987, can be seen as the successor to *Black Phoenix* and was also founded by Araeen. Published four times a year, it has become a major international periodical and the only British journal to devote itself to international and post-colonial visual art (see **visual and plastic arts**).

From its inception the periodical has carried the description 'Third World Perspectives on Contemporary Art and Culture' on its cover. Araeen explains in the editorial of the first issue that, despite the fracturing of the term, it can still be seen to refer to particular geographical areas and cultures, as long as these cultures are not treated as a homogenous whole. Araeen argues for the specificity and differences of culture, implicitly aligning himself against conventional multicultur-alism without espousing conventional anti-racism. Instead he states that the magazine will seek to examine the particular configurations of power and ideology operating in the sphere of visual art, offering a critical account of dominant discourses from the periphery.

Jean Fisher joined as associate editor in 1989 and subsequently took over as editor. The period-ical has published the work of many important scholars such as Benita Parry, Okwui Enwezor, Paul **Gilroy**, Geeta Kapur, Laura Mulvey and Griselda Pollock. It has also served as the locus for many of the debates that framed black art in the UK in the 1980s and the formation of more recent concepts such as New Internationalism and hybridity. Many articles have appeared on indivi-dual black and Asian British artists, as well as reviews of relevant exhibitions and books. The editorial policy has supported a variety of dis-courses, and artists' own writings have often been printed. Special issues have covered specific exhibitions such as '**The Other Story**', which Araeen curated, and 'Magiciens de la Terre', or wider themes such as autobiography and new technologies. While the periodical has remained true to the spirit of its initial remit, its scope has widened to deal with changes in the art world, covering for instance the growth of young British art.

Third Text has successfully connected the prac-tices of British black and Asian artists – which tended to be insular in the 1980s – to the wider world of international practices and debates. In this way it prefigured later critical discourses that have stressed the global as well as the local. It has also transformed itself into a truly international journal, which seeks not to homogenise or celebrate, but to explore the increasingly complex waters of global artistic practices. Fisher departed as editor in 1999, succeeded by Ziauddin Sardar. An international advisory board and an editorial board both operate, and include a number of well-regarded academics and writers.

Further reading

Araeen, R. (1987) 'Why *Third Text?*', *Third Text* 1: 3–5.

NIRU RATNAM

Tippa Irie

b. 1965, London, England

singer, producer

Tippa Irie (Anthony Henry) first came to promi-nence as a member of the influential London-based Saxon Sound Studio International during the early 1980s, along with performers such as **Smiley Culture**, Papa Levi and Maxi **Priest**. Tippa Irie, nicknamed 'Mr Versatile' due to his ability to incorporate both humorous and serious 'reality' lyrics into his sets, was part of a wave of British MCs and performers who were successfully able to challenge the dominance of the Jamaican perfor-mers upon the **music** scene from the mid-1980s on. In 1986, Tippa Irie released *Is it Really Happening to Me?*, his debut album. Since then he has recorded over ten albums, working in colla-boration with a diverse range of producers and performers including the **Mad Professor**, who produced 1994's *Rebel on the Roots Corner* and the ground-breaking *JA To UK Clash* (1988) with the Jamaican MC Papa San. Tippa Irie has toured the world as a solo artist and with the band UB40 and the solo performer Pato Banton, as well as with the Saxon Sound System, while remaining based in Britain, having built his own studio in London.

ANDY WOOD

Transforming the Crown

'Transforming the Crown' (1997) was the first major attempt on the part of a US institution to present a wide-ranging selection of the work of black British visual artists (see **visual and plastic arts**) to a US audience. The exhibition was organised by the Caribbean Cultural Centre, known for presenting exhibitions about Africa and the African diaspora, in conjunction with the

Studio Museum in Harlem and the Bronx Museum of the Arts. The exhibition was curated by Mora Beauchamp-Byrd who had initially wished to organise a group show of around twelve black British artists she admired, including Ronald **Moody**, Aubrey **Williams** and Keith **Piper**. Subsequent visits to the UK persuaded her that a larger exhibition would be both desirable and possible. The result was 148 works by the fifty-eight artists who agreed to exhibit. The list of participating artists ranged from some of those who practised in the 1950s through to young, relatively unknown artists. A number of artists turned down the opportunity to exhibit.

'Transforming the Crown' was divided thematically around the three venues. Byrd attempted to tease out the main preoccupations of black British artists, rather than following a historical approach; organising categories included 'the body' and 'the flag'. Major installations during the exhibition included David **Medalla**'s *A Stitch in Time* and Yinka **Shonibare**'s *Sun, Sea and Sand*. A film (see **film and cinema**) and video programme by black British film-makers was screened at intervals during the exhibition's run. The wider exhibition also contained two smaller mini-exhibitions, one on the **Caribbean Artists' Movement**, and one on the **photography** of Vanley **Burke**, which took up the whole of the smallest of the venues. Burke's photojournalism provided a pictorial context of the recent history of multicultural Britain. The exhibition catalogue was also designed to set the scene for the US viewer with both historical accounts and more broad-brushed theoretical essays.

Byrd repeatedly stresses in her catalogue essays that the exhibition ought to be seen as a US take on black British art rather than an attempt at an overall survey. The possible links between black British art and black US art had not been explored in any exhibition up until that point, although writers such as Eddie **Chambers** had argued that the influence of the Harlem Renaissance and the Civil Rights movement had been important for British black artists. It is perhaps possible to draw a parallel between the function of this exhibition in the USA with the role that 'Rhapsodies in Black: Art of the Harlem Renaissance' played in Britain. Although it was received moderately well in the USA, the exhibition was subsequently criticised by British commentators. Critics argued that the layout and structure of the show replicated mid-1980s British group shows, when 'black art' was used as a monolithic funding category by bodies such as the **Greater London Council**.

Further reading

The Franklin H. Williams Caribbean Cultural Center (1997) *Transforming the Crown*, exhibition catalogue, New York: the Franklin H. Williams Caribbean Cultural Center.

Ratnam, N. (1998) 'Transforming the Crown', *Third Text* 41: 85–8.

NIRU RATNAM

Transglobal Underground

More of a collective of musicians and DJs than a straightforward band, Transglobal Underground formed around the release of the single 'Templehead' on **Nation Records**. The single was to be a one-off but its success saw the band being signed to Deconstruction, but then dropped. The band re-signed to Nation and released a series of eclectic and stunning records including 1996's *Psychic Karaoke*, and vocalist Natacha Atlas, who is of Arabic origins, released several highly acclaimed solo albums, most of which featured members of Transglobal Underground, including *Diaspora* (1995), which was described upon its release as being 'more or less an unofficial Transglobal Underground release'. Prior to joining Transglobal Underground, Atlas, having relocated to Northampton from Brussels, had enjoyed success collaborating with Jah Wobble on five songs on his critically acclaimed 1991 album *Rising Above Bedlam*. Transglobal Underground's live shows are a colourful and exciting spectacle, moving away from the non-performance performances of traditional dance acts, and their **music** reflects the bands multi-racial line-up with influences from Arabic, Indian and African music, producing a style that breaks away from stereotypical views of **dance** and world music, while being influenced by both.

ANDY WOOD

Traynor, Joanna

b. London, England

novelist

Traynor came into prominence with her debut novel *Sister Josephine*, which won the **Saga Prize** in 1996. Her second novel *Divine* was published in 1998. Her first two novels have heroines who are feisty characters and they explore the terrain of growing up and living in Britian, where the assumption of ethnicity and identity is drawn without any self-consciousness. The novels are largely sketched from the circumstances of her own life experience, first as a nurse and then as a student of psychology. *Sister Josephine* tells the story of a young mixed-race woman who trains to be a nurse in the National Health Service, and the novel contains much comedy about the manner in which bodies come together and fall apart. *Divine* details the life of a black woman immersed in a world of drug abuse, bad trips, an encounter with the law, rejection and rape. Traynor has a wonderful ear for dialogue, and the world of her novels may be harsh but her characters are resilient and often funny. As Traynor herself said in an interview, 'You just run into these things. It's a reflection of society, and that's why they're in my novels. There are always mad things going on in my life. But not always bad.' Her latest novel *Bitch Money* (2000) is a crime thriller.

Select bibliography

Traynor, J. (2000) *Bitch Money*, London: Bloomsbury.
—— (1998) *Divine*, London: Bloomsbury.
—— (1996) *Sister Josephine*, London: Bloomsbury.

GAIL CHING-LIANG LOW

Tricky

b. 1964, Bristol, England

artist, performer, producer

Adrian Thaws (Tricky) was involved with Bristol's Wild Bunch and was a fringe member of **Massive Attack**, appearing on both *Blue Lines* and *Protection*, before signing to Island as a solo artist. His debut album *MaxinQuaye* (1995) is unique, both musically and lyrically, taking similar influences to those of Massive Attack but utilising them in a starkly contrasting way. Tricky's second album *Pre-Millenium Tension* (1996) and the *Nearly God* project (1996, featuring collaborations with a number of artists Tricky admired, including Terry Hall of the Specials) were also ambitious and impressive releases, as is 1998's *Angels with Dirty Faces*. Tricky has worked with US rappers Gravediggaz, and set up his own label Durban Poison to release artists from both sides of the Atlantic. A number of Tricky's lyrics appeared in the poetry collection *The Fire People* in 1998 and Canongate plan to publish a book by Tricky entitled *All I Hear Is Words*. **Channel 4** filmed a documentary on Tricky for their *Arthouse* series called 'Naked and famous', which was broadcast in 1997. *Juxtapose*, with DJ Muggs and Grease, was released in 1999.

ANDY WOOD

Trojan Records

Trojan Records took its name from the vehicle Arthur 'Duke' Reid used to bring his sound system to dances in 1950s Jamaica, and Reid's Trojan label initially brought out a number of calypso singles. In 1967, the British Trojan label released its first single 'Judge sympathy', which was credited to Duke Reid's All Stars. Island allowed Trojan to peter out after less than a dozen releases but it re-emerged in 1968 as a company in its own right. The revitalised Trojan issued a mixture of new Jamaican- and British-produced records as well as issuing a series of budget-priced **reggae** compilations, which over eight albums helped introduce Jamaican music to a much wider British audience. In 1969, the label had several notable chart hits including the Upsetters' 'Return of Django' and Jimmy Cliff's 'Wonderful world beautiful people'. During the 1970s, the emphasis of Trojan was focused more upon the UK, which produced a number of successes. In 1975, the label was sold off and for the next decade existed in a rather haphazard form, lacking a coherent direction. In recent years, Trojan has re-emerged and has begun a wide-ranging re-issue campaign utilising its extensive catalogue.

ANDY WOOD

Tyson, Cathy

b. 1965, Liverpool, England

actress

Tyson was raised by her father, a barrister, and her mother, a social worker, in Liverpool. In her early teens, she attended the Rathbone Theatre work-shop on a Government Training Scheme. After a year, she joined the Everyman's Youth Theatre, where she appeared in *The Blitz Show*. In the mid-1980s, she won admission to the renowned Royal Shakespeare Company and took the lead role in their production of *Golden Girls*. Her Shakespearean credits now include: Kate in *The Taming of the Shrew*, with Regent's Park Open Air Theatre; Cleopatra in *Anthony and Cleopatra*, with the English Shakespeare Company; and Regan in *King Lear*, directed by Yvonne **Brewster** at the **Talawa Theatre Company**. Tyson's film (see **film and cinema**) debut occurred in 1986 when she won the role of Simone, a prostitute, in Neil Simon's *Mona Lisa*, which brought her critical acclaim. Further film work followed (*Serpent and the Rainbow*, 1987; *Business as Usual*, 1988; and *Priest*, 1994), along with **television** work in Britain and the USA, where she starred in a mini-series based on Barbara Taylor Bradford's *Remember* (1993). In Britain, her face is well known from popular television dramas including the series *Band of Gold* with Granada Television. Tyson is one of the celebrities featured in the return of *Jackanory* on BBC 1, where she will star in 'The Unknown Chef' written by Diran **Adebayo**.

YINKA SUNMONU

U

Uzzaman, Badi

b. 1939, Uttar Pradesh, India

actor

Badi Uzzaman is familiar on the British **televi-sion** landscape as a 'bit part' actor in popular programmes such as *The Bill*, *The Singing Detective*, *Inspector Morse*, *Boon*, *Casualty* and *London's Burning*. His self-deprecating approach to being a jobbing actor is summed up by his motto: 'Your buddy, everybody's buddy.' He has, however, played several noteworthy character parts. One was that of the rival restaurant owner opposite Saeed **Jaffrey** in *Tandoori Nights*, while another was as Puran Kapoor, the much put-upon husband in *Firm Friends*. He appears as Mr Ganatra in BBC's landmark drama, *In a Land of Plenty* (2001). Uzzaman has an extensive film career and credits include: *Kevin and Perry Go Large* (2000); *Immaculate Conception* (1992); ***My Beautiful Laundrette*** (1985); *Mad Cows* (2000); and a touching portrayal of an elderly immigrant, 'Old Ram', in Udayan **Prasad**'s, *Brothers in Trouble* (1995).

Uzzaman always wanted to act and walked from India to Rawalpindi, where his brother was a radio producer, to work as a child actor in radio drama. His big break came in 1977 when he moved to Lahore and began working for Pakistan Television (PTV), the public service broadcaster, in many of the country's high-quality television dramas and serials. Uzzaman was already a star when director Salman Peerzada approached him to act in his film (see **film and cinema**), *Mela*, in which he played five characters. The film, an allegorical political tale about the military regime, fell foul of the authorities and had to be completed in London. Uzzaman arrived here in 1982 and has built his career in the UK.

SUMAN BHUCHAR

V

Verma, Jatinder

b. 1954, Dar-es-Salaam, Tanzania

writer, artistic director

Jatinder Verma was born in Tanzania but grew up in Kenya. He arrived in the UK in 1968, as part of the Kenyan exodus and lived in South London. He has a first-class history degree from York University and an MA in South Asian studies from Sussex.

In 1977, he co-founded **Tara Arts**, and has since been its artistic director and driving force. He has written, adapted and directed most of the company's seventy-five productions. His main focus has been to evolve a distinctive theatrical performance style for Tara, which he has termed 'Binglish' and which he has argued for in several publications.

In 1990, he was the first Asian director to be invited to stage a play at the Royal National Theatre. He chose *Tartuffe*, and its resounding success led to other collaborations, including *Cyrano de Bergerac*, a version written by Verma and Ranjit Bolt. Verma is a major personality on the arts scene in the UK and lectures and speaks widely on **theatre**. He has also produced several radio documentaries and plays. *Ashes to the Ganges* deals with Verma taking his father's ashes back to India, while *The Great Sentinel and the Great Soul* is on the relationship between Tagore and Gandhi. In 1997, Verma was a member of the Poverty Commission set up by **Channel 4** to examine social exclusion in the UK.

Select bibliography

Verma, J. (1998) 'Binglishing the stage: a genera-tion of Asian theatre in England', in R. Boon and J. Plastow (eds) *Theatre Matters*, Cambridge: Cambridge University Press, pp. 126–34.

—— (1996) 'The challenge of Binglish', in P. Campbell (ed.) *Analysing Performance*, Manchester: Manchester University Press.

SUMAN BHUCHAR

Vir, Parminder

b. 1955, India

film-maker, television producer

Vir took up the post of Producer and Advisor on Cultural Diversity with Carlton Television in September 2000. She started as an Arts Administrator with the **Minorities' Arts Advisory Service** before moving on to the Commonwealth Institute. Her expertise in race equality, together with her artistic and creative knowledge, was recognised when she joined the **Greater London Council** as Head of the Race Equality Unit for Arts and Recreation. Vir worked for the BBC before joining Carlton, a few years later, as a Consultant to the Director of Programmes, implementing a strategy to encourage and achieve diversity on and behind the screens. She has also written a report examining inclusion in the media.

In 1986, she moved into film-making, producing a show reel of black and Asian talent for the BBC. In 1987, she founded Formation Films with her husband, the director Julian **Henriques**. Importantly, she was one of the organisers of 'Shooting from the Hip', a one-day celebration of the contributions of black and Asian women to the film (see **film and cinema**) and **television** industry. An award-winning drama and documentary producer, Vir is on the board of directors for the Film Council, Women in Film and Television and the Tricycle Theatre. She was a member of the Cultural Diversity Committee of the Arts Council of England. Vir produced *Single Voices* (2000), a series of comedy broadcasts, and is developing feature films with new writers through her company. She produced ***Babymother*** (1998).

YINKA SUNMONU

visual and plastic arts

The past forty years have seen a transformation in black British art. This section will look at some of the key themes, exhibitions and artists from that period. This is not a complete survey nor an encyclopedic view, but the beginnings of a map. We shall look at significant developments in the following areas: institutional developments and changes; differences and convergences in artistic practices; independent organisations; globalisation and internationalism; the role of the curator; and social and political events. More research needs to be done on black artists and black cultural practice in Britain. Some work has been done on black artists since the post-war period, but much more archaeological work is required on the pre-1945 era, with artists like Ronald **Moody**, who was exhibiting in Europe and America during the 1930s. Indeed, it is important to consider this earlier period when looking at developments from 1970 onwards.

In the 1950s and 1960s, England was the place where artists came together from the newly formed 'Commonwealth'. These included Iqbal Geoffrey, Avinash **Chandra** and Francis N. **Souza** from India, and Sam Ntiro and Ben Enwonwu from Tanzania and Nigeria. One crucial gathering was the formation of the **Caribbean Artists' Movement** (CAM) in London in 1966. This formation was an important moment that influenced events in the 1970s, 1980s and 1990s. Formed by Kamau (Edward) Brathwaite, John **La Rose** and Andrew

Salkey, its visual arts membership included Aubrey **Williams**, Karl Craig, Clifton Campbell, Ronald Moody, Errol **Lloyd**, Althea McNish, Art Derry, Winston Benn, Carlisle Chang, Edmund Gill, Peter Minshall, Ronald Savory, Karl Broodhagen and the young painter Paul **Dash**. Like the Harlem Renaissance that emerged in New York during the 1920s and 1930s, CAM was a diverse collection of writers, critics and artists who were interested in developing a modern Caribbean aesthetic; an aesthetic that explored colonial histories as well as a newly formed black British identity. By the 1970s CAM had initiated a journal, ***Savacou***, and exhibitions such as 'Caribbean Artists in England', which featured Althea Bastien, Winston Branch, Daphne Dennison, Karl Craig, Art Derry, Errol Lloyd, Althea McNish, Ronald Moody, Ricardo Wilkins (now Kofi Kayiga) and Aubrey Williams. This show took place in 1971 at the Commonwealth Institute and a subsequent exhibition, 'Four Black Artists at the Keskidee Centre', happened in London in 1977. There were other international movements in Britain like the Indian Artists UK (IAUK), whose membership included prominent artists like Balraj Khanna.

The 1970s was also a rapidly changing period for African and Asian artists in Britain, who were making important contributions to global art movements. F.N. Souza was included in the 'Commonwealth Artists of Fame' exhibition alongside Henry Moore. The works of Ronald Moody, Aubrey Williams, Emmanuel **Jegede**, Uzo Egonu and Winston Branch were representing Britain in the 'Second World Black and African Festival of Arts and Culture' (Festac 77) in Lagos, Nigeria. There were also those that challenged the modernist paradigm with activities that took art out of the pristine 'white cube' gallery space to alternative spaces and on to the streets with happenings, activism and conceptual art. The **Drum** Arts Centre was an alternative space, established to promote the art of black people in Britain with exhibitions that included the work of Donald **Locke** and Frank **Bowling**. It was during this period that Avtarjeet **Dhanjal** displayed his kinetic aluminium sculptures and David **Medalla** formed the 'Artists Liberation Front' and 'Artists For Democracy' in London. Artists for Democracy had an international membership that included

Rasheed **Araeen**, who performed *Paki Bastard* (1977), one of the first critiques into the positive/ negative imagery debates. Later, Araeen launched the art magazine *Black Phoenix* with an article entitled 'Black manifesto'. The events of the 1970s led to the first major report on black arts in Britain, or what was then termed Ethnic Minority Arts. With institutional support from the Community Relations Committee (CRC), the highly influential *The Arts Britain Ignores* by Naseem **Khan** was published. This report heralded support for the arts from diverse cultures by organisations like the Arts Council of Great Britain and the Gulbenkian Foundation, and enabled the setting up of the **Minorities' Arts Advisory Service** in London, with regional bodies in the West Midlands, Manchester and Cardiff, and CHROMA, a Nottingham-based group that stimulated and supported black art activity within this region.

The 1980s became a period of intense activity from a new generation of 'raised in Britain' artists, writers and critics. Civil disruptions across the country seemed to go hand in hand with the Thatcherite era, which in turn had its influence on artistic production and policy. There was mass movement within the arena of black curatorial practice, independent publishing (see **publishing, books**), forums, mainstream exhibitions, collaborative ventures and organisational developments. One of the most influential public bodies in the 1980s was the **Greater London Council**. Between 1982 and 1986, through funding, institutional support and changes in legislation, practitioners and community groups were brought together to advise and shape local government initiatives, thus transforming the cultural landscape. For the arts some of the key events included the Ethnic Arts Conference in 1982, which established the Ethnic Arts Sub-committee; as well as the Anti-Racism Year Programme in 1984; 'Reflections For A Different World' (1984); 'Staying On' (1985); 'New Horizons' (1985); the Black Visual Arts Forum (1985); 'Black Artists – White Institutions' conference (1985); the Black Experience Programme in 1986; 'The Colours of Black' (1986); 'Darshan' (1986); 'Twelve Days At The Roundhouse' (1986); and 'Aurat Shakti' (1986). By 1986, the Arts Council had begun to adopt some of

the initiatives developed by the GLC, through the Directorship of Sandy Nairne

In the 'Black experiences' issue of *Ten.8*, Stuart **Hall** made the point that black subjectivities in the 1980s entered 'the Age of Innocence', ensuring visibility and central positioning at the heart of artistic discourses. If the 1970s was about a politicisation and mobilisation around blackness, then the 1980s' use of the term 'Black' was at the forefront of exhibitions, events and publications, with exhibitions like: 'Black Art an' Done'; '**Black Women Time Now**'; 'Radical Black Art'; '**The Thin Black Line**'; 'Black Skin/Blue Coat'; 'The Black Triangle'; 'The Black Bastard As A Cultural Icon'; 'Black Edge'; '**Black Art: Plotting the Course**'; 'No More Little White Lies'; 'White Power Black Sexuality'; and 'Young, Black and Here'. Publications such as *Making Myself Visible*, conferences like 'Black Artists – White Institutions', artists-led groups such as the **Black Art Group** and organisations called the **Black Art Gallery** all gave the impression that the narrative theme and mode of address was one of confrontation and opposition to whiteness. However, as Hall concludes, within this moment of visibility and positioning there has to be an 'opening up' to the question of the complexity and heterogeneity of the black experience; an opening up that requires a critical framework.

This idea of a radical critical framework took place among the multitude of voices and differing styles of writing around black art in Britain: from the art historical, to questions of psychoanalysis centring/de-centring the subject, and to post-colonial approaches that foregrounded the 'other' and colonial discourses on the body. This establishment of a critical framework was clearly central to the writings of Stuart Hall, Paul **Gilroy**, Pratibha **Parmar**, Homi **Bhabha**, Kobena **Mercer**, Eddie **Chambers**, Lubaina **Himid**, Rasheed Araeen, Sarat Maharaj, Gilane Tawadros and Guy Brett. This is illustrated in the range of published journals, magazines (see **publishing, newspapers and magazines**) and catalogues of the period: *Camerawork*, *Block Magazine* and *Arts Review*. In some cases there were special issues where editorial control was given to black practitioners: the 'Creative camera drum issue' of *Ten.8* (1984); *The Struggle For Black Arts In Britain, Storms of The Heart: An Anthology of Black Arts and Culture* (1988) by Kwesi **Owusu**; and *FAN* (1988) by **Sulter** and Himid. This was also the period where independent journals and publications were established: *Artrage* (1982); *Blackboard* (1984); *Making Myself Visible* (1984); *The Black Triangle* (1985); *Third Text* (1987); *BAZAAR (South Asian Arts Forum)* (1987); *Polareyes* (1987); *The Art Pack* (1988); *Autograph Newsletter* (1988); *Black Arts In London* (1985–6); *Revue Noire* (1991); *Race Today Review* (1986–7); Urban Fox Press (*Passion*, 1989) and *Mukti* (1983). There were mainstream institutional interventions by organisations who published material that explored black art practices, such as the **Commission for Racial Equality**'s *The Art of Ethnic Minorities* (1985), *State of The Art* (1986), *Aperture: Towards A Bigger Picture* (1988) and *Black Male/White Male* (1988).

The question of the black body and autobiography became a contested debate in the 1980s among a range of artists from differing generations. These cross-generation moments took place at the First National Black Art Convention (1982), organised by the Pan-Afrikan Connection; Vision and Voice Conference (1985); Creation For Liberation – Open Submission Exhibition, where Errol Lloyd and Aubrey Williams discussed 'Hearts In Exile' (1983), the inaugural show of the Black Art Gallery; 'Caribbean Expressions In Britain' (1986); and 'Seeking a Black Aesthetic' (1987). These discussions culminated in the exhibition '**The Other Story**' in 1989. The question of the black body and history was explored further in Stuart Hall's essay 'Reconstruction work' (1991); in **Black Audio Film Collective**'s *Expedition* (1983) and *Signs Of Empire* (1983); in SAAAC – Southall Afro-Caribbean Asian Arts Collective's 'Forces and Figures In Asian History' (1986); as well as in the exhibition 'Sojourner Truth Association Black Perspectives' at the South London Art Gallery (1987). By the end of the 1980s the question of documentation and historical legacy led to the development of the Chelsea School of Art Collection, the **African and Asian Visual Arts Archive** (1988), **Panchayat** (1988), the George Padmore Institute at **New Beacon Books** and the **Black Cultural Archives**.

The 1980s saw a wealth of exhibitions, including Creation for Liberation's Open Submission Exhibitions, and galleries were producing exhibitions that showcased a diverse range of artists: the Mappin Gallery's 'Into the Open', Camerawork's 'Testimony' and the Whitechapel show, 'From Two Worlds'. The years 1982 and 1986 also saw the celebration of art from India and the Caribbean in two major festivals. The first was the Festival of India, in which Avinash Chandra, F.N. Souza and Balraj Khanna were invited to participate ('In The Image of Man' at the Hayward Gallery; 'Between Two Cultures' at the Barbican Art Gallery, organised by Indian Artists United Kingdom; 'Six Modern Indian Painters' at the Tate Gallery; 'Contemporary Indian Art' at the Royal Academy; and 'India: Myth and Reality' at the Museum of Modern Art, Oxford). The second festival, Caribbean Focus, saw the re-emergence of the Commonwealth Institute as a focus for key activities in the 1980s with 'Caribbean Art Now' (1986). 'Caribbean Expressions In Britain' included the work of Simone Alexander, Frank **Bowling**, Sonia **Boyce**, Pogus Caesar, Denzil **Forrester**, Anthony Jadunath, Errol Lloyd, John **Lyons**, Bill **Ming**, Ronald Moody, Colin Nichols, Eugene **Palmer**, Veronica **Ryan**, Gregory Whyte and Aubrey Williams. There were other mainstream developments that positioned white artists alongside black artists: 'State of the Art' at the **Institute of Contemporary Arts** (1986), 'Critical Realism' (1987), 'Art History' at the Hayward (1987), 'Along the Lines of Resistance' (1988) and 'Through the Looking Glass' (1989). International exhibitions abroad showed works by British black artists, such as 'US/UK' (1989), 'Havana Bienal' (1989) and 'Les Magiciens de la Terre' (1989).

In addition, a range of black curatorial practices began to emerge in the 1980s. The work of three people stands out as particularly significant: Lubaina Himid (arts reviewer for journals such as *City Limits* and curator of 'Five Black Women', 'Black Women Time Now', 'The Thin Black Line', 'Unrecorded Truths' and 'Elbow Room'); Eddie Chambers ('Black Art and Done', 'Pan-Afrikan Connection', 'The First National Black Art Convention', 'Radical Black Art', '**D-Max**' and 'Black Art: Plotting The Course'); and Rasheed Araeen ('Third World Within', 'Essential Black Art' and 'The Other Story').

The 1990s was a period of celebration but also of closure. It was celebration because black artists were being selected in major public shows like 'The

British Art Show' and nominated for the prestigious Tate Gallery Turner Prize (Anish **Kapoor** in 1991, Chris **Ofili** in 1998 and Steve **McQueen** in 1999). It was closure for organisations that helped to put black art on the British art scene: *Ten.8*, the Black Art Gallery, MAAS, *Artrage*, Horizon Gallery, Bazaar, Camerawork Gallery and Magazine. However, this period sees the launch of new organisations like **Institute of International Visual Arts** (inIVA), with publishing and exhibition franchises that go to Sunil **Gupta** (OVA), Rasheed Araeen (Kala Press) and Eddie Chambers. By 1994, under the Directorship of Gilane Tawadros, inIVA's output is multifaceted. They instigate innovative collaborations with a range of critics, curators, artists, art historians, galleries, museums and arts organisations on exhibition and publishing projects, like *Recordings: a Select Bibliography of Contemporary African, Afro-Caribbean and Asian British Art*, and the Annotations series. The 1990s saw the merging of film (see **film and cinema**) and visual art practices with artists like Isaac **Julien** and Steve McQueen. It also saw the re-emergence of **live art** and performance (Susan Lewis, Ronald **Fraser-Munro** and Keith **Khan**) led by Edge, **Moti Roti** and the curatorial work of Catherine Ugwu and Lois Kegan, who established the **Live Art Development Agency**. New technology in the form of computer, CD-ROM, video art and Internet-based projects became a key element in the work of Keith **Piper** (the founder of Digital Diaspora), Roshini **Kempadoo**, Rita **Keegan**, Derek **Richards** (the founder of Displaced Data) and Simon **Tegala**.

Major public and private collections produced exhibitions such as: 'Shocks to the System: Social and Political Issues in Recent British Art' from the Arts Council Collection (South Bank Centre, 1991, with Sonia Boyce, David Medalla, Sunil Gupta, Gavin **Jantjes**, Tony Phillips, Keith Piper and Donald **Rodney**); 'Prints and Photographs by Artists of African Descent' (V. and A., 1995); 'Picturing Blackness in British Art' (Tate London, 1995); and 'Sensation' at the Royal Academy. Black British art was also gaining attention abroad with Anish Kapoor representing Britain at the Venice Biennale (1990). There is also 'Disputed Identities' (1990); 'Interrogating Identity' (1991); 'Houston Fotofest' (1992); Arles Photography Festival: 'Rencontres au Noir' (1993); the Second Johannesburg Biennale (1997); '**Transforming the Crown**' (1997); and 'The Unmapped Body' (1998). One of the biggest events of the 1990s, in terms of mainstream intervention, was the AFRICA 95 festival, a season celebrating the arts of Africa. The visual arts programme offered a wide range of arts, from painting, sculpture and **photography** to performance and installation-based work. Concentrating on art from North Africa, the Sub-Saharan regions and the African diaspora, there were major shows throughout England. Exhibitions included: 'Africa: the Art of a Continent' (Royal Academy), 'International Sculpture Workshop' (Yorkshire Sculpture Park), 'Self-Evident'; 'The Impossible Science of Being: Dialogues between Anthropology and Photography'; 'Play and Display: Masquerades of Southern Nigeria' and 'Original' (Gasworks Studios), which highlighted work by Yinka **Shonibare** and Virginia **Nimarkoh**.

Like the 1980s, the 1990s saw the proliferation of black curatorial practices. Sunil Gupta emerged as an independent curator, while Eddie Chambers got into serious production mode ('Let the Canvas Come to Life with Dark Faces', 'History and Identity' and 'Frank Bowling'). Other important curators and projects include Virginia Nimarkoh ('Exotic Excursions' and 'The Phone Box'), Richard **Hylton** ('Imagined Communities'), Bisi Obsilva ('Heads of State' and 'Hair Project') and Donald Rodney ('White Noise'). Other shows produced in this curatorial period explored postcolonial themes, such as 'Black Markets' (1990), 'Hysteria' (1991), 'Trophies of Empire' (1992), 'Fine Material for a Dream' (1992), 'Black People and the British Flag' (1993), 'Disrupted Borders' (1993), 'Time Machine' (1994), 'G. **Donkor** Slave to Champ' (1998), 'Mirage' (1995), 'The Impossible Science of Being' (1995), 'Empire and I' (1999) and 'Africa by Africa' (1999). Sexual politics was addressed in 'Ecstatic Antibodies' (1990), 'Taboo' (1994), 'Blackbodyscapes' (1994), 'The Attendent' (1992) and 'Rotimi Fani-Kayode – a Retrospective' (1990). The black body, portraiture and the autobiographical are explored in 'Autoportraits' (1990) and 'Let The Canvas Come to Life with Dark Faces' (1990). Significant installation-based practices included '4 × 4' (1991), 'Four Rooms' (1993) and 'Beyond Destination' (1993).

Exhibitions that explored cross-generational dia-sporic themes included 'The Elders' (1999); 'The Caribbean Connection' (1995); 'Crossing Black Waters' (1992), 'An Economy of Signs' (1990), 'In Focus' (1991), 'Hysteria' (1991), 'The Circular Dance' (1991), 'Home and Away' (1994), 'Seen/Unseen', 'Prints and Photographs by Artists of African Descent' (1995) and '000ZeroZeroZero' (1999).

Although New Labour came into office with a political spin on the arts, with phrases like 'YBAs' (Young British Artists) and 'Cool Britannia', there is no acknowledgement that young black artists like Chris Ofili are the product of the changing developments of the British art scene since CAM in the 1960s, or that the roots of the word 'cool' lay in the black vernacular language of the 1940s and 1950s. The 1990s was also a period of reflection with a number of projects attempting to document the past. Nation-wide projects included **Windrush** (1998); the *Ten.8* publication, 'The critical decade' (1992); Anne Walmsley's *The Caribbean Artists' Movement, 1966–1972 – a Literary and Cultural History'* (1992); Pratibha **Parmar**'s film, *The Colour of Britain*; the **Commission for Racial Equality**'s *Roots of the Future: Ethnic Diversity in the Making of Britain'* (1996); the African and Asian Visual Arts Archive conference, the 'Living Archive' (1997) and Gen Doy's book, '*Black Visual Culture, Modernity and Postmodernity'* (1999).

Further reading

Araeen, R. (ed.) (1993) *The Other Story*, Manchester: Southbank Centre, Cornerhouse Publications.

Bailey, D.A. and Hall, S. (eds) (1992) 'Critical decade: black British photography in the 80s', special issue, *Ten.8* 2(3).

Beauchamp-Byrd, M.J. (1997) *Transforming the Crown: African, Asian and Caribbean Artists in Britain 1966–1996*, New York: Franklin H. William Caribbean Cultural Center/African Diaspora Institute.

Chambers, E. (1988) *Black Art: Plotting the Course*, Oldham: Oldham Art Gallery.

Chambers, E, Lamba, J. and Joseph, T. (1985) *The Artpack: a History of Black Artists in Britain*, London: Haringey Arts Council.

Day, P. and Chambers, E. (1990) *Let the Canvas Come to Life*, Coventry: Herbert Art Gallery.

Doy, Gen (1999) *Black Visual Culture, Modernity and Postmodernity*, London: IB Tauris.

Hall, S. (1991) 'Reconstruction work: images of post-war black settlement', in J. Spence and P. Holland (eds) *Family Snaps: the Meanings of Domestic Photography*, London: Virago, pp. 152–65.

Khan, N. (1976) *The Arts Britain Ignores: the Arts of Ethnic Minorities in Britain*, London: Arts Council of Great Britain.

Sulter, M. (ed.) (1990) *Passion: Discourses on Black-women's Creativity*, Hebden Bridge: Urban Fox Press.

Walmsley, A. (1992) *The Caribbean Artists' Movement 1966–1972*, London: New Beacon Books.

DAVID A. BAILEY

Voice, The

Since its launch in 1982, the *Voice* has become the biggest selling black newspaper (see **publishing, newspapers and magazines**) in Britain, with a readership in excess of 200,000. Started by chair-man Val McCalla, it was the first newspaper to address issues concerning British-born black peo-ple. Its significance was that it published stories on race relations and black issues that were not often tackled by the mainstream press. Most importantly, news came from a black perspective at a time when race relations was a topic generating a lot of debate and discussion. The newspaper, published weekly, started as a London-wide publication and filled a void for black Britons. In 1984, it began circulation outside of London.

The paper has started to lead the field in education and fostering and adoption. A *Voice* adoption survey, the first of its kind in a black newspaper, was featured in **Channel 4**'s *Adoption on Trial* series and led to an item on *Channel 4 News*. The Voice Group also publishes the monthly colour supplement *Woman 2 Woman* and was responsible for the *Journal*, formerly the *Weekly Journal*. The paper is a training ground for journalists. The paper has supported numerous campaigns, notably the Stephen **Lawrence** Trust and the Dr Joan Francisco Foundation. The *Voice*'s fifteenth anniversary, in 1987, was marked by the launch of an Annual Community Awards event. Publications aside, the *Voice* participates actively in outreach work. It has established a Fellowship Scheme, which has presented scholarships to students at the University of Warwick, and helps charities and foundations. It has also registered the McCalla Voice Charitable Trust. Ex-journalists include Dotun **Adebayo**, who went on to found **X Press** Publishing and novelist Leone **Ross**.

NYANTAH

W

Wadia, Nina

actor, comedian

Wadia has worked in **theatre**, radio and **television**. She has made guest appearances on several popular television shows, including *Holby City*, and the comedy sitcoms *Vicar of Dibley* and *Kiss Me Kate*. In 1997, she played Dolly Kotwal in *The Sixth Happiness* and she played Maggie in the 2000 television series *Perfect World*. Since 1998, Wadia has become best known as part of the enormously popular ***Goodness Gracious Me*** comedy team, along with Meera **Syal**, Kulvinder **Ghir** and Sanjeev **Bhaskar**. Perhaps her most notable character is Mrs Bedi, who can make anything at home with one small aubergine. In 1997, Wadia hosted the BBC Asian Success, Innovation and Achievement Awards.

ALISON DONNELL

Walker, Maxine

b. 1962, Birmingham, England

artist

Beginning in the mid-1980s, Maxine Walker, a photographer who currently lives and works in Birmingham, emerged as an important artist in the UK. In her well-known early series, such as *Auntie Lindie's House* (1987), Walker critically interrogates and eschews documentary **photography**'s claim to present an unmediated reality. While employing the serial format and prompting viewers to piece together the fragmented lives that evolve in her photographic narratives, Walker refutes the historic perception that photographs have the ability to objectively present an uncontested truth.

More recently, as demonstrated in series photographs, such as *Black Beauty* in the 1980s and the untitled photographs that were featured in the 'Self-Evident' exhibition in 1995, Walker has created compelling self-portraits that investigate identity, genealogy, the construction of racial difference and related concerns that have become central to the perception of belonging in Britain. By donning wigs, clothes, jewellery and make-up, Walker departs from traditional representations of black women, provocatively challenging the idea of racial purity and theatrically examining black women's ability to transform and re-invent themselves. Moreover, by conveying the multiple dimensions of black women and self-representation, Walker asserts that histories are artificial and ultimately rooted in fiction.

Further reading

Mercer, K. (1995) *Self-Evident*, Birmingham: Ikon Gallery.
Tawadros, G. (1992) 'Redrawing the boundaries', *Ten.8* 2(3): 86–91.

ANDREA D. BARNWELL

Walker, Rudolph

b. 1939, Trinidad

actor

Rudolph Walker's long career is decidedly varied. On stage, he has played the lead in Mustapha **Matura**'s *Play Mas*, Jenny **McLeod**'s *Victor and the Ladies* and three productions of *Othello*. He has played cameos in a number of films (see **film and cinema**), including ***Bhaji on the Beach*** (1993). He first appeared on **television** in 1965 in *The Wednesday Play*, and since then has done everything from an appearance in *Doctor Who* to playing Trade Union leader Bill Morris in **Channel 4**'s *Dockers*. He is still best known, however, for *Love Thy Neighbour*, an extremely popular sitcom, which ran for eight series from 1972 to 1976, in which he played the black next-door neighbour of a white bigot. While claiming to be a satire on racism, this show was largely built on an exchange of racial insults, and some of the jokes were positively sinister. On the other hand, it put Walker and Nina Baden-Semper (who played his wife) slap bang in the middle of a show that topped the viewing figures at a time of limited opportunities for black actors. Since then, Walker has appeared in less controversial sitcoms like *A Perfect State*, and *The Thin Blue Line*, in which he played a delightfully world-weary police constable. In 1999, he received a lifetime achievement award at the Black Entertainment Comedy Awards.

OLIVER DOUBLE

Wall, Akure

b. 1970, Nigeria

poet, singer, musician, performance artist

Daughter of a Nigerian mother and an English father, Wall grew up in Croydon. Professionally based in London but with frequent visits to Lagos and extended stays in New York, her creative life spans three metropolitan cities. This international dimension is reflected in her work, which responds to the **music** of Nigerian Fela Kuti just as readily as to spoken poetry by black American Paul Beatty.

Formerly associated with the Urban Poets Society, London, Wall has developed a strong story-telling approach for her poetry performances, exploring political issues in terms of personal experience, like the search for black female role models or the situation of a double outsider. Her debut album *Afromorph Text* presents a wide range of musical styles including **hip hop**, funk and free jazz, with instruments like the talking drum or the cello as symbols of her African and British heritage. Anthologised by Lemn **Sissay** and Karen McCarthy, Wall's texts always argue for the fluidity of blackness and identity.

Select bibliography

McCarthy, K. (ed.) (1998) *Bittersweet*, London: the Women's Press.
Sissay, L. (ed.) (1998) *The Fire People*, Edinburgh: Payback Press.

Select discography

Wall, A. (1997) *Afromorph Text*, Freakstreet Records.

TOBIAS DÖRING

WALLEN, MICHELLE *see* Paris, Mica

Wambu, Onyekachi

b. 1960, Nigeria

journalist, editor

Onyekachi Wambu came to the UK in 1970 after the Biafran civil war in Nigeria. He was educated in London and at the Universities of Essex and Cambridge. Since 1983, he has worked as a journalist and was editor of the ***Voice*** in the late 1980s, where he launched the 'Innervision' column. His 'World's Eye' column for the ***New Nation*** is similarly popular. Wambu has also produced and directed for **television**, making documentaries and factual programmes for the BBC and **Channel 4**. He wrote the Literary Essay for the BBC's ***Windrush*** website and has edited *Empire Windrush: Fifty Years of Writing about Black*

Britain (1999). His other publications include *A Fuller Picture* (1999) on black British film (see **film and cinema**) and *Lord John Taylor of Warwick* (Tamarind Ltd) in 2000.

Select bibliography

Wambu, O. (1999) *A Fuller Picture*, London: BFI.
—— (1999) *Empire Windrush: Fifty Years of Writing about Black Britain*, London: Phoenix Press.

ALISON DONNELL

Wasafiri

Founded in 1984 by Susheila **Nasta**, *Wasafiri* is a magazine-style journal of literary criticism, imaginative writing and research on African, Asian and Caribbean writings. Originally published by the Association for the Teaching of Caribbean, African and Asian Literatures, the journal was initially established with the objective of publishing new writers and fostering an awareness of multicultural literature. Now an established and international literary magazine, supported by a well-known community of writers and critics worldwide, *Wasafiri* continues to make an important intervention into literary and cultural studies, placing African, Asian, Caribbean and diasporic writers at the forefront of debates in contemporary **literature**. It has published several useful special issues including 'Black Writing in Britain', 'Migrant Writing in Europe' and 'Film'.

ALISON DONNELL

Wee Papa Girl Rappers

London-born rap-pop duo Wee Papa Girl Rappers consisted of sisters Timmie (TV Tim) and Sandra (Total S) Lawrence. Although massively influenced by US **hip hop** culture, like their contemporaries the **Cookie Crew**, Wee Papa Girl Rappers mixed their rap influences with other styles. Their debut release was a rather novelty affair, a cover of George Michael's hit 'Faith', but their follow-up release, a collaboration with the dance–pop group Two Men and a Drum Machine, was a success.

Like Cookie Crew's rap–house fusion 'Rok da house', 'Heat it up' charted in Britain and also in the USA. When they released their third single 'Wee rule' and debut album *The Beat, the Rhyme, the Noise* in 1988, both were Top 10 hits as indigenous British rap seemed for a time to displace the hegemony of its US counterpart. Wee Papa Girl Rappers delayed releasing a second album until 1990 and despite *Be Aware* utilising an astute array of contemporary producers, including Coldcut and C + C Music Factory, it was a flop. Wee Papa Girl Rappers split up a year later.

ANDY WOOD

Weekly Journal, The

The *Weekly Journal* was first launched by black media entrepreneur Val McCalla in April 1992 under his Voice Communications publishing umbrella, which also included the renowned black women's magazine (see **publishing, newspapers and magazines**) *Pride*. The *Weekly Journal* was the first black broadsheet aimed specifically at African-Caribbean professionals and was also a sister paper to the **Voice**. The first editor of the paper was the British-Nigerian journalist Isabel Appio, who had previously worked at both the *Voice* and *Time Out* magazine. At its peak, the *Weekly Journal* had an estimated readership of 115,000 and official circulation of 26,000. It was widely considered to be the first newspaper to tap fully into the black British socially and politically aware readership and it was also noted for its high advertising revenue among the black community, particularly from the public sector. Although the *Weekly Journal* folded in the late 1990s, it is still regarded as one of the best quality black newspapers (see **publishing, newspapers and magazines**) and the top-selling weekly black broadsheet.

Further Reading

Benjamin, I. (1995) *The Black Press In Britain*, London: Trentham Books.

RAYMOND ENISUOH

Wek, Alek

b. 1977, Sudan

supermodel

In a profession where black women are still in the minority, Alek Wek has earned the title 'supermodel'. At the age of fourteen she fled Sudan, which was engulfed in civil war, taking her sister with her. They were granted asylum-seeker status in Britain. She was later joined by her mother and two other siblings. Wek was pursuing a course in fashion (see **fashion and design**) and business when she was discovered by a scout from the Models 1 agency in London. She has appeared on the covers of international magazines (see **publishing, newspapers and magazines**) from *Vogue* to *Elle*. Ralph Lauren chose her to open his spring 1997 show and she is in demand by the world's most famous designers. She has appeared in campaigns for Nars, Clinique, Moschino and Joop. Wek did attract comment when she appeared in *Elle* magazine with devil horns sticking out and a painted red tongue. Her importance is that she is a 'natural' and is one of the few models who has stayed true to her African roots and heritage. It is said that Wek is at the forefront of re-inventing what is defined as beauty. Her accolades include being named as MTV Model of the Year, Model of the Decade from *I-D* magazine and Best New Model at the Venus de la Mode Fashion Awards, Paris. She is a member of the US Committee for Refugees Advisory Council and participates in charity work throughout the world.

YINKA SUNMONU

White Town

White Town essentially consists of only one person, Jyoti **Mishra**. Although White Town have existed in many forms since 1989, sometimes as a full band, other times as a solo artist, they took until 1994 to release a debut album *Socialism, Sexism and Sexuality*. White Town/Mishra remained largely unknown until 'Your woman' became a surprise hit, bringing the Derby-based Mishra to a wider audience. 'Your woman', which was released as a

song on the e.p. *Abort, Retry, Fail....* and the subsequent album *Women in Technology*, were largely recorded in Mishra's bedroom. The single became a hit without much record company hype, instead slowly building up masses of radio airplay, reaching number one while the album made the Top 10, both in 1997. Despite this success, Mishra shied away from excessive publicity, and he avoids having his picture appear on the artwork of his records, in his videos or in promotional material. Despite the prominence gained by White Town on the radio and in the media, Mishra has not since achieved anything like the same level of success, although he continues to record and release material as White Town.

ANDY WOOD

Williams, Aubrey Sendall

b. 8 May, 1926, Georgetown, Guyana;
   d. 27 April, 1990, London, England

Artist

In 1952, during rising political tension in Guyana, Williams left for London to pursue a career as a painter, becoming a founding member of the **Caribbean Artists' Movement**. In the late 1980s, he took part in major exhibitions in Tokyo, Jamaica, Chicago and London, including **'The Other Story'**. Williams's abstract oil paintings feature those based on the symphonies of Shostokovich (1969–81). His both figurative and abstract works include the Olmec-Maya series (1981–5), using glyphs of pre-Columbian writing; murals based on Carib, Warrau and Arawak mythology; and a group showing tropical birds in response to the destruction of the natural environment.

Despite living and practising as an artist for almost forty years in Britain, during his lifetime, Williams's contribution was never considered part of the history of British art. In 1998 a large exhibition of Williams's works was staged at the Whitechapel Art Gallery, London. His understanding of pre- as well as post-coloniality, and his artistic presence in multiple contexts – that of Guyana, the Caribbean diaspora, and British society – show Williams as a complex figure.

Further reading

Dempsey, Tawadros and Williams (eds) (1998) *Aubrey Williams*, London: inIVA.

Walmsley, A. (ed.) (1990) *Guyana Dreaming: the Art of Aubrey Williams*, Coventry: Dangeroo Press.

LEON WAINWRIGHT

Williams, Fred

b. 1947, Jamaica

performance poet

Fred Williams came to England in 1963 at the age of sixteen. He has worked in public transport for much of his life. A performance poet in his spare time, he was particularly productive in the late 1970s and early 1980s. Williams's publications include *Me Memba Wen* (1981), *Movin Up* (1978) and *Leggo De Pen* (1985).

Select bibliography

Williams, F. (1985) *Leggo De Pen*, London: Akira Press.

—— (1981) *Me Memba Wen*, Nottingham: Broadsheet Press.

—— (1978) *Movin Up*, Nottingham: Broadsheet Press.

JAMES PROCTER

Wilmot, Gary

b. 1954, London, England

actor

Wilmot was born into a show-business family and has made his own mark on the industry with innumerable appearances on **television**, including several of his own television programmes. In 1989, he made his West End **theatre** debut as Bill Snibson in *Me and My Girl* at the Adelphi Theatre, where he received critical acclaim. He played the role in the award-winning musical for two years and received a Best Actor nomination for the national tour. Critical success followed with a number one theatre tour of the comedy *Teething Troubles*, the award-winning *Carmen Jones* at the Old Vic Theatre, London, and an appearance in the world première of *Copacabana* at the Prince of Wales Theatre, London. In 2000, he appeared at the Churchill Theatre, Bromley, in the Alan Ayckbourn play *Confusions*, where the cast played more than twenty roles between them. Renowned theatre critic Jack Tinker has described him as a 'Musical Talent of the Highest Order'. As a singer, Wilmot has recorded six television shows with the BBC Concert Orchestra and a one-hour television special – *Showstoppers*. Apart from recording albums of his musical appearances, his solo **music** work includes *The Album*, recorded at the Abbey Road Studio with the London Symphony Orchestra. Wilmot has worked behind the scenes as a director and producer, and he is the recipient of a Variety Club Silver Heart 'in recognition of his contribution to the world of entertainment and The Variety Club Children's Charity'. In 1996, he hosted the Laurence Olivier Awards.

YINKA SUNMONU

Wilson, Amrit

b. 1941, Calcutta, India

feminist, anti-racist activist, journalist

Amrit Wilson grew up in India and came to Britain as a student in 1961. She became a freelance journalist in 1974 and has contributed articles to the *Guardian*, *New Statesman and Society*, *Spare Rib* and *Feminist Review*. Wilson took an active role in the first waves of militant anti-racist struggles in the 1970s, and her book *Finding A Voice: Asian Women in Britain* was one of the first to document the collective struggles of Asian women workers and it remains influential for black British feminists. Although best known for her work on Asian women's rights within and outside their communities, racism in the workplace and immigration procedures in Britain, she has also written about the role of women in the long struggle for Eritrean independence, as well as critiques of hegemonic US foreign policy. More recently, Wilson has been concerned to expose advanced capitalist countries' attempts to control world resources and the World Bank's policies of target population controls, enforced in the name of health and women's rights. She edited the magazine (see **publishing, newspapers and magazines**) *Poverty and Power*, published by War on Want, in the 1980s.

Select bibliography

Wilson, A.(1991) *The Challenge Road: Women and the Eritrean Revolution*, London: Earthscan.

—— (1989) *US Foreign Policy and Revolution: the Creation of Tanzania*, London: Pluto.

—— (1978) *Finding a Voice: Asian Women in Britain*, London: Virago.

Wilson, A. and Lal, S. (1986) *'But My Cows Aren't Going to England': a Study in How Families are Divided*, Manchester: Manchester Law Centre.

RUVANI RANASINHA

Wilson, T-Bone

b. Guyana

actor, dramatist, poet

T-Bone Wilson came to Britain in 1962 to study engineering, but shortly afterwards decided to pursue an artistic career. In the early 1970s, Wilson acted in Mustapha **Matura**'s series of four short plays, *Black Pieces*, which formed one of the foundations of black British theatre. He was so inspired by this experience that he went on to write for the theatre himself. His publications include *Counterblast* (1980).

Select bibliography

Wilson, T. (1980) *Counterblast*, London: Karnak House.

JAMES PROCTER

Windrush

On 20 June 1948, the *SS Empire Windrush* docked at Tilbury; among the 1,024 passengers of the liner, a group of 492 Jamaicans, Trinidadians, Barbadians and Guyanese disembarked. The Nationality Act (1948), which was designed to encourage migration from the colonies and former colonies in order to help with labour shortages, formed the background to their arrival. This group represented the beginning of large-scale post-war migration from the Caribbean and 1948 is often assumed to be the starting point of black British history. The Passenger List, which is held at the Public Record Office, was displayed at the Museum of London in the 1998 exhibition 'Windrush – Sea Change'. It hints at a network of migrant workers from places other than the Caribbean, but the history, for example, of twenty Polish citizens who relocated from Mexico to Britain is regularly overlooked in accounts of the *Windrush*. The ship's arrival was widely viewed as a return to the Mother Country and the *Evening Standard* printed 'Welcome Home' on its front page on 21 June. Nevertheless, almost 300 of those arriving had to be housed in the Clapham Deep Shelter, which had previously accommodated German and Italian POWs. Moreover, race riots in Liverpool in the same year indicate that a different message was also on the streets.

A wide range of events was staged in 1998 to mark the fiftieth anniversary of the arrival. These ranged from a special issue of the journal *Kunapipi*, to a lecture ('A Dream Deferred: 50 years of Caribbean Migration to Britain') delivered by Caryl **Philips** at Leeds University, to an African-Caribbean fun day in Huddersfield and to a Black Workers Conference in Southampton. Perhaps most notable was the broadcast of a four-hour **television** documentary by the BBC, which was supplemented by the publication of an oral history compiled by Trevor and Mike **Phillips**. This companion piece contained interviews with *Windrush*-veterans, their friends and children, and was interspersed with short expository passages, plus letters and excerpts from newspaper (see **publishing, newspapers and magazines**) articles. However, if on the one hand the festivities celebrated the development of the black British community, on the other it relegated them to the position of 'arrivants' in a way that neglects the pre-1948 history of black Britain. Also, the *Windrush* celebrations tended to privilege black Caribbean settlers and neglect South Asian and African black British traditions.

Further reading

Dabydeen, D. (ed.) (1998) *Kunapipi. The Windrush Commemorative Issue: West Indians in Britain. 1948–1998* 20(1).

Fryer, P. (1984) *Staying Power. The History of Black People in Britain*, London: Pluto Press.

Phillips, M. and Phillips, T. (1998) *Windrush. The Irresistible Rise of Multi-Racial Britain*, London: HarperCollins

Procter, J. (ed.) (2000) *Writing black Britain 1948–1998*, Manchester: Manchester University Press.

Sewell, T. (1988) *Keep on Moving*, London: Voice.

Wambu, O. (ed.) (1998) *Empire Windrush. Fifty Years of Writing About Black Britain*, London: Gollancz.

MARK STEIN

Wolf, Rita

b. 1960, India

actress

Following involvements with various London youth **theatre** groups including the Royal Court Youth Theatre, Wolf began her professional career in Hanif **Kureishi**'s *Borderline*. A co-production between the Royal Court Theatre and Joint Stock Theatre Company, the strongly political play focused on the 1981 race riots. Wolf's subsequent theatre work involved **Tara Arts**' first professional production and other fringe and repertory work from Shakespeare to Ibsen. Wolf founded the Kali Theatre Company with writer Rukshana **Ahmad** in 1989 to produce and promote Asian women's writing. Wolf directed the company's first production *Song for a Sanctuary*, written by Ahmad, with the company continuing to tour productions, stage readings and writing workshops. In 1984, Wolf played a young Pakistani woman abandoned by her husband in Britain in **Retake Film and Video Collective**'s *Majdhar*. A year later, she played her most memorable role to date as Tania in *My Beautiful Laundrette*. **Television** and film (see **film and cinema**) parts as various manifestations of feisty young British Asian womanhood continued through soaps including *Albion*

Market and *Coronation Street* (as Felicity 'Flick' Khan), **Channel 4**'s comedy/drama *Tandoori Nights*, BBC productions such as Farrukh **Dhondy**'s *Romance Romance* and *Calling the Shots* and barrister Yasmin Jamal in Channel 5's *Wing And A Prayer*. Wolf's film credits include Jack Gold's *The Chain* (1984), Steven Lisberger's *Slipstream* (1989) and Pratibha **Parmar**'s *Khush* (1991). Based between New York and London, Wolf is writing her first feature-film screenplay, to be directed by Parmar.

SATINDER CHOHAN

WOLVERHAMPTON YOUNG BLACK ART GROUP *see* Black Art Group

WOMAD

The original concept for the World of Music, Arts and Dance (WOMAD) came about in 1980, but it was not until 1982 that the first festival took place in Bath. WOMAD's organisers aimed to 'bring arts of different cultures before the widest possible audience', bringing together a diverse range of musical styles, cultures and genres in the one event. Although the initial WOMAD festival was a financial disaster, the organisers continued to build upon their initial concept and WOMAD is now a truly international organisation. During the year 2000, WOMAD festivals were staged in the USA, Brazil, Australia, Singapore and Sicily, as well as in Britain, where WOMAD remains firmly based. The British WOMAD festival featured artists and performers from thirty-two different countries including British acts such as Pato Banton, Zion Train and State of Bengal playing to crowds of over 20,000 people. As well as running the highly successful festivals, WOMAD also runs an educational charity, the WOMAD foundation, and is involved in the Real World record label based at Peter Gabriel's studio of the same name in Bath. A compilation album celebrating ten years of WOMAD was released on Real World in 1992.

ANDY WOOD

womanism

Womanism is a term coined by Alice Walker as a unifying theme for her essay collection *In Search of Our Mothers' Gardens*. Walker supplies four definitions of the concept at the front of the collection and these include: (1) 'From *womanish*...a black feminist or feminist of colour': the opposite of 'girlish' or 'not serious'; (2) a 'woman who loves other women sexually and/or non-sexually'. The first of these definitions notes Walker's resolve to find a concept that identifies **feminism** with a black feminine genealogy: a narrative of black women's knowledge that bypasses conventional patriarchal epistemologies. Womanism, for Walker, derives from the 'black folk expression of mothers to female children' (Walker 1984: xi). Philosopher Helen (**charles**) has rejected the notion of womanism in favour of black feminism. (charles) suggests that 'Here in Britain, the term womanism is barely recognized or used' ((charles) 1997: 280) despite being taken up in the 1980s by Buchi **Emecheta** and the **Camden Black Sisters**. Her major concern with the concept is its aspiration to an all-embracing universal world that denies difference in black feminist identity ((charles) 1997: 285). Yet Kadiatu Kanneh, writing on Jackie **Kay**'s *Adoption Papers*, finds Walker's concept critically enabling. While acknowledging the 'heterogeneity of Black cultures' Kanneh claims, in the light of Walker's study, that '[f]or many Black feminist and women's texts, understanding one's mother, learning her story, becomes an act of racial and historical reassertion and self-understanding' (Kanneh 1994: 29).

References

(charles), H. (1997) 'The language of womanism: rethinking difference', in H.S. Mirza (ed.) *Black British Feminism: a Reader*, London and New York: Routledge, pp. 278–97.

Kanneh, K. (1994), 'When our mother's garden is unfamiliar', in Sally Ledger, Josephine McDonagh and Jane Spencer (eds) *Political Gender: Texts and Contexts*, New York and London: Harvester Wheatsheaf.

Walker, A. (1984) *In Search of Our Mothers' Gardens: Womanist Prose*, London: Women's Press.

LYNNETTE TURNER

women theatre collectives

Britain's first black women's **theatre** company, **Theatre of Black Women**, was founded in 1982 by Patricia Hilaire, Paulette Randall and Bernardine **Evaristo**. The three women met at drama school and their experience of devising their first play together, *Coping*, directed by Yvonne **Brewster**, inspired them to form a company to address the lack of plays and roles by and for black women. In 1982 they presented a triple-bill of one-woman shows that they had written, which explored the experience of being young, black and female in Britain. In 1983 Evaristo and Hilaire staged the two-hander *Silhouette* in which a slave woman performs a duet with a modern black woman in an exploration of black identity and oppression. Not only did *Silhouette* treat the under-represented issue of mixed-race identity, but it also engaged in an exploration of what **feminism** (identified with white women's experiences) might mean for black women. The group later began to work with playwrights and in 1986 performed Jackie **Kay**'s *Chiaroscuro*. Despite the company's success, Theatre of Black Women were forced to disband in 1988 when their annual funding from the Greater London Arts Council was not renewed.

In 1983, the year after the founding of Theatre of Black Women, dramatist Jacqueline **Rudet** set up her company Imani-Faith, which was similarly dedicated to theatre by and for black women. Rudet's objection to the male (mis)direction of her own work at the Royal Court raised an important point: the need for black women to have artistic control over their work. The company Munirah formed as a response to this need. *On the Inside*, their 1986 production, stressed the social and cultural invisibility of black women's experiences. The difficulty, however, as the company histories of Theatre of Black Women, Imani-Faith and Munirah demonstrate, is how to keep a 'space' open for black women's theatre to grow and to develop. None of these groups survived into the 1990s.

Theatre director Denise **Wong** tried a different approach. Rather than inaugurate a new women's company, Wong founded a 'sister' group under the umbrella of the established **Black Mime Theatre Company**, which had begun in 1984. Wong, who joined as an actress, began directing for the group in 1986 and formed Women's Troop, the 'sister' company, in 1990. The Women's Troop's first show, *Mothers*, was similar to the early work of Theatre of Black Women in that it drew on the personal experiences of company members to create theatre through a process of collective devising. Stylistically Wong aims at creating 'living cartoons' in which the physical playing of images is intercut with song and dialogue (Evaristo, 1993b). In 1991 the Women's Troop presented *Total Rethink*, which satirised the macho adventure film (see **film and cinema**), and in 1992 tackled the issue of women and alcohol in *Drowning*. From 1992 Black Mime continued under Wong's direction as a mixed ensemble. However, for *Mourning Song*, Black Mime's 1997 production, which examined death and grieving and incorporated lyrical poetry and gospel **music**, the company returned to an all-female cast. Wong linked the energy of *Mourning Song* to its all-female composition, which she described as 'a return to the women's troop' (Wong, 1997).

Also creating the space and support for women's work, without being exclusively by and for women, is the Asian theatre company **Tamasha Theatre Company**. Co-founded in 1989 by Kristine **Landon-Smith** and Sudhar **Bhuchar**, Tamasha's repertoire reflects a strong commitment to issues of race and gender – especially, for example, in their highly acclaimed production of Ruth Carter's *Women of the Dust* (1993), a dramatic treatment of the plight of women migrant workers on construction sites in Delhi. Landon-Smith's direction of *A Yearning* (1995), Carter's adaptation of Lorca's *Yerma*, which relocates from rural Spanish society to a Punjabi community in Britain today, showed a sensitive approach to the cross-cultural, social pressures on young British-Asian wives to become mothers.

Like Tamasha, **Talawa Theatre Company**, founded in 1985 by Yvonne Brewster, was headed by a strong team of women: Brewster, Inigo Espejel, Mona Hammond and Carmen Munroe. Ironically, in the 1980s Talawa could not find pieces by women that suited the 'epic' style which Brewster was keen for the company to develop. In 1992, however, Talawa, together with Jean 'Binta' **Breeze**, staged their first piece by a woman playwright: African American Shange's choreopoem *The Love Space Demands*. The company has since gone on to perform other work by women writers.

Despite the poor levels of subsidy in the 1990s for new (and existing) theatre companies, young black women, in the wake of the pioneering Theatre of Black Women, try to found new companies to give voice to their experiences, which would otherwise be culturally and theatrically invisible. Siren Theatre was set up in 1990 to perform new plays by black women and produced Shange's *For Coloured Girls* under Paulette Randall's direction. In the 1990s, Evaristo cites the formation of Assati, a new black women's theatre group in Liverpool, and the founding of the first ever all-female, black comedy troop, Bibi Crew. That said, given the diversity of racial communities, identities, cultures and experiences in Britain, set against the very small number of companies who manage to keep their commitment to racially and gender-aware theatre financially afloat, it is not surprising that, overall, black women writers and practitioners experience difficulty in finding the 'space' necessary for the sustained development of their creativity in the theatre.

Further reading

Aston, E. (1995) 'Black women: shaping feminist theatre', in *An Introduction to Feminism and Theatre*, London and New York: Routledge.

Kadija, G. (ed.) (1993) *Six Plays by Black and Asian Women Writers*, London: Aurora Metro.

Ponnuswami, M. (2000) 'Small island people: black British women and the performance of retrieval', in E. Aston and J. Reinelt (eds) *Companion to Modern British Women Playwrights*, Cambridge: Cambridge University Press.

Wong, D. (1997) 'Interview', in *Mourning Song* programme notes.

ELAINE ASTON

women's writing

Writing by black women in Britain dates back at least as far as 1831 with the publication of *The History of Mary Prince, A West Indian Slave, Related by Herself* in London and Edinburgh. Mary Prince's narrative, which documented her life as a slave and, importantly, as a woman, needed to assert its authentic authorship ('written by herself') because the very proposition that black women could write, or should write, was extremely contentious. Although black women's writing is now recognised as an exciting and intellectually vigorous field, the pathway leading to literary acknowledgement has not been free from obstacles.

Beryl **Gilroy**, whose 1970 autobiographical publication *Black Teacher* was one of the first pieces of black women's writing to be published and circulated in the UK, has spoken about the difficulty of achieving writer status as a woman in the 1950s and 1960s. Although several male writers who had settled in the UK from the Caribbean (Sam **Selvon**, George **Lamming** and V.S. **Naipaul**) were beginning to shape successful literary careers during these decades, women's writings seldom found their way into print. It is perhaps not surprising that those writers who did manage to locate a space within the predominantly white and male world of publishing often wrote with the authority of their own experience. These authhobiographically influenced texts interestingly took up the trail that Mary Prince had blazed.

Like Beryl Gilroy, who published eight major creative works, Buchi **Emecheta**, from Nigeria, is one of the UK's best-known and best-established black women writers. Like Lauretta **Ngcobo**, Emecheta is often still considered an African woman writer, and it would appear that these two writers have managed to speak to both continents through their work. Nevertheless, Emecheta's first novel, *In the Ditch* (1972), documents the life of a bright, young Ibo woman who must endure the hardships and degradations of her life with five children in a council flat in North London. In *Second Class Citizen* (1976), Emecheta continues Adah's life narrative with a careful and bleak description of the profound disillusionment and social decline, that she experiences when she leaves a secure job in Lagos in order to join her husband who is studying in London. Although the metropolitan heartland of empire promises only discomfort and prejudice to Adah, the narrative affirms her ability to negotiate a space for her own survival and that of her children within this hostile environment.

A strong element of autobiography also informs the work of black women's writing in the UK in the 1980s. *Sumitra's Story* by Rukshana Smith (1982) draws on the author's own life in order to tell the 'story' of a young East African Asian woman who must culturally relocate herself in British society. Several of Joan **Riley**'s novels also draw on autobiography in order to powerfully articulate the experience of being a black woman in Britain – the experience of discrimination, of isolation and of the need for belonging and a positive sense of self. Riley's *The Unbelonging* (1985), *Waiting in the Twilight* (1987) and *Romance* (1988) in many ways echo Emecheta's two novels set in the UK in their emphasis on the psychological consequences of living in an antagonistic society, in which the pathology of power is not only racist but sexist. Riley also joins Emecheta in seeking to represent both the depression and the resourcefulness of her black female subjects. In a 1994 piece, 'Writing reality in a hostile environment', Riley outlined the political project that informs her work: 'Writing a reality out of step with perception carries a high emotional and intellectual price.... But questions which create debate, however hostile, keep a normally hidden reality uncovered and raise the possibility of change.'

The political charge of black women's writing is strongly evident in the works of Lauretta Ngcobo and Merle **Collins**. Ngcobo, who fled to the UK in the 1960s from South Africa, where certain of her works were, until recently, banned, has continued a literary dialogue with her homeland through her searching novels of political and sexual revolution. Collins, who was active in the National Women's Organisation in Grenada until the 1983 US invasion, has also continued to engage with Caribbean politics through her creative work. Her poetry collection *Because the Dawn Breaks, Poems Dedicated to the Grenadian People* (1985) was followed in 1987 by the superb first novel *Angel*, which spans the life of three generations of women in Grenada. Although both Ngcobo and Collins had achieved some critical acclaim for their own work in the 1980s, both sought to foster an awareness of, and positive reception for, writing by other black women in the UK.

The year 1987 saw the publication of *Watchers and Seekers*, edited by Rhonda Cobham and Merle Collins, as well as of *Let it Be Told*, edited by Lauretta Ngcobo. These two collections, along with *Charting the Journey: Writings by Black and Third World Women* (1988), were able to bring diversity and the talent of a significant number of women writers to wider public attention. As Ngcobo pointed out in her editor's note to *Let it Be Told*: 'We have been writing for a long time; it is now that these writing are beginning to come out into the open.' However, while these anthologies presented an important opportunity for publication for many black women writers, they were also convenient publications for mainstream publishing houses (see **publishing, books**) whose woman-centred lists were still predominantly white, and who would not risk the publication of single volumes by 'unknown' black women writers.

Certainly, the 1985 poetry collection *A Dangerous Knowing: Four Black Women Poets*, edited by Barbara **Burford** with poems by Barbara Burford, Jackie **Kay**, Grace **Nichols** and Gabriela Pearse, enabled poets who were lesser known at that time to be launched alongside Grace Nichols. Nichols had won the Commonwealth Poetry Prize for *i is a long memoried woman* in 1983 and published *The Fat Black Woman's Poems* with Virago in 1984, and the consciously irreverent but playful iconoclasm of her works had raised the serious issue of what it meant to be identified as a black woman in the UK. This was a crucial issue that Asian women's publications were also beginning to address at the time. As the titles of the collective publications *Breaking the Silence* (Centerprise, 1984) and *Right of Way* (**Asian Women Writers' Collective**, 1988) suggest, these collections provided an important forum for both testimony and self-representation by enabling the voices and experiences of British Asian women to be heard. Some of the writers included went on to publish novels with the Women's Press (Ravinda **Randhawa**'s *A Wicked Old Woman*, 1987 and Leena **Dhingra**'s *Amritvela*, 1988).

Although black women's writing in the UK is still most commonly associated with African-Caribbean voices, several interesting literary works have emerged from Asian communities, for example *The Red Box* (1991) by Farhana **Sheikh**, and the recently published *Tomorrow is Another Day* (1994) by Narmala Shewcharan, who has settled in Britain from Guyana. As Shewcharan and Janice **Shinebourne** (Caribbean born, of Chinese and Indian ancestry) remind us, many black women writers in the UK have a complex cultural and ethnic identity, and defy reductive attempts to categorise writers and writings according to simple ethnic boundaries.

Indeed, it could be argued that black women's writing has positively stretched the boundaries demarcating concepts of both writing and identity in late twentieth-century Britain. Although the poetry of Jackie Kay connects to that of many other black women writers in its exploration of a creativity that is intimately involved with lived experience, the crafted honesty of *The Adoption Papers* (1991) and *Other Lovers* (1993) is enlivened by the more radical Scottish and lesbian elements that also inform her work. Perhaps with the need to break a silence or to address racist stereotypes less urgent in the late 1980s and 1990s, several women writers have confidently written across a range of issues. Aware of their ethnic identities, but unwilling to allow themselves and their writings to be constrained by limited notions of what it means to be black, Suniti **Namjoshi**, Amryl **Johnson** and Bernardine **Evaristo** have created texts in which multiple identities (cultural, sexual, creative) find expression.

A creative response to literary orthodoxies is also demonstrated in the performing poetry (see **performing poets**) of Valerie **Bloom** (*Touch Mi, Tell Mi*, 1983) and Jean 'Binta' **Breeze**. Breeze, who had already gained a reputation alongside male dub poets in the Caribbean when she moved to London in 1985, has staked her claim in this traditionally 'male' form through her several works, which powerfully reclaim a female body and voice, as well as through her strident essay which asks: 'Can a dub poet be a woman?' (1990). A second generation of performing poets has now established itself, with Patience **Agbabi**, **SuAndi** and Akure **Wall** among others offering new works that bring together aesthetics, politics and performance in complex and interesting ways.

In the 1990s, women writers also gained recognition in the area of popular fiction, previously perceived as an aggressively male genre dominated by cult novels such as Victor **Headley**'s *Yardie*. The **X Press**, the largest black popular fiction publishing house in the UK, now has a number of titles written by women. Yvette Richard's, *Single Black Female* (1994), Andrea Taylor's *Baby Mother* (1996) and Naomi King's *Other People's Property* (1993, with a **television** series adaptation) all address the issues of male and female relationships, sexuality and motherhood. Possibly the most challenging texts within this broad genre of popular fiction are the erotic fictions, such as Sheri Campbell's *Wicked in Bed* (1995) and *Rude Gal* (1996), which powerfully reclaim black female sexuality in texts written by and for black women.

Further reading

Asian Women Writers' Workshop (ed.) (1988) *Right of Way*, London: the Women's Press.

Centerprise Trust (eds) (1984) *Breaking the Silence*, London: Centerprise.

Cobham, R. and Collins, M. (eds) (1987) *Watchers and Seekers*, London: the Women's Press.

'Many Voices, One Chant. Black Feminist Perspectives' (1984) Special Issue of *Feminist Review* 17 (autumn).

Nasta, S. (ed.) (1991) *Motherlands*, London: the Women's Press.

Ngcobo, L. (1987) *Let it Be Told: Black Women Writers in Britain*, London: Virago.

Grewal, S., Kay, J., Landor, L., Lewis, G. and Parmar, P. (eds) (1988) *Charting the Journey: Writings by Black and Third World Women*, London: Sheba.

ALISON DONNELL

Wong, Denise

b. 1958, Bedford, England

freelance theatre director

Denise Wong trained in Community Theatre at Rose Bruford's and the Circle in the Square, New York. She worked as an actress with Shared Experience, the Young Vic and Kaboodle, before joining the **Black Mime Theatre Company** when it was founded in 1984. She became Artistic Director in 1986, and thereafter directed all fifteen of the company's productions between 1986 and 1997. In 1990, she formed the Black Mime Women's Troupe, and the Mixed Ensemble in 1992. She was instrumental in presenting notions of a black British mime aesthetic and in establishing and leading an annual two-week black women's training project to teach women the art of mime and physical **theatre**. An accomplished theatre director, Denise Wong directed the drama aspect in shows for Union Dance Company (*Driving Force*, 1993), and Adzido Pan-African Dance Ensemble (*Oya's Choice*, 1994; *Thand 'Abantwaana*, 1995; and *Shango the God of Thunder*, 1996), as well as winning an Arts Council bursary to work as an associate director at the Birmingham Repertory Theatre from 1997 to 1998.

Further reading

Goodman, L. (1996) *Feminist Stages: Interviews with Women in Contemporary British Theatre*, London: Routledge.

—— (1993) *Contemporary Feminist Theatres: to Each Her Own*, London: Routledge.

LYNETTE GODDARD

Working Group against Racism in Children's Resources

The Working Group against Racism in Children's Resources (WGARCR) is a registered charity, founded in 1986 by Gerry German and originally funded by the **Commission for Racial Equality** (CRE). Originally concerned with addressing the absence of images of black communities in the toy industry, WGARCR has also taken on many of the activities of the National Committee on Racism in Children's Books, which lost its funding in 1994. Verna Wilkins, children's author and the force behind Tamarind Books, chaired the organisation during a period of expansion and it is currently supported by its growing membership, in addition to some Lottery funding. Stating its central aim: 'to combat and eradicate racism in the children's world', the Working Group provides information and training for childcare workers, toy manufacturers, publishers, teachers, librarians and others to encourage the elimination of racism through the promotion of positive images. By confronting the extent to which racist and stereotypical imagery is still common in play and learning materials, and addressing the predominance of white, European communities and the subsequent absence of images of black people, the Working Group's activities aim to increase awareness of the damaging consequences of this practice and seek to ensure that children's resources offer 'positive and authentic representations of black people'.

In addition to workshops for parents and professionals which are designed to enable those who work with children to evaluate resources and select those which support an anti-racist framework, the organisation is also concerned with confronting racism in schools by supporting and training advocates who work with children and their families in resisting exclusions. The need to protect the rights of all children in school has led to the inception of the advocacy programme which, again, emphasises positive action.

WGARCR also publishes a series of guidelines and resource lists for schools, libraries and childcare facilities. These include lists of organisations that supply toys and educational materials. In co-operation with the CRE, these information packs aim to reinforce the legislation of the 1989 Children Act and encourage anti-racist practice in a pre-school setting. Demand for information about children's books is met by guidelines and selections of picture books titles that meet the strict criteria of an anti-racist perspective for **children's literature**. The Group also promotes the celebration of Kwanzaa and publishes a booklet of information, including lists of suppliers of relevant resources, emphasising the importance of such festivals to help children of the African diaspora to acknowledge and celebrate African identity.

From 1978 until its closure in 1994, the National Committee on Racism in Children's books published an anti-racist children's books magazine, called *Dragon's Teeth*. This quarterly journal was principally concerned with promoting an awareness of racism in children's books, identifying good educational practice and providing a forum for debate surrounding issues of race, gender and education. WGARCR continues to supply back issues of this magazine and has recently opened a website, in order to increase access to its materials and activities.

DEBBIE THACKER

Workshop Declaration, the

The Workshop Declaration was signed in 1981 as part of a concerted effort to put film (see **film and cinema**) and video workshops on a more secure financial footing. The Declaration was an industrial agreement signed by the Association of Cinematograph Television and Allied Technicians union (ACTT), regional arts associations such as Greater London Arts, the **British Film Institute** and **television** companies. It was intended to facilitate grant approval via franchises to film and video workshops wanting to produce non-commercial and grant-assisted film and video. The rationale for the Declaration was to develop and sustain an independent film sector that might begin to evolve on the basis of a more permanent funding structure than had been possible before. While the Declaration had not been drawn up specifically with **Channel 4** in mind, the relentless reduction in funding from every other source meant that Channel 4 became the principal sponsor almost by default. Five black workshops were franchised under the Declaration, including **Sankofa Film Collective** and **Black Audio Film Collective**, all of which then became eligible to bid for funding for a term of up to five years. After this initial period, further funding was to be provided at the discretion of the Declaration signatories, and a number of franchised workshops continued to be sponsored after 1986. The more progressive period of the 1980s gave way to a far more ruthless and commercialised environment in the 1990s, and funding for small film collectives was never again organised in the way originally envisaged by the Workshop Declaration.

KAREN ROSS

WriteOnLine

The WriteOnLine Publishing Company was conceived in 2000 by a group of black British writers and artists as a forum for promoting their work and reaching a global audience. Using the Internet as a tool that does not require the approval of councils, publishers, production companies and the 'one-black-writer-a-year' policy, Paul **Boakye** and others decided to take matters into their own hands. Initially a London-based black British project, WriteOnLine soon reached international participants and audiences. Boakye, Topher **Campbell**, Terence Facey, **Ajamu** and Charles Kwesi Sagoe were joined by writers, academics and artists from around the world, including writer and critic Bonnie Greer, actess and ex-*EastEnders* Joan Hooley, Brooklyn performance poet Ayin Adams, Radhika Gajjala, Elaine Starkman and others from places as varied as Costa Rica, Poland, India, Israel, the Philippines, Canada and the USA. WriteOnLine publishes electronic books in all genres and styles, and explores new approaches to new media and independent creativity from all sections of the multicultural international community. Its appeal to diversity and communication has made it popular with researchers, talent seekers and the general public. A collection of writing *On the Move: the Net, the Street and the Community* is one of their first projects.

KRIS KNAUER

WRITERNET *see* New Playwrights Trust

X

X Press

Founded by Steve Pope and Diran **Adebayo** in 1992, X Press began after the two left their jobs at the *Voice* newspaper and were pursuing other ideas. Together they published Victor **Headley**'s *Yardie* on a home computer. The novel gained both interest and a market, and Pope and Adebayo sold the rights to Pan enabling them to set up a publishing house specifically for black popular fiction. Many of their titles are on subjects that have a good PR angle, such as Patrick Augustus's *Baby Father* and Yvette Richards's *Single Black Female*, but this concentration on issues associated with sex and violence has left X Press open to accusations of negative profiling. At the beginning of the venture, they consciously courted publicity and notoriously mailed bullets as part of their marketing campaign for Gorgon's *Cop Killer*. They have now focused more on the **literature** itself and have diversified their market with three more lists: X Press Black Classics, which reprints classic African American texts and is commercially strong; 20/20 for speculative fiction, not exclusively by black writers; and Nia for their literary (rather than popular fiction) authors. The Press has made several charitable donations, including to SCAR, the sickle cell charity, and the Stephen **Lawrence** Fund. With a strong and diverse list X Press has both proven the market for black fiction in Britain and has also helped to lead and shape it.

ALISON DONNELL

Y

Yashere, Gina

comedienne, writer

Yashere made a striking appearance on the comedy scene by taking second place at the Hackney Empire 'New Act of the Year' awards in 1996 – the highest place ever to be won by a black woman. She followed up this success with a place on London Weekend Television's *Big, Big Talent Show*, hosted by Jonathan Ross, and was the only comedian to make it to the final, winning by more than 15,000 votes. She has made regular **television** appearances on Channel 5's *The Comedy Store*, **Channel 4**'s *Gas* and *Planet Pop*, and most notably on the late-night panel show *Blouse and Skirt*. As well as performing, Yashere has written a number of sketches for BBC Radio and is one of the head writers for the Richard **Blackwood** show. She won Best Female at the 2000 Black Comedy Awards.

ALISON DONNELL

Young, Lola

b. 1951

academic

Although formerly a professional actor, Lola Young is Professor of Cultural Studies at Middlesex University. Her work focuses on representations of race, gender and sexuality in **television** and media, and she has also written about black British cultural expression, especially in **photography**, film (see **film and cinema**) and video. Her book, *Fear of the Dark. 'Race', Gender and Sexuality in the Cinema* (1996) concentrates on the portrayal of black female sexuality in film, and the extent to which both black and white film-makers have challenged stereotypes of black femininity. By examining a selection of films made between 1959 and 1986, Young traces the impact of a generation of post-war black settlement on representations of racial **difference**, and she analyses the terms in which ideologies of racial and sexual difference are expressed in the cinema.

For the last decade, Young has been an important presence in the British media. This was recognised in 1998 when she featured in Donald MacLellan's 'Black Power' exhibition of photographs of prominent black British figures at the National Portrait Gallery, and in 1999 when she was Chair of Judges for the Orange Prize for Fiction.

Select bibliography

Young, L. (1996) *Fear of the Dark. 'Race', Gender and Sexuality in the Cinema*, London: Routledge.

SARA SALIH

Young Soul Rebels

After the art-house success of films such as *The Passion of Remembrance* and ***Looking for Langston***, *Young Soul Rebels* (1991) represents a determined assault on the mainstream by director Isaac **Julien**.

Set during the Silver Jubilee celebrations of 1977, the film (see **film and cinema**) depicts the relationship of Chris and Caz, **soul** DJs and pirate broadcasters. The murder of a young black man raises tensions in the neighbourhood, though, for some, sympathy and solidarity are complicated by the fact that he was killed in a local park noted for being a gay meeting place. The film underlines, and undermines, issues of identity and identification, loyalty and community, whether based on race, sexuality, locality or social marginality. The Silver Jubilee also situates these more 'local' identities within the even more problematic context of the nation. Chris and Caz's friendship is tested to the limit as Chris (like the film) heads for a position in mainstream media, while Caz (also like the film) courts disapproval and rejection by the black community by being openly gay. The film ends with the murder solved, Chris and Caz's relationship reaffirmed, and with the image of the ideal microcosmic community of friends – black and white, male and female, gay and straight.

PATRICK WILLIAMS

youth culture

The development of a distinctive black youth culture in Britain can be traced to the post-war period of the 1950s and 1960s when migration to the UK from its former colonies was at its peak, and families joined working fathers. Subsequently, the 1970s saw young people who had grown up in the UK and who were not prepared, as their parents had been, to accept the racism and prejudice that greeted them in so many areas of their daily lives. Youth culture offered them an avenue both through which to express themselves and to escape the prejudices of British society.

Young people frequently have to negotiate an environment that was largely unknown to their parents but this was a particularly pertinent phenomenon for young black people growing up in the UK. Many forms of adaptation, negotiation and resistance used to address issues such as prejudice and other negative forms of dominant white British culture are incorporated from the culture of their parents. A site of both contestation

and creativity, black youth culture is the source of a plethora of subcultures inspired and maintained by young people. Young black people have undoubtedly contributed to the dynamics of mainstream British youth culture, particularly through **music** and style. However, while research has highlighted the problematics of class, gender and economics in locating youth culture, young black people, and specifically the role of 'race', have frequently been side-stepped. **Hall** and Jefferson's *Resistance through Rituals* (1975) was one of the first texts that examined youth cultures, including black youth culture, to any extent.

Youth culture has always been noted for its ability to define and influence the mass consumption of entertainment, art and culture, particularly since young people tend to have the highest percentage of 'free' money. Black youth are no exception to this. Youth cultures tend to utilise those materials (**fashion**, **music**, talk) and contexts (dance halls, youth centres, nightclubs, pubs) most readily available to them in order to construct subcultural identities. Even so, some youth cultures stand out as 'other' from 'mainstream' culture far more than others. This has often been the case for black British youth, growing up in a culture alien both to themselves and to their parents. In such a position they similarly utilise and rebel against elements from both the majority culture and the peripheral culture of their parents, subsequently constructing cultural identities that reflect their own unique position.

Faced with a high level of disillusionment with established arts venues and arts forms (see **art forms**), many young black people look for alternatives. Increasingly, demand is not being met by 'established' popular culture. The Avebury Youth Review (1988) highlighted how 'traditional' arts venues attracted only 2 per cent of young people and have virtually no attendance from black young people or the young unemployed. While access slightly increased in the 1990s, the figure remains exceptionally low. For black youth in Britain historically there have been few opportunities to experience non-mainstream cultural forms in safe spaces that allowed free expression. The 1950s and 1960s were a time when black youth culture was strictly underground. While **reggae** and **ska** were regularly played in dance halls and at blues parties, there was little opportunity for their mass consumption since record companies held them of no consequence. Equally, it was the lack of access to music such as **bhangra** and reggae that encouraged small recording companies such as Star (part of **Oriental Star Agencies**) and West Indian Records to set up.

However, ska music was one of the first forms of music not confined to the black community and the Ram Jam nightclub in Brixton one of the few clubs where black and white youths mixed in any number. Dick Hebdige and Ian Chambers were at the forefront of theorists who examined the dynamics taking place between black and white youth. Chambers highlighted the manner in which black cultural forms became a resource upon which white youth drew, thus providing an alternative to the dominant culture; skinhead culture was one aspect of this. Counter to Chambers, Hebdige suggested that the development of youth cultures highlighted some of the ongoing tensions within race relations. So, while skinhead culture drew heavily on Jamaican forms of music (ska) and dress (the crombie), it also propagated 'white power'. Partly due to the lack of profile given to black youth culture, the 1970s seemed to be dominated by the skinhead and punk movements. Many aspects of the skinhead movement were so heavily influenced by Caribbean styles that cultural integration was seen as desirable, although only with African/Caribbeans. Such integration was only ever superficial, however, since the prejudice and racism that followed young black youth was never to apply to white skinheads. The 1980s saw some of the first obvious re-definitions of youth culture by black youth.

Following on from ska, two tone was dominated by groups such as the Specials, who highlighted the fusion between black and white audiences and music styles. **Hip hop** also came to the fore as young people drew on this hybrid musical form hailing from the USA. Alongside were rap, break-dance and bhangra, all of which utilised their hybrid backgrounds and influenced black British lifestyles.

In the 1990s, black youth culture continues to draw heavily on countries such as the USA and the Indian subcontinent, while proclaiming the Brit-ishness of black youth. Hence, bands such **Asian Dub Foundation** reflect Britishness, Asianness and utilise sound system culture as a means of representation, while an artist like **Apache Indian** combines reggae with creole and Punjabi lyrics, and is accepted both by African-Caribbean and Asian youth. We increasingly see a youth culture that draws both on being British and on the multiple dimensions of being black in Britain.

Further reading

Back, Les (1996) *New Ethnicities and Urban Culture: Racisms and Multiculture in Young Lives*, London: UCL Press Ltd.

Hall, S. and Jefferson, T. (eds) (1975) *Resistance through Rituals: Youth Subcultures in Post-war Britain*, London: Routledge.

Hebdige, D. (1979) *Subculture: the Meaning of Style*, London: Methuen.

Jones, S. (1988) *Black Youth, White Culture: the Reggae Tradition from JA to UK*, London: Macmillan.

SAMINA ZAHIR

Z

Zaidi, Ali

b. 1963, Bombay, India

visual artist

Born in Bombay, Ali Zaidi's family moved to Pakistan in 1967. He grew up in Lahore and graduated in graphic design and **photography** from the National College of Art. Later, he worked with an advertising agency and lectured in photography at the art college. He came to the UK on a British Council Fellowship in 1988 and gained his Masters in alternative media from Chelsea School of Art. Zaidi works in a range of art forms: film (see **film and cinema**), **theatre**, **live art**, installation, site-specific design and new technologies. In 1988, he met designer Keith **Khan** and together they have created many projects including: *Flying Costumes, Floating Tombs*, a large-scale outdoor spectacle inspired by the Islamic Festival of Muharram. They also presented *Moti Roti Puttli Chunni*, combining live action and film sequences on stage. Both the projects won the *Time Out* London Dance and Performance Award in 1991 and 1993 respectively. Zaidi and Khan set up **Moti Roti**, in 1991, an artist-led organisation pushing the boundaries of artistic and cultural discourse. They produced the play *Maa* (written by Ash Kotak) in 1995, as part of Barclays New Stages, and *One Night* (written by Dolly Dhingra) in 1997. *Wigs of Wonderment* (1996, 1998 and 1999), a performance installation commissioned by the **Institute of Contemporary Arts**, challenges dominant notions of beauty. Single audience members meet with seven performers individually on a sensory journey, looking at the politics of black hair and gender in a humorous and non-confrontational way. Zaidi worked on the LIFT spectacles, *Factory of Dreams* (1996) and *Un Pu plus de lumiere* (1997), collaborating with the French pyrotechnics artist Christophe Berthenou. In 1995, he directed *The Seed the Root*, a series of installations and performances around Brick Lane in East London. He also directed *Fresh Masaala*, an installation at Warwick Arts Centre, where three artists and 150 participants take a closer look at issues of perception. It is an exhibition in flux, adapting as it absorbs images, voices, thoughts and ideas. His lastest work, *Reality Bytes*, is an interactive new-technology piece working with young Asian women. Zaidi's pieces are held in the New Walsall Museum and Art Gallery, and the Walsall and Cartwright Hall and Museum in Bradford.

SUMAN BHUCHAR

Zephaniah, Benjamin

b. 1958, Handsworth, Birmingham, England

poet, writer, actor, presenter

Benjamin Obadiah Iqbal Zephaniah finished his formal education at the age of thirteen but by then was already a poet, having used words to help express his thoughts on the 'street politics' of his youth, as well as the Jamaican **music** and speech of his parents. Always engaged with the reality of injustice, both local and global, Zephaniah has performed subversive and often humorous poems on the issues of racism, gender identity, green issues and animal rights. Although nearly a dozen collections of his poems have been published to date, including three for children, his energetic performative style means that his poetry is best experienced on stage (see **performing poets**). His work can also be heard on his albums, including *Dub Ranting* (1982), *Free South Africa* (1986) and *Belly of De Beast LP* (1996). Zephaniah has written plays and his latest, *Listen to Your Parents*, was broadcast on Radio 4 in 2000. He is a regular **television** and radio presenter with credits including *Dread Poets' Society* in 1991 and *Crossing the Tracks* in 1993. His first novel, *Face*, was published in 1999 and *Refugee Boy* in 2001. Zephaniah is also active in human and animal rights movements and, after his tribute to the then imprisoned Nelson Mandela, was asked to work in the South African townships and later to host the President's Two Nation Concert in London in 1996. There was much controversy in 1991 when he was nominated for a Chair of Poetry at Cambridge University. He did not get the post, but he has been asked to select his *Desert Island Discs*.

Select bibliography

Zephaniah, B. (2001) *Refugee Boy*, London: Bloomsbury.

—— (2000) *Wicked World*, London: Puffin.

—— (1999) *Face*, London: Bloomsbury.

—— (1995) *Talking Turkeys*, London: Puffin.

—— (1993) *City Psalms*, Newcastle upon Tyne: Bloodaxe Books.

ALISON DONNELL

Index